Que's MS-DOS® 5
User's Guide
Special Edition

Que® Development Group

Que's MS-DOS® 5 User's Guide, Special Edition

Copyright© 1991 by Que® Corporation.

Library of Congress Catalog No.: 90-63648

ISBN 0-88022-671-4

94   93   92   91   4   3   2   1

Interpretation of the printing code: the rightmost double-digit number is the year of the book's printing; the rightmost single-digit number, the number of the book's printing. For example, a printing code of 91-1 shows that the first printing of the book occurred in 1991.

This book is based on MS-DOS Version 5.0 and can be used with all versions of DOS after 3.0.

Publisher: Lloyd J. Short

Associate Publisher: Karen A. Bluestein

Acquisitions Manager: Terrie Lynn Solomon

Managing Editor: Paul Boger

Product Development Manager: Mary Bednarek

Book Designer: Scott Cook

Production Team: Jeff Baker, Martin Coleman, Sandy Grieshop, Denny Hager, Betty Kish, Bob LaRoche, Howard Peirce, Tad Ringo, Louise Shinault, Bruce Steed, Johnna VanHoose, Lisa Wilson, Christine Young

Product Director
Walter R. Bruce III

Production Editor
Kelly D. Dobbs

Editors
Gail S. Burlakoff
Kelly Currie
H. Leigh Davis
Donald R. Eamon
Barbara K. Koenig
Mike La Bonne
Tim Ryan

Technical Editor
James T. Karney

Composed in Garamond and Macmillan
by Que Corporation

Phil Feldman
Caroline Halliday
Rick Hellewell
David H. Longstreet
Mark Schulman
David Solomon
Timothy S. Stanley

Phil Feldman received his B.A. degree in physics from the University of California in 1968 and did graduate work in computer science at UCLA. He has written and coauthored many articles in engineering journals and personal computer magazines; with Tom Rugg, he has coauthored more than a dozen books, including *Using QuickBASIC 4* and *QuickBASIC Programmer's Toolkit*. Feldman is chairman of 32 Plus, Inc., a software development and consulting firm.

Caroline Halliday is an electrical engineer with High Tech Aid in the Chicago area. Her company specializes in technical documentation and teaching for the PC environment. She has a Bachelor of Science (Hons) degree from the University of Manchester, England, and is a former technical editor for *PC Tech Journal*. She is the principal author of *Using OS/2*, published by Que Corporation. She now contributes articles to various magazines including *PC Week* and *InfoWorld*.

Rick Hellewell is a micrcomputer specialist for the City of Sacramento and is a consultant to business and home users. He has served as president of the Sacramento PC Users Group, the fifth largest users group in the United States, and is the associate editor of *Sacra Blue*, their monthly newsletter.

David H. Longstreet is an information systems project leader for Sprint/United Corporation in Kansas City, MO. He specializes in the measurement and maintenance of software systems. His PC specialization includes WordPerfect, DOS, database management, and spreadsheet applications. He is the author of *Tutorial on Software Maintenance and Computers* published by IEEE Computer Society Press. He has a Bachelor of Science degree from Texas A&M University.

Mark Schulman is a computer programmer and instructor with Cincinnati Bell Information Systems. He has worked with a wide range of computer hardware and operating systems from micros to mainframes, running under UNIX, XENIX, MS-DOS, OS/2, and others. Since 1983, most of his work has involved writing software for a variety of applications and teaching classes in UNIX and the C and C++ programming languages.

David Solomon is product development director for New Riders Publishing and specializes in operating systems, database management, and programming. He has developed and written custom software for scientific and business applications on a worldwide basis. Solomon also is the author of *Using DOS, MS-DOS QuickStart,* and *Using UNIX* and the coauthor of *Using dBASE IV* and *Using Turbo Prolog*, all published by Que Corporation.

Timothy S. Stanley, a product development specialist for Que Corporation, also has served as technical editor and author for several of Que's titles. Specializing in operating systems/environments and spreadsheet and database applications, Stanley has contributed to *Using 1-2-3 Release 3.1*, 2nd Edition; *Using dBASE IV*; *Using DOS 5*; *Upgrading to DOS 5*; *Windows 3 Quick Reference*; and *Batch Files and Macros Quick Reference*.

Que Corporation has made every effort to supply trademark information about company names, products, and services mentioned in this book. Trademarks indicated below were derived from various sources. Que Corporation cannot attest to the accuracy of this information.

1-2-3, Blueprint, Lotus, Lotus Manuscript, and Magellan are registered trademarks of Lotus Development Corporation.

Apple, Macintosh, and Mac are registered trademarks of Apple Computer, Inc.

COMPAQ Personal Computer is a trademark and COMPAQ and COMPAQ DeskPro 386 are registered trademarks of COMPAQ Computer Corporation.

CompuServe Information Sevices, dBASE IV, and dBASE III Plus are registered trademarks of Ashton-Tate Corporation.

DisplayWrite 4, IBM Personal Editor, IBM ProPrinter, IBM Token Right, Micro Channel, OS/2, Systems Application Architecture (SAA), and TopView are trademarks and IBM, PC XT, PS/2 Models 25, 30, 50, 50Z, 60, 70, and 80, and QuietWriter are registered trademarks of International Business Machines Corporation.

Dow Jones News/Retrieval is a registered service mark of Dow Jones & Company, Inc.

DUMP.EXE is a trademark of Phoenix Technologies, Ltd.

EPSON is a registered trademark of Epson America, Inc.

FLASH is a trademark of Software Masters, Inc.

Hercules Graphics Card is a trademark of Hercules Computer Technology.

Keyworks is a trademark of ALPHA Software Corporation.

GW-BASIC, Microsoft Excel, Microsoft QuickBASIC, Microsoft Windows/386, Microsoft Windows Development Kit, Microsoft Windows Write, Microsoft Word, MS-DOS, and XENIX are registered trademarks of Microsoft Corporation.

Mouse Systems is a trademark of Mouse Systems Corporation.

NU and the Norton Utilities are registered trademarks of Symantec Corporation.

Novell is a registered trademark of Novell, Inc.

PageMaker is a registered trademark of Aldus Corporation.

Paradox and Query By Example are registered trademarks of Borland/Ansa Software.

PC Paintbrush is a registered trademark of ZSoft Corporation.

Post-It is a registered trademark of 3-M Corporation.

ProKey is a trademark of RoseSoft, Inc.

RamQuest 50/60 is a trademark of Orchid Technology, Inc.

ACKNOWLEDGMENTS

Thanks to the following people who provided invaluable help during the revision of this book: Kelly Dobbs, Gail Burlakoff, Kelly Currie, Don Eamon, Mike La Bonne, Tim Ryan, and the rest of the editorial and production staff at Que who asked challenging questions and made many good editorial suggestions.

CONTENTS AT A GLANCE

Part V Command Reference

TABLE OF CONTENTS

I   Understanding the Fundamentals of DOS

Part II   Working with the Core Commands

Part III   Expanding Your Use of DOS

Part V   Command Reference

Introduction

S ince its introduction in 1981, MS-DOS has grown to be the most widely used operating system in the world. Thousands of applications programs have been written for MS-DOS operating systems. With more than 10 million users worldwide, DOS affects more people than any software product ever written.

As DOS has evolved, Que Corporation has helped hundreds of thousands of personal computer users get the most from MS-DOS. *Que's MS-DOS 5 User's Guide*, Special Edition, represents Que's continuing commitment to provide the best microcomputer books in the industry. This book is a comprehensive learning tool and reference volume for users of MS-DOS and PC DOS. This Special Edition reflects the maturity of DOS and the far-reaching impact that DOS-based microcomputing has had on people and the way in which they work.

DOS is the operating system of choice for the majority of personal computer users. *Que's MS-DOS 5 User's Guide*, Special Edition, offers DOS users a source of information to organize their work with the PC more effectively and to make their hardware respond more efficiently.

Who Should Read This Book?

This book is written and organized to meet the needs of a large group of readers. The book is especially well-suited for readers who are proficient with applications programs, but who can benefit from a better understanding of DOS. *Que's MS-DOS 5 User's Guide*, Special Edition, also is for those people who have grown beyond elementary tutorials.

Perhaps you have upgraded your hardware to a more powerful PC with more memory and disk capacity or have upgraded your version of DOS and want to take advantage of its new or expanded features. Maybe you are just beginning to use a PC, but you would like to get up to full speed quickly. If you find that you fit into any of these categories, this comprehensive edition is a "must have" volume.

What Hardware Is Needed?

This book applies to the family of IBM personal computers and their close compatibles, including the IBM Personal Computer, the IBM Personal Computer XT, the IBM Personal Computer AT, and the IBM PS/2 series. Dozens of other computers that use DOS and are manufactured or sold by COMPAQ, Zenith Data Systems, EPSON, Leading Edge, Tandy, Dell, Northgate, CompuAdd, and others also are covered by this book. If your computer runs the DOS operating system, you have the necessary hardware.

What Versions Are Covered?

Special attention is given to the features new with DOS Version 5, but this book covers from Version 3 on. Users of Version 2 also can benefit from the discussions, but many useful DOS features and commands included in the newer versions are not available.

What Is Not Covered?

This book does not include the DEBUG or LINK commands, nor does it include a technical reference to the applications programming interface that DOS provides programmers. If you are interested in programming at the operating system level, Que offers a complete line of books that cover DOS programming.

Also not included in this book are computer-specific setup or configuration commands, such as IBM's SETUP for the PS/2 and Toshiba's CHAD for laptop displays. Although these commands often are distributed with the same disks as DOS, they are too variable to be covered adequately here. Your computer-supplied manual and your PC dealer are the best sources of information about these machine-specific features.

How Is This Book Organized?

You can flip quickly through this book to get a feeling for its organization. *Que's MS-DOS 5 User's Guide*, Special Edition, approaches DOS in a logical, functionally defined way. The material in this book is arranged into five main parts and a set of appendixes.

Part I—Understanding the Fundamentals of DOS

Part I is devoted to explaining the fundamental role of DOS in a working PC.

Chapter 1, "Understanding the Role of DOS," looks at the common uses of the term DOS and builds a definition of the layered PC. This chapter demonstrates that DOS is not a software entity but a set of modules, each specializing at its own level in a PC.

Chapter 2, "Understanding the DOS File System," is a tutorial on DOS's extensive provisions for using disks. An entire range of topics is covered—from why disk drives are the primary storage media to how DOS tracks your files in a multidisk filing system.

Chapter 3, "Understanding the Command Processor," covers the general rules and considerations for all DOS commands, keyboard keys, and key combinations. The commands are categorized and described in several useful tables.

Chapter 4, "Gaining Control of Hardware," looks at the nature of device drivers and their role in DOS. Important considerations—such as how programs operate and how memory is divided—are covered in this chapter. System configuration concepts are explained, and the concept of redirection and piping is introduced within the context of DOS's device-independent commands.

Chapter 5, "Using the DOS Shell," shows you how to use the DOS Shell to access programs and perform file maintenance. By adding your own program groups and objects, you can create your own menu system of commands and programs. This chapter also covers the Switcher, which enables you to move from one task to another among several programs without having to exit and reload each program.

Part II—Working with the Core Commands

The core commands of DOS are presented in Part II. Familiar commands are explained so that you can glean some new insights into their operation. Commands that you are less likely to use are treated in a slightly more tutorial way. With this approach, you can use Part II to get the most from what you know—and expand your base of daily DOS commands.

Chapter 6, "Preparing and Maintaining Disks," concentrates on disk-level commands. Partitioning, formatting, disk copying, and disk comparison are covered. Examples and exercises help you understand these disk-level commands.

Chapter 7, "Managing and Navigating the Directory Hierarchy," reviews the important hierarchical directory file-management system. The commands presented in this chapter enable you to manage DOS directories in an effective fashion.

Chapter 8, "Managing Your Files," illuminates the file-level DOS commands. Because you likely spend most of your time with DOS working with files, this chapter offers an in-depth view of the file-level commands. Each command includes examples that help you appreciate the full power of these important commands.

Chapter 9, "Working with System Information," covers the commands that set and retrieve system information in your DOS-based computer. These commands often are neglected, but they key you into the control panel of DOS. These commands are helpful whether you oversee one PC or help other users with their PCs.

Chapter 10, "Gaining Control of Devices," explains the DOS commands that control the behavior of logical DOS devices. By using these commands, you can control the way DOS sees your system's drives and directories. You learn how to use your printer while doing other computer work, and you see how to use DOS pipes and filters effectively.

Part III—Expanding Your Use of DOS

Part III provides the information you need to tap the expanded power available with batch-file processing and screen and keyboard control. Creating and editing your own batch files is a sure way to become a more proficient DOS user—these chapters show you how.

Chapter 11, "Using the DOS Editor," provides a tutorial approach to DOS's built-in text-file editor. The examples developed in this chapter show you how to use the DOS Editor as a day-to-day utility. With the careful attention given to the Editor's practical use, you learn the skills needed to quickly compose a text file. Practical examples of using the DOS Editor to create memos and batch files also are presented.

Chapter 12, "Understanding Batch File Basics," guides you through the process of creating batch files. The commands related to batch files are explained in a tutorial style. Useful examples help make mastering the basics of batch files easier.

Chapter 13, "Understanding ANSI.SYS," shows you how to make DOS screens look colorful and controlled. The details of the ANSI.SYS driver are presented in workshop fashion. You learn how to reassign keys, control the cursor's position on-screen, display the date and time, and more.

Chapter 14, "Learning Advanced Batch File Techniques," builds on what you learn in Chapters 11, 12, and 13. You learn how to automate utility DOS work in a batch-file environment. The batch files presented in this chapter are useful, but they also serve as models for designing your own advanced batch files. Whether you are customizing your own DOS work or providing an easy-to-use set of utilities for a DOS beginner, this chapter shows you how.

Part IV—Advancing Your DOS Capabilities

Chapter 15, "Configuring Your Computer," is a comprehensive collection of DOS commands and directives that are explained to help you get the best performance from your PC. You learn several useful techniques—from creating a CONFIG.SYS file to using disk-caching software and extended memory.

Chapter 16, "Understanding the International Features of DOS," steps you through the complicated, but sometimes necessary, configuration of a PC to various international language standards.

Chapter 17, "Understanding QBasic," teaches you about DOS 5's full-featured version of the BASIC programming language. You learn how to write simple programs, how to interact with the DOS Editor, and how to print a program listing.

Chapter 18, "Programming with QBasic," teaches you how to custom design programs to fit your needs. QBasic offers a full-screen editing environment and many important language enhancements.

Part V—Command Reference

Part V contains the comprehensive command reference. The commands, which are arranged alphabetically, are shown with syntax, applicable rules, and possible screen messages. You can use this section as a reference and as a source of practical advice and tips. The command reference is a complete, easy to use, quickly accessed resource on the proper use of DOS commands.

Appendixes

Que's MS-DOS 5 User's Guide, Special Edition, also includes six appendixes containing useful information. Appendix A lists the changes and additions among the various DOS versions. Appendix B is an ASCII code chart. Appendix C shows the DOS control and editing keys. Appendix D provides the information you need to install DOS 5. Appendix E provides the ANSI control sequences supported by DOS through ANSI.SYS. Appendix F gives you vital information for using Edlin, DOS's mini-text editor.

Conventions Used in This Book

Certain conventions are followed in this edition to help you more easily understand the discussions.

Uppercase letters are used to distinguish file names and DOS commands.

Ctrl-Break indicates that you press and hold down the Ctrl key while you press the Break key. Other hyphenated key combinations, such as Ctrl-Z or Alt-F1, are performed in the same manner.

Words or phrases defined for the first time appear in *italic*. Words or phrases that you type (when following the tutorials and examples) are in **bold**.

Screen displays and on-screen messages appear in a `special` typeface.

Different conventions are used to distinguish between optional and mandatory parts of a command. Items displayed in bold are mandatory; you always must give this part of a command. For some mandatory items, you must substitute the appropriate information such as a file name, a device name, a drive name, or a path name. In the example, **ASSIGN** *d1=d2* ..., you must substitute the appropriate drive letters for *d1* and *d2*.

Items in *italic* are optional or are variable names that appear in the discussions; you supply and/or substitute values for these items only when needed. In most cases, the text also helps you distinguish between the optional and mandatory items.

Uppercase letters usually are used in the examples, but you can type commands in upper- or lowercase letters.

Part I

Understanding the Fundamentals of DOS

Includes

Understanding the Role of DOS

Understanding the DOS File System

Understanding the Command Processor

Gaining Control of Hardware

Using the DOS Shell

Understanding the
Role of DOS

Not many years ago, most people never got to see a real computer. Computers were large, expensive, and rare. Most people who worked in a computerized environment had no knowledge of how the machine worked. Keypunch operators entered source documents into machines to produce cards. These punch cards then were fed into the mysterious mainframe computer by a card reader. The mainframe used the data from the cards to do math-intensive calculations and output the results onto green-bar paper. Screen displays were rare and expensive.

Science fiction movies, such as *2001: A Space Odyssey*, depicted computers of the future as semihuman thinking machines with columns and rows of blinking lights, input devices that looked like crystal cylinders, and output in the form of a man's monosyllabic voice.

In those days, computers were predicted to become more complex and mysterious. The expense and expertise required for everyday people in everyday jobs to have their own computers (and know how to use them) seemed as possible as the belief that people would abandon commercial aviation and begin flying their own airplanes.

Despite a fear of input devices and blinking lights, people continued to move closer to the computer. Video display terminals replaced punch cards and green-bar paper. Screen messages in plain English nearly replaced cryptic numbers. Minicomputers appeared where mainframes had been supreme. In the computer's mysterious insides, thousands of transistors were replaced by dozens of integrated circuits, which in turn were replaced by a small microprocessor and a handful of support-circuit components. Microcomputer hobby shops opened next to model airplane shops. The microcomputer industry was born.

Cue:
The MITS Altair introduced in early 1975 was the first widely available microcomputer.

In the past few years, the microcomputer field has grown from a cottage industry to a multi-billion-dollar business. A computer for each user has become a reality. You now live in the era of the personal computer. Much of the credit for this transition is due to International Business Machines, Inc. (IBM), for designing and marketing the IBM Personal Computer, and to Microsoft, Inc., for producing operating system software for the IBM PC. These companies benefitted from the growing wave of acceptance for personal computers that began with the CP/M operating system and the Apple Computer.

In this chapter, you get a clearer view of the world's most popular operating system, MS-DOS, as well as its role in the personal computers that you use today.

Explaining DOS

Cue:
DOS is an acronym for Disk Operating System.

DOS is an acronym for Disk Operating System. Nearly every computer has a disk operating system. Those computers that do not are severely limited in reliable data storage. Disk operating systems manage many of the technical details of computers and disk-file storage. Disk management, however, is perhaps the most important service these operating systems provide.

Many computers, from laptops to large, multiuser machines, use DOS as part of their operating system's name. Microsoft's MS-DOS, IBM's PC DOS, and Apple's DOS Version 3.3 and ProDOS are just a few examples.

Cue:
Various other operating systems are called DOS.

Although all these systems are DOS systems, more people associate the term DOS with MS-DOS than with any other disk operating system. When you read about *DOS* in this book, you are reading about MS-DOS. MS-DOS is a single-user, single-tasking disk operating system that provides the framework of operation for millions of today's computers.

Comparing Variations of MS-DOS

MS-DOS is an operating system that accommodates variation in its exact makeup while retaining its core characteristics. This capability for variation enables computer manufacturers to adapt MS-DOS to their computers. IBM PC DOS and COMPAQ DOS, for example, are variations of MS-DOS. Today, commonly available variations of MS-DOS are close in design and operation.

Cue:
Variations of MS-DOS are close in design.

MS-DOS works with computers designed around Intel's 8086 microprocessors, including the 8088, 80286, 80386, and 80486. The original IBM PC's great influence on the PC market convinced other 8086 PC manufacturers to closely follow IBM's design. Because IBM used an open approach to design its PC, other companies configured their computers to use programs and hardware designed for the IBM PC. From a DOS standpoint, these various computers virtually are alike, even though the PCs may be more advanced than the original IBM PC.

The closeness of its design to the IBM PC determines to what degree a PC is *IBM-compatible*. The buying public has demanded a high degree of IBM compatibility in PCs. Most PCs not designed after the IBM PC no longer are being produced or are sold in specialty markets and countries other than the United States. Most compatible PCs successfully operate by using a version of IBM's PC DOS, even though most compatible manufacturers usually offer their own variation of MS-DOS.

Most users consider variations in MS-DOS minor and usually limited to the names of a few commands or the way parameters are given. Some manufacturers include in their MS-DOS packages additional utilities that work only with their product. If you are proficient with one variation of MS-DOS, however, you are proficient with all variations.

As MS-DOS evolved, the core product was enhanced several times. Each enhancement is a distinct version of the program. Since its appearance in the summer of 1981, DOS has evolved through five major versions. (Changes between versions are summarized in Appendix A.) Even with the introduction of Microsoft's OS/2 and the presence of several versions of the UNIX operating system, DOS remains strong. You can expect your investment in learning DOS to continue paying dividends in any future computing. Most industry experts predict that DOS will remain in the PC picture for years to come. Even if you move to OS/2 or UNIX, much of your DOS expertise can be used with these operating systems.

Cue:
DOS has evolved through five major versions.

Understanding DOS in Context

Depending on the context of activity and use, the exact meaning of DOS can vary greatly. Most users read about DOS and talk about DOS in ways familiar to them.

Consider the PC buyer who asks the dealer, "Does this computer come with DOS?" If the dealer's answer is "Yes," that affirmation doesn't necessarily mean that the buyer receives a set of master DOS disks and manuals in a bound package. To the buyer, DOS means the DOS *package*. The dealer, on the other hand, may answer "Yes" because the hard disk on the PC includes MS-DOS Version 2.2 and utility files already loaded. Buyer and dealer are using the term DOS in different contexts.

An applications software package also may include a help screen that flashes the message `Press F10 to return to DOS`. The message doesn't mean, "Return to the DOS manuals and master disks." This message is the software's way of telling you how to finish your work with the package.

Agreeing on a common definition of DOS is easier when everyone concerned knows the context in which DOS is being discussed. The next sections look at some of the common contexts of DOS. Each context helps you build a definition of DOS.

Figure 1.1 illustrates the use of DOS in different contexts. Each picture can represent DOS in the right context. As the contexts progress from top to bottom, the meaning of DOS becomes less literal and more abstract. You can touch and see a DOS package, but you must conceptualize the idea of DOS working in a computer.

The DOS Package

The buyer's question to the dealer, "Does this PC come with DOS?" usually means "Does it come with a DOS package?" This meaning is product-oriented for DOS. Dealers and manufacturers usually supply or sell DOS as a stand-alone package or as an accessory package to a PC. Most often the DOS package includes one or more manuals and two or more disks. The DOS software is on the disk(s).

MS-DOS Version 5.0, for example, comes on four or five disks. PC DOS Version 4.0 comes on two or five disks depending on the model of computer intended for the software. PC DOS Version 3.3 comes on one or

Cue:
Some DOS packages include supplemental programs.

two disks. COMPAQ supplies DOS Version 4.0 on two DOS disks and one supplemental disk. DOS packages supplied by other computer manufacturers may have more or fewer disks. The disks may contain supplemental programs for the PC such as GW-BASIC and MS-LINK. These supplemental programs often are part of DOS because the manufacturer includes them in the physical DOS package. Depending on the context, supplemental programs may be associated with the term *DOS package*, but for the purpose of this book, you should consider such supplemental programs to be outside of DOS.

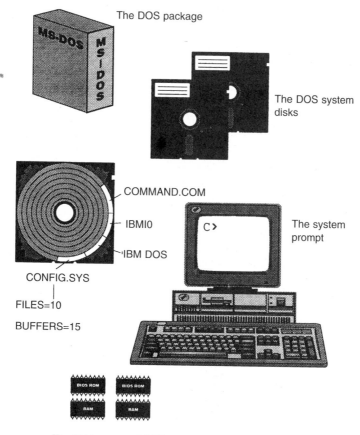

The DOS package

The DOS system disks

COMMAND.COM

IBMI0

IBM DOS

CONFIG.SYS

FILES=10

BUFFERS=15

The system prompt

The hidden core of DOS

Fig. 1.1. *The term DOS in context.*

The DOS package normally contains a DOS reference manual, which is an important supplement because it contains specific information about your version of DOS. Many PC users, however, prefer to use another book, such as this book or other books about DOS published by Que Corporation, for their daily DOS reference.

Many manufacturers include in the package other manuals that look similar to the DOS reference manual and contain information specific to the computer model or its auxiliary software. The topics in these specialty manuals are not covered in this book, so keep those additional manuals at hand for reference.

The Bootable Operating System Disk

Bootable DOS disks, like the DOS package, are physical products. The disks contain specific DOS operating files, which contain the computer-level instructions that provide the functional aspects of DOS. The PC doesn't have these computer-level functions built in. The instructions are logical—not physical. Because a physical definition is incomplete, the role of the instructions and the operation must be viewed conceptually.

Each time the PC is turned on, it must restart itself by importing the DOS instructions from the DOS system files on the PC's start-up disk to the PC's working memory. The PC then is ready to run software.

Disks must be prepared by DOS before they can be used. Only disks prepared with the DOS system files can start the PC. Disks that include DOS system files are DOS boot disks. Many people refer to a bootable disk as DOS.

Don't use the master DOS disks for everyday work. The manufacturers intended for you to make copies of these master disks; the copies then can be used. Store your masters in a safe place. You should have at least one good (tested) set of working DOS floppies even if the computer has a hard disk that contains the DOS files.

With versions of DOS before 4.0, you can use the DOS command DISKCOPY to duplicate and prepare working copies of the packaged DOS disks. With versions after 4.0, you can use the Select program to install DOS on a hard disk and a floppy disk. The Select program runs when you start the PC with the package's Install disk. The Install program eliminates the need to use DISKCOPY by guiding you through the creation of DOS working disks.

Even if DOS is installed on your hard disk, keep on hand floppy-based copies of the DOS disks. You may need them if your hardware experiences problems.

The System Prompt

A certain company's procedure book includes the following instructions for downloading a file from the mainframe computer: "When the file is downloaded, exit to DOS and start the translation program." In this context, DOS has another meaning. Many users think they are in DOS when they see the system prompt. Being in DOS is the same as being at the operating system level.

Many applications programs provide messages that tell you they are `Returning to DOS`, `Exiting after a fatal error to DOS`, or `Temporarily invoking DOS`. These messages mean that the program is turning control over to COMMAND.COM, which then displays the system prompt on-screen. You recognize the system prompt as `A>` or `C>` or perhaps other text followed by the `>` symbol. COMMAND.COM is the DOS program that processes the commands you issue.

COMMAND.COM is an important part of DOS. Many PC users think COMMAND.COM is the essence of DOS because it is so visible and because they equate issuing commands with performing DOS-level, PC-management work. Chapter 3 discusses COMMAND.COM more fully, and Part II of this book is devoted to the DOS commands users most often issue. Issuing commands is only a part of using DOS. Many of the commands you issue at the DOS prompt work with the file system. Chapter 2 provides an inside view of the file system that makes using disk- and file-related DOS commands more meaningful.

Cue:
COMMAND.COM is the most visible part of DOS.

The Hidden Core of DOS

An instructor of C-language programming for the PC tells his students: "You can use the INT86( ) function to get directly at DOS." In the context of the instructor's statement, DOS is the collection of services that DOS offers in the form of built-in groups of related instructions or software routines. These routines provide the core of the services DOS provides to your applications programs. The extensive file-system management provided by DOS, for example, is made up of these routines. Programmers can access these software routines to perform a variety of internal operations with the PC.

Cue:
Programmers can access the internal operations of DOS.

These functions are common and repetitive actions that operating system designers have included in DOS to make life easier (and programs more uniform) for PC programmers. DOS commands rely on these service routines to do standard low-level computer work. Most computer languages provide built-in access to DOS service routines so that a programmer (or a program) doesn't see the details of how DOS works with the PC. With the interface to DOS service built-in, computer languages and the programs they produce use DOS uniformly.

The programming aspects of DOS often are as invisible to DOS users as interaction with COMMAND.COM is obvious. If you ask an assembly-language programmer to tell you about DOS, however, you may hear about interrupts, BIOS services, registers, file handles, returns, and other aspects of working with the DOS core.

Fortunately, you do not have to know about these programming concerns to operate the PC. Knowing what goes on at the program level, however, may give you more insight into how a DOS command or the word processor works. Programming at the DOS level is fascinating and rewarding to many, but this book does not attempt to teach you the programming aspects of DOS. To find out more about programming at the DOS level, refer to one of the books published by Que Corporation on this topic: *DOS Programmer's Reference*, 2nd Edition by Terry Dettman or *Using Assembly Language* by Allen Wyatt.

Most DOS users generally are uninformed about programming, and they do well. As your DOS skills increase, however, you may find that having a general notion of programming enables you to become a more self-reliant PC user.

The Configuration Capability of DOS

The error-correction instructions in a popular spreadsheet manual say, "If the message `Too many open files` appears, you may need to make adjustments in DOS." In this example, the spreadsheet-software manual is interpreting DOS to mean "the configuration aspects of DOS." Although most computers that use MS-DOS as an operating system are highly compatible with each other, individual aspects of each PC's hardware and software components can vary.

Some operating systems make configuration decisions for you. Fortunately, DOS is flexible, and many of the DOS parameters are under your control.

Cue:
The flexibility of DOS enables you to tune the PC to your needs.

The flexibility of DOS enables you to tune the system to your needs. The configuration aspects of DOS also keep you from being locked into a rigid PC design. You need not use a parallel printer when a serial printer serves your purposes just as well. As you learn in Chapters 15 and 16, the configuration aspects of DOS include many variables, ranging from the amount of memory in your PC to the country's character set you use.

Many DOS users overlook the configuration capabilities of DOS because someone else (usually the dealer) set up the PC for them. Others overlook the capabilities because the PC seems to work well as it is. As software becomes more complex and hardware continues to make technical strides, however, the ability to use these capabilities becomes increasingly important in fine-tuning the PC for maximum efficiency.

Examining the Layers of DOS

DOS is designed in modular parts that cooperate with other software and hardware parts to produce the effect called computing. Between the fundamental electrical signals that make the hardware function and the user-friendly screens of the applications programs, the parts divide into layers of responsibility. No one layer is totally responsible for the job of computing: not the program, not DOS, and not the hardware that sits on your desk.

As a PC user, you see the surface layer of the PC as the program that prepares a memo or budget spreadsheet. When you are at the system prompt or using the DOS Shell to do DOS work, you can get the feeling that you are in a lower layer of the PC where you manipulate directories and files.

Occasionally, you catch a glimpse of lower layers of responsibility. In these glimpses, you see a more hidden layer of DOS. You see system information or error messages reporting lost clusters in a file allocation table or memory parity errors. These messages originate from hidden layers of the system that DOS passes to the surface for you to see. The hidden layers are responsible for the fundamental tasks that comprise the low-level support system of the computer.

The DOS layers work on the surface with you and your programs as well as with a layer of low-level support routines permanently programmed into the PC. To understand this concept of layers and how DOS fits in, think of the hardware as the core or innermost level of the working PC system. The circular diagram in figure 1.2 helps you follow the levels outward.

When IBM designed the IBM PC, hardware designers integrated other manufacturers' hardware components into a personal computer design specification. This hardware design was the core of a working computer. The core of the circle in figure 1.2 represents the hardware as the core of a working PC.

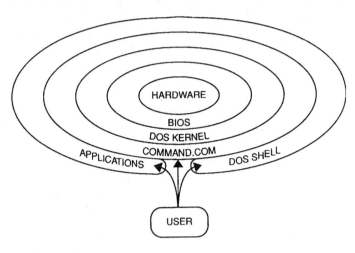

Fig. 1.2. The modular layers of a working PC.

With a core hardware design specified, IBM designed the low-level BIOS (Basic Input/Output System) software routines. The BIOS routines handle the specifics of the hardware at a detailed level. An operation as seemingly simple as translating a key press from the keyboard is a complicated elemental task. The BIOS carries out this complicated task and many others. Because it must work directly with the PC's hardware, the BIOS is built directly upon the hardware's requirements and capabilities. The BIOS is modular because it can be adapted to changing hardware designs and still provide the same elemental task. The BIOS is a modular layer of a working computer that connects to the hardware and acts as a basis for the DOS kernel layer.

Cue:
The DOS kernel is the core of the DOS software.

The next level of the circle is the DOS kernel, which is the core of the DOS software. In a working PC, the kernel is insulated from the hardware by the BIOS. The kernel relies on the elemental services of the BIOS layer to access the features of the hardware. The kernel is modular because it can evolve into higher level services such as device redirection. The BIOS, on which the kernel is built, remains relatively unchanged. Figure 1.2 shows the DOS kernel layer connecting to the BIOS layer and providing a foundation for COMMAND.COM.

COMMAND.COM, the DOS command processor, acts as a module of DOS. COMMAND.COM is best known for providing a user-interactive interface to commands. COMMAND.COM provides a means for entering commands and communicating with the DOS kernel. Because it protects the user from dealing directly with the kernel, COMMAND.COM often is called a *shell*. Figure 1.2 shows the COMMAND.COM layer of a working computer built upon the DOS kernel.

Other programs can be written that serve the same purpose as COMMAND.COM—accepting user commands and instructing the kernel to take the appropriate action. Any such program that serves as an interface between the user and the kernel can properly be called a shell. Many such programs have been written, including the DOS Shell, which was introduced in Version 4. (See Chapter 5 for more information on the DOS Shell.)

The Hardware

PC hardware is a collection of electronic and electro-mechanical components. Some components operate at the system level, and others operate at the peripheral level. System-level components are integral to the PC's computing architecture. The CPU (Central Processing Unit) is an example of a system-level component. System memory, control components, and circuits are other examples. System-level hardware in IBM PC, PC AT, PS/2, and compatible computers have CPUs that belong to the Intel 8086 microprocessor family.

The number of memory locations or addresses that an 8086 (or its counterpart, an 8088) can directly access is 1M (1,048,576 locations). DOS uses up to 640K (655,360) of these addresses for executing programs and reserves the remaining 384K for accessing the operating system. Computers with the more advanced 80286 microprocessor used in the IBM PC AT can address more memory than those with an 8086 or 8088 microprocessor. The 80386 and 80486 microprocessors have even greater addressing ranges. Even on a PC with one of these advanced microprocessors, DOS uses the 1M address range to ensure that it can be used with any member of the 8086 family of microprocessors.

Having an 8086 microprocessor is the common hardware characteristic of all DOS-based PCs. In other respects, the system-level hardware of compatible computers can vary considerably. Even with this variation, system-level hardware provides a uniform function.

Peripheral hardware, which connects to the system hardware, provides input and accepts output. Disk drives, keyboards, modems, mice, display terminals, and printers are types of peripheral hardware. Peripherals provide input for computing and display the output.

Although the system-level hardware computes, it needs input from the outside world for the computing to be useful. Even a simple keyboard entry is an input for computation. When a computational result is passed from the system hardware, the peripheral hardware outputs the result. If the result is intended to be visual, the peripheral hardware displays the result on a printed report or on-screen.

Hardware deals with data at the *binary* or two-state level, and the programs the hardware understands are binary, machine-level instructions. Binary data is ideal for electrical components because the two binary states can be represented by the presence and absence of a voltage. By understanding the interpretation of patterns of on-and-off binary states, computer hardware components can communicate meaningful information electrically. The various display adapters, such as the CGA, EGA, VGA, Hercules, and MDA, require specific binary instructions to produce output through a display's CRT (Cathode Ray Tube).

Many other peripheral-hardware components and their associated controlling circuitry add to the number of distinct ways that peripheral-controlling software must be configured. At the hardware layer, the electronic specifics of the components can vary from PC to PC. DOS cannot be responsible for all of these specifics, so it relies on an intervening layer to handle hardware specifics.

PCs can have floppy and hard disk drives. Within drive types, a wide variety of configurations can exist. The drives' electronic controllers may follow varying standards and require various control programs for proper operation.

The Basic Input/Output System

The logic that drives and controls the peripheral hardware is the *Basic Input/Output System*, or *BIOS*, which is a set of low-level, programmed routines. The BIOS deals with hardware specifics. BIOS routines are well-defined, binary-program segments that use the peripheral hardware's features and provide a uniform access to hardware functions. Higher level programs can be built on these BIOS functions. In fact, DOS is built on these BIOS functions. BIOS routines provide an interface between the hardware and programs such as DOS. This interface frees DOS from the need to know exactly how to use the hardware at the binary level.

Cue:
BIOS routines reside in permanent ROM.

BIOS routines reside in permanent *ROM (Read Only Memory)*, which is located at predetermined addresses within the address range of the CPU. Most ROM is located on the PC's main system circuit board, but some ROM also can be located on adapter boards plugged into the PC's expansion connectors. DOS supplements the ROM BIOS with extensions, corrections, and additions during the boot process. These extensions are in a hidden file on a DOS disk and are loaded during the boot process.

After they are loaded, the BIOS extensions are located in reserved address areas of the system's *RAM (Random Access Memory)*. Each version of DOS can include new BIOS extensions to incorporate new hardware or features. The BIOS routines provide DOS with a foundation of elemental operating functions that handle hardware-specific details at the machine level. With machine-level details provided by the BIOS, DOS can concentrate on providing higher level operating system services.

The DOS Kernel

The DOS layer of the PC system is a collection of program routines and data tables that provides higher level programs, such as applications programs, with standardized and unified PC-operating services. This functional nucleus is the *DOS kernel*. The kernel resides as a file on the DOS boot disk and is read into reserved areas of RAM during system booting. This hidden file usually is named IBMDOS.COM or MSDOS.SYS. You do not see the DOS kernel in action; it does its job behind the scenes. The kernel manages the file system, handles character input and output, oversees memory allocation, provides basic networking functions, and performs other operating system tasks. At its lowest level, the DOS kernel calls on the services of the BIOS layer where the kernel uses the BIOS routines as building blocks to supply operating system services to programs. To access the services of the kernel to copy a file or make a directory, you must go through the next outer layer, COMMAND.COM.

The Command Processor (COMMAND.COM)

COMMAND.COM, the command processor program, is a layer of services that rides above the DOS kernel. COMMAND.COM provides a standard set of commands that gives users access to file-management, device-management, configuration, and miscellaneous functions, such as maintaining and verifying the time and date. COMMAND.COM deals with user commands as a separate module from the kernel and is the kernel's command-interpreting shell. You can recognize this layer of a working computer by the > prompt.

The executable COMMAND.COM file loads during the boot process and accepts commands from the user. COMMAND.COM can execute internal DOS commands, load external DOS commands from program files, and execute the external commands. COMMAND.COM loads and executes DOS batch files and applications programs and provides the DOS house-keeping utilities and commands. Chapter 3 discusses COMMAND.COM in more detail and explains other functions of this layer of the system. Part II of this book discusses the internal and external DOS commands. The command reference section of this book includes the use and syntax of all the standard DOS commands.

The DOS Shell

DOS 4.0 introduced a keyboard- or mouse-driven graphical user interface that provides many of the functions of the command processor but with a point-and-shoot approach. This windowed graphical user interface is the DOS Shell. The DOS Shell does not replace COMMAND.COM; instead, it provides a substitute for typing commands to COMMAND.COM.

Reminder:
Include the DOSSHELL command in your AUTOEXEC.BAT file.

The DOS Shell isn't the same shell used to describe COMMAND.COM. The DOS Shell is a program that can be loaded and executed like other programs and is activated by the DOSSHELL command. The program is not loaded during the boot process, however, unless you include the DOSSHELL command in your AUTOEXEC.BAT file. You need not know how to issue DOS commands at the system prompt to use the DOS Shell. The program provides a visual shell that displays DOS-related commands in its windows and enables the user to pick a desired action. Chapter 5 provides a detailed look at the DOS Shell.

The Applications Programs

The applications programs layer is the highest level of the PC system. Applications programs include word processors, spreadsheets, database managers, games, and others. You use many of the programs for daily computer tasks. Applications programs are written in programming languages such as C, Pascal, BASIC, and Assembler. Programming languages using DOS rely on the services provided by COMMAND.COM and the DOS kernel to provide repetitive file-and-device services and critical-error handling.

Applications programs usually use the DOS kernel interface to access lower layers of the computer. These programs call on DOS to display characters on-screen, access the correct file, and manage the PC's memory resource. DOS, in turn, calls on the BIOS for assistance. Some programs misbehave and call BIOS services or access hardware directly. Bypassing the uniform platform provided by DOS may cause these programs to operate incorrectly (or not at all) on PCs that have some hardware or BIOS variance.

The main reason you use the PC is to run applications programs. These programs seem independent and diverse when they are running. However, they are only a visible, outside layer of the whole operation. Behind the scenes, the applications programs use DOS and the deeper layers of the PC.

Chapter Summary

In this chapter, you learned about the role of DOS. Following are the key points to remember:

- DOS is an acronym for Disk Operating System. Many computer operating systems use DOS in their names.

- MS-DOS is the name of an operating system for IBM PCs and close compatibles. To most PC users, DOS means MS-DOS.

- When PC users use the term DOS, they may be referring to only one contextual part of the whole of DOS.

- DOS works with the Intel 8086 family of microprocessors.

- A working PC can be viewed as consisting of cooperative layers.

- The core of a working PC is the system and peripheral hardware.

- The BIOS layer of a PC is contained in permanent ROM, which works with the hardware and provides a foundation of services for DOS.

- The DOS kernel layer of a working PC is located in RAM and provides the functional nucleus of an operating system.

- COMMAND.COM executes DOS commands and relies on the kernel for operating system services.

- The DOS Shell program available with DOS Version 4.0 provides a windowed interface that enables the user to execute DOS commands by selecting an item from a menu.

- Applications programs rely on lower layers of the working PC to provide a uniform platform of control and support.

In the next chapter, you get a close-up view of the DOS file system. You examine the hardware, see how DOS does its file bookkeeping, and gain a fresh perspective on hierarchical directories.

Understanding the DOS File System

One of the primary roles of a disk operating system is to provide the service of storing and retrieving data to and from disks. Providing this service involves many factors. The operating system must not only oversee the many technical details of the disk hardware but also provide a framework of organization for file storage on disks. This framework includes the way the operating system shows you what is stored and where it is stored.

The operating system must have an internal bookkeeping system to account for unused disk space as well as the contents of used disk space. The operating system should offer a full complement of commands that enable you to manage all aspects of data storage, ranging from disk preparation to doing safety backups. Finally, the disk operating system should provide these services without your needing to know the internal details of the operation.

You shouldn't be burdened with technical details just to save a memo produced during a session with your word processor. Your word processor also should not have to supervise elemental disk-output tasks to save that memo. A disk operating system assumes responsibility for getting data, in the form of files, to and from a disk. The operating system determines how the data is organized on disk and provides commands for manipulating the data. A disk on which this organization has been imposed is a *file system*. Disk hardware and file commands are linked closely to this file system. These fundamental disk operations are discussed in this chapter. The disk and file commands are discussed in Part II of this book.

Since its introduction, DOS's file system has evolved from simple to more complex (and more versatile). DOS commands that give users access to disk services also have evolved. Commands have been added to each new version of DOS; most current disk-oriented commands take parameters not available as a part of the original command.

When working with files, many DOS users rely on the older, simpler, and more familiar forms of commands; some avoid learning new commands. These users don't take advantage of the full complement of commands DOS provides for dealing with disks, drives, directories, files, and file-like devices. People are understandably reluctant to master new commands when the techniques they already know are sufficient to get the job done. Perhaps they don't fully understand how DOS manages the file system and the disks. After you gain a thorough understanding of the DOS file system, DOS commands that once seemed cryptic become more useful.

This chapter does not tell you how to use the disk, file, and directory commands; you do not need to memorize its content. Rather, this chapter is a layperson's guide to understanding the DOS file system. First, you examine files and the disk drives that store them. You learn about the different disk formats used by DOS. Finally, you get an inside look at the way DOS manages file allocation, directory entry, and partitions. By the end of the chapter, you should feel confident about how DOS commands define and manage the file system and its related support components. While you use these commands, you should develop greater insight into the hidden DOS kernel layer discussed in Chapter 1.

Examining Files and File Systems

Cue:
A file system is an organized collection of files.

A file system is an organized collection of files. As a user, you see the DOS file system at work in the files you organize into directories and subdirectories on your disks. Each file is a named group of data that DOS appears to manipulate as one continuous unit. Behind the scenes, however, DOS uses a structured management strategy whose complexity is hidden from you. The DOS file system reflects this strategy. A file system includes the files, the internal tables that record the file organization, and the built-in rules that ensure the consistency of file organization.

Understanding Files

A *file* is a variable-length collection of related information referenced by a name. In a concrete sense, you can think of a file cabinet full of file folders, each with a name on the tab. The cabinet and the individual pieces of paper in the folders are not files. Only the named collection in one folder is considered a file (see fig. 2.1).

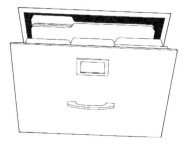

Fig. 2.1. *A file represented as a collection of related pieces of paper in one folder.*

In a computer setting, a file can contain data (information), programs (instructions that guide computer tasks), or both. A file can exist on a disk, on magnetic tape, on punch cards, and even in a computer's memory. Files are made up of elements of data or programs. The individual elements can be stored as patterns of holes in a paper tape, as patterns of magnetic fields on the surface of a disk, or in many other ways. Physical storage techniques for files vary greatly, but in all likelihood, when you reach for some stored files, you reach for a disk. Disks are the predominant means of data storage for DOS.

DOS uses file names to identify files. Full file names consist of up to eight characters of a name prefix followed by an optional period character (.) and up to three optional characters of suffix or extension. The full file name often is referred to as the *file name plus extension*.

The prefix or root of a file name usually describes the contents of the file. Extensions, on the other hand, traditionally are used to describe the type of file. Suppose, for example, that you want to use your word processor to write a memo to a Mr. Duncan. DUNCAN.MEM is a good name for this memo file. The extension DOC commonly is used for word processing document files. A monthly policy statement may be named JAN.DOC. DOS enables you to use a wide variety of full file names.

You can develop your own file-naming conventions as long as you stay within the character limits imposed by DOS. Particular extensions, however, are especially convenient in some situations. For example, many word processors assume that document file names end in DOC unless specifically told otherwise. If such a word processor is told to find a file called MEMO, the program actually looks for MEMO.DOC. Most spreadsheets and databases have similar defaults.

DOS imposes no structure on the contents of a file. To DOS, a file is a stream of binary information. Because DOS has no way of knowing whether a file is a spreadsheet or memo produced by a word processor, the operating system relies on applications programs to apply structure to the contents of files.

Understanding the File System

DOS is an operating system for personal computers, and personal computers are designed for ordinary people. Ordinary users want to use the computer as a tool to make their jobs easier. The computer should enable the user to focus on the user's work; the computer should not become the object of the user's work.

DOS provides an operating environment that is easy to use for the novice and powerful and versatile enough for the experienced user. To attain this versatility, the internal structure of the file system is more complex than its surface appearance. This versatility is due to the internal structure of the file system, which is more complex than it seems. In this chapter, you see below the surface of the DOS file system.

Cue:
Each disk for-matted by DOS has its own file system.

In the strictest sense, each disk formatted by DOS has its own file system. Because DOS commands use a drive-name specifier (such as A:, B:, C:, and so on), you can have the benefit of a multidisk file system without the headache. For example, some multidisk file systems such as UNIX require you to have a much greater understanding of the file system and require you to use special commands to attach an additional disk's file system to the main file system. DOS can use all available disk drives without requiring you to take any specific action, saving you time and the responsibility of remembering to perform these commands.

All disks prepared by DOS are given the essential ingredients for their own independent file system. This disk independence enables DOS to manage a PC with one disk or many disks. By incorporating named disk drives, DOS can effectively use their file systems as one larger file system.

By hiding the internal complexity of the file system from the user, DOS enables a beginner to use the basic file commands. The COPY command, for example, completely hides the complexity of disk input and output; whereas the DIR command completely hides the way DOS stores files on a disk. In fact, most DOS commands free the user from the need to know what is going on below the user-friendly surface. Just as you don't need to know how the Bendix enables the starter gear to engage the flywheel to start your car, you don't need to know DOS bookkeeping techniques to copy a disk or a file.

Cue:
Many DOS commands hide the internal complexity of the file system from the user.

Not every DOS command, however, hides all the details and complexity of DOS. One example is the CHKDSK command, which reports problems with the tables that DOS uses internally to store important file information. After finding a problem, CHKDSK asks the user to decide whether to alter the tables. Some of the complexities of the file system's details are presented by CHKDSK on-screen, as in the following message:

```
237 lost allocation units found in 29 chains.
Convert lost chains to files (Y/N)?
```

or

```
Cannot recover . . . entry,
Entry has a bad link.
```

Without some knowledge of what CHKDSK is reporting, you cannot give CHKDSK an informed response.

Examining Disks and Drives

Storing data in files requires a physical medium on which to record the files' data along with bookkeeping information maintained by DOS. Disks are the PC designers' file-storage medium of choice. Disks, removable and fixed, have a virtual monopoly on file storage in PCs. Tape and CD ROM (Compact Disk Read-Only Memory) finish a distant second and third. Disk drives, DOS's warehouse for file storage, are convenient, reliable, reusable, and provide rapid access to files. Because disks are the primary storage media for files, you need to understand how disks perform this storage job.

Cue:
Disks have a virtual monopoly on file storage in PCs.

Understanding the Disk's Magnetic Storage Technique

Disk drives are electro-mechanical components that record and play back data, using the magnetic surfaces of a disk. Normally, the data is in the form of a file. During the recording or *writing* of a file, an electronic circuit translates the PC's electrical data into a series of magnetic fields. These magnetic fields are mirrored (weakly) by the oxide coating of the disk in the drive. In effect, the original data is magnetically imprinted on a disk.

Caution:
Magnetic fields, such as those produced by motors, magnetic paper-clip holders, ringing telephones, and televisions, can ruin a disk.

During the playback or *reading* of data from the disk's surface, an electronic circuit translates the magnetic fields back into electrical signals, and the data is again in electrical form. The disk's original magnetic imprint is not destroyed by the reading operation. Under normal use, the imprint is changed only by recording over it, a process called *overwriting* the disk. The recorded magnetic imprint on the disk is resistant to weakening and will last for years. Other magnetic fields, however, such as those produced by motors, magnetic paper-clip holders, ringing telephones, and televisions, can weaken the magnetic imprint on a disk, quickly rendering a disk unreadable.

Magnetic recording of electrical signals is not new technology. Computer data and programs are recorded on disk in much the same way that music information is recorded on cassette tapes. In both cases, tiny particles of magnetic material are magnetized in certain ways. Later the information can be retrieved by a device (a *head*) that detects magnetism and transforms it back into an electrical signal.

Although the techniques of recording on disk and tape are similar, the mechanical equipment that moves disks and tapes is quite different. The expected quality of operation is different. A cassette player retrieves music imperfectly at best, enabling small errors to creep in. In good cassette decks, however, these errors are so small that most people don't notice them, and the music, even with the errors, is considered acceptable.

The situation with computers, however, is quite different. No errors are acceptable. One misread bit can change the meaning of data or the actions performed by a program. A computer disk or tape drive must be able to retrieve billions of bits of data without an error.

Although designers of cassette tape recorders can be satisfied with high-fidelity music reproduction from the tape, disk and disk drive designers must strive for perfect data reproduction from computer disks. One bad spot on a disk can result in a `General Failure error reading drive A:` message and the unrecoverable loss of all data on a disk.

Understanding Disk Drives

Disk drives are electro-mechanical computer components. Their mechanical parts and electrical circuits are complex. Although disk drives are parts of PC systems, the drives are machines in their own right. DOS relies on the driver programs of the BIOS to signal a drive's electronic circuitry to control the actions of the drive's mechanical components.

All disk drives have in common certain components: read/write heads, head positioning mechanisms, and disk spinning motors. Disk drives all record on disks. Some disks are removable; some are built into the drive. Fixed disks and removable disks are spun on a center spindle in the disk drive.

Many of today's PCs have fixed disks and removable disks installed in their system units. DOS's BIOS extensions provide for both types of disks. In addition to their shared features, fixed and removable disk drives have some important distinctions. If you know what these differences are, you can better understand the way each drive type operates in your system.

Hard Disk Drives

Drives with built-in disks are called *fixed disk drives* or, because their disks are made of a hard, rigid metal, *hard disk drives*. These names often are shortened to *fixed disk* or *hard disk*. Many users refer to hard disks as *Winchester* disks. (The name Winchester is derived from an IBM code name for the sealed disk-drive technology developed by IBM.) In this book, the term *hard disk* is used to describe the built-in, fixed disk drive.

Figure 2.2 shows a cut-away view of a typical hard disk. The circular platters in the figure are the drive's magnetic disks. A head-positioning arm holds the read/write heads above and below each surface of each platter. When the drive leaves the factory, the inner components are not open; the drive is sealed closed.

A hard disk drive can contain more than one hard disk or *platter*. Multiple platters are arranged in a stack, with space between the individual platters.

The advantages of hard disks are quick operation, high reliability, and large storage capacities. The disadvantage of hard disks is that because the hard disk's platters cannot be removed, data stored on the disk is tied to the PC in which the drive is installed. Hard disks are installed in a PC with mounting hardware and interconnecting power and data cables. To move an entire hard disk to another computer just to use the hard disk's data is

Cue:
Drives with built-in disks are called hard disk drives.

impractical. When you need to move data between the hard disks of two computers, you can use DOS's XCOPY command, or the BACKUP and RESTORE commands.

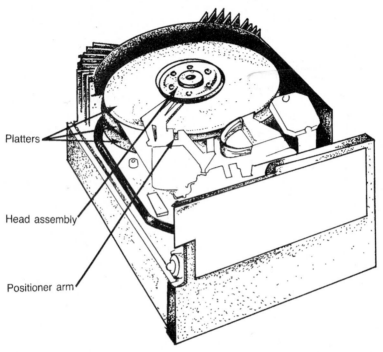

***Fig. 2.2.** An inside view of the main components of a hard disk.*

Floppy Disk Drives

In a PC system, the floppy disk drive offsets the disadvantage of tying data to the hard disk. By far the most common class of removable disk is the *floppy* disk. Floppy disks are protected by a permanent jacket that covers the flexible mylar disk. The first floppy disks were 8 inches in diameter. By today's standards, the early 8-inch floppy disks didn't store much data, considering their size. Some 8-inch floppies could store only 320K of data.

Some early microcomputers used these 8-inch floppies as their standard. For three or four years, the pioneering microcomputer makers offered 8-inch floppy drives as the alternative to such primitive off-line file storage as paper tape and cassette recording.

Because of its size, a smaller version of the 8-inch floppy—the 5 1/4-inch *minifloppy*—quickly became the PC designers' floppy of choice. The 3 1/2-inch *microfloppy* is yet another departure from its larger, older cousins; this type of disk incorporates a rigid plastic case (its jacket) as a protective cover. The 3 1/2-inch mylar circular medium inside a microfloppy disk is flexible like the media in 8-inch and 5 1/4-inch floppies.

Cue:
A 5 1/4-inch disk is a mini-floppy; a 3 1/2-inch disk is a microfloppy.

Figure 2.3 shows a microfloppy disk being inserted into a drive. You cannot interchange disks between different size (diameter) classes of floppy drives.

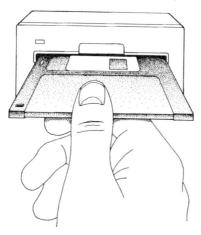

Fig. 2.3. Inserting a microfloppy (3 1/2-inch) disk into a drive.

Officially, the two smaller sizes of floppy disks are *diskettes*; the 8-inch version is a *disk*. The term *floppy disk* (or just *floppy*) refers to any lower capacity disk that you can remove from your PC's drive. *Minifloppy* always refers to 5 1/4-inch floppy disks; *microfloppy* always refers to 3 1/2-inch floppy disks. The term *disk* commonly is used to mean any floppy or hard disk when the disk type is clear in context. (This book uses the term floppy disk, rather than floppy diskette.)

Understanding the Dynamics of the Disk Drive

Disk drives are constructed from several electronic components, and these components are discussed in the following sections.

Disk Drive Heads

Cue:
*Disk heads
convert magnetic
energy to
electrical data.*

Disk drives use one or more record/pickup or read/write *heads*. The heads of a disk drive are like the pickup cartridge of a phonograph. The cartridge picks-up vibrations from the stylus riding in the track and converts them to electrical energy. Disk heads convert magnetic energy to electrical data. Although several heads can be used in a disk drive, the electronics of the disk drive accept data from one head at a time.

Disk drive heads come in different shapes. Figure 2.4 illustrates two common head configurations. The heads are held in position by flexible metal head-holder assemblies. A set of wires carrying electrical signals connects to the head and passes through the head-holder assembly, where the set connects to a flexible ribbon cable. The ribbon cable absorbs wire movements when the head assembly moves. The hard disk head assembly is low in mass to allow for greater start-stop control during high-speed head positioning.

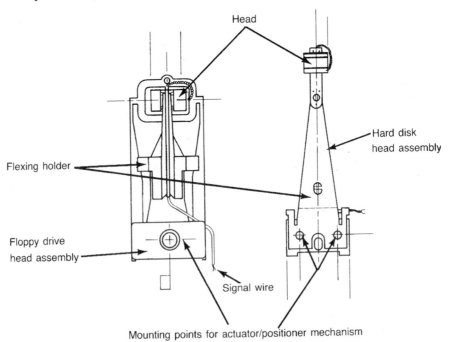

Fig. 2.4. Typical disk drive head assemblies.

On most floppy disks, data is recorded by a head on each of the disk's two sides or surfaces. Floppy drives that use a head on each side of the floppy disk are called *double-sided* drives. Hard disk drives can accommodate more than one double-sided platter because the drives incorporate heads on both sides of each platter. Using both sides of a disk or platter doubles its capacity. Incorporating multiple platters in a hard disk further multiplies its capacity by the number of heads used.

Disk Tracks

Regardless of the type of disk drive, all disks spin on a center axis, like records spinning on a phonograph. A floppy disk spins at 360 revolutions per minute. The rotational speed of a hard disk is 10 times higher (approximately 3,600 RPM). The heads, which are positioned above the spinning surface of the disk, are held and moved in distinct steps by an actuator arm and head positioning. The heads of a floppy disk drive touch the medium's surface; the heads of a hard disk ride above the surface of the disk platter on a cushion of air. At each step position, the alignment of the head and the spinning disk produces a circular track.

The track is not a physical track like the groove in a record, but rather a ring of magnetically recorded data. Unlike the phonograph, which plays a record's contents by following a single, spiraling track, the disk drive steps from track to track to retrieve data. Figure 2.5 gives an idea of the position of the tracks. Notice that the tracks are not depicted as a spiral. All the tracks on disk's surface are perfect concentric circles. The number of concentric tracks available on the surface of one disk is determined by the mechanical movements of the head positioning device. The smaller the stepping distance, the tighter the track pattern, and consequently, the greater the number of tracks.

Cue:
All the tracks on a disk's surface are perfect concentric circles.

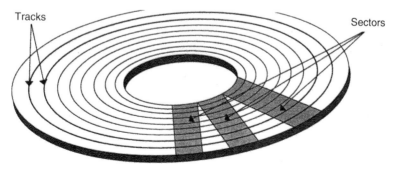

Fig. 2.5. Concentric tracks on a disk's surface.

Cylinders

A disk drive's multiple heads are affixed to one positioning mechanism. When one head moves one track on its side of a platter (or floppy), the other heads all move one track on the respective sides of their respective platters. Picture a top head riding over track 10 of side one of a platter while the bottom head is riding under track 10 of side two. If the disk has more than one platter, all the heads of that disk are positioned on track 10 of their associated side and platter. This conceptual alignment of heads on the same track position on different sides (and platters) of the same disk is called a *cylinder* (see fig. 2.6).

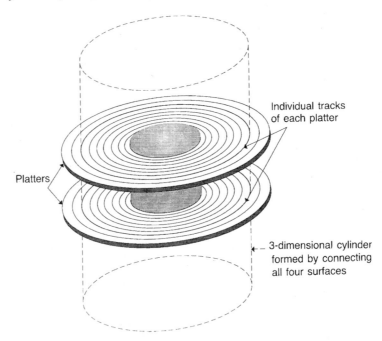

Fig. 2.6. A cylinder on two disk platters.

Because only one head can be active at one time, the drive must activate all of its heads in sequence to write (or read) all tracks at the cylinder position. To fill a cylinder, a 4-head drive writes a track with head 1; then head 2; then head 3; and finally head 4. The head positioning moves one cylinder, and the sequence repeats.

Seek Time

The time a drive takes to move the heads from one cylinder to another cylinder is the drive's *seek time*. Hard disk drives have low seek times because they can move the heads quickly from one cylinder to another. The amount of time a hard disk requires, on average, to seek to a cylinder often is used as a measure of its speed. Slower disks may require 65 milliseconds; faster disks may seek in 10 milliseconds. Most disks fall between these numbers, with 18 to 25 milliseconds being common for good disks. The seek times of floppy disk drives can be more than 10 times slower than the seek time of a slow hard disk.

Seek time is an important measure of disk drive performance. Often, the heads must seek several nonadjacent cylinders to collect the parts of a file. You may have noticed that many applications programs seem sluggish when they use a floppy for file operations but seem quite speedy when they use a hard disk. Seek time, rotational speed, and the nature of the drive's interfacing electronics affect a drive's relative access-time performance.

Disk Drive Alignment

Floppy disks do not leave the manufacturer with their tracks (or cylinders) identified. The disk drive is responsible for putting the data in tracks, but the disk drive has no grooves or markings to use as a guide for recording and locating tracks. To ensure interchangeability of floppies between different drives (of the same type), the drives must be aligned to a standard.

To achieve this standardization, technicians use alignment disks, which contain carefully positioned tracks. With the alignment disk in the drive, the technician adjusts (mechanically or electrically) the positioning mechanism of the drive until the heads are one-to-one with the special tracks of the alignment disk. Drives are designed so that once aligned, they resist drifting out of alignment. A drive that is out of alignment lays down tracks of data on a new disk and reads them back with no error. The alignment problem usually becomes apparent when a disk from an improperly aligned drive is placed in another drive. When this different drive attempts to read the disk, heads do not align to track positions, and read errors may result.

Applying Drive Dynamics to Data Storage

Disk drives have undergone significant evolution since the IBM PC was introduced. Storage capacities have increased, and new technologies have been developed. However, DOS still organizes information in much the same way as it has since the introduction of MS-DOS 2.0. Regardless of the underlying dynamics of the disk, DOS uses a consistent organization for all disks. As you work with the computer, you see all disks as file systems. The higher levels of DOS provide this uniform organization.

Track Density

Getting more storage capacity from a disk is useful. One way to get more capacity from the same disk size is to put the tracks closer together so that the disk has more tracks or cylinders. With more tracks, the disk can hold more data. Why not, then, dramatically increase the number of tracks on the disk's surface? The number of tracks can be increased, but there are limits.

To understand how the drive head records information as a track on the disk's surface, picture the drive's recording head as a tiny spray-painting nozzle whose paint is a spray of magnetic energy. As the disk spins, the spray nozzle directs a narrow stream of paint onto the surface of the wheel.

After the wheel has turned one complete revolution and the spray nozzle turns off, a perfect circle has been painted on the wheel's surface. It is in this manner that the drive's head(s) magnetically alter the disk's surface. The nozzle is stepped-in a small amount toward the wheel's center, and the spraying process is repeated. By continuing the step-in-and-paint process, the wheel eventually will have its surface completely painted with concentric circles. Likewise, a disk will have its available surface divided into distinct data tracks.

To double the number of rings on the wheel's surface, you can repeat the entire operation of painting and stepping to the center of the wheel. You can step the paint nozzle toward the center by one half the distance per step that you used the first time. The process includes twice as many steps and results in twice as many painted rings. A analogous technique can be used with disks; by reducing the step size between tracks of data on a disk, the capacity of the disk is effectively doubled. The disk becomes a double-density disk.

The number of distinct rings this capacity-increasing trick enables is limited. The rings eventually get so close together that you cannot tell where one ring ends and the next ring begins. The rings blur together and lose their individual identity. On the surface of a disk, the magnetic fields of the tracks begin to interfere with adjacent tracks. In the disk drive, you can use a head with a smaller magnetic gap designed to produce a narrower magnetic field, or you can use disks with fine-grained magnetic particles that resist magnetic bleeding. By using more precise technology, you can get more tracks on the disk. The more precise head and disk surface produces a weaker magnetic imprint that requires more electronic and mechanical alignment precision to read the weaker data tracks. Even with the additional precision, the tracks reach a point where they begin to blur together as a drive makes smaller steps between tracks.

Data Density

Unlike a constant spray of paint, however, data is not recorded in tracks as a constant stream of magnetic signals. Rather, data is written as a series of magnetic energy pulses that represent the data. During data reading, the magnetic fields created by the pulses are deciphered by the drive's electronics and reconverted into data.

When the drive is writing (recording) data, the pulses are like magnetic bursts created by the head. These bursts are registered in a track as it spins by the head. The information in a file is encoded as a series of off-and-on patterns of these magnetic pulses. If the magnetic pulses were paint, they would resemble dots. In theory, if you increase the number of pulses in a track, you increase the disk's capacity. If you want more dots, put the dots closer together. By packing two pulses into the track space that holds one, you double the capacity of a disk.

Just as spraying shorter bursts of paint produces smaller dots that can be painted closer together, so reducing the duration of each pulse enables you to pack more pulses into a track. If you reduce the space needed to hold one bit of information, you can hold more bits of information in any given space.

You are limited, however, to how tightly you can pack magnetic fields in a track before an individual field begins to blur into its neighboring fields. If the magnetic information is packed too tightly, the drive's electronics cannot read the data properly. Precision heads and special magnetic coatings help increase data density in each track, but even with these precision components, disk technology has its limits.

Disk Sectors

When a disk is blank, as it is when it comes from the factory, the disk contains no tracks. DOS has to prepare the disk to accept data; the process is called *formatting*. As the name implies, formatting puts a uniform pattern of format information in all tracks as the process steps through each cylinder of the disk. With this format information in each track, DOS can slice each track into smaller, more manageable, fixed-size component parts called *sectors*. In figure 2.7, the sectors of a floppy disk are represented as slices of the disk's surface. The figure shows the boundaries for every other sector. The concentric arcs between the indicated sectors are the disk's tracks. Notice that each track has the same number of sector boundaries (and therefore sectors) as every other track.

Fig. 2.7. A visual representation of sectors.

DOS always reads and writes data in groups of one or more sectors. Each sector contains 512 bytes. Even when a program requests that smaller amounts of data be read or written, the layer of DOS that performs the disk access must rearrange the operation to work on whole sectors. For example, if a program attempts to read 10 bytes, DOS may read a full sector, pass the desired 10 bytes to the program, and ignore the remaining 502 bytes.

Although DOS always has used 512-byte sectors, the operating system actually can use other sector sizes. However, the 512-byte sector has been used for so long that future versions of DOS probably will use the same sector size.

The number of sectors formatted into each track is tied to the data density the drive uses when it reads or writes data. The denser the recording in a track, the greater the number of sectors that can be formatted. The more tracks, the greater the number of sectors per disk.

Designers select the number of tracks and the number of sectors per track with reliability in mind. Floppy disk drives are designed with more margin for error than hard disks. Clearly, some margin for error is desirable for a drive that must ensure the mechanical alignment of each disk a user shoves in the door. Floppy disk drives must read disks that may have been stored in a place where the disk's magnetic information has been weakened. Even with the protective jacket, the magnetic-coated surfaces of many floppy disks become contaminated with smoke, dust, or finger prints. The drive must be able to tolerate some contamination on a disk and still function without numerous errors. Of course, no disk drive can avoid errors if the floppy disks it uses are abused. Drive heads cannot read through liquid spills or ball-point pen dents.

Hard disk drives have higher capacities than their floppy cousins. The higher capacity is due in large part to the precision of the drive's critical components in conjunction with the special oxides used to coat the platters magnetically. The working parts of the drive also are sealed at the factory in a way that protects the platters, head positioning devices, and heads from particles and contamination. With outside influence over these critical components sealed out, the hard disk drive can offer more tracks and sectors in the same physical space. When you consider that most hard disks have more than one platter, each capable of two-sided operation with more tracks, you can begin to understand how hard disks get their large storage capacities.

Disks as Binary Storage

You may recall that disk drives store data on disks as magnetic changes of polarity or pulses. Digital computers are designed to work with data made up of binary digits, or *bits*. Bits are the most fundamental representations of data. Computers can store and change data in two (binary) stable states: on and off. At any given moment, each data bit in a computer is on or off.

Cue:
Binary digits or bits are the representations of data in a computer.

All computer data is composed of a number of bits. Bits can be converted conveniently to magnetic pulses and stored reliably as magnetic fields on the surface of a disk. Magnetic fields have two poles: north and south. When a disk drive head cuts through the polarized magnetic fields of data on the disk, a positive or negative voltage is produced in the head's coil. The drive electronics treat this induced voltage as binary 0 or 1. Although this explanation is a simplified view of disk magnetics, you can see that the data in a magnetic field relates directly to the binary data in a computer. The coils in the head change the state of, or *transduce*, the magnetic energy to binary data through the drive's electronics.

Bytes and Disk Capacity

Computers generally store data in groups of eight bits. The eight-bit group of data is a *byte*. By design, digital computers are most efficient when they work with numbers as some power of 2. Numbers that are powers of 2 can be represented directly in a binary notation.

Computer programmers and designers apply this power-of-2 convention to the expression of a quantity of bytes. A kilobyte is 2^{10}, or 1,024 bytes, for example. 2 kilobytes = 2,048 bytes, or 2K. A megabyte, or 1M, is 1,024K. All you need to know about numbers in the power of 2 is that capacity in kilobytes or megabytes has this 1,024 multiplier rather than a 1,000 multiplier. For scaling purposes, think of 1K as approximately 1,000 bytes.

The capacity of disk drives is stated in bytes, as kilobytes or megabytes. The storage capacity of a hard disk is in the order of millions of bytes; megabyte is the usual capacity descriptor. The capacity of floppies is in the order of hundreds of thousands to just over a million bytes. Kilobyte (K) and megabyte (M) can be used as a multiplier to describe the capacity of a floppy.

The sectors in an individual disk store a fixed number of bytes of data. This fixed number can vary from operating system to operating system or even from disk to disk. In DOS, the size of the sectors on all disks is 512 bytes. 512 bytes just happens to be 1/2K, or 2^9. DOS provides for other sector sizes, but 512-byte sectors are the rule. During formatting, each cylinder is segmented into 512-byte sectors, starting with the first sector of the first track (the top head) and working to the last sector of the last track (the bottom head). Remember that a drive is more efficient if it completes all track work on each cylinder stop before moving its heads.

To find the correct location of the first sector, the disk drive needs some additional help. Remember that a blank disk has no track or sector divisions. To locate sector 1, the drive relies on an index pulse from a sensor in its circuitry. In a 5 1/4-inch floppy, the small hole you sometimes see in the disk surface helps provide this index pulse (see fig. 2.8). As the hole is rotated under a sensor, light passes through the hole to actuate a response in the sensor. This electrical response then is relayed to the drive's electronics for use as a start-of-track indicator. With this reliable indicator, the drive can begin to record information for sector 1.

Although 3 1/2-inch and hard disk drives also rely on index pulse indicators, the method of sensing isn't the same as with 5 1/4-inch drives. By detecting sector 1 of track 1, the disk drive can extract some specially coded data that helps DOS determine how to manage the disk. The one location that DOS is guaranteed to find on every disk is this first track and sector, which is always at cylinder 1, head 1, and immediately after the index pulse. When the special data is known, DOS can determine the location of any other sector on the disk.

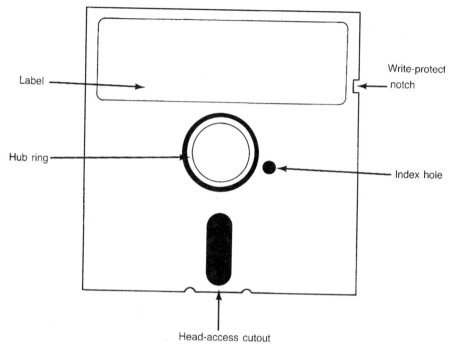

Fig. 2.8. *A 5 1/4-inch floppy disk.*

Understanding Disk Formats

Disk drives have a universal way to divide a disk's available physical space in a logical manner. The number of platters, the number of sides, the number of tracks, the number of bytes per sector, and the number of sectors per track are the specific details that enable this logical division of a disk's physical space. The specification for a disk's use of its physical space is its *format*. PCs use a variety of disk drive sizes and formats; some PCs are equipped with 5 1/4- and 3 1/2-inch floppy drives as well as hard disk drives. Most PC users and software manuals differentiate between formats by stipulating the byte-capacity figure for the desired format. Each new version of DOS has maintained support for disk formats supported by its predecessors. This support ensures that disks made with older drive formats can be used with current versions of DOS.

Floppy Drive Formats

The first DOS-supported disk drives allowed for double the number of tracks on a 5 1/4-inch floppy disk than the standard 5 1/4-inch disk formats of the time. These DOS formats were *double-density* formats. The original PC disk size and format was 5 1/4-inch, single-sided, 40 tracks with 8 sectors per track, and 512 bytes per sector. These disks were single-sided, double-density disks, or SSDD. The capacity of this 8-sector single-sided format was 160K.

Cue:
During formatting, data is recorded onto both sides of a double-sided disk.

The early format was extended by making the disk format double-sided in DOS Version 1.1. All floppies are double-sided in the sense that they have two sides. The term *double-sided* in the formatting sense means that data is recorded onto both sides of the disk. Only drives equipped with a second head can accommodate double-sided recording. Clearly, recording on both sides of the disk doubles disk capacity. To differentiate between these two-sided disks and those disks that used only one side for storage, disk makers called these disks double-sided, double-density disks, or DSDD. With both sides used for storing data, the format capacity became 320K. Today, a PC with a single-sided disk drive is rare. Most 5 1/4-inch floppy drives are equipped with two heads.

As disk drives became more sophisticated in design and magnetic materials improved, the number of sectors per track was increased from 8 to 9 in DOS Version 2.0, with no reliability problems. DSDD and SSDD formats got the extra sector per track. More data could be stored in the new 9-sector-per-track format than in the earlier DSDD and SSDD formats. The new format quickly became popular with users. An easy way to keep from confusing the different formats is to think of the 8-sector formats as DSDD-8 and SSDD-8, and to think of the 9-sector formats as DSDD-9 and SSDD-9. The single-sided, 9-sector version has a capacity of 180K; the double-sided version has a capacity of 360K.

The evolution of DOS to Version 3.0 provided for drives with quadruple the number of tracks of the early standard disks. These new 80-track quad-density formats were applied to 5 1/4-inch drives and to the newer 3 1/2-inch drives. DOS provided one quad-density format of 9 sectors per track, used primarily on 3 1/2-inch drives. This quad-density, 9-sector format is QD-9 (or *quad*). The QD-9 disk capacity is 720K.

At the same time, a second quad-density, high-capacity quad format of 15 sectors per track was incorporated by DOS designers. This high-capacity format is used primarily on 5 1/4-inch drives. Called *HC*, for *high capacity*, the quad-density, 15-sector format also can be called QD-15. The QD-15 format, with a capacity of 1.2M, was popularized by the IBM PC/AT.

A high-capacity format for 3 1/2-inch drives, added with DOS Version 3.3, supports the 80-track quad density but provides 18 sectors per track. This QD-18 format, sometimes called 3 1/2-inch HC, offers 1.44M of storage space from a microfloppy. DOS 5.0 adds support for 3 1/2-inch drives that offer 2.88M of storage.

Table 2.1 summarizes the common floppy disk formats. In some versions of DOS, you can use the FORMAT command to format a disk differently than the normal format.

Table 2.1
DOS Floppy Disk Formats

Format	Tracks	Sectors/Track	Total Sectors	Usable Capacity
SSDD	40	8	320	160K
DSDD	40	8	640	320K
SSDD-9	40	9	360	180K
DSDD-9	40	9	720	360K
QD-9	80	9	1440	720K
QD-15	80	15	2400	1.2M
QD-18	80	18	2880	1.44M
QD-36	80	36	5760	2.88M

Most disks have a *write-protect tab* that prevents data from being erased or changed accidentally. 5 1/4-inch disks have a notch cut on the side of the disk. Covering this notch with a piece of opaque tape (provided with blank disks) tells the disk drive that the contents of the disk should not be erased or altered. A light beam or a mechanical sensor within the drive detects whether or not the notch is covered. 3 1/2-inch disks work similarly—a tiny plastic square slides forward or backward to cover or uncover a hole. If the hole is covered, data may be written to the disk; an open hole indicates that the disk is write-protected.

Raw and Usable Capacity

Not all of the recording area on a disk is available to you for recording data. A 1.44M disk, for example, actually has space for more than 1.44M of information. DOS uses this space for sector identification and error-checking information. High-capacity disks, which enable you to record 1.44M of data, may be labeled as 2M disks.

To understand this apparent discrepancy, you need to understand the difference between total (raw) capacity and usable (formatted) capacity. The larger of the two numbers for the same disk is considered the disk's *raw* capacity. Raw capacity includes the storage space that the formatting information uses at format time. The smaller of the two numbers for the same disk is the disk's *usable* capacity; this number of bytes is available for storing files after the formatting information has been put on the disk. In this book, *disk capacity* refers to usable capacity after the disk has been formatted.

Hard Disk Drive Formats

Formats for hard disks nearly always use seventeen 512-byte sectors per track. Each track has seventeen sectors, and each sector is made up of 512 bytes.

Cue: The DOS FORMAT command can perform a high-level format on a hard disk.

DOS does not provide the low-level format data for a hard disk as it does for a floppy disk. Normally, hard disks are prepared with a low-level format at the factory; end users seldom (if ever) need to initiate a low-level format on a hard disk. In a discussion of hard disk formatting, the term *format* refers to the high-level format initiated by the DOS FORMAT command. During the formatting of a hard disk, DOS initializes its book-keeping tables and then writes dummy data into the disk's tracks. From your point of view, formatting a hard disk is the same basic operation as formatting a floppy. DOS keeps the details of the low-level format hidden and out of your way.

Table 2.2 shows some typical hard disk formats. An increasing number of hard disk sizes are being used in PCs.

Table 2.2
Hard Disk Formats

Typical Disk	Sectors per Track	Heads	Cylinders	Capacity
IBM PC/XT	17	4	306	10M
IBM AT	17	4	615	20M
IBM AT (late model)	17	5	733	30M
IBM PS/2 Model 60	36	7	583	70M

Examining How DOS Manages Disks and Files

You can think of blank disks as empty warehouses in which DOS intends to store files. Floppy disks are relatively small file warehouses; hard disks are large warehouses. To DOS, receiving a new file is like receiving a shipment of a particular product. The quantity of the file's data bytes is like the quantity of the shipment. When DOS stores files, DOS places the bytes in empty disks (bins) for future retrieval. DOS uses one sector as one bin. Some files can require hundreds of sectors as data storage bins.

DOS doesn't use every sector on the disk for storing files, however. DOS reserves a small part of the disk (normally, the sectors on track 0) as its own bookkeeping space, leaving most of the disk available for data storage. Although the exact make-up and the amount of space reserved on a disk can vary, the amount is never significant. You will see more clearly what DOS does with the reserved area as components of the reserved area of a disk are introduced in this chapter.

Understanding Storage Allocation Logging

To keep track of which sectors it has used, DOS keeps a log of all available sectors. DOS uses the log of a disk's sectors to allocate storage space on the disk for new file data. The sector log keeps DOS from searching the disk for sectors available for allocation.

Figure 2.9 illustrates a simple allocation log. Because of its role in storage allocation, DOS's sector log is the *FAT (File Allocation Table)*. Each disk formatted by DOS has at least one FAT stored in the reserved area of the disk. DOS also provides for a backup FAT in the reserved area, but its inclusion is not a fully supported feature of DOS.

The disk type determines whether DOS assigns sectors individually, in adjacent pairs, or in units of four, eight, or more sectors per unit. The FAT lists the storage locations of the disk in these sector units, rather than in individual sectors. Each unit is a *cluster* or an allocation unit, whether it contains one sector or more than one sector. DOS always uses adjacent sectors to make a cluster. The number of sectors in a cluster always is a power of 2. Table 2.3 lists the common cluster sizes for different disks.

Cue:
Each disk formatted by DOS has at least one FAT stored in the reserved area.

Cue:
Each sector unit is a cluster.

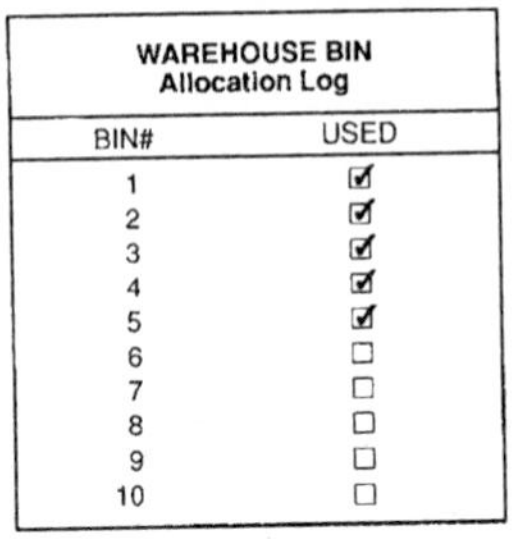

```
         WAREHOUSE BIN
          Allocation Log

   BIN#               USED
    1                  ☑
    2                  ☑
    3                  ☑
    4                  ☑
    5                  ☑
    6                  ☐
    7                  ☐
    8                  ☐
    9                  ☐
   10                  ☐
```

Fig. 2.9. A simple allocation log for a typical warehouse.

Table 2.3
Typical Disk Cluster Sizes

Disk Type	Capacity	Sectors per Cluster
5 1/4-inch floppy	360K	2
	1.2M	1
3 1/2-inch floppy	720K	2
	1.44M	1
PC/XT hard disk	10M	8
PC/AT hard disk	30M	4

If DOS needs to store additional bytes in a file, the last cluster of the file may have space to hold these additional bytes. DOS does not always have to allocate additional storage space when a user adds to a file. Multiple-sector clusters reduce the number of FAT entries. A disk with 1,000 sectors and 2 sectors per cluster, for example, needs only 500 FAT entries.

A FAT with 1,000 available entries can track 8,000 sectors if each cluster has 8 sectors. Multiple-sector clusters increase the number of sectors a given FAT can track. If DOS must allocate space for a 2,048-byte file, DOS needs to make just one FAT entry if the cluster size is 4 sectors ($512 \times 4 = 2,048$). Larger clusters make DOS more efficient. When multiple-sector clusters are used with the same amount of space devoted to a FAT, more disk space can be allocated to data for each FAT access.

On a typical PC-operator's disk, many clusters are partially filled with bytes because the files are small; the unfilled portion of these bytes is wasted. In a disk with a 4-sector cluster, DOS allocates at least four times the 512-byte sector size, or 2,048 bytes. With a 4-sector cluster, even a file that contains

1 byte of data reduces the available disk space by 2,048 bytes. (This system is as efficient as storing one screw in each bin in a warehouse.) If most of the files stored on the disk are smaller than 512 bytes, one sector per cluster is the most efficient ratio. Generally, because people frequently save large files or add to many small files, such as memos, clusters of more than one sector are space-efficient.

DOS uses a coded indicator in the FAT for each cluster the operating system allocates. DOS can tell immediately whether a cluster has been used (or is defective) or whether it is free. During each search of the FAT for available clusters, DOS searches from the first cluster toward the last cluster. DOS marks and uses for storage the first available cluster in the FAT's list of all the disk's clusters. This process is DOS's "first-found, next-used" cluster-search method.

In the case of a newly formatted disk, all clusters (except the first two, which are used by DOS) are available for storing files. As successive clusters are allocated, the disk begins to fill from sector to sector and from cylinder to cylinder in a uniform fashion. Cluster entries in the FAT are marked from the start downward in a uniform fashion. All files receive as much contiguous cluster space as they need—perhaps a little extra, if the files are smaller than the cluster size.

DOS marks the cluster entries being used in the FAT in order, from the top of the list down. When all new files have been allocated, the FAT has an entry that is the point at which DOS allocated the last cluster to the last file. The remaining cluster entries in the FAT are not yet marked as used. Files stored in consecutive clusters in this way are *contiguous*. Figure 2.10 demonstrates this concept. In the simplified version of the FAT shown in figure 2.10, the first three clusters belong to LETTER.1. Clusters 4 and 5 belong to MEMO.1. Clusters 6 and 7 are allocated to BUDGET.YTD. In this example, clusters 8, 9, and 10 have not been allocated.

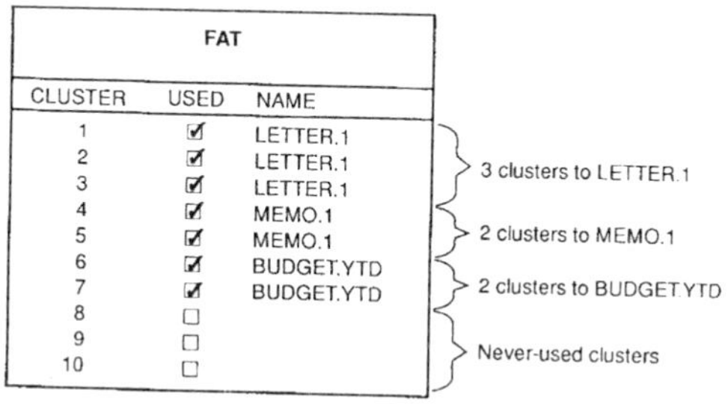

Cue:
Files stored in consecutive clusters are contiguous.

Fig. 2.10. *Allocating contiguous clusters to each file in the FAT.*

If the addition of a new file is the next disk activity, some of the never used clusters are used. Storing a file's bytes in one contiguous block of clusters isn't always possible.

When a file is erased (removed from the disk), the clusters the file occupied are available for DOS to reuse; the FAT reflects their availability. Conceptually, DOS indicates the availability of the freed clusters by erasing from the FAT the check mark for the removed file's clusters (see fig. 2.11). The left side of figure 2.11 shows MEMO.1 being deleted from the FAT; clusters 4 and 5 are returned to DOS for later use. Notice in the resulting right view that BUDGET.YTD sits between two blocks of available cluster entries. The freed clusters are higher on the FAT's list than the empty block of clusters farther down the list where files have not been allocated.

FAT During file deletion				FAT After file deletion			
CLUSTER	USED	NAME		CLUSTER	USED	NAME	
1	☑	LETTER.1		1	☑	LETTER.1	
2	☑	LETTER.1		2	☑	LETTER.1	
3	☑	LETTER.1		3	☑	LETTER.1	
4	☒	MEMO.1		4	☐		Next available
5	☒	MEMO.1		5	☐		cluster
6	☑	BUDGET.YTD		6	☑	BUDGET.YTD	
7	☑	BUDGET.YTD		7	☑	BUDGET.YTD	
8	☐			8	☐		
9	☐			9	☐		
10	☐			10	☐		

Fig. 2.11. Erasing a file and freeing clusters.

When you need to store a new file (or additions to an existing file), DOS scans the FAT for free clusters, starting from the top of the list. First, DOS finds the reusable clusters and allocates them, in order, to the new file. If all the freed clusters are used for the new file before the new file is completely allocated, DOS resumes allocating clusters—this time using the never-used clusters farther down the FAT (see fig. 2.12). In this figure, DOS has to allocate 3 clusters to the file NEWFILE.ADD. Clusters 4 and 5 are the first available clusters; part of NEWFILE.ADD is entered in these clusters. The remaining part of NEWFILE.ADD is recorded in cluster entry 8, the next available cluster. NEWFILE.ADD is fully allocated, but another file sits between the parts of NEWFILE.ADD.

Not only the FAT entries for the new file but also the sectors of the storage area are noncontiguous. The file and its FAT entries exist in chunks, or *fragments*. The process of allocating a file in fragments doesn't pose a problem for DOS, but file storage isn't always as simple as keeping a group of papers tucked neatly inside a file folder. A highly fragmented file easily can be spread all over the disk (see fig. 2.13).

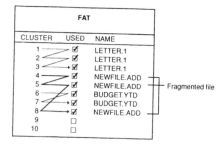

Fig. 2.12. Reallocating previously freed clusters.

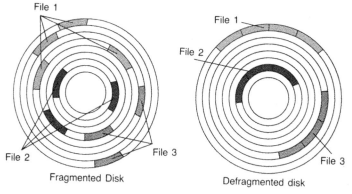

Fig. 2.13. Disk fragmentation.

Understanding Coordinates and Logical Sectors

On floppy and hard disk drives, DOS uses the cluster numbers of each disk's FAT to locate a cluster of data. Remember that each disk is arranged according to the head-cylinder-track coordinate system built into the formatting directions for that particular disk. A 360K floppy disk has 2 heads, 40 cylinders, and 9 sectors per track. DOS formats other types of disks differently, using other formatting directions. In all cases, any given data can be located where the specified head, cylinder, and sector intersect.

Remember, however, that disk drives have different numbers of heads, cylinders, and sectors per cylinder. DOS doesn't try to track disk data by coordinates. DOS views a disk at a higher level.

The warehouse manager uses a bin log with bin numbers instead of aisle, shelf, and bin coordinates. He uses the numbered bins because all warehouses finally come down to bin space. DOS disks finally come down to clusters. DOS "sees" all disks as a number of clusters made up of a number of sectors. To DOS, the disk is an addressable group of logical sectors. As long as DOS knows the ordering method of the sectors and clusters, DOS doesn't need to log storage information in terms of cylinders and heads.

Cylinders and heads are disk-drive specific; sector numbers are general. All DOS-formatted disks, whether removable 160K floppies or 80M hard disks, have a first sector and a last sector. By numbering the sectors from one and counting the sectors cylinder-by-cylinder and from head-to-head in cylinders, DOS can use the same basic space-allocation strategy without regard to the disk's physical attributes.

The low-level driver routines are programmed to deal with disk specifics. DOS relies on the low-level routines in the BIOS layer to interface directly with the disk drive's electronics. DOS merely communicates file needs to the driver. At the point where DOS and the driver communicate, cluster numbers are translated to disk coordinates of cylinder, head, and sector and passed on by the driver to the disk drive. Because each driver routine is familiar with the disk type that it supports, DOS doesn't need to know the disk's hardware details. The lower-level service that the go-between driver provides enables DOS to view the disk in a more generic way. The lower-level service keeps DOS from being bogged down with details such as starting the drive's motor, activating a particular head, or determining when the correct sector is passing under the activated head. DOS doesn't have to memorize every disk type and predict future disk types just to make a simple disk access. The same basic numbered-cluster allocation system works for DOS whether the disk is small or large.

Knowing What DOS Stores— the Directory

Cue:
Every disk formatted by DOS has a directory.

So far, this discussion of DOS's storage management has focused on allocating storage space from a record kept in a file allocation table. How does DOS find what it has stored? Although the use of a FAT indicates that *something* is being stored in the appointed clusters, there is no record of *what* is being stored. On the surface, DOS shows you a file as a named collection of data. DOS doesn't record the file's name in the file's disk storage area, so it must be stored somewhere else. DOS needs some convenient means to tie a file name to where it can be found quickly on the disk. Most disk operating systems incorporate some sort of catalog or directory that indicates what is being stored as well as storage location(s). Every disk formatted by DOS has a directory.

The directory is stored in a portion of the disk's reserved space in the sectors in the first track. Each file stored in the directory is listed once by name. The DOS file directory includes provisions for other information about each file. In addition to the file's name, the total number of bytes of storage space occupied by the file is listed. Also listed is some status information such as the time and date of creation or last modification of the file.

Table 2.4 summarizes some important inclusions in DOS directories. This directory information is handy, but the directory seems to have no way to indicate which of the disk's clusters holds a file. DOS, however, provides an even better method. The FAT and a directory are linked so that they can work together to locate named files.

Table 2.4
The Main Features of DOS Directories

Feature	What Is Stored	Example
File name	Eight-character file prefix	THANKYOU
File-name extension	Three-character file suffix	THANKYOU.OLD
Time	The time of creation or last modification	10:22
Date	The date of creation or last modification	11-14-91
Starting cluster	The number of the first cluster allocated to this file by DOS in the FAT	576
File attributes	Special status information about this file used by DOS	Read-only/Hidden

You will recall that the FAT contains a list of cluster numbers, one for each cluster on the disk. In a simplistic view of a FAT, you might picture that there is a box beside each cluster number. The resulting FAT would be similar to the one represented in figure 2.9. If the cluster is in use, the box is check-marked; if the cluster is available, the box is empty (not check-marked). DOS can allocate clusters with this FAT because DOS can determine easily the first free cluster by looking for an unmarked box. Now, if you replace the box with an entry blank beside the cluster, DOS can enter a variety of information in the blank. DOS, for example, can enter a binary value represented here by the word "free" if the cluster can be allocated. The meaning signified by "free" is the same as the meaning signified by the absence of check mark in a box in figure 2.9.

Figure 2.14 shows the visualization of the improved FAT with its entry blank as a link status. Each cluster in the FAT has an entry for a link status. When a cluster logs part of a file, the link status shows the cluster number of the next cluster allocated to the file. Clusters that are available because they are no longer part of a linked list of clusters (in this case, clusters 4 and 5) are "free" clusters. You can presume that clusters 4 and 5 once were allocated to a file which has since been erased. Clusters that have never been part of a linked list also are "free." In figure 2.14, clusters 9, 10, and those that would follow in the complete FAT, have never been allocated. "Free" clusters are not part of a linked list of clusters belonging to a file. DOS is responsible for marking a usable FAT entry as being "free."

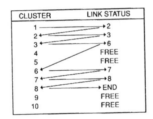

Fig. 2.14. The concept of linked clusters in DOS's FAT.

DOS has two ways of using the entry in the FAT to indicate that the cluster is part of a file. The first way is by placing the linking number to the next cluster used for the file in a FAT entry. The other way is to put a value that indicates the "end" in the file's last cluster entry. Not only do the linking number and the "end" entries indicate that the clusters are unavailable for allocation, they also form a traceable chain for each file allocated.

In practice, DOS allocates a cluster to a file and then determines whether the entire file will fit into the cluster. If the entire file will not fit, DOS stores as much as it can in the cluster. DOS then finds and allocates another cluster. When the next cluster is found, DOS puts the number of the second cluster back in the entry blank of the preceding cluster. DOS has chained the two clusters together by using the entry in the first to point to the location of the second. If the remaining bytes of the file do not fit in the second cluster, DOS again stores what it can and finds another cluster. DOS repeats this partial store-and-allocate process until the entire file is allocated to clusters. Each cluster except the last has the number of the next cluster as its entry. Because the last cluster is the end of the file's chained allocations, the last cluster has a value of "end" in its entry.

The example in figure 2.14 shows the linkage of clusters 1-3 and 6-8 for a file allocated by DOS. You can assume that clusters 4 and 5 were allocated to some other file when the rest of the clusters were allocated. Even with the fragmentation of the file between two blocks of clusters, the entry in cluster 3 which points to cluster 6 as the next cluster leaves DOS a trail.

Using this "point-to-the-next-cluster" method, the contents of the blank for any cluster number in the FAT is free, end, or the number of the cluster to examine to find additional bytes of the file. One file's sequence of FAT entries forms a chain of cluster numbers; any link of the chain ties to another link (cluster) or is the end link in the chain (the file's last cluster). Using this chain, DOS can start at the first cluster number entry for a file in the FAT and quickly trace that file's other clusters through the chain to the end cluster. DOS knows where all of the bytes of the file were stored. This use of the FAT is a sort of scavenger hunt with each clue giving the exact location of the next clue. DOS needs to know only where the first entry for a file is located in the FAT, and it can access the entire file. DOS needs a link between the FAT's "where" values and the directory's file names.

Remember that the directory entry for each file contains the starting cluster number for the file. DOS makes these entries when files are allocated. Figure 2.15 shows the same FAT as the preceding example, but also shows the directory's link to the FAT through the directory's starting cluster number for the file.

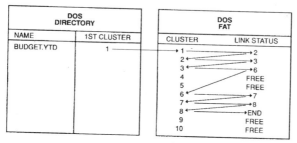

Fig. 2.15. *The directory linked to the FAT by starting cluster.*

DOS enters the directory information for BUDGET.YTD and then allocates the first available cluster in the FAT to the file. DOS puts that first cluster number in the directory for future access. DOS allocates the rest of the space for the file and chains the allocated clusters together in the FAT. DOS's method for file allocation and access is the same for all files.

With this system, DOS allocates free space quickly and finds all the bytes of a file—regardless of where the file is stored—by using the FAT. The file name, file status, and the pointer to the first entry in the FAT are available for each file with the directory.

Now apply this FAT-plus-directory system to DOS file management. Every disk formatted by DOS has some space reserved in the first track of the disk to serve as a directory table. DOS also uses some of this space to create a FAT that matches the number of clusters on the disk. Each file stored on a disk is entered in the directory table by DOS. When a new file is added to the disk, DOS consults the FAT to find the first cluster that can store the file and puts the first cluster number in a field in the directory entry for that file.

As clusters are allocated to store the file, the current cluster number is entered into the preceding cluster's pointer entry. If the file has been completely stored on the disk, the final cluster entry for that file in the FAT is marked with a value DOS takes as "end." When DOS gets a request for a file (such as from a COPY command), DOS looks for the file's name in the directory. When DOS finds the name, it uses the first cluster entry to directly access that cluster's entry in the FAT. DOS calls for low-level service from the BIOS routines to read the cluster's data at the cylinder, head, and sector coordinate that the disk understands. If the cluster entry in the FAT points to another cluster, DOS consults that other cluster's entry in the FAT and repeats the read steps. DOS continues to move to each cluster in the chain until the last cluster's data is retrieved. If the file is fragmented (in noncontiguous sectors), the disk drive has to work a little harder, but DOS has no problem following the file's cluster chain. The directory and the FAT work together to make DOS more efficient.

The directory is good for storing file names and associated status information. If the disk capacity is small, the number of entries in the directory is small because the directory's "living quarters" in the reserved area of the disk is limited. The dedicated reserved space for the directory accommodates all of the limited number of entries; searching the entries for a file name is therefore reasonably fast. If the disk capacity is huge, however, the number of files the disk can accommodate is proportionally huge. The space reserved by DOS for the directory on a large capacity disk may become filled before the disk becomes filled.

DOS designers faced this limited directory problem in Version 1 when hard disks began to catch on with users. The DOS designers facing the larger disks solved the directory limitation problem. But, before you see how they solved the problem, you should see how they could have solved the problem and why some solutions were not implemented.

Enlarging the reserved space would allow more directory entries, but establishing how much directory space is enough is an arbitrary judgment call. If DOS designers provided for 5,000 files to be stored in the directory, those users who needed 10,000 files would be disappointed. If the designers provided for 10,000 entries in the directory, those users who needed only 1,000 entries would be sacrificing usable disk space to hold a directory that couldn't be fully utilized.

Unless some cap were established on the number of entries, the directory could take the lion's share of the disk. Besides, because DOS makes directory entries on a first-come, first-serve basis, file names will not be in any particularly useful order in the directory. To find a file, DOS has to search from the start of the directory until it finds the name it is looking for. This long search would be cumbersome with a filled, over-sized, disk directory.

In addition, there wouldn't be a way to instruct DOS to divide files into categories by their purpose, what programs normally use them, what special functions they support, or other categories. Searching a category is much faster and to the point than searching every entry in a large directory.

Considering the disadvantages of expanding the directory size to accommodate more files on a hard disk, DOS designers had to answer one question: How can you use the same basic directory system and gain the benefits of categories of your choosing without having a confusing, slow-to-use directory that may fill with file entries long before the disk fills with files? The DOS designers answered this question in Version 2.0 by introducing hierarchical directories.

Understanding the Root Directory and its Subdirectories

To maintain the functionality of a directory-based system, DOS designers designed one master directory with a predetermined number of entries to keep the reserved space small. The designers first established a cap on the number of entries in this master directory to fix its size. The cap number was proportional to the capacity of the disk the designers were dealing with. Floppies had fewer file entries in the master directory (less bytes) than hard disks.

The master directory was not intended to list the names of every file on the disk (unless the disk was a floppy used to store a few files). The master directory, as the *root* of the system, was called the *root directory*. Many of

Cue:
The main directory of a disk is the root directory.

the disk's files could be entered into subcategory expansion directories or *subdirectories*.

Ideally, the subdirectory system would not limit the number of files it could manage. Like a single directory system, the subdirectory system was efficient and easy to use. This subdirectory system had the root directory as its only required directory and optional subdirectories subordinate to the root.

An earlier mainframe operating system, UNIX, solved the directory problem by enabling users to create their own subdirectories as expansions of the main directory. Borrowing this UNIX-like directory system, DOS incorporated subdirectories into its file system.

In the root directory or in a subdirectory, DOS can still enter the name and the first cluster number of a file's FAT entry. The DOS subdirectory is a special file that DOS uses like the root directory. On the surface, you can't tell that the root directory is a reserved section of the disk and that the subdirectory is a special file. DOS manages the root directory and subdirectory difference internally and provides uniformity on the surface. For this reason, it is quite common for DOS users to call subdirectories "directories." Unless the context of the term dictates otherwise, subdirectories can be called directories.

DOS can implement an entire system of subdirectories and still retain the general advantages of a single directory. From a space-economy point of view, a subdirectory system overcomes many of the drawbacks of a single-directory system such as an excessively large number of dedicated file entries. Of course, DOS has to provide a few commands to manage the subdirectory system. Commands to create, remove, and change the current directory are examples.

On a freshly formatted disk, you have access to the disk's only directory, the root directory. With the MKDIR (Make Directory) command, you can create a subdirectory called LETTERS. You can use the name LETTERS as the subdirectory name to categorize the letter files that you will keep in this new subdirectory. To focus DOS's attention on the LETTERS subdirectory as though it were the only directory on the disk, you can use the CHDIR (Change Directory) command to change the current directory to LETTERS. To remove the LETTERS subdirectory, you can use the RMDIR (Remove Directory) command to do so. DOS's subdirectories, as well as the commands that support them, are a great advancement over the single fixed directories of Version 1.

Subdirectories as Files

DOS can use subdirectories while maintaining a fixed-size reserve area on a disk because DOS is in charge of files. DOS makes a subdirectory out of a file. A subdirectory can be considered DOS's personal file.

A subdirectory is not placed in the reserved area like the root directory. Instead, it is located in the main storage area of the disk just like other files. Unlike the master directory, which is fixed in size, a subdirectory can grow as more file's entries are added to it. All subdirectories have names similar to files, and to DOS, a subdirectory's name is a modified file name. Because there is only one root directory and its space is reserved, it has no recorded name and is always known as the root. DOS attaches no special meaning to your choice of a subdirectory's name.

A Hierarchy of Directories

The first subdirectory you add can be considered an "offspring" of the root directory. You create it from the root. It is the child of its parent (root) directory. Your first subdirectory is not, however, the end of the parent-child relationship. Subdirectories can contain other subdirectories as child directories. A child-expansion directory is subordinate (lower in the ordering) to its parent directory in the file system. Figure 2.16 shows a typical hierarchy of the DOS file system.

When viewed from the parent-child perspective, the typical DOS file system resembles a family tree with the root directory branching through generations of subdirectories with files as leaves coming from each branch (see fig. 2.16). There is a natural hierarchical ordering to this type of tree structure. Using this hierarchical ordering approach to file-system management, DOS enables you to specify a directory structure as elaborate as necessary.

Cue:
The directory system of DOS is organized in a hierarchical fashion.

Yet DOS always can keep file names and their physical disk locations in order. When you tell DOS to create a directory, DOS handles the details of making a new file and marking it as a directory. DOS also makes an entry in the new directory for the starting cluster of the parent directory and another entry for the starting cluster of the new directory itself. These two directory entries in the newly created subdirectory are useful to DOS when DOS needs to find its way back to a parent or grandparent directory. The DOS designation for the parent directory entry is called . . (dot, dot), and the designation for the directory itself is called . (dot). Because the root is the top level of the hierarchy and has no parent, the root has no . or . . entries. The hierarchical directory structure of the DOS file system provides large storage capacity, subdirectory privacy, and efficiency for DOS's disk related services.

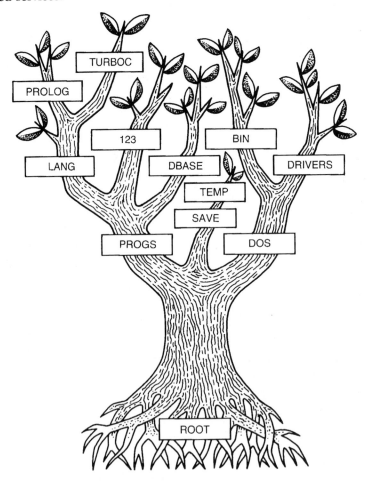

Fig. 2.16. The DOS tree-structured directory system.

Directory Paths

When you want to access files in a particular subdirectory, you can give the full path name down the directory hierarchy starting at the root. The path name consists of the \ (backslash) specifier for the root; backslashes also separate subdirectory names that trace the family tree to the files. The file name is the eight-character name plus an optional period and a three-character extension. In the LETTERS directory in a previous example, the full path name of the MOM.LET file is \LETTERS\MOM.LET.

A full path name is the path name plus the file name and extension. Every file in the file system has a full path name, even if the file belongs to the root directory. The file CONFIG.SYS in the root directory has a full path name of \CONFIG.SYS. No full path name can appear more than once in a disk's file system. The full path name is DOS's positive identifier for a file. A duplicate full path name would eliminate this positive ID method.

The same full file name (file name plus extension) can appear in every directory, because every directory has a unique path name. The file MOM.LET can appear in \LETTERS and \MAIL at the same time. The full path names \LETTERS\MOM.LET and \MAIL\MOM.LET make the two files unique to DOS even if their contents are exactly the same.

DOS always considers the path name when doing its internal bookkeeping. Because each disk has its own file system (and therefore bookkeeping provision), file and path names can be duplicated from one disk to another. The files A:\LETTERS\MOM.LET and C:\LETTERS\MOM.LET are two distinct files in DOS's view even though they both have a full path name of \LETTERS\MOM.LET.

DOS keeps this duplication straight by relying on the drive name (the letter, such as C) to distinguish your intent.

Understanding Defaults

To make entering commands more efficient, DOS provides for predetermined values, *defaults*, to be used when you omit certain parts of a drive and path name in a command. The default disk drive is established by the boot process and becomes the drive that your PC boots from. The default directory is set to the root directory of the boot disk.

You can change the default drive and directory to the drive and directory that contain your desired files. Changing to a new disk or directory makes it the *current* drive or directory. When you boot your computer from drive A, the current drive is A, and the current directory is \. If you enter **C:** at the DOS prompt, you current drive is then C. If you then enter **CD \LETTERS**, your current drive and directory become C:\LETTERS.

DOS assumes that files are accessible on the default drive in the default directory unless you use a drive name and a path name in a command.

If you don't clearly understand the concept of using defaults in commands, don't worry. Part II of this book explains defaults in detail. For now, just understand that through defaults, DOS can accept commands that treat a disk and a directory as if it were the only disk and directory in the file system. The commands that use DOS defaults look simple, considering the potentially complicated hierarchical file system that DOS is tracking below the surface.

Understanding Disk Partitions

The growing storage capacity of hard disks offers an opportunity for people to use their PCs as a hardware platform for operating systems in addition to DOS. Many hard disks today have the storage capacity to support the files of more than one operating system. Without some provision to host more than one operating system on the same hard disk, however, a PC needs a different hard disk for each operating system.

Cue:
A partition is a subsection of a disk.

Luckily, such a provision is available. It is the *disk partition table*. The disk partition table is located at the start of a hard disk's sectors where it is available for any operating system to examine. The disk partition table has entries to log up to four partitions. Each partition is a number of cylinder and head units of the hard disk. In other words, a partition is a subsection of the disk. Of course, if the disk is given only one partition, the entire disk is devoted to the operating system that controls that partition.

IBM introduced the concept of a partitionable disk with PC DOS Version 2.0. The provision for partitions was introduced to coincide with the introduction of the IBM PC XT computer. Every version of DOS introduced since Version 2.0 has included provisions for partitions.

Earlier versions of DOS had a more important reason for introducing hard disk partitions. Earlier versions of DOS could not handle a hard disk larger than 32M. (*Note:* DOS 4.0 and higher can create partitions larger than 32M. DOS 3.3 and higher can break large hard disks into multiple logical partitions, each no larger than 32M.) Partitioning enabled the user to divide a large hard disk into several partitions, each smaller than 32M. DOS worked with each partition as though it were a separate drive, even though the partition actually was a piece of a much larger drive. Any size of hard disk could be used, as long as the disk was partitioned into pieces of 32M or less.

The hard disk partition table is located in the track(s) of the disk reserved for operating system tables. DOS cannot really claim to own the partition table as one of its bookkeeping features. The partition table is a hard-disk-level bookkeeping provision to which all operating systems have equal access. The partition table indicates which cylinders are controlled by which operating system.

QNX, a UNIX-like PC operating system, can access the partition table of an IBM PC or compatible's hard disk. When you "mount" the hard disk's QNX partition, QNX accesses the disk partition table and scans the entries to find the first QNX partition. Other PC operating systems access partition table data in a way similar to DOS and QNX. The XENIX operating system also honors the disk partition table's entries.

Two or more tenants who share a warehouse facility may draw a yellow line down an agreed line to divide the warehouse space. On a hard disk, the disk partition table formalizes this type of imaginary line. The physical space of the hard disk can be divided into partitions. Figure 2.17 will help you visualize this division.

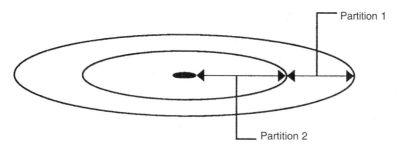

Fig. 2.17. *The physical division of a single disk through partitions.*

Partition 1 in figure 2.17 is on the outer cylinders of the disk. Partition 2 begins at a cylinder boundary and extends to the centermost cylinder of the disk. Although one disk is present, the two partitions defined in the partition of the disk act as two.

Unlike the warehouse example, however, only one operating system can be active at a time. The division of the hard disk, however, is still respected by the active operating system. The active operating system confines its file-management activities to its partition. Each operating system has a utility to access and maintain its part of the partition table. DOS uses the FDISK utility to manage its partition definitions. QNX, as well as other operating systems, also names its partition-table maintenance command FDISK.

Reminder:
Only one operating system can be active on a disk at any one time.

When DOS gets its starting and ending cylinders from the partition table, it uses the starting cylinder of the partition as though it were the first cylinder on a physical disk. The FAT and root directory tables, as well as other DOS-reserved information, starts in the first cylinder. QNX lays out its partition as though the partition was the entire disk. Internally, QNX uses the first cylinder of its partition as though that cylinder were the first cylinder of the disk. QNX also can read DOS's partition table information and mount the DOS partition to the QNX file system. With a special command, you can convert DOS files to QNX files.

Although you may never use the flexibility that the partition table offers in multioperating system operation, the partition table is there on the hard disk should you need it.

Cue:
DOS Version 3.3
introduced the
capability of the
extended parti-
tion.

A hard disk's flexibility is further enhanced when this same partitioning concept is extended so that DOS can manage more than one partition. Starting with Version 3.3, this extended partition capability was included with DOS. The physical hard disk can include a standard or *primary* DOS partition as well as an *extended* DOS partition. The extended DOS partition can be one or more logical drives. The concept of logical drives is seen in figure 2.18. Logical drives are not real disk drives; rather, they are defined sections of a real disk drive.

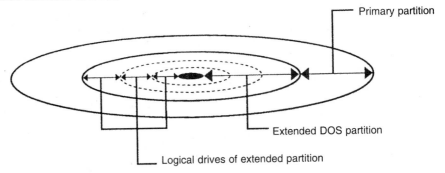

Fig. 2.18. *An extended partition with logical drives.*

In figure 2.18, the outer cylinders of a hard disk have been allocated to the primary DOS partition. The extended DOS partition begins after the last cylinder of the primary partition. The extended partition extends to the last cylinder of the disk. Notice the two dotted circles further dividing the secondary DOS partition. Each of the dotted circles marks the beginning of a logical drive. In this example, drives C, D, E, and F have been created through the partition table.

The commands that work with disks and files behave in the same way on logical and physical drives. DOS is the agent that makes the behavior of the logical drive appear the same as it would if the drive were a physical drive. Each logical drive contains its own file system and has its own disk name.

The extended DOS partition is similar to a primary or standard DOS partition. The big difference is that DOS cannot boot from an extended partition. The FDISK partition-maintenance command provided by DOS has no provision to designate the extended partition (or its logical drives) as a bootable partition. Other operating system partitions, such as a QNX partition, are not affected by DOS's extended partition.

Only the primary DOS partition can be bootable. At the command-issuing level of DOS, no practical difference exists between physical and logical drives. Files stored on a logical drive D appear to you as though they were on their own drive, but they are on the same physical hard disk as the files on logical drive E. Each logical disk has no log of what is stored on another disk or logical disk. From DOS's bookkeeping point of view, logical drives are totally separate entities.

Reminder:
Only the primary
DOS partition can
be bootable.

Starting with Version 4.0, DOS can create partitions larger than 32M. For example, you can create a 100M partition for your 100M disk. You still may choose to create multiple logical partitions that are a more manageable size.

Looking at DOS's File System from the Ground Up

The DOS file system and its related mechanics aren't as simple as they appear on the surface. At the DOS command prompt, you issue commands and rightfully don't expect to be responsible for the success or failure of the command's execution. Command execution is the responsibility of DOS. Needless to say, DOS cannot be responsible for failed commands that are poorly formed or inaccessible. But there is a big difference between your learning to issue commands correctly and your learning to control hardware at the binary level.

Through the hardware, the driver software, and through DOS's own internal organization, the complexities of the file system remain in the capable hands of DOS. When you have some insight into what DOS is up to behind the scenes, you stand a better chance of mastering those aspects of DOS that you are responsible for. Figure 2.19 puts in perspective the role of DOS in disk-based activity. The figure shows a series of transformations or refinements of organization that become the structure for your disk and file work.

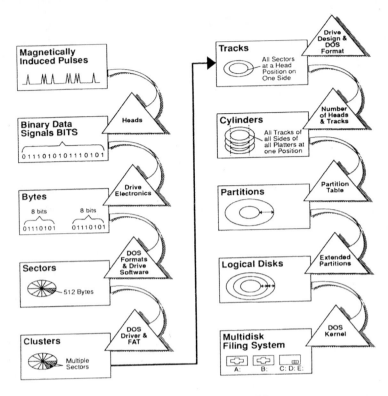

Fig. 2.19. The underlying organization of the DOS file system.

Figure 2.19 shows boxes containing a level of data organization. Connecting the boxes are a series of arrows. Each arrowhead references the method used to transform the level of data organization from the preceding box to the next box. Follow the transformation of magnetic pulses and fields through to the multidisk file system that DOS offers.

From magnetic pulses, the drive head extracts the electrical signals that the drive electronics can transform into electrical binary data. The drive electronics, in cooperation with the disk-driver program, package these binary signals into bytes and deliver them to the PC's memory in 512-byte sectors. DOS's format-defined clusters keep the bookkeeping of the sectors efficient. The sectors give rise to tracks; tracks give rise to cylinders.

DOS keeps a logical map of this disk real estate in the FAT and matches file names to their location on the disk through the directory. DOS knows a disk's organization as soon as it reads the disk's boot record. DOS transparently treats one hard disk as many disks when DOS finds the disk's division into partitions in the partition table. DOS uses names for physical and logical drives so that you can manipulate a multidisk filing system using hierarchical directories. When you consider that DOS manages this range of details from magnetic pulses to multidisk filing systems, it is hard to believe that DOS has its "disk act together" in the moment it takes the drive light to glow.

Chapter Summary

In this chapter, you learned some of the fundamentals of the DOS file system. Following are the key points to remember:

- DOS tracks named collections of data in files.

- Disk drives are the principal file storage devices for DOS.

- Disk drives appear logically the same to DOS because DOS accesses disk drives through the services of drivers.

- DOS provides formats that use the capability of a disk drive to produce a number of tracks for each of a number of heads; each track then is divided into a number of sectors.

- Although the DOS formats usually are applied to specific disk sizes, the formats are logical and can be applied to different disk sizes.

- DOS allocates disk space to files in cluster units. Clusters are logged in the File Allocation Table or FAT.

- DOS tracks file names in the directory. Each DOS formatted disk has one primary or root directory. All DOS directories link a file's starting cluster number to the FAT.

- Because each disk formatted by DOS has its own FAT and root directory, each DOS disk has its own file system.

- DOS Version 2.0 introduced subdirectories to the DOS file system. You manage subdirectories by using DOS commands.

- DOS subdirectories enable the file system to be arranged in a tree-like hierarchical structure of your design.

- The FDISK command manages DOS's entry in the disk-level partition table.

- DOS Version 3.3 introduced the extended DOS partition. FDISK can divide the extended partition into additional logical drives.

An understanding of the concepts presented in this chapter better equips you to understand the commands DOS provides for managing disks, directories, and files and for optimizing file systems. Chapter 3 introduces the DOS command processor, COMMAND.COM, and the organized computer environment in which it operates.

3

Understanding the Command Processor

The most visible part of DOS is its command processor, which is a program named COMMAND.COM. At the DOS level, the command processor presents the familiar C> prompt and waits for the keyboard command. Behind the scenes, the command processor is prepared to handle the critical interrupts generated by the PC when processing is in jeopardy, such as when a disk file is unreadable. Information interpreted by the command processor may be DOS commands or the names of programs. The command processor oversees the execution of the command.

Cue:
The DOS command processor is a program called COMMAND.COM.

When you turn on the PC, it cannot process DOS commands. In fact, the steps that a PC goes through before DOS commands can be processed are numerous. The hardware must be prepared and the PC's resources must be assessed and brought under control before the command processor can do its job.

This chapter provides descriptions of the boot process and COMMAND.COM's control of the PC. To make COMMAND.COM's role clearer, the chapter discusses the computer's hardware and software and the invisible layers of an operating PC. You learn about syntax, parameters, and switches, and understand the difference between internal and external DOS commands. Through the discussion of COMMAND.COM, you gain a more thorough understanding of the role of the command processor in DOS.

Examining the Role of Hardware

A PC's hardware is the collection of electronic and electromechanical components that make up the physical computer. All of computing is an attempt to make the hardware do something useful, whether you are trying to print a letter, store information for later retrieval, or display sales figures on the computer's screen. To many people, the nature of hardware seems complex and forbidding. You may have seen a television comedy in which a naive handyman takes the cover off a neatly covered box, and springs, gears, and wires fly out of the box in chaos. Many people believe that a similar fate awaits anyone who removes the case from a PC's system unit. Reading *Upgrading and Repairing PCs* (published by Que Corporation) may convince you that a useful understanding of PC hardware is within your reach. Fortunately, you don't have to disassemble the PC to see how the hardware works. Hardware can be divided into two general categories: system-unit and peripheral.

System-Unit Hardware

System-unit hardware represents the brain of the computer. This hardware enables the computer to do what most closely resembles "thinking." System-unit hardware includes the microprocessor, memory, and various control chips. What it does not include is access to the outside world, or communication with people—that task is handled by peripheral hardware.

Cue:
The circuits and components typically on the PC's main circuit board are system-unit hardware.

In the past, the components comprising the system-unit hardware could be easily identified inside the computer because they consisted of the circuits and components that traditionally appeared on a PC's *main circuit board* (*motherboard*). Newer PC designs, however, make greater use of large-scale integration and pack more components into a smaller space. Many different types of hardware that once were classified as peripherals now are often found on the main circuit board, with their circuits next to system-unit-hardware circuits. A built-in Video Graphics Array (VGA) circuit that controls the color monitor in an IBM PS/2 or some COMPAQs is an example of large-scale integration. Today, function rather than physical location determines whether hardware is peripheral or system hardware.

The Central Processing Unit

The *central processing unit*—or CPU—is the part of the computer that examines, manipulates, and transfers data from one place to another in the computer. In effect, the CPU is the master controller for the computer. In large computers, the CPU may be comprised of many circuit boards containing dozens of chips. In PCs, however, the CPU essentially is contained in one chip, or integrated circuit. When a chip contains a CPU, the chip also is a microprocessor. The IBM PC and compatible PCs use the Intel 8086 family of microprocessor chips (which includes the 80286, 80386, and 80486, with new additions under development).

Cue:
The micro-processor is the CPU.

Microprocessors by themselves know how to perform only a limited number of simple operations, such as adding two numbers together or storing a number in a memory location. To make a microprocessor do something useful, it must be given a detailed description, or program. A *program* is a list of instructions, often quite long and complex, that tells the microprocessor what to do, step-by-step. Each *step* is an instruction and represents one of the simple things the microprocessor inherently knows how to do. The microprocessor performs, or executes, each instruction in order, unless the instruction tells the microprocessor to skip to a different instruction.

Cue:
A program consists of instructions that perform a general task.

Advertisements and specifications for a computer sometimes include a rating in megahertz (MHz). *Megahertz* is a unit of measurement equal to 1 million electrical cycles or instructions per second. A computer rated at 16 MHz can process about 16,000,000 instructions per second.

Programming Languages

Each instruction consists of a series of memory locations that form a pattern of on and off signal levels (logical 0s [zeros] and 1s) that are meaningful to the microprocessor. The instructions are called *machine instructions* or *machine code* because they exist at a level that the machine (the PC) understands. Think of machine code as a language spoken in the CPU's native tongue.

Although the computer understands machine code, people find working with such a collection of 1s and 0s difficult. In the early days of computing, people had no choice; if they wanted to program a computer, they had to compose cryptic lists of instructions in machine code.

Today, programmers rarely write machine code programs. Programmers today use assembly language, in which *mnemonic* (devices to aid the memory) abbreviations represent the instructions. For example, SUB may represent a subtraction instruction, or MOV may represent a move instruction to move data from one place to another. Although the computer cannot directly understand these mnemonics, a program called an *assembler* translates mnemonics into the 0s and 1s that the computer has to have.

The assembler exercises a one-to-one relationship between what the programmer writes and what the microprocessor eventually sees in the program. The assembler translates every assembly language instruction into a machine code instruction.

Cue:
*High-level
languages enable
you to write
programs in
English-like text.*

However, programmers today more often make use of high-level languages. Although still somewhat cryptic to nonprogrammers, high-level languages are much more English-like. Each high-level language statement describes some relatively complex operation to be performed. For example, to compute an employee's gross pay, a programmer using the COBOL language may write the following formula:

MULTIPLY HOURS BY RATE GIVING GROSS-PAY.

A programmer using the C language expresses the same formula slightly differently, as shown in the following example:

gross_pay = hours * rate;

Among dozens of additional common high-level languages are BASIC, FORTRAN, PL/I, LISP, C++, Smalltalk, Ada, and Prolog.

As with assembler, the computer cannot directly understand a high-level language, and a *compiler* is necessary to translate programs into the machine code that the computer understands. However, because high-level language statements usually represent relatively complex operations, a compiler may translate a high-level statement into many machine code instructions.

Keep in mind that the computer has no understanding of what a particular program is supposed to accomplish. Rather, the computer rigidly follows the instructions that make up the program. If the program contains an incorrect instruction or if an instruction tells the computer to perform the wrong operation, the computer blindly does as it is told. Contrary to the public perception, computers are quite dumb, and although they can perform millions of instructions per second, they cannot reason or think. They can cope only with situations anticipated by the people who wrote the programs and for which instructions are included.

RAM and ROM Memory

Memory refers to the chips in which the computer stores the instructions and data currently being used. This kind of memory most closely parallels a person's short-term memory. In all cases, the values that memory stores are binary values, or patterns of 0s and 1s. Each 0 or 1 is a *binary digit*, or bit. For convenience and design efficiency, bits are grouped together in collections of 8, and each collection is a *byte*.

Cue:
The values stored in memory are binary.

Many computers use several different types of memory. Common to all computers is *random-access memory,* or RAM, so called because the computer can use different sections of RAM in any order (randomly) dictated by a program. RAM cannot be used to store information long-term, because it cannot retain information when the computer's power is turned off. For the most part, RAM is loaded with program and data values from a disk drive. Some specialized RAM is powered by a backup battery that supplies power when the PC's main power is off. This type of RAM is *nonvolatile* RAM, or NV RAM. The memory that retains the setup parameters of an AT-class computer is an example of NV RAM. If NV RAM's battery power is turned off, NV RAM loses its contents.

Cue:
The CPU uses RAM for reading and writing data.

Another type of memory has instructions and data permanently encoded into its byte contents. This permanent encoding ensures that this type of memory does not lose its contents when the power is switched off. As with RAM, this memory also is randomly accessible by the CPU. Because the content of this type of memory is permanent, the CPU cannot use this memory to store new information or instructions; the CPU can read but cannot write to the memory. This permanent memory is *read-only memory*, or ROM. Most of the PC's basic input-output system, or BIOS, is contained in ROM.

Cue:
The CPU cannot write to ROM.

Although many ROM chips have information permanently encoded within them, some ROM chips can be erased by ultraviolet light and reprogrammed with new information. This erasable type of programmable ROM is called EPROM. In a working PC, ROM and EPROM function in an equivalent fashion.

In the early days of computing, memory was expensive—the rule of thumb for many years was "a buck a byte"—so that computers with even a few thousand bytes of memory capacity were expensive. By the time the first PCs came out, computers commonly contained many thousands of bytes of memory capacity, so the term *kilobyte*, or K, was adopted (from the Greek for thousand) to keep the numbers more manageable. Although in other disciplines (finance and electronics) K means exactly 1,000, in the world of computers a K is actually 1,024. However, thinking of a kilobyte as 1,000 is good for mental approximations. A computer with 256K of memory, therefore, can store 262,144 bytes.

When the original PCs were designed by IBM, memory was still expensive enough that 64K or 128K seemed like a great deal of memory. The PC was designed in such a way that it could not make use of more than 640K of memory. At the time, nobody believed PCs would ever need more. Today, however, far from buying only a byte, a buck buys several K. Various schemes have been developed to break the 640K limit, and the memory in many PCs is no longer measured in kilobytes, but in megabytes (Greek for great or mighty). One megabyte is 1,024K. Many PCs today come with a megabyte or more of memory.

Buses and Control Chips

Although the CPU supervises the activities of the PC, the CPU relies on a collection of support circuits to perform many tasks. The CPU communicates with these support circuits by signalling them over electrical pathways called *buses*. Most computers have several buses. The bus through which the CPU coordinates computer activity is the *control bus*. When the computer wants to access a memory location, it specifies the location via the *address bus*, and the data is transferred through the *data bus*. Many components are connected to the buses in a party line-like arrangement. Part of the function of the control components is to ensure that the correct device is the recipient or sender of information transferred from place to place within the computer.

With numerous components connected to the three buses, successful computing requires a high degree of internal coordination among components. Control components, through the supervision of the CPU, provide this coordination. All the components in the system-unit hardware step in time to a system clock. At regular intervals, the system clock sends pulses that synchronize the work cycles of the components. Like soldiers marching, all of the system hardware inside the computer steps through its tasks by using the beat of the system clock as a timing cue.

While the system clock keeps things synchronized inside the computer, things can happen outside the computer at almost any time. Events such as your pressing a key have no way of falling into step with the smooth flow of clock-controlled activity. Outside events happen in their own time frames, not in the time frame of the system clock. Outside events are *asynchronous* to the system clock.

To service an outside event, the CPU must interrupt what it is doing and give immediate attention to the outside event, or *interrupt*. As soon as possible, the CPU executes a special block of instructions designed to handle the outside event that has occurred. A special control component, the *interrupt controller*, is tasked with detecting external events and informing the CPU that the current series of instructions must be put on hold. The interrupt controller then informs the CPU where the instructions that process the outside event can be found. The CPU then can begin executing the interrupt service routine to process the interrupt condition. When the outside event is handled, the CPU picks up where it left off and continues processing. In effect, the interrupt controller has taken an asynchronous outside event and made possible the handling of that event by the synchronous system hardware. When more than one outside event needs the attention of the CPU, the interrupt controller can determine the order in which the outside events are to be handled.

Peripheral Hardware

Peripheral hardware is hardware not immediately associated with a PC's system circuits; rather it is equipment attached to the system-unit hardware. Peripheral hardware is often equipment that enables the computer to communicate with the outside world, such as a printer, keyboard, or screen. Peripheral hardware also may be some type of equipment controlled by the computer—such as laboratory equipment—or long-term data storage devices such as a disk drive or an optical disk. Because peripherals provide the computer with *input* (items such as a keyboard or mouse) or *output* (items such as a screen or printer), they are sometimes called input/output (I/O) devices.

Cue:
Peripheral hardware is not directly associated with a PC's system circuits.

Booting DOS

When you switch the PC on, you have begun a procedure called *booting* the computer. The term *booting* is derived from the old concept that someone with no external help can "pull himself up by his bootstraps." Someone can start with nothing and turn it into something useful. Initially, the computer has no data and no instructions in its CPU. How does the computer obtain the instructions to enable it to become useful?

Cue:
PCs initiate a boot procedure when you turn them on.

The business of getting the computer started is done in stages by a series of increasingly sophisticated bootstrap programs, or boot programs. The first and simplest of these programs is stored permanently in ROM. The microprocessor is designed so that when power is first turned on, it executes this bootstrap program. The program tests the computer's memory and then instructs the computer to access track 0 of the boot disk (the floppy drive, if there is a floppy in it; otherwise the hard disk). This track contains another boot program, somewhat more complex than the ROM program, that finds and loads the final boot program from disk. This last program is complex enough to complete the task of getting the computer started.

The boot program then looks for a special file called CONFIG.SYS. This file contains information about how DOS should be configured. Most importantly, CONFIG.SYS specifies which device drivers should be loaded. *Device drivers* are pieces of the operating system required to control certain types of hardware. Rather than waste memory on device drivers that may not be needed, only device drivers specified in CONFIG.SYS are used. This feature enables the PC to operate in a configuration tailored to the specific needs of the PC's individual hardware and running requirements.

When configuration is complete, the boot program loads from disk and turns over control to COMMAND.COM—the command interpreter. COMMAND.COM does not immediately display the system prompt and await input, however. First, COMMAND.COM relocates part of its own instructions to another location in memory. In effect, COMMAND.COM splits itself into two parts. One part remains in memory at all times. Another part, a transient part, is overwritten by incoming programs that need the memory occupied by the transient part to fit into memory completely. The part of COMMAND.COM that stays in memory can reload the transient part from disk and be a whole program again.

COMMAND.COM searches the root directory of the boot disk for a file named AUTOEXEC.BAT. If the AUTOEXEC.BAT file is found, its contents are executed as a series of DOS commands. By providing for this special batch file to be executed at boot time, DOS can tailor the start-up of every PC to meet the specific needs of the user. AUTOEXEC.BAT can contain any DOS command but normally contains commands such as PROMPT, PATH, TIME, and DATE. The PATH command is discussed in detail in Chapter 7, and the PROMPT, TIME, and DATE commands are discussed in Chapter 9.

When AUTOEXEC.BAT has been executed by COMMAND.COM, you see the DOS prompt, or *system prompt* (assuming that one of the commands in AUTOEXEC.BAT does not start a program). COMMAND.COM then is ready to receive the command.

Understanding Commands

The lines that you type and enter at the DOS prompt are commands. They tell DOS what task to perform and what information should be used in accomplishing that task. COMMAND.COM examines the commands that you type and determines what actions should take place. In this section, you are introduced to the categories and syntax of DOS commands.

Reminder:
Commands may be DOS commands or executable program names.

Views of Command Names

DOS commands may be divided into two categories: internal and external. Some commands are built into COMMAND.COM. These *internal commands* are commands that DOS directly understands. As an example, to view a list of files in a directory, you type the following command:

Cue:
Commands may be internal or external.

DIR

COMMAND.COM does not have to look to another program to accomplish that task; the machine instructions are an integral part of COMMAND.COM.

The following is a list of DOS 5.0's internal commands.

BREAK	DEL (ERASE)	PATH	TIME
CALL	DIR	PAUSE	TYPE
CHCP	ECHO	PROMPT	VER
CHDIR (CD)	EXIT	REM	VERIFY
CLS	FOR	RENAME	VOL
COPY	GOTO	RMDIR (RD)	
CTTY	IF	SET	
DATE	MKDIR (MS)	SHIFT	

Other commands are not inherently understood by COMMAND.COM and are called *external commands*. These tasks are too complex for COMMAND.COM to handle without help. Rather, COMMAND.COM looks to other programs on disk to do the work that the task requires.

For example, to format a floppy disk, you probably type the following:

FORMAT A:

COMMAND.COM does not directly understand this command and does not contain the instructions to perform the task. Instead, it searches the hard disk for a program called FORMAT. When FORMAT is found, COMMAND.COM transfers control to that program, which then begins the task of formatting a floppy.

Because they are not built into COMMAND.COM, external DOS commands don't have to be as conservative in memory use as internal commands. Although some external commands such as SHARE and MODE stay in memory after they are loaded by COMMAND.COM, the majority of the external commands are loaded, do their jobs, and exit completely. The following list shows the external commands that come with the generic version of DOS 5.0. As with internal commands, the external commands included in different versions of DOS vary.

APPEND	DOSSHELL	KEYB	SETVER
ASSIGN	EDLIN	LABEL	SHARE
ATTRIB	EXE2BIN	MEM	SORT
BACKUP	FASTOPEN	MODE	SUBST
CHKDSK	FC	MORE	SYS
COMMAND	FDISK	NLSFUNC	TREE
COMP	FIND	PRINT	UNFORMAT
DEBUG	FORMAT	RECOVER	XCOPY
DISKCOMP	GRAFTABL	REPLACE	
DISKCOPY	GRAPHICS	RESTORE	
DOSKEY	JOIN	SELECT	

The actual programs that represent these external commands have extensions of COM or EXE; the full name of FORMAT, for example, is FORMAT.COM; CHKDSK is CHKDSK.EXE. (The difference between a COM and EXE command is subtle and unimportant here.) In either case, you don't have to type the extension; COMMAND.COM understands that the proper program, when found, will include one of these extensions.

Cue:
A batch file is an executable text file.

Besides COM and EXE, one other extension can signal an external command: BAT. Called *batch files*, files ending in BAT are text files that contain DOS commands. When looking for an external command, if DOS finds a file ending in BAT, the operating system executes all the commands contained within that file. BAT files can cause a long list of commands to be performed when only one command name is typed. Chapter 12 is dedicated to explaining batch-file basics.

Note that COMMAND.COM does not turn control over to a batch file as it does an EXE or a COM file. In the case of the latter two, COMMAND.COM completely gives up all control over the PC to the executing program. In the case of BAT files, however, COMMAND.COM remains in control as it interprets each line in the batch file and carries out the action associated with each line. From your point of view, you enter a batch file's root file name at the DOS prompt, and the computer does the file's intended work. The outward appearance of the executing batch file is not much different from the outward appearance of an executing COM or EXE program file. Because of this similarity in appearance, you can think of a batch file as an executable command file. Remember that COMMAND.COM steps through each line of a batch file as it executes individual command lines along the way but that COMMAND.COM turns over control of the PC to a COM or EXE file.

DOS locates external commands through one of the following methods:

1. External command names can be preceded by a path name, drive name, or both. Suppose that you type the following command: **C:\DOS\CHKDSK**. DOS looks only on the drive and directory specified; if the command is not found, an error message appears.

2. If no path or drive is specified, COMMAND.COM looks in the current directory.

3. Finally, if a PATH was previously specified with a PATH command, COMMAND.COM searches the directories specified in the PATH.

Sometimes a directory may contain more than one file with the same name but different extensions. For example, you may create a text file called FORMAT.BAT and place it in the same directory as the DOS command FORMAT.COM. When some combination of files with the BAT, COM, and EXE extensions exist, COMMAND.COM uses the following hierarchy:

1. If a COM file exists, it is used.

2. Otherwise, if an EXE file exists, it is used.

3. If neither a COM nor EXE file exists, a BAT file is used.

Reminder:
You can issue internal commands at the DOS prompt at any time; external commands are supplied to COMMAND.COM from disk files.

DOS includes internal and external commands because both types have advantages and disadvantages and are appropriate for some commands and not others. Internal commands are faster than similar external commands, because COMMAND.COM does not have to perform a disk search when running internal commands. Internal commands also are always available on floppy-based systems. In contrast, the floppy on which external commands reside may be removed from the system and become unavailable. However, the instructions that make up the internal commands continuously occupy precious memory, because they are an integral part of COMMAND.COM. DOS designers had to make a decision about each command: internal commands are faster but take up memory; external commands are slightly slower but do not permanently occupy memory. Generally, commands that are relatively simple and heavily used are internal; commands that are more complex and less-often used are external.

From a practical standpoint, often it does not matter whether commands are external or internal. However, you may care when one or both of the following conditions exist:

- The PATH is incorrectly set. Because internal commands are directly understood by COMMAND.COM, you still may be able to use them. However, COMMAND.COM depends on the PATH to find external commands, and these commands may temporarily be inaccessible to you.

- You use a floppy-based system with no hard drive. Typically one of the floppy drives may contain DOS, including the external commands. If you remove this floppy, the external commands become inaccessible. Many users of floppy-only systems use drive A for DOS and the external commands and drive B for programs and data.

A hard disk almost always has enough capacity beyond normal program and data files to accommodate all the external DOS command files. With a search path established to external commands, most hard disk users do not see much difference between internal commands and external commands. However, note that hard disk users should have a bootable floppy with the external command files on it; you can never tell when a hard disk failure is going to occur, and in such a situation, you may need a floppy disk with which to rebuild the hard disk.

Categories of DOS Commands

DOS commands can be categorized as internal or external, but other types of groupings also are useful. When you have a general DOS function in mind, you can choose from a selection of commands that share common characteristics of that function. The following are functional categories of DOS commands:

Cue:
DOS commands may be categorized according to function.

Disk management (*see Chapter 6*)

Directory management (*see Chapter 7*)

File management (*see Chapter 8*)

System-information management (*see Chapter 9*)

Input-output-device management (*see Chapter 10*)

Batch-file management (*see Chapter 12*)

System configuration (*see Chapter 15*)

Country-information management (*see Chapter 16*)

Tables 3.1 through 3.8 summarize the commands included in each of the functional categories.

Table 3.1
Disk Management Commands

Command	Action
CHKDSK	Analyzes disk directories and the disk's internal bookkeeping areas (the file allocation table, or FAT); helps detect disk problems; also shows disk space and memory status report
DISKCOMP	Compares two disks for differences
DISKCOPY	Copies an entire disk to a different disk with the original disk's format
FDISK	Creates and maintains the partition table for DOS partitions on a hard disk
FORMAT	Prepares a blank or recycled disk to receive files; creates DOS's bookkeeping records on the disk

continues

Table 3.1 *(continued)*

Command	Action
LABEL	Creates, changes, or deletes a disk's volume label
RECOVER	Recovers one or all of a disk's files when a file or directory has a bad sector
REPLACE	Updates a disk with files of the same name from another disk
SELECT	Installs DOS on a disk with country-specific information; configures the DOS Shell in Versions 4 and 5
SYS	Installs the hidden DOS system files from one disk to another
UNFORMAT	When executed immediately after a FORMAT command, restores a hard disk to its previous condition (Version 5 only)
VOL	Reports a disk's volume label on-screen

Table 3.2
Directory Management Commands

Command	Action
APPEND	Locates files needed by programs outside the current directory
CHDIR (CD)	Changes the current working directory
MKDIR (MD)	Creates a directory in a disk's directory tree structure
PATH	Establishes directory search list for COMMAND.COM to use to load programs or external commands when the programs or commands are not located in the current directory
RMDIR	Removes an empty directory from the directory tree structure
TREE XCOPY	Displays the directory tree structure of a disk; copies files in a selective manner; includes the provision to create directories on the destination disk

Table 3.3
File Management Commands

Command	Action
ATTRIB	Reports and modifies the archive and read attributes of a file or group of files
BACKUP	Copies files in a special format from one disk to another to be restored when needed by RESTORE
COMP	Compares two files or sets of files and reports differences among files
COPY	Copies a file or a group of files; concatenates (joins) multiple files into one file
DEL (ERASE)	Releases a file or group of files from a disk and returns the space occupied by the files to DOS
EDLIN	Creates a text file or makes modifications (edits) to an existing file
FC	Compares two binary or text files and reports differences in selectable formats
RENAME	Changes the name or extension of a file or group of files
RESTORE	Reads specially formatted backup files produced in a BACKUP operation from a backup set disk to another disk
TYPE	Sends the content of a file to the screen for viewing
VERIFY	Turns DOS's internal read-after-write file verification routines on or off; reports the current VERIFY setting

Table 3.4
System Information Commands

Command	Action
CHCP	Displays and changes the current code page
COMMAND	Starts a secondary command processor. This feature enables programs to execute DOS commands.
DATE	Sets or displays the system date

continues

Table 3.4 *(continued)*

Command	Action
DEBUG	Enables programs to be examined in great detail; used by programmers to find mistakes
DIR	Displays the directory information for files in a directory
DOSKEY	Installs the command history mechanism that enables you to re-execute previous commands without retyping them
DOSSHELL	Starts the Version 4 or 5 graphical interface program
EXIT	Returns from a secondary command processor to the one started below it
MEM	Displays the current status of system memory
MODE	Sets the operational parameters of many devices
PROMPT	Sets the appearance of the system prompt
SET	Establishes or displays the command processor's environment values
SETVER	Sets the current DOS version number
TIME	Sets or displays the system date
VER	Reports the version number of the DOS program that booted the computer

Table 3.5
Input-Output-Device Commands

Command	Action
ASSIGN	Directs disk requests from one disk to another disk
CLS	Clears the screen and places the cursor in the upper left corner
CTTY	Provides for a serial device to be the standard input-output device
FIND	Locates all lines in a file that contains a given parameter string; displays the line(s) on-screen

Command	Action
JOIN	Connects a drive to a directory on another drive to produce one logical directory; in effect, this feature fools the computer into thinking that a set of directories is on another disk drive.
MORE	Enables data to be viewed a screenful at a time
PRINT	Sends files to the printer device
SORT	Rearranges data in alphabetical or numeric order
SUBST	Enables use of an alias drive name in place of the drive's true name

Table 3.6
Batch File Commands

Command	Action
CALL	Enables the nesting of batch files
ECHO	Displays predefined text to the screen; used to display prompts from within batch files
FOR	Marks the repeating of DOS commands in a batch file
GOTO	Causes batch-file processing to continue on the line following a given label
IF	Causes a line in a batch file to execute conditionally
PAUSE	Temporarily pauses the execution of a batch file
REM	Enables the addition of nonexecuting remarks in a batch file
SHIFT	Enables the use of more than 10 replaceable parameters in a batch file

Table 3.7
System Configuration Commands

Command	Action
BREAK	Controls the checking of the Ctrl-Break key press
BUFFERS	Sets the number of system disk buffers allocated
DEVICE	Names a device driver to be used at boot time

continues

Table 3.7 *(continued)*

Command	Action
FCBS	Specifies the number of Version 1 file control blocks allowed to be open at the same time
FILES	Specifies the number of files that can be open at one time
FASTOPEN	Enables the internal FAT buffering feature and the directory read-ahead feature
INSTALL	Enables CONFIG.SYS processing to load a command
LASTDRIVE	Sets the maximum number of drives that can be accessed
SHELL	Sets the name and location of the command processor that DOS uses during a boot in place of COMMAND.COM
STACKS	Enables the overriding of the default stack allocation
SWITCHES	Makes an extended keyboard appear as a standard keyboard to DOS
SHARE	Loads and enables disk-change checking

Table 3.8
Country Information Commands

Command	Action
CHCP	Selects character-set code pages for I/O devices
COUNTRY	Modifies country-dependent settings
DISPLAY.SYS	Supports code-page switching on certain displays
GRAFTABL	Accommodates national language characters displayed in graphics mode
KEYB	Selects a special keyboard key layout
NLSFUNC	Supports country-specific information
PRINTER.SYS	Supports code-page switching on certain printers

Understanding the Command Line

When you enter a DOS command, you often must type more than just the name of the command. Many commands require additional information that specifies what data is to be manipulated or exactly how a task is to be performed. Each DOS command has a set of rules, or *syntax*, that specifies what information is to be entered when the command is used.

The following sections discuss the rules for entering commands and provide information relating to all commands. This discussion is fundamental to later chapters. If you already are comfortable with the information presented here, read the following sections for a quick review. If you find the information new, be sure that you understand it before you move on.

Note that the rules discussed in the following sections apply to most commands but not all. The designers of DOS found it impossible to adhere to every rule throughout all the DOS commands. The command reference section of this book gives the detailed syntax for each command.

Cue:
The syntax of a command line is the way in which the command line is phrased.

Examining the Command Line

A DOS command may contain the following elements:

- Command name

- Parameters

- Switches

All commands must include the command name; the other parts may be optional, depending on the rules for a specific command.

In most situations, DOS doesn't care whether you type the commands in upper- or lowercase or any combination. For example, you can type the following command three ways, but all three ways do exactly the same thing:

DIR/W

DIR/w

dir/w

This rule has exceptions. The FIND command, for example, can perform differently if a particular parameter is in uppercase rather than lowercase.

Understanding Parameters

All DOS commands require a command name: something that tells DOS what type of operation you want to do. For some commands, the command name is all the information they need to do their job. For example, the VER command tells you which version of DOS you are using. The command does not require any additional information to do its job.

However, for most commands, the name of the command is usually not enough; additional information often is required. For example, you may type COPY to copy a file, but the name of the command by itself is not enough to tell DOS which file you want to copy and to where. Most DOS commands require that you provide supplemental information on the command line. The text you supply to indicate the objects of a command's actions contains the *parameters*. Parameters are used to specify files or disk drives to be used by the command. Parameters are separated from the name of the command and from each other by one or more spaces, or *delimiters*, as shown in the following example:

COPY *OLDFILE NEWFILE*

In this example, COPY is the command name; OLDFILE and NEWFILE are parameters and tell COPY the name of the file to be copied (OLDFILE) and the name that should be given to the copy (NEWFILE).

The number of parameters required by each command, and what those parameters mean, varies from one command to another. For common commands, such as COPY and DIR, you may memorize the rules that specify what parameters are possible. For other less common commands, such as APPEND and SUBST, you may not want to remember the rules. If an occasion arises to use these commands, consult the command reference in the back of this book to refamiliarize yourself with the appropriate rules.

COMMAND.COM uses rules to parse commands that contain file parameters, as well as to parse commands that contain other types of parameters. When you issue DOS commands, you must form the command line properly for COMMAND.COM to parse the parameters of the command line correctly. In addition to parameters, some commands include optional modifiers of the command's basic action. These modifiers are *switches*.

Understanding Switches

A switch is designed to slightly alter the way the command works. Switches do not normally change the fundamental action performed by the command. Switches usually follow the parameters on a command line and are delimited (separated from the parameters) by a leading / (forward slash) character (not to be confused with the \ [backslash] used to separate directory and file names). In most cases, only one character follows the switch's / delimiter. Some commands include switches that may have several characters following the /. In all cases, the text that accompanies the / character in the command line has no space characters within the switch text. DOS interprets an intervening space as a delimiting character and misreads the switch.

The DIR command has several switches available. By itself, DIR lists the contents of the current directory. Switches do not change this basic action; they modify how the directory contents are shown. For example, the DIR /W switch displays a directory listing in a *wide* format. The DIR /P switch displays a directory listing one screen *page* at a time and prompts you before displaying another page. The DIR /S switch specifies that subdirectories should be listed. You can issue the DIR command with none, all, or any combination of these switches.

Most commands with multiple-switch capability can be issued with more than one switch appearing in the command line. Some command's switches are mutually exclusive, however, which means that they cannot be used together in the same command line. DOS responds with an error message when certain command's switches are issued together. Other commands have switches that make sense only when paired with other switches. The BACKUP switch /T for *time* makes sense when used with the /D *date* switch. The BACKUP /T switch alone doesn't produce any meaningful modification of the BACKUP command, because basing a backup on the time of day that a file was created or modified is rather random.

Many commands share the same switch letters, although in most cases these switches actually have different meanings for different commands. For example, in DOS 5.0, the FORMAT and DIR commands have a /S switch. In the case of FORMAT, the /S switch causes system files to be copied onto the formatted disk; for DIR, the /S causes subdirectories to be listed. This duplication is unfortunate and leads to some confusion. The duplication is necessary because the alphabet has only 26 letters, but hundreds of switches are needed by all the DOS commands. You may memorize a few of the more common switches; the command reference in this book can provide you with a comprehensive list of the switches available for each command. When you use switches, make sure that you understand the meaning of each switch as it applies to the particular command you are using.

Understanding Defaults

For most DOS commands, DOS must know many pieces of information before the command can do its job. For example, when you list a directory with the DIR command, DOS must answer the following questions:

- Do you want regular format or a wide listing?

- Should subdirectories also be listed?

- Should the display pause after each screenful?

- Which directory should be listed?

Clearly it would be tedious if every DIR command had to supply all of this information. Fortunately, almost every piece of information has a *default* value. A default is a value that DOS uses if you do not specify a value.

In the case of DIR, the following default values are used for the preceding questions:

- A regular listing is used.

- Subdirectories are not listed.

- The screen does not pause.

- The current directory is listed.

If you type DIR with no other information, therefore, these default values apply. They can be changed by adding parameters or switches to the command. Knowing the defaults for a command is crucial to using DOS comfortably, because you can save typing time by letting DOS make assumptions about what you want to do.

One of the most important defaults is the disk drive used by a command. When you start the computer, DOS notes the drive from which it booted. On a hard-disk system, this drive is most often drive C; on a floppy system, it is drive A. When waiting for a command, DOS shows you the familiar C prompt:

```
C>
```

This prompt indicates that drive C is the default drive; if you do not specify otherwise, DOS assumes that all files are to be found on drive C. To make a copy of a file, therefore, you may type the following command:

COPY *OLDFILE NEWFILE*

Here both files, OLDFILE and NEWFILE, reside on drive C. If you want NEWFILE to be placed on drive A, you must explicitly tell DOS by overriding the default, as shown in the following example:

COPY *OLDFILE A:NEWFILE*

You change the current disk drive to another disk drive by typing the desired drive's letter, followed by a colon, and pressing Enter. At the command prompt, the process looks like the following:

```
A>C:

C>
```

You can have only one default drive at any time (the default drive, the current drive, and the logged drive all refer to the same drive).

Each disk has its own file system. When you boot the PC, DOS places you in the root directory of each disk on the system. Assuming that you have created subdirectories on each of the system's disks, you can change each disk's default directory to a different directory. Changing directories is similar to switching to a new drive except that although only one drive can be DOS's default drive, each drive has its own default or current directory. The current drive's current directory is the working directory. If you omit the optional drive specifier and the optional path specifier from a command, DOS uses the current working directory. If you include a drive specifier but omit the optional path specifier, DOS uses the specified drive's current directory.

Defaults help to make command lines look simpler. If you mainly use a hard disk, you may seldom use a drive specifier in a command line; if you mainly work in a particular subdirectory, you may seldom use a path specifier in a command line. In such a case, DOS supplies default values for the command line. COMMAND.COM still parses the command line according to the rules of syntax, however. If COMMAND.COM finds that you have specified an optional specifier, the specifier that you supplied is the one used.

Using the Keyboard

Normally, you issue DOS commands from the keyboard and view the commands' messages on-screen. COMMAND.COM gets command lines from the standard input device: the keyboard. COMMAND.COM issues system messages through the standard output device: the screen. Error messages produced by DOS during command execution also appear on-screen. However, DOS provides for input or output to be associated with a device other than the standard device. You can instruct DOS to redirect the standard inputs and outputs to other logical DOS devices. Chapter 4 discusses redirection. For now, consider the keyboard the input device for DOS commands.

Cue:
The keyboard is the standard input device; the screen is the standard output device.

Like a typewriter, the keyboard of a computer contains all the letters of the alphabet. The numbers, symbols, and punctuation characters are virtually the same. The computer keyboard has the familiar QWERTY layout. (The name QWERTY comes from the letters found on the left side of the top row of letters on a standard typewriter.) A computer keyboard is different from a typewriter keyboard in several important ways.

The most notable difference is the extra keys—the keys that do not appear on a typewriter. These keys are described in table 3.9. Depending on the type of computer you use, you also may find 10 or 12 special function keys.

Table 3.9
Special Keys on the Computer Keyboard

Key	Function
Enter	Signals the computer that you have finished typing a command and that the command should now be executed; also functions as a carriage return in many programs such as word processors
Cursor keys	Changes your location on-screen. Included are the arrow, PgUp, PgDn, Home, and End keys.
Backspace	Moves the cursor backward one space at a time, deleting any character in that space
Del	Deletes, or erases, any character at the location of the cursor
Ins	Inserts any character at the location of the cursor
Shift	Enables you to capitalize letters when Shift is held down and the letter is typed. When pressed in combination with another key, Shift can change the standard function of that key.
Caps Lock	When pressed to the lock position, capitalizes all characters typed. This step is slightly different from holding the SHIFT key down, however, because only letters are capitalized.
Ctrl/Control key	When pressed in combination with another key, changes the standard function of that key

Key	Function
Alt/Alternate key	When pressed in combination with another key, changes the standard function of that key
Esc	The meaning of Esc varies, depending on what you are doing. Typically, this key enables you to escape from a current operation to a preceding one.
Num Lock	Changes the numeric pad from cursor-movment to numeric-function mode
PrtSc	Used with the Shift key to send the characters on the display to the printer
Print Screen	Found on Enhanced Keyboards; same as Shift-PrtSc
Scroll Lock	Locks the scrolling function to the cursor-control keys. Instead of the cursor's moving, the screen scrolls.
Pause	Suspends display output until another key is pressed (not provided with standard keyboards)
Break	Stops a program in progress from running
Numeric	A cluster of keys to the right of the standard keypad keyboard. The keypad includes numbered keys from 0 to 9, cursor-control keys, and other special keys.

Many of these extra keys are designed for use with other keys. For example, pressing the Shift key and the PrtSc key in combination causes DOS to print what currently appears on-screen. Pressing the Ctrl and PrtSc keys simultaneously causes DOS to continuously print what you type and what DOS sends to the screen. On some keyboards, pressing only the Print Screen key causes the contents of the screen to be printed. Pressing Ctrl and PrtSc a second time turns off the printing.

The function keys are shortcuts. Not all programs use these keys, and some use only a few of them. When used, they carry out common operations for you. For example, the F1 key often is used for on-line help in application programs. On-line help displays instructions from the computer's memory to help you understand a particular operation. The DOS Shell uses the F3 key to back out of one operation and move into another. The F10 key moves the cursor to various parts of the screen in the DOS Shell.

Many early PC-compatible computers use a standard keyboard like that of the IBM PC. Other machines use Personal Computer AT keyboards. IBM's PS/2 computers use the 101-key Enhanced Keyboard. You can determine whether the computer has a standard keyboard, a Personal Computer AT-style keyboard, or an Enhanced Keyboard. Certain keys are found only on specific keyboards. For example, you find the Print Screen and Pause keys only on the Enhanced Keyboard. You can, however, simulate these keys by using a combination of keys on the standard keyboard.

Some new keyboards enable you to change key caps and to switch key definitions for the Caps Lock, Ctrl, Esc, and ~ (tilde) keys. Northgate Computers, for example, not only offer these options but also offer an enhanced keyboard. On this enhanced keyboard, the first 10 function keys are to the left of, instead of across the top of, the alphabet and number keys. The arrangement requires one more key than do the 101-key enhanced keyboards.

Small computers, such as lunchboxes and laptops, may use nonstandard keyboards to conserve space. On some computers, space is so restricted that you need an external numeric keypad for use with software that performs advanced calculations.

DOS acts on combination keys in predefined ways. Table 3.10 lists key combinations and the action that DOS takes when you use a key combination.

Table 3.10
DOS Key Combinations

Keys	Function
Ctrl-Num Lock	Freezes the display; pressing Ctrl-S or any other key restarts the display.
Shift-PrtSc	Prints the contents of the video display (print-screen feature)
Ctrl-PrtSc	Sends lines to the screen and the printer; giving this sequence a second time turns this function off.
Ctrl-C	Stops the execution of a program; usually the same as Ctrl-Break
Ctrl-Alt-Del	Restarts DOS (warm boot)

DOS uses some of the function and editing keys for editing a command line. This feature enables you to enter a new command similar or identical to the last command without having to retype the entire command. To re-execute the last command without any changes, you need only press F3 to recall the command and press ENTER to execute it. Alternatively, by using the arrows, INSERT, DELETE, and the other function keys, you can make changes to the command and execute the changed version. Table 3.11 lists the function keys and the action the keys take at the command line prompt. These keys are available in all versions of DOS.

Table 3.11
DOS Command-Line Editing Keys

Key	Action
Tab	Moves cursor to the next tab stop
Esc	Cancels the current line
Ins	Enables you to insert characters in the line
Del	Deletes a character from the line
Backspace	Moves the cursor back one character
F1	Copies one character from the preceding command
F2	Copies all characters from the preceding command line up to the next character you type
F3	Copies all remaining characters from the preceding command line
F4	Deletes all characters from the preceding command line up to, but not including, the next character typed (opposite of F2)
F5	Moves the current line into the buffer but does not enable DOS to execute the line
F6	Produces an end-of-file marker when you copy from the console to a disk file

Editing Commands with DOSKEY

The keys in table 3.11 provide simple editing and re-execution of the last command. Version 5 of DOS introduces a much more sophisticated facility called *DOSKEY*. DOSKEY enables you to recall, edit, and re-execute any command recently typed. The command also contains a macro facility, which enables you to define short-hand notations for commands you use frequently. Anyone who spends a great deal of time entering DOS commands may find DOSKEY helpful.

Cue:
DOSKEY records the commands you type for reuse at a later time.

Installing DOSKEY

DOSKEY's features are not automatically available; you must tell DOS that you want to use them in one of the following ways:

1. Type **DOSKEY** at the DOS prompt.

2. Place the command *DOSKEY* in the AUTOEXEC.BAT file so that it is installed when the system starts up.

3. Install DOSKEY from within the CONFIG.SYS file by including the following command:

   INSTALL=*C:\DOS***DOSKEY.COM**

The actual command on the system may be slightly different to indicate the drive and directory in which DOSKEY can be found.

DOSKEY records every command you enter into DOS (up to a maximum limit that the user sets; the default limit is 512 characters), until you turn the computer off. At any time, you can use special keys to list all preceding commands, recall a particular command, make desired changes to a previous command, and re-execute the command. Unlike the regular DOS command editing features described in the preceding section, DOSKEY does not limit you to the most recent command.

When DOSKEY is loaded, it must reserve part of the computer's memory for its use, to record the commands you type. This memory then is unavailable for use by the word processor, spreadsheet, or other application. The amount of memory used by DOSKEY is small, but if you do not type many DOS commands—if you spend most of the time in a word processor, or if you use the DOS Shell instead of COMMAND.COM—you may find DOSKEY of little use to you and may choose not to waste the memory.

Accessing Previous Commands

DOSKEY records the commands that you type, up to a maximum of 512 characters (although this amount can be increased). After DOSKEY is loaded, most of the special keys are available from the command prompt to recall, edit, and re-execute commands. Notice that some of these keys are the same ones used by the standard DOS command editor; when DOSKEY is loaded, it replaces the standard DOS command editor.

At any time, you can press F7 to list the commands that DOSKEY has recorded. To recall, change, and execute one of these commands, press F9.

DOSKEY asks for the number of the command you want to recall. When you press ENTER, the specified command appears on the command line. Pressing ENTER executes the command.

Alternatively, you can recall a recent command by typing the first few letters of the command and pressing F8. DOSKEY looks for the most recent command that begins with the letters you typed and then recalls that command.

When a command appears on the command line, pressing ENTER causes it to be executed. To make changes to the command before it is executed, most of the usual editing keys are available: the left-arrow key moves the cursor one character to the left; the right-arrow key moves the cursor one character to the right. In addition, Home moves the cursor to the beginning of the line; End moves the cursor to the end of the line; Ctrl-left arrow moves the cursor left one word; Ctrl-right arrow moves the cursor one word right.

When the cursor appears on the character you want to change, type over it or press Delete to delete the character. To add new text, press Insert. The size of the cursor increases to indicate that you are in Insert mode. Now when you type new characters, they are inserted instead of replacing existing characters.

The up-arrow and down-arrow keys enable you to browse through recorded commands. The up-arrow key recalls the preceding command. Each time the up-arrow key is pressed, the preceding command appears on the command line. By pressing the up-arrow key repeatedly, you can recall commands farther back; you move backward through the list of recent commands. If you go too far, the down-arrow key moves you forward in the list.

Other keys are sometimes useful: PgUp recalls the oldest recorded command; PgDn recalls the most recent. ESC clears the current command—useful if you accidentally recall the wrong command and do not want to execute it. ALT-F7 erases all recorded commands.

Using Macros with DOSKEY

The DOSKEY macro facility enables you to define a shorthand notation for any commonly used commands. Suppose that you often want to list the names of all the documents in a current directory; perhaps such files have the extension DOC. You can accomplish this task by typing the following command:

DIR *.DOC

Cue:
DOSKEY macros enable you to create shorthand notations for commands.

You can use the following DOSKEY macro to create a shorthand notation for this command:

DOSKEY LD=DIR *.DOC

This command tells DOS that from now on the letters LD (for List Documents) are shorthand for DIR *.DOC. Now when you type LD, it is as though you had typed the longer command.

Several special characters cannot appear in a macro definition, so DOSKEY uses the following special key combinations to represent these special characters:

In place of	Use instead
>	$G
<	$L
|	$B
;	$T
$	$$

Macro definitions often are included in the AUTOEXEC.BAT file so that commonly used macros are defined every time the computer starts.

Setting the DOSKEY Buffer Size

By default, DOSKEY remembers the last 512 characters-worth of commands typed, which typically averages about the last 50 commands. You can save computer memory by setting this limit lower or increase the number of commands recorded by increasing this limit. This action can be achieved with the /bufsize= switch when DOSKEY is installed, as shown in the following example:

DOSKEY /bufsize=2000

This command installs DOSKEY with space to remember the last 2,000 characters.

Stopping a Command

Reminder:
Pressing Ctrl-C or Ctrl-Break stops a command.

DOS monitors the status of the Ctrl-C and Ctrl-Break key combinations to see whether one of the combinations has been pressed. If DOS detects that one of these combinations has been pressed, it stops the command that is executing and presents a new command prompt. If you are entering a command from the keyboard, COMMAND.COM throws out the current line and issues a fresh prompt on the next line.

Some commands can be effectively stopped. For example, a long directory listing resulting from a DIR command can produce several screens of output. If you press Ctrl-C during the listing, the listing operation stops, and COMMAND.COM prompts for the next command.

Other commands can be stopped, but doing so may leave you with a job that is half-done. For example, if you mistakenly issue a FORMAT command with the wrong drive specifier, you can stop FORMAT. However, there is a good chance that FORMAT operated long enough to overwrite some of the DOS tables on the target disk. The disk is not usable, and the disk's previous contents are lost. Issue commands carefully. Ctrl-C or Ctrl-Break may be unable to stop a DOS operation quickly enough to keep some commands from overwriting DOS tables or user files.

Understanding the Environment

When each program is loaded into memory, the program is given a set of values—pieces of information—that DOS stores in reserved memory locations. Collectively, this information is the *environment*. Each piece of information is a *variable* and has a name associated with it that programs can use to access the information.

Cue:
The environment is a DOS storage area for values held in named variables.

For example, perhaps several related pieces of business software all need to know the name of the company using the software. They may obtain this information by requiring you to provide an environment variable called COMPANY that contains the value "Acme Widgets, Inc."

Actual examples of environment variables are *PROMPT*, which determines how DOS prompts you for a command, and *PATH*, which determines in which directories DOS looks to find commands. PROMPT and PATH commands set the values associated with these environment variables. Other environment variables are assigned by you when you use the SET command. Consider the following sample SET commands:

SET *COMPANY=Acme Widgets, Inc.*

SET *FINDIT=C:\DOS*

The first example sets a mythical company. In the second example, the variable named FINDIT is assigned the character value of C:\DOS. The variable FINDIT and the variable's value C:\DOS are then part of the environment.

You don't just arbitrarily place variables in the environment; rather you assign values to variables required by the programs you are using. The documentation for a specific program usually explains any environment variables it requires. A database program, for example, may need to know in which directory the data files are located. The program can search the environment string, looking for the predetermined variable FINDIT. On locating FINDIT, the program can extract FINDIT's value. The program then can use the variable's value as the directory to search. Programs must know how to use the environment, and you must know how to assign values to variables that programs expect.

Because some DOS commands use environment variables, you may see references to the environment throughout this book. Chapter 9 has specific references to the environment in discussions of the SET and COMMAND commands. For now, just be aware that one of COMMAND.COM's important jobs is to make the environment available to the programs and commands that COMMAND.COM starts.

Using the DOS Shell

This chapter has examined the command interpreter, COMMAND.COM. COMMAND.COM repeatedly asks you what you want to do (by displaying a prompt), waits for you to type an explanation of the next task you want to perform (in the form of a command), and loads the appropriate program or executes the appropriate block of machine instructions to carry out the task.

Such a scheme places something of a burden on the user to know what the possible tasks (commands) are and how to formulate the commands so that COMMAND.COM can understand them. Experienced users who also are fast typists find this a very satisfying way to communicate with the computer. Other users, who are less experienced or less-capable typists, may prefer another approach.

Since Version 4, DOS has incorporated an alternative way of communicating with the operating system: the DOS Shell. Rather than asking, "What do you want to do?" as COMMAND.COM does, the DOS Shell asks in a much more friendly way: "Here are the things you may want to do; pick one." By using the keyboard or a mouse, the user then selects the task to be performed and the parameters that apply to the task.

As you learn more about COMMAND.COM, keep in mind that an alternative exists. Chapter 5 discusses the DOS Shell in detail; you then may be able to pick the method of communicating with DOS that is most natural for you.

Chapter Summary

This chapter discussed COMMAND.COM, the DOS command processor. The information presented in this chapter may help you as you work with commands. When you read about the core DOS commands in Part II and about other commands in Parts III and IV, you may be better equipped to use COMMAND.COM's universal concepts with those commands. In this chapter, you learned the following information:

- The CPU processes data as it executes instructions retrieved from RAM and ROM. The data is stored in RAM.

- The CPU can interrupt its current instruction sequence and execute other blocks of instructions when outside events occur.

- Programs and service routines are written in computer languages. The lowest-level language is machine code that the CPU directly understands.

- Booting DOS involves a series of operations during which the PC initializes and tests the hardware, loads the DOS files, and executes COMMAND.COM.

- Commands can be categorized according to whether they are internal or external and according to the command's general DOS-management function.

- COMMAND.COM examines a command line to extract the command, the parameters, and the switches.

- Many commands use default values for specifiers if you omit the specifiers in the command line.

- DOS commands use the keyboard for standard input and the screen for standard output.

- Besides the typewriter keys, a PC keyboard has keys and key combinations that mean something special in DOS.

- DOSKEY enables you to record the commands you enter, for reuse at a later time.

- COMMAND.COM passes the values of environment variables to programs when COMMAND.COM loads the programs.

- An alternative method for communicating with DOS is available through the DOS Shell.

In the next chapter, you learn about an alternative method of communicating with DOS.

4

Gaining Control
of Hardware

Chapter 1 discusses the many contexts of DOS and the layered computer. In Chapter 2, you learn how DOS, through the kernel, implements a multidisk hierarchical file system. Chapter 3 discusses COMMAND.COM as the command processor layer of DOS. Chapter 3 also demonstrates how the CPU steps through instructions for entire programs or for service routine blocks. This chapter provides a basic understanding of how DOS deals with devices. In DOS, a discussion of devices can include topics that range from how COMMAND.COM accommodates redirection to how CONFIG.SYS expands the device base of the PC to your peripheral hardware and memory expansion. Understanding devices not only returns DOS benefits but also helps you understand personal computing in the context of networks, window environments, and future operating systems.

Reviewing the Layered PC

In Chapter 1, you learned that the instructions that make up the MS-DOS operating system are arranged in layers. Higher levels are more abstract and less technical and deal with ideas that concern humans. Lower levels, less abstract and more technical, deal with issues oriented toward the computer hardware.

When you run programs, you interact with a highest layer of the PC. In this layer, you see computing as spreadsheet cells, word processor function keys, and modem links to on-line data services. This surface activity

105

between you and your keyboard and screen is an abstraction from the logical and electro-mechanical activity at lower layers of the PC. Your primary interest is with the activity on-screen. When you hit a golf ball or return a tennis lob, you don't often stop to consider the underlying physics involved at the moment of impact. You only want to place the ball close to (or in) the hole or hit the ball over the net, in bounds, and in a strategic area of the far court. In computing, you want to create an accurate financial model of next year's sales or reformat a block of text for a manual. That you can use a personal computer as a useful tool and not worry about how the computer operates is a tribute to the improvements brought to computers in the past decade. The internal processes of the machine, however, are hidden from view.

When you type commands at the DOS prompt to manage disk directories, files, and devices, you are at a slightly lower and slightly less abstract level of the computer. When working with COMMAND.COM, you are more aware of the file system and of the devices on your PC. At the DOS prompt, you maintain the PC to become more orderly and useful for your computing work. Just as you maintain your tennis racket or your golf clubs, you maintain your files and the PC configuration.

Cue:
The kernel translates higher layer requests into requests for lower layers.

DOS maintains organizational order in your PC under the surface of COMMAND.COM. This core layer of operating system organization is the DOS kernel, which is less abstract than COMMAND.COM. The kernel deals with requests from COMMAND.COM and other programs for data from files and devices. Ordinarily, you have no direct contact with the kernel. From file and device names that you or the program provide, the kernel translates these requests to the hardware values necessary to access data. The kernel translates input or output requests from the higher layers into uniform requests of a predetermined form for lower layers. The higher layers do not know the details of how the kernel handles the higher layer requests. The kernel, in turn, does not know how the lower layers go about fulfilling the kernel's request. Thanks to the kernel, however, a program can be totally independent of the overhead of managing the file system and can count on its requests—for file input, printer output, and so on—to be fulfilled in a constant and reliable fashion.

Cue:
The BIOS is responsible for getting input from and output to the peripheral hardware.

Beneath the kernel layer, a layer of basic input-output services, or BIOS, is built into the hardware. The BIOS layer is the PC's device-dependent layer. The responsibility for getting input from and output to the peripheral hardware rests on the BIOS. Because the BIOS processes kernel requests through uniform service routines, the kernel is device-independent. Any new peripheral hardware that the BIOS supports is available for kernel requests. The BIOS, the least abstract layer, deals with peripheral hardware at the binary level. BIOS routines are the glue that attaches hardware to the basic computer in a fashion that disguises the seams.

Understanding Device Drivers

To be properly used, all peripheral equipment—printers, modems, and disk drives—connected to your computer must communicate with the computer. This communication usually involves special electronic circuitry and software within DOS. From DOS's point of view, however, different techniques are required for each piece of equipment. Even types of equipment that seem similar—such as two different brands of disk drives—may require different techniques from DOS. DOS is designed to use the appropriate techniques for all possible types of equipment by using *device drivers*.

A device driver is a specialized program *module* (a section of a program) that provides DOS with the information to control and communicate with a particular type of equipment. When the DOS kernel needs to control a device, the device driver does the actual work. The kernel tells the device driver what to do, and the device driver handles the details of the job. When your computer starts, appropriate device drivers are loaded from disk into the computer memory and are available to control the device.

Cue:

Device drivers enable you to attach peripheral hardware to the DOS kernel.

Figure 4.1 shows how a typical program's I/O request is fulfilled by a device driver. The program, represented by the top block, makes a request of the DOS kernel. This request can be to read a track from disk, to print a character on the printer, or to send a byte through a modem. The kernel consults a list of device drivers to determine which handles the request. The device driver translates the kernel's request into a set of control and transfer actions by dealing directly with the device. The device's output data is transferred to the program through the device driver and the kernel. No one block knows exactly how the next block works. Each block relies on a uniform interface to adjacent blocks to complete the I/O service.

The following list explains how DOS device drivers enable you to create a more efficient and flexible computing environment:

- DOS is not built to understand every possible piece of equipment. Because device drivers are separate program modules, new device drivers can be written and installed on your computer as new types of hardware are made available.

- Because you choose the device drivers that you use, you waste no precious computer memory for code that controls devices that you do not use. When properly configured, your computer knows how to handle only your hardware.

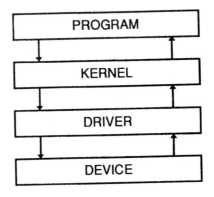

Fig. 4.1. How program I/O requests are filled.

Understanding Controllers

Software needed to control a device often is not an integral part of DOS; this software often is contained in a separate module called a *device driver*. A similar situation applies to the circuits that control peripheral devices. Usually, a special piece of equipment, a *controller*, handles the hardware requirements of communicating with a device. The controller can be located in the same cabinet as the computer, within the controlled device, or in a separate container. The device drivers previously mentioned are programs written to manage the activities of the controllers.

Display adapters are examples of controllers. A computer can have one or more display adapters, based on the type of monitor you use, such as a Monochrome Display Adapter (MDA), Color Graphics Adapter (CGA), Enhanced Graphics Adapter (EGA), or Video Graphics Array (VGA). When characters are displayed to the monitor, the DOS kernel doesn't really care which type of monitor is connected. The kernel tells the device driver to print the desired text. The device driver understands the type of monitor you use and sends the appropriate signals to the controller (display adapter). The controller sends the appropriate electrical signals to make the characters appear on-screen.

Notice that each part of the machine doesn't worry about details that are the responsibility of some other portion. The CPU knows how to communicate with controllers; the controllers know how to communicate with peripheral hardware.

Another common example of a controller is found in disk drives. Most disk drives contain little intelligence; they require precise direction from another piece of equipment to perform a useful function. The disk controller supplies much of the underlying logic or intelligence of disk operations. Although disk drives are fundamentally alike, each type of drive has its own electro-mechanical personality. The controller (hardware) and disk device driver (software) are adapted to the drive's electro-mechanical personality. When the kernel requests that data be read from the disk, the driver manages the controller to ensure that the drive is ready for transfer and was given the correct head, track, and sector information. When the drive controller returns the data, the device driver supervises the placement of the returned data into memory. The kernel is unaware of the nature and the number of individual tasks that the driver carries out to make the data available. When the kernel calls on a disk device driver, the kernel can make a generic request for sectors and count on the driver to be responsible for the variations that can occur from one type of disk to another.

If a programmer is sufficiently familiar with how a new item of peripheral hardware works, the programmer can write a device driver for the hardware (or its adapter), and the PC can incorporate the new device. DOS clearly defines the rules that must be followed if the kernel can communicate with the driver. If a programmer strictly follows the rules, DOS can use the device.

Grouping Device Drivers

For convenience, the designers of DOS grouped physical devices into two categories: *character* device drivers are designed for devices such as the keyboard and printer that tend to deal with data as individual characters; *block* devices are designed for devices such as disk drives and tape drives that tend to view data as chunks (blocks) to be manipulated.

Character Device Drivers

Character devices perform I/O one character or byte at a time. Typical character devices in PCs are the keyboard, the display, serial ports, and printer ports. Usually, one device driver controls one character device. Serial ports transfer data one bit at a time in series, and printer (parallel) ports transfer data 8 bits, or one byte, at a time

Device drivers have names that the kernel uses to refer to the device. The names can be one to eight characters, like file names. Unlike file names, however, device names do not include extensions.

Cue:
Character devices perform
I/O one character at a time.

DOS uses the names of device drivers like file names, except that when used, the drivers activate the associated device rather than storing or retrieving data to or from a disk. For example, the printer may be named LPT1. If you copy data to LPT1, the data is printed on the printer.

Character devices tend to be the less complex devices—a printer, for example, is a simpler device than a disk drive. Character device drivers also tend to be simpler than block device drivers. The block devices are the more complex disk, tape, and network control equipment that move massive amounts of data in and out of the computer. Such devices are not well served by device drivers and controllers that operate on one character at a time.

Block Device Drivers

To deal with the movement of massive amounts of I/O data, DOS incorporates block device drivers. Unlike character device drivers, block device drivers transfer data to and from the kernel in large units of data called *blocks*. Block devices are given names that are letters, such as A, B, and C. These letter names are the same kind of names that DOS gives to your disk drives.

Unlike character devices, which DOS treats much like files, block devices are considered by DOS to be logical disk drives. The drive designator D: may not actually represent a physical disk drive within your computer. Depending on which type of driver is named D in your computer, you can access one of the following devices:

- *A portion of a disk drive.* Some device drivers are written so that one disk drive is divided into several pieces, each with its own name. Several different drives—for example, C, D, and E—actually may be different pieces of the same disk drive.

- *A network controller.* Disk drives on a network file server appear to be disk drives on your local system, thanks to the device driver. When you copy a file to a network device, you actually request that your computer transmits the file across the network to the file server, for storage on the file server's disk drives.

- *Memory masquerading as a disk drive.* A device driver called *VDISK* enables you to pretend that some of your system RAM can store files like a disk drive. This area of memory, called a *RAMdisk*, appears to operate like a regular disk drive except that RAMdisks operate very fast, and you lose files stored on the disk when you turn off the computer. RAMdisks are good for storing files temporarily.

Character and block device drivers form the backbone of the PC's input-output system. These drivers enable the operating system to deal with a multitude of different types of devices in a uniform manner, because the details of exactly what kind of equipment is connected to the computer is hidden from DOS. This modularity is why the same program can run on an IBM PS/2 Model 80 or a Dell 310 and why the same serial port can operate an optical-character-recognition device in one instant and a modem in the next.

Defining Resident and Installable Device Drivers

Among the files provided on the DOS system disks are a selection of device drivers. Not all possible device drivers are supplied with the DOS package; DOS cannot possibly anticipate the kinds of hardware you may have. You can add additional device drivers at any time, however, as long as these drivers are written by knowledgeable programmers or supplied with new equipment. On the DOS disk, the hidden system file IO.SYS (IBMBIO.COM in IBM DOS) contains the device drivers that load into memory at boot time. Because IO.SYS is part of the DOS-supplied software, the device drivers included in IO.SYS are *resident drivers*.

In Version 2.0 and later, the DOS package includes other device drivers; however, these drivers are provided in separate files, and you can decide when to load them. These device driver files use SYS extensions and include ANSI.SYS, VDISK.SYS, PRINTER.SYS, and others. Not all versions of DOS have these drivers. The SYS files are loaded into memory as part of the boot process of the CONFIG.SYS file. (Note that CONFIG.SYS is not a device driver, even though the file extension is SYS. CONFIG.SYS is the file that determines the device drivers that are loaded.) The controlled way that the drivers load into memory is called *driver installation*. The device drivers with the SYS extensions are *installable device drivers*. In a DOS environment, device drivers are resident or installable.

Cue:
Device drivers are resident or installable.

Resident Device Drivers

Resident device drivers reside in the hidden system file IO.SYS (IBMBIO.COM). Each version of DOS uses its own selection of resident device drivers. Different implementations of DOS from PC vendors may

Cue:
Resident device drivers reside in IO.SYS.

modify the list of IO.SYS-included device drivers to include a particular hardware feature. If a manufacturer is particularly proud of a piece of equipment available exclusively through them, the device driver for that equipment may be resident. Usually, each version of DOS comes with a distinct set of device drivers in IO.SYS. Figure 4.2 depicts the resident device drivers available to the DOS kernel. The kernel views these devices drivers as logical devices that provide input, output, or both.

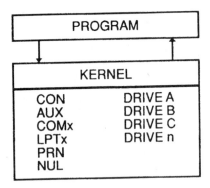

Fig. 4.2. The resident device drivers available to the DOS kernel.

The disk device driver supports the standard disk devices of the PC. As newer, higher capacity floppy drives became standard equipment, new versions of drivers are added to DOS to support these disks. If you use Version 3.1 and want to install a 720K 3 1/2-inch disk drive, for example, DOS does not support the added drive. Your computer is not the problem; the older DOS is the problem because this version does not include a device driver for that type of disk. As newer devices are added to PCs, the resident drivers are modified to keep pace.

DOS provides many resident character device drivers. As is the rule with character device drivers, the resident character device drivers reserve names for the devices they control. Table 4.1 lists the resident character device drivers for DOS 5.0. Other versions and implementations have most of these resident device drivers.

Because these resident device drivers are defined by DOS, their names are reserved. DOS first tests file parameters to ensure that the parameters are device names. When using a file name, especially with an extension that uses the root name of a reserved device, DOS assumes that you refer to the device, not a file. To avoid naming conflicts, don't use file names similar to reserved device names. A file named DON is one keystroke away from the device name CON. In a COPY command line, typing C instead of D sends file output to the screen, not to DON.

Table 4.1
DOS 5.0 Resident Character Device Drivers

Device Name	Meaning
CLOCK$	The system clock device driver
CON	The keyboard as input and the display as output
AUX or COM1	The first serial communications port
COMn	The nth serial communications port up to 4
LPT1 or PRN	The first parallel printer port (output only)
LPTn	The nth parallel printer port up to 3
NUL	A nonexistent (dummy) device used to discard output when output is unwanted, often used in batch files to suppress (throw away) screen output

Installable Device Drivers

After the arrival of DOS 2.0, your computer's device complement is no longer limited to those devices supported by IO.SYS. DOS provides for additional device support to be added at startup time. Figure 4.3 shows the installable device drivers made available with DOS. DOS inspects the contents of the special file CONFIG.SYS in the boot disk's root. If CONFIG.SYS contains device installation commands, DOS installs the indicated device driver or drivers from the indicated disk. Figure 4.3 shows CONFIG.SYS as a pathway from the disk file device drivers to their installed locations in the system. The broken line that divides the device driver box indicates that the number of installed device drivers varies based on CONFIG.SYS. A more detailed description of CONFIG.SYS appears in the next section. By providing a means to load additional device support at boot time, DOS makes the kernel interface to the hardware much more versatile than the one provided for by IO.SYS.

Cue:
Installable device drivers are loaded from CONFIG.SYS.

DOS provides some installable device drivers on the master DOS disks. Again, different versions supply different numbers of device driver files. Table 4.2 shows the installable device drivers that come with DOS 5.0.

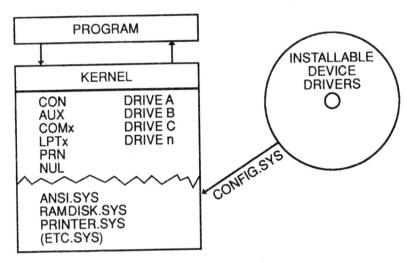

Fig. 4.3. CONFIG.SYS, loading installable device drivers.

Only DRIVER.SYS can support additional hardware on the PC. DRIVER.SYS can be configured to support an additional disk device that does not conform to the design of the disk devices supported by the resident disk driver routines.

The other installable device drivers in table 4.2 don't add new devices to the computer. Instead, the rest of the device drivers modify or enhance the resident drivers and add logical devices created from existing system resources. If you don't need to enhance the standard devices, you don't need to install the device driver that enhances. Some of the installable device drivers are for special purposes.

EMM386.SYS, for example, is useful for owners of 80386 CPU-equipped computers like the IBM PS/2 Model 80. Through the addressing modes of the CPU and the device driver translation, RAM that surpasses the 1M addressing range of DOS appears to be an expanded-memory adapter board. Expanded and extended memory are covered in a subsequent section of this chapter.

Although some installable device drivers included with DOS are for special purposes, others have a general appeal. ANSI.SYS, for example, replaces the resident keyboard device and display device driver. ANSI.SYS enables the device's character stream to encode device control sequences that position the cursor, change the screen colors, give keys new definitions, and more.

Table 4.2
DOS 5.0 Installable Device Drivers

Device Driver	Action
ANSI.SYS	Replaces the standard console device driver with a device driver that incorporates ANSI terminal control sequences
DISPLAY.SYS	Enables code-page switching to the screen
DRIVER.SYS	Operates an external disk drive through a block device letter name
EGA.SYS	Saves and restores an EGA screen when using DOSSHELL and the Task Swapper
EMM386.EXE	Emulates expanded memory in extended memory (XMS memory); useful with applications that need expanded memory when only extended memory is available; also provides upper memory blocks
HIMEM.SYS	Manages extended memory
PRINTER.SYS	Supports code-page switching for the parallel printer ports
RAMDRIVE.SYS	Enables the use of computer memory to simulate a hard disk
SETVER.SYS	Establishes a version table that lists the version number DOS 5.0 reports to named programs
SMARTDRV.SYS	Enables the use of RAM as cache memory, usually speeds disk accesses

RAMDISK.SYS adds one or more virtual drives or RAM disks to a system. Because RAM disks are actually system memory and not a mechanical disk drive, they are very fast. Many users create RAM disks to speed operations that involve heavy file searches, such as spell-checking a document from a dictionary file.

DISPLAY.SYS and PRINTER.SYS accommodate DOS's capability to configure the international character sets. Versions 3.3, 4.0, and 5.0 have extensive provisions for international configuration. Chapter 16 explains how to use the international configuration considerations of DOS.

Third-party software vendors and hardware manufacturers offer a wide variety of installable device drivers that enhance existing hardware or accommodate new peripheral hardware. DOS also can install these device drivers at boot time. The key to installing device drivers lies in CONFIG.SYS. Pointing devices, such as mice and digitizer pads, often include device driver files. MOUSE.SYS and KOALA.SYS are examples of pointing device drivers. External add-on disk drives often come with special block device drivers. The 5 1/4-inch add-on floppy drive from Sysgen for IBM PS/2 systems is delivered with a driver named BRIDGE.DRV. Note that the DRV extension is used for the disk drive's driver file name. DOS can use other driver file extensions besides SYS. IBMCACHE.SYS is a disk-caching driver that uses extended memory in PS/2 computers to speed disk operations. IBM supplies IBMCACHE.SYS with some of IBM's computers. The variety of third-party installable device drivers is great. At some point, you may use a third-party installable device driver in your system. Thanks to the CONFIG.SYS file, installing a device driver is easy.

Understanding CONFIG.SYS

CONFIG.SYS is an optional file that DOS looks for during system booting. The DOS 5.0 Setup program creates a default CONFIG.SYS, but DOS does not come packaged with a CONFIG.SYS file in earlier versions. You can create CONFIG.SYS by using a COPY CON command line or by using a text editor such as the DOS Editor. Part IV of this book covers CONFIG.SYS and the configurable aspects of your PC. Read Part IV before you change the CONFIG.SYS file or add a new one. The following section gives you a brief overview of the process. To see how CONFIG.SYS is used, take a moment to review the boot process.

When you power up the computer for a cold boot or press the Ctrl-Alt-Del key combination for a warm boot, DOS loads from the boot disk with the aid of the bootstrap ROM and the boot disk's bootstrap loader routine. The DOS kernel and the BIOS extensions are loaded from the MSDOS.SYS and IO.SYS (in IBM DOS, IBMDOS.COM and IBMBIO.COM) disk files into memory. The system is initialized, and DOS looks for CONFIG.SYS in the root directory of the boot disk. DOS cannot look in other directories on other disks for CONFIG.SYS. If CONFIG.SYS is present, DOS opens the file and executes the directives found in the file.

DOS looks for configuration commands and parameters as directives to carry out. DOS encounters directives similar to the following:

```
FILES=15
BUFFERS=20
```

The first of these two directives tells DOS how many files to accommodate at one time. DOS sets the number of files to 8 if CONFIG.SYS is missing. The default eight files accommodate DOS's five resident character devices with room to open three additional files. The second of the two directives tells DOS how many RAM buffers to set aside out of memory for temporarily housing of transient I/O data. These two directives are not device driver directives, but they do affect the operation of data interchange between the disk device drivers and the kernel's transient data buffers.

You also may see a line in the CONFIG.SYS file that looks similar to the following:

```
SHELL=C:\COMMAND.COM /P
```

This line tells DOS where to find COMMAND.COM, the command processor. In special cases, a non-DOS command processor can be used for unusual applications. In all likelihood, your command processor is COMMAND.COM.

You also may see several lines that contain the DEVICE directive. These lines look similar to the following:

```
DEVICE = ANSI.SYS
DEVICE = MOUSE.SYS
DEVICE = RAMDISK.SYS
```

DOS looks for these lines to install device drivers during the boot process. When DOS encounters a DEVICE = line in CONFIG.SYS, DOS finds the file named in the assignment and installs the content of the file as a device driver. When the installable device driver is in RAM, DOS adds the driver to the list of available drivers. The driver is then available for use.

When CONFIG.SYS is processed completely, DOS completes the boot process by loading COMMAND.COM and finding and executing commands in AUTOEXEC.BAT. AUTOEXEC.BAT contains any sequence of DOS commands that should be executed each time the computer boots. These commands may load special utilities, load resident programs (called *TSRs*), or execute any other commands. In the absence of AUTOEXEC.BAT, DOS prompts for the time and date. DOS then displays the system prompt.

If you use a hard disk as your boot disk, don't forget to include necessary CONFIG.SYS directives in your bootable working DOS copy. In most cases, you want the same device configuration when booting from a floppy as when you boot from the hard disk. You can select for a boot floppy CONFIG.SYS directives that install a varying set of devices from the normal set. Booting from a floppy with a specially prepared CONFIG.SYS file gives you device flexibility without requiring that you edit the CONFIG.SYS file in the root of the hard disk. Make sure that any device drivers are available on the disk or in a PATH statement.

Understanding Extended and Expanded Memory

The presence of extended memory managers, such as XMAEM.SYS in Version 4 and HIMEM.SYS in Version 5, shows that DOS is modernizing to keep up with the developments in memory-addressing capabilities of the 80286 and 80386 members of the Intel 8086 microprocessor family, on which DOS is based. DOS can address only 1M of memory in a normal way. The 1M limit is caused by the number of address lines available on the 8086 microprocessor. The 8086 supports 20 binary address lines. Because binary condition consists of 2 states, 2 to the 20th power is 1,048,576, or 1M. To address just one byte more of data than the 1M of data that 20 address lines support, a microprocessor must have 21 or more lines. When DOS was designed, the Intel microprocessors supported only 20 lines. The subsequent 80286 and 80386 have more than 20 address lines and can address far more memory than 1M.

Programs and data reside in memory. The more memory in a PC, the more program instructions and data the PC can accommodate. Without some electronic intervention, this larger memory, larger capacity axiom is not true for DOS. When DOS was designed, the 80286 and 80386 processor chips were not used in PCs. The 8086 and 8088 chips, with a memory limit of 1M, were the top Intel microprocessors of the era. DOS designers placed DOS routines at specific locations within the 1M of memory space. You can use DOS's internal tables to manipulate addresses within 1M.

When the 80286 and 80386 microprocessors appeared in PCs, DOS already had a huge installed base. The designers of DOS faced a dilemma: how to increase the memory capacity of DOS without abandoning the large number of DOS installations already in use. DOS designers chose not to change the basic arrangement of DOS and to keep DOS uniform with the installed base. Still, the lure of larger memory capacities gave third-party vendors the incentive to find a way for DOS to break the 1M memory barrier.

Two basic methods are used to give programs access to more memory:

- *Extended memory* uses a facility available to the 80286 and 80386 microprocessors called *extended-memory addressing*. The memory beyond 1M is accessed by programs much like the memory below 1M; this memory is an extension of the memory already in the machine.

- *Expanded memory* creates an area of memory. The computer views this area as more than an extension of the memory already in the computer. Expanded memory is not accessed like regular memory; programs must access the memory through a device driver.

When additional memory—more than 1M—is installed in your computer, you must install the memory as extended or expanded. Because extended and expanded are similar terms, you easily can confuse the two. Extended and expanded memory are part of today's PC life, however, and you benefit from understanding the difference between them.

Understanding Extended Memory

The Intel 80286 has 24 address lines and can address 16,777,266 locations, or 16M, of memory. The 80386 and 80486 CPUs have 32 address lines and can address 4,294,967,296 locations, or 4G, (gigabytes) of memory. (A gigabyte is 1,024 megabytes.) The first 1M of this address range addresses the system's conventional memory. The first 1M is called *conventional memory* because the 8086 chip uses only 1M and because DOS is designed around this 1M convention. Addresses above the 1M point are *extended-memory addresses*. Figure 4.4 shows the addressable memory of the various Intel 8086 family members. The figure shows that the 80286 and 80386 can address a significant number of extended addresses.

Memory at these extended addresses is extended memory. Only the 80286, 80386, and 80486 can use extended memory. The 80286, 80386, and 80486 address conventional memory like an 8086 by using an internal operating mode called *real* mode. In real mode, the microprocessors are restricted to the same 1M address range as the 8086. Unlike the 8086, however, the newer microprocessors can enter another mode to address the extended-memory locations. This extended-memory mode is *protected* mode. DOS became a standard before the advent of protected mode and cannot effectively take advantage of protected mode's extensive address range. Figure 4.5 shows how conventional memory is divided. DOS addresses the first 640K of memory as conventional low memory. DOS addresses the remaining 384K of the 1M conventional memory as high conventional memory (also called reserved memory).

Cue:
The 80286, 80386, and 80486 can use extended memory.

Some DOS utility programs and drivers can use extended memory. The programs switch the CPU from real mode to protected mode. The DOS kernel has nothing to do with the switch. Because the kernel is DOS's administrative bookkeeper, the kernel is unaware of how the extended memory is used or what programs use the memory. The programs that use extended memory in protected mode must indicate to each other which program is using what portion of memory. Unless the programs agree to cooperate, a program can steal the extended memory of another program, creating a conflict. The DOS device drivers that can use extended memory cooperate in memory use, but outside programs that use extended memory may not cooperate.

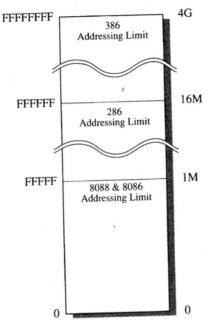

Fig. 4.4. A map of memory addressable by the various CPUs. The 386 addresses 4,000 times more memory than the 8088/8086.

Protected mode and extended memory have some operational disadvantages when used with a real-mode operating system such as DOS. The switch from real to protected mode is not easy for a programmer to code. The DOS kernel and the BIOS offer little functional support for protected mode. Programs that use extended memory must do some careful checking in special memory locations to determine which programs use which extended memory. Unfortunately, not all extended-memory programs check thoroughly, and memory conflicts arise. Some memory conflicts make a program work erratically. Some conflicts crash a program so badly that you must reboot. Still, the lure of additional memory beyond the limits of 1M keeps programmers trying the extended-memory protected-mode method.

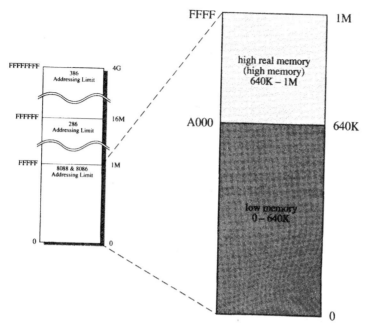

Fig. 4.5. *The first 1M of real memory in all personal computers is broken into low memory, from 0K to 640K, and high memory, from 640K to 1M.*

Understanding Expanded Memory

Although the term expanded sounds like extended, expanded memory is not extended memory. By using expanded memory, all CPUs in the 8086 family can break the 1M conventional-memory barrier. The way expanded memory provides access to memory besides conventional memory marks the true difference between expanded and extended memory.

Expanded memory is accessed through a device driver as though the expanded memory were a device. Through the device driver, a program can make a chunk of expanded memory look like conventional memory. This defined portion of expanded memory is a *page*. The predefined portion of conventional memory is a *page frame*. Figure 4.6 illustrates the paged-memory concept. Notice that more than one memory page is associated with a page frame.

When the CPU addresses the page frame, the CPU actually accesses the values in a page of expanded memory. The expanded-memory device driver locates unused portions of conventional memory in 16K blocks and uses the blocks for page frames. Normally, the number of 16K pages of expanded memory on the expanded-memory adapter far exceeds the

Cue:
Expanded memory is divided into portions called pages.

number of page frames established in conventional memory by the driver. To access all the pages of expanded memory, the driver must swap pages of memory in and out of the available page frames.

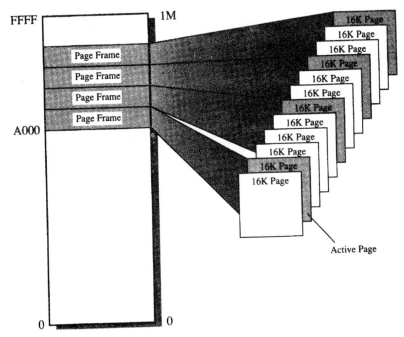

***Fig. 4.6.** EMS memory works by swapping 16K pages of physical memory on the EMS board into page frames in conventional memory.*

When a program needs to access a page of expanded memory not in the page frame, the device driver must establish the new page in the page frame. This swapping of page frames is a processing overhead that extended-mode addressing lacks. Expanded-memory operation offers the capability for specially designed programs to have access to more than 1M of memory through page frames. Expanded memory also has the advantage of following recognized standards that make memory conflicts rare.

Cue:
EMS comes in two versions: LIM 3.2 and LIM 4.

All programs that use expanded memory must do so in an identical fashion; the Expanded Memory Specification (*EMS*) describes how this usage is accomplished. Two versions of EMS exist. LIM 3.2 and LIM 4 use the paged switching of expanded memory. LIM 4 provides for more flexible page-frame location and greater expanded-memory access. If you add expanded memory, check your system documentation to determine whether the EMS version is LIM 3.2 or LIM 4. Applications software that uses expanded memory is usually configurable to either type. Because of the additional flexibility, LIM 4. is more desirable.

The 80386- and 80486-based computers can take advantage of the advanced memory-management features of the processor and emulate an expanded-memory adapter board. DOS 4 and 5 provide various programs to trick extended memory into following the EMS convention. These two device drivers create a logical bridge between extended-memory- and expanded-memory-capable programs.

Understanding Standard Input and Output

Most programs require some kind of input and produce some kind of output. If you do not specify otherwise, many commands assume that input comes from text typed at the keyboard and that output is displayed on-screen. Collectively, the keyboard and screen are known as the CON device.

Some commands prompt you for information. Other commands wait for you to supply information in the form of a keyboard response. Supplying information to a DOS command is an example of supplying standard input. For example, the SORT command takes lines of input and then outputs the lines in an alphabetically sorted order. You issue the command as follows:

SORT

When you issue the command, the cursor drops to the next line, and SORT waits for standard input from the keyboard. You provide input, such as the following:

BRAVO

CHARLIE

ALPHA

After entering ALPHA, press Ctrl-Z or F6 to tell SORT that you completed input. SORT alphabetizes the lines that you input and shows the list on the standard output device, your screen, as the following:

```
ALPHA
BRAVO
CHARLIE
```

SORT is not handy when you need to provide the standard input from the keyboard. Fortunately for SORT (and for you), DOS's treatment of devices enables standard input and output to be redirected from and to other devices. You can tell commands to take input from some source other than the keyboard and to send output to some place other than the screen. The input can come from a file or another command's output; the output of SORT can go to a file, device, or another command's input. The temporary reassignment of inputs and outputs is *redirection*.

Understanding Redirection

Cue:
The less-than (<) symbol indicates input to come from a file or device.

Because the DOS kernel processes I/O requests from programs through a uniform set of calls to device drivers, the kernel can view all sources of data in a universal way. With only minor programmatic intervention, the kernel can accommodate the substitution of a different input device for the standard input device. The same substitution capability applies to an output device. DOS knows when to substitute or redirect input and output by recognizing special characters in the command line syntax. On the command line, the special redirection symbol < tells DOS that input comes from the file or device name that follows the symbol.

Suppose that a text file named TODO.TXT in the working directory contains the following lines:

```
03-22-91... Go to doctor's appointment at 3:30
03-17-91... Dinner with Bill
01-01-91... Resolution: Use BACKUP regularly
04-04-91... Buy David's birthday present
03-20-91... Get chemicals for spa
```

These lines obviously make up a reminder file, but the dates are out of order. Thanks to SORT and redirection, you can show them in order. Issue the SORT command, using the input redirection symbol to show that input is from TODO.TXT instead of the keyboard. The command resembles the following line:

```
SORT <TODO.TXT
```

SORT alphabetizes the lines and, in doing so, arranges the dates in order. The screen output shows the following lines:

```
01-01-91... Resolution: Use BACKUP regularly
03-17-91... Dinner with Bill
03-20-91... Get chemicals for spa
03-22-91... Go to doctor's appointment at 3:30
04-04-91... Buy David's birthday present
```

The same alphabetized lines can be written back to a file through output redirection. The special symbol **>** in the command line syntax tells DOS to redirect output to the file or device that follows the output redirection symbols. In the SORT example, the command line syntax looks like the following:

SORT <TODO.TXT >BYDATE.TXT

DOS does not show the sorted lines on-screen. Instead, the output is redirected to the file named BYDATE.TXT. If BYDATE.TXT does not exist, DOS creates the file. If the file does exist, the previous contents of the file are lost, and the results of the SORT command are placed in the file.

The symbol **>>** also enables you to add new output to a file without erasing existing data, as in the following example:

CHKDSK >>DISKDATA

This command runs the CHKDSK utility and places the output in the file DISKDATA. However, unlike **>**, if the file already exists, the previous contents are retained, and the output from CHKDSK is added at the end of the file.

Devices often are used in redirection. Type the following example to first produce and then send a directory listing to the printer:

DIR >PRN

PRN is the special name for the printer device driver. Similarly, to execute the MEM command and send its output to the serial communications port, type the following:

MEM >COM1

The MEM, CHKDSK, SORT, and DIR commands are discussed more in Part II.

Cue:
The symbols >
and >> indicate
output to come
from a file or
device.

Understanding Piping

Often, the results of one command are used as the input to another command. Suppose that you want an alphabetical listing of the current directory. DOS 4's DIR command lists your files but not in alphabetical order. (DOS 5's DIR command now provides the /0 switch for listing file names in sorted order.) If you use a method to tell SORT to sort the output from DIR, you can approximate the results you want.

By using redirection, you can accomplish this sort, although in several steps. You may first type the following line to place the output from DIR—a list of files—in a file called list:

DIR >LIST

Next, type the following to read the data from LIST and to display an alphabetized list to the screen:

SORT <LIST

Don't forget to remove LIST when you're done by typing the following command:

DEL LIST

Figure 4.7 shows how the process looks. Note that the output shows all lines from the DIR output, including the headers and statistics. Although probably not what you want, the result may do for now. Also, notice that the temporary file LIST that you used to hold the intermediate data is included in the listing.

```
C:\BELINDA>dir >list

C:\BELINDA>sort <list


                    23091200 bytes free
           9 file(s)      292499 bytes
Directory of C:\BELINDA
Volume in drive C is DOS500
Volume Serial Number is B0AB-ABA0
          <DIR>      09-08-90  12:42a
          <DIR>      09-08-90  12:42a
DRAW     BMP    141558 09-09-90   3:35p
HOMEWORK DOC      2429 10-11-90   8:41p
LETTERS  <DIR>         09-23-90   2:52p
LIST               0 10-20-90   9:30p
NEWSPPR  DOC      4536 10-16-90   6:26p
PARTY    BMP    141558 09-16-90   6:42p
SHANNON  DOC      2418 10-04-90  11:11p

C:\BELINDA>del list

C:\BELINDA>
```

Fig. 4.7. Using intermediate files to produce a sorted directory listing.

A better way exists to accomplish this task. DOS's logical method of viewing devices makes possible another form of input and output substitution: piping. *Piping* is named from the concept of coupling commands like pieces of pipe, in which the output of one command flows into the next command to be used as input. The symbol | indicates that two commands are joined. The output of the first command goes to the input of the second command.

You can accomplish the same task by using piping. Type the following line:

DIR | SORT

DIR produces a directory listing, but rather than sending the output to the screen, DOS feeds the listing as input into the SORT command. SORT alphabetizes and displays the data. Figure 4.8 shows this command in use.

```
C:\BELINDA>dir | sort


                         23091200 bytes free
             8 file(s)      292499 bytes
   Directory of C:\BELINDA
   Volume in drive C is DOS500
   Volume Serial Number is B0AB-ABA0
                  <DIR>      09-08-90   12:42a
   ..             <DIR>      09-08-90   12:42a
   DRAW     BMP    141558 09-09-90    3:35p
   HOMEWORK DOC      2429 10-11-90    8:41p
   LETTERS        <DIR>      09-23-90    2:52p
   NEWSPPR  DOC      4536 10-16-90    6:26p
   PARTY    BMP    141558 09-16-90    6:42p
   SHANNON  DOC      2418 10-04-90   11:11p

C:\BELINDA>
```

Fig. 4.8. Using pipes to produce a sorted directory listing.

Pipes have several advantages over the use of temporary files to hold intermediate data. Pipes involve less typing; using them is faster than using temporary files; and no intermediate files are created that you must remember to delete.

Chapter Summary

Understanding how DOS relies on device drivers enables you to see how you can use DOS commands to gain control of your hardware. Although the detailed operation of DOS devices is hidden, DOS configuration commands and concepts like redirection and piping give evidence that DOS controls the devices. DOS, through COMMAND.COM, views devices in a logical way.

- Device drivers add new hardware or modify the operation of existing hardware.

- DOS uses two types of device drivers: character and block.

- Resident device drivers are loaded during booting from the hidden DOS file IO.SYS (IBMBIO.COM).

- Installable device drivers are optional and are loaded during booting from directives in the CONFIG.SYS file.

- Programs can overcome DOS's 1M real-memory limit by accessing extended memory and expanded memory.

- Extended memory is memory above 1M accessed by the CPU in protected mode.

- Expanded, or EMS, memory is additional memory accessed through page frames. EMS memory is LIM 3.2 or LIM 4.0.

- Through redirection and pipes, you can change commands' standard inputs and standard outputs. Redirection most often is used with devices; pipes are used to connect commands.

The information in this chapter and in the three preceding chapters provides a good framework for understanding DOS. The material in Part I covers aspects of DOS's operation that give you a view beneath DOS's surface. You don't have to be a computer or software designer to use DOS competently. Becoming too technical runs counter to the spirit of personal computing. If you understand the material presented in Part I, you will be more confident and capable when you use the DOS commands presented in Parts II, III, and IV.

Chapter 5 covers the DOS Shell, which gives you an alternative, more intuitive way of interacting with DOS.

Using the DOS Shell

The DOS Shell is a user interface that replaces the DOS command line with easy-to-use and easy-to-understand menus. Although DOS 4's Shell is helpful, Version 5's Shell is an outstanding improvement. (The more functional Shell in DOS 5 is a good reason to upgrade.) Because of the many changes to the Shell in DOS 5, this chapter discusses only that version.

The Version 5 Shell is more like Windows and offers several commendable features: you don't need a graphics monitor; you can use your mouse; and you don't need much memory. The Shell also enables you to switch among programs, up to the limit of your system's memory.

Learning to use the DOS Shell can serve as an introduction to more complex systems like Windows. You can use the Shell to learn to install programs, manage the file system, and use pull-down menus. You use many of these DOS 5 concepts with Windows or another shell. If you don't understand any aspect of the Shell, you can get help by pressing the Shell's Help key, F1.

Cue:
Use the F1 (Help) key to get help on the current command.

Even if you don't intend to use the Shell, you probably should learn how to use it. As a standard part of the latest version of DOS, the Shell is likely to see widespread use. This chapter explains what you need to know if you encounter the Shell.

Understanding the DOS Shell Window

You may have instructed the DOS installation program to run the DOS Shell each time you start your computer. Setup places the command C:\DOS\DOSSHELL at the end of the AUTOEXEC.BAT file. (The DOS programs are stored in the C:\DOS directory by default, unless you specify another directory.) This line causes the Shell to be run each time you start the computer. If this line is not in the AUTOEXEC.BAT file or if you want to restart the Shell program, use the following command:

C:\DOS\DOSSHELL

When you start the Shell, you see a screen like the one in figure 5.1, the DOS Shell window. (**Note:** This screen is shown in graphics mode. Your screen looks different if displayed in text mode, the default. Refer to the "Setting Options" section later in this chapter for more about changing display modes.) This screen has four major parts: the menu bar, the files area, the main program area, and the keyboard prompts.

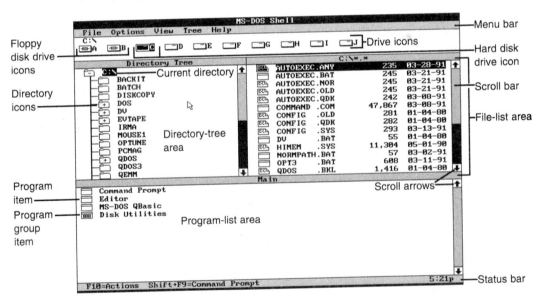

Fig. 5.1. The DOS Shell window.

The menu bar shows you the command choices available for the files and main program areas. The top half of the Shell window is divided into three sections: the current directory and the available drives, which appear just under the menu bar; the directory-tree area, listing directories for the selected drive; and the file-list area, listing files for the selected directory.

The selected drive is highlighted on-screen. The lower half of the screen, the program-list area, is used to show a list of available program choices. These choices can start programs or access groups of programs that you can select from submenus.

The keyboard prompts at the bottom of the screen alert you to some of the available shortcut keys that perform various functions. These shortcut keys are available if you don't have or don't want to use a mouse.

Cue:
Look for the shortcut keys listed at the bottom of the screen.

A fifth area of the screen, the Active Task List Area, is shown only if you enable the Shell's Task Swapper. With the Task Swapper, you can use several programs at the same time, switching from one to another with a keystroke. You learn more about the Task Swapper later in this chapter in the section entitled "Using the Shell's Task Swapper." Each of the areas of the screen is headed by a *title bar*.

Using the Keyboard in the DOS Shell

Many shortcut keys are available to perform various Shell functions. As each Shell function is discussed in this chapter, you learn how to use the mouse and the keyboard to access that function. Table 5.1, however, lists Shell keyboard commands common to all screens in the DOS Shell.

Table 5.1
Keyboard Commands for All Shell Screens

Key	Function
Enter	Executes the currently selected item
Esc	Cancels the current command or operation
F1	Accesses help information on the current area, command, or dialog box option
Alt-F4 or F3	Exits the Shell and returns you to the MS-DOS command prompt
Shift-F5	Redraws the screen but does not update the file lists
Shift-F9	Temporarily exits to the DOS prompt

After you use Shift-F9 to exit to the DOS prompt, you can return to the Shell by typing **EXIT** and pressing Enter.

Moving around in the Shell Window

Before learning about the various functions of the Shell and how to access them, you need to learn how to move around the Shell window.

You can use the keyboard or the mouse to move to and select various items in the Shell window. Using the mouse is somewhat easier because all you have to do is move the mouse pointer to the item and click the left mouse button. If you don't have a mouse (or don't want to use your mouse), you can use keystrokes to perform the same functions. Table 5.2 lists the keys you can use for moving the cursor in the Shell window.

Table 5.2
Using the Keyboard To Move the Cursor

Key	Function
F10 or Alt	Activates the menu bar at the top of the screen
Tab	Moves to the next area of the Shell window; in a dialog box, moves to the next choice
Shift-Tab	Moves to the preceding area of the Shell window; in a dialog box, moves the cursor to the preceding choice
Home	Moves to the beginning of a line or list
End	Moves to the end of a line or list
Ctrl-Home	Moves to the beginning of a list
Ctrl-End	Moves to the end of a list
↑	Moves up a list one item at a time
↓	Moves down a list one item at a time
Any letter	Moves to the next item in the list that begins with the letter you press

Scrolling the Screen

Cue:
Use the scroll bars with the mouse to move quickly through the file list.

The various Shell window areas each have scroll bars at their right edges. In figure 5.1, these scroll bars are shown for the directory tree, the file list, and the main windows. You use the scroll bars with the mouse to scroll additional information into a window. Each scroll bar has two main components:

- A scroll arrow is located at each end of the scroll bar. Clicking the mouse pointer on the arrow moves the text or window display up or down one row at a time.

- A scroll box is located between the scroll arrow boxes. The scroll box enables you to move quickly through the display. Move the mouse pointer to the scroll box and drag the box up or down to scroll the text in the area. To drag a box, hold down the left mouse button and move the mouse up or down.

If you don't have a mouse, you can use the up- and down-arrow keys or PgUp and PgDn to scroll the information in the selected area. Use the up- and down-arrow keys to move the information up or down one row at a time. Use the PgUp and PgDn keys to scroll quickly through the display.

Selecting Different Areas of the Shell Window

You can use the mouse or keystrokes to move from one area of the Shell window to the next. As you press the Tab key, the next area is highlighted on-screen and is the selected area. The Shift-Tab key moves to the preceding area. You also can use the mouse to select the active area by moving the mouse pointer anywhere in the desired area and clicking the left button. As you select a different area, that area's title bar is highlighted.

Reminder:
Tab moves you to the next window. Shift-Tab moves you to the preceding window.

Selecting Menu Items

You can activate a menu by pressing the F10 key, which highlights the File menu name on the menu bar. You then can use the cursor-movement keys to select another menu name, such as the View menu name. You also can select a menu by holding down the Alt key and pressing the first letter of the choice. To select Options from the menu bar, for example, press the Alt key and the O key together or in sequence.

Cue:
Select commands with the Alt key plus the high-lighted letter of the commands.

If you have a mouse, move the mouse pointer to the desired menu name on the menu bar and click the left mouse button once.

When you select a menu name from the menu bar, the DOS Shell displays a menu of commands. Figure 5.2, for example, shows the pull-down menu that appears when you choose File from the menu bar with the directory-tree area as the selected area.

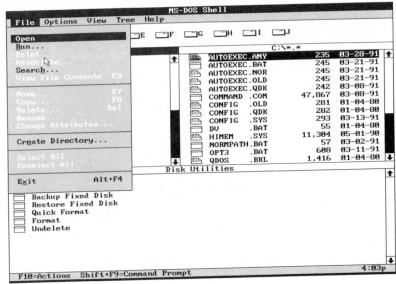

Fig. 5.2. The pull-down menu displayed when you select File from the menu bar.

Cue:
*Dimmed com-
mands indicate
an unavailable
command.*

Cue:
*Press the
highlighted letter
of a menu option
to select that
choice.*

Some of the menu commands are displayed differently than others. Notice, for example, that the Print command is shown with dimmed characters. This display tells you that the Print command is not available with the current operation.

Each of the available menu commands has a highlighted or underlined letter. You can press the highlighted letter to select that choice. If you are using a mouse, click the option you want to choose. An ellipsis (...) after a menu choice indicates that the command accesses a dialog box that must be completed before you are finished with the command.

Some menu choices can be set on or off. The dot (•) in front of a menu choice shows that the option is toggled on. If you select that choice again, the dot is removed, indicating that the option is turned off (not active).

Some commands have corresponding shortcut keys displaying after the command name. You can use these shortcut keys to perform various functions without having to select from the menu.

As you use the Shell, you probably will find yourself using the mouse and the keyboard to perform the various functions.

Using Dialog Boxes

As you work with the Shell, various dialog boxes are displayed. The DOS Shell uses these boxes to ask for additional information needed to complete a command. As mentioned previously, a menu choice followed by an ellipsis (...) indicates that you have to complete a dialog box or specify additional choices to complete the operation.

Cue:
The ellipsis (...) reminds you that additional choices are available for a command.

A dialog box can contain different types of information. The Advanced dialog box is shown in figure 5.3.

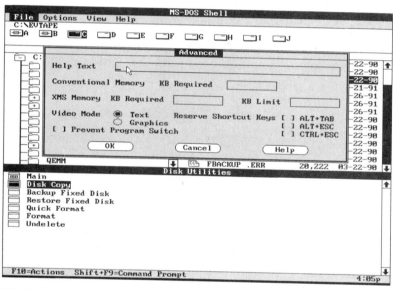

Fig. 5.3. *An example of a dialog box with options to complete.*

This dialog box includes some areas (text boxes) in which you can enter text. Some dialog boxes list a group of mutually exclusive options called *option buttons*. You can choose only one option at a time from a group of option buttons. Each option button is denoted by a circle to its left (a pair of parentheses in text mode). The selected option has a black dot in the circle. Some Shell dialog boxes enable you to select the desired command settings by clicking the appropriate option check boxes. An option check box is a pair of brackets followed by a command setting. A selected check box is marked with an X; unselected check boxes are blank.

Every dialog box has at least three command buttons at the bottom of the box:

OK   Tells the Shell that all information is OK; finish the operation. For Help dialog boxes, the OK button is used to close (remove) the box.

Cancel   Tells the Shell to cancel the current operation

Help   Tells the Shell that you want to enter the Help system and receive information about the currently selected item

When you see a dialog box, fill in the needed information. Dialog boxes have up to three choices that you can select: Yes or OK to complete the action, No or Cancel to cancel the action, or Help to display additional help about the action. (The Esc key also is used to cancel an action.) You can tab to the desired choice and press Enter or click the left mouse button on the choice.

Getting To Know the Shell's Icons

Four kinds of icons (pictures) are shown in the Shell window (in graphics mode). The following paragraphs describe the icons identified in figure 5.1.

Cue:
Use the Tree Expand All command to show all directories.

The directory icon, shaped like a file folder (a pair of square brackets if the screen is in text mode), is shown in the directory-tree area. Each icon can have a + or − character inside the folder. The + indicates that additional subdirectories exist. If you press the + key on the keyboard, the additional directories are shown, and the + on the icon changes to a −.

The program icon is shown in the file-list area and appears for all EXE, COM, and BAT files.

In the file-list area, the data icon is shown for all nonprogram (not EXE, COM, or BAT) files in the file-list area.

The drive icons show the available disk drives. Notice the difference between the icons for drives A and B and the ones for drives C and D.

The selected drive is shown by an icon in reverse video, as is the selected directory or file. You can select drives or directories by clicking on the drive, directory, or file icon or by clicking on the name of the directory or file.

Examining the Shell Menus

The menu bar at the top of the screen offers five choices: File, Options, View, Tree, and Help. Each of these choices accesses a pull-down menu (see fig. 5.2).

The menus are listed following this paragraph. Some menu choices also have their own shortcut keys.

```
FILE (drive-icon, directory-tree, and file-list areas)
     Open
     Run...
     Print
     Associate...
     Search...
     View File Contents (F9)
     Move...(F7)
     Copy...(F8)
     Delete...
     Rename...
     Change Attributes...
     Create Directory...
     Select All
     Deselect All
     Exit (Alt-F4)

OPTIONS
     Confirmation...
     File Display Options...
     Select Across Directories
     Show Information...
     Enable Task Swapper
     Display...
     Colors...

FILE (Program-list and Active Task List areas)
     New...
     Open (Enter)
     Copy
     Delete...(Del)
     Properties...
     Reorder
     Run...
     Exit (Alt-F4)
```

```
VIEW (drive-icon, directory-tree, and file-list areas)
      Single File List
      Dual File Lists
      All Files
      Program/File Lists
      Program List
      Repaint Screen (Shift-F5)
      Refresh (F5)

VIEW (program-list and Active Task List areas)
      Single File List
      Dual File Lists
      All Files
      Program/File Lists
      Program List
      Repaint Screen (Shift-F5)

TREE (drive-icon, directory-tree, and file-list areas)
      Expand one level (+)
      Expand branch (*)
      Expand All (Ctrl-*)
      Collapse Branch (-)

HELP
      Index
      Keyboard
      Shell Basics
      Commands
      Procedures
      Using Help
      About Shell
```

The File menu enables you to perform file-oriented commands, such as showing a directory list, moving or copying files, or viewing or printing files. You also can start programs by selecting a program file (BAT, COM, and EXE files) and then choosing Open or Run from the File menu.

Remember, you can select a menu item in one of three ways:

Cue:
Select the menu item with a mouse click or by holding down the Alt key and pressing the command's highlighted letter.

- Move the mouse pointer to the item and click the left mouse button.

- Press F10 and the highlighted letter of the item.

- Hold down the Alt key and press the highlighted letter of the item. For example, to select the File menu name, press Alt-F (together or in sequence).

To cancel a menu choice, press the Esc key or use the mouse to click an area outside the pull-down menu.

Getting Help

The Shell's help system is contextual: it provides information about the currently highlighted menu item. You also can use the help system to get help about any other topic. Figure 5.4 shows the Help menu.

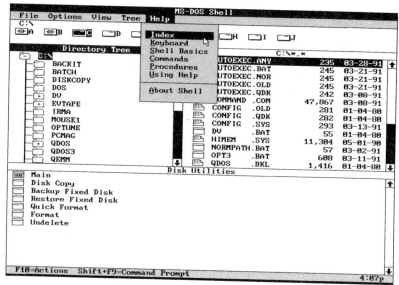

Fig. 5.4. The Help menu.

The Help menu contains seven options:

Index	Accesses an index of help topics
Keyboard	Lists the keyboard commands available in the Shell
Shell Basics	Provides information about how to use the basic Shell functions
Commands	Provides information about the various menu commands
Procedures	Provides information on various tasks performed with the Shell

Using Help   Provides information on how to use the Shell's Help system

About Shell   Displays the current version information about the Shell

You select a Help topic by highlighting the choice and pressing Enter or by double-clicking the mouse on the desired topic. Figure 5.4 shows that the Help Index is being selected.

The Help dialog box lists five command buttons at the bottom:

Close   Exits the Help system. You also can use Esc to exit Help.

Back   Displays the previously viewed Help screen

Keys   Shows the Keyboard Help screen

Index   Shows the Help Index screen

Help   Explains how to use the Help system

Reminder:
Use the F1 key to
get Help.

The Help system is available to you at any time in the Shell. Some dialog boxes provide a Help button to give you further information. You also can press the F1 (Help) key to get information about the selected menu item.

Setting Options

The Options menu enables you to set various options used in the Shell. The following commands are available from the Options pull-down menu.

Confirmation is used to specify whether you want the Shell to ask you to confirm actions when you delete, replace, or perform mouse operations.

File Display Options enables you to cause the Shell to display file names that match a certain file-name specification, such as *.* (the default), *.EXE, and so on. By selecting different file-name specifications, you can limit the list of files that you want to display in the file-list area.

Cue:
Change the sort
order to rearrange
the file list.

You also can specify the sort order of the displayed files. With your mouse or keyboard, select Options and then select File Display Options. A dialog box appears, as shown in figure 5.5. In the Sort By group of option buttons, click the option button for the sort order you want to use: Name, Extension, Date, Size, or DiskOrder. (Name is the default.) An ascending sort is the default; if you want a descending sort, select the Descending Order check box.

The Name text box in the File Display Options dialog box enables you to specify which files you want displayed. The default file-name specification for the Name text box is *.*. This pattern indicates all files. You can change the pattern to indicate the files you want displayed, and you can use the * and ? wild cards. To see only those files with an extension of TXT, for example, type *.**TXT** as the file-name specification in the Name text box. You can select only one file-name specification at a time.

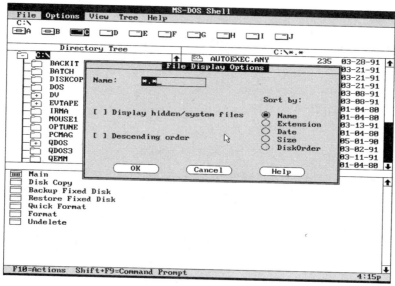

Fig. 5.5. *The File Display Options dialog box.*

After you have set the appropriate file specification and changed the sorting parameters, select OK to save your new settings. The file-list window then displays the selected files in the order that you specified. The first line of the window shows you the file selection pattern.

Select Across Directories is a toggle that enables you to select files only in the selected directory (the default) or enables you to select files from multiple directories of the selected drive.

Show Information enables you to view additional information about the currently selected files. After you choose Show Information, you see a window showing the current file name and attributes; the number of selected files and their total size; and information about the currently selected drive and directory. Figure 5.6 shows an example of the Show Information window with six files selected.

Enable Task Swapper is a toggle that enables the task-swapping feature of the Shell. When this toggle is turned on, a dot appears next to the choice, and the Active Task List Area appears on-screen.

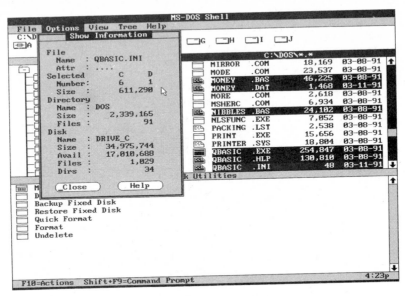

Fig. 5.6. The Show Information window.

Display enables you to select from several text- or graphics-based display modes.

Your choices for text-based display modes are as follows (depending on your system setup and monitor type):

- 25 lines, Low Resolution

- 43 lines, High Resolution 1

- 50 lines, High Resolution 2

Your choices for graphics-based display modes are as follows (depending on your system setup and monitor type):

- 25 lines, Low Resolution

- 30 lines, Medium Resolution 1

- 34 lines, Medium Resolution 2

- 43 lines, High Resolution 1

- 60 lines, High Resolution 2

The default choice is 25 lines, Low Resolution. Use the Preview button to see the effects of a display mode selection. When you find the one you like, select OK. To cancel changes to your display mode, select the Cancel button or press Esc.

Colors enables you to select the colors to be shown on-screen. The available choices depend on your system but include the following:

Basic Blue	Blues and grays
Ocean	Blues, bright cyan, and grays
Monochrome-2 Colors	Black and white
Monochrome-4 Colors	Black, white, and grays
Reverse	White on black with grays
Hot Pink	Pink, purples, black, and white
Emerald City	Greens, black, and white
Turquoise	Blues, black, white, and grays

As in other areas of the Shell, you can select the color choice you want by using the mouse pointer, or you can use the cursor-movement keys. Select the Preview button to see the color choices on-screen. When you find the color scheme you like, select OK. Pressing the Cancel button or the Esc key does not change the current color scheme.

Controlling Windows with the View Menu

The View menu enables you to specify the areas shown in the Shell window. When you first start the Shell, the directory-tree, file-list, and program-list areas are shown. You can change the displayed areas by using the commands on the View menu, which include the following:

Single File List shows only one directory-tree area and one file-list area. When this option is selected, the program-list area is removed.

Dual File Lists shows two directory-tree areas and two file-list areas. This setup enables you to look at two directories and file lists at the same time. When this option is enabled, the program-list area is removed.

All Files shows a list of all files in all directories for the currently selected drive.

Program/File Lists shows one directory-tree area and one file-list area along with the program-list area. This setting is the default value when you start the Shell.

Program List shows only the program-list area. The directory-tree area and file-list area are removed.

Repaint Screen redraws the screen but does not refresh the file or directory list.

Refresh redraws the screen and refreshes the file and directory list.

Try the various commands on the View menu. The Single File List choice is useful, for example, when you want to see more files listed on-screen.

Controlling the Directory Tree with the Tree Menu

The options on the Tree menu enable you to determine the way the directory-tree area displays directories. The menu offers these four choices:

Expand One Level shows the next level of directories of the selected directory. Remember that the + symbol on a directory icon indicates that the directory has subdirectories.

Expand Branch shows all levels of directories beneath the selected directory.

Expand All shows all directory levels for all directories of the selected drive.

Collapse Branch removes the display of the subdirectories of the selected directory.

Remember, if a displayed directory has any subdirectories, that directory's icon shows a + symbol inside it. A – sign in a directory icon tells you that subdirectories of the selected directory have been collapsed. The default setting when you start the Shell is to show only the first level of directories.

Using the Shell for Maintaining Files and Accessing Programs

When the directory-tree area or the files-list area is selected, the File menu enables you to perform operations on listed directories or files. These operations can be grouped into two areas:

- *File maintenance*: search for files; copy, rename, move, or delete files; and create directories

- *Program access*: start programs by selecting the program file name and associate files with programs

Each of these types of operations is covered in the following sections. For your convenience, the keyboard shortcuts for various file- and directory-manipulation commands are listed in table 5.3.

Table 5.3
Using File- and Directory-Handling Shortcut Keys

Key	Function
File-Directory Keys	
F7	Moves the selected file or files from one directory to another; equivalent to the Move command on the File menu
F8	Copies the selected file or files from one directory to another; equivalent to the Copy command on the File menu
Del	Deletes the selected file(s) or directory(s)
File-Selection Keys	
Shift-F8	A toggle that turns add mode on or off (When add mode is on, ADD displays in the lower right corner of the Shell window, and you can select multiple files from the file-list area.)
Shift-↑	Adds the preceding file in the file list to the selection
Shift-↓	Adds the next file in the file list to the selection
Shift-PgUp	Adds to the selection all files listed above the current file in the selected directory
Shift-PgDn	Adds to the selection all files listed below the current file in the selected directory
Ctrl-/	Selects all files in the selected directory
Ctrl-\	Clears all selected files in the selected directory
Shift-space bar	In add mode, selects the group of files between the previously selected file and the selected cursor
Space bar	In add mode, adds to the selection the file at the cursor location

continues

Table 5.3 *(continued)*

Key	Function
Directory-Tree Keys	
↑ or Ctrl-↑	Moves to the preceding directory level
↓ or Ctrl-↓	Moves to the next directory level
Ctrl-*	Displays (expands) all directories in the tree
−	Hides (collapses) the directories below the selected directory
+	Displays (expands) one level of directories below the selected directory
*	Displays (expands) all directories below the selected directory
Drive-Selection Keys	
←	Moves selection cursor to preceding drive
→	Moves selection cursor to the next drive
space bar	Selects the drive at the selection cursor
Ctrl-drive letter	Moves the selection cursor to the drive specified by the drive letter, reads the drive, and displays its directories; equivalent to moving the selection cursor to the drive letter and pressing the space bar
Enter	Rereads the selected drive and displays its contents
File-Display Keys	
F5	Updates (refreshes) the file list for the selected drive by rereading the disk
Ctrl-F5	Updates the file list for the current directory only
F9	With a file selected, displays the contents of a file; while viewing a file, switches between displaying ASCII text and Hexadecimal display.

Using the Shell To Maintain Files

When you start the Shell, it looks for all the available drives. These drive letters are listed on the fourth line of the screen. Then the Shell scans the current drive, getting a list of all the directories and files. A box in the center of the screen shows the progress of this scan.

When the scan is complete, the directory-tree area displays a list of the first level of directories. If a directory has subdirectories, the directory icon shows a + symbol. The current directory is highlighted and shown on the third line of the screen. The file-list area displays a list of the files in the currently selected directory.

The File Maintenance choice on the File menu enables you to copy, move, delete, and search for files. To perform these operations, you need to learn how to select directories and files.

Selecting the Current Directory

After the directory-tree and file-list areas are displayed, you can select the directory to be displayed by clicking that directory with your mouse. Use the mouse and scroll bar or the keys described in the "Directory-Tree Keys" section of table 5.3 to move through the directory tree.

To display additional directory levels, you can click a directory icon with a + symbol. This process is called expanding the directory. With the keyboard, you can press the + key when the directory is highlighted. You also can use the Expand One Level command from the Tree menu when a directory having a + symbol in its icon is selected.

Selecting Files

As you select the various directories, the file-list area shows you a list of files in the currently selected directory. To select a file, you need to make the file-list area active. Press the Tab key or use your mouse to click anywhere in the file-list area.

The list of files in this window normally is sorted by file name. You can change the way the files are sorted and control which files are displayed by using the Options menu. For more information on sorting and displaying files, see "Setting Options."

Select a file in the file-list area by clicking the file name or by highlighting the file name and pressing Enter. After the appropriate file is selected, you can perform the necessary file-maintenance functions, such as copying and deleting files or starting a program.

Searching for Files

If you cannot find the file in the file-list area, you can search for the file. With the File, Search option, you can specify a search pattern. For example, to locate a file called PARTS.LST, use the following steps:

1. Select the drive-icon area, the directory-tree area, or the file-list area.

2. Select File, Search.

3. Enter the name of the file you are looking for (**PARTS.LST**) in the Search for text box.

4. Check the Search entire drive check box (the default is set to on) to look for the file in any directory of the current drive. Remove the check to search only the current directory.

5. Select OK to begin the search.

The results of the search are displayed in the Search Results list, as shown in figure 5.8. You then can select the file from the list as needed.

If you have forgotten part of the file name, you can use the * and ? wild cards to look for the file. **INV*.DBF**, for example, looks for all files with INV as the first three characters of the file name and DBF as the extension.

Figure 5.7 shows the Search File dialog box in which *.BAT was specified as the Search For pattern. Figure 5.8 shows the results of the search. All files in all directories on the current drive are searched. You can tell the Shell to search only in the current directory by selecting the Search Entire Disk option in the Search dialog box. Selecting this option turns it off and removes the X that precedes the option.

Viewing the Contents of a File

After you have selected a file with the mouse or keyboard, you can use the View File contents command from the File menu to look at a file. Usually, only ASCII text files are comprehensible. Shell does, however, enable you to view files in hexadecimal values format.

For practice, try viewing your AUTOEXEC.BAT or CONFIG.SYS file, because they are text files. First select the root directory. With the keyboard, use the up- or down-arrow key to highlight the C:\ directory. With a mouse, use the scroll bars to display the C:\ directory in the Directory Tree window. Then select the AUTOEXEC.BAT or CONFIG.SYS file in the file-list area. To look at the file, choose File and then View File or press the F9 shortcut key.

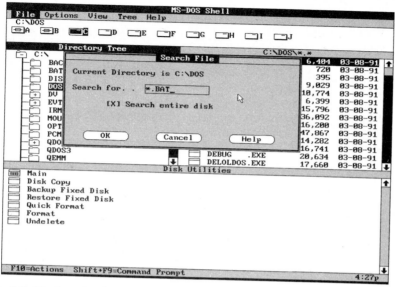

Fig. 5.7. *The Search File dialog box.*

Fig. 5.8. *The results of the search.*

The contents of the file are shown full screen (see fig. 5.9). If the file is too big for the window, you can use the PgUp and PgDn keys to move through the file. ASCII files are shown in text mode. To look at the hexadecimal display of the file, press F9 or select Display Hex. Change the file display back to ASCII with the F9 key or the Display Ascii command. Press the Esc key or click the View, Restore View command to close the View window.

Figure 5.9 shows the View window displaying the \DOS\README.TXT file. The Display pull-down menu is shown.

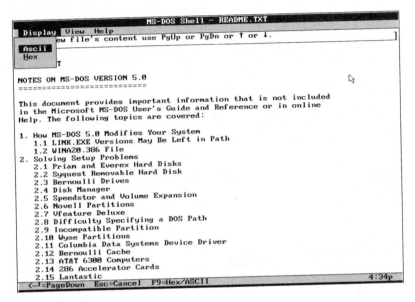

Fig. 5.9. The View window in ASCII display mode.

Printing Files

If you need to print the contents of a file, you first need to select it. (You normally want to select a text file because program files contain nontext characters that confuse your printer.) After the appropriate file is selected, choose File from the menu area and then choose Print.

For the Print command to work, you must run the DOS PRINT program *before* you start the Shell. If the PRINT program is not installed, and you choose File Print from the Shell, the Shell displays a dialog box reminding you to exit the Shell and start the PRINT program. If your AUTOEXEC.BAT file starts the Shell, you need to add a PRINT command on a line before the DOSSHELL command.

To see how the Print command works, try printing the DOSSHELL.INI file. (Exit the Shell and run PRINT, if needed.) This file contains information about the current Shell settings, including the color settings, and normally is stored in the \DOS directory of your boot disk. After selecting the file, choose File and then **Print**. When you select the Print command, the file is added to the PRINT queue. The PRINT program runs in the background and spools the file to the printer. This program is equivalent to the DOS command **PRINT <filename>**.

Creating Directories

Creating directories with the Shell is quite easy. First, select the parent directory under which you want to create a directory. To create a directory off of the root directory (C:\), you first must select the C:\ directory in the directory-tree area. Then choose File, Create Directory, and enter the name of the new directory. The new directory is created as a subdirectory of the selected directory. Do not include a backslash as the first character of the new directory name—a dialog box reminds you to select the root directory before creating a subdirectory off of the root.

To practice, select the \DOS directory, choose File, and choose Create Directory. Type **DOSTEMP** as the new name. The resulting directory is \DOS\DOSTEMP. In the directory-tree area, the directory icon for \DOS shows a + symbol to indicate that additional directory levels exist for the \DOS directory. With the \DOS directory selected, press the + key to display the \DOS\DOSTEMP directory. You can use this new directory in the next sections as you practice moving, copying, and deleting files.

Copying Files

The Copy command is used to make a copy of a file. This command is useful if you need to make a temporary duplicate of a file, such as the DOSSHELL.INI file. By making a copy of a file that you are about to change, you can ensure that you can recover from any errors that you make to a file. If you make some changes to the DOSSHELL.INI file, for example, and then find that the file doesn't work properly, you can copy the backup copy of the file from the \DOS\DOSTEMP directory back to the \DOS directory.

Just select the file you want to copy (DOSSHELL.INI, for example), select File, and then select the Copy command. The Shell shows the From and To text boxes, with the From text box already filled in with the name of the selected file. In the To text box, type the name of the new file—it can be another file name or a different directory. When you have specified the To name, select OK, and the file is copied. If the file name already exists, a dialog box appears, showing the existing file name and the file you want to copy, along with the date and size of each file. To replace the file, select Yes; otherwise, select No or Cancel. (Note that the Confirm or Replace check box of the <u>O</u>ptions <u>C</u>onfirmation command determines whether the Replace File Confirmation dialog box appears.)

Be careful about copying files. You may inadvertently copy over a needed file. If you see the Replace File Confirmation dialog box, make sure that you want to proceed with the operation. (Keep your hard disk backed up in case you make a mistake.)

Practice the Copy command by copying the DOSSHELL.INI file to the \DOS\DOSTEMP directory. Make sure that you leave the original DOSSHELL.INI file in the \DOS directory.

Cue:
To copy a file, press the Ctrl key and use the mouse to drag the file to its new directory or drive.

Another way to copy files is by using the mouse to drag a file to its new directory or disk drive. Use the mouse to select the file you want to copy. Press the Ctrl key and then hold down the left mouse button as you move the mouse pointer to the directory-tree area or the drive-icon area. The mouse pointer changes to a little file icon in reverse video as you move the mouse. Move the icon (keep Ctrl and the left mouse button pressed) until the appropriate directory or drive is highlighted. When you release the button, the Shell asks you to confirm the operation. Click the Yes button to copy the file. Click the No button to abort the copy procedure.

Cue:
Use the F8 key to copy a file.

A keyboard shortcut to the <u>F</u>ile, <u>C</u>opy command is F8. Select the file you want to move, press F8, and specify the To directory.

Moving Files to Another Directory

As you work with the files on your hard disk, you may find that you need to reorganize the files into different directories. Using standard DOS commands, you have to copy the file into the new directory and then delete the file from the old directory. By using the <u>F</u>ile <u>M</u>ove command in the DOS Shell, you can place a file in a different directory in one step.

As with other File functions, moving files is a quick process:

1. Select the files you want to move.

2. Select the <u>F</u>ile, <u>M</u>ove command or press the F7 shortcut key.

3. The names of the selected files are shown in the From text box.

4. Type the new directory name in the To text box.

5. Select OK to move the files.

To try this procedure, select the README.TXT file from the \DOS directory. Then select the <u>F</u>ile, <u>M</u>ove command. The command asks for the name of the destination directory. Because the \DOS directory is the current directory, type **C:\DOS\DOSTEMP**. (You create the C:\DOS\DOSTEMP directory in the "Creating New Directories" section.) Click or select OK, and the file is moved. You should see the README.TXT file listed in the file-list area, in the C:\DOS\DOSTEMP directory.

Another way to move files is by using the mouse to drag a file to its new directory or drive. Use the mouse to select the file you want to move. Press the Alt key and then hold down the left mouse button as you move the mouse pointer to the directory-tree area or drive-icon area. The mouse pointer changes to a little file icon in reverse video as you move the mouse. Move the icon (keep the Alt key and the left mouse button pressed) until the appropriate directory or drive icon is highlighted. When you release the button, the Shell asks you to confirm the operation. Click the Yes button to move the file. Click the No button to abort the move.

Cue:
Use the mouse to drag a file to its new directory or drive.

A keyboard shortcut to the File, Move command is F7. Just select the file you want to move, press F7, and specify the To directory.

Cue:
Use the F7 key to move a file.
Caution:
Don't move files needed by your programs. Move only your data files.

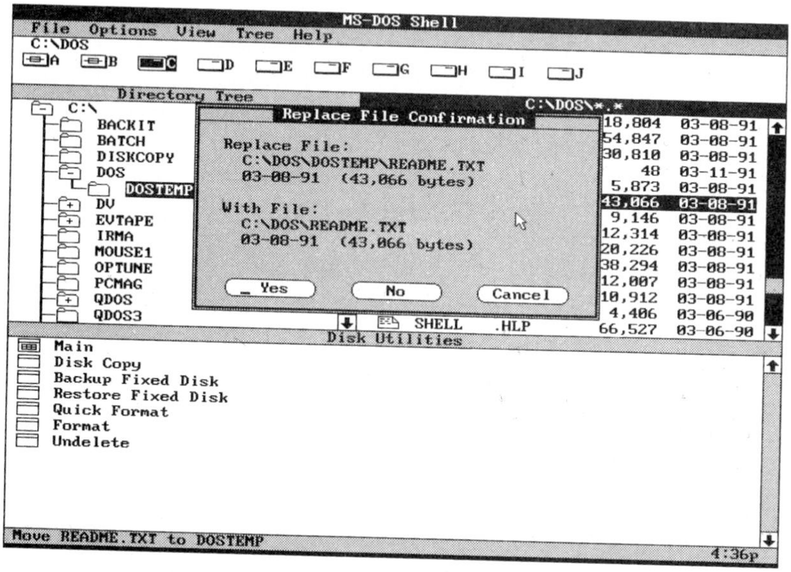

If you try to move a file with the same name as a file in the target directory, the Shell program displays the Replace File Confirmation dialog box (see fig. 5.10). Notice that the dates and sizes of the source and target files are shown. To complete the move, select the Yes button; otherwise select No or Cancel. Look at the file name in the target directory to make sure that you want to replace the file.

Fig. 5.10. *The Replace File Confirmation dialog box.*

You also can rename a file as you are moving it by specifying the file's complete new name when the Shell asks for the new directory—type the drive letter, directory, file name, and extension.

Deleting Files

After a period of time, you probably will find that you don't need certain files any longer. The Shell enables you to delete files quickly with the File Delete command. Select the file you want to delete, select File, and then select Delete. (You also can use the Del key to delete a selected file.) After you indicate that you want to delete a file, the Shell displays the Delete File Confirmation dialog box, asking for confirmation of the Delete command. Select the Yes command button to delete the file or use the No or Cancel button to cancel the Delete command.

Caution:
Make sure that you don't make any changes to other files before trying to undelete a file.

After a file is deleted, you may not be able to recover (undelete) it. DOS 5 has an undelete utility. Several commercial disk utility programs also include an undelete command. If you do delete a file accidentally, you need to undelete the file before you perform any other functions.

Another use for the Delete command is to delete empty directories. Make sure that the directory is indeed empty before you try to delete it. If you try to delete a directory that contains files, a dialog box displays an error message explaining that you cannot delete a nonempty directory.

Renaming Files and Directories

To give a file or directory a new name, you can use the File Rename command. Select a file or directory, select File, select Rename, and enter the new name. Press Enter or select OK to complete the command.

Caution:
Rename only your data files.

Be careful about renaming program files—your program may not work properly afterwards. Rename only the files that you create: documents, spreadsheets, database files, and so on.

Selecting a Group of Files

Up to this point, you have worked with only one file at a time. You can select a group of files, however, with the mouse or the keyboard.

To select a group of files in consecutive order, move to the first file in the group. Then hold down the Shift key as you use the cursor-movement keys or the mouse to move to the last file in the group.

To select a group of files scattered throughout the list, move to the first file and then hold down the Ctrl key as you use the mouse to click each item. From the keyboard, press the Shift-F8 key to turn on add mode (ADD appears at the bottom of the screen). Use the cursor-movement keys to move to the first file you want to select and press the space bar to select the file. Then use the arrow keys to move to the next item and press the space bar to select that item. When you finish selecting files, press Shift-F8 to toggle out of add mode. You can combine the two methods to select a group of files in the current file list. An easier way to select groups of files is to hold down the Ctrl key as you select files with the mouse or keyboard.

Cue:
The Add function enables you to work with groups of files.

To select all files in the file list, select <u>F</u>ile and then choose <u>S</u>elect All or press Ctrl-/.

To cancel or clear a selected file, hold down the Ctrl key while you click the file. You also can press Shift-F8 (if add mode is not active), use the cursor-movement keys to move to the selected file and press the space bar to unselect the file. To unselect all files, select File and then choose Deselect All or press Ctrl-\.

Using the Shell To Access Programs

The second group of functions available on the File menu enables you to start programs by selecting a file. This file can be a program name (COM, EXE, or BAT file) or a file associated with a particular program. Although this group of commands can be useful, you may want to create program menu entries. By creating program menu entries, you can ensure that the program starts properly. Running a program is easier from the program menu because all the start-up parameters already are specified.

Using the File Run Command

The <u>R</u>un command on the <u>F</u>ile menu enables you to run programs that you don't use often. You need to know the exact file name of the program you want to run, along with the directory in which the file is stored.

You have two ways to run a program with the <u>F</u>ile <u>R</u>un method. You can select the program's file name from the file list and then select the <u>F</u>ile <u>R</u>un command. You also can type the program's file name when you select the File Run command. When the program has finished, you are returned to the Shell window.

Associating Groups of Files with a Program File

With the Associate command from the File menu, you can correlate a particular file with a specific program. When you select that file and use the File Open command, the specified program starts and loads the file into the program.

One limitation to the Associate command is that a particular file extension can be associated with only one program. You cannot associate a group of files with the TXT extension in one directory with one program and a different group of files with the TXT extension in another directory with another program. For example, if you consistently name all WordPerfect documents with a WP5 file-name extension, you shouldn't use the WP5 extension for any other type of program's data files.

With one Associate command, you can specify up to 79 characters in the dialog box. First, highlight the file name of the program you want to associate, such as WP.EXE for your WordPerfect program. Next, select File and then Associate. The Associate File dialog box appears.

Type the extension name of the files you want to associate with the WP.EXE file, such as

   *.WP5

You can specify more than one file extension by separating each one with spaces, as in

   *.WPS *.DOC

When you are done, select the OK button to store the file association. Use the Cancel button to cancel the association.

A second way to associate files is by selecting the file from the file-list area. For example, the Shell program is set up to associate all TXT files with the EDIT program. You can determine an existing file association by highlighting a nonprogram file (program files are BAT, COM, or EXE files) and selecting the File, Associate command. The Associate File dialog box is shown on-screen. This dialog box shows that the EDIT program has been associated with all TXT files. The program name is placed in the text box.

To create file associations, select the file in the file-list area. Then use the File Associate command and fill in the complete program name (including drive and directory) in the text box of the Associate File dialog box. Select OK to save the file association or Cancel to cancel the process.

To remove a file association, select the program file name. Then select File, select Associate, and remove the file extensions from the dialog box. Select OK to save the changes, and the file is no longer associated with those file extensions.

Using the File Open Command

After you have associated a file extension with a particular program file, you can use the File Open command to start the selected file's associated program. Select the file, select File, and select Open. If the file you have selected does not have an extension associated with a program, the system beeps, and the command is ignored.

The Open command works by starting the program with the file name. If you have associated all WP5 file extensions with the WordPerfect program and have selected the MOMLETTR.WP5 file, the Shell program enters the following command at the DOS prompt:

```
C:\WP51\WP.EXE MOMLETTR.WP5
```

The WordPerfect program starts, and the MOMLETTR.WP5 document is retrieved to the screen. This procedure works because the WordPerfect program enables you to specify at the DOS prompt the name of the document that you want to retrieve. Not all programs have this capability, however, so you need to check your program's documentation.

Reminder:
Not all programs can specify a data file on the command line.

Exploring the Program-List Area

The program-list area of the Shell window enables you to set up your own menu of programs. These menu options can access individual programs or groups of programs. The initial main program group in the program-list area, for example, includes four default items:

Command Prompt   Temporarily exits to the DOS prompt. Type **EXIT** and press Enter to return to the Shell.

Editor	Starts the DOS Editor program. A dialog box asks you for the name of the file to edit. You can enter the file name or press Enter to start a new text file.
MS-DOS QBasic	Starts the MS-DOS QBasic program. A dialog box asks for the name of the QBasic file you want to edit. To create a QBasic program, press Enter.
Disk Utilities	Displays another menu that lists various disk-based commands

Of the preceding four items, the first three are individual program items. The Disk Utilities is a program group consisting of the following program items:

Disk Copy	Makes a copy of a floppy disk using the DISKCOPY command
Backup Fixed Disk	Performs a backup of the hard disk by using DOS's BACKUP command
Restore Fixed Disk	Restores the hard disk backup by using DOS's RESTORE command
Quick Format	Exits to DOS to perform a FORMAT /Q command. A dialog box asks you for additional parameters, such as the drive letter, which defaults to A.
Format	Formats new floppy disks
Undelete	Recovers deleted files by using the UNDELETE command. A dialog box asks you for the UNDELETE parameters, with the /LIST parameter as the default.

Warning: If your disk is close to full, refrain from using Undelete from within the Shell. When you use this command from the Shell, DOS temporarily writes a file to disk. This file contains the contents of memory. This action can overwrite the data you intend to recover. Instead, press F3 or Alt-F4 to exit from the Shell and execute the UNDELETE command from the command line.

Each of the standard program items has a short Help screen. If you highlight the command by using the arrow keys or the Tab key and then press F1, a dialog box explains the function of each command. These help messages are contained in the menu item's properties, as explained in the next section.

When the file-list area is selected, four menu names appear in the menu bar: File, Options, View, and Help. Only the File menu is different; the others are the same as when the directory-tree or file-list area is active.

Using the File Command in the Program-List Area

The commands listed on the program-list area's File menu enable you to create or modify your own program items; copy, delete, or move program items; or run a program associated with the items. Figure 5.11 shows the File pull-down menu for the program-list area.

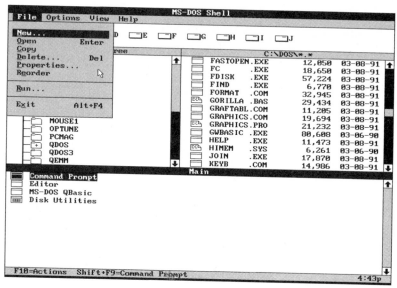

Fig. 5.11. The program-list area File menu.

Creating Program Items

With the File New command, you can set up a new program group or program item. Remember that an individual menu item running one program is a program item, and a group of program items are placed in a program group. You can think of a program group as a menu choice that leads to other menu choices.

Cue:
A program group is a collection of individual program objects.

When you select File and then New, the Shell asks whether you want to create a program group or a program item. Select the Program Item option button. The Shell displays the Add Program dialog box similar to the one in figure 5.12.

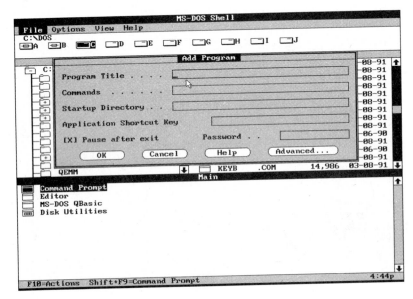

Fig. 5.12. The Add Program dialog box.

In the Program Title text box, type the title that you want shown in the Shell window. You can type up to 23 characters. Use the Tab key or Shift-Tab key combination to move to the next or preceding text box.

The Commands are needed to start the program. You can type multiple commands in this text box, using up to 255 characters. The commands you enter here should be the same commands you enter at the DOS prompt to start the program. In this manner, the commands you specify are similar to those you place in a batch file.

To specify multiple commands, separate each command sequence with a semicolon (;) preceded and followed by one or more spaces. Suppose that you need to enter the following three commands to start your spreadsheet program:

D:

CD \LOTUS3

LOTUS

To use these commands in the Add Program dialog box's Commands field, enter

D: ; CD \LOTUS3 ; LOTUS

When you select this program from the Shell's Main window, the Shell executes each command in sequence.

To use batch files as the program commands, use the CALL command to run each batch file. That method enables additional commands to be completed, and control returns to the Shell.

Startup Directory is normally the directory that contains the program you want to start. If you are creating a program to start WordPerfect, for example, you type the WordPerfect directory in this field.

Application Shortcut Key enables you to specify a shortcut key to use to switch to the program when using the Task Swapper. You have to start the program, but if you start or switch to a second program, the shortcut key is available to switch back to the first program. Use the Alt, Shift, or Ctrl key with a letter key to specify the shortcut key. Several combinations are reserved.

Pause after Exit is a check box that specifies whether a pause should follow the program's completion. When this option is checked (turned on), a Press any key to continue message appears after the program finishes and before the Shell window reappears. Your program may display some information that you need to see before the Shell window is redisplayed.

Password is an optional field in which you can type a password to be required before the program starts. You can specify a password with up to 20 characters.

If you have specified a password for the program you select from the Shell window, you must enter the password successfully before the program starts. If a program has a password, you also need to supply the password if you have to change the program's properties.

Caution:
Enter the correct password to run the settings of the program object or group.

Using Replaceable Parameters in the Command Line

You can use replaceable parameters in the command line. A replaceable parameter is additional information you enter with a command. When you specify replaceable parameters in the Command box, as in **CHKDSK %1**, selecting the program displays a dialog box that asks for the value to use for *%1*.

You can specify up to 9 replaceable parameters (%1 through %9), just as you can in batch files. For each parameter you specify in the command line, you need to complete the Program Item Properties dialog box (see fig. 5.13). This dialog box is shown when you select OK when creating or modifying a menu program item. The Program Item Properties dialog box contains the following text boxes:

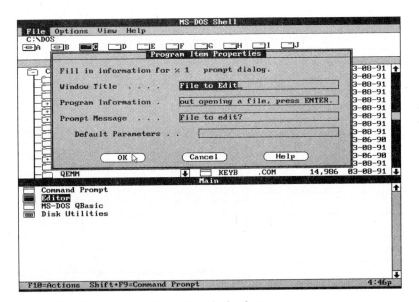

Fig. 5.13. The Program Item Properties dialog box.

Window Title. Type the title that you want to display at the top of the dialog box, which appears when the program is selected.

Program Information. Type a descriptive message about the replaceable parameter, such as **Disk Drive Statistics** for a CHKDSK command.

Prompt Message. Type the message that should appear in front of the parameter entry area of the dialog box that appears when the program item is selected.

Default Parameters. This field enables you to specify a parameter that can be overridden by the user's entry.

The entries in the Program Item Properties dialog box, shown in figure 5.13, produce the same dialog box that displays when the Editor program item is selected from the main program group (see fig. 5.14).

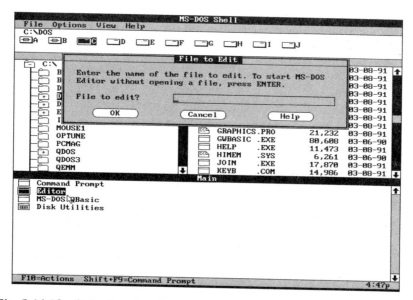

Fig. 5.14. *The dialog box that displays when the Editor program item is selected.*

Setting Up Advanced Program Object Properties

You can specify additional program properties by selecting the Advanced button in the Program Item Properties dialog box. The Shell then presents you with the Advanced dialog box, shown in figure 5.15.

The elements of this dialog box are described in the following paragraphs.

Help Text. Type a message of up to 255 characters that should be displayed when the user selects the program and then chooses Help. The message information is displayed in a Help dialog box. To start a new line in the help message, use the ^ and M characters at the spot at which you want a line to break. The Help Text field is not required but can be useful to a user.

Reminder:
Use the Help Text field to set up your own help screens for a program group or item.

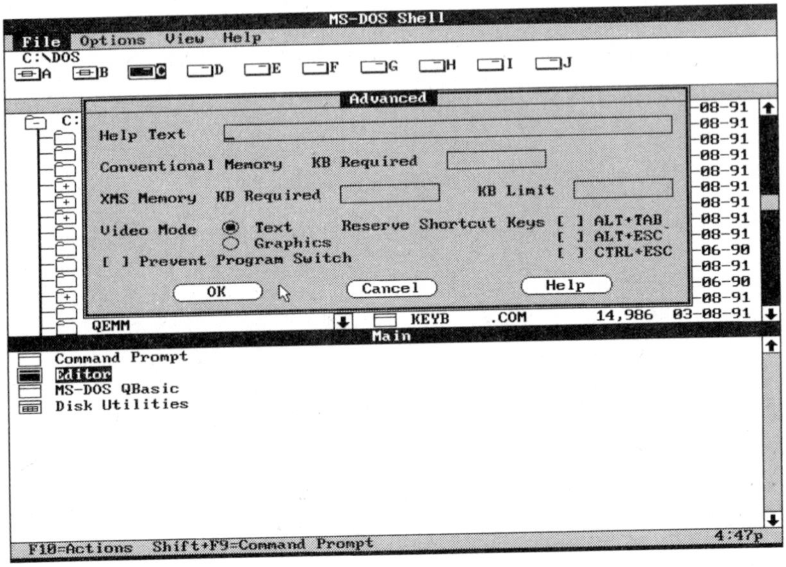

Fig. 5.15. *The Advanced dialog box.*

Cue:
*Make sure that
the memory
values are
sufficient for the
program's
requirements.*

Conventional Memory KB Required. Indicate the amount of conventional memory required by the program. The default setting is 128K; change this setting according to your program's needs. This memory value is the minimum amount of memory needed by the program; DOS provides all the available conventional memory when you select the program. If the available memory is below this amount, the program does not start, and a dialog box alerts you to the lack of available memory.

XMS Memory. This field represents the amount of extended memory that is made available to the program. The XMS memory is used according to the Lotus-Intel-Microsoft-AST extended Memory Specification. Two values are included here: KB Required is the amount of extended memory that must be available before the program is started. Normally, you leave this value at the default 0, as most programs can get along without extended memory. KB Limit is the amount of extended memory that the program is allowed to use. This setting enables you to limit a program's use of extended memory, because some programs try to grab all the extended memory they can find. Set the limit value to 0 to prevent the program's access to extended memory. A value of –1 enables the program to grab all the available extended memory. The default is 384, if your system has that amount of available extended memory.

Video Mode. This field specifies how the program uses the video display and controls the amount of conventional memory that DOS reserves for storing display images. This amount of memory is part of the total amount of memory specified by the program's KB Required field. If you choose Text, the Shell runs the program in text mode. Because text mode doesn't use much memory, most of the memory is available to the program. If you choose Graphics, the Shell runs the program in graphics mode. This mode uses more memory than text mode, because an amount of memory must be reserved for the text and graphics screens of the program.

Reserve Shortcut Keys. These check boxes specify the key combinations used by the program rather than by the Shell Task Swapper. The available options are Alt-Tab, Alt-Esc, and Ctrl-Esc. When you have reserved these keys, the Task Swapper (if enabled) ignores those keystrokes.

Prevent Program Switch. This check box disables the use of the Task Swapper to switch to another program. Enable this option for communications programs, for example, to prevent your communications sessions from being interrupted.

After you have specified the advanced parameters of the program you are adding, select OK to save the changes. Select Cancel to cancel any changes you have made to the Advanced dialog box. Then verify the information on the Add Program screen and select OK to save the information. Selecting Cancel cancels the entire Add Program command.

Changing a Program's Properties

After you have defined the properties of a program item, you may need to change that information. Select the program that you want to change, select File, and then select Properties. If a password was specified for the program, the Password dialog box appears. You need to enter the correct password to change the program information.

Caution: Enter the password to change the program's properties.

The Program Item Properties dialog box contains the same dialog box elements as the Add Program dialog box (see fig. 5.12).

Deleting a Program Object

If you no longer need a program item, select that item and choose the File Delete command (or press the Del key). If the item has a password, you need to enter the correct password in the Password dialog box. Then a dialog box appears asking you to confirm the deletion. Select OK to confirm the deletion; select Cancel to cancel the deletion.

Creating a Program Group

Grouping similar programs is sometimes helpful. To create a program group, select File and then New. When the Shell asks whether you want to create a program item or a program group, select the Program Group option button and then choose OK. The Shell displays the dialog box shown in figure 5.16.

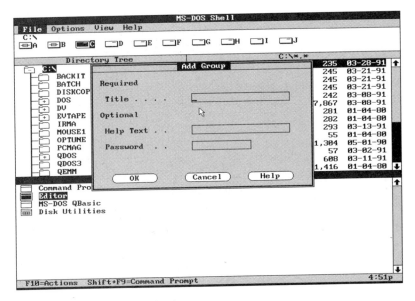

Fig. 5.16. The Add Group dialog box.

This dialog box has one required text box (Title) and two optional text boxes (Help Text and Password). The Title text box contains up to 23 characters of text that you want to display as a group menu item. The help text is displayed in a dialog box when you highlight the group menu item and press the F1 Help key. You can enter up to 255 characters in the Help Text text box. Use the ^ and m characters to indicate a line break. The Password box can contain up to 20 characters that must be entered to select the group menu item. The password also must be entered correctly to change the properties of the group menu item.

To create programs and add them to a group, select that group. For example, the Disk Utilities program group is a subgroup of the Main program group. Selecting the Disk Utilities item displays the menu items that have been defined as part of the Disk Utilities group. A double-click on the group name (or pressing the Enter key with the group highlighted) brings you to the group's program list. Then you can use the File New command to add programs (or groups) to that group.

You can create any number of levels of program groups, although you may want to limit the number of levels to two or three. Any more levels can cause you extra work getting back to the main level.

Cue:

Limit the number of program group levels to three.

When you select a program group from the Main group, the Shell shows you a new program group in the file-list area. The program group's name appears in the title bar of the file-list area. One group already is installed in the Shell when you begin using it: the Disk Utilities group. This group contains the program items shown in figure 5.17.

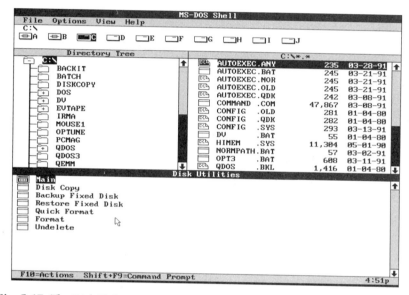

Fig. 5.17. *The Disk Utilities program group.*

The first item in the list is the Main program group. After you are through with any programs in the Disk Utilities group, select Main (or press Esc) to return to the initial program-list area.

Copying a Program Item to Another Group

After you have set up a program item, you may decide to make that program available in several different groups. By selecting the program item and using the File Copy command, you can copy the program item to another group. After the program item is copied, you can make additional changes to the program item with the File Properties command. Note, however, that a change to one copy of a program item's properties does not affect the other copies.

Reordering Program Items in a Group

As you add program items, you may decide to reorder them in a more logical manner. Select the program item you want to move, select File, and then select the Reorder command. The Shell asks you to select the new location; double-click the new location with the mouse or move to the new location and press Enter. The program moves to the new location, which also moves all other items down the list. If you want to cancel the Reorder operation, press the Esc key, and this item is not moved.

Moving Program Items from Group to Group

Cue:

To move a program item, copy it to its new location and delete it from the old location.

To move a program item from one area to another, you need to copy the program item to its new location and then delete the program item from its old location. Select the program item you want to copy and then choose File and Copy.

If the program item has a password, you need to enter the correct one. Then open the destination program group by double-clicking or highlight the group and press Enter. After the correct destination program group is displayed, press the F2 key to complete the move. (To cancel the copy, press Esc.) The program item then is added to the bottom of the group's list. You can use the File Reorder command to change the order of the program items in the group.

After you have copied the program item to its new location, you need to delete the program item from its original location. Use the File Delete command to do so. If you don't delete the original program item, you have a duplicate menu item.

Deleting a Program Group

To delete a program group, the group must be empty. Use the File Delete command to delete each program item. When all the program items in a group are deleted, you see only the name of the parent program group in the program-list area. Press Esc to get back to the parent group; then select File and Delete to delete the now empty group. You also can press the Delete key. A dialog box appears asking you to confirm the deletion. If you attempt to delete a program group that still contains one or more program items, a dialog box reminds you that you cannot delete a nonempty group.

Running a Program

After you have created various program items and groups in the program-list area, you can test the new programs (or the default programs) by running them. With the mouse, double-click the item you want to run. With the keyboard, highlight the menu item or group, press Enter or select File, and select Open.

If the menu item or group has a password assigned to it, you need to enter the correct password to run the program or group. An incorrect password causes a bell to sound, and the program does not run. You also need to have the amount of memory specified by the program's properties before you can run the program.

After the item's commands have completed, you are returned to the Shell window. If the program has the Pause after Exit check box enabled, you first see the message `Press any key to continue.`

Using the Shell's Task Swapper

The new Task Swapper enables you to start several programs at the same time. You then can switch among them with a keystroke.

The Task Swapper is a task-switching utility. The Task Swapper is not a true multitasking environment like Windows or DesqView. When you have one program running and want to switch to a second program, the first program is frozen and saved to disk. That computer's memory then is released so that you can start the second program. If you then switch back to the first program, the second program is frozen and saved to disk, freeing up the memory space it was using. The first program then is loaded back into memory, continuing where it left off.

After you have added all the program items you may need, select Options and then select Enable Task Swapper to open up the Active Task List area, which is shown in figure 5.18.

To run a program, double-click the program name (or highlight the program in the Main window and press Enter or select File Open). To switch, use one of the following keys:

Ctrl-Esc   Switches back to the Shell from the current program

Alt-Tab   Cycles among active tasks

Shift-Enter   Adds a task to the Active Task list without switching to the program

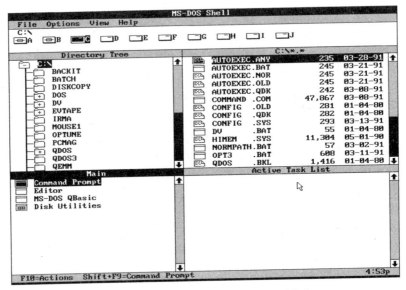

Fig. 5.18. The Shell window with the Task Swapper enabled.

Exiting the Shell Temporarily

If you need to go to the DOS prompt temporarily, you can select the MS-DOS Command Prompt choice in the Main program group. (Another method is to press Shift-F9, which is shown on the bottom of the Shell window.) You then can run any command that you want. While you are at the DOS prompt, the Shell program has been suspended. When you are finished at the DOS prompt and want to return to the Shell, type **EXIT** and press Enter.

Quitting the Shell

Reminder:
You cannot exit the shell without closing all active tasks.

To quit the Shell and return to the DOS prompt, make sure that you have exited all programs properly. You shouldn't see any programs listed in the Active Task List area. If you do, press Alt-Tab to switch to any running programs and exit them properly. After you have exited all programs, choose File and then choose Exit (or press the F3 shortcut key) to quit the Shell.

The Shell doesn't enable you to exit without first closing all active tasks.

Customizing the Shell

The DOSSHELL.INI file is the Shell's configuration file. This file contains information about the following Shell settings:

- The program items and program groups that have been defined

- The toggle settings such as the screen mode and resolution

- The current color choice and the color settings for each color choice

- The associations of file extensions to programs

These parameters are stored when you make changes to the various settings. When you use the Options Colors command to select a different color scheme, for example, the *currentcolor* parameter is changed.

The format of the DOSSHELL.INI file is very specific. Although you can make changes to the file, you must be careful to preserve its format. Before you make any changes to the file, make a copy of it, calling the copy something like DOSSHELL.IBK. If the changes you make don't work properly, you can copy the DOSSHELL.IBK file to DOSSHELL.INI, and things are back to normal. You also can create several copies of the INI file and use a COPY command to install the appropriate INI file before you start the Shell.

Caution:
Make a backup copy of the DOSSHELL.INI file before you make any changes.

Although some of the parameters are beyond the scope of this text, you can make simple changes to the color settings or add your own. The following is an extract of the DOSSHELL.INI file that details the settings of the Basic Blue color choice.

Caution:
Don't make changes to the format of the DOSSHELL.INI file.

```
selection =
{

    title = Basic Blue
    foreground =
    {

    base = black
    highlight = brightwhite
    selection = brightwhite
    alert = brightred
    menubar = black
    menu = black
    disabled = white
    accelerator = cyan
```

```
        dialog = black
        button = black
        elevator = white
        titlebar = black
        scrollbar = brightwhite
        borders = black
        drivebox = black
        driveicon = black
        cursor = black
    }
background =
    {
        base = brightwhite
        highlight = blue
        selection = black
        alert = brightwhite
        menubar = white
        menu = brightwhite
        disabled = brightwhite
        accelerator = brightwhite
        dialog = brightwhite
        button = white
        elevator = white
        titlebar = white
        scrollbar = black
        borders = brightwhite
        drivebox = brightwhite
        driveicon = brightwhite
        cursor = brightblack

    }

    }
```

Because DOSSHELL.INI is an ASCII text file, you can change the file with the DOS Editor program. Select Editor from the Main program group in the file-list area and type the name of the file (C:\DOS\DOSSHELL.INI).

Use the scroll bar or the PgDn key to get to the `color=` section of the file. You can see that the various items on the list enable you to set the colors for all of the parameters used in Shell. For example, if a menu choice is not available, the disabled parameter displays the menu choice in white text on a bright cyan background.

Table 5.4 shows a list of the available colors used in the Shell.

Table 5.4
Color Words Used by the Shell

black	brightblack
white	brightwhite
blue	brightblue
red	brightred
cyan	brightcyan
green	brightgreen
magenta	brightmagenta
yellow	brightyellow

Cue:
Make sure that you spell the color names correctly, or they will not work properly.

You can change any of the color settings. You also can create your own color scheme. Using the DOS Editor program, block the text from the selection to the } character just before the next selection text. Then carefully copy the block to the area between the } and selection text. Change the Title line to the name of your color scheme. Make any other changes to the color settings for each parameter.

When you create a color scheme, make sure that you carefully follow the format of the color selection area, including the { and } characters.

When you have verified all the color settings, save the file and return to the Shell window. To select the new color scheme, use the Options Colors command; the color setting you defined appears in the menu.

To make changing the INI file easier, enable the Task Swapper. Start the DOS Editor, editing the DOSSHELL.INI file. While in the Editor, save the file and then press Alt-Esc to switch back to the Shell window. Select your color setting again, and you should see the results of your work. If some of the colors are not what you wanted, switch back to the DOS Editor, make the changes, and switch back to the Shell window to see the results.

To return things back to normal, you can copy the backup copy of the INI file (DOSSHELL.IBK) that you made before you changed the file.

Table 5.5 includes brief descriptions of the terms used in the color settings section of the DOSSHELL.INI file.

Table 5.5
Color Settings Items

Term	Colors used on:
base	Directory-tree list, file list, program list, and task list
highlight	Shell title and all items highlighted but not chosen
selection	Chosen items
alert	Warning messages
menubar	Menu bar, nonselected menus, and status line
menu	The selected menu
disabled	Dimmed commands
accelerator	Underlined letters in menu commands
dialog	Dialog boxes
button	Dialog box buttons
elevator	Scroll boxes
titlebar	Area title bars
scrollbar	Scroll bars
borders	Dialog list box borders
drivebox	Disk drive area
driveicon	Disk drive icon
cursor	Color of cursor

Chapter Summary

The DOS 5 Shell gives you a great deal of power in an easy-to-use package. Using the Shell to access different programs and perform file maintenance enables you to become more productive in the use of your computer. By adding your own program groups and program items, you can create your own menu system of commands and programs. The Task Swapper, by enabling you to start several programs, gives you the convenience of moving from one task to another without having to exit and reload each program. Although the Task Swapper is not a true multitasking system like Windows, it can increase your productivity a great deal.

Part II

Working with the Core Commands

Includes

Preparing and Maintaining Disks

Managing and Navigating the Directory Hierarchy

Managing Your Files

Working with System Information

Gaining Control of Devices

6

Preparing and Maintaining Disks

Chapter 2 presents a short course in the fundamentals of the DOS file system and related topics. This chapter describes the commands that directly relate to the preparation and maintenance of disks. All the commands presented in this chapter can be viewed as disk-level commands; REPLACE, RECOVER, and CHKDSK, however, have file-level options. If you are like most DOS users, you spend more time managing files than you do managing disks, so you are likely to be more comfortable working with file-level DOS commands than you are with disk-level DOS commands. You don't format your hard disk, for example, just for practice. These disk-level commands, however, put you in the driver's seat of disk preparation and maintenance. Knowing when and how to use these commands enhances your PC competence.

Each disk-level command, its possible parameters, and any optional switches also are listed in the command reference section of this book. This chapter provides general information about the disk-level commands, such as how they do their job within DOS and what rules apply in their usage.

The commands covered in this chapter include the following:

- FDISK
- FORMAT
- LABEL
- VOL
- SYS

- UNFORMAT

- MIRROR

- DISKCOPY

- DISKCOMP

- REPLACE

- CHKDSK

- RECOVER

Issuing External Commands

Cue:
The commands built into COMMAND.COM are the DOS internal commands.

Because this chapter introduces the first DOS commands of the book, take a moment to review the difference between internal and external commands. Chapter 3 discusses COMMAND.COM and its built-in commands—the internal DOS commands. You can issue an internal command whenever you see the DOS prompt; COMMAND.COM executes the internal command immediately. External commands, however, require some extra consideration.

Reminder:
External DOS commands must be loaded by COMMAND.COM.

Because external DOS commands are programs that COMMAND.COM loads and executes, they must be accessible to the command processor. This section discusses the process of making these commands accessible to COMMAND.COM.

As an example of an external command, look at the FDISK command. The full syntax is as follows:

*dc:pathc***FDISK**

dc:pathc is the optional full path name, which consists of a drive name and path name on the drive in which the external command is located. You can omit the drive name if the command is on the default drive, and you can omit the path name if it is the current path on the drive that contains the command. You also can issue the command without a full path name if the full path name is included in the latest PATH command.

If your external DOS command programs reside in a directory named \\DOS on drive C, for example, you can issue the following command:

PATH=C:\\DOS

This command tells DOS that some external commands can be found in the directory \\DOS on drive C. When you enter an external command, DOS searches the \\DOS directory on drive C if the external command is not in the current directory. If you have not yet used the PATH command, look over the information on PATH in Chapter 7 before you continue with this chapter. Your computer may have an AUTOEXEC.BAT file that sets the path.

Dividing a Hard Disk with FDISK

A hard disk can be divided logically into partitions. (See Chapter 2 for more information on partitions.) A *partition* is a section of the storage area of a hard disk. Many operating systems, including DOS, can use disk partitions, and most have some utility program that creates and manages partitions. DOS's utility program for partition creation and management is the external command FDISK.

Cue:
The FDISK command creates and manages disk partitions.

Issuing the FDISK Command

The syntax for FDISK is as follows:

FDISK

Notice that FDISK has no parameters. Because this command handles the partitions of any hard disks on your system sequentially, a drive parameter is not needed.

Understanding Hard Disk Partitions

The concept of dividing one real or physical disk into more than one apparent or logical disk drive can be traced back to pre-DOS operating systems. In earlier minicomputer disk operating systems, dealing with disks of different sizes often was inconvenient. Utilities may be available to copy all files from one disk to another, for example, but only if the disks were the same size. If a minicomputer system had one 32M removable platter disk drive and one 64M hard disk, the size differential of the real disks precluded the use of disk-level copying utilities. If the system allowed partitioning, however, the storage space of the 64M disk could be split in half. In effect, the system could be tricked into thinking that it had two 32M disk drives. Copying from any 32M "drive" on the system to any other therefore was possible.

The operating system wasn't really tricked, however. During the boot process of the minicomputer, the operating system loaded the disk partition table into memory reserved for data-file management. Each time a program made a disk request, the disk address (head and cylinder numbers) for the file on the logical 32M disk volume was intercepted by the data-file manager section of the operating system. The data-file management system used the table to transform the logical disk address into a real or absolute disk address. The applications program and the higher levels of the operating system were no more the wiser to the switch. Because no operating system was dominant across computer manufacturers' lines, most manufacturers added their own innovations to the process of creating logical disks out of a physical one.

Cue:
Version 2.0 was the first DOS version to support hard disk partitioning.

DOS started out supporting floppy disks only, so prior to Version 2.0, DOS did not need to worry about hard disk partitioning. As hard disk drive innovation and competition drove hard drive prices lower, however, the IBM PC/XT with its 10M hard disk and DOS Version 2.0 brought DOS out of the floppy disk category and into the high-capacity storage category. Partitioning a hard disk became an issue for two reasons:

- Early versions of DOS could not accommodate disks with more than 32M of space. As larger disks became common, partitioning provided a way to make use of them. A disk with 40M could be split into 30M and 10M partitions, and DOS was tricked into believing that it had two smaller hard disks attached. Later versions of DOS made this type of partitioning unnecessary.

- The larger disk drives invited the use of other operating systems, such as UNIX and XENIX. Users who wanted to run XENIX and DOS, however, found out that the two file systems were incompatible; each needed its own drive. Partitioning provided a way to accomplish this pairing on a single drive.

Microsoft and other operating system suppliers uniformly leave a reserved area of the hard disk available for the partition table, which contains information on how the partitions are arranged on the disk. A large disk can contain one partition or many. Operating system vendors understand that a user may want to install an additional operating system on the hard disk, but most operating systems are not compatible with other operating systems. An operating system such as DOS wants to establish the disk as its own. Fortunately, most operating systems consult the hard disk's partition table when booting from the hard disk. The partition table establishes the boundaries of the physical disk that each operating system can call its own. Each operating system uses the partition table information to coexist peacefully on the same physical disk with other operating systems.

Chapter 2 describes the disk-level boot record and bookkeeping tables that DOS places in track 0. If another operating system "owns" track 0 as part of that system's partition, DOS cannot use track 0 without damaging the internal tables of the other operating system. DOS avoids the problem by consulting the partition table at start-up. If DOS does not "own" track 0, DOS uses the first track that it does own as its track 0. DOS also considers the last physical cylinder of the DOS partition as the logical end of the hard disk.

The partition table, therefore, supports multioperating systems. With DOS Version 2.0, the concept of the DOS partition was born. The tool that created and maintained the DOS partition was FDISK.

Understanding the Operation of FDISK

The primary function of the FDISK program is to provide the DOS user with access to the disk's partition table. FDISK enables DOS to participate in a multioperating system disk-sharing arrangement. Other operating systems, such as XENIX, have their own versions of FDISK to manage the partition table. You can use FDISK to create a DOS partition of the size you specify, to make DOS's (or another operating system's) partition active, and to delete an existing DOS partition. You also can use FDISK to define partitions for up to four different operating systems.

Caution:
To install another operating system, use the instructions supplied with FDISK.

> *Note:* If you have another operating system to install on your hard disk, use the instructions supplied with FDISK or a similar command of the other operating system.

With DOS Version 3.3, you can use FDISK to create more than one DOS partition. After you define a primary DOS partition with FDISK, you can define an extended DOS partition, which you divide into one or more logical drives. All primary DOS partitions and logical drives must be formatted properly with the FORMAT command before they can be used. When DOS is the active operating system as reflected in the partition table, DOS boots from the active DOS partition. You then can log on to one of the logical drives. The primary DOS partition normally is assigned the drive name C.

Cue:
You can use FDISK Versions 3.3 and later to create more than one partition: a primary DOS partition and an extended DOS partition.

Caution:

Before you format a new hard disk, you must ensure that the disk has been prepared with FDISK.

Before you format a new hard disk, you must ensure that the disk has been prepared with FDISK. DOS 5.0's installation program, SETUP, runs FDISK when you are installing DOS on a new computer with an unpartitioned hard disk. DOS cannot work with a hard disk that has no DOS values in its partition table. In fact, if you have in your computer system another physical hard disk that has been partitioned, DOS moves the drive letter that would apply to the unpartitioned drive to the next physical drive's primary DOS partition. Remember that DOS uses drive letters as names for drives in a multidisk system.

Caution:

The presence or absence of primary or extended DOS partitions affects the drive letters that DOS assigns to physical or logical drives.

Suppose that in your system you have two hard disks, each with one DOS partition. Their DOS-assigned drive names are C and D. Suppose that drive C fails, and you replace it with a new unpartitioned drive in the failed drive's position. DOS detects that the new drive lacks a DOS partition and assumes that the second hard disk is drive C or the next usable disk in line. Because you have used the first hard disk as C and the second hard disk as D, you may decide to format the new first drive with the command FORMAT C:/V/S. If you don't catch the mistake at the warning prompt, DOS formats the second hard disk that you usually refer to as D. The result is disaster. The second hard disk is wiped out because the first hard disk was not partitioned. Remember that the presence or absence of primary or extended DOS partitions affects the drive letters that DOS assigns to physical or logical drives. The drive-name movement also can occur when you delete an extended partition or logical drive or if you run a DOS window under another operating system.

Cue:

FDISK provides confirmation prompts and warnings during its operation.

After you partition your hard disk(s), DOS respects the logical drives and creates a file system for each drive when it is formatted. If you use FDISK to delete a partition and subsequently create another partition, all the data in the original partition is destroyed. You see warnings when you are electing to do something with FDISK that destroys data. To proceed beyond the warnings, you must answer a confirmation prompt.

Before FDISK deletes a partition, for example, you see the following warning message:

```
Warning: Data in the DOS partition
will be lost. Do you wish to
continue (Y/N). . . . . . . . . . . . . ? [N]
```

Respond N if you do not want to continue with the partition deletion operation. Respond Y if you are sure that deleting the partition is your intention.

Because of its potentially dangerous effects, FDISK is one DOS command with which you should not experiment. You will have some opportunities, however, to work with FDISK. If you decide to reformat your disk, for example, and you have one DOS partition on the whole disk, you can run FDISK first and experiment. If you are upgrading to a hard disk from a floppy-only system, you can experiment with FDISK before you make your "official" partition decisions. Just remember that you need a bootable floppy disk that contains the FDISK and FORMAT programs. As always, you should have a working copy of your DOS master system disks. Deleting partitions can cause you to rely on the system's floppy disk until the hard disk is again partitioned and formatted. For this reason, keeping a formatted floppy with DEBUG, FORMAT, and SYS available is a good idea.

Formatting Disks with FORMAT

Before receiving files, disks must be initialized by the external DOS command FORMAT. DOS 5.0's installation program, SETUP, runs FORMAT when you are installing DOS on a new computer with an unformatted hard disk. From a user's point of view, formatting a disk consists of issuing a properly constructed FORMAT command and letting the computer do all the work. After you run FDISK on a hard disk, FORMAT is the most essential disk-level command. In fact, the only thing that DOS can do with an unformatted disk is format it!

Before you read on, remember the following caution: You should think of FORMAT as destroying all files and directories on a disk. Although in some cases this statement is not true, and the UNFORMAT command often can be used in DOS 5 to "unformat" a disk, always use care and caution when formatting disks. You should consider FORMAT a dangerous command to misuse.

Caution: FORMAT destroys all files and directories on a disk.

Issuing the FORMAT Command

The syntax for FORMAT is as follows:

FORMAT *drive: /switches*

drive: is the drive that holds the disk you want to format; */switches* are one or more of the optional switches listed in table 6.1.

Table 6.1
FORMAT Switches

Switch	Action
/1	Formats a floppy disk as a single-sided disk. /1 often is used with the /8 switch to format 8-sector-per-track disks to be compatible with Version 1.0 and Version 1.1 systems.
/4	Formats a 5 1/4-inch floppy disk with 40 tracks per side in an HC (1.2M) drive. The resulting disk may be unreadable by a standard 360K (double-sided, double-density) drive.
/8	Formats a 5 1/4-inch floppy disk with 8 sectors per track rather than 9 or 15
/F:size	Formats a disk to the capacity specified by *size*. The possible values for *size* include the following: 160, 160K, 160KB 180, 180K, 180KB 320, 320K, 320KB 360, 360K, 360KB 720, 720K, 720KB 1200, 1200K, 1200KB, 1.2, 1.2M, 1.2MB 1440, 1440K, 1440KB, 1.44, 1.44M, 1.44MB 2880, 2880K, 2880KB, 2.88, 2.88M, 2.88MB
/N:nn	Formats a floppy disk with the number of sectors specified by nn. The disk drive, controller electronics, and driver must support the specified number of sectors.
/T:nn	Formats a floppy disk to the number of tracks (per side) specified by nn
/Q	Quick format; performs a safe format but does not scan the disk for bad sectors; can be used only with previously formatted disks.
/S	Produces a bootable DOS system disk that contains the hidden DOS system files and COMMAND.COM
/u	Formats a floppy disk so that it cannot be unformatted using the UNFORMAT command (DOS 5.0 only)

Switch	Action
/V	Causes FORMAT to prompt for a volume label of up to 11 characters. When you have entered the volume label, press Enter. (In DOS 4.0 and 5.0, FORMAT always prompts for a volume label.)
/V:label	Causes FORMAT to label the disk being formatted with the volume label specified in label.

Understanding the Operation of FORMAT

From the standpoint of disk management, FORMAT initializes a disk. In other words, FORMAT prepares a disk to accept files. FORMAT prepares a disk for the maximum capacity in tracks and sectors that the drive can support (unless optional switches included with the command indicate otherwise). DOS knows the number of heads, cylinders, sectors per track, and bytes per sector from the drive type. DOS also knows the number of sectors per cluster and the size in sectors of the root directory and the FAT (see Chapter 2 for more information on the FAT).

Cue:
The FORMAT command prepares a disk to accept files—a process known as initialization.

FORMAT divides its work between two main tasks. First, FORMAT records the DOS bookkeeping information on the disk in a control area. Then, on new disks, or if certain switches are specified (see table 6.1), FORMAT writes "dummy" data into the remaining part of the disk (called the files area). If you use the optional /V and /S switches, FORMAT additionally writes a volume label you designate and copies the hidden system files along with COMMAND.COM to make the disk bootable. (The Version 4 and 5 FORMAT commands prompt for a volume label automatically and create a unique disk serial number.) The following sections look at FORMAT's operation in the control area and the files area. The disk's volume-label and system files also are covered.

Formatting the Control Area

DOS, through FORMAT, reserves some early sectors of every disk for recording information the system needs to manage the disk. These sectors (usually track 0) are called collectively the control area of the disk.

Cue:
Every DOS disk has a boot record.

The first sector on the disk (or partition) is used for the boot record. The boot record tells DOS the size and number of FATs contained on the disk and the number of entries that the disk's root directory can accommodate. Details about a disk's heads, sector number, sectors per cluster, and other details that give the disk type its unique BIOS "fingerprint" are recorded here. The boot record contains a brief program that enables the BIOS to begin loading DOS into the system. Every DOS disk has a boot record even if that disk is not bootable. As you may recall from Chapter 3, a disk's DOS bootability is determined by the presence of the DOS hidden system files and COMMAND.COM on the disk.

After creating the boot record, FORMAT creates the primary and secondary file allocation tables—the FATs. (See Chapter 2 for an extended discussion of the FAT.) Remember that every cluster on the disk has an entry in the FAT and that the amount of disk space given to the FAT depends on the capacity of the disk. Generally, larger capacity disks receive more space for a FAT because they have more clusters.

After initializing the FAT, FORMAT creates the disk's root directory in the control area. The root directory is the last of the FORMAT-created control area entries. (But DOS Versions 4 and 5 place a volume label in the control area as well.)

Cue:
Each disk's root directory is fixed in length.

Each disk's root directory is fixed in length. A root directory cannot shrink or grow because of file activity. Different formats of disks, however, may fix the length of the root directory to a size different from other formats. Disk formats with more capacity allot more sectors to a root directory than do formats with lesser capacity.

Each entry in the root directory consists of a 32-byte record describing either a file, a subdirectory, or a disk volume label. Chapter 2 explains the function of a directory as a basic DOS "bookkeeping" tool. Table 6.2 lists the number of entries available with different disk formats.

The control area normally is located in track 0 of cylinder 0 in any disk, partition, or logical disk. DOS does not format a disk if its track 0 contains any bad sectors. DOS needs to extract the control area's bookkeeping information from expected points. If FORMAT "skips around" a bad sector, DOS does not find the necessary information in the control area.

Table 6.2
Capacity of Root Directory

Disk Format	Number of Entries
5 1/4-inch Floppy Disk	
180K	64
360K	112
1.2M	224
3 1/2-inch Floppy Disk	
720K	112
1.44M	224
Typical Hard Disk	512

When FORMAT finds a bad track 0, it displays a message similar to the following:

```
Invalid media or track 0 bad—disk unusable
```

You can take one of several courses of action when FORMAT displays such a message. If the disk is a floppy, you can try to reformat or make sure that the disk is right for the drive capacity. If the disk is a logical drive or partition, you can delete the partition and move its boundaries so that a different track becomes its track 0. You learn about these alternatives in later sections of this chapter. For now, just remember that the control area of a disk or a disk partition must be free of bad sectors.

Reminder:
The control area of a disk or disk partition must be free of bad sectors.

Managing Disks Larger than 32M

Until the introduction of Version 4, DOS used 16 bits (binary digits) to represent sector numbers internally. A 16-bit binary number can have a maximum value of 65,536. In order to use the 16-bit sector numbers, DOS must hold the number of sectors on a disk to 65,536 or fewer. Because all versions of DOS have used 512-byte sectors, the largest drive capacity (or partition) DOS could manage was 512 bytes for each of 65,536 (64K) sectors, or 32M. The introduction of the extended partition in Version 3.3 enables DOS to support an extended partition of more than 32M, even though no logical drives of the Version 3.3 extended partition can be larger than 32M.

Cue:

Versions of DOS starting with 4 accept disks or partitions larger than 32M.

With DOS Versions 4 and later, a disk or partition can be larger than 32M. Versions 4 and 5 add a second field in the boot record for disks or partitions that have more than 64K sectors. If a disk is formatted with more than 64K sectors, the new sector number field is used, and the preceding sector number field is set to 0. When building the disk's FAT, DOS 4 adjusts the cluster's sector multiple upward as disk capacity increases. By adjusting the cluster, DOS can keep the FAT's size constant while covering the additional sectors of a disk larger than 32M.

Caution:

Before using a disk optimizer or rapid backup program with Version 4 or 5, be sure that the application's version can handle that version of DOS.

Because DOS versions prior to Version 4 are not designed for extensions that accommodate disks larger than 32M, you cannot expect to find everything you stored on a large-capacity disk (larger than 32M) if you boot your PC with an earlier version of DOS. Some third-party disk utility applications programs also do not support DOS Version 4's extensions to the boot sector. If you have DOS Version 4 or 5, before you use a disk optimizer such as the Norton Utilities or a rapid backup program such as FASTBACK, be sure that the application's version expressly handles disks for your version of DOS.

Formatting the Files Area

FORMAT writes sector identification numbers, filler data, and cyclic-redundancy-check data in every sector space on a disk. The sector identification is used by DOS when reading a sector of data to ensure that the correct sector was read by the drive. Without this test, the drive can return the wrong sector and cause the requesting program to lock up or cause a disk crash.

If you do an unconditional format of a floppy disk, or if you are formatting a new disk, FORMAT writes filler data into each sector after the sector identifier. This operation is what destroys the previous data stored on the disk. The filler data is reread immediately by FORMAT to test that sector's capability to record data faithfully. FORMAT considers a sector bad (unusable) if the sector area on the disk has a flaw, and the filler data is not written properly. If FORMAT finds a bad sector in the files area of the disk, the sector's cluster is marked as bad in the FAT. DOS does not allocate the bad cluster to any file. A hard disk containing one or two bad clusters is not uncommon. Remember, however, that if the bad sector is in the reserved control area of the disk (usually track 0), FORMAT must reject the disk as being unusable. The reserved area of the disk contains data whose position is fixed by FORMAT.

Writing a Volume Label

If you use the /V switch with FORMAT, you are prompted for a volume label. (The /V switch is built into FORMAT Versions 4 and 5.) In versions prior to Version 4, a volume label refers to a name stored in a special root directory entry. The volume label reduces the total available root directory entries by one. In DOS Versions 4 and 5, the volume label is stored in the boot record along with a volume serial number.

You can use the VOL command to identify a disk by its volume label. Versions 3.2 through 4 require you to give the volume label of a hard disk that you are trying to reformat if the disk currently has a label as a safety precaution. The DIR command gives the volume label of the disk specified (or the default) in the command. Volume labels do not serve, however, as positive identification because you freely can give two disks the same volume label.

For identifying Version 4 and 5 disks, DOS has implemented an additional identifier besides the volume label. The DOS serial number is positive identification because it is generated by FORMAT and is based on the time and date the disk is formatted. The SHARE command in Versions 4 and 5 checks the serial number of a disk before accessing an open file to make sure that no disk swap has occurred. FORMAT gives serial numbers to all disks.

Copying the System Files

The command FORMAT /S copies the DOS hidden system files along with COMMAND.COM from the default disk and directory, or the disk and directory named in the CONFIG.SYS COMSPEC directive, to the disk being formatted. The capacity of the newly formatted disk is reduced by the size of these files, and the disk is bootable. If you know that you want to make a disk bootable, use the /S switch with FORMAT. You also can use the SYS command later. DOS 5.0's SYS command transfers the system files even if you have copied files to the formatted disk.

Reformatting a Disk

You also can format disks that already have been formatted. Prior to DOS 5.0, reformatting a disk effectively erased the previous contents of the disk. DOS 5.0's FORMAT command first determines whether the disk contains data. If the disk does contain data, FORMAT saves file information to a safe place on the disk where UNFORMAT can find it. You can unformat a disk that has been formatted with DOS 5.0, but only if you have not created or copied other files to the disk.

DOS 5.0's FORMAT command clears the disk's file allocation table (FAT) and the first character from each file name in the root directory but does not erase any data. (The program does scan the entire disk for bad sectors.) FORMAT then saves the first letter of each file name to a safe place on the disk.

Using the Quick Format

The /Q switch available in DOS Version 5's FORMAT command enables you to perform a quick format on a disk that has been formatted previously. FORMAT /Q clears out the FAT and root directory, thus effectively erasing all files on the disk, but takes no other action. The command does not check for bad blocks, and you cannot change the storage capacity of a disk during a quick format. You gain the advantage of a speedier format but lose the ability to spot any blocks that have become bad since the disk was last formatted.

Understanding the General Rules of FORMAT

The general rules of the FORMAT command are as follows:

- A hard disk must be partitioned before you can format it even if the entire disk is used as one partition.

- FORMAT cannot prepare a disk that is being rerouted by an ASSIGN or SUBST command.

Formatting a Floppy Disk

To see an example of using the FORMAT command, try formatting a bootable floppy disk. If you already are comfortable with formatting disks, you can skim this exercise. Be sure not to include the drive letter of your hard disk in the command line; you do not want to format your hard disk by mistake. Because FORMAT is an external command, you must include its directory in your PATH, make its directory your current directory, or log on to drive A and use your working DOS disk. As with other external DOS commands, you can include the path name as part of the full command and therefore directly specify to DOS where the FORMAT command is located.

Type the following command line and press Enter. (If you are using a version of DOS prior to 4.0, add the /V switch.)

FORMAT A: /S

After you type the FORMAT command line, the red light on the disk drive may go on briefly. You see the following message:

```
Insert the diskette for drive A:
and strike ENTER when ready
```

If you are using a floppy disk system and have the DOS working disk in drive A, take the disk out of drive A. Place a blank or reclaimed disk (a disk containing no useful files) in drive A and press Enter. You can abort the command at the prompt by pressing Ctrl-C instead of Enter.

Reminder:
To abort the
FORMAT,
press Ctrl-C.

After you press Enter, the red light on the first disk drive goes on again, and the following message appears if you have DOS Version 3:

```
Head:    0 Cylinder:   1
```

If you have DOS Version 4 or later, you see this message:

```
1 percent of disk formatted
```

The numbers on-screen change as the formatting precedes. For DOS Version 3, the number after the word Head flips between 0 and 1. The number after the word Cylinder starts at 1 and increases to either 40 (for 360K minifloppies) or 80 (for high-density floppy disks). DOS Versions 4 and 5 give you a continual update of what percentage of the disk has been formatted.

After 20 to 40 seconds, the line with the numbers disappears, and the following message appears in its place:

```
Format complete
```

After a few more seconds, you see another message:

```
System transferred
```

Then DOS asks the following:

```
Volume label (11 characters, ENTER for none)?
```

Type any volume label that you think is appropriate, using up to 11 characters. For this example, type **DOS_Disk_01** and press Enter. Alternatively, you can type DOS DISK 01 and press Enter. Spaces are allowable in volume labels.

The floppy disk spins, and DOS tells you how much total information the disk can hold, how much space is taken up by DOS, and how much free space is on the disk. For DOS Version 3.3, for example, the figures are

Disk Size	Message
360K	362496 bytes total disk space
	78848 bytes used by system
	283648 bytes available on disk
1.2M	1213952 bytes total disk space
	78336 bytes used by system
	1135616 bytes available on disk
720K	730112 bytes total disk space
	78848 bytes used by system
	651264 bytes available on disk
1.44M	1457664 bytes total disk space
	78336 bytes used by system
	1379328 bytes available on disk

Remember that the numbers for various versions of DOS Version 3 are slightly different.

DOS 4 and 5 users see slightly different results, such as the following results from a 1.44M disk:

```
1457664 bytes total disk space
 107520 bytes used by system
1350144 bytes available on disk
    512 bytes in each allocation unit
   2637 allocation units available on disk
Volume Serial Number is 3952-0BE4
```

Note that these versions also report the number of bytes taken up by each allocation unit, which is the cluster size in bytes. By dividing the number of bytes in each allocation unit (cluster) by 512 (the sector size in bytes), you can determine the number of sectors in a cluster for the disk type being formatted. This screen report also tells you the number of allocation units or clusters available on the disk. Remember that these information items are part of DOS's internal bookkeeping tables for the disk's file system.

In addition, DOS Versions 4 and 5 assign to each disk a unique serial number, which is calculated from an internal algorithm. As you learned in a previous section, this unique serial number enables DOS to keep track of disk changes, even if many disks have the same volume number or name.

You may see one of the following messages on-screen:

```
1024 bytes in bad sectors
```

or

```
Invalid media or track 0 bad—disk unusable
```

The first message means that DOS found on the disk some bad sectors that cannot be used to hold information. Your disk is usable, but the total amount of free space on the disk is reduced by the number of bytes in bad sectors.

The second message means that the areas on the disk that hold key DOS information are bad, and the disk cannot be used at all. Chances are good that you will not see one of these messages. If, however, one of these messages appears, answer Y to the following question to try the process again with the same disk:

```
Format another (Y/N)?
```

Press Y and then press Enter. You see a repetition of the messages that instruct you to insert a floppy disk to be formatted. You are using the same disk that showed problems but don't press Enter at the prompt yet. First, take the disk out of the drive, reinsert the disk, and close the door if necessary. The disk may not have been seated correctly in the drive the first time, or a piece of dust may have gotten between the disk and one of the drive's heads. Some floppy disks that do not format correctly the first time do so the second time. Press Enter to confirm that you are ready, and the format process repeats.

Reminder:
Some floppy disks that do not format correctly the first time do so the second time.

If the disk does not format properly the second time, something may be wrong with either the disk drive or the disk (most likely the disk). You can take a guaranteed disk that has some bad sectors back to the dealer for a replacement, or you can use the disk, knowing that you have less storage space than you should have. If the disk is old, it may be starting to deteriorate, and FORMAT has detected the bad sectors. Throw the old disk away. If you use a deteriorating disk, files stored on the disk may become corrupt; you then cannot use the files.

The message `Invalid media` can appear if you try to format a 360K disk in an HC disk drive or a 720K disk in a 1.44M disk drive. If you used the wrong type of disk, get the right type and try this exercise again. HC and 1.44M disks have special magnetic coatings designed to work with higher data densities. (Data densities and drive designs are discussed in Chapter 2.) If you used the right type of disk and got this message, take the disk back to your dealer for a replacement. If the message `Invalid media` often appears while you are using valid media, you may have a faulty drive. Two or three failed disks per box is excessive when you are buying good-quality disks. The problem may be with your hardware.

FORMAT next asks the following question:

```
Format another (Y/N)?
```

Caution:
Never use a ball-point pen to write on the label after it is attached to a 5 1/4-inch floppy disk.

Press N and then press Enter. The DOS prompt reappears. Even if you have formatted bootable floppy disks before, use this exercise to help you look closely at the process. As always, label the newly formatted disk, using a label specially designed to adhere to floppy disks. A Post-it note has a life expectancy of 30 seconds when used as a disk label. The same Post-it note, when dislodged in your drive, can jam up your drive's mechanical parts intermittently for years. Also remember never to use a ball-point pen to write on the label after it is attached to a 5 1/4-inch disk. Use a felt-tip pen only.

Performing a Safe Format

If a disk already contains data and the /U switch is not specified, FORMAT performs a "safe" format. The control area is cleared to indicate that all parts of the disk may be reused, but no data is erased. If you later realize that the disk was formatted in error, you can use the UNFORMAT command, discussed in a subsequent section of this chapter, to retrieve data from the disk. As time passes and you create files on the disk, however, old data is destroyed.

Alternatively, the /U switch causes FORMAT to erase all data a floppy disk as it formats.

Formatting a Floppy Disk with the DOS Shell

Cue:
DOS Versions 4 and 5 users can access the FORMAT command from the DOS Shell.

Using the DOS Shell to format a bootable floppy disk is much like formatting from the DOS command line. The DOS Shell requires you to type the command line parameters just as you did in the preceding exercise (see fig. 6.1).

To format a floppy disk with the DOS Shell, follow these steps:

1. Insert into drive A a fresh disk to be formatted.

2. Use the cursor keys or mouse to highlight the Disk Utilities program group in the program list area. Press Enter or double-click the mouse button.

3. Select Format from the Disk Utilities program group list. The Shell displays the Format dialog box, shown in figure 6.1, which includes a text box labeled Parameters. Because FORMAT is used

most often to prepare a floppy disk, DOS supplies the drive name A as a default value in the Parameters text box. To prepare a bootable floppy disk, add the /S switch.

4. Type **/S** and press Enter or click the OK command button.

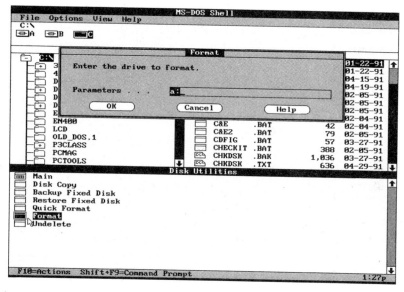

Fig. 6.1. The Format dialog box.

The menus are erased from your screen, and you see the same screen display as when you format a disk from the DOS prompt. When DOS is finished, DOS displays the following message:

```
Press any key to return to the MS-DOS Shell
```

This method is not much faster than pressing Shift-F9 and typing the **FORMAT** command from the DOS prompt. You may find, however, that knowing how to perform this task within the Shell is helpful.

Formatting a Hard Disk

Formatting a hard disk is similar to formatting a floppy disk but takes more time. Remember that formatting a hard disk or partition is going to render inaccessible any data that exists on that disk or logical drive. Check any instructions that came with your version of DOS. Some manufacturers include some specialized instructions for preparing a hard disk.

Reminder:
Appendix D contains instructions for preparing and formatting hard disks.

Completing Preliminary Steps

Before formatting a hard disk, you should complete some preliminary steps that make your hard disk formatting experience more predictable. Because you will not be formatting your hard disk often, refer to this section each time you format a hard disk.

Before you can format a new hard disk, you must partition it. You format separately the primary DOS partition and any logical drives of an extended DOS partition. Some hard disks are partitioned by the dealer before users get them. If you have any doubt about your hard disk's partition status, run FDISK from your floppy drive to check for partitions. See the section on FDISK in this chapter.

Caution:

Always have available a working copy of the master DOS disks before you use FORMAT on a hard disk.

Always have available a working copy of the master DOS disks or the DOS Version 4 or 5 working disks before you format your hard disk. If you format the active DOS partition, chances are good that you will be destroying the external DOS commands that reside on your hard disk. The directory that holds the external DOS commands (usually \DOS or \BIN) will not be there when the format is completed. Without the DOS working copy, you will not have access to the external DOS commands. Also make sure that your floppy drive is in reliable condition before you begin the format. Run CHKDSK on your working copy of the DOS disk(s) to ensure that the disk is all right. (For instructions on using CHKDSK, see the command reference and the section on CHKDSK in this chapter.)

If you are using DOS Version 3.2 through 4.0, log on to the drive you want to format and issue the DIR command to see the current volume label. If you cannot remember the label easily, write it down with its exact spelling (including underscores and spaces). Before formatting the disk, FORMAT Version 3.2 and later versions ask for this label for confirmation as a safety precaution. This step is not necessary for Versions 3.0, 3.1, and 5.0. If the drive has never been formatted, it has no volume label, and you can skip this step.

Issuing FORMAT for the Hard Disk

In this example, assume that the hard disk (or logical disk) that you are going to format is drive C. If you are formatting another drive, use its drive name (letter) in place of C. Note that if your drive is not the primary DOS partition, you do not need the /S switch because DOS boots from the primary DOS partition only. Put your working copy of the DOS master system disk in drive A, log on to that drive by typing **A:**, and then type the following:

FORMAT C:/S

If the drive already has been formatted, it has a volume label; if you are using Version 3.2 through 4.0, FORMAT displays the following prompt:

```
Enter current Volume label for drive C:
```

Enter the current volume label for the drive. If the volume label does not match what FORMAT found on the disk, you see the following message:

```
Invalid Volume ID
Format failure
```

If this message is displayed, make sure that you are formatting the correct drive. Check the volume label again and type the correct label.

FORMAT next issues the following warning message and confirmation prompt:

```
WARNING, ALL DATA ON NON-REMOVABLE DISK DRIVE C:
WILL BE LOST!
Proceed with Format (Y/N)?
```

Examine this prompt to confirm the disk drive name (letter) before you answer Y. If you get in the habit of answering Y to the confirmation prompts of less dangerous commands, you may make a serious mistake with this final FORMAT confirmation prompt. If the drive is the one you intend to format, press Y and then press Enter. If not, press N and then press Enter to terminate FORMAT.

FORMAT then updates the display with progress reports on its initialization activity. The process can take from a few minutes to more than a half-hour; the length of time is related to the capacity of the disk being formatted. Larger disks take more time. When the disk has been formatted, FORMAT issues the following message:

Cue:
The time required for the complete FORMAT process varies.

```
Format complete
```

But FORMAT may not be finished. If you used the /S switch, you see the following message:

```
System Transferred
```

FORMAT prompts for the volume label with the following line:

```
Volume label (11 characters, ENTER for none)?
```

Enter the label text you want to assign to the hard disk. The discussion of LABEL in this chapter includes a list of allowable volume-label characters. If you need to change this label, you can use the LABEL command in Version 3.1 (PC DOS Version 3.0) and later versions.

Finally, FORMAT displays a report showing the disk space formatted, the bytes used by the system files, defective sectors marked (if any), and the number of bytes available on the disk. Don't be surprised if your hard disk shows some bad sectors in the report. A hard disk with a few bad sectors is not uncommon, especially if the formatted capacity exceeds 21M. These bad sectors are marked in the FAT and are not allocated to a file.

Naming Disks with LABEL

The external command LABEL adds, modifies, or changes the volume label of a disk. In DOS, a volume label is a character name given to a physical or logical disk. The LABEL command is available with PC DOS Version 3.0 and later versions and MS-DOS Version 3.1 and later versions. If a disk's volume label is blank (if the user pressed Enter when FORMAT or LABEL prompted for the label), you can use the LABEL command to add a volume label. Volume labels are passive. They do not affect any DOS operation. Labels merely show the identity that the disk was given during formatting or the last entry of the LABEL command. Some installation programs for DOS applications check the volume label of each disk inserted during the installation process to ensure that you haven't inserted a disk out of order.

Cue:

Give each disk (physical and logical) a volume label so that you more easily can identify the disk later.

DOS displays the volume label when you issue commands such as VOL, CHKDSK, DIR, and TREE. The DOS Version 3.2 FORMAT command asks for a hard disk's volume label before reformatting the disk. DOS Versions 4 and 5 also store the volume label in an extended field of the boot record in the disk's control area where the label can be accessed speedily without a directory search. Giving each disk (physical and logical) a volume label is a good idea. You can identify the disk more easily when it has a unique volume label.

Issuing the LABEL Command

The syntax for the LABEL command is as follows:

```
LABEL d:volume_label
```

Cue:

The LABEL command can accept up to 11 characters of volume-label text.

d: is the drive name that holds the disk to be labeled. *volume_label*, the optional label text that you supply as the new volume label, can include from 1 to 11 characters. If you do not supply the *volume_label* parameter, LABEL automatically prompts you for a new label.

Understanding the Operation of LABEL

When you issue a LABEL command alone or with an optional drive specifier, DOS accesses the special file entry in the root directory of the default or specified disk and finds the volume-label characters in the file-name field.

When you issue a LABEL command with the optional label parameter of from 1 to 11 characters, DOS immediately updates the specified or default drive's label with no warning prompt. If you enter an incorrect volume label, enter the LABEL command for the drive again and correct the label.

Understanding the General Rules of LABEL

The general rules of the LABEL command are as follows:

- Volume labels can include from 1 to 11 characters.

- The label can contain any alphabetic (upper- and lowercase) character (letter) or any numeric character. DOS translates lower-case letters into uppercase letters before storing them in the label.

- The following special characters and punctuation symbols are allowed: $ # @ ! ( ) { } " _ ~

- The extended (ASCII 128 and greater) characters produced when you hold down the Alt key and then select a number from the numeric keypad are allowed.

- The space character is allowed, but for Version 3.2 and earlier versions, you must use the LABEL command with no label parameter so that you can enter the label when prompted. DOS does not interpret the space as a part of the label parameter in the command line as you intend it to. In the command LABEL A:MY FLOPPY, for example, DOS sees the space between Y and F as a command-line delimiter and concludes that the label is formed incorrectly. The same label entered at the prompt `Volume label (11 characters, ENTER for none)?` is accepted with no objections.

- You cannot use the LABEL command on a networked drive.

- You cannot use LABEL on a disk in a drive that is affected by the SUBST or ASSIGN command.

Labeling a Disk

If you formatted without a volume label a floppy disk that you intend to use as a work disk, you can place a volume label on the disk by placing the disk in drive A and issuing the following command:

LABEL A:WORK_DISK1

DOS immediately attaches the volume label WORK_DISK1 to the disk in drive A.

If you have a floppy disk with an existing label and want to identify the disk as a work disk, place the disk in drive A and issue the following command:

LABEL A:

Then you see the following prompts:

```
Volume in drive A: is SAMPLE
Volume label (11 characters, ENTER for none)?
```

Type **WORK_DISK2** and press Enter. The volume label of the floppy disk in drive A is changed to WORK_DISK2.

To delete an existing volume label, press Enter without typing a new name.

DOS displays the following prompt:

```
Delete current volume label (Y/N)?
```

Press Y and then Enter; the volume label of drive C is deleted.

Examining Volume Labels with VOL

Cue:
The VOL command displays the volume label.

The internal command VOL is a convenient command for seeing a disk's volume label or verifying that a label exists. VOL is a display-only command. It does not modify the current volume label. VOL shows the volume label created during the disk's formatting or modified by a subsequent LABEL command.

VOL accesses the disk's volume label from the root directory and displays the label. VOL does not change any files or the label name, so you can use the command freely.

Issuing the VOL Command

To see the volume label of the disk in drive A, enter the following command:

VOL A:

DOS responds with a message similar to the following:

```
Volume in drive A: is WORK_DISK1
```

Understanding the General Rules of VOL

The general rules of the VOL command are as follows:

- If you do not specify a drive parameter, the current drive is assumed.

- You add a volume label to a disk during formatting or after formatting with the LABEL command.

- The VOL command displays the same volume label for a disk as the DIR, CHKDSK, and TREE commands do.

Transferring the DOS System with SYS

All DOS disks have a DOS file system, but only disks with the hidden DOS system files and COMMAND.COM can be used to boot DOS. The external command SYS transfers (copies) the hidden system files from a bootable system disk. When using a version of DOS prior to 4.0, you must use COPY to transfer COMMAND.COM to the target disk.

Cue:
The external command SYS transfers the hidden system files from a bootable disk.

Issuing the SYS Command

The syntax for the SYS command is as follows:

SYS d:

If you are using DOS Version 4 or 5, you also can provide the source drive for the system files, as in the following command:

SYS d: d2:

The drive specified by d: is the target drive for the system files. You must include a drive name (letter) for drive d:; the drive specified by d: (Versions 4 and 5 only) is the drive that is used for the source of the system files.

Understanding the Operation of SYS

SYS can make bootable a disk that was not formatted with the /S switch. In addition, SYS can transfer a new version of the operating system to existing bootable disks.

As you may recall from Chapter 3, DOS loads the two system files from the boot disk into memory, where they act as the default system drivers and the operating system kernel. You do not see these files when you use a DIR command, because they are hidden. The two system files also are marked with a system attribute and read-only attribute.

Understanding the General Rules of SYS

The general rules of the SYS command are as follows:

- SYS requires the destination disk to be formatted.

- With Version 3.3 or earlier versions, if a disk already contains user files and does not contain the two system files, DOS issues the following error message:

  ```
  No room for system on destination disk
  ```

  If the existing system files are too small to allow a new version's system files to take their space, DOS issues the following error message:

  ```
  Incompatible system size
  ```

- SYS Version 4 and later versions can transfer the system files as long as two root directory entries are available on the disk on which you are putting the system.

- You cannot use SYS on a networked drive. If you want to use SYS on a networked drive, you must either log off the network or pause your drive. For exact restrictions, consult your system's network documentation.

- You must give the destination drive parameter for the SYS command. SYS is a command that does not use the default drive for the destination parameter. The source drive for the system files is always the default drive unless you specify a source drive parameter when using SYS Version 4 or 5.

Using SYS To Transfer DOS to a Floppy Disk

Assume that you are using DOS Version 5 with a hard disk and have an empty floppy disk that you want to make bootable to use with another computer. Put the formatted floppy in drive A and be sure that your current PATH setting includes the directory that contains SYS. Then enter the following command:

SYS C: A:

The C: is optional. If you are logged on to drive C, it already is the default source for the system files. SYS replies with the following message:

```
System transferred
```

The system files are now on the disk in drive A. DOS 5.0's SYS command also copies COMMAND.COM from C to the disk in A. The disk in drive A is now a bootable disk.

Recovering Data from a Formatted Disk with UNFORMAT

Virtually every PC user accidentally formats a disk. The UNFORMAT command enables you to recover some or all of the data on a disk that is accidentally reformatted under DOS Version 5.

UNFORMAT also can be used to rebuild a damaged partition table but only if you issued the MIRROR /PARTN command before the partition table was damaged.

Ideally, you will never need to use the UNFORMAT command. Because it completely rebuilds your disk's File Allocation Table (FAT), root directory, and boot record, you should use the UNFORMAT command as a last resort. If you accidentally delete a file, use the DOS 5.0 UNDELETE command to recover your data. If you accidentally format an entire disk, you have to use UNFORMAT to attempt to recover the data that was on the disk. The degree of success you have in recovering all files depends partly on whether and how recently you ran the MIRROR command. Successful recovery of an accidentally formatted floppy disk also depends on which program you used when you accidentally formatted the disk.

> *Caution:* If the disk you accidentally formatted contains the DOS files, you need to use a copy of UNFORMAT on another disk. DO NOT install DOS on the problem hard disk as the DOS files would overwrite files that you want to recover. Indeed, do not copy or save files of any kind to the reformatted hard disk. If you have to reboot the computer, use a bootable floppy disk.

The discussions that follow in some cases assume that you have run the MIRROR command. The MIRROR command makes a copy of your hard disk's FAT, root directory, and boot record and saves this information as a disk file in a safe place on the disk. This file is referred to as the mirror-image file. MIRROR gives this file the name MIRROR.FIL. The second and each subsequent time you run MIRROR on a particular disk, MIRROR renames the existing MIRROR.FILE to MIRROR.BAK and creates a MIRROR.FIL. MIRROR also creates a hidden file named MIRORSAV.FIL which contains information needed to rebuild the root directory.

The DOS 5.0 FORMAT command also creates a mirror-image file during its safe format procedure, but this file is visible only to the UNFORMAT command and cannot be listed by the DIR command. If you use the /U switch with FORMAT, however, no mirror-image files are created.

Issuing the UNFORMAT Command

The syntax for UNFORMAT, when used in connection with an accidental format, is as follows:

UNFORMAT d: */J /L /P /TEST /U*

d: is the drive that contains the disk to be unformatted.

/J causes UNFORMAT to verify that MIRROR.FIL, created by MIRROR, accurately reflects the current disk information.

/L searches a formatted disk and lists file and directory names found.

/P sends all output to a printer.

/TEST provides a test run to indicate whether UNFORMAT can successfully unformat a disk.

/U attempts to unformat a disk without the benefit of a mirror-image file.

When used to rebuild a hard disk partition table, the UNFORMAT command syntax is as follows:

    UNFORMAT /PARTN */L /P*

/PARTN causes the command to attempt to rebuild the hard disk partition.

/L displays the current partition table.

/P sends all output to a printer.

Verifying the Mirror-Image File

After you run MIRROR and create the file MIRROR.FIL, you may want to satisfy yourself that the program made a valid copy of the system information. UNFORMAT provides the */J* switch for this purpose. To verify that the mirror-image file created by MIRROR on drive C contains the current FAT, root directory, and boot record information, type the following command and press Enter:

    UNFORMAT A:_/J

UNFORMAT first instructs you to insert a disk in the specified drive and press Enter. When you follow these instructions, your computer beeps and displays the following warning message:

```
Restores the system area of your disk with
the image file created by MIRROR

WARNING!!   WARNING!!

This should be used ONLY to recover from the inadvertent
use of the DOS FORMAT command or the DOS RECOVER command.
Any other use of UNFORMAT may cause you to lose data!
Files modified since the last use of MIRROR may be lost.
```

Just checking this time. then is displayed. This message is your assurance that you are performing a test only. You can ignore the warning this time. Next, UNFORMAT displays the following messages:

```
The LAST time MIRROR was used was at hh:mm on mm-dd-yy.
The PRIOR time MIRROR was used was at hh:mm on mm-dd-yy.

If you wish to use the LAST file as indicated
above. press 'L.' If you wish to use the PRIOR
file as indicated above, press 'P.' Press ESCAPE
to terminate UNFORMAT.
```

UNFORMAT substitutes for **hh:mm** and **mm-dd-yy** in these messages the times and dates that MIRROR.FIL and MIRROR.BAK were created. These are the files created the last and most recent times you ran MIRROR. Press l to cause UNFORMAT to compare the contents of MIRROR.FIL to the actual FAT and root directory on the specified disk. Press p to cause UNFORMAT to compare the preceding mirror-image file to the actual SYSTEM area of the disk. UNFORMAT then displays the message The MIRROR image file has been validated.

Finally, if UNFORMAT finds that the contents of MIRROR.FIL matches the hard disk's FAT and root directory, the command displays the following message:

```
The SYSTEM area of drive d has been verified
to agree with the image file.
```

Otherwise, UNFORMAT displays the following message:

```
The SYSTEM area does NOT agree with the
image file.
```

When the image file, MIRROR.FIL, does not agree with the system area (the FAT, root directory, and boot record), one or more files have been changed or added since you last ran MIRROR. If you had to use UNFORMAT to recover from an accidental format, the files that have been changed or added would be lost.

Recovering from an Accidental Format Using the Mirror-Image File

Assume that you accidentally have formatted a hard disk (or incorrectly used the DOS RECOVER command). Assuming that you have been routinely running MIRROR on the disk or that you formatted the disk with DOS

5.0's safe format feature, UNFORMAT uses the information stored in the file MIRROR.FIL to restore the FAT, root directory, and boot record.

To use the UNFORMAT command to unformat an accidentally formatted disk, type the following command at the DOS command line:

UNFORMAT d:

Substitute the drive letter for *d* in this command. UNFORMAT first instructs you to insert a disk in the specified drive and press Enter. When you follow these instructions, your computer beeps and displays the following warning message:

```
Restores the system area of your disk with
the image file created by MIRROR

             WARNING!              WARNING!

This should be used ONLY to recover from the inadvertent
use of the DOS FORMAT command or the DOS RECOVER command.
Any other use of UNFORMAT may cause you to lose data!
Files modified since the last use of MIRROR may be lost.
```

Next, UNFORMAT displays the following messages:

```
The LAST time MIRROR was used was at hh:mm on mm-dd-yy.
The PRIOR time MIRROR was used was at hh:mm on mm-dd-yy.

If you wish to use the LAST file as indicated
above, press 'L.' If you wish to use the PRIOR
file as indicated above, press 'P.' Press ESCAPE
to terminate UNFORMAT.
```

UNFORMAT substitutes for **hh:mm** and **mm-dd-yy** in these messages the times and dates that MIRROR.FIL and MIRROR.BAK were created. These are the files created the last and most recent times you ran MIRROR (or performed the safe format operation). Press l to cause UNFORMAT to use MIRROR.FIL to rebuild the formatted disk. If you inadvertently have run MIRROR since you accidentally formatted the disk, press p to use MIRROR.BAK instead.

After you press l or p, UNFORMAT again causes your computer to beep and then displays the following messages:

```
The MIRROR image file has been validated.

Are you SURE you want to update the SYSTEM area
of your drive d (Y/N)?
```

UNFORMAT substitutes the drive letter for **d**.

Press Y to indicate that you want to continue and update the SYSTEM area of the formatted disk or press N to quit UNFORMAT and return to the command line.

If you choose to update the SYSTEM area, UNFORMAT writes to the disk's system area the FAT, root directory, and boot record that have been stored in MIRROR.FIL (or MIRROR.BAK). This operation effectively unformats the disk and recovers all its files, except files added or changed since the last time you used MIRROR (or performed the safe format operation).

Assume that someone in your office accidentally formats drive C but uses DOS 5.0's safe format feature. You can use UNFORMAT to restore the disk to the same state as when MIRROR was last ran. Type the following command at the DOS command line:

UNFORMAT C:

When UNFORMAT prompts you to press L or P, press l to cause UNFORMAT to use MIRROR.FIL to restore drive C, and when UNFORMAT asks whether you are sure you want to do this, respond Y. UNFORMAT uses MIRROR.FIL to rewrite the FAT and root directory, restoring the hard disk to its status the last time you ran MIRROR.

Recovering from an Accidental Format without a Mirror-Image File

Even if a mirror-image file is not available for a formatted disk, the UNFORMAT program may be able to recover most of the data.

In this case, the syntax for UNFORMAT is as follows:

UNFORMAT d: */U /L /TEST /P*

Replace the **d:** with the drive designator of the accidentally formatted hard disk. The */U* parameter stands for unformat and tells UNFORMAT that you are not using a mirror-image file created by MIRROR or FORMAT. The optional */L* parameter causes UNFORMAT to list on-screen all files and directories it finds during the unformat operation. Similarly, */P* causes UNFORMAT to print the entire UNFORMAT process to your printer. Use the */TEST* option to run a simulation of the process, to check to see which files UNFORMAT can recover before you cause any changes to be written to the hard disk.

After you execute the command, UNFORMAT displays the following messages in succession:

```
CAUTION !!

This attempts to recover all files lost after a
FORMAT, assuming that you have NOT been using MIRROR. This
method cannot guarantee complete recovery of your files.

The search-phase is safe: nothing is altered on the disk.
You'll be prompted again before changes are written to the
Disk.

Using drive d:

Are you SURE you want to do this?
If so, type in 'Y'; anything else cancels.
```

To continue with the unformat operation, press Y and Enter. Press any other key to abort the process.

While UNFORMAT searches the disk, it displays the following messages:

```
Examined nn root entries
Files found in the root: x
Subdirectories found in the root: y
Searching disk...
pp% searched, mm subdirs found.
```

UNFORMAT substitutes the number of root-level entries it finds for nn, the number of root-level files it finds for x, and the number of root-level subdirectories it finds for y ($nn=x+y$). As UNFORMAT searches the disk, it continually updates the last message, substituting the percentage of the disk read for pp and the number of subdirectories found for mm.

When UNFORMAT completes its search of the hard disk data, it lists the subdirectories found. Because the DOS FORMAT command erased root-level directory names, UNFORMAT gives each of these root-level directories the name SUBDIR.nnn where nnn is a number from 1 to 999. The first subdirectory is SUBDIR.1; the second is SUBDIR.2; and so on. UNFORMAT also indicates how many files are found on the disk.

UNFORMAT next displays the following warning:

```
Warning! The next step writes changes to disk.
Are you SURE you want to do this?
If so, type in 'Y'; anything else cancels
```

To proceed with the unformat operation, press Y and Enter. UNFORMAT then begins checking for file fragmentation. If you have not used a program such as the PC Tools program Compress to unfragment the files on your hard disk, many files on the disk are stored in several different sections. When UNFORMAT locates such a fragmented file, it has no way to find the next segment of the file and offers you the following two choices: Truncate or Delete. UNFORMAT tells you the total size of the file and the number of bytes in the first fragment. Press t and Enter to at least recover this fragment of the file, or press d and then Enter to cause UNFORMAT to omit this file in the new directory.

After UNFORMAT deletes or truncates all fragmented files, it rebuilds the FAT, root directory, and boot record using the information found during the search. When finished, UNFORMAT indicates the number of files recovered and displays the following message:

```
Operation completed.
```

When UNFORMAT is finished, most files not truncated or deleted are intact. UNFORMAT may have included data in a file that didn't belong to that file. This problem can happen when a previously deleted file was fragmented into two blocks of data separated on the disk by data from another file. The unallocated space appears to UNFORMAT to be a part of the existing file. The only way to discover this type of error is to use the file—run the program or display the file's contents.

Rebuilding a Partition Table

UNFORMAT also enables you to recover from a corrupted hard disk partition table. Such an error normally generates the DOS message Invalid drive specification. To recover from this problem, you first must run UNFORMAT with the /PARTN parameter and then run UNFORMAT without this parameter to restore the FAT, root directory, and boot sector.

To recover from a corrupted hard disk partition table, boot your computer (with a floppy disk, if necessary) and display the DOS command line. Change to a disk drive that contains the UNFORMAT program, UNFORMAT.COM. If your only hard disk is inaccessible because of partition table corruption, use a copy of the program on a floppy disk. (UNFORMAT.COM is contained on the Startup disk, which is one of the disks created during DOS 5.0 installation). Type the following command at the DOS command line:

UNFORMAT/PARTN

UNFORMAT prompts you to insert the disk containing the file PARTNSAV.FIL and to enter the name of that disk drive. Place in drive A the disk that contains the copy of the partition table created by MIRROR. Press A and then press Enter. MIRROR rebuilds the partition table from the file PARTNSAV.FIL found on the floppy disk.

After UNFORMAT has rebuilt the partition table, the program prompts you to insert a master DOS disk in drive A and press Enter. UNFORMAT causes your computer to reboot. Finally, use the copy of UNFORMAT to restore the FAT, root directories, and boot record.

Understanding the General Rules of UNFORMAT

The general rules of the UNFORMAT command are as follows:

- The UNFORMAT command is effective only if used immediately after the disk is formatted, before new files are created. If a disk is formatted and then files are created on the disk, these new files overlay the old data, and the old files become unrecoverable.

- Data on floppy disks formatted with the /U switch cannot be recovered.

Creating a Mirror-Image File

To create a mirror-image file on drive D, type the following command at the DOS prompt and press Enter:

MIRROR D:

MIRROR makes a copy of the hard disk's FAT, root directory, and boot record and saves this information to disk in the file MIRROR.FIL. The following message appears on-screen:

```
MIRROR, UNDELETE, and UNFORMAT Copyright (C) 1987-1991
Central Point Software, Inc.
Creates an image of the system area.
Drive D being processed.
The MIRROR process was successful.
```

The UNFORMAT command can use the mirror-image file, MIRROR.FIL, to recover from an accidental FORMAT or RECOVER command.

For MIRROR to be most effective, you should run MIRROR at least every time you turn on the computer. UNFORMAT cannot recover files added since the last time you ran MIRROR. The easiest way to run MIRROR is to add the command to your AUTOEXEC.BAT file. For example, if your system has two hard disk drives, C and D, add the following command to AUTOEXEC.BAT:

MIRROR C: D:

Every time you turn on your computer, MIRROR creates a mirror-image file on each drive.

The parameter /1 in MIRROR'S start-up command enables you to turn off the default feature that normally causes MIRROR to keep two copies of MIRROR.FIL. By default, when you run MIRROR, it renames the most recent copy of MIRROR.FIL to MIRROR.BAK and deletes any previous copy of MIRROR.BAK. Unless you are running severely short on disk space, do not use the /1 parameter. The earlier copy of MIRROR.FIL, stored as MIRROR.BAK, provides additional insurance that you can restore the hard disk after an accidental erasure.

> *Warning:* If you accidentally format a hard disk, do not run MIRROR again before using UNFORMAT to recover the deleted files. However, if you do run MIRROR, you still can run UNFORMAT using MIRROR.BAK.

Fortunately, DOS 5.0's FORMAT command poses less danger than previous versions of FORMAT because DOS 5.0 performs a safe format by default, creating its own mirror-image file. This mirror-image file enables DOS 5.0's UNFORMAT command to recover your files and directories if you format the disk by mistake.

> *Note:* When you perform a safe format with DOS 5.0's FORMAT command, FORMAT creates a mirror-image file that contains the same type of information as the MIRROR.FIL. Unlike MIRROR.FIL, the mirror-image file created by FORMAT is not listed in the disk's directory. UNFORMAT can use either mirror-image file to recover data on a formatted disk.

DOS 5.0, however, provides an unconditional format option that can render UNFORMAT ineffective, depending on whether you accidentally format a floppy or a hard disk.

If you mistakenly format a floppy disk using DOS 5.0's unconditional format switch (/ U), you cannot recover the files and directories on the formatted floppy disk even if you ran MIRROR just before formatting the disk. When FORMAT unconditionally formats a floppy disk, the command writes the hexadecimal value F6 to every byte on the disk, erasing all data on the disk. Nothing remains for UNFORMAT to recover.

The unconditional format option does not, however, erase data from a hard disk. When DOS 5.0'S FORMAT command performs an unconditional format of a hard disk, the command does not destroy existing data. Rather, FORMAT clears the FAT, root directory, and boot record, leaving all data intact, and then does a surface scan of the hard disk, looking for bad sectors. The only difference between this procedure and the unconditional format procedure is the absence of a mirror-image file. If you run MIRROR immediately before doing an unconditional format of your hard disk, you have in effect performed the safe format operation. UNFORMAT can recover your hard disk successfully.

Performing Delete Tracking

Adding the optional /Td switch causes MIRROR to load the delete-tracking memory-resident program. Replace *d* in this switch with the drive to be monitored.

The *–entries* parameter is a number from 1 through 999 preceded by a minus sign (–). This parameter sets a maximum on the number of deleted files you want to track and indirectly determines the maximum size of the delete-tracking file (PCTRACKR.DEL). The default number of files tracked varies depending on the size of the disk MIRROR is tracking. Table 6.3 lists the default number of files tracked for each disk size and the resulting maximum delete-tracking file size.

Table 6.3
Default Number of Files Tracked and
Maximum Delete-Tracking File Sizes

Disk Size	Number of Files Tracked	Maximum File Size
360K	25	5K
720K	50	9K
1.2M	75	14K
1.44M	75	14K
20M	101	18K
32M	202	36K
Larger	303	55K

To cause MIRROR to start delete tracking for drives C and D each time you turn on the computer, include the following command in AUTOEXEC.BAT:

MIRROR /TC /TD

To start delete tracking and to create a mirror-image file for both drives, add the following command to the AUTOEXEC.BAT file instead:

MIRROR C: D: /TC /TD

This command creates a mirror-image file for drives C and D and causes MIRROR to load the memory-resident delete-tracking program. The delete-tracking program then saves separate PCTRACKR.DEL files for drives C and D, tracking deletions on both disks.

You may want to unload all memory-resident programs from your computer's memory. To unload MIRROR's delete-tracking feature, type the following command at the command line and press Enter:

MIRROR /U

Saving the Partition Table

As a part of the initial setup of your computer, the DOS program FDISK creates one or more partitions on your hard disk. A *partition* is a section of the hard disk set aside for use as a unit. You must have at least one DOS partition on your hard disk. You can have one or more partitions set up for use with another operating system, such as UNIX. DOS stores partition information in the *partition table*. If this table is damaged, DOS cannot locate any files on the disk. The third purpose for MIRROR, therefore, is to save a copy of the partition table to a file on a floppy disk for safekeeping. The UNFORMAT command can restore the contents of the file to the hard disk in case of damage to the partition table.

Note: MIRROR saves standard DOS partition tables only. Some hard disk manufacturers distribute with large hard disks special setup programs that create nonstandard partitions. Disk Manager by On-Track and SpeedStor by Storage Dimensions are examples of programs that create partitions that MIRROR cannot save to a floppy.

To save partition information to a floppy disk, type the following command at the DOS command line and press Enter:

MIRROR /PARTN

When you execute this command, MIRROR displays the following messages:

```
MIRROR, UNDELETE, and UNFORMAT Copyright (C) 1987-1991
Central Point Software, Inc.

Disk Partition Table saver.

The partition information from your hard drive(s) has
been read.

Next, the file PARTNSAV.FIL will be written to a floppy
disk. Please insert a formatted diskette and type the
name of the diskette drive.

What drive? A
```

Place a formatted disk in a floppy disk drive, type the letter of the floppy drive, and press Enter (for drive A, just press Enter). MIRROR saves the partition table to the floppy disk in the file PARTNSAV.FIL and displays the following message:

```
Successful
```

Put this disk in a safe place so that it is available if the hard disk partition table is damaged.

You need to repeat this partition-saving routine only if you later use FDISK to change your hard disk's partition information.

Copying Disks with DISKCOPY

You can use the external command DISKCOPY to copy an entire disk's contents to another disk of the same size that has a like disk format. DISKCOPY works with floppy disks only; you cannot use DISKCOPY on a hard disk. Unlike the file-based COPY command, DISKCOPY is a sector-based command. DISKCOPY reads and writes in sectors rather than in files. The destination (target) disk of a successfully completed DISKCOPY is a mirror image of the source disk. After you issue the DISKCOPY command, DOS waits for you to get the appropriate disks in the drives. Then, when you press any key, the disk copying process begins.

Reminder:
You can use DISKCOPY with floppy disks only; you cannot use DISKCOPY to copy the contents of a hard disk to another hard disk.

If the source disk is bootable, DISKCOPY makes a bootable destination disk. DISKCOPY does not know that the system files on a source disk are hidden files. DISKCOPY never consults the source disk's directory. You can use DISKCOPY on a disk that contains no files or 100 files. The DISKCOPY operation is exactly the same regardless of the number of files on a disk.

Issuing the DISKCOPY Command

The syntax for DISKCOPY is as follows:

DISKCOPY d1: d2: /1

d1: is the drive that contains the disk you are using for the source of the copy (the original).

d2: is the drive that contains the disk targeted for the resulting copy (the duplicate).

The optional /1 switch specifies that the disk copy should be single-sided rather than double-sided. The /1 switch assures compatibility with DOS Version 1.0 single-sided disks.

Understanding the Operation of DISKCOPY

Normally, the type of drive used for the DISKCOPY source and destination disks is the same. You can use DISKCOPY on a 5 1/4-inch disk to copy to a 5 1/4-inch disk or on a 3 1/2-inch disk to copy to a 3 1/2-inch disk. The source and destination disks must have the same logical DOS format. DOS consults the disk's boot record to ensure that the formats are the same before the DISKCOPY operation. The key here is the disk's format, not the disk's physical size.

If the destination disk is not formatted, or if its format is not the same as that of the source disk, DISKCOPY tries to produce the source disk's format on the destination disk as a preliminary step in the copying process. DISKCOPY's capability to produce target formats is linked directly to the formats supported by the disk-driver routines.

DISKCOPY cannot produce a destination format that the destination drive (or driver routine) does not support. You cannot, for example, use DISKCOPY to copy a 1.2M disk to a disk in a 360K drive.

DISKCOPY reads as many of the source disk's sectors as available system memory allows before writing those sectors to the destination disk. In a single floppy disk system, this all-sector-read method results in fewer disk swaps of the source and destination disks than the command COPY *.* would require. COPY reads and writes one file at the most before requiring a disk swap on a one-floppy system. In a system with 640K of available memory, DISKCOPY reads an entire 360K floppy into memory in one read operation before the command writes the source disk's contents to the destination disk.

DISKCOPY transfers to the target disk any hidden and system files that may be on the source disk.

Any files present on the target disk before a DISKCOPY operation are overwritten by DISKCOPY. Write-protecting the source disk is a good idea; you easily can get the source and destination disks reversed when using DISKCOPY on one disk drive.

Reminder:
DISKCOPY cannot produce a destination format that the destination drive (or driver routine) does not support.

Caution:
Always write-protect the source disk when using DISKCOPY.

Understanding the General Rules of DISKCOPY

The general rules of the DISKCOPY command are as follows:

- DISKCOPY works only with floppy disks. DISKCOPY cannot copy to or from hard disks.

- If the target disk originally is formatted differently than the source disk, DISKCOPY formats the target with the same format as the source.

- If you do not supply source and target parameters, DISKCOPY uses the current drive for both the source disk and the target disk, and you may have to swap the disks more than once during the copy process.

Comparing Floppy Disks with DISKCOMP

Cue:
DISKCOMP is useful for determining whether a working copy of an original disk has been modified or has errors.

The external command DISKCOMP is a sister command to DISKCOPY. DISKCOMP compares each sector of one floppy disk with the same sector of another to determine whether the two disks are identical. DISKCOMP is useful for determining whether a working copy of an original disk has been modified or has errors. DISKCOMP is primarily useful to compare disks copied with DISKCOPY. Due to the nature of first-available, first-used file allocation, two disks that contain the same files transferred by COPY or XCOPY probably will not compare as identical.

Like DISKCOPY, DISKCOMP works at the sector level, not at the file level. When a difference is detected by DISKCOMP, only the fact that the compared sectors are different is implied. DISKCOMP does not indicate which disk is "correct" and which is "incorrect." Remember that DISKCOMP is a disk-level command. To compare individual files or sets of files, use the FC or COMP command.

Issuing the DISKCOMP Command

The syntax for DISKCOMP is as follows:

DISKCOMP d1: d2: */1 /8*

d1: is the name of the drive that holds the first disk of the comparison; *d2:* is the name of the drive that holds the second disk of the comparison.

The optional */1* switch tells DISKCOMP to compare the disks as single-sided formats only.

The optional /8 switch tells DISKCOMP to compare only the first 8 sectors per track, even though the disks may have a 9-, 15-, or 18-sector-per-track format.

Understanding the Operation of DISKCOMP

DISKCOMP determines the format of the first disk and then reads as many sectors from the first disk as available system memory can accommodate.

DISKCOMP then examines the second disk's format. If it is compatible with the first disk's format, DISKCOMP compares each sector of the first disk to each sector of the second disk. This read-and-compare process repeats until the two disks are entirely compared. If sector-comparison errors are detected on the second disk, they are reported. If the second disk has a bad sector marked in its FAT that does not match the first disk's, DISKCOMP terminates the comparison and reports the bad sector.

Because DISKCOMP, like DISKCOPY, works below the layer of DOS that performs file-system bookkeeping, sectors marked as being bad (and therefore not used by DOS for file allocation) may be reported as being part of a bad disk rather than a non-comparing sector. DISKCOMP is blind to DOS's provisions to keep bad sectors from being allocated. Remember that DISKCOMP reports comparison failures as errors. You shouldn't automatically think that the second disk has file-system errors.

Reminder:
DISKCOMP reports comparison failures as errors; do not assume that the second disk has file-system errors.

Understanding the General Rules of DISKCOMP

The general rules of the DISKCOMP command are as follows:

- DISKCOMP uses the default drive for both disks in the comparison if you do not give a drive parameter in the command.

- You cannot use DISKCOMP to compare hard disks.

- Disk formats of the disks to be compared must be the same.

- Drives participating in a JOIN, ASSIGN, or SUBST command cannot be used in a comparison.

- You cannot use network drives in a comparison.

Using DISKCOMP To Compare Floppy Disks

On a system with one 3 1/2-inch drive and one 5 1/4-inch drive, you must use the same drive to compare two like-sized floppies. Assume that drive B is a 5 1/4-inch drive and that you have two minifloppies to compare. First issue the following command:

DISKCOMP B: B:

DOS responds with the following prompt:

```
Insert FIRST diskette in drive B:
Press any key when ready . . .
```

Place the first disk in drive B; then press the space bar once. DOS reports on the first disk's format. If the disk is a 1.2M disk, the message reads as follows:

```
Comparing 80 tracks   15 sectors per track, 2 side(s)
```

DISKCOMP reads as much of the disk as possible into available RAM and then displays the following prompt:

```
Insert SECOND diskette in drive B:
Press any key when ready . . .
```

Caution:
With using DISKCOMP, do not mix up the disks when swapping them.

Remove the first disk from drive B and insert the second disk in the drive. Press the space bar; the comparison continues. You are asked to swap the disks several times. Be sure that you don't mix up the disks.

When the comparison process is done, DISKCOMP displays the following message:

```
Compare OK
```

The command then prompts you with the following question:

```
Compare another diskette (Y/N)?
```

Press N and then press Enter to terminate DISKCOMP. Press Y to compare other disks.

Each track that fails comparison is reported on-screen as follows:

```
Compare error on
side  x  track  yy
```

The actual side and track numbers appear in place of x and yy.

Selectively Updating a Disk with REPLACE

The external command REPLACE was introduced in Version 3.2 as a utility for updating files with different versions of the same files. REPLACE is a real boon for people who must update a disk or directory from another disk or directory.

You can add selectivity to the command with switches and make the updating of the target disk files conditional on date (and time with Version 4 and later versions) and the absence of a file. REPLACE even performs an optional search of the target disk directory's subdirectory for a replaceable file.

You can use REPLACE to collect the most recent versions of common files from a group of PCs to a floppy disk. You can use REPLACE to upgrade to a new version of some software package. REPLACE is more versatile than COPY because REPLACE offers conditional copying of source files to the destination. Without switches, REPLACE transfers from the source only files that already exist on the destination. COPY issued with the *.* wild-card designation transfers all files from the source to the destination.

Issuing the REPLACE Command

The syntax for the REPLACE command is as follows:

> **REPLACE** *d1:path1***filename.***ext* **d2:***path2* */switches*

d1: is the optional source drive. If you omit the source drive specifier, the current drive is assumed.

path1 is the optional path of the source files. If you omit the source path specifier, the current directory is assumed.

filename.ext is the required file name and optional extension of the source file(s). Wild cards are allowed.

d2: is the required target drive specifier, which tells the command where the files should be replaced.

path2 is the optional target path name where the files are replaced. If the target path specifier is omitted, the current directory of the specified (or current) target disk is assumed.

/switches are optional switches shown in table 6.4.

Understanding the Operation of REPLACE

The external command REPLACE is a useful file-copying command that works at the directory level. This command is included with disk-level commands in this chapter because REPLACE lends itself nicely to updating one disk from another.

Table 6.4
REPLACE Switches

Switch	Action
/A	Copies source files that do not exist on the target; enables you to add files without overwriting existing files with the same names. /A cannot be used with /S or /U.
/P	Prompts for confirmation before copying each file
/R	Enables you to overwrite read-only files on the target
/S	Searches all subdirectories of the target directory for a file matching each source file. /S cannot be used with /A.
/U	Copies source files that have a more recent date and time than files with the same names on the target. /U cannot be used with /A. (Versions 4 and 5)
/W	Causes REPLACE to wait for you to press a key before the command executes, to enable you to change disk(s) to the correct source and target

Reminder:
Unlike COPY, REPLACE cannot rename files as they are copied to the destination.

When issued with no parameters, REPLACE reads the source disk and directory for files matching the command line's source-file specifier. All files meeting the conditions of the source specification are transferred to the destination disk and path. Unlike COPY, REPLACE cannot rename the files as they are copied to the destination; therefore, no file specifier is allowed (or needed) in the destination parameters.

REPLACE uses DOS's standard file-allocation method. File space is allocated using the destination disk's FAT, and the destination directory is updated. Files present on the destination disk that are not part of the replacement files remain intact.

If you give any optional switches on the command line, REPLACE performs a compatibility check of the switches to determine disallowed switch combinations. If any are found, REPLACE issues the message `Parameters not compatible` and then terminates (see table 6.4 for switch actions and compatibilities).

If you issue REPLACE with the /W switch specified in the command line, REPLACE prompts you to press any key before any replacement or adding begins. This waiting condition enables you to change disks to those appropriate for the files you want to update.

The /U switch adds date and time selectivity to REPLACE. /U causes REPLACE to update destination files with source files having a more current date and time.

The /A switch can be used to copy new files. This switch causes REPLACE to copy only files that do not already exist on the destination drive. Existing files are not replaced, even if the source version is newer.

If you specify the /A, /U, or /P switch in the command line, REPLACE tests the appropriate conditions of the source file against the destination. If the test passes, REPLACE proceeds with replacing the file. If the test fails, REPLACE moves to the next source file candidate and tests again. With /P, the test checks the user's response to REPLACE's prompt.

If you specify the /P switch in the command line, REPLACE prompts you before copying the candidate source file to the destination. You can confirm the replacement by pressing Y or reject it by pressing N. If you answer N, REPLACE skips that replacement and moves on to the next candidate file.

Use the /R switch to allow replacement of read-only files in addition to normal destination files.

The /S switch enables REPLACE to search all subdirectories of the destination directory for the files to update. You cannot use the /A (add a new file) switch with the /S switch. If /A were allowed with /S, REPLACE would be unable to determine to which destination subdirectory it should add the file.

When you use two or more (allowed) switches with the command, REPLACE considers their effects additive. The actions or selections implied by each switch are carried out by REPLACE at the point at which each switch would have been carried out if it were the only switch in the command line.

Understanding the General Rules of REPLACE

The general rules of the REPLACE command are as follows:

- You must include a source parameter with REPLACE. The source parameter may be a drive, a path, or a file name and can include all three. The file-name parameter may contain wild cards.

- If you omit the source drive or path name, REPLACE assumes the current value for the omitted item.

- In the destination parameters, you can include a drive and a path name but not a file name. If you omit the destination drive, path, or both, REPLACE assumes current values.

- You cannot use the /A switch with the /U, /D, or /S switch. All other switch combinations are allowed.

Analyzing a Disk with CHKDSK

The external command CHKDSK analyzes the FAT, the directories, and, if you want, the fragmentation status of the files of a disk. Optionally, CHKDSK repairs problems in the FAT occurring because of lost clusters and writes the contents of the lost clusters to files. CHKDSK also provides an option to display all of a disk's files and their paths. Upon completion, CHKDSK displays a screen report of its findings. If you are not familiar with the structure of DOS's FAT and directories or do not understand fragmentation, you should review Chapter 2.

Running CHKDSK periodically on your hard disk and important floppies is good practice. Because the FAT and the hierarchical directory system work together to manage file allocation, identification, and status, a problem in either the FAT or one of the directories is always a serious one.

Issuing the CHKDSK Command

You issue the CHKDSK command with the following syntax:

CHKDSK *d:path\filename.ext* /F/V

d: is the optional drive name to be checked. If you omit the drive name, CHKDSK assumes the current drive.

path is the optional path to the directory containing the files to be analyzed for fragmentation. If you omit a path and give a file specifier in the command line, CHKDSK assumes the default directory.

filename.ext is the optional file name and extension for the file(s) to be analyzed for fragmentation. If a file-name specifier is not present on the command line, CHKDSK does not check for fragmentation.

/F is the optional "fix" switch, which instructs CHKDSK to repair any problems encountered.

/V is the "verbose" switch, which instructs CHKDSK to provide file names as the files are being analyzed.

Understanding the Operation of CHKDSK

CHKDSK checks for the following problems in the FAT:

- Unlinked cluster chains (lost clusters)
- Multiple linked clusters (cross-linked files)
- Invalid next-cluster-in-chain values (invalid cluster numbers)
- Defective sectors where the FAT is stored

CHKDSK checks for the following problems in the directory system:

- Invalid cluster numbers (out of range)
- Invalid file attributes in entries (attribute values DOS does not recognize)
- Damage to subdirectory entries (CHKDSK cannot process them)
- Damage to a directory's integrity (its files cannot be accessed)

CHKDSK then produces a screen report that summarizes disk and system RAM usage.

Following is a typical report produced by CHKDSK with no parameters.

```
C:\>chkdsk

Volume QUE BRUCE   created 02-28-1991 1:04p
Volume Serial Number is 48A6-0000
Errors found, F parameter not specified
Corrections will not be written to disk

     1420 lost allocation units found in 14 chains.
  2908160 bytes disk space would be freed

104515584 bytes total disk space
   401408 bytes in 4 hidden files
   290816 bytes in 119 directories
 85069824 bytes in 2847 user files
 15845376 bytes available on disk
```

```
        2048 bytes in each allocation unit
    51033 total allocation units on disk
     7737 available allocation units on disk

   655360 total bytes memory
   571680 bytes free


C:\>
```

A report similar to the following appears when CHKDSK is issued with an optional path to check for fragmentation:

```
C:\>chkdsk \dos\*.*

Volume QUE BRUCE   created 02-28-1991 1:04p
Volume Serial Number is 48A6-0000

  04515584 bytes total disk space
    401408 bytes in 4 hidden files
    290816 bytes in 119 directories
  85071872 bytes in 2848 user files
  18751488 bytes available on disk

      2048 bytes in each allocation unit
     51033 total allocation units on disk
        7736 available allocation units on disk

    655360 total bytes memory
    571680 bytes free

C:\DOS\EGA.SYS Contains 3 non-contiguous blocks
C:\DOS\FORMAT.COM Contains 4 non-contiguous blocks
C:\DOS\FDISK.EXE Contains 3 non-contiguous blocks
C:\DOS\UNDELETE.EXE Contains 2 non-contiguous blocks
C:\DOS\DOSSHELL.EXE Contains 3 non-contiguous blocks

C:\>
```

Reminder:
Take advantage of CHKDSK's "dry run" capability to assess reported problems on a disk.

Note that you should issue the CHKDSK command without the /F (fix) switch before you subsequently use the /F switch. CHKDSK can make a "dry run" of its checking routines. CHKDSK with no /F switch prompts you if it finds a problem, just as if you had used the /F switch. Take advantage of CHKDSK's "dry run" capability to assess reported problems. After you have assessed the findings of CHKDSK and have taken remedial actions (such as those that follow), you can issue CHKDSK with the /F switch so that the command can fix problems it finds.

CHKDSK performs much of its analysis using information read from the FAT and directories. DOS's file-allocation method gives CHKDSK its method.

Every file on the disk has its sectors allocated as clusters from the FAT. Each file's directory entry should contain a starting cluster that points to the first cluster allocated to this file by DOS in the FAT.

CHKDSK processes each directory by starting at the root and following each subdirectory. The command checks the indicated cluster chain by using the directory entry's FAT pointer. The size of the file in bytes also is compared with the size of the FAT's allocation in clusters.

CHKDSK expects to find enough chained clusters in the FAT to accommodate the file, but not more than necessary. If CHKDSK finds too many clusters, it issues the following message:

```
Allocation error, size adjusted
```

CHKDSK makes sure that each of the FAT's clusters are allocated only once. In rare circumstances such as power problems or hardware failures, DOS can give two different files the same cluster. By checking each cluster chain for cross-linked files, CHKDSK can report "mixed-up" files. Each time you see the message filename cross-linked on cluster X, copy the file reported in filename to another disk. You will find that CHKDSK reports another file with the same message. Copy the second file to another disk also. The two files are probably mixed up, but you have a better chance of recovering them if you save them to another disk before CHKDSK "fixes" the problem.

Unfortunately, if CHKDSK encounters a file-allocation chain that loops back to itself, CHKDSK runs in a circle reporting errors. You can press Ctrl-C to stop the process. If you detect that a circular reference episode is taking place with CHKDSK, don't reissue the command with the /F switch. Try erasing the file and restoring it from your backup.

If CHKDSK encounters any clusters or cluster chains to which no directory entry points, CHKDSK issues the following message:

```
x lost clusters in Y chains
```

CHKDSK then prompts as follows:

```
Convert lost chains to files (Y/N)?
```

If the /F switch is active, CHKDSK turns each cluster chain into a file in the root directory. Each created file has the name FILEnnnn.CHK, where *nnnn* is a number that increments for each file created by the CHKDSK command's current execution. You then can delete these files to free up the space that was being used by the lost clusters.

Understanding the General Rules of CHKDSK

The general rules of the CHKDSK command are as follows:

- CHKDSK repairs problems found during operation only when you issue the /F switch in the command line.

- If you answer Y to the `Convert lost chains to files (Y/N)?` prompt, CHKDSK converts lost clusters to files by placing the files in the disk's root directory with a FILEnnnn.CHK name (but only if the /F switch is used).

Using CHKDSK To Repair an Allocation Size Error

For this example exercise of CHKDSK, suppose that you are copying a group of files from your hard disk to a floppy. During the copy, the lights flicker and then go out completely. In a few seconds, power is restored to normal. Your computer reboots DOS Version 4 and awaits your input.

Power problems during file operations such as COPY can cause DOS's bookkeeping job to be interrupted. The directory and the FAT can contain errors. To ensure that no errors go undetected, you issue the CHKDSK command on the floppy disk:

CHKDSK A:

CHKDSK analyzes the floppy disk in drive A and then reports as follows:

```
Volume SCRATCH DISK created 09-12-1989  11:23a
Volume serial number is 1982-BA9A
Errors found, F parameter not specified
Corrections will not be written to disk

A:\DBASE1.OVL
Allocation error, size adjusted

  730112 bytes in total disk space
  415744 bytes in 4 user files
  314368 bytes available on disk

    1024 bytes in each allocation unit
     713 total allocation units on disk
     307 available allocation units on disk
```

```
655360 total bytes memory
409856 bytes free
```

Because you did not specify the /F switch, CHKDSK did not repair the problem. You have the opportunity to examine the problem further before reissuing CHKDSK with the /V switch. You look at a directory listing of the files on drive A to see whether you can determine the nature of the allocation problem. Suppose that the directory listing shows the following:

```
Volume  in  drive  A  is  SCRATCH  DISK
Volume Serial Number is 1982-BA9A

Directory of  A:\

DBSETUP   OVL    147968 10-21-88    12:22a
DBASE3    OVL     85024 12-28-88    9:04p
DBASE6    OVL    114832 10-20-88    11:22p
DBASE1    OVL         0 09-12-89    1:46a
          4 File(s)     314368 bytes free
```

The last directory entry, DBASE1.OVL, shows a file size of 0 bytes. A 0-byte file size should never result from a COPY operation. The file's directory size entry is suspicious. To clarify further the nature of the allocation error, you compare the CHKDSK report with the directory listing for the same files.

The CHKDSK report shows 415,744 bytes in the four files. When you total the bytes in the directory listing, you can account for only 347,824 bytes in the four files. Both CHKDSK and DIR report 314,368 bytes available on the disk. CHKDSK and DIR both report available disk bytes as the number of bytes in unallocated disk clusters—not the difference between the capacity of the disk and the number of bytes in the disk's files. Both commands get the disk's remaining capacity indirectly from the FAT.

Because both commands agree on the FAT's calculation, you must assume that the directory entry for DBASE1.OVL is incorrect in its reflection of the file's size. CHKDSK can repair the directory entry. Issue the CHKDSK command again, using the /F switch:

CHKDSK A: /F

CHKDSK then reports the following:

```
Volume SCRATCH DISK created 09-12-1989  11:23a
Volume Serial Number is 1982-BA9A

A:\DBASE1.OVL
Allocation error, size adjusted

730112 bytes in total disk space
415744 bytes in 4 user files
314368 bytes available on disk
```

```
1024 bytes in each allocation unit
 713 total allocation units on disk
 307 available allocation units on disk

655360 total bytes memory
409856 bytes free
```

To confirm that the problem you suspected in the directory is repaired, list the directory of the disk again. You see the following:

```
Volume in drive A is SCRATCH DISK
Volume Serial Number is 1982-BA9A
Directory of  A:\

DBSETUP  OVL    147968 10-21-88    12:22a
DBASE3   OVL     85024 12-28-88    9:04p
BASE6    OVL    114832 10-20-88    11:22p
DBASE1   OVL     65536 09-12-89    1:46a
         4 File(s)     314368 bytes free
```

Notice that DBASE1.OVL shows 65,536 bytes rather than 0. The available capacity of the disk remains unchanged. Now the figure for total bytes shown in the directory listing is within a few thousand bytes of the difference between the disk's capacity and the bytes-free total. You can account for this small difference by considering that some of the files do not fill their last allocated cluster. The error in the directory is corrected, and the disk is ready for use again.

Recovering Files and Disks with RECOVER

The external command RECOVER is DOS's "tool of last resort" for file and directory recovery. RECOVER "dismantles" a file or a disk one sector at a time. RECOVER then rebuilds as much of the file or the disk as the command can recover. The need for a RECOVER command stems from the possibility that a disk will develop bad sectors in a file or directory.

CHKDSK works with the FAT and root directory; RECOVER works with one file or with a complete disk of files and subdirectories. When CHKDSK cannot complete its processing because of a damaged directory, you can use RECOVER. When a program or a data file has DOS-reported problems, you can use RECOVER to salvage as much of the file as it can. As always, however, the best defense against file and directory damage is making full and incremental backups.

The syntax form of RECOVER that recovers a complete disk dismantles all the files and directories on the disk. You should never experiment with the form of RECOVER that works on complete disks unless the disk is unimportant.

After RECOVER has "fixed" the disk or directory, you may spend hours trying to recover from RECOVER. Don't get the idea that RECOVER is a weak command or that it is an incomplete command. A more proper approach is to think of RECOVER as a "last resort" command whose job is to reduce the total damage to directories and files. The form of RECOVER you use on a single file, however, is not risky. Each form of RECOVER is covered separately in the following paragraphs.

Caution:
Think of RECOVER as a "last-resort" command whose job is to reduce the total damage to directories and files.

Using RECOVER on a Defective File

As its name implies, RECOVER enables you to recover a file that contains defective sectors. Defective sectors may develop on a disk because of wear and tear, loss of magnetic fields, electronic problems in a drive, or other problems. In any event, one bad sector can make an entire file inaccessible to DOS.

The recovery, however, is partial. With RECOVER, you can make a new copy of a file, minus the data held in the bad sectors. Depending on the file being recovered, you may or may not be able to use the recovered file. If the file is a program file, you almost are guaranteed that the recovered program will malfunction. If the file is a data file, especially a text file, you may be able to use its contents. Even if the file is not usable after recovery, rest assured that the bad sectors are marked in the FAT as being defective so that they are not used again.

The syntax for the file form of RECOVER is as follows:

dc:pathc\RECOVER d:path\filename.ext

dc:pathc is the optional disk drive and path name to the RECOVER command.

d: is the optional disk drive name if the file is not on the current disk drive.

path is the optional path name if the file is not in the current directory.

filename is the root name of the file to recover, and *.ext* is the optional extension. You cannot use wild cards (* or ?).

After you use RECOVER on a file, the file has the same name as before. The bad sectors on the disk are "removed" from use, and the data in them is lost. This recovery method reduces the total capacity of the disk by the number of bytes contained in bad sectors that have been removed.

For practical reasons, the only files you should recover and try to use are text and data files. Do not bother recovering program files. When information is lost from such a file, the program may not run or, worse, the program may run erratically and do some file damage on its own. Copy a backup copy of the program to the disk after you erase the damaged file. You then can use the new program file.

You need to edit text or data files after you recover them. For text or ASCII data files, use a text editor to remove any spurious characters or to add lost information. You may need special programs to restore non-ASCII (binary) data files to their original states. Some applications programs refuse to read data files that have been recovered, because essential header or internal pointer information may have been deleted.

You have little reason to rely on RECOVER. If you make frequent backup copies of your hard disk or disk copies of your floppy disks, you usually can restore files easily from the backup copies and then re-edit as necessary.

Using RECOVER When a Directory Is Damaged

Bad sectors can develop in directories. This problem is a serious one. If a bad sector is in the root directory, the problem is grave. The root directory is in a fixed position on the hard disk or floppy disk. Because DOS cannot move the root directory, this condition can be "fatal." The second form of RECOVER, the potentially dangerous form, recovers damaged root directories.

If a subdirectory has bad sectors, the problem is serious but not fatal. CHKDSK can cope with it. Before you run CHKDSK, take the following steps for copying the floppy disk or hard disk. If CHKDSK does not work, RECOVER is your final choice.

> *Caution:* Use this command only as a last resort; then use RECOVER to recover files one at a time. You should never use RECOVER to recover your entire hard disk. Several excellent utility programs are available that do a much better job of recovering data from a damaged disk. (PC Tools Deluxe, Norton Utilities, and Mace Utilities are three examples.)

Taking Preliminary Steps

First, you should copy or back up all the files from the problem disk that you can. Use a different set of floppy disks than the set you used for your last backup copies. Your last backup set is important insurance. Keep your last backup floppy disks intact. You may need to use them if all else fails.

For a faulty floppy disk, use the COPY command to copy each file to a second floppy disk. Then use the DISKCOPY command to copy the bad floppy disk to a third floppy disk. If the offending disk is your hard disk, use a different set of backup floppy disks. Run BACKUP, keeping your master backups and last daily backups intact.

Because you do not know at this point the cause of any bad sectors, you should suspect that the same problem exists in the backed-up or copied files you have just made. Whatever caused the directory to develop bad sectors may have damaged other areas on the floppy disk or hard disk. Make sure that the files you just copied or backed up are correct before you fully trust them.

(If the problem is in a subdirectory, use CHKDSK first. If CHKDSK does not work, use the disk-level form of RECOVER.)

Issuing RECOVER To Recover a Directory

The next step is to use RECOVER. The syntax for this form of RECOVER is as follows:

dc:pathc\RECOVER d:

dc:pathc is the optional disk drive and path name to the RECOVER command.

d: is the optional disk drive name. If the current drive does not hold the disk you want to recover, give the appropriate disk drive name.

DOS runs through the file allocation table (FAT). Remember that the FAT knows the disk clusters (sectors) where each file is stored. But the FAT does not know the preceding file name, the file's attributes (system, hidden, and so on), or the file's date and time, because these details were lost in the defective directory.

DOS first re-creates the root directory. Then DOS begins to create files with the name FILEnnnn.REC in the root directory. *nnnn* is a number from 0000 to 9999. Each file that DOS creates represents one of the recovered files from the disk. Every file on the disk becomes a FILEnnnn.REC file: program files, data files, and subdirectories.

Identifying the Recovered Files

Now your detective work begins. Each FILEnnnn.REC file can be any-thing—a normal file or a subdirectory. You must find which FILEnnnn.REC files hold the information you need to keep and which FILEnnnn.REC files (such as subdirectories) hold information you can discard. The files' previous names are lost. Their dates and times also are lost. The best indicator of what is in each file is the content of the file itself. A regular printout of the output of TREE would remind you of the file names.

You need several tools to help you. The TYPE command can display on-screen the characters in a file. This command can help you identify ASCII text files. Program files and subdirectories, however, are different. Most of their information is displayed as gibberish. To display the contents of these files, you need DOS's DEBUG, NU from the Norton Utilities, DUMP.EXE from Phoenix Associates, or a similar program. You also can use the DOS Shell's View File Contents command.

With one of these tools, you can find the files you were not able to copy or back up. Copy these files to another floppy disk and change their names back to what they were. Make sure that the files are intact. There is a small chance that whatever caused the directory to develop bad sectors may have affected other areas of the floppy disk or hard disk, making other files bad.

Cue:
*Before using
RECOVER on a
directory, practice
first on a copy of
any floppy disk.*

Before you use RECOVER, you may want to practice first on a copy of any floppy disk. Use DISKCOPY to replicate the problem on another disk. Then you can see how RECOVER works without risking the disk you want to recover. If you botch up the copy, you still have the unaltered original and have lost nothing except time.

When you try to recover a floppy disk that has a flawed directory, again use a copy. If you make a mistake recovering the copy, you can make another copy of the original flawed floppy disk. If you work with the flawed floppy disk and do not have a copy, a mistake can be costly.

After you have re-created your files, you should reformat your floppy or hard disk. FORMAT gives a message when it cannot properly format any system area, including the areas for the boot record, the root directory, and the FAT. If you use FORMAT's /S switch, the system files' areas are checked also, and DOS gives error messages if these areas are bad. The error messages indicate that the floppy or hard disk is currently unusable. You can retire a floppy disk, but you must have a hard disk repaired or purchase a new one.

Remember to back up your data frequently. You will have less work and experience less frustration if you back up your floppy disks and hard disk instead of trying to re-create them with RECOVER.

Understanding the General Rules of RECOVER

The general rules of the RECOVER command are as follows:

- The single-file form of RECOVER retains the recovered file's name and directory entry.

- With the disk form of RECOVER, files and directories are recovered to the disk's root directory with FILEnnnn.REC file names.

- Before RECOVER begins execution, you see the following prompt:

```
Press any key to begin recovery of the file(s)
on drive x

x is the drive that will hold the disk to be
recovered.
```

- RECOVER terminates execution when the root directory of the recovered disk fills with FILEnnnn.REC entries. If the root directory fills, RECOVER warns you with the following message:

```
Warning—directory full
```

- If you issue RECOVER with a path specifier and no file-name specifier, RECOVER responds File not found.

Chapter Summary

The disk-level DOS commands covered in this chapter provide you with a means to manage and maintain the disks and drives that you use with your PC. The following key points were covered:

- FDISK manages DOS partitions in the hard disk partition table.

- FORMAT initializes disks and places DOS bookkeeping tables on disks.

- LABEL adds and changes a disk's volume-label text.

- VOL displays a disk's volume-label text.

- SYS transfers DOS system files from one disk to another.

- DISKCOPY replicates one floppy disk to another floppy disk with the same format.

- DISKCOMP compares two floppy disks track by track and reports comparison errors.

- REPLACE selectively updates a disk's or directory's files from another disk's or directory's files.

- CHKDSK analyzes a disk's FAT, root directory, and file fragmentation. With the /F switch, CHKDSK repairs defective directory entries and the FAT.

- RECOVER salvages directories and files that contain bad sectors on a disk.

In the next chapter, you learn about commands that manage disks at the directory and subdirectory levels. These important commands are your tools for structuring your individual version of the DOS hierarchical directory system.

Managing and Navigating the Directory Hierarchy

O ne of the primary features of DOS is its hierarchical directory system. Chapter 2 explains how DOS uses directories in conjunction with the file allocation table (FAT) to log the physical location of files on a disk. DOS uses internally related directories and the FAT to provide a framework for the management of the hierarchical file system.

Ideally, as long as DOS provides you with the commands to organize directories, you shouldn't be bothered with what is going on behind the scenes. An understanding of some of these internal details, however, helps you get the most from any discussion of the DOS directory system.

The chapter's main focus is the external view of the file system. From this external point of view, a freshly formatted disk is ready for you to give it a tree-structured file system. DOS directory commands enable you to design, manage, and modify the directory tree.

Many DOS commands deal with directories. For example, you can copy a file from one directory to a different directory with COPY, a file-level command that deals primarily with files. The directory commands have a definite connection with directories. This chapter explains how you can use the directory-level commands. The commands presented in this chapter include the following:

- MKDIR (MD)

- CHDIR (CD)

- PATH

- APPEND

- TREE

- XCOPY

- RMDIR (RD)

The chapter also offers some suggestions for efficient management of the hierarchical directory system on your hard disk.

Understanding the Hierarchical Directory System

A hierarchy is an organization of entities. What makes hierarchical organization useful is that its entities are arranged by some method of relationship into branching series of dependencies.

DOS entities are directories in a directory system. The hierarchy begins with the essential core, or root, entity. In a family tree, the core entity may be great-great-grandfather John Materson. In DOS, this core entity is the root directory. Subdirectories can trace their paths back to the root directory.

Understanding the Directory Entry

Cue:
The DOS FORMAT command creates a root directory on any disk.

Every DOS-created disk has a root directory, which is created by the DOS FORMAT command. The root directory is a table, fixed in length, that is placed in the control area of each disk. As part of the file-allocation process, DOS makes directory entries that consist of file names, locations, and status information about each file. Figure 7.1 shows the main components of each directory entry. The directory entry is DOS's essential file identifier.

File Name	Extension	Attributes	Reserved	Time	Date	Starting Cluster	Size

***Fig. 7.1.** A directory entry.*

The directory entry is a description of the file in DOS's own annotation. DOS uses this description to locate a file's content, manipulate the content, and provide you with information about the file.

Fields in a directory entry store information about a file. Figure 7.1 shows the fields of a file entry. The 8 characters of the file's root name are stored in the root-name field; the 3 characters of the extension are stored in the extension field. Subdirectory names also are stored in the root-name and extension fields. The disk volume label is stored in a directory entry in the root directory. The 11 characters of the volume label are stored in the 8 characters of the root name and the 3 characters of the extension. Unlike entries for file names, no period is assumed between the root name and the extension.

A file's attribute status is stored in the attribute field. The attribute field is one byte long; each attribute uses one bit as the attribute indicator. If the bit is set to on, the attribute is true. Two of the eight attribute bits are reserved for future use. DOS uses the remaining six attributes: archive, subdirectory, volume label, system file, hidden file, and read-only file.

A reserved field follows the attribute field in the directory entry. This field is reserved for future use. The time field stores the time at which the file represented by this entry was created or last modified. DOS stores the time as hours, minutes, and seconds. The date field stores an encoded date that indicates when the file was created or last modified. DOS stores the date as the year (relative to 1980), the month (1–12), and the day (1–31).

Following the date field, DOS stores the starting cluster number for the entry's chain of allocated clusters. The starting cluster number points to the FAT entry that begins the file's cluster chain. This piece of information enables DOS to access the data within the file; without this starting cluster field in the directory entry, DOS has no link to the file's physical storage locations on the disk.

The final directory-entry field is the file-size field, which stores the actual number of bytes contained in the file. Normally, because DOS allocates space in cluster units, the file size is different from the size of the disk space allocated to the file. *Cluster units* are multiples of a 512-byte sector. A 1-byte file shows 1 byte of file size in the directory entry, but the file uses at least 512 bytes of disk storage space. You can see that the directory entry DOS makes for a file provides a great deal of information for DOS's bookkeeping functions.

Understanding the Root Directory

Cue:

The root directory is designated in the command line by a backslash (\).

To show the root directory in a command line, you designate the root by using the backslash symbol (\).

Every DOS disk has a root directory. To differentiate between the roots of different disks, DOS recognizes drive names. Each of the following designations names the root directory of a different disk:

A:, **B:**, and **C:**

Hard disks can be partitioned into more than one logical drive, and each logical drive has its own root directory.

Cue:

DOS uses certain files and directory entries for internal purposes.

A file is a part or by-product of your computing work. Normally, DOS enables you to access, manipulate, and execute files. DOS uses some files and directory entries, such as system files, volume labels, and subdirectories, for internal manipulation. Special files are on the disk because DOS places them on-disk, not necessarily because you want them there.

When you add the first subdirectory to the root directory, you are introducing a hierarchical directory structure on the disk. The root directory now has an offspring, and DOS manages your creation. Without your overview, DOS prepares a special subdirectory file and gives the file the same basic capability to receive file entries as its parent directory, the root.

Understanding Subdirectories

A subdirectory is a file that DOS uses like it uses the root directory. The root directory is a fixed-length directory table in the control area of each disk. Subdirectories share the common 32-byte entry size used to record information about a file with the root directory.

When you are working with files, you easily can get the impression that DOS keeps the files themselves, rather than entries about the files, in directories. This is an erroneous impression. A disk is not divided physically into subdirectories of files. A directory's files may be spread randomly across the disk.

Even though only file entries are located in directories, and not the files themselves, most people think of files as being located in directories. This view of files, although not accurate, works under most circumstances.

Specifying a Path in a Command Line

When DOS was introduced, you could use drive specifiers and file specifiers—but not directory specifiers—with the commands that dealt with files. DOS Version 1 did not need to know how to find the directory that contained the entry for a specific file. Version 1 had just one directory per disk. That directory was to become Version 2's root directory. Even though subdirectories were added, users were not required to use them. Many floppy-only users continued to issue the same commands with the same parameters as they had when using Version 1. By the time Version 3.0 was introduced, hard disks were in common use, and the subdirectory capabilities that hard disks justified finally caught on with DOS users.

Dealing with subdirectories necessitated a new element in syntax lines—the directory specifier or parameter. Because DOS logs to the root directory as the default directory, file commands without directory parameters look like DOS Version 1 commands.

In symbolic form, a command line that includes the directory directions as an element of syntax looks like the following:

COMMAND *drive:path directory_name\full_filename*

In this syntax line, **COMMAND** is the symbol for the DOS command.

drive: is the drive specifier—the symbol for the name of the disk drive that holds the disk this command uses.

path is the path specifier—the symbolic placeholder for the chain of related directories that lead to the final element of the syntax: the directory name or the file. *path* is optional in the command line. If you don't supply a path, DOS uses the path to and including the current directory of the indicated drive as a default value for *path*. DOS Version 1 did not have this syntax element. Version 2 and later versions include the path element of syntax in many commands.

> **Cue:**
> The path specifier in a syntax line symbolizes the chain of related directories that lead to the object of the command's action.

directory_name (the directory specifier) and/or *full_filename* (the file specifier) are the objects of **COMMAND**'s action. Commands that manage files (such as COPY) may have sets of full file names (file names plus extensions) to reflect source and target parameters. The object of commands that manage directories (such as MKDIR) is a *directory_name*. This chapter discusses many commands that use directory names as the objects of the actions of commands.

The notion of using a path in a command line can be a slippery concept to grasp. You can think of the path as the listing of every directory required to get to a file. In this context, examine the following command:

DIR C:\DIR1\DIR2\FILE.111

The command is DIR; the drive specifier is C:; and the path specifier is \DIR1\DIR2. The final \ delimits the path from the file name on which DIR is reporting—FILE.111.

The symbolic syntax of this command is as follows:

DIR *d:path\filename.ext*

In these DIR examples, the path is a listing of directories DOS needs to find FILE.111 and make its report. The path points to the object of the command.

When the object of the command is a directory name rather than a file, the syntax representation is different. Look at the subdirectory-management command MKDIR. To make a directory called DIR2 as a subdirectory of DIR1, you issue the following command:

MKDIR C:\DIR1\DIR2

The command is MKDIR; the drive name is C:; and the path is \DIR1. If the directory name DIR2 is the object of the command's action, the directory name is listed in a syntax line as a separate element called *directory_name*. If DIR2 is a syntax element called *directory_name*, \DIR1 is the path that leads to the point at which the MKDIR command is to carry out its action—adding the DIR2 directory. MKDIR's syntax representation looks like the following:

MKDIR *d:path\directory_name*

Reminder:
Read the text that accompanies the syntax lines for an explanation of each element.

Good syntax representation is always accompanied by an explanation of each element of the syntax. If you have any doubts about how to form a command line with a path included, read the explanation of each element of the syntax. The following guidelines may help you interpret and specify paths:

- If the path specifier begins with the backslash character (\), DOS interprets the path as starting at the root.

- If the path specifier does not begin with \, DOS interprets the path as starting at the current directory.

- If the path specifier is omitted, DOS assumes that the path is the path of the current directory and that you are supplying the object of the command's action in a command-line parameter. The object may be a file name and extension, or in the case of the directory commands, a directory name.

Using PROMPT To Display a Full Path

While you are reading about directory-level commands, you may want to confirm that your DOS prompt is displaying the current full path (drive and path) of your current directory. To give you visual confirmation of your current logged drive and any logged directory, DOS provides the PROMPT command. With PROMPT, you can display the full path as part of the DOS prompt. Enter the following command at the DOS prompt:

Cue:
The
DOS PROMPT
command
displays the full
path.

> **SET**

DOS displays the current setting of the prompt string. Look at the string and determine whether the string contains the characters *pg*.

If the string contains these characters, you can see the current drive and path in the DOS prompt. If the string does not contain these characters, you may want to change the prompt string so that you can see the current full path. To do so, issue the following command:

> **PROMPT pg**

When you reboot, the prompt returns to the system default. You can cause the new prompt to become your standard DOS prompt by adding the preceding PROMPT command to the batch file AUTOEXEC.BAT. Refer to Chapter 12 for a full discussion of batch files and to Chapter 15 for more information about AUTOEXEC.BAT.

With the prompt established as pg, you can log to the \DOS directory of drive C, for example, and see the following prompt:

```
C:\DOS>
```

Making Directories with MKDIR (MD)

Because the root is the only directory available on a DOS disk, the user must add any additional directories. To tell DOS to make a new directory, you use the DOS MKDIR, or MD, command. You can use either name for the command; MKDIR and MD are identical in operation.

When you issue the MKDIR command, you instruct DOS to add a new subdirectory to some part of the file-system tree.

Issuing the MKDIR Command

Remember that any time you can use MKDIR, you can use MD in its place. The following syntax and examples use the MKDIR version of the command. The syntax for the MKDIR command is as follows:

MKDIR *d:path***dir_name**

d: is the specifier for the optional target drive containing the disk on which the new directory is to be added. If the *d:* parameter is omitted, the default drive is used.

path\ is the specifier for the optional path to which the new directory is added.

dir_name is the name for the new directory; a directory name must be given.

Reminder:
The length of the full path must not exceed 63 characters.

The length of the full path (drive, path, and new directory name) must not exceed 63 characters. If you are creating a directory relative to your current directory, you must count your current directory's full path length from the implied root \ character as being part of the 63 limit.

Understanding the Operation of MKDIR

When you issue the MKDIR command, DOS verifies that the given (or default) parent directory exists. Then DOS confirms that the new directory has a unique file name. The parent directory cannot contain an entry for a file with the same name as the proposed directory's name.

After confirming that the new directory name is unique in the parent directory, DOS allocates a file for the new directory. Technically, the directory is created when the new directory file is allocated.

DOS completes two entries in the new directory. The first entry named . (dot) includes the new directory's starting cluster number in the FAT.

The second entry named .. (dot-dot) contains information about the parent directory, including the directory's starting cluster in the FAT. Every subdirectory, except those whose parent directory is the root directory, has a valid starting cluster that points to the subdirectory's parent directory.

These two constant named entries are sometimes referred to as *alias* entries. The alias entries are directory entries that don't "own" the files they point to. Disk-level "analyze-and-fix" commands, such as CHKDSK and

RECOVER, know that these alias entries point to starting clusters that other directory entries point to at the same time. CHKDSK and RECOVER do not get confused by the seeming cross-linking of clusters that aliases exhibit.

The usefulness of the aliases may not be immediately obvious. For example, COMMAND.COM accepts the aliases as legitimate path specifiers. By using the dot-dot alias as a path specifier, you can access the parent directory of your working directory no matter where in the directory tree your working directory is located. (This same shorthand mechanism also is available to DOS for internal use.)

Reminder:
DOS accepts the .
and .. directory
entries as
legitimate path
specifiers.

Understanding the General Rules of MKDIR

- MKDIR and MD are different names for the same command.

- All characters allowed in a normal file name can be used in a directory name.

- A directory name can include as many as eight characters; the name may be followed by a period (.) and as many as three characters of extension. DOS users have, by convention, established that DOS directories normally do not include extensions.

- A directory name cannot be the name of a standard DOS device, such as AUX, PRN, and CON.

- A directory name cannot duplicate any file name in the intended parent directory.

- The specified or implied parent directory of an intended directory must exist. MKDIR cannot create more than one directory at a time.

Creating a Directory with MKDIR

Assume that you currently are logged onto the root directory of a newly formatted floppy disk in drive A. To create the directory \DATA on the disk in drive A, type the following command:

MKDIR \DATA

To confirm that DOS created the directory—DATA—on the disk in drive A, enter the CHKDSK command from the DOS directory of your hard disk. For a report of the disk in drive A, type the following command:

C:\DOS\CHKDSK

DOS displays the following:

```
Volume Serial Number is 114B-15cc

730112 bytes total disk space
  1024 bytes in 1 directories
729088 bytes available on disk

  1024 bytes in each allocation unit
   713 total allocation units on disk
   712 available allocation units on disk

655360 bytes total memory
603152 bytes free
```

The available space on this disk has been reduced by 1K because DOS allocated a two-sector cluster (allocation unit) to the \DATA directory. You can achieve the same result while logged onto the root directory by issuing the MKDIR command, using the following form:

MKDIR DATA

Cue:
If you do not specify a path with the MKDIR command, DOS makes the current directory the parent directory.

The directory is created directly from the root, even though no disk name or beginning backslash is given in the command line. DOS uses the default current drive, drive A, and makes the directory relative to the current directory, the root. If you do not specify a path, DOS makes the current directory the parent directory of your new directory.

Changing the Current Directory with CHDIR (CD)

Cue:
Use the CHDIR (CD) command to change the current directory.

DOS remembers the current directory path and the current drive name. To change the current directory, making another directory current, you issue the CHDIR or CD command. The directory you make current with CHDIR becomes the directory DOS searches first for files. CHDIR and CD are the same command; their usage is identical. Use these commands to navigate the directory system.

If you use the CHDIR command with no parameters, DOS displays the current directory's path name for the current drive.

Issuing the CHDIR Command

The syntax for CD or CHDIR is as follows:

CHDIR *d:path*

d: is the optional drive name specifier. Specifying a drive in the CHDIR command does not cause that drive to become the current logged drive.

path is the name of the directory you want to make the current directory on the disk in drive *d:*. If no drive is specified in the command line, the path specifier is assumed to be on the current drive. The path specifier can begin with the .. alias.

Understanding the Operation of CHDIR

Each drive that DOS recognizes on your system has its own current directory value stored by DOS. When you issue CHDIR with a path specifier but no drive specifier, DOS first consults the logged-drive storage area to determine which drive is the current one. DOS verifies that the path from the CHDIR command exists. If the path is not found, DOS issues the invalid directory message and does not change the current directory, which is stored internally. If the path does exist, DOS stores the path's name in the internal storage area as the current directory.

If the CHDIR command is issued with no parameters, DOS displays the current directory name. Issued with only a drive parameter, CHDIR reports the current directory name on the specified drive.

Reminder:
Each drive that DOS recognizes on your system has a current directory value stored by DOS.

Understanding the General Rules of CHDIR

- CHDIR and CD are different names for the same command.

- If the path specifier begins with a \, CHDIR assumes that the directory specified in the path starts from the root.

- If the path specifier does not begin with a \, CHDIR assumes that the directory given in path starts from the current directory.

- When the path specifier is omitted from the command line, CHDIR reports the current working directory for the disk in the drive specified.

- When the path specifier and the drive specifier are omitted from the command line, CHDIR reports the current working directory of the current drive.

- When only a drive is specified in the command line, CHDIR reports the current directory of that disk but does not log that disk as the current disk.

Using the Two Forms of CHDIR To Change Directories

CHDIR has two operational forms. One form returns a report of a disk's logged directory's path name. The second form of CHDIR replaces a disk's logged directory with the directory given in the command line.

Suppose that the current directory on drive A is \DIR1. To receive a report of the default directory of the A disk, type the following command and parameter:

CHDIR A:

CHDIR reports the following:

```
A:\DIR1
```

Suppose that the logged disk is C and that the current directory of C is \KEEP. To see the default directory, type the following:

CHDIR

CHDIR reports as follows:

```
C:\KEEP
```

To change the default directory of the disk in drive A to \FILES when the logged disk is C:, type the following command and parameters:

CHDIR A:\FILES

DOS changes the current directory in drive A to \FILES. To confirm the change, type the following command:

CHDIR A:

CHDIR replies as follows:

```
A:\FILES
```

The subdirectories \WP\MEMOS and \WP\DOCS have \WP as their parent directory. To change the directory in the current drive (drive C) from \WP\MEMOS to \WP\DOCS, issue the following command:

CHDIR ..\DOCS

Notice that the alias for the current directory's parent directory (.., with no leading \) acts as a shorthand substitute for the same full command you issue in the following form:

CHDIR \WP\DOCS

To change from the \WP\DOCS directory on the current drive to the \WP (the parent directory of \WP\DOCS), you issue the command:

CHDIR ..

DOS logs \WP as the current directory of the current disk drive.

The use of the .. alias as the only parameter of the command always logs to the parent of the current directory, unless the current directory is the root. The root directory has no parent.

Reminder:
The root directory has no parent.

Defining the Program Search with PATH

The PATH command enables you to define a search path that DOS uses to locate programs not located in the current directory. A search path defined by PATH remains in effect until you issue the PATH command with another search path.

Executing programs (files with COM, EXE, or BAT extensions) in a single-directory file system is no problem. You issue the command or program name, and COMMAND.COM loads and executes it. In a hierarchical directory system, however, especially one that includes a hard disk, your current working directory may not be the directory that contains the entry for the program you want to run. You can include the drive and path specifiers as part of the command line, directly before the name of the program you want, but typing the additional specifiers can be a cumbersome process.

DOS provides an alternative to issuing drive and path specifiers in front of a command by enabling you to define alternate search paths. DOS uses these alternate search paths if the current directory does not contain the COM, EXE, or BAT file you want.

Cue:

You can use the PATH command to specify which disks and directories DOS searches.

The PATH command specifies the disks and directories that DOS searches if the command or program is not located in the current directory of the specified (or default) drive's disk. Most users provide a PATH command with alternative search paths in their AUTOEXEC.BAT file so that the search path is defined when the computer is booted. The PATH command also can be executed at the DOS prompt.

Issuing the PATH Command

The syntax for the PATH command is as follows:

PATH *d1:path1;d2:path2...*

Each alternative search path consists of a drive and path pair represented by *dn:pathn*, in which *n* shows the corresponding position of the pair—in this case, 1 or 2.

If you issue **PATH** with no parameters, a report of the current search path is displayed.

The optional drive parameters *d1:* and *d2:* can be any drive names, such as A, B, or C. The current drive is the default.

The optional parameters *path1* and *path2* are path names on the corresponding drives. If one of the path parameters is omitted from the command line, the specified disk's root directory is assumed.

The semicolon (;) separates multiple drive and path pairs in the command line. If a semicolon follows the PATH command as the last character of the command line, DOS eliminates the defined search path. No spaces separate drive and path pairs and the semicolon.

The ellipsis (...) indicates that the number of drive and path pairs can vary. You can specify several alternate drive and path pairs.

Understanding the Operation of PATH

Normally, the external DOS commands are copied from the DOS master disk to a directory named \DOS on the hard disk (usually drive C). You can issue one of these commands (CHKDSK, for example) from any directory on any disk by including the full path to the command in the following form:

C:\DOS\CHKDSK A:

This command tells DOS that the command program, CHKDSK, is located on drive C in the \DOS directory. Although giving command-path specifiers makes commands accessible from any directory, the extra keystrokes mean additional work (and possible typos). External commands issued with command paths are not as convenient to use as internal DOS commands in which no characters precede the command name. Typing **COPY** is simpler than typing **C:\DOS\XCOPY**. In a DOS work session, you can issue dozens of external DOS commands from different directory locations. You can use the PATH command to eliminate the cumbersome process of including the command's path from the command line.

By defining the search path for programs as C:\DOS, you ensure that every DOS command will execute from any point in the directory tree of any disk. You do not have to think about which command is internal and which is external. You type the name of the DOS command and then focus on providing the correct parameters and switches. If the external command you use is located in C:\DOS, the PATH definition of C:\DOS gives DOS an alternate directory to search for the command if the working directory does not include the command. The PATH command is not limited to just one alternative for the current directory. You can define several alternate paths; DOS searches the alternate paths in the order in which they are listed in the PATH command, from left to right.

Reminder:
You can define several alternative paths with the PATH command.

Understanding the General Rules of PATH

- Alternative search paths defined by PATH remain in effect until another PATH command modifies the current definition.

- When you turn off the computer or use the Ctrl-Alt-Del sequence to warm boot the computer, you must re-establish the defined search path. (Many AUTOEXEC.BAT files set the search path.)

- If directories defined by the PATH command do not exist, the nonexistent path(s) are ignored when the alternate search paths are searched. DOS does not issue any message or warning about nonexistent search-path alternatives.

- DOS uses the search paths defined by PATH in the order the alternatives are defined.

- The search path string defined by the PATH command is passed to executing programs as part of the environment.

Reminder:
Unless a path is set in AUTOEXEC.BAT, you must re-establish the defined search path when rebooting.

- To remove the search path, issue the PATH command followed by a semicolon (**PATH;**).

Using PATH To Search Directories

To establish a search path to the \DOS directory on drive C, enter the following command:

PATH C:\DOS

To confirm the new search path, type **PATH**. DOS then displays the following:

```
PATH=C:\DOS
```

To confirm that the new search path is in the environment, use the SET command. DOS reports as follows:

```
COMSPEC=C:\COMMAND.COM
PROMPT=$P$G
PATH=C:\DOS
```

You can use the equal sign to separate the command from the parameters. DOS accepts the following command:

PATH=C:\DOS

To include the root directory of drive C as the first alternative in the search path, reenter the search path, using the following command:

PATH C:\;C:\DOS

To remove a search path, enter the PATH command with a semicolon, as follows:

PATH ;

Type just the command name **PATH** to confirm that no search path is in effect. DOS responds as follows:

```
No Path
```

Using Aliases with PATH

Remember that DOS accepts the (..) directory name as an alias for the current directory's parent directory. You can include the parent alias in the PATH command as a path parameter; DOS searches the current directory's parent directory if the program you want to run is not in the current directory. The logic of aliases as PATH parameters is based on how many of the applications programs' directories are nested.

Many applications programs create subdirectories when you install the programs on your hard disk. If several of your applications programs include their default directories in the search path, the number of directories and directory entries within each directory can become quite large. DOS can search a large number of directory entries in a search path, but the efficiency of the search is reduced. DOS may have to wade through hundreds of directory entries before locating a program. Because most applications programs that create their own subdirectories are never more than one or two levels away from their subdirectories, you can improve efficiency by placing a path relative to the current directory—rather than to the root directory—into the search for programs.

Reminder:
Many applications programs create subdirectories during installation.

For example, you can issue the PATH command in the following form:

PATH ..;..\..;C:\;C:\DOS;\C:\DBASE

The first two directories in line for a search always are the parent of the current directory and the parent of the parent of the current directory (the grandparent directory). In this example, DOS can find DBASE.EXE from any subdirectory of \DBASE and even from any subdirectory of a \DBASE subdirectory. The aliases in the search path find the DBASE.EXE program.

With the same search path, you can start the program Reflex from the \REFLEX\DATA\Y_1991 directory and not even need the \REFLEX directory in the search path. DOS finds the REFLEX.EXE program because the search path is relative and reaches backward from the current directory.

Using aliases with PATH is a good example of how these .. directory entries can be used to improve your efficiency with the PC.

Simplifying Data-File Searching with APPEND

The external command APPEND is a program that gives users of DOS Version 3.2 and later versions a search path to data files similar to PATH's search path to program files. APPEND is a memory-resident program that loads when you issue the APPEND command and remains in memory until you reboot.

Reminder:
APPEND is a memory-resident program.

PATH enables DOS to locate program files—those with COM, EXE, and BAT extensions—found in the search path. But PATH cannot help locate data files in other directories.

APPEND can be considered the PATH command to use with data files. The way the command operates was changed slightly for DOS Version 4. The APPEND command is more complex and has somewhat more complicated syntax requirements than the PATH command.

Issuing the APPEND Command

The syntax for APPEND is as follows:

APPEND *d1:path1\;d2:path2\... /X /X:ON /X:OFF*
/PATH:ON /PATH:OFF /E

d1: is the optional drive specifier of the first alternative of the APPEND search path.

path1 is the optional path specifier of the first alternative of the APPEND search path.

; separates APPEND search path but a semicolon (;) used alone cancels the current APPEND search path, as in **APPEND;**.

d2: and *path2* are additional optional APPEND search-path alternative specifiers.

/X redirects programs that use the DOS function calls SEARCH FIRST, FIND FIRST, and EXEC. This switch works much like the PATH command, enabling programs to run executable files that are not in the current directory. This switch can be used the first time you issue the APPEND command during a DOS session.

/X:ON is the alternate form of /X (DOS 4 and 5).

/X:OFF disables the /X search feature (DOS 4 and 5).

/PATH:ON enables programs to search the APPEND search path for a file even when a file name is specified with a drive and/or full path name.

/PATH:OFF disables the capability for programs to search the APPEND path for a file when a path is specified with the file name.

/E creates an environment variable named APPEND that stores the APPEND search path. This switch can be used only the first time you issue APPEND during a DOS session. After you use the /E switch, you can use the SET command to display and/or change the APPEND search path.

Understanding the Operation of APPEND

Normally, a program's request for DOS to find a file fails if the file is not in the specified directory. APPEND detects when the requested file has not been located. When the standard routine fails, APPEND looks for the file in the first APPEND search path. If the first path fails, APPEND tries the next. APPEND searches each path until the file is found, or until no path remains. If APPEND locates the file, the file is turned over to the calling program as though the program's original request for the file was successful. If AP-PEND cannot locate the file, APPEND returns a "failed" code to the requesting program as though the program's original file-service request failed to find the file.

If your program writes information to files, be careful when you use APPEND to enable a program to find a data file. Your program may write information to files in the current directory, rather than in the directory that contains the original files. For example, if the current directory is \WORDS, and APPEND has tricked a program into finding the file RALEY.TXT in the directory \WORDS\CONTRACTS, the program will save the file in \WORDS. The original file in \WORDS\CONTRACT remains unchanged. You can be tripped up when you are not aware that a program is saving files in the current directory. For example, your word processor may find the old version of the RALEY.TXT file when you request a printout.

If you misspell a path that you use with APPEND, or if you delete the directory, APPEND does not notice the error until DOS attempts to use the paths. You do not see any error messages if you specify invalid paths. DOS simply skips any missing or misspelled path names and proceeds to the next path. If you use an invalid path name, APPEND may skip the directory you intended APPEND to use.

Understanding the General Rules of APPEND

- APPEND is initially an external command. After you issue the first APPEND command, subsequent APPEND commands act as an internal command because APPEND is memory resident.

- The /X and /E switches can be used only the first time you issue the APPEND command.

- The command APPEND; cancels the APPEND search path, but APPEND remains memory-resident.

- The /X switch instructs DOS to search the APPEND search path when attempting to execute a program that is not found in the current directory.

Caution:
Use the APPEND command before you use the ASSIGN command.

- APPEND must be started before ASSIGN is used. ASSIGN "hides" the true nature of the assigned drive from most commands; if ASSIGN is issued first, APPEND will behave erratically.

Using APPEND with the /X Switch

The sample session in this section demonstrates how **APPEND** works. Place a blank, formatted disk in drive A and issue the following command:

TYPE AUTOEXEC.BAT

DOS responds with the following message:

```
File not found -- AUTOEXEC.BAT
```

Next, issue the following commands:

TYPE AUTOEXEC.BAT

APPEND C:

This time, DOS displays the contents of the AUTOEXEC.BAT file from your C drive. APPEND causes DOS to search the root directory of the C drive (C:\) and the current directory of the B drive. To cause DOS to search additional directories when looking for data files, you can add additional paths to the APPEND command. For example, to cause DOS to search the \DOS directory and \DATA directory on the C drive (in addition to the root directory), type the following command and press Enter:

APPEND C:\; C:\DOS; C:\DATA

> *Caution:* If you use APPEND with the /X switch, some programs may react in unexpected ways. A program that has always worked perfectly may no longer perform correctly. If you encounter this problem, restart DOS and use the APPEND command without the /X switch (or, if you have DOS Version 4 or a later version, turn off the feature by typing **APPEND /X:OFF**). If the program then works correctly, remember not to use APPEND with the /X switch with that program.

Listing Directories with TREE

Your floppy disks and the files in your hierarchical directories probably are organized in much the same way. Perhaps you have subdirectories for letters, for applications programs, for memos, and for many other categories just as you would keep disks with categories of files. As the number of directories and files increases, however, your ability to remember which directory holds which file decreases. Instead of asking yourself which disk holds your file, your question becomes "Which directory holds my file?"

DOS provides an external command—TREE—that lists all the directories of a disk. TREE also can list the files in the directories. If your computer has a hard disk, the TREE command is especially useful.

Cue:
The TREE command lists the directories, and optionally, the files on a disk.

Note: You also can use the DOS shell to see a graphical view of the directory tree.

Issuing the TREE Command

TREE's command syntax is as follows:

> **TREE** *d:path\ /F/A*

d: is the optional name of the disk drive that holds the directories you want to list. If you omit *d:*, TREE lists the directories on the current disk drive.

TREE Version 3.3 and earlier versions accept only the single switch */F*, which directs TREE to list the *files* in the directories. Use this switch if you are trying to locate a file. If you do not give the switch, TREE displays a list of the disk's directories only—not the disk's files.

In MS-DOS 3.3 and later, TREE accepts the optional *path* specifier. The path specifier names the directory in which TREE starts processing the listing. If the path specifier is omitted, TREE begins processing from the root directory.

In Versions 4 and 5, TREE's output displays the directory tree with line graphics characters. The */A* switch uses nongraphics characters to draw the tree.

Understanding the Operation of TREE

With the TREE command, unlike the DIR command, you do not specify a path or file name with the drive name. The TREE command—available with PC DOS through Version 3.3 and MS-DOS through Version 3.2—always starts its listing with the root directory of the specified or current disk drive. You do not give TREE a choice of where to start, and you cannot specify a file to search for. With TREE, you get an all-or-nothing listing of the disk's hierarchical directory structure.

MS-DOS Versions 3.3, 4, and 5 accept an optional path specifier that causes TREE to list the directory structure for a specific directory and subordinate directories.

In the MS-DOS Versions 3.3, 4, and 5 TREE listing, the tree structure is drawn with graphics characters (see fig. 7.2). If you specify the /A switch with Version 4 or 5, TREE uses nongraphics characters to draw the tree (see fig. 7.3). The characters produced by the /A switch, although not as well suited to drawing lines as TREE's default characters, can be printed on any printer. If your printer does not follow the IBM printer character set for extended characters (ASCII 128 or greater), use the command **TREE /A >PRN** to direct the output to your printer.

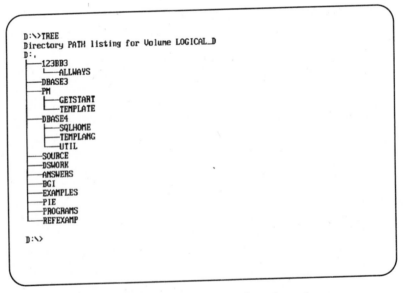

```
D:\>TREE
Directory PATH listing for Volume LOGICAL_D
D:.
├──123BB3
│  └──ALLWAYS
├──DBASE3
├──PM
│  ├──GETSTART
│  └──TEMPLATE
├──DBASE4
│  ├──SQLHOME
│  ├──TEMPLANG
│  └──UTIL
├──SOURCE
├──DSWORK
├──ANSWERS
├──BGI
├──EXAMPLES
├──PIE
├──PROGRAMS
└──REFEXAMP

D:\>
```

Fig. 7.2. The TREE command, showing line graphics characters.

```
D:\>TREE /A
Directory PATH listing for Volume LOGICAL_D
D:.
+---123BB3
|    \---ALLWAYS
+---DBASE3
+---PM
|    +---GETSTART
|    \---TEMPLATE
+---DBASE4
|    +---SQLHOME
|    +---TEMPLANG
|    \---UTIL
+---SOURCE
+---DSWORK
+---ANSWERS
+---BGI
+---EXAMPLES
+---PIE
+---PROGRAMS
\---REFEXAMP

D:\>
```

*Fig. 7.3. The output of **TREE** /A, showing nongraphics characters.*

Comparing CHKDSK and TREE

Remember that you can use CHKDSK to produce a report similar to those produced by TREE (see Chapter 6). The CHKDSK command accepts the /V switch, which gives a *verbose* listing of the disk's directories and files. The command syntax for the TREE-like version of CHKDSK is as follows:

CHKDSK *d:* /V

CHKDSK /V is like the TREE command. *d:* is the optional name of the disk drive to be checked. The /V switch lists the directories as well as the files.

Reminder:
CHKDSK /V produces a listing similar to that of TREE.

Controlling the Output of TREE with Filters and Redirection

The output of the TREE (and CHKDSK /V) commands can be lengthy. This type of output is ideally suited for redirection. You can, for example, use the MORE filter to display one screen full of information at a time. The command syntax for using MORE for output redirection with TREE is as follows:

TREE | MORE

You can redirect the output of TREE to the printer with this command:

TREE > PRN

You can place TREE's output in a disk file with this command:

TREE > treelist.txt

If you store the output in a disk file, you can print the output at any time. Occasionally running TREE on your hard disk is a good idea; you can keep the printed copy of your disk's entire contents near your computer. This type of output is a good road map of your hard disk's structure and can help coworkers or friends when they must use your computer.

Combining Copying and Directory Management with XCOPY

The external command XCOPY is used to copy files and can be used also to create directories. Because XCOPY can create directories, the command is included in this chapter with the other directory-management commands.

The XCOPY command, introduced with DOS Version 3.2, addresses the needs of three principal types of computer users: those who have more than one computer, those who have hard disks, and those who need more selectivity than the standard COPY command offers. Because almost all PC users fit one or more of these categories, XCOPY is an important command to know and use.

Issuing the XCOPY Command

XCOPY's syntax is similar to COPY's syntax, but the switches are more complex. XCOPY's syntax is as follows:

XCOPY *ds:paths\filenames.exts*
    dd:pathd\filenamed.extd /V /P /W /S /E /A /M /D:*date*

The *source* files, designated by an *s*, are the files to be copied. If you omit the disk drive name (*ds:*), the current disk drive is used. If you omit the path name (*paths*), the current directory on the drive is used. You can use wild cards in the file name (*filenames.exts*). If you omit the file name, XCOPY assumes that you want to specify wild cards (*.*); all files in the given path will be copied. If you do not specify a path and file name, XCOPY issues an error message.

With XCOPY, the *destination* files are designated by the *d* in the name. File names, disk drive names, and path names follow the *rule of currents*. This means that if you do not specify a drive name (*dd:*), XCOPY uses the current disk drive. If you do not specify a path name (*pathd*), XCOPY uses the current disk's directory. If you omit the file name (*filenamed.extd*), the copied files retain their previous names.

Cue:

With the XCOPY command, file names, disk drive names, and path names follow the rule of currents.

If you give a destination name that may be a path name or a file name, and the potential path does not exist, XCOPY asks whether the destination is a file name or path name.

As an example, look at the following command:

    XCOPY C:\WORDS*.* A:\WORDS

If you use this command to copy the files from C:\WORDS to the disk in drive A, and that disk does not have a directory called WORDS, XCOPY displays this message:

```
Does WORDS specify a filename
or directory name on the target
(F = file,D = directory)?
```

If the destination is a file name, press F. If the destination is a directory, press D. Unlike COPY, XCOPY creates directories on the destination disk as they are needed.

Understanding XCOPY's Switches

XCOPY has eight switches, all described in this section. A table of XCOPY's switches can be found in the Command Reference section.

/V is the familiar *verify* switch. XCOPY verifies that it has copied the files correctly.

/W causes XCOPY to prompt you to insert the source disk. This switch is particularly important to users of floppy disk drives. XCOPY is an external program that must be loaded from a disk; the copying process normally starts after the program loads. If you want to copy files between disks—none of which have the XCOPY program—use the /W switch. After XCOPY starts, the program prompts you to insert the correct disk. Remove the disk that holds XCOPY, insert the correct disk, and press any key to start the actual copying process.

Reminder:

XCOPY is an external program that must be loaded from a disk.

/P is the *pause*-and-ask switch. XCOPY displays the name of the file it will copy and asks whether the file should be copied. For the file /MYFILE.123, for example, XCOPY displays the following prompt:

```
/MYFILE.123 (Y/N)?
```

Answer Y to copy the file or N to skip it. When you answer Y, XCOPY immediately copies the file.

Reminder:
*XCOPY can
traverse the
subdirectory tree
and copy
complete directory
branches.*

The /S and /E switches affect how XCOPY handles additional subdirectories. These two switches show the true power of XCOPY. COPY is limited to handling the files from one directory; XCOPY starts with the named or current directory and can process the files in all additional subdirectories of that directory, all lower subdirectories of these subdirectories, and so on. XCOPY traverses the subdirectory tree and can copy complete directory branches from one disk to another.

The /S switch affects the source and destination directories. The /S switch instructs XCOPY to copy all designated files from the current and subsequent *subdirectories* to a parallel set of subdirectories on the destination disk drive. As an example, look at the following command:

XCOPY C:\WORDS*.* A: /S

The command executes in the following sequence:

1. XCOPY copies all files in \WORDS to the current directory on drive A.

2. XCOPY copies all files from \WORDS\LETTERS to a subdirectory of the current directory called \LETTERS on drive A.

3. XCOPY copies all files from the subdirectory \WORDS\CONTRACTS to the subdirectory of the current directory on drive A called \CONTRACTS.

In essence, XCOPY lifts a copy of the subdirectory tree, starting at the source directory, and transplants the copy to drive A.

Note that XCOPY does not place the copied files from the subdirectories into a single directory. XCOPY places files from one subdirectory into a parallel subdirectory. If the subdirectory does not exist on the destination, XCOPY creates the subdirectory.

The /E switch affects the operation of the /S switch. If XCOPY encounters an *empty* subdirectory on the source drive, XCOPY /S skips the empty subdirectory. If you give the /S and /E switches, XCOPY also creates empty subdirectories on the destination drive. If you give the /E switch without giving the /S switch, the /E switch has no meaning. You also must use /S to get any action from /E.

The switches /M, /A, and /D:date control which of the files that match the source-file name will be copied. The /M switch tells XCOPY to copy any *modified* file. /M tells XCOPY to copy a file that you have not backed up or copied with XCOPY.

In Chapter 8, you learn more about the archive attribute stored in the directory with each file name. When you create or change a file, this attribute is turned on. XCOPY checks to see whether the archive attribute has been set. (The set (on) archive attribute is shown as an A to the left of the file name reported by the ATTRIBUTE command.) DOS turns on the archive attribute when a file is created or modified. When you give the /M switch, XCOPY processes this file. If the attribute is not set, XCOPY skips the file.

The /A switch works like the /M switch; XCOPY processes only files that have the *archive* flag turned on. But after XCOPY has copied a file, /M clears the archive attribute; /A does not. This difference can be important. The BACKUP command selects files by considering the archive attribute. If XCOPY has cleared this flag, however, BACKUP will not process the file. Therefore, if you use XCOPY /M and BACKUP /M (the meaning of the switches is identical for both commands), the backup you make using BACKUP may not be complete. Unless you customarily use XCOPY as a backup program, avoid using the /M switch; use the /A switch instead.

The /D:date switch selects files according to their *directory date*, which is the date of the file's creation or modification. XCOPY copies files created or modified on or after the date specified.

Understanding the Operation of XCOPY

XCOPY is best described as a hybrid of COPY and BACKUP/RESTORE, the disk-backup commands discussed in Chapter 8. Both XCOPY and COPY copy files between disks but XCOPY, unlike COPY, does not copy files to other devices, such as the printer (PRN) or the console (CON). Like BACKUP and RESTORE, XCOPY can copy files selectively and traverse the directory tree to copy files from more than one directory. XCOPY also can make a destination directory when one does not exist.

Like COPY but unlike BACKUP, the files XCOPY copies are directly usable: you cannot use files processed by BACKUP until you have processed them with RESTORE.

Understanding the General Rules of XCOPY

- If a file specifier is omitted in the XCOPY syntax, XCOPY assumes the *.* full wild-card pattern as the file specifier.

- If you include the /D switch, the date specifier must be entered in the format of the system's DATE command or in the format indicated by the latest COUNTRY command.

Cue:
XCOPY /V
performs the
same read-after-
write checking as
SET VERIFY ON.

- The /V switch performs the same read-after-write checking as the SET VERIFY ON global-verify flag.

- To use XCOPY to copy empty source subdirectories, you must specify both the /S and the /E switches.

Using XCOPY Effectively

Cue:
XCOPY can be
used as a quick
hard disk backup
command.

Because XCOPY can control which files should be copied by date or archive attribute, can copy complete subdirectory trees, and can confirm which files should be copied, the command has several ideal uses. One use is to copy files selectively between disks or directories. A second major use is as a hard disk backup command if you want to back up only a few critical files in several subdirectories.

Cue:
XCOPY can be
used to keep the
directories of
more than one
computer
synchronized.

With COPY, your control is limited. With its all-or-nothing approach, COPY copies all files that match the given name. If you use the /P switch with XCOPY, however, you can select all the files that match the source file's name; XCOPY asks you whether to copy each file. You can give a single "larger" file name (a name that selects more files than necessary but covers all the files you may want to copy); then you can select the individual files you really want to copy.

XCOPY is practical to use if you want to make backup copies of less than a disk full of files from several directories. Rather than using BACKUP, you may prefer to use XCOPY /M/S to select files that have changed since the last backup across all subdirectories of the specified directory.

XCOPY copies only files with the archive attribute. When XCOPY successfully copies a file, the /M switch causes XCOPY to turn off the file's archive attribute. Replace the floppy disk with an empty formatted disk and issue the XCOPY command again with the /M/S switches. XCOPY picks up where it left off. Continue this procedure until all files are copied. When the destination disk fills, XCOPY stops. XCOPY, however, cannot handle a file that is too large to fit on one disk. If you need to back up such a file, use BACKUP.

A favorite use of XCOPY is to keep synchronized the contents of the hard disks of two computers. Many people have one computer at work and another at home. If both computers have hard disks, keeping the copies of programs and data files current is a major task. Which files did you change today? Which machine has the more current version?

Removing an Unneeded Directory with RMDIR (RD)

When you need to remove a directory from your directory tree structure, use the RMDIR (or RD) command. (The effect is the same, no matter which name you use.) RMDIR removes directories that are at the end of a path branch of the directory tree. Just as you can create a directory structure with MKDIR, you can remove a directory structure with RMDIR.

Reminder:
RMDIR removes directories that are at the end of a path branch of the directory tree.

Issuing the RMDIR Command

RMDIR and RD are different names for the same command. You can issue the command with either name. The syntax for RMDIR is as follows:

RMDIR *d:path***dir_name**

d: is the optional disk drive holding the disk the command searches for the directory to be removed. If *d:* is omitted from the command line, DOS assumes that the current (logged) disk holds the directory to be removed.

path is the valid, existing path to **dir_name**. If the path specifier is omitted, DOS assumes that **dir_name** is a subdirectory of the current directory of *d:*. If *path* begins with a backslash (\\) character, DOS assumes that the path to the directory name is absolute from the root. If the path specifier does not begin with a backslash, DOS assumes that the path to the directory name is relative from the current directory of *d:*.

dir_name is the name of the directory to be removed. The directory name is required in the command line.

Understanding the Operation of RMDIR

Deleting a subdirectory is similar to deleting a file. Subdirectory entries are special files to DOS. Unlike user files, however, subdirectories may contain user files *and* subdirectory entries. DOS does not "orphan" a subdirectory's files and subordinate subdirectories by simply deleting the subdirectory as it does a user file.

When you issue the RMDIR (RD) command to delete a subdirectory, DOS checks to ensure that the subdirectory is empty. The subdirectory will contain the . and .. file entries, but DOS knows that these two entries are part of the subdirectory bookkeeping function. The presence of only the . and .. files in the directory tells DOS that the directory is empty. DOS also checks to ensure that the current directory is not the directory you are deleting or one of its subordinate directories.

Reminder:
Use the CHKDSK command to check for the presence of hidden files in a directory.

Hidden files that do not appear in a DIR command listing of the directory are considered user files; the directory cannot be removed if it contains hidden files. (*Note:* You can use the ATTRIB command to "unhide" hidden files.) The CHKDSK command will show the presence of hidden files on a disk. A directory that contains even one subdirectory is not an empty directory.

Having determined that the subdirectory to be deleted is empty and is not the current directory, DOS marks the subdirectory's parent-directory entry with a deletion indicator. The deletion indicator tells DOS that the subdirectory is no longer in the file system. A deleted subdirectory entry's indicator in the parent directory tells DOS that the subdirectory entry can be recycled. The deleted subdirectory's allocated space on the disk as tracked in the FAT is then available for DOS reallocation.

Understanding the General Rules of RMDIR

- The directory you remove must be empty.

- A directory affected by a SUBST command cannot be removed.

- Do not remove directories from a drive affected by a JOIN or ASSIGN command.

- The directory to be deleted cannot be the current directory of any disk.

Deleting an Empty Directory with RMDIR

As an example of deleting a directory with RMDIR, assume that drive E of your system includes the \PROLOG\DSWORK\DONE directory, which contains program files that have been checked by their author. The files and the directory are no longer needed, and can be removed. By logging to drive E and changing to the \PROLOG\DSWORK directory, you log to the parent directory of \PROLOG\DSWORK\DONE. From the parent directory of the directory to be deleted, you can issue the RMDIR command with no drive and path specifiers, as follows:

    RMDIR DONE

DOS responds with the following message:

```
Invalid path, not directory,
or directory not empty
```

This message tells you that one of the following situations exists:

1. The path name you gave is not on the disk.

2. The path name you specified names a file, not a directory.

3. The directory you are asking DOS to delete contains files.

To determine which message applies to your situation, use the process of elimination.

By checking the current directory with the CHDIR command, or by looking at the prompt (if you have incorporated a current directory in the PROMPT command), you can verify that the path is valid. By looking at the parent directory and seeing that \DONE is listed as a directory, you can be assured that the directory name you are using really is a directory name, not a file name. Now you know that the path is valid and that the directory is a directory; the remaining possibility is that the directory is not empty. To determine whether the DONE directory contains user files or subdirectories, you can change to that directory by using the following command:

    CHDIR DONE

Then issue the DIR command.

If the directory listing of the DONE directory shows that the directory is not empty, you can erase all files to empty the directory; then verify that it is empty by again issuing the DIR command.

When only the . and .. alias directory entries remain, you can change to the parent directory by using the following shorthand command:

CHDIR..

From DONE's parent directory, you can remove the now empty DONE with the following command:

RMDIR DONE

You have removed the E:\PROLOG\DSWORK\DONE directory.

Taking Advantage of the Hierarchical Directory System

DOS supplies each disk with a root directory. Beyond the root, you can use the directory-management commands to create a directory tree in any architecture you want. You can control the external look of your directory tree while DOS manages the internal bookkeeping tasks of the DOS hierarchical directory system. Still, some planning on your part will help make your directory system design easy to use. The following sections suggest some directory structures that you may want to consider. If you already have your directories arranged, keep these suggestions in mind for the next time you reorganize your hard disk.

Keeping a Clean Root

Because DOS defaults to the root directory of the boot disk, the root is a likely place for you to save some of your files. If you have a floppy-only system, the boot disk may leave little room for additional files and you may normally swap the boot disk for a work disk. If you have a hard disk, consider keeping the root directory as clean as possible. Keep in the root only the few files DOS needs to get started.

If you are using an AUTOEXEC.BAT file, it must reside in the root directory of the boot disk. The same rule applies to the CONFIG.SYS file, if you include one. If the disk is bootable, the hidden DOS system files also are located in the root, but the FORMAT command puts them there.

COMMAND.COM is normally in the root by virtue of the FORMAT command's /S switch. But you do not have to leave COMMAND.COM in the root. You can move COMMAND.COM to another directory (\DOS, for example), provided that you first make an entry in the CONFIG.SYS file. In your CONFIG.SYS file, add the following line:

```
SHELL=C:\DOS\COMMAND.COM C:\DOS /P
```

When DOS boots, the operating system loads COMMAND.COM, the command processor, from the C:\DOS directory. Be sure not to misspell any parts of the full path name. DOS locks up at boot time if the assignment to SHELL is a nonexistent file. Clearly, a working copy of DOS on a floppy makes any SHELL error (or any other hard disk boot failure) easier to recover from. After you put this line in CONFIG.SYS, do not reboot until you have copied COMMAND.COM to \DOS. You now are free to delete COMMAND.COM from the root directory of drive C.

Caution:
DOS will lock up at boot time if you name a nonexistent file in the SHELL directive.

Some users keep *device drivers*, the programs specific to the operation of input/output devices, in the root directory. If you have these types of files in your root directory, you can move them. The next section discusses driver files.

Finding some batch files in a root directory is not uncommon. Batch files are ideal for relocation from the root. You can put these files in another directory and use the PATH command to lead DOS to them. The next section also discusses a home for batch files.

Including a Directory To Store DOS Programs

The DOS external commands and other DOS programs, such as EDLIN and DEBUG, have one important element in common: these programs are all files that directly relate to the functions of DOS. Including a directory to hold these programs and their associated files is a good idea. The name for this DOS directory can be \DOS; as the name implies, the \DOS directory is a subdirectory of the root. Some users follow the UNIX operating system's convention of keeping the utility commands in a directory called \BIN. Either name works from an organizational standpoint.

Cue:
Include a separate directory for the purpose of storing the DOS program files and associated programs.

Note: The DOS 5.0 installation program, Setup, by default places your DOS files in the \DOS directory of your hard disk.

When you issue a PATH command on the command line or in an AUTOEXEC.BAT file, position the \DOS entry to immediately follow the root entry. Don't forget to include the drive specifier with each alternative search path in the PATH command line. Because all external DOS commands are located in the second alternative search path, you should get a good response when you are working in DOS.

Cue:
Keep your driver
programs
in a separate
directory.

Many users prefer to create a subdirectory called \DOS\DRIVERS and use it to store the drivers included with DOS (the files with SYS extensions) and drivers included with applications programs or hardware. Because drivers are loaded during the processing of CONFIG.SYS, you can place in the CONFIG.SYS file the full path name to the drivers you need, thus eliminating the need to include a search path to the drivers with PATH. An example of a CONFIG.SYS line follows:

```
DEVICE=\DOS\DRIVERS\MOUSE.SYS
```

If you separate the drivers from the DOS commands, listings from the TREE command indicate more clearly the function of each subdirectory's file group in the \DOS tree branch.

If the PATH command includes an alternative search path for utility batch files, you can execute these files from any point in the directory tree.

Ensuring Uniform Directories for Applications Programs

Many of today's applications programs use subdirectories to store sample files, tutorials, auxiliary utilities, and your data for the applications. Although most of these programs include default directory names used when you install the software, most programs also enable you to substitute names you choose for the subdirectories instead of using the default names. In most cases, you can let the package install with the default names for directories. In one situation, however, you may not want to use the default names. If you have an older version of the package and want to keep that older version, you may want to control the names of the package's directories.

If you need to keep operating an older version of a software package (to maintain older data or program files, for example), you invite disaster by allowing the defaults to decide where the program and associated files will load. The new version may copy files with the same names as old files into the default directories, because the new version's default directories and your old directories have the same names.

Carefully read the installation information for a package before you install the software. You will not be happy if you "return" your way through the installation default directories and find that you cannot start your old version of dBASE or 1-2-3. The old version can be overwritten in installation. Pick a new set of directory names for the new package, such as \DB4 for dBASE IV or \123R3 for Lotus 1-2-3 Release 3. The installation process will not alter the contents of the earlier versions' directories.

If you have an applications package that does not create directories during installation, you should think about how you want to structure your own directories for the package and its data. WordStar Release 4, for example, can be copied to a directory named \WS4. The directory or directories for your document files should be subordinate to the \WS4 directory so that all of WordStar's associated files will form a branch of the directory tree instead of being spread across branches of a directory tree. You can create a \WS4\MEMOS directory for your memo documents and a \WS4\FORMS for office-form master documents.

Keeping associated files in the same branch of the directory tree also makes the job of backing up files easier. The command **BACKUP /S** backs up all files from the named directory and its subdirectories. You can make convenient partial interim backups of one branch of the directory tree if all associated files you want to back up are in that branch.

Using a Temporary Directory

On many occasions, a temporary directory is handy for holding files you are readying for a final disposition. An example is the use of a temporary directory for recovering from an errant COPY command that deposited files in the wrong directory. You can create a directory called \TEMP to act as a temporary storage location for such files. A single-floppy-disk system is not a good system on which to copy floppy disks. The drive gets the job done, but the COPY command, using the same drive for the source and the target, asks for many disk swaps. You can use the DISKCOPY command, which may require fewer swaps, but any fragmentation of the original disk is mirrored on the copy.

A simple and speedy way to make several copies of an original is to copy the source files to the \TEMP directory and then copy the files from the \TEMP directory to the destination floppy in the sole floppy drive. The process reduces disk swapping, and the copies are finished faster because of the hard disk's extra speed. When the copies are finished, you can erase the contents of \TEMP so that it is ready to be used again. Watch out for other programs, such as Windows, that require a temporary directory. Check your AUTOEXEC.BAT file for a `SET TEMP=` statement.

Keeping Files in \KEEP

Sometimes a file is like a favorite old shirt. You just aren't sure that you want to get rid of it. You leave it in a subdirectory like an old shirt in the corner of your closet. You may need it some day, but then again, you may not. In either case, you may be too distracted by other issues to make a decision about what to do with this file when you stumble across it yet another time. You will change directories and forget about the file—until you're short on disk space. Then you will dig through the dark corners of your subdirectory closets, looking for a file or two to discard. And at "disk-space-running-out" time, feeling less equipped than ever before to make a decision about the file's importance, you decide to erase the old file.

If this scenario seems familiar, you may want to create a \KEEP directory. When you find a file that has questionable future use, and you don't want to have to decide at the moment what to do with the file, copy it to \KEEP. As always, make sure that the file will not overwrite another file with the same name. You should always give your files descriptive names and avoid generic names like TEMP and SAVE. Remember that you can always rename files when you use COPY.

After copying the file to \KEEP, erase the copy of the file from the subdirectory in which you found it. At the end of a week, \KEEP may hold several files.

At this point, you may not have saved any disk space, but you have done some housecleaning in a few directories. Now comes the hard part. Before \KEEP contains more bytes of files than one floppy disk can hold, sit down and decide which files stay and which go. You probably will copy some files back to their original directories. Some you will erase, and others you will copy to a "just-in-case" floppy disk as archive copies. Before you store the floppy, issue the following command:

DIR *d:*/W **>PRN**

d: is the name of your floppy disk. This command with the /W switch sends a wide directory report to your printer. Put the printed copy in the envelope with the disk, for reference. Now, with the \KEEP "keepers" safely stored on a floppy disk, you can erase the contents of \KEEP. Using this method regularly helps you develop a better sense of which files are important; you can erase those that are not important. Floppy disks are so inexpensive that the cost of a year's worth of \KEEP files on floppies is offset the first time a \KEEP floppy contains a file you spent hours creating.

Chapter Summary

This chapter covers the commands used to manage the hierarchical directory structure. The hierarchical directory system is an important feature of DOS. Computing is more productive when you understand and manage your directory tree effectively.

The following are key points in this chapter:

- DOS manages the directory structure internally; you manage the directory structure externally with commands.

- All DOS disks have a root directory.

- The MKDIR (MD) command makes new subdirectories.

- The CHDIR (CD) command changes the default (working) directory.

- Use the PATH command to have DOS search for program and batch files.

- Use the APPEND command to have DOS search for data files.

- The XCOPY command can make new subdirectories while copying.

- The TREE command reports the structure of your directory tree.

- The RMDIR command removes empty directories.

- Directories for applications software packages should be uniform in structure.

- Using a \TEMP directory can simplify the process of copying files on a single floppy drive system.

- Using a \KEEP directory as part of a file's housekeeping routine can reduce clutter in directories.

You are more likely to use the directory-level commands presented in this chapter than you are to use the disk-level commands presented in Chapter 6. The directory-level commands lend themselves to practice and experimentation. You can use your existing directory layout to try variations of these commands. The concept of the path is important to understanding the disk-level commands presented in the next chapter. You may want to refer to this chapter from time to time as you work with the commands that take directory parameters.

8

Managing Your Files

Chapter 6 examines the commands you use to manage your PC at the disk level. Chapter 7 presents a discussion of the DOS hierarchical file system and the commands that manage the file system's directories. This chapter advances the disk and directory theme of the preceding two chapters to managing files. You probably spend more time in DOS activities that manage files than you do in all other DOS activities combined.

File-management commands are fundamental to even the most primitive use of a PC. Most elementary-level texts tutor DOS beginners in the use of file-level commands in early chapters. You probably learned the basics of copying, deleting, and renaming files before you learned about directories and partition tables. Now that you have gained some DOS experience, you can take the time to review the fundamentals of the file-management commands and to expand your understanding of files and their management.

This chapter leads off with a review of files, from the DOS point of view and from your point of view. The chapter then focuses on the commands used in file management. The commands covered in this chapter include the following:

- ATTRIB
- RENAME (REN)
- ERASE (DEL)
- UNDELETE
- TYPE
- COMP and FC

275

- COPY
- VERIFY
- BACKUP
- RESTORE

Reviewing the Concept of Files

A file is the smallest unit of disk-based information that you can manage without special tools. Every file has a name; DOS uses the file name to identify the information that the file contains. As a user, you view a file as a single named group of information. As a disk operating system, DOS views a file as a collection of allocated clusters that are accessible through a directory entry and the file allocation table. As a user, you concentrate on creating and using files as an extension of your applications programs. As a disk operating system, DOS concentrates on providing a uniform set of file-level services to applications programs and to DOS commands.

Reminder:
The DOS operating system occupies the middle of the layered computer, between the innermost layer of physical hardware and the outermost layer of applications programs.

The innermost layer of the computer is comprised of physical hardware; the outermost layer is comprised of applications programs. DOS, with its file services and commands, falls in the middle of this layered computer. When you use DOS commands to manage files, you do not need to know how the inner layers of DOS support those commands. Yet, the details of these inner workings manage to come to the surface in the form of rules and syntax. The rules governing DOS file names, for example, are mandated by the way DOS lays out its directories and by the way COMMAND.COM reads the commands from the keyboard. Rules are easier to understand and remember when you understand the underlying logic. The following sections explain file rules as well as the underlying logic of those rules.

Selecting File Names

Reminder:
Every file created by DOS is given a name that is placed in one of the directories.

DOS ensures that every one of your files has a name. In fact, DOS provides no method of putting file data on a disk without a file name. When a file is created, either by your applications software or a DOS file-service routine, DOS places the name of a file in one of its directories.

DOS provides room in a directory entry for eight characters of a file-name prefix and three characters of a file-name suffix. The file-name prefix is what you think of as the root file name; the suffix is the file-name extension or simply extension. When you include a file name in a command, you place a period between the file name and extension. In the directory, DOS does not store the period character. DOS separates the file name from the extension internally by knowing the position of the extension in the directory field.

The designers might have written DOS so that a file name consisted of seven characters of file name and four characters of extension—or nine characters of file name and two characters of extension. The UNIX operating system, for example, does not treat extensions differently from the rest of the file name; extension and file name can be any length, as long as the total is not more than 14 characters. The OS/2 operating system allows file names that can include dozens of characters. DOS, however, allows up to eight characters of file name and up to three characters of extension because a DOS directory can accommodate those number limits. DOS uses the file-naming convention of the once-dominant CP/M operating system. DOS designers felt that staying with the CP/M file-name convention enabled an easier transition from CP/M computers to DOS computers.

Recall that characters are the ASCII-code representations of a byte of data. The name field of a directory entry is 11 bytes long (8 for file name plus 3 for extension). DOS accepts for file names most characters that you use for "everyday" names. You can use in file names the upper- and lowercase letters *a* through *z*; DOS automatically stores them in uppercase format in a directory entry. The numeric characters 0-9 can be used as well as the alternate graphics characters of a PC's keyboard. (The alternate characters, ASCII values 128-255, are produced by holding down the Alt key while pressing the number keys on the numeric keypad for the desired ASCII value.) Also, many punctuation characters are allowed in file names.

Reminder:
DOS stores all alphabetic letters in uppercase format in the directory entry.

A DOS file name *must* have the following:

- A root name of one to eight characters. Also, you can add an optional extension of one to three characters.

- A period between the root name and the extension, if you use an extension.

The following characters are *allowed* in a file name:

- The letters A to Z. (Lowercase letters are transformed automatically to uppercase.)

- The numbers 0 to 9.

- The following special characters and punctuation symbols:

  $ # & @ ! & ( ) - { } ' _ ~ ^

The following characters are *not allowed* in a file name:

- Any control character, including Escape (27d or 1Bh) and Delete (127d or 7Fh).

- The space character.

- The following special characters and punctuation symbols:

  + = / [ ] " : ; , ? * \ < > |

  If an illegal character is found in a file name, DOS usually stops at the character preceding the illegal one and uses the legal part of the name. (Some exceptions are noted in this chapter.)

- A device name can be part of a root name but cannot be the entire root name. For example, CONT.DAT or AUXI.TXT are acceptable; CON.DAT or AUX.TXT are not.

- Each file name in a directory must be unique.

- A drive name and a path name usually precede a file name. (Path names are discussed in Chapter 7.)

Avoiding Reserved Names

Caution:
Avoid using file names that are reserved for DOS devices.

DOS reserves names for its built-in character devices. You recall from Chapter 4 that DOS can treat some devices in a PC in a high-level way by accepting their names as input or output parameters in a command line. Before DOS looks for a file that uses the file name parameters from a command line, DOS checks whether the name is a device name. Table 8.1 lists the DOS character device names and their purposes.

Table 8.1
DOS Device Names

Device Name	Purpose
COMx or AUX	Identifies the serial communication port(s)
LPTx or PRN	Identifies the parallel printer port(s)
CON	Identifies the screen and keyboard
NUL	Identifies the "throw away" or "do nothing" device

Reminder:
Use a device name only as a device parameter in a command.

If you try to make DOS use one of these device names as a file name, you may be disappointed with the outcome of your command. Even if you add an extension, DOS intercepts the device name and tries to use the device—not the file that you intend—to complete the command. The rule on the reserved device names of DOS is simple: use a device name *only* as a device parameter in a command. Never expect to write a disk file with a root file name that also is a device name.

Observing File-Naming Conventions

A convention is an informal rule not explicitly enforced. DOS file names follow a certain convention. Although you can use any file name that passes character rules and device-name rules, you want to observe file-name conventions when possible. You can, for example, name a memo file and use a BAT extension; DOS does not know that you are not saving a conventional batch file. As long as you do not try to execute the memo as a batch file, DOS is happy. If you try to execute the memo file, however, DOS sees the BAT extension and tries to execute the file as a BAT. Of course, the memo cannot be executed.

You also can name an EXE file with a COM extension. Although both file types are executable, EXE and COM files have internal differences unique to each file type. DOS does not interpret the extension's name to mean that the file is an EXE or COM file. DOS inspects a key part of the file before deciding how to load and execute the program file. If you name a spreadsheet file as an EXE or COM file, for example, DOS is not fooled into trying to execute a nonprogram file.

Many software manufacturers use certain extensions for special files in their applications programs. To avoid confusion as to the contents of a file, avoid using certain extensions, especially if they are used by software you use. For example, dBASE III uses the DBF extension for some of its files; if you use dBASE III, you should not use DBF as an extension on any other type of file. Table 8.2 lists conventional file-name extensions and their meanings.

Reminder:
Avoid giving your file names extensions used by DOS programs and other applications programs.

Table 8.2
Common File-Name Extensions

Extension	Common Use
ARC	Archive (compressed file)
ASC	ASCII text file
ASM	Assembler source file
BAK	Backup file
BAS	BASIC program file
BAT	Batch file
BIN	Binary program file
C	C source file

continues

Table 8.2 *(continued)*

Extension	Common Use
CBL	COBOL source file
CFG	Program configuration information
CNF	Program configuration information
CHP	Chapter file (Ventura Publisher)
COM	Command (program) file
CPI	Code page information file (DOS)
CPP	C++ source file
DAT	Data file
DBF	Database file (dBASE III)
DCT	Dictionary file
DEV	Program device driver file
DIF	Data Interchange Format file
DOC	Document (word processing) file
DRV	Program device driver file
DTA	Data file
EXE	Executable program file
FNT	Font file
HLP	Help file
IDX	Index file (Q&A)
IMG	GEM image (graphics) file
INI	Initialization file
KEY	Keyboard macro file (ProKey)
LET	Letter
LST	Listing of a program (in a file)
LIB	Program library file
MAC	Keyboard macro file (Superkey)
MAP	Linker map file

Extension	Common Use
MEU	Menu file (DOS visual shell and SELECT)
MOS	Mouse drive file (DOS visual shell)
MSG	Program message file
NDX	An index file (dBASE III)
OBJ	Intermediate object code (program) file
OLD	Alternative extension for a backup file
OVL	Program overlay file
OVR	Program overlay file
PAK	Packed (archive) file
PAS	Pascal source file
PCX	A picture file for PC Paintbrush
PIF	Program Information File (TopView/Windows)
PRO	Profile configuration file (DOS GRAPHICS)
PRN	Program listing for printing
PS	PostScript program file
RFT	Revisable Form Text (Document Content Architecture)
SAV	Alternative extension for a backup file
SYS	System or device driver file
STY	Style sheet (Ventura Publisher)
TIF	A picture file in tag image format
TMP	Temporary file
TST	Test file
TXT	Text file
$xx	Temporary or incorrectly stored file
WK1	Worksheet file (1-2-3, Release 2)
WK3	Worksheet file (1-2-3, Release 3)
WKQ	Quattro spreadsheet file
WKS	Alternative extension for a worksheet file

Finding the End of a File

Reminder:
A byte can be classified into two general types: ASCII and binary.

Knowing how DOS finds the end of a file may seem like an unnecessary technical detail, but this knowledge can help you understand the concept of copying from devices and copying from files. As discussed in Chapter 2, DOS does not impose any form on the contents of a file. To DOS, a file is simply a stream of bytes. Remember that a byte can represent more than one kind of value. A byte can be encoded to represent a number, a computer instruction, a table, or even an ASCII character. Usually, computer professionals divide the representation categories of a byte into two general types: ASCII and binary.

An ASCII byte contains a bit code in its 8 bits that represents one of 256 possible ASCII characters. Files that are composed of bytes, all of which are ASCII representations, are called ASCII text files. Not all ASCII codes, however, represent readable text characters, such as letters, numbers, and punctuation symbols.

Some ASCII characters represent device-control codes, which a device detects and uses to control its operation. Ctrl-S is such a control code; a device that detects Ctrl-S in a character stream stops sending its stream of characters. You use Ctrl-S to stop displayed information from scrolling off the screen. When the control characters are not being used for controlling a device, they can represent special characters on-screen, such as a smiling face or musical notes. Other ASCII representations make special characters on your screen, but have no device-control representations.

Reminder:
ASCII text is not always readable when displayed by the TYPE command.

ASCII text is not always readable on your PC monitor. To DOS, a file is a stream of bytes. The TYPE command makes the assumption that the bytes are ASCII representations.

When the most significant bit (the one with the highest value) in a ASCII byte is set (has a value of 1), the 128 distinct combinations of the lower 7 bits can represent special graphic-like characters. Some word processors set the eighth bit of a byte to transform a printable character into a special character. The word processor does not print the special character as a special character, but rather uses the eighth bit internally to indicate that the special character is the final character of a word or paragraph. When the character is printed, the eighth bit is ignored, and the printable character represented by the remaining 7 bits is printed.

Cue:
In ASCII mode, the ^Z character represents the end of the file.

Programs and commands like COPY can instruct DOS to internally work with input and output bytes in an ASCII mode. In ASCII mode, DOS recognizes one ASCII control character—the ^Z—as meaning "the end of the file." Applications programs that create ASCII text files send a stream of characters to DOS for DOS's file service. The applications place a Ctrl-Z in their character-output stream to indicate that the end of the characters that make up the file is reached. In ASCII operations, DOS uses the Ctrl-Z character as a signal to close the file and update the file's directory entry.

If an application uses these file services in a non-ASCII or binary mode, the application must explicitly tell DOS to close the new file even if the application sends DOS a Ctrl-Z. The application can send additional bytes of file data to DOS following a Ctrl-Z character. The application is not obligated to place the Ctrl-Z at the end of the physical file (the point in the data stream where DOS is told to close the file). In fact, between the Ctrl-Z and the end of the physical file, the application can pad several hundred bytes with filler values. In the binary mode, DOS does not care when it encounters a Ctrl-Z character.

Most DOS file commands, by default, deal with files in binary instead of ASCII mode to avoid a case of mistaken identity. Remember that numeric values, instructions, and other data are alternative representations of the value of a byte. The chances are good that a byte from a numeric value or instruction has the same value of the Ctrl-Z in its ASCII representation. A binary file might contain several bytes that represent an ASCII Ctrl-Z, but are actually data or instructions in binary representation. In ASCII mode, DOS can mistake these values as the end-of-file marker and prematurely close the file. The result of this mistaken identity is the loss of file data.

Cue:
Most DOS file commands deal with files in a binary mode instead of an ASCII mode to avoid a case of mistaken identity.

Understanding Devices and the End-of-File Marker

Recall from Chapter 4 that DOS's built-in character devices can be used as source and destination parameters in command lines. When an input device, such as CON, is used for direct or redirected input in a command, DOS needs some way to know when the input character stream is finished and the file should be closed. The device drivers for the built-in devices of DOS work in ASCII mode; they use the Ctrl-Z character as the end-of-file indicator when the devices are used as parameters in DOS commands.

The use of the COPY command with the CON keyboard device is a good example of the need for an end-of-file marker. Although the COPY command is covered in a following section of this chapter, a brief example here can help you see the role of ^Z. When you issue the command **COPY CON MYFILE.TXT**, DOS uses the console device, CON, as the source file and expects to copy ASCII characters from keystrokes entered in the target file. As you press the characters that you want included in the new MYTEXT.TXT file, DOS buffers the characters internally.

At some point, you finish providing characters for the new file and want to issue more DOS commands. Unless you signal DOS that you are finished with the COPY command, DOS continues to fill the internal buffer with every letter that you type. Without pressing a Ctrl-Z (or F6, which sends Ctrl-Z and then Enter), you remain in the COPY command. When you press Ctrl-Z and then Enter, DOS creates the new file's directory entry and copies your keystrokes out of its internal buffer to the file. DOS's final step is to close the file and update the directory for the time, date, and file size entries.

Keep the topics introduced in these first few sections in mind when you are working with files in DOS. Knowing what DOS expects in a file name is important. Additionally, knowing how some DOS commands work with Ctrl-Z and ASCII is necessary for understanding the more advanced commands.

Manipulating File Attributes by Using ATTRIB

Cue:

The external command ATTRIB enables you to manipulate the file's read/write and archive attributes.

Remember that each directory entry provides some fields to record a file's attributes. The external command ATTRIB enables you to manipulate the file's read/write and archive attributes. Both of these attributes are given default values by DOS when the file is added to the directory.

Issuing the ATTRIB Command

You can issue the ATTRIB command in three basic ways.

1. Use the following syntax form to receive a screen report of a file's current attribute values:

   ATTRIB *d:path***filename.ext**/*S*

2. Use the following syntax form to set (turn on) a file's attribute(s):

   ATTRIB +*R* +*A* +*S* +*H d:path***filename.ext**/*S*

3. Use the following syntax form to reset (turn off) a file's attribute(s):

   ATTRIB –*R* –*A* –*S* –*H d:path***filename.ext**/*S*

d: is the optional drive that holds the disk that contains the selected files, and path\ is the optional directory path that contains the selected files.

filename.ext, the selected file specifier, can contain wild cards. A file name must be specified.

The optional */S* switch (Version 3.3 and subsequent versions only) instructs ATTRIB to additionally process files that match the file specifier in all subdirectories of the path directory.

The options beginning with a + instruct ATTRIB to set (add) the read-only and archive attributes respectively.

The options beginning with a – instruct ATTRIB to reset (clear) the read-only and archive attributes respectively.

The R, A, S, and H attributes can be specified individually or together in the command line. The same command can turn on some attributes while turning off others.

If no attribute specifiers are included in the command line, the ATTRIB command produces a screen report showing the attribute status of desired files.

Understanding the Operation of ATTRIB

DOS provides an attribute in the directory entry of each file to indicate the archive status of the file. By DOS's action, each file has its archive attribute turned on when the file is stored in the directory. Whenever DOS writes data to a file or shortens (truncates) a file, DOS turns on the archive attribute. DOS Version 3.2 and subsequent versions enable you to use the ATTRIB command to manipulate the archive attribute. If your version of ATTRIB manipulates archive attributes, you can use this command on files created with earlier versions of DOS.

Establishing Read-Only Files

The read/write attribute controls the capability of DOS to overwrite or erase a file. When DOS (or an application through DOS) adds a file to a directory, the read/write attributes are established so that the file can be overwritten or erased. The default value of the read/write attribute enables DOS commands to perform destructive operations on the file. If you

Cue:
The read/write attribute controls the capability of DOS to overwrite or erase a file.

change the read/write attribute of a file to make the file "read-only," the DOS commands that normally overwrite or erase files cannot affect the read-only file.

After you use the ATTRIB command to mark a file as read-only, you can use the ATTRIB command again to mark the file as read/write. The file is then subject to DOS commands that can overwrite or erase the file.

Marking a file as read-only protects the file in a similar way to the manner in which write-protecting a disk protects the contents of a disk. You can use the ATTRIB command effectively to write-protect important files and to ensure that an errant COPY or ERASE command does not destroy the marked files.

Displaying Archive Attributes

ATTRIB is one of the DOS commands that can report information. ATTRIB reports the current attributes of a file when you issue the command without an attribute specifier. The resulting file list shows the read/write and archive attribute settings of specified files. When you issue ATTRIB in a report syntax, all attributes of reported files remain unchanged.

The attribute-report syntax of ATTRIB is useful for determining which files are processed or which files have their attributes modified by a BACKUP, RESTORE, XCOPY, or ATTRIB command. You should view a reported list of file attributes before you issue a command that can change those attributes.

Understanding the General Rules of ATTRIB

- The A attribute can be modified with DOS Version 3.2 and more recent versions.

- The H and S attributes can be modified in DOS 5 only.

- The /S switch is available with DOS Versions 3.3 and later.

- You must include the A, H, S, or R attribute specifier to modify a file's existing attributes with the ATTRIB command.

- The ATTRIB command does not affect a file's data. ATTRIB affects only a file's specified attributes.

- You must provide a file specifier, but drive and path specifiers can be omitted. The current values of drive and path are used by default if either specifier is omitted from the command.

- If a file has the system or hidden attribute set, you must clear those attributes before you can change the read-only or archive attribute.

- The /S switch enables ATTRIB to process all subordinate directories in addition to the specified (or default) directory.

- You can mix the set (+) and reset (−) attribute indicators in the same command.

Using Archive Attributes with XCOPY, BACKUP, and RESTORE

An important benefit of archive attributes is their capability to tell XCOPY, BACKUP, and RESTORE that a file should be processed. The XCOPY command covered in Chapter 7 and the BACKUP and RESTORE commands covered in a following section of this chapter can optionally use the archive attribute of a file to select files for inclusion in their operation. Both XCOPY and BACKUP can clear the archive attribute of a file when the commands process a file. (For details of how each command works, see the appropriate chapter or the command reference.)

Cue:
The archive attributes work with the XCOPY, BACKUP, and RESTORE commands to determine whether a file can be processed.

XCOPY and BACKUP both accept the /M switch, which means "operate on *modified* files." In other words, either command issued with the /M switch limits the source files to those files that have the archive attributes set (turned on). Remember that DOS turns on the archive attribute of a file when the file is created or modified.

You can use XCOPY and BACKUP with the /M switch to copy or back up changed files. You do not need to check directory dates or remember your work activities to determine the files that you should place in another directory or disk for safekeeping. The archive attribute and the /M switch make the decision for you. After the files are processed by using the /M switch, the archive attributes of the source files are reset (turned off).

Reminder:
You can use XCOPY and BACKUP with the /M switch to copy or back up changed files.

You might use XCOPY several times between backups. When **XCOPY /M** resets (turns off) the archive attributes of the files copied, **BACKUP /M** cannot find those files. Your next use of BACKUP might miss files that changed since the last backup. To avoid this possibly confusing situation, you can use **XCOPY /A**, which also copies files whose archive attribute is set. **XCOPY /A**, however, does not reset the archive attributes of the files copied. A subsequent **BACKUP /M** command finds and includes the files although **XCOPY /A** processed the same files first.

RESTORE uses the /M switch to selectively restore files from a backup set by examining the archive attribute of the target file. If the archive attribute is set, RESTORE with /M restores the file from the backup. If the archive attribute is not set, **RESTORE /M** will not restore the file from the backup. The RESTORE command is discussed in detail in a following section of this chapter.

You directly can manipulate the archive attribute of a file with the ATTRIB command. In modifying a file's archive attribute, you can override the default setting of the file's archive attribute. Even if XCOPY or BACKUP clears a file's archive attribute, ATTRIB can set the attribute manually.

In fact, a useful way to approach the BACKUP and XCOPY commands is to select files that you want to include in their operation through the changing of the file's attributes. To include all MEM files in the \MEMO subdirectory in an XCOPY /M operation, you first turn off the archive attribute for all files in the \MEMO directory. Then turn on all archive attributes for the MEM files in the \MEMO directory. Use the following commands:

ATTRIB –A \MEMO*.*

ATTRIB +A \MEMO*.MEM

XCOPY /M copies only the files with the MEM extension.

Using ATTRIB To Write-Protect Applications Program Files

Cue:
You can use the ATTRIB command to "write-protect" certain files.

If you created a \DOS directory for your DOS external program files, you can use the ATTRIB command to "write-protect" with one command the external command files. Because you probably don't want to erase an external command from the \DOS directory, you can issue the following command:

ATTRIB +R C:\DOS*.*

This command assumes that the default search path can locate the external ATTRIB command. Because the disk and path specifiers are included in the command, you can issue this command from any disk or directory.

The *.* wild-card file specifier tells ATTRIB to process all files in C:\DOS. The +R attribute tells ATTRIB to mark all processed files as read-only. All files in C:\DOS are bypassed in an ERASE or COPY command that specifies the files. If you try to erase files from the \DOS directory, the following message appears:

```
Access Denied
```

To enable a COPY or ERASE command to modify or erase a read-only file, you can issue the ATTRIB command by using the file's name and the –R attribute specifier. To make the RECOVER.EXE command erasable after the previous command, you can log to C:\DOS and issue the following command:

ATTRIB –R RECOVER.EXE

You can now erase or overwrite the RECOVER.EXE file in C:\DOS.

Many applications programs, such as dBASE IV, copy the main program and support files to a specific directory during the installation process. These core package files are seldom modified after installation. An applications program's core files are ideal candidates for read-only protection.

Cue:
Use the ATTRIB command to write-protect the core files of your applications programs.

To set the read-only attributes of all dBASE IV core package files after you install the package, first log to the dBASE IV directory or the directory in which your files are stored. Then issue the following command:

ATTRIB +R *.*

The same basic command can change any directory's files to read-only. Be sure that you are in your intended directory.

When the command is executed, the files in the \DBASE directory are protected. You can verify that the read-only attribute is set by issuing the ATTRIB command for an extension that shows a sampling of the files. For dBASE, the OVL files are a good choice. From any directory on drive C, you can issue the following command:

ATTRIB \DBASE*.OVL

You then see the following screen report:

```
A    R   C:\DBASE\DBSETUP.OVL
A    R   C:\DBASE\DBASE3.OVL
A    R   C:\DBASE\DBASE6.OVL
A    R   C:\DBASE\DBASE1.OVL
A    R   C:\DBASE\DBASE2.OVL
A    R   C:\DBASE\DBASE5.OVL
A    R   C:\DBASE\DBASE4.OVL
A    R   C:\DBASE\PROTECT.OVL
A    R   C:\DBASE\RUNTIME1.OVL
A    R   C:\DBASE\RUNTIME3.OVL
```

```
A     R   C:\DBASE\RUNTIME2.OVL
A     R   C:\DBASE\RPROTECT.OVL
A     R   C:\DBASE\RUNTIME4.OVL
```

Notice that each file is listed with its full path name and that both the archive and read-only indicators are shown for all files. If either reported attribute is not set (is cleared), that attribute will not be indicated beside the file name.

> *Note:* Many applications programs maintain one or more configuration files whose contents may change as you operate the program. Be careful not to write-protect such a configuration file or your program may not work properly.

Using ATTRIB with the XCOPY Command

The archive attributes of the files in a directory can be useful when you use XCOPY to maintain a current set of files on a floppy disk. In any directory in which data files or program source files are changed frequently, you can use XCOPY to copy only the changed files to a floppy disk. Of course, you must have enough capacity on the disk to hold all the files XCOPY can copy.

This example illustrates the use of the archive attribute in XCOPY. Suppose that you installed a PROLOG programming language package on your hard disk. A directory named \PROLOG\PROGRAMS holds the PRO program source text files and some miscellaneous files. Suppose that you want to keep a current version of all the PRO source files on a floppy disk. Before you leave work, you copy to the disk PRO files that change in the course of a day. You do not alter all the source files each day, so you want to copy only the files that changed during the day. When you first decide to make a daily copy, you can look at the archive attributes of all the \PROLOG\PROGRAMS files by using the following command:

ATTRIB \PROLOG\PROGRAMS*.*

DOS reports the files with a listing similar to the following:

```
A          C:\PROLOG\PROGRAMS\BROWSER.PRO
A          C:\PROLOG\PROGRAMS\DBATEST.PRO
A          C:\PROLOG\PROGRAMS\DIFF.HLP
A          C:\PROLOG\PROGRAMS\DIFF.PRO
```

```
A        C:\PROLOG\PROGRAMS\DUMPDBA.PRO
A        C:\PROLOG\PROGRAMS\D_CURVE.PRO
A        C:\PROLOG\PROGRAMS\FWGC.PRO
A        C:\PROLOG\PROGRAMS\GENI.GNI
A        C:\PROLOG\PROGRAMS\GENI.HLP
A        C:\PROLOG\PROGRAMS\GENI.PRO
A        C:\PROLOG\PROGRAMS\GEOBASE.DBA
```

As you see, all files in the directory have their archive attribute set. To copy only the PRO files with their archive attributes set (in this instance, all PRO files) to the floppy disk in drive A, type the following command:

XCOPY \PROLOG\PROGRAMS*.PRO A: /M

The XCOPY command copies the PRO files to the disk in drive A and resets the archive attribute of each file as the file is copied. When XCOPY completes the copy process, you can verify that the source files with PRO extensions in \PROLOG\PROGRAMS have their archive attributes reset and that all other files' archive attributes are unchanged. You then type the following command:

ATTRIB \PROLOG\PROGRAMS*.*

DOS reports with the following listing:

```
         C:\PROLOG\PROGRAMS\BROWSER.PRO
         C:\PROLOG\PROGRAMS\DBATEST.PRO
A        C:\PROLOG\PROGRAMS\DIFF.HLP
         C:\PROLOG\PROGRAMS\DIFF.PRO
         C:\PROLOG\PROGRAMS\DUMPDBA.PRO
         C:\PROLOG\PROGRAMS\D_CURVE.PRO
         C:\PROLOG\PROGRAMS\FWGC.PRO
A        C:\PROLOG\PROGRAMS\GENI.GNI
A        C:\PROLOG\PROGRAMS\GENI.HLP
         C:\PROLOG\PROGRAMS\GENI.PRO
A        C:\PROLOG\PROGRAMS\GEOBASE.DBA
```

Notice that only the PRO extension files have their archive attributes reset. The other files' attributes remain unchanged because XCOPY did not process the non-PRO files.

During the day, suppose that you use the EDLIN text editor to edit the BROWSER.PRO file. When DOS updates the file's contents, DOS updates the archive attribute in the file's directory entry by turning the attribute back on. You can confirm that the file's archive attribute was set by issuing the following command:

ATTRIB \PROLOG\PROGRAMS\BROWSER.PRO

DOS reports with the following message:

```
A        C:\PROLOG\PROGRAMS\BROWSER.PRO
```

The archive attribute is set because the file was modified by EDLIN. At the end of the day, type the following daily copy command that you established:

XCOPY \PROLOG\PROGRAMS*.PRO A:/M

As the XCOPY command is executed, you see the following:

```
Reading source file(s). . .
BROWSER.PRO
        1 File(s) copied
```

Of all the PRO extension files in the directory, only BROWSER.PRO was processed by the XCOPY command.

Making COMMAND.COM Read-Only by Using ATTRIB

COMMAND.COM is an important program file. To protect the file against accidental erasure or overwriting, you can make COMMAND.COM read-only. Assume that COMMAND.COM is in your root directory, and then issue the following command:

ATTRIB +R \COMMAND.COM

COMMAND.COM is now a read-only file. To verify that the file has its read-only attribute set, issue the following command:

ATTRIB \COMMAND.COM

DOS responds with the following message:

```
R  C:\COMMAND.COM
```

If you then issue the ERASE command with COMMAND.COM as the file specifier, DOS reports with the following message:

```
Access Denied
```

DOS does not erase the file. The same type of command can make another file read-only. By using wild cards in the file specifier, you can make groups of files read-only. To return a file's read-only status back to read-write, you reverse the process. In the case of COMMAND.COM, you issue the following command:

ATTRIB –R \COMMAND.COM

The file can now be erased or overwritten.

Changing File Names with RENAME (REN)

Cue:
The RENAME command changes the name of an existing file.

File renaming in DOS is a straightforward process. If you aren't satisfied with a file's name, you simply change the name. The RENAME command is your DOS tool to alter the name of an existing file. The two command names, RENAME and REN, work in identical ways.

RENAME is useful in situations other than the occasional renaming of a file when the current name isn't right. When used with wild cards, RENAME can be a powerful command.

Issuing the RENAME Command

The command name RENAME and REN are identical in operation; you can use either name in a command. The following line shows the syntax for the RENAME command:

RENAME *d:path***filename1**.*ext1* **filename2**.*ext2*

The file to be renamed is on the disk in the default drive or the optionally listed drive *d:*.

The file to be renamed is in the default directory or the directory listed in *path*.

The file is currently named **filename1**.*ext1*. Wild cards are enabled in the full file-name specifier in the file name, the extension, or both.

filename2.*ext2* is the new name for the file. The new file name can be literal (an actual new name) or can contain wild cards. You cannot specify a drive or a path for **filename2**.*ext2*.

Understanding the Operation of RENAME

RENAME changes the name in a file's directory entry. The file itself and its physical location on the disk, however, remain unchanged. RENAME takes the new file name either literally from the command line or by filling in wild cards and scanning the directory that holds the file(s) to be renamed for duplicate file names. Because DOS does not support duplicate file names in a directory, RENAME will not change a file to the new file name if the new file name already exists.

If you use wild cards in the old file name, and more than one existing file matches the pattern you specify, RENAME processes the old files in order. In other words, when DOS performs a top-down search of the directory, DOS renames the files in the order that the REN command encounters each one. Before each renaming of two or more files that match the wild-card pattern of the previous file specifier, DOS ensures that the file name that is being processed has a unique new name.

Understanding the General Rules of RENAME

- You can use the command names REN and RENAME interchangeably. Both command names produce identical results.

- You *must* supply an old file name and a new file name on the command line. Both the old file name and the new file name can contain wild cards for pattern matching.

- The renamed old file remains on the same disk in the same path after renaming.

- You cannot use RENAME to move a file from a directory or a disk to another directory or disk. To move a file, copy it to the new destination and erase the original file from the source location. (Note: Alternatively, you can use the DOS Shell to move files.)

- RENAME does not issue a message if the file-renaming is successful. RENAME does issue messages in the following three instances:

  1. You included an invalid parameter on the command line.

  2. The old file name does not exist in the optional specified full path or the default full path.

  3. The new file name duplicates an existing file name.

Renaming Files

The most controlled way to use the RENAME command is to issue the command with a literal old file name and new file name. You then do not need to worry about wild cards causing unwanted renaming of pattern-matching file names. Suppose that you prepared with your word processor a sales report backup file called SALES.BAK. To give the file a more descriptive name, you can type the following command:

RENAME SALES.BAK SALES_08.REP

You can be sure that only the desired file is renamed because you literally specified the name of the file that you wanted renamed.

Perhaps you want to change the name of a file EXPENSE.YTD to a more descriptive extension with the same root name. You can specify the entire old name and an entire new name in the command line as in the previous example. An easier way, however, is to use an * wild card for the root file name and change only the extension. You then issue the following command:

RENAME EXPENSE.YTD *._89

The new file name for EXPENSE.YTD becomes EXPENSE._89. You can confirm that only the extension of the EXPENSE.YTD file was renamed by using DIR to list the directory. These file names appear as follows in the directory listing:

```
SALES_08 REP      1664    8-01-89    2:51p
SALES_09 REP       128    9-23-89    1:34p
```

Suppose that you decide to change the names of the two files to reflect that they are month-to-date reports. You want to keep the same extension for both files, so that the extension specifier should be an * in both the old file name and the new file name. You want the new file name for both files to take the form of MTD_S_nn, where nn is the month. Because both REP files use the two-number month as a unique set of characters in the current file name, you can use a combination of * and ? wild cards to form the old and new file parameters. You can issue the command in the following manner:

RENAME *.REP MTD_????.*

The old file specifier matches both REP files in the current directory as candidates for renaming. If you specify **MTD_????**, the RENAME command selectively changes the first four characters of the old file names from SALE to MTD_ and keeps the next four characters—represented by the ? wild card—intact. The * in the extensions of the new files enables the new names to keep their old extensions:

```
MTD_S_08 REP      1664   8-01-89   2:51p
MTD_S_09 REP       128   9-23-89   1:34p
```

Deleting Files with ERASE (DEL)

The ERASE and DEL commands remove files from the disk. Both command names produce identical results; you can use ERASE and DEL interchangeably. When you erase a file with ERASE or DEL, the file is no longer accessible by DOS, and the file's directory entry and storage space is available to DOS for additional storage of another file. Because ERASE destroys files, use the command with caution. ERASE is a necessary file-management command, however. Unless you erase unwanted or unnecessary files from a disk, the disk can eventually reach full storage capacity. If the disk is a hard disk, you need to erase files in order to use the hard disk for your primary data storage.

Issuing the ERASE Command

You can use either form of this command—ERASE or DEL. The following show the syntax for both versions of the command:

ERASE *d:path***filename.ext**/*P*

DEL *d:path***filename.ext**/*P*

d: is the optional drive containing the disk that holds the file(s) to be erased. If you omit the drive specifier, the logged drive is used.

path is the optional directory path to the file(s) to be erased. If you omit the path specifier, the current directory is assumed.

filename.ext is the specifier for the file(s) to be erased. Wild cards are permitted in the file name and extension. A file specifier or a path specifier is required.

The */P* switch is available with Versions 4 and 5. You can use the optional */P* switch to pause the ERASE command and to display on-screen the name of each file that may be erased—before you delete the file. You answer Y to delete the file or N to leave the file intact.

Understanding the Operation of ERASE

When you issue an ERASE command, DOS locates the file's entry in the directory and marks the directory entry with a special internal indicator. DOS uses this indicator to search for available directory entries when a new file is added to the directory. By reclaiming a deleted file's directory entry, DOS can control the expansion of a subdirectory or reclaim one of the limited root directory entries.

ERASE does not affect the contents of the file's allocated clusters. ERASE does not "record over" the file's data as erasing a cassette tape records over existing audio. The entire operation of ERASE involves altering DOS's bookkeeping records in the directory and the file allocation table (FAT). The directory entry for the file receives its special indicator, and the FAT cluster chain for the file is de-allocated. DOS marks the file's clusters as being "free." Until another file is added to the directory or another file in any directory is expanded or added, the DOS bookkeeping records for the deleted file remain relatively intact.

DOS Version 5 includes the UNDELETE command, which can recover a file that you accidentally erase, if you realize your mistake quickly. In earlier versions of DOS, no such command is included. However, utilities are widely available from third-party companies that can "undelete" a file in ways similar to the Version 5 UNDELETE command. Both the UNDELETE command and the third-party utilities take advantage of DOS's internal file-erase methods by "fixing" the erased file's directory entry and reconstructing the erased file's cluster chain. If DOS already has allocated the erased file's sectors to another file before you attempt recovery, however, these unerase utilities cannot recover the erased file. Keeping proper backup files is the best insurance against the accidental file erasure.

Cue:
DOS 5 includes the UNDELETE command for recovering accidentally erased files.

Understanding the General Rules of ERASE

- ERASE cannot erase files marked with the read-only attribute.

- ERASE cannot erase a directory file, volume label, or a hidden or system file.

- If you type **DEL subdirectory name**, DOS tries to delete all the files in **subdirectory name**.

- When a file is erased, you cannot access the file through DOS. The file is effectively removed from the disk.

- Unless you use the /P switch (Version 4 and later), ERASE silently erases a file and issues no messages.

- If you attempt to delete all the files in a directory, DOS prompts
  `Are you sure (Y/N)?`

  You answer Y to delete all erasable files in the directory or N to cancel the command. Files marked read-only, system, or hidden are not erased.

- The DOS Version 5 UNDELETE command can recover a file that is accidentally deleted, if the command is used before the erased file's sectors are reallocated by DOS.

Using ERASE

Suppose that in the process of working in dBASE, you added the file PROG.BAT to the dBASE directory. Now you no longer need the file. You can erase the PROG.BAT file while you work in any directory on the same disk by issuing the following command:

ERASE \DBASE\PROG.BAT

DOS erases the PROG.BAT file without issuing a message. You can erase PROG.BAT from \DBASE when dBASE is your current directory with the following command:

ERASE PROG.BAT

Recovering Deleted Files with UNDELETE

DOS 5 includes the UNDELETE command, which enables you to recover files that you accidentally erase. When working with DOS, sooner or later you may accidentally delete a file. You also may realize that, seconds after you delete a file, the erased file contained important data. You also can delete all the files in the current directory with DEL *.* and then realize that one or two of the files in that directory held needed information. Such a catastrophe can—and probably will—happen.

Your best protection against accidentally deleting valuable data is to make full backups of your data. In this chapter, you learn proper backup procedures. Despite your best efforts, however, you may delete a file for which you have no backup.

Issuing the UNDELETE Command

The syntax for the UNDELETE command follows:

UNDELETE *d:path\filename.ext /LIST/DT/DOS/ALL*

d: is the optional parameter that specifies the drive containing the disk that holds the deleted file(s).

path is the optional parameter that specifies the path to the directory that contains the deleted file(s).

filename.ext specifies the file(s) you want to undelete. You can use wild cards to indicate multiple files. By default, if you do not specify a file name, DOS attempts to undelete all deleted files in the current directory or in the directory specified by the *path* parameter.

The */LIST* parameter causes UNDELETE to list the deleted files that can be recovered.

The */DT* switch instructs DOS to use the delete-tracking method of recovering the specified file(s). This method is described in the next section. If no delete-tracking file exists, the command will not proceed. By default, UNDELETE uses the delete-tracking method when no switch is specified; but when no delete-tracking file exists, the program uses information in the DOS directory to recover files.

/DOS causes DOS, in its attempt to undelete files, to rely on the information still stored in the DOS directory instead of using the delete-tracking method.

The */ALL* switch attempts to recover all deleted files without further input from you. When used with this switch, UNDELETE first looks in the delete-tracking file for information about the deleted files and then uses information from the DOS directory.

Understanding the Operation of UNDELETE

Because of the way DOS deletes files, reversing the process is relatively easy—but only if you do so promptly. When DOS deletes a file, DOS changes one character in the file name recorded in the directory area of the disk so that the target file is no longer listed. As far as DOS is concerned, the file is gone. DOS does not erase the modified file name from the directory, however, nor does DOS erase any data from the disk. Eventually, as you add new files to the disk, DOS reallocates the disk space assigned to the deleted file, thus causing new data to overwrite the old data. Soon, the file and its data are gone permanently. If you use the DOS 5 UNDELETE command before DOS has a chance to overwrite a deleted file's data, however, DOS can reverse the DELETE operation.

The UNDELETE command has two approaches to recovering a deleted file: the *delete-tracking* method and the *DOS* method. The sections that follow discuss these methods.

Understanding the General Rules of UNDELETE

Remember these points when using DOS 5's UNDELETE command.

- To successfully recover a file, you must realize your mistake and use the UNDELETE command before DOS reallocates the disk space that had been assigned to the deleted file.

- Remember that some commands, such as MORE, create temporary files. Such commands can overwrite the data you want to recover. You should avoid all DOS commands and application programs except UNDELETE until you recover your files.

- UNDELETE cannot recover a directory that was deleted nor undelete any files whose directory was removed.

- MIRROR (DOS 5) can be installed to keep an on-disk record of all files deleted. If used, MIRROR increases your chances of recovering deleted files.

Using the Delete Tracking Method

Ideally, your AUTOEXEC.BAT file contains a command that causes the DOS 5 MIRROR command to load its delete-tracking option, which is a memory-resident program. MIRROR's delete-tracking option constantly tracks and maintains a list of all files deleted from your computer. MIRROR saves the delete-tracking information in the *delete tracking file*. Note that this file (PCTRACKR.DEL) is assigned the system attribute and is not listed by the DIR command. Using this small but powerful program, MIRROR, is crucial if you want to provide maximum protection against accidental file deletions. (See Chapter 6 for more about the MIRROR command. See Chapter 4 for more about AUTOEXEC.BAT).

By default, UNDELETE tries to read the MIRROR delete-tracking information. If no delete-tracking file exists, UNDELETE attempts to recover files through the DOS directory. You also can use the /DT switch to force UNDELETE to use the delete-tracking file. When the /DT switch is used, the command terminates when no delete-tracking file can be found.

Suppose that you want to recover a file by using the delete-tracking method. If your AUTOEXEC.BAT file has loaded MIRROR's delete tracking into memory, change to the directory that contains the deleted file. Type the following command:

UNDELETE *filename.ext*

Be sure to substitute *filename.ext* for the name of the file you want to recover. When you press Enter, DOS displays a message similar to the following:

```
Directory of C:\SPREADSH\QPRO2DAT
File Specs: BUDGET.WQ1

Delete Tracking file contains 1 deleted files.
Of those,    1 files have all clusters available
             0 files have some clusters available.
             0 files have no clusters available.

MS-DOS Directory contains 1 deleted files.
Of those,    1 files may be recovered.

Using the Delete Tracking file.
   BUDGET  WQ1    4037   1-29-91     4:58p


                              ...A Deleted 2-5-91 1:32a
All of the clusters for this file are available.

Do you want to recover this file? (Y/N)
```

Reminder:
The delete tracking method is the most reliable way to recover an erased file.

This message generated by the UNDELETE command indicates first, in place of *filename.ext*, the name of the file you specified. The message then indicates the total number of deleted files by this name listed in the delete-tracking file, the number of files by this name that have all clusters available and are therefore recoverable, the number of partially recoverable files, and the number of files that are not recoverable.

Next, the DELETE command's message may indicate that the deleted file is still listed in the MS-DOS directory. Such a file may have been deleted when MIRROR's delete-tracking option was not loaded in memory as well as when delete tracking was active. The UNDELETE command's message then indicates the number of files that meet the file name criterion and may be recoverable by using information stored in the DOS directory rather than in the delete-tracking file.

Finally, the UNDELETE message lists the first file (matching *filename.ext*) found in the delete-tracking file. If this file is recoverable (that is, if the file's clusters have not yet been reallocated to another file), DOS asks you to confirm that you want to recover the file. To recover the file, press Y. DOS recovers the file and displays the following message:

```
File successfully undeleted.
```

Reminder:
UNDELETE lists the most recently deleted files first.

The UNDELETE message also lists any other files by the same name found in the delete-tracking file. The files are listed one by one, starting with the most recently deleted files. For each file, UNDELETE asks whether you want to recover the file.

If recovering a file will cause a duplicate file name in the directory, UNDELETE displays the following message:

```
The filename already exists. Enter a different
filename.
Press "F5" to bypass this file.
```

If you want to recover this file, type a unique file name (one that does not already exist in the current directory). Otherwise, press F5 to skip this file.

Occasionally, by the time you realize that you need to recover an accidentally deleted file, other files may have reused some of the file's clusters. In this case, UNDELETE displays the message:

```
Only some of the clusters for this file are
available. Do you want to recover this file
with only the available clusters? (Y/N)
```

Press Y to recover the available bytes or N to skip the file.

If you wait too long before attempting to recover a file, the file may not be recoverable because all its clusters are being used by other files. When this is the case, UNDELETE tells you so and instructs you to Press any key to continue.

If you want to know which deleted files are still available to be recovered, type the following command:

UNDELETE /LIST

UNDELETE displays, from the delete-tracking file, a list of deleted files from the current directory. Partially recoverable files are listed with an asterisk (*) to the left of the file name; unrecoverable files, with two asterisks (**) to the left of the file name.

If a delete-tracking list is longer than one page, you can use Ctrl-S to pause the display. Press any key on the keyboard to resume scrolling. Do not use redirection or the MORE filter, because these tricks create disk files that may overwrite some or all of the data you want to recover.

If you delete all the files in a directory and then remove the directory, you cannot recover any of the deleted files from that directory. UNDELETE cannot recover a directory that has been removed.

Reminder: UNDELETE cannot recover a removed directory.

The UNDELETE command is a product of Central Point Software, licensed by Microsoft for distribution as part of DOS 5. Another program from Central Point Software, PC Shell, is capable of recovering a removed directory. (PC Shell is a part of the PC Tools Deluxe utility package.)

Using the DOS Directory Method

If you were not using MIRROR's delete-tracking option when you accidentally deleted the file you want to recover, you can try to recover the file by using the information stored in the DOS directory. Type the following command:

UNDELETE *filename.ext* **/DOS**

Substitute for *filename.ext* the name of the file you want to recover.

UNDELETE displays a message similar to the following:

```
Directory of C:\SPREADSH\QPRO2DAT
File Specs: BUDGET.WQ1

    Delete Tracking file not found.
    MS-DOS Directory contains 1 deleted files.
    Of those,  1 files may be recovered.
```

```
Using the MS-DOS Directory.

  ?UDGET    WQ1    4037   1-29-91    4:58p   ...A
Do you want to undelete this file? (Y/N)
```

Press Y to recover the file or N to skip the file. After you press Y, UNDELETE displays the following prompt:

```
Enter the first character of the filename.
```

Because the DOS directory no longer has any record of this first character, you must supply the letter. Type the letter you want UNDELETE to use as the beginning letter of the file name. UNDELETE recovers the file and displays the following message:

```
File successfully undeleted.
```

Viewing a File's Contents with TYPE

When you need to see the contents of a text file, you can use the TYPE command. TYPE gets its input from a file (or a device) and sends the ASCII interpretation of the file's content to the screen. You can use the MORE filter with TYPE to keep the file's text from scrolling off the screen as you view the file. You also can redirect the output of TYPE to your printer to produce a hard copy of the file.

Cue:
The TYPE command produces screen output of any character-based file.

Because TYPE enables you to see the contents of a file, TYPE is an important file-management command. When you are cleaning up a directory or a floppy disk, you can use TYPE to refresh your memory about files whose names don't "ring a bell." When you are configuring your system, you can use TYPE to see the contents of your CONFIG.SYS and AUTOEXEC.BAT files. When you are installing a new applications program, you can use TYPE to see the latest instructions in the package's README.DOC or equivalent file. TYPE produces screen output of any file that contains ASCII characters.

Issuing the TYPE Command

The following line shows the syntax for the TYPE command:

TYPE *d:path***filename.ext**

d: is the optional drive that holds the disk that contains the file to be typed. If you omit the drive, the current drive is assumed.

path is the optional path to the file to be typed. If you omit the path, the current directory is assumed.

filename.ext is the name of the file to be typed. You must name the file in the command line. Wild cards are not permitted.

Understanding the Operation of TYPE

TYPE is designed to display the content of a text file that contains ASCII characters. When you issue a TYPE command, DOS opens the specified file and sends the file's content to the output (normally the screen) as a stream of bytes. The bytes are shown as ASCII characters. When DOS encounters a Ctrl-Z, the end-of-file character, the input file is closed and the output terminates.

TYPE can be filtered by MORE as in this example:

TYPE AUTOEXEC.BAT | MORE

The output-character stream is interrupted when the screen fills. Pressing any key starts the output again. (Chapter 4 discusses MORE and other pipes and filters.)

If you use DOS redirection to send the output stream to a printer, the printer may store characters faster than the character stream can handle. As a consequence of the printer's buffering of yet-to-be-printed characters, Ctrl-C or Ctrl-Break may not stop the printer immediately.

Your computer screen wraps a text-line output produced by TYPE to the following line if the number of characters in the line exceed 80. The same line, when redirected to a printer, may not wrap to the next print line after 80 characters, if the printer is capable of printing a line in excess of 80 characters. In such a circumstance, the printer-redirected output of TYPE can print off the page. TYPE is faithfully sending the output stream with the stream's embedded line feed and carriage return characters, but the line's format doesn't match the printer's paper width.

Understanding the General Rules of TYPE

- The output of TYPE stops when the first Ctrl-Z is encountered.

- TYPE does not accept wild cards in the file specifier.

- You can pause the output of TYPE by pressing Ctrl-S or Pause.

- You can terminate the output of TYPE by pressing Ctrl-C or Ctrl-Break.

Viewing the Contents of CONFIG.SYS with TYPE

You can use the TYPE command to view the contents of a short text file. In this example, suppose that you want to view the contents of your CONFIG.SYS file. Issue the following command:

TYPE \CONFIG.SYS

DOS sends the character content of CONFIG.SYS to the screen for you to view:

```
DEVICE=\DOS\DRIVERS\SETVER.EXE
DEVICE=\DOS\DRIVERS\HIMEM.SYS
DEVICE=\DOS\DRIVERS\EMM386.EXE
BUFFERS=15
FILES=15
SHELL=C:\DOS\COMMAND.COM C:DOS\ /P
STACKS=-0,0
```

Using TYPE and Redirection

Cue:
You can use the MORE filter to control TYPE's output to the screen.

Many text files are too large to fit on the display at one time. You can control TYPE's output to the screen by using the MORE filter. To view a 30-line README.TXT file, issue the following command:

TYPE README.TXT | MORE

DOS types the first screen of text from the README.TXT file and adds the following prompt:

```
-- More --
```

When you press any key, TYPE displays the next screen of the README.TXT file.

To print a simple copy of a text file's content, you can redirect the output of the TYPE command to the printer. Because TYPE does not format the text into pages, the printed output can not "break" at page boundaries. To print the contents of README.TXT, you can ensure that your printer is on-line and issue the following command:

TYPE README.TXT >PRN

The file is then printed by your printer. You also can redirect TYPE to another device, such as COM1 or COM2 (see Chapter 4 on redirection).

Comparing Files with COMP

The external command COMP compares two files or two sets of files to find differences in the files. Any differences are reported on-screen. MS-DOS includes a similar command, FC, which is discussed in the next section.

Cue:
The COMP command is available with some versions of DOS.

When a copied file is extremely important, you can use COMP to compare the file with the original. If any difference exists, you know on the spot that something is wrong with the copy. Normally, DOS will detect data integrity even while reading and writing files. But if you want to be sure that two files are the same, you can ease your mind by using COMP.

Issuing the COMP Command

The syntax for the COMP command follows:

COMP *d1:path1\ filename1.ext1 d2:path2\filename2.ext2 /D /A /L /N=xxx /C*

d1: is the optional drive that contains the first file or set of files (the primary set) to be compared. If you omit the d1: specifier, the current drive is assumed.

path1 is the optional path to the file(s) to be compared. If you omit the *path1* specifier, the default directory is assumed.

filename1.ext1 is the optional file specifier for the file to be used as the basis of comparison. Wild cards are allowed in both the file name and extension. If you omit the file specifier but include a drive or a path, COMP assumes that the file specifier is *.*.

d2: is the optional drive specifier that has the second file or set of files (the secondary set) to be used in the comparison. If you omit the d2: specifier, but include a path or file-name specifier, the logged disk is assumed.

path2 is the optional path to the secondary set of files. If you omit the path2\ specifier, COMP assumes the default directory.

filename2.ext2 is the optional file name and extension of the secondary set of files. Wild cards are allowed in the file name and extension. If you omit the secondary set file-name specifier, COMP assumes that the secondary set files are the same name as the primary set files.

No switches are available in versions prior to Version 5. The following switches are valid in DOS 5.0 only:

/D causes COMP to list file differences in decimal format.

/A causes COMP to display differences in character (ASCII) format.

/L causes COMP to display the line numbers of a discrepancy, rather than a byte of fact.

/N = *number* causes COMP to compare files only up to the line in the files indicated by the *number* parameter.

/C causes the comparison to ignore the case of ASCII text in the files.

If you issue COMP without parameters, DOS prompts you for parameters.

Understanding the Operation of COMP

COMP reads one file and compares each byte to another file. Bytes are compared based on their relative position in the file. COMP is not aware if the bytes represent ASCII-character data or binary data. COMP does check both files for the Ctrl-Z end-of-file markers. If an end-of-file marker is not found, COMP displays the message `EOF mark not found`. The end-of-file marker message is informational only and not an indication of a problem.

After the COMP program is loaded into memory, you can continue to conduct file comparisons by answering Y to the prompt `Compare more files (Y/N)?`. COMP then prompts you for parameters.

You can redirect the output of COMP to the printer, but the final prompt of a comparison, `Compare more files (Y/N)?`, prompts for parameters redirected to the printer. If you use redirection, you need to read the prompts from the redirection device. When you redirect the output of COMP to a file, you need to anticipate any prompting messages, because prompts are not visible.

Understanding the General Rules of COMP

- If you do not specify parameters, COMP first prompts for the primary set specifier and then for the secondary set specifier.

- As COMP compares each file in the set, the file-compared names are displayed.

- If the two files being compared are different sizes, the only report issued for those files by COMP is Files are different sizes. No further comparison of the two files is made.

- If COMP detects differences in two files of the same size, the differences are reported to the screen as byte offsets (positions in the file) and values of the differing bytes. By default, byte offsets and values are given in ASCII hexadecimal (base 16) notation. In DOS 5, options are available to change this behavior. The /D switch causes the values of the differing bytes to display as the ASCII decimal notation. The /A switch causes the ASCII characters to display.

- COMP reports the first 10 differences in the two files and then reports 10 Mismatches - ending compare.

- When all sets of files are compared, COMP prompts for additional comparisons.

Comparing Two Text Files with COMP

Suppose that two text files identical in size, ORIGINAL.TXT and ANOTHER.TXT, are located in the default directory of the logged drive A. Assume that the original text file contains the following list of numbers:

```
1
2
3
4
5
```

```
6
7
8
9
```

Also assume that the file ANOTHER.TXT contains the following numbers:

```
9
8
7
6
5
4
3
2
1
```

To compare the two files, issue the following command:

COMP ORIGINAL.TXT ANOTHER.TXT

The following listing shows the COMP report:

```
Comparing ORIGINAL.TXT and ANOTHER.TXT...
Compare error at OFFSET 0
File 1 = 31
File 2 = 39
Compare error at OFFSET 3
File 1 = 32
File 2 = 38
Compare error at OFFSET 6
File 1 = 33
File 2 = 37
Compare error at OFFSET 9
File 1 = 34
File 2 = 36
Compare error at OFFSET F
File 1 = 36
File 2 = 34
Compare error at OFFSET 12
File 1 = 37
File 2 = 33
Compare error at OFFSET 15
File 1 = 38
File 2 = 32
Compare error at OFFSET 18
```

```
File 1 = 39
File 2 = 31

Compare more files (Y/N)?
```

To compare the two files by displaying the mismatches as ASCII characters (rather than hexadecimal) and displaying the locations of the mismatches as line numbers (rather than byte offsets), issue the following command:

COMP ORIGINAL.TXT ANOTHER.TXT /A/L

COMP found 8 mismatches in the files. Because the number sequences in the files are reversed, you may expect to see 9 mismatches reported. Remember, however, that the number 5 is in the same position in both files.

Performing a Full-File Comparison with FC

The external FC command is similar to the COMP command in that both compare files. FC, however, is a more versatile command than COMP. FC generally provides more information than COMP, has more options that enable you to control the command's output, and can compare files of different lengths.

Reminder:
The FC command is not available with all versions of DOS.

Issuing the FC Command

The FC command has two general syntax forms. One form uses the /B switch to force a binary comparison. The other form uses the remaining switches in an ASCII comparison. The following two form lines show the syntax of the FC command:

FC */B d1:path1***filename1.ext1** *d2:path2***filename2.ext2**

or

FC */A/C/L/LBn/N/nnnn/T/W d1:path1***filename1.ext1**
*d2:\\path2***filename2.ext2**

Note: All switches must precede the other parameters.

d1: is the optional drive that contains the first file to be compared. If the first drive specifier is omitted, the current drive is assumed.

path1 is the optional path of the directory that contains the first file. If the first file's path is omitted, the current directory is assumed.

filename1.ext1 is the file name of the first file. A file name must be entered. Wild-card characters are *not* allowed.

d2: is the optional drive that contains the second file to be compared.

If the second drive specifier is omitted, the current drive is assumed.

path2 is the optional path of the directory that contains the second file. If the second file's path is omitted, the current directory is assumed.

filename2.ext2 is the file name of the second file. A file name must be entered. Wild-card characters are *not* allowed.

The switches are explained in table 8.3.

Table 8.3
FC ASCII Mode Switches

Switch	Action
/A	Instructs FC to *abbreviate* its output (Version 3.2 and later)
/C	Instructs FC to ignore the *case* of alphabetic characters
/L	Instructs FC to do a *line-by-line* comparison on files in ASCII mode even when the files have EXE, COM, SYS, OBJ, LIB, or BIN extensions (Version 3.2 and later)
/LBn	Sets the number of *lines* in FC's *buffer* to *n*. The default number is 100 (Version 3.2 and later)
/N	Instructs FC to include the line *numbers* of lines reported in the output (Version 3.2 and later)
/nnnn	Establishes as *nnnn* the number of lines that must match after a difference to resynchronize FC
/T	Instructs FC to view *tab* characters as literal characters rather than tab-expanded spaces (Version 3.2 and later)
/W	Instructs FC to ignore *white space*—tabs, empty lines, and spaces

Understanding the Operation of FC

FC works in two modes. FC compares two files in the ASCII mode or compares two files in the binary mode. Each mode reports its own formatted output. FC defaults to ASCII mode comparison unless the files to be compared have EXE, COM, SYS, OBJ, LIB, or BIN extensions.

In ASCII mode, FC compares two files on a line-by-line basis. Lines from both files are held internally in a line buffer. FC uses the lines in the buffer to compare the first file to the second.

If a difference is detected by FC, the first file's name is displayed, followed by the last matching line from the first file. The first mismatching line and subsequent mismatching lines from the first file are displayed on the screen. FC then produces output that contains the first matching line from file 1 that synchronizes the matching of file 2.

After displaying mismatch information about file 1, FC repeats the same sequence for file 2. The file 2 name is displayed first, followed by the last matching line to file 1, followed by the mismatched lines to file 1, and ending on the first resynchronizing line of the two files.

The result of this output is a tool to identify the point of difference detection, the difference itself, and the point that the detected difference ended. You use this output as a short-cut alternative to a side-by-side comparison of the files' contents.

In the ASCII mode, FC offers several switches to modify the operation or output format of FC. Table 8.4 describes the action of each switch available in ASCII mode.

In binary mode, FC compares two files byte for byte. At the first difference, the byte offset position in the first file is reported along with the value of the two files' bytes at the position. The offset as well as the byte values are reported in hexadecimal (base 16) form.

In binary mode, FC does not attempt to resynchronize the two files by finding an adjusted point of byte agreement. If one file has an additional byte at one offset only, not only does FC report the difference, but all subsequent bytes of the file also are likely to be reported.

If one file is longer than its comparison file, the binary mode compares as many bytes as are present and then report that one file is longer. When a binary file comparison results in a long listing of differences, you may want to stop the FC operation with Ctrl-C.

Only one switch is available in the binary mode. The /B switch causes the comparison to be binary even if file extensions indicate that the files are not binary. You use the /B switch to compare two text files in binary mode. You may find situations in which you prefer the binary mode output format of FC over the ASCII mode format. Binary mode format reports differences as pairs of hexadecimal values. You then can see the values of characters, such as Ctrl-G (bell), that do not produce printed output.

Understanding the General Rules of FC

- The internal buffer defaults to 100 lines for comparison, but can be changed with the /LBn switch. If the number of nonmatching lines exceeds the buffer size, FC aborts the compare operations.

- The default number of lines that must match in an ASCII comparison after a difference has ended is 2. The files are then considered to be resynchronized. You can change the number of "must match" lines by using the /nnnn switch to set nnnn to the desired value.

- Unlike the COMP command, FC requires file-name specifiers that consist of literal file names. Wild cards are not allowed.

Using FC To Compare Two Versions of a Memo

Suppose that the file C:\WP\REPLY.MEM is a text file that contains a brief memo. The content of the file is as follows:

Dear Mr. Smith,

I want to thank you for considering me for the position of Senior Buyer at Smith Industries. I have spent much time deciding between staying at Aberle Manufacturing and joining your firm. I hope you appreciate that my decision was not easy.

I have decided to join Smith Industries. I feel that my decision is the best for my career.

Again, thank you for your consideration.

Sincerely,

Megan Sue Heichelbech

The originator of the memo, Megan Sue Heichelbech, revised the memo and saved a copy to the file A:\REPLY.MEM. Later, Ms. Heichelbech elected to send the memo, but first compared the two files with the same name by issuing the following command:

FC /N/W REPLY.MEM A:REPLY.MEM

FC reports with the following message:

```
***** reply.mem
5:  your firm. I hope you appreciate that my decision was
not easy.
6:  I have decided to join Smith Industries. I feel that my
decision
7:  is the best for my career.
***** a:reply.mem
5:  your firm. I hope you appreciate that my decision was
not easy.
6:  I have decided to decline your offer. I feel that my
decision
7:  is the best for my career.
*****
```

FC found a difference in line 6 of the two files. The final matching line was line 5 and the next matching line after the difference (where FC resynchronized the comparison) was line 7. FC ignored blank lines because the /W switch was included. FC added line numbers because the /N switch was included.

Tapping the Power of COPY

The COPY command is the DOS workhorse. Copying files is a fundamental job for disk operating systems. DOS provides COPY with the capability to copy files as well as the capability to copy to and from logical devices. Figure 8.1 shows the COPY command used with a variety of possible inputs and two possible outputs. Three of the possible inputs consist of more than one file or logical device. DOS can join two or more inputs into one output in a process called concatenation.

When COPY concatenates two files, the files are joined in the output file. Concatenation is not new in disk operating systems. The UNIX operating system uses the command cat (for concatenate) to copy files and devices. The DOS COPY command can concatenate a device's output and a file, a file and a file, or even a device's output to another device's output. The resulting output can go to a file or a device. COPY is versatile when accepting inputs and providing outputs.

Cue:
The DOS COPY command has the capability to copy files as well as copy to and from logical devices.

Cue:
When COPY concatenates two files, the files are joined in the output file.

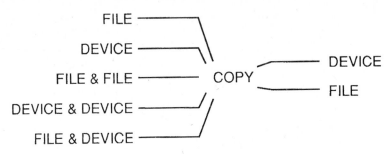

Fig. 8.1. The possible inputs and outputs of the COPY command.

COPY can selectively use either ASCII or binary mode for input and output. Switches given with the command control COPY's mode selection. In ASCII mode, COPY interprets a ^Z (end-of-file marker) as the logical end of file and considers the current input file or device as finished. In ASCII mode, COPY places a ^Z as the last character in the output file or device data stream. Applications programs and DOS commands that use the ^Z end-of-file marker are accommodated by COPY.

The COPY command accepts wild cards in file specifiers to provide a versatile syntax. With drive and path parameters, COPY can reach any user file on a system, from every logged drive and current directory. With *.* file name parameters, COPY can take every file from a fragmented floppy disk and copy each file to a newly formatted disk. By doing so, COPY eliminates the fragmentation on the second disk.

Even with the presence of the related commands DISKCOPY and XCOPY, COPY is the most widely used file-system command. If you are not taking full advantage of COPY's range of features, this discussion of COPY shows you how.

Issuing the COPY Command

In a symbolic representation, the COPY command looks like this:

COPY *from this source or these sources to this destination*

COPY always orders the parameter requirements in a direction of source to destination or target. When you include the mode of reading and writing the files (or devices), COPY symbolically looks like this:

COPY *from source in this mode to destination in this mode*

The symbolic mode for this example is either ASCII or binary for both the source and the destination.

If you incorporate the symbolic view of COPY into syntax lines, you see the following syntax forms:

> COPY *d1:path1***filename1.ext1** */A/B*
>   *d0:path0***filename0.ext0** */A/B/V*

or

> COPY *d1:path1***filename1.ext1** */A/B* +
>   *d2:path2***filename2.ext2** */A/B* +. . .
>   *d0:path0***filename0.ext0** */A/B/V*

d1: and *d2:* are the optional source disk drive specifiers. If you omit a source disk specifier, the current drive is assumed.

path1 and *path2* are optional source path specifiers. If you omit a source path specifier, the current directory is assumed.

The + character delimits source files that are to be concatenated.

filename1.ext1 and **filename2.ext2** are source file-name and extension specifiers. You must give a source file specifier.

The ellipsis (…) signifies that other drive, path, and source file name parameters can be included in a concatenation.

The */A* switch invokes *ASCII* mode and affects the file specified directly preceding the switch and all files following the switch up to the file preceding a subsequent /B switch.

The */B* switch invokes *binary* mode and affects the file specified directly preceding the switch and all files following the switch up to the file that precedes a subsequent /A switch.

The */V* switch causes COPY to perform a read-after-write *verification* of the output sectors of the destination file. The destination file is not compared to the source file(s) directly. Instead, the memory-resident working buffer portion of the file being written is compared to the same data that is read back from the destination file after being written to the file by COPY. The result of this memory-to-file comparison is an effective file-data validity check.

Understanding the Operation of COPY

COPY approaches its work serially; the command's operations occur one step at a time. The flow of COPY proceeds from source to destination. Internally, DOS assures that affected directories and FATs are updated correctly. COPY's initial act is determining the first source file or device.

Cue:
COPY's operation proceeds from source to destination.

If the first source has a reserved device name, COPY enters the ASCII mode, reports the device's name on-screen, and awaits input from the device. If the first source is not a device, COPY assumes that the source is a file. Unless a previous /A switch, an associated /A switch, or an associated + operator is present, COPY enters the binary mode. If the current source is a file, COPY determines the full path specification for the source file.

COPY scans the source parameter for the first drive, path, and file name. If any of these specifiers is missing, COPY consults DOS's internal log for current settings to use in the parameter. When COPY finds the intended directory of the source file(s), COPY reads the source directory from the top entry downward to find the file or a file that matches a wild-card pattern. When the file is located, COPY reports the file name on-screen and begins to read the file.

Data that is read from the input file or device is temporarily stored in a RAM buffer, which fills during the input to COPY. When the buffer first fills or the end of the source file is encountered, COPY establishes the destination parameter.

If the destination is the device, COPY begins to write the contents of the buffer to the device until the buffer is empty. COPY then reads more data from the source, and the cycle repeats until all data is copied from the source to the destination device.

Reminder:
COPY uses
current values if
drive and path
specifiers are
omitted.

If the destination is a file, COPY establishes the destination file's directory. COPY uses the given destination drive and path specifiers to locate the destination directory. Again, COPY uses current values if drive and path specifiers are omitted. The destination directory is searched from the top downward, using the name of the destination file. If the destination file-name specifier contains wild cards, COPY uses the characters from the source file to match the wild-card patterns in forming the destination file specification.

If COPY finds a duplicate full file specification as the destination parameter (same drive, directory, and full file name), COPY determines whether the operation is a concatenation or a straight copy. If a + operator is given in the source parameter or if a wild card is given in the source file name while a literal destination file name is given, COPY assumes that a concatenation operation is taking place. Otherwise, COPY assumes that a straight file-to-file copy operation is taking place. If a concatenation operation is taking place and a duplicate source/destination file name is not the first source file name, COPY issues a warning message that the contents of the destination file are lost before the copy operation executes. If the operation is a straight file-to-file copy, COPY issues a message that the file cannot be copied to itself and then aborts the operation.

When COPY finds the destination file's entry in the destination directory during a concatenation operation, or if the destination file name is different from the source file name, COPY truncates the current file and writes the contents of the buffer as the new contents of the truncated file. COPY retains the same directory entry and name for the new contents of the truncated file.

When COPY finds that the destination file is a new file (not currently in the destination directory), COPY establishes an entry in the destination directory for the new file and begins to write the temporarily buffered source data to space allocated for the new file.

If the /V switch is given in the command, sectors that are written to the destination file are read back from the new file and compared to the data in the buffer for verification. If the original buffer information and the read-after-write information do not agree, COPY issues an error message and aborts the operation.

COPY continues reading source information into the buffer and writing the full buffer to the destination until the source file is completely read to the end of file. If the destination file is affected by the /A switch, COPY appends the Ctrl-Z character to the end of the destination file. COPY then closes the destination file and updates the directory.

If the source parameter contains wild cards or the + concatenation operator, COPY repeats the entire process by moving to the next source for the copy.

If no other source parameters remain for COPY to process, COPY issues a message indicating the number of destination files and devices processed. With its job complete, COPY returns control to COMMAND.COM.

Understanding the General Rules of COPY

- The source parameter must contain at least one of the following: a drive specifier, a path specifier, a file specifier, and a device specifier.

- If the source file specifier is omitted, all files in the specified (or default) directory of the specified (or default) drive are copied. This situation is equivalent to supplying *.* (the source-file specifier).

- Additional source parameters can be specified by using the + operator for concatenation.

- If the source file parameter contains a wild card and the destination parameter is a literal file name, the destination file will be the concatenation of source files matching the pattern of the wild card.

- If COPY detects an attempt to copy a single source file to itself (same drive, directory, file name, and extension), the copy operation is aborted.

- When a device is used as a source, no drive or path specifiers should be used in the source specification.

- When multiple source files are concatenated to a destination file that is one of the source files, the contents of the destination file is its own source file at some point in the copy operation. Unless the destination file is specified as the first source file, the contents of the doubly specified source file will be lost before the copy is made. DOS produces an error message to this effect.

- The optional destination parameter consists of a combination of drive, path, and file-name specifiers. An omitted drive or path specifier assumes the value of the default drive or directory. An omitted file-name specifier assumes the value of the source file-name specifier.

- COPY uses the ASCII mode by default for multiple source files (concatenation), device sources, and device destinations. All other operations use the binary mode by default. The /B operator is not allowed for source devices and produces an error message. Source device input must end with Ctrl-Z (F6 function key).

- The /A (ASCII) and /B (binary) switches affect the file specified directly preceding them and affect subsequent files specified up to and not including the file specification, which is directly followed by another /A or /B switch.

- When the /A switch is applied to a source file, the file is copied up to, but not including, the end-of-file marker (Ctrl-Z) or the physical end of file (as indicated by the byte count in the directory), whichever comes first.

- When the /A switch is applied to the destination file, COPY appends the Ctrl-Z character as the last character in the file.

- When the /B switch is applied to a source file, all bytes in the file, including Ctrl-Z characters, are copied to the destination file.

- When the /B switch is applied to a destination file, COPY does not append its own Ctrl-Z character to the destination file.

Respecting the COPY Command

COPY is certainly a versatile file-management workhorse. Yet even with its versatility, an errant COPY command can do nearly as much damage as an errant ERASE command, so be sure that you treat COPY with respect. Many programs provide warnings regarding their internal file-copying commands. The DOS COPY command does not warn when an existing file is about to be overwritten; COPY simply overwrites the files. If you confuse the source and destination when you are copying a file to a standby floppy, you can easily copy yesterday's standby file over today's work. You might not even notice the error until you need today's work. Not all mistakes with COPY, however, overwrite current data. Some mistakes just create file-management messes.

Relying on default drive and directory values when using COPY is convenient. Yet, if you mistake your current drive or directory for another drive or directory, you can copy many files to the wrong disk or directory with one COPY command. The aftermath of cleaning the misplaced files from the erroneous directory or disk and getting the files into the correct directory or disk can be a tedious process. If the misplaced files have no common root name or extension that differs from the ones of the proper file residence of the disk or directory, you need to copy these errant files one by one to their correct home.

To avoid sending files to the wrong directory, check the name of the logged disk or directory. Don't forget to check the name of the current directory on other drives on your system. You may forget that you changed floppies before a coffee break. Use the DIR command with drive and path parameters for the source and destination of your next COPY command. Viewing the directories takes a bit longer but not as long as copying misplaced files one by one. For complete control of COPY, give the command drive, path, and file-name specifiers for source and destination files.

Reminder:
For complete control of COPY, give the command drive, path, and file-name specifiers for both source and destination files.

Watch out for wild cards. You can select a source wild-card pattern that results in the inadvertent overwriting of destination files. For example, suppose that you have three reports and one graph in the files REPORT1.TXT, REPORT2.TXT, REPORT3.TXT, and REPORT3.PIX. You decide to save a standby copy of each file by using a SAV extension and issuing the following command:

Caution:
Be careful when using wild cards with COPY.

COPY REPORT?.* *.SAV

You intend for the ? wild card to differentiate the files by number after they are copied. The error in this reasoning is that both REPORT3.TXT and REPORT3.PIX fit this source wild-card pattern and that both files will write to a file named REPORT3.SAV. The REPORT3.PIX copy overwrites the existing REPORT3.SAV, which was created as a standby copy of REPORT3.TXT. As a result, REPORT3.TXT no longer has an equivalent standby copy. If you erase the TXT extension files because you think that the file's contents are covered by the SAV extension files, you lose the information represented by REPORT3.TXT.

Many COPY problems can stem from the way you develop patterns or habits when entering commands. If you are accustomed to copying a file from the default directory of your hard disk to the floppy disk in drive A, you're not unlikely to develop a rhythm of entering the COPY parameters. When a different COPY situation arises, the conditioning of the previous rhythm can cause you to enter the accustomed parameters and rely on the accustomed defaults. Without thinking, you can press Enter and rapidly overwrite your good data with old data. Perhaps you pause before pressing Enter and review the command line for accuracy. If you do, you're to be congratulated. But if you get hasty from time to time, you might destroy some data with COPY.

Using COPY in a Variety of Operations

To get a full view of COPY, this section presents straight file-to-file COPY commands as well as COPY commands that are concatenation operations. COPY commands that include devices as source and destination parameters are included. Use these examples as templates for your own COPY needs and watch out for included traps.

Copying Directory to Directory

With today's hard-disk-based PCs, you can find file management difficult if you avoid directory-to-directory COPY commands. This set of examples shows three command lines that copy a file from one directory to another while giving the file a new destination name. Each command takes full advantage of DOS defaults by omitting current values in the command. The source file's full path name on drive C is as follows:

    \DBASE\DATA\BUDGET.DBF

The destination full path name for the copied version of the file on drive C is as follows:

    \KEEP\BUDGET89.DBF

To copy the file while logged to the \DBASE\DATA directory, issue the following command:

COPY BUDGET.DBF \KEEP\BUDGET89.*

Because C is the logged drive, and \DBASE\DATA is the current directory, only the file name and extension are offered as the source parameter. The drive specifier is omitted from the destination parameter because C is the logged drive. The path to the \KEEP directory is given as well as the changed root file name. The * wild card is given for the destination extension; the command defaults to the DBF extension of the source parameter when copied.

The same COPY operation is performed while logged to the destination directory of \KEEP by using the following form:

COPY \DBASE\DATA\BUDGET.DBF BUDGET89.*

This command gives the full path name for the source file in the \DBASE\DATA directory so that DOS can find the file. The destination parameter is simply the changed root file name and the * wild-card extension. Because \KEEP is the current directory of the logged drive C, the drive and path parameters are omitted from the destination parameter.

The same COPY operation can be performed from another directory other than the two directories involved in the command's source and destination. In this case, assume that the logged directory is the root. From the root, you issue the following command:

COPY \DBASE\DATA\BUDGET.DBF \KEEP\BUDGET89.*

In this command, the source and destination drives are omitted because C is the logged disk drive. The full path specifiers are given for the source and destination files because neither the source nor the destination directory is the current working directory.

To illustrate the use of the .. (dot-dot) shorthand name for a parent directory, the following example copies the same file as in the preceding example to the \DBASE directory from the \DBASE\DATA directory. You log to the \DBASE\DATA directory as the current directory and issue the following command:

COPY BUDGET.DBF ..\BUDGET89.*

Notice that the destination parameter includes the .. specifier. From the point of view of the current directory, the command says, "Copy my BUDGET.DBF to my parent directory (\DBASE) and then change the file's name to BUDGET89.DBF." The .. specifier can be used in a file-level command to refer to any subdirectory's parent directory.

Cue:
When using the COPY command, use the .. specifier to refer to any parent directory.

Copying from Disk to Disk

Cue:

Use the COPY
command to copy
files from one
hard disk to
floppies that can
then be copied to
another hard disk.

With word processors, spreadsheets, and database managers providing much of the useful work on PCs, moving data from one PC to another is a common activity. Unless you work in a networked PC environment, you most likely move data files to or from another computer by way of floppy disks. The transportability of floppies is one of their strong features. Whether the task is transporting data to another computer or copying standby files as a "just-in-case" measure between backups, the task requires disk-to-disk copying.

For the first disk-to-disk COPY example, assume that the hard disk drive C contains three memos with a date in Julian-calendar style as their common extension. (A day's Julian date is the number of days passed since January 1.) The files are located in the \WP\MEMOS directory. The files are named MEETING.233, ESTIMATE.233 and CHKLIST.233.

In order to print these three memos on the department's laser printer, you must copy the files to a floppy and take the floppy to another computer. You do this task as part of your daily computer work, and you always add today's Julian date as an extension to your memos for tracking purposes. To copy the files from their directory on drive C, you first log to their directory by using the following command:

CD \WP\MEMOS

Now, issue the following COPY command:

COPY *.223 A:/V

COPY uses the default disk and the default directory to find all files matching the 223 extension as the source parameter. COPY finds the three memos of the day in the directory. The source files are copied to the disk in drive A. Notice that the drive name is the only destination specifier. The files are copied to the root directory of the floppy disk and retain their original full names. The /V switch causes read-after-write verification as the file is copied.

To copy a file from one disk to another on a single floppy system, you issue the COPY command with a destination drive name of B although a drive B isn't physically included in your system. DOS uses the existing drive A as a logical drive B for the operation. To copy the REPLY.MEM file from one floppy to another in a single floppy drive system, issue the following command:

COPY A:REPLY.MEM B:

DOS reads the source file into its file buffer and, with the following prompt, asks you to swap disks in the drive:

```
Insert diskette for drive B:
and press any key when ready
```

First, you remove the source disk from drive A and insert the destination disk in drive A. When you press a key, COPY writes the buffer contents to the second disk. Depending on the size of the file you are copying, DOS can prompt you to swap disks more times. After COPY completes the writing of the destination file, you see the following message:

```
      1 File(s) copied

Insert diskette for drive A:
and press any key when ready
```

You can change either the disk in drive A back to the source disk or leave the destination disk in the drive. When you press a key, the DOS prompt appears.

Concatenating Text Files

Although you can use COPY to concatenate any two or more files, the concatenation operation is most effective when the files are ASCII text files. Concatenating binary files results in a destination file that is not usable in most cases.

Reminder:
Use COPY to concatenate ASCII text files; concatenating binary files can result in an unusable destination file.

For the concatenation examples, assume that three text files exist in the current directory. All three have TXT extensions. The first file is named INTRO.TXT, the second BODY.TXT, and the third is ENDING.TXT. The contents of each file is as follows:

File	Contents
INTRO.TXT	Once upon a time,
BODY.TXT	there was a file.
ENDING.TXT	And the file was copied.

To join the three files into a third file, you separate the source files with the + operator by using the following command:

COPY INTRO.TXT+BODY.TXT+ENDING.TXT ALL.TXT

The resulting file, ALL.TXT, contains the text from the three source files. To verify ALL.TXT, issue the following command:

TYPE ALL.TXT

TYPE sends the contents of ALL.TXT to the screen; you see the following:

```
Once upon a time, there was a file. And the file was copied.
```

You can concatenate the same three files into ALL.TXT in another way. First you must determine if the files are in the correct order in the directory. Use the DIR command in the following form:

DIR *.TXT

DOS reports with the following message:

```
Volume in drive C is LAP TOP
Volume Serial Number is 1599-2045
Directory of  C:\WS

INTRO    TXT      17    8-31-89    3:36p
BODY     TXT      18    8-31-89    3:37p
ENDING   TXT      27    8-31-89    3:37p
         3 File(s)             62 bytes
                   1648640 bytes free
```

The files are in order, and are the only files in the directory that contain the TXT extension. To concatenate the files without using the + operator, you use a wild card in the source-file name that matches only the three desired text files. You also give the destination file a literal name. The command takes the following form:

COPY *.TXT ALL.ALL

COPY works down the source directory and finds the three text files with the TXT extensions. The screen report resembles the following:

```
INTRO.TXT
BODY.TXT
ENDING.TXT
       1 File(s) copied
```

To confirm that the wild-card form of concatenation has joined the three source files, use the following TYPE command:

TYPE ALL.ALL

Again, the screen shows the following:

```
Once upon a time, there was a file. And the file was copied.
```

If you named the destination file in the preceding example ALL.TXT instead of ALL.ALL, the source wild-card parameter would find the destination file's directory entry at the end of the directory while the operation was in progress. The screen then shows the following messages:

```
INTRO.TXT
BODY.TXT
ENDING.TXT
ALL.TXT
Content of destination lost before copy
Content of destination lost before copy

      1 File(s) copied
```

Because COPY created the ALL.TXT entry in the directory to accommodate the destination file name, the destination file name also was in the directory for the source wild card to match. In carrying out the command as specified, DOS has no choice but to truncate ALL.TXT after reading the file's contents. Fortunately, ALL.TXT was completely read into the buffer before COPY had to truncate the source version of ALL.TXT to create the destination version of ALL.TXT. The final content of ALL.TXT is the same as ALL.ALL. If ALL.TXT is too large to fit in the buffer at once, the unread portion of the source version of ALL.TXT is lost. The unread portion is never included in the destination version of ALL.TXT.

For added insurance against destroying part of the destination file of a concatenation, use the + operator rather than wild cards to generate an explicit list of the files or give the destination file a unique full name.

Copying from a Device to a File

A common and handy use of the COPY command is to copy keystrokes entered from the CON device to a file. The resulting text file can be a batch file, a configuration file, a memo, or any kind of short ASCII file.

The use of COPY with the CON device as a source parameter is so popular that many users refer to the COPY CON command when talking about the operation. For an example of copying the console device to a file, you can create a simple batch file that changes the current directory to \123R3 and starts Lotus 1-2-3 Release 3. The batch file is copied to the \DOS directory, so that you can access the batch file from any directory, if you include \DOS as a search-path alternative. The destination file's name is RUN123.BAT. After the COPY operation, you can start LOTUS from any disk or directory. The following command creates the batch file:

COPY CON C:\DOS\RUN123

When you press Enter, DOS displays the word CON on the next line of the screen. This message is DOS's indicator that CON is the source device and that DOS is awaiting input from the keyboard.

Cue:
Use the COPY
CON technique to
copy the contents
of the keyboard
device to a file.

When you see the word CON, enter the following line; be sure to press Enter:

C:

The cursor drops to the next line, and you enter the following line (remember to press Enter):

CD\123R3

The cursor drops to the next line; enter the following:

LOTUS

The cursor drops to the next line, and you press the F6 function key or the Ctrl-Z key combination. Now press Enter one last time. DOS responds with the following:

```
1 File(s) copied
```

To confirm that the new file is correct, you can use the TYPE command to review the contents of the file. If you try this example on your system, be sure to use the appropriate directory names for DOS and Lotus 1-2-3. Also make sure that the start command for Lotus 1-2-3 is LOTUS on your system.

Turning Verification On with VERIFY

Cue:

The DOS VERIFY command controls DOS's internal verification system.

The VERIFY command controls DOS's internal verify indicator. The verify indicator controls the read-after-write checking of data written to disk. If the verify indicator is on, data written to a disk is verified. If the verify indicator is off, the data written to disk is not verified.

DOS does not perform the actual verification but simply maintains the setting of the verify indicator. Data verification is the job of the device driver. The exact method a device driver uses to verify data written to a disk varies. Thorough device drivers can read a written sector to compare with the contents of the disk buffer in memory. The device drivers supplied as a part of the BIOS extension layer of DOS check the written data by rereading the data to verify that the data can be read and that the data's CRC is correct. The DOS BIOS device drivers do not compare the reread data with the contents of the buffer.

You can verify operations with the COPY command by including the /V (verification) switch in the command. This switch turns on the verify indicator for the duration of the copy operation. XCOPY also has a /V switch. Other commands, however, must rely on the action of the DOS VERIFY command to take advantage of the read-after-write verification of data written to disk. Commands such as BACKUP, RESTORE, XCOPY, DISKCOPY, and REPLACE benefit from the VERIFY command.

Verifying data during disk writes is inherently slower than not verifying data. Each disk write is reread when VERIFY is on. The reread sector's CRC is checked for correctness. The CRC is a reliable indicator of write errors. Even the fact that the written sector can be found is a verification of correct operation. If the sector cannot be found or if the CRC is erroneous, DOS assumes that the data is incorrectly written. This extra verification activity takes extra time. In most disk-intensive activities, a program can run 20% to 40% slower during disk I/O. For extra insurance of data verification, however, the slower disk operation is a small price to pay.

Reminder:
You can verify operations with the COPY and XCOPY commands by using the /V switch with those commands.

Reminder:
Although time-consuming, performing data verification provides extra insurance for your files.

Issuing the VERIFY Command

The VERIFY command can be issued in any of the following three forms:

VERIFY ON

VERIFY OFF

VERIFY

When you boot the computer, the default setting of VERIFY is off. Use the first form of the VERIFY syntax to turn VERIFY on.

When VERIFY is on, use the second form of the VERIFY syntax to turn VERIFY off.

To see the current setting of VERIFY on-screen, use the VERIFY command with no parameter.

Understanding the General Rules of VERIFY

- If you issue VERIFY with a parameter other than ON or OFF, DOS issues the message `Must specify ON or OFF`.

- If you issue VERIFY with no parameter, DOS responds with
  `VERIFY is ON` or `VERIFY is OFF`.

- If VERIFY is on, specifying a /V switch in a COPY command has no
  additional verification effect.

- You cannot use VERIFY to cause verification of a network drive.

Verifying a Critical BACKUP Operation with VERIFY

If you plan to perform a critical backup operation on your hard disk, you can add some extra insurance to the operation by turning the verify indicator on. DOS verifies each sector that is written to the backup disk(s). To turn VERIFY on, type the command **VERIFY ON**.

You can confirm the setting at any time from the DOS prompt by issuing the command **VERIFY**. DOS responds with the following message:

```
VERIFY is ON
```

When you no longer want verification, you can turn the feature off with the command **VERIFY OFF**.

Caution:
*Don't confuse
VERIFY with SET.*

You easily can confuse the VERIFY command with a SET command variable. If you issue the command **SET VERIFY OFF**, DOS issues the following error message:

```
syntax error
```

No syntax error message is reported, however, if you issue the command **SET VERIFY=OFF**.

Although the command that you gave to DOS was accepted, you did not affect the current setting of VERIFY. Instead, you assigned the value of OFF to an environment variable named VERIFY. You can see the environment variable with the other variables by issuing a SET command. (The SET command is covered in Chapter 8.) DOS displays the following:

```
COMSPEC=C:\COMMAND.COM
PATH=C:\DOS;C:\DOS\DRIVERS;C:\
PROMPT=$P$G
VERIFY=OFF
```

The last variable displayed seems to indicate that VERIFY is OFF. The real meaning of the line is that the environment variable called VERIFY has a string value of OFF. This environment variable is *not related* to the internal verify indicator controlled by the VERIFY command. To prove that VERIFY is still on, issue the VERIFY command with no parameters; DOS responds with the following message:

```
VERIFY is ON
```

Unlike PROMPT and PATH, VERIFY does not export its current setting to the environment. When you issue a PROMPT or PATH command, the command's parameter is placed in the environment. DOS uses the environment string to get the setting of the prompt or the search path. VERIFY is an internal indicator or flag. DOS does not look in the environment for a VERIFY variable. DOS (or the device driver) checks the internal flag.

Making Backup Sets with BACKUP

Compared to floppy disks, hard disks have many advantages. Hard disks are faster, have greater storage capacities and larger root directories, support multiple partitions, and never require a disk swap. A file on a hard disk can be many times the size of a file on a floppy disk. DOS provides the external BACKUP command and its counterpart, the RESTORE command (discussed in the previous section of this chapter) to enable you to maintain floppy disk backup sets of a hard disk's contents.

BACKUP is a modified COPY command that copies files from one disk, normally a hard disk, to another disk, normally a floppy disk. The "copies" of the files on the second disk are held in a modified format, which cannot be accessed by DOS commands, other than the RESTORE command. BACKUP does not use the normal file format on the backup disk. Only the BACKUP and RESTORE commands can use this special file format.

Reminder:
BACKUP and
RESTORE use a
special format
when storing files.

Backup disks not only contain special copies of files; they also contain directory information about each file that enables RESTORE to copy the backup files to their original locations in the directory tree. In a way, the backup disks are a picture of the original files and directories held in suspended animation.

BACKUP can spread a single file across more than one floppy disk. No other DOS command can cross a disk's FAT boundary with a single file. BACKUP's capability to cross disk boundaries with a single file enables BACKUP to "copy" files that are too big to fit on a single floppy disk to additional disks. If a BACKUP operation uses more than one floppy disk, each disk is internally linked to the next disk to form a backup set.

Backup set disks are related by the order in which they were created by BACKUP. Each disk in a set is filled to capacity until the files from the disk being backed up are complete. If a file is only partially written to a backup disk when the disk reaches full capacity, the remainder of the file is written to the next disk in the set.

BACKUP is a selective command. You can specify a directory or branch of directories, a file name, a file name patterned after a wild card, and additional selection switches. By taking advantage of BACKUP's selectivity, you can maintain more than one set of backup disks at one time, with each set having a logical purpose.

You can, for example, keep one backup set that contains every file on your hard disk. This set is insurance against data loss resulting from a hard disk failure or crash. You can have another backup set that contains only the files that have their archive attributes turned on. With an archive set for each day of the week, you can recover a week's worth of data between complete backups. When your hard disk fails, replace the unit, restore the data by using the full set, and then update with the daily set. Whatever the logical method for using BACKUP, the very presence of the BACKUP and RESTORE commands indicates that a reason exists to replicate your data.

Determining a BACKUP Policy

Reminder:
Every PC user should develop a backup policy.

The first question every computer user must ask is: How often should I perform a backup, and what kind of backup do I want to do? This question has more than one correct answer.

The cost of backups is time. Nobody likes doing backups, and few find the task intellectually challenging. The benefit of backups is data security, and the safety of knowing that a major catastrophe won't cost you everything stored on your computer. Determining a backup policy requires a delicate balancing of benefits with costs. You can approach perfect security by spending all your time doing backups, but this overly cautious approach leaves no time to do work. At the other extreme, you can become optimally productive by never performing a backup, but then you are completely unprotected if a catastrophe strikes. You must determine a balance that leaves you productive and secure.

No one is immune to the need for backups. You can lose data from your computer for many reasons:

- Almost any type of hardware failure, including disk drives, disk controllers, RAM, or ROM failures.

- Bad floppy disks.

- Program bugs.

- Human error, such as deleting the wrong file.

- Deliberate nastiness, such as sabotage, so-called "computer viruses," and theft.

- Lightning strikes and power surges.

- Other catastrophes, ranging from fires to spilling coffee on the keyboard (liquid spills can crash a computer and result in major repairs).

All of these events can destroy data on your hard disk. If you did not replicate the data, you can be forced to recreate the data and suffer the consequences of permanent data loss where you cannot recreate data. Just because you haven't experienced a disk-related failure, don't be overconfident. With 10 million hard-disk-based DOS users working with their computers for an average of eight hours per day, over 250,000 computer owners will experience a hard-disk-related failure this year. You can be next.

Determining How Often To Back Up

How do you determine how often to perform a backup? Typically, you may want to consider the following questions:

1. How much risk do you run of suffering a catastrophe? If you live in a high-crime area or an area that is subject to lightning strikes, if you have a flaky power company and no surge protector, and if you run old hardware that breaks down a lot, you probably want to perform more backups than those who work in a good area (no lightning, reliable power), running top-notch equipment with a perfect track record.

2. What is the cost of a catastrophe? For some, losing any data is a tragedy. For an author who pours his or her blood, sweat, and tears into creating each paragraph, losing a week of work can be truly crushing, and frequent backups probably are justified. For a clerk who spends about an hour a day entering sales figures from printed reports, losing a week's worth of data probably entails retrieving the printed reports and re-entering the data. This work may be time-consuming, but much less tragic than the first case.

Time-Saving Backup Techniques

You can use a number of techniques to minimize the inconvenience of performing backups. In most cases, a trade-off of some kind is involved; in exchange for easier backups, you must pay additional costs or suffer inconvenience at some other time.

1. **Back up only data, not programs.** In most cases, you do not need to back up the entire hard disk every time you perform a backup. For example, suppose that you installed WordPerfect on your computer. The programs that make up WordPerfect do not change (unless WordPerfect sends you updates), and copying these programs every day is pointless. A sensible technique is to make a few copies of the original WordPerfect floppy disks that came with the package, store them safely, and then back up only the documents that you create. If you ever experience a catastrophe, you can retrieve your documents from the backups and reinstall WordPerfect from the original disks. *Advantage:* Usually a huge savings in time required to perform a backup. *Disadvantage:* In the event of a loss, requires each software package to be reinstalled.

2. **Mix full backups with incremental backups.** An incremental backup makes copies of only those files that changed since the last backup. DOS can determine which files are changed by examining the archive flag for each file, discussed previously in this chapter. On many systems, only a relatively few files change between backups, and only these files need to be backed up. For example, you can perform a full backup each Monday and an incremental backup on Tuesday through Friday. Most backup programs, including the BACKUP command provided with MS-DOS, enable you to specify that only changed files are backed up. *Advantages:* Because relatively few files change on some systems between backups, incremental backups tend to go fast and require significantly fewer disks. *Disadvantages:* Because incremental backups contain only those files that changed, if a file is lost, you may not be able to find the file on your most recent backup. You may be forced to search backward through the incremental backups to find the backup that contains the most recent copy of the file.

3. **Faster backup package.** Many companies sell programs, such as Central Point Backup and FASTBACK, which can produce backups faster than the DOS BACKUP command. Many programs also compress files so that more data fits on fewer floppy disks. *Advantages:* Many of these packages are faster, require fewer disks, and

are easier to use than BACKUP. *Disadvantages:* You must purchase these programs, and you must be sure that you keep a floppy disk that contains these programs in order to restore your files in the event of a catastrophe.

4. **Faster backup medium.** This chapter assumes that you are making your backups to floppy disks, but other avenues are open to store backup data. Many companies make cartridge tape units, which are ideal for backups. You even can consider optical disks that can be written to; one optical disk can hold months of backups. *Advantages:* For most systems, one tape or optical disk is more than sufficient to hold a full backup. This method enables you to start a backup before going home at night; the backup runs unattended for as long as necessary and is finished when you return the next morning. *Disadvantages:* Tape and optical disk units are expensive and require special software (usually provided with the unit).

Increasing Backup Safety

You can employ several tactics to increase the reliability of your backups. After all, when a catastrophe occurs your backups can be your only hope for recovering data. After a disaster is no time to find out that your backup disks are unusable.

1. **Rotate backups.** Many PC users perform backups conscientiously, but they use the same set of floppy disks to perform every backup. These disks can wear out and, in a moment of crisis, these users turn to their backup disks and find that one of the disks has errors. A better method is to create several sets of disks and use a different set each time until you use each set. If you do daily backups, for example, you may have ready five sets of disks, one for each day of the week. In this way, if your most recent backup set turns out to be bad, you can go back to the preceding day's set—a loss of only one day's work.

2. **Store some backup sets off-site.** What good are backups if your office burns down, destroying both the computer and the backups? For maximum effectiveness, an extra set of backups should be made and stored away from the computer—at home, at a friend's house, or in a safe-deposit box.

Issuing the BACKUP Command

The following line shows the syntax for the BACKUP command:

BACKUP *d1:path\filename.ext* **d2:** */switches*

d1: is the optional name of the source drive that you are backing up. If you omit the drive source name, the default drive is assumed.

path is the name of the optional path that holds the files you are backing up. If you omit the path name, the current directory of the specified (or default) drive is assumed.

filename.ext is the optional name of the source file(s) that you are backing up. You can use wild cards in the root file name as well as in the extension. If you omit the file-name specifier, the *.* wild-card pattern is assumed.

d2: is the required name of the destination drive where the backup disks are written. If the destination drive name is omitted, DOS issues an error message.

/switches are optional switches that add additional selectivity and control to the command. Table 8.5 outlines each switch and the DOS versions with which the switch can be used.

Table 8.5
BACKUP Switches

Switch	DOS Version	Action
/S	2.0 or later	Includes files from the specified directory and all subsequent *subdirectories* of the specified directory
/M	2.0 or later	Includes files whose archive attribute is turned on
/A	2.0 or later	*Adds* the files to be backed up to the files existing on the backup set
/F	3.3 or later	Formats destination disks as part of the *backup operation*
/F:size	4.0 and later	Optional *format size* is given as /F:size
/D:date	2.0 or later	Includes files created or modified on or after the *date* specified with the /D switch in the form /D:mm-dd-yy or /D:mm/dd/yy

Switch	DOS Version	Action
/T:time	3.3 or later	Includes files created or modified on or after the *time* specified as /T:hh:mm:ss
/L	3.3 or later	Writes a backup *log* entry in the file specified as /L:d:path\filename.ext or in a file named \BACKUP.LOG in the source disk when /L with no file specifier is used

Understanding the General Rules of BACKUP

- Files backed up are selected by the drive, path, and file specifiers or their default values. Further selection of files is based on the optional switches.

- Unless the destination disk is a backup disk and you use the /A switch, the contents of the destination disk's root directory will be lost in the backup operation.

- If the destination disk is a hard disk, BACKUP checks for a directory named \BACKUP to store the backed up files in. The BACKUP command creates the \BACKUP directory if the directory does not already exist.

- If \BACKUP contains previously backed-up files, they are erased as part of the backup operation unless the /A switch is used. If the /A switch is used, and the destination disk is a hard disk, the current backup files are appended to existing backup files in \BACKUP.

- The DOS Versions 4 and 5 BACKUP command automatically formats a destination floppy disk that is not yet formatted, as if you were using the /F switch in a previous DOS version.

- If BACKUP is formatting destination disks, the FORMAT command must be available in the current directory or accessible through a search path specified by the PATH command. The specified search path in the PATH command cannot be the destination drive.

- BACKUP cannot format a hard disk, even if you add the /F switch.

- The source disk cannot be write-protected because BACKUP resets each backed-up file's archive attribute.

- BACKUP does not back up the hidden DOS system files or COMMAND.COM in the root directory.

- You cannot use RESTORE Version 3.2 or earlier to restore files backed up by BACKUP Version 3.3 or more recent versions.

BACKUP Procedures

As you learned in the preceding sections, most users do not back up all their files each time; they try to find a workable mix of partial (or incremental) backups and full backups.

Caution:
Uninstall all copy-protected software before you perform a full backup.

When you perform a full backup, all your files are backed up. If disk disaster should strike, you can recover your data from your full backup set. You can restore the full backup set to your existing hard disk or even to a new replacement disk.

Unless you use DOS Version 3.2 or earlier, you don't need to format the destination disks. The number of disks you need is derived from the number of bytes you are preparing to back up. When you run CHKDSK, DOS reports the number of bytes in various categories of files. A sample CHKDSK report can resemble the following:

```
Volume LAP TOP     created Aug 17, 1989 6:41p
Volume Serial Number is 162F_BA9A
21204992 bytes total disk space
   51200 bytes in 3 hidden files
   98304 bytes in 42 directories
19404800 bytes in 1150 user files
 1650688 bytes available on disk

    2048 bytes in each allocation unit
   10354 total allocation units on disk
     806 available allocation units on disk

  655360 bytes total memory
  598784 bytes free
```

Two lines in this report apply to a disk-count calculation for BACKUP: the hidden files line and the user files line. If the number of hidden files is 2 or 3, and the space that the hidden files occupy is less than 150,000 bytes, you can ignore the line. Otherwise, add the number of bytes in hidden files to the number of bytes in user files. The result is the approximate number of bytes in files that you are backing up. In the preceding case, the number of bytes is 19,404,800, which is about 18.5M (M=1,048,576 bytes).

Divide the number of megabytes (M) of one file by the capacity of the destination drive (in megabytes). For 360K disks, divide by 0.35 (360 ÷ 1,024); for 720K disks, divide by 0.7; for 1.2M disks, divide by 1.2; and for 1.44M disks, divide by 1.44. In this example, you need about fifty-three 360K disks, twenty-seven 720K disks, sixteen 1.2M disks, or fourteen 1.44M disks. You also can use the information in table 8.6 to derive an approximation of your disk requirements.

Table 8.6
Number of Floppy Disks Required for a Full Backup

Bytes to Back up	Disk Capacity			
	360K	720K	1.2M	1.44M
10M	29	15	9	7
20M	57	28	17	14
30M	86	43	25	21
40M	114	57	34	28
70M	200	100	59	49

Issuing the Full BACKUP Command

Unless you use Version 4 or later, or intend to use the /F switch with Version 3.3, format all your backup floppies the first time you intend to use them. Label each floppy disk as "Full Backup Set." After you format and label all disks, you can start the full BACKUP with the following command:

BACKUP C:\ A:/S

This command tells BACKUP to start in the root directory of the hard disk and process all subdirectories on the disk. BACKUP issues the following warning message:

```
Insert backup diskette 1 in drive A:
Warning! Files in the target drive A:\ root directory
will be erased.
Strike any key to continue.
```

Write the words "disk 1" on the first floppy disk's label as indicated in the screen message. Then insert the disk and press a key. DOS reports file names on-screen as they are being backed up. When the first disk is filled, BACKUP repeats the message that asks for the next disk. Again, mark the next disk's label with the sequential number that appears in the message.

The process repeats until the final file from the hard disk is processed by BACKUP. When you complete the full backup, store the destination disks in order and in a safe place. Be sure that you do not mix this set with another backup set; you may try to restore a disk from the wrong set.

Following Up with Incremental Backups

An incremental backup is a method of backing up only the files that are no longer current on the full backup set. You use a second set of disks for the incremental backup set. The number of disks in the incremental backup set depends on the number of bytes in files that were modified since the last BACKUP. The key to making an incremental backup is the archive bit.

BACKUP turns the archive attribute off for any file backed up. When you modify or create a file, DOS turns on the archive attribute for the modified or created file. BACKUP uses the /M switch to select files with their archive attribute in the on (set) state. Unless you issue the ATTRIB command with the +A parameter or the XCOPY command with the /M switch, DOS sets only the archive attributes of changed or modified files.

You can use either of two basic strategies for making incremental backups. Either strategy can be combined with the full backup to comprise your backup strategy. Either incremental backup strategy uses the /M switch available with all versions of BACKUP.

The first incremental strategy or method is maintaining several small backup sets and using different sets over time. The second incremental backup method is maintaining one incremental backup set and adding files to the set over time. If your version of BACKUP supports the /A switch, the additive method is for you.

If you use the multiset incremental backup method, you need to ensure that you formatted enough backup disks to complete any given incremental backup. If you always keep on hand a few spare formatted backup disks, you will not be caught short when BACKUP prompts you to insert one disk more than you expect.

If you use PC DOS Version 4, you need only blank disks; PC DOS Version 4 BACKUP detects blanks and formats them on the fly. With MS-DOS Version 3.3 and later versions, you always can specify the /F switch and format every disk during the backup operation. Using the /F switch slows the BACKUP operation, however, but at least you will not be caught with only blank, unformatted disks and no way to complete the backup.

If you perform an incremental backup every Tuesday and Friday, and you run a full backup every two weeks, you have four incremental backup sets accumulated before you need to repeat the backup cycle and reuse the disks. If you perform an incremental backup every Friday and a full backup on the final Friday of every month, you need four sets of incremental backup disks, although most months can require only three disks. Note that the number of disks in each set can vary with each incremental time period's file-modification activity. The second backup set, for example, can be two disks for one month and three disks for the next month. You may need to renumber some disks from one set to another to accommodate the peaks and valleys of each set's disk requirements.

If you use the additive incremental backup method, you use just one incremental backup set. You add files to the end disk in this set when you perform the incremental backups. An exception to adding files to the set occurs during the first incremental backup operation after a full backup. For this first incremental backup in a backup cycle, you start with the first disk in the set by omitting the /A switch from the BACKUP command line. By using this switch, you effectively reclaim the disks for reuse. The number of disks your set requires depends on the worst case file-modification load for your full backup cycle. If your full backup cycle is one month, you may need five disks in your additive incremental backup cycle for 11 months out of the year, but you may need as many as ten disks during a month during high file-creation or modification activity. Remember that you can scan the archive attributes of the files in your most heavily-used directories to get a sense of the number of bytes awaiting backup.

Issuing the Multiset Incremental Backup Command

You start a multiset incremental backup with the following command:

BACKUP C:\ A: /S/M

The /S switch includes all directories on the hard disk in the operation, and the /M switch selects only those files with their archive attribute switch set. The backup proceeds as the full backup described previously. Mark each disk in the set with the number and the date that belongs to the increment for this backup. Store the completed set in a safe place and avoid mixing the disks with disks from another backup set.

If you use the additive incremental method, you can use the same command as the multiset backup method just described for the first incremental backup following a full backup. For the first incremental backup of the cycle, insert disk 1 of the set first.

For every other additive incremental backup besides the first backup of the cycle, issue the following BACKUP command:

BACKUP C:\ A: /S/M/A

BACKUP sees the /A switch and knows to add the files to the end of the backup set. BACKUP issues the following prompt:

```
Insert last backup diskette in drive A:
Strike any key when ready
```

You now insert the final disk from the last incremental backup operation. Don't start with the next reclaimed (unused in this cycle) disk. BACKUP /A needs to start up exactly where the command left off at the last backup operation. When you insert the correct disk, press a key. The operation proceeds in the same manner as the full backup described previously.

Restoring Backed-Up Files with RESTORE

Cue:
RESTORE reads the special file format copied with the BACKUP command and restores the files to regular format.

The external command RESTORE is the functional counterpart of the BACKUP command. RESTORE is the only command that can read the special control information associated with files that are copied with the BACKUP command. When you need to recover backup files from a backup set, RESTORE is the command that you use.

By issuing a literal file-name parameter with RESTORE, you can restore a single file from a backup disk. With a directory parameter and a wild-card file-name parameter, you can restore selected files to the named directory. With the /S switch, you can restore an entire hard disk with only a source drive specifier. RESTORE puts the selection of files in your control.

Like BACKUP, the RESTORE command provides additional control and selectivity through the use of numerous switches. With RESTORE's switches, you can use time, date, presence, and absence as selection criteria for files to be restored.

Issuing the RESTORE Command

The following line shows the syntax of the RESTORE command:

RESTORE ds: *dd:path\filename.ext /switches*

ds: is the required source drive that holds the file(s) to be restored.

dd: is the drive that receives the restored files.

path is the optional path to the directory that receives the restored files. If the path specifier is omitted, the current directory of the destination disk is assumed.

filename.ext is the optional name of the file(s) to be restored. You can use wild cards in the file name's root and extension.

/switches are optional switches.

Table 8.7 displays the optional RESTORE switches, their actions, and the applicable versions of DOS.

Table 8.7
RESTORE Switches

Switch	DOS Version	Action
/S	2.0 or later	Restores files to the specified (or default) directory and *subdirectories*
/P	2.0 or later	*Prompts* to confirm the restoration of a read-only file or a file modified since the last backup
/M	3.3 or later	Restores files *modified* or deleted since the last backup
/N	3.3 or later	Restores files that *no* longer exist on the destination disk
/B:date	3.3 or later	Restores files created or modified *before* or on the *date* given as /B:mm/dd/yy or /B:mm-dd-yy
/A:date	3.3 or later	Restores files created or modified *after* or on the *date* given as /A:mm/dd/yy or as /A:mm-dd-yy
/L:time	3.3 or later	Restores files created or modified *later* than or at the *time* given as /L:hh:mm:ss
/E:time	3.3 or later	Restores files created or modified *earlier* than or at the *time* given as /E:hh:mm:ss
/D	5.0	*Displays* a list of files on the backup disks that match the file names in the command. No files are actually restored

Cue:
Time and date entries used with RESTORE are given in the format of your country code.

Note that time and date entries used with applicable systems are in the format of your country code. United States formats are presented in table 8.7. More information about providing country information can be found in Chapter 15.

Understanding the Operation of RESTORE

Reminder:
RESTORE always restores files to the directory in which they were located when the files were backed up.

RESTORE is the only command with the capability to read the special file format of files "copied" by the BACKUP command. RESTORE always restores files to the directory in which they were located when the files were backed up. RESTORE cannot restore files to another directory other than to the files' original directory.

If RESTORE is restoring a file whose original directory is no longer on the destination disk, RESTORE creates the directory before restoring the file. RESTORE makes directory entries for files that are no longer on the destination disk and allocates the next available space in the FAT for the restored file's allocation. If the destination disk is newly formatted, the restored files on the disk are, in most cases, contiguous. Files with the same full path name but different sizes from an additive backup set can result in a fragmented destination file after RESTORE allocates the first file of a duplicate name pair and subsequently allocates additional clusters for a larger file with the same name.

Like the BACKUP command, RESTORE prompts you for the disks of the backup set. If you know the disk number that contains the file(s) that you want to restore, RESTORE accepts that disk as the first disk. You can use the /L switch with BACKUP to create a log file showing the names and disk numbers of files in a backup set.

Understanding the General Rules of RESTORE

- RESTORE Version 3.2 or earlier versions cannot restore files created by BACKUP Version 3.3 or more recent versions. DOS 5.0's RESTORE command, however, can restore files backed up with any version of the BACKUP command.

- You must give a source drive name in the command line.

- All files restored from the backup set are placed in their original directories on the destination disk. If a source directory does not exist on the destination disk, DOS creates the directory.

- You select files for restoration with the destination drive, path, and file specifiers. Further selection is based on the included switches.

- The destination disk must already be formatted. RESTORE, unlike BACKUP, offers no provision to format the destination disk.

- Files restored to a freshly formatted disk are not fragmented.

Note: Copy-protected files cannot properly restore to the destination disk. Uninstall all copy-protected files prior to BACKUP and reinstall the files after RESTORE.

Using RESTORE following a Disk Failure

For the examples of the RESTORE command, assume that your backup policy includes a weekly full backup on Friday and an incremental backup each Wednesday. You have two backup sets. The first set from Friday contains all files. The second set contains only files that are modified or created after Friday, but before Thursday.

On Thursday morning, suppose that, in the middle of saving a worksheet file, a workman begins to use a large drill next door. You notice that DOS reports the following message:

```
General Failure on drive C
```

You abort the spreadsheet session and run CHKDSK to ensure that your FAT and directory system are in order. (The operation of CHKDSK is covered in Chapter 5.) DOS reports hundreds of lost clusters, and CHKDSK fills your root directory with reclaimed clusters. CHKDSK aborts after the root directory of your hard disk fills up.

You just experienced an electrical noise-induced hard disk failure. Your hard disk most likely wrote errant information over valid information in the FAT. Your only choice is to reformat your hard disk and then fall back on your backup disks. After you format your hard disk, copy the external DOS commands back to the hard disk, from the DOS master disk or from a working copy. Use the PROMPT command to set a search path to the DOS directory so that DOS can locate the RESTORE command.

In the case of total disk failure, restore your backup sets in chronological order. The first set to restore after you format your hard disk is your full backup set. Locate the disks from your full backup set and ensure that they are in proper order. Then issue the following command:

RESTORE A: C:\ /S

DOS prompts you with the following message:

```
Insert backup diskette 1 in drive A:
Strike any key when ready. . .
```

Put the first disk in drive A and press a key. DOS responds with the following message:

```
*** Files were backed up mm/dd/yy ***
```

The actual message shows mm/dd/yy as the date of the backup, in the format used by your country code. DOS prompts:

```
*** Restoring files from drive A: ***
```

You see the full path names of the files as they are restored. When all the files from the first disk are restored to the hard disk, DOS prompts you for the next disk in the backup set. Repeat the restoration disk prompt cycle until you complete the restore operation.

With the full backup set restoration complete, you now must restore the incremental backup set. Because you want to restore all the files in the incremental backup set, use the same command that you used to restore the full backup set. The operation proceeds in the same fashion.

With both backup sets restored, run CHKDSK to ensure that the hard disk is in order. Keep both of your backup sets intact until you determine that your hard disk is performing correctly. Run CHKDSK several times during the day. If all is in order, perform a full backup at the end of the day.

Using RESTORE following an ERASE *.* Command

In another example of the use of RESTORE, assume that you accidentally issue an ERASE command with a *.* wild card parameter. You thought you were logged to the temporary directory \TEMP, but you were actually logged to your \REFLEX\DATA directory. Now, all your Reflex data files are erased. In DOS Version 5, you can use the UNDELETE command to recover the files if you realized your mistake immediately. But imagine that you are either using an earlier DOS version, or that you did not realize your mistake immediately. To recover your lost data, you must perform a selective restoration operation from your two backup sets. To restore only the files in the \REFLEX\DATA directory from the full backup set, issue the following command:

RESTORE A: C:\REFLEX\DATA*.*

As in the complete restoration example, RESTORE prompts you to insert the first disk. You can insert the first disk or, if you know the starting disk number that holds the Reflex files, you can insert the disk that holds the Reflex files. RESTORE bypasses all files on the source disk that are not included in the destination parameter that you gave in the command. When RESTORE does encounter a \REFLEX\DATA file, that file is restored to the \REFLEX\DATA directory of the hard disk.

When you are sure that all files are restored to the erased directory, you can press Ctrl-C or Ctrl-Break to abort the RESTORE operation. For safety's sake, insert all disks from an additive backup; a few files can be backed up toward the end of the set.

Again, you must restore all files from the incremental set that belong in the \REFLEX\DATA directory. To restore from the incremental backup set, use the same command that you issued to restore the \REFLEX\DATA files from the full backup set.

If you maintain more than one incremental backup set, you should restore desired files from each of the incremental backup sets you created since the last full backup and before the incident that caused the need to restore. Always restore backup sets in the order that they were created. Restore the oldest set first and the newest set last. If you restore the sets out of chronological order, you can overwrite more recent versions of files with older versions of the same files.

Caution: Always restore backup sets in chronological order.

In situations that lend themselves to BACKUP and RESTORE, and that do not involve data loss (such as moving data from a work PC to a home PC), you can use the various RESTORE switches to ensure that you aren't moving older data to a PC that contains newer data. You can, for example, restore older files to a PC while preserving files modified or created after a specified date. Use the switches available with RESTORE to get the most from the command.

Chapter Summary

This chapter covered the DOS file-management commands. Files are an essential "way of life" in personal computing. The more competent you are at managing your files, the better your computing experience becomes. In this chapter, you learned about the following key file-management points:

- DOS allows a defined set of characters in "legal" file names.

- DOS device names are reserved. If you use a reserved name for a file specifier, DOS uses the specifier as a device.

- Some file extensions conventionally are used to indicate the type of file that the extension implies.

- The ^Z character marks the end of many ASCII files.

- The ATTRIB command lists and manages a file's archive and read-only attributes.

- The RENAME command changes the name of an existing file.

- The ERASE (DEL) command removes files from a directory. Erased files are no longer available to DOS.

- The COMP and FC commands compare files for differences.

- The TYPE command displays a file's content in ASCII on the screen.

- The COPY command concatenates and copies files and devices in binary and ASCII modes.

- The VERIFY command manages the DOS internal verify indicator that device drivers check to determine whether the device drivers need to perform write verification of data.

- The BACKUP command is used to produce special backup disks. Backup disks usually are used for recovering lost data.

- The RESTORE command reads files from backup sets and restores the files to their original directories on another disk.

In the next chapter, you learn the commands that DOS provides to access, display, and change system information. These commands are generic to all phases of PC operation.

9

Working with System Information

Chapters 1 through 5 of this book introduce the DOS fundamentals and detail how they relate to the user and the hardware. Chapters 6 through 8 show you the commands associated with the disks, directories, and files. This chapter covers commands that enable you to control how DOS interfaces with you.

These commands can change system information, such as the date and time assigned to files. If you use DOS 4 or 5, you may issue a command to invoke the DOS Shell. If you use an earlier version of DOS, several commands enable you to adjust how the screen looks.

The system information commands covered in this chapter are described in the command reference. The command reference includes the parameters and switches. The following commands are covered in this chapter:

- DATE
- TIME
- VER
- SETVER
- MEM
- DIR
- DOSSHELL
- PROMPT

- MODE
- COMMAND
- EXIT
- SET

Changing the Date and Time

When DOS saves a new file to disk, the operating system assigns a date and time stamp to the file. This stamp is placed in the directory entry with the file name, attributes, and starting cluster information for the FAT. The date and time assigned to a file are read by the computer as the current date and time.

If you use an AT-class (286-based) or a 386-based computer, a battery-backed clock keeps the date and time in an area of memory after the date and time are set. Even when the computer is turned off, this small area of memory receives power from the battery, and the date and time remain current. In a PC or XT, an add-on, battery-backed clock can serve a similar function. The PC-style clocks require you to run a program, supplied with the clock; to transfer to DOS the date and time; and to store the information.

Setting the date and time becomes increasingly significant as you create more files on your computer. The DOS file-naming rules enable you to use only eight characters in the root name and three characters in the extension. The convention of using the extension to indicate the file type leaves a limited choice of names for the root name. On computers without a clock or with a clock and a dead battery, the date and time are set to the same value each time the computer is switched on. Unless you enter the current date and time each time you start the computer, you end up with many files assigned similar date and time stamps.

Caution:
All clocks in personal computers lose time.

Checking your computer's date and time occasionally is worthwhile. All batteries eventually fail and need replacing. All clocks in personal computers lose time. How much time your clock loses depends on the particular programs you run on your computer.

The clock that you use to keep the date and time in a PC is controlled by an electronic component in the computer—the system timer. This chip is the heartbeat of the computer. Everything the computer does takes a known amount of time. The system timer provides a regular pulse that controls all the functions occurring in the computer.

One of these functions is to update the clock that DOS uses to tell the time (and consequently the date). Functions that cannot afford to be interrupted while they are working, however, tell DOS not to interrupt them until they finish that operation. A typical example is a communications program that waits for a character to be sent from another computer. If DOS is busy doing other things, such as updating the clock, the character may be missed. This program type disables the interrupts—the program tells DOS to do nothing else for the period of time that it needs full control. During these times, the clock is not updated. These periods are only a few seconds, but the effect is cumulative, and eventually the time loss is noticeable.

If you do not have an AUTOEXEC.BAT file, which runs when you start your computer, DOS prompts you for the date and time when you boot the computer. DOS shows the current settings and enables you to change them. On an AT-class or 386-based machine, you probably can accept the current settings because the date and time are loaded from the battery-backed memory.

Cue:
If you lack an AUTOEXEC.BAT file, DOS prompts you for the date and time.

If you have an AUTOEXEC.BAT file that lacks DATE and TIME commands, DOS uses its current settings. You can change the current settings by using the DATE and TIME commands.

Cue:
Use DATE and TIME to change the current settings.

Issuing the DATE Command

The syntax for the internal DATE command is as follows:

DATE *actual_date* or **DATE**

If you type **DATE** at the DOS prompt, DOS returns the current setting and prompts you for a new date. You can change the date without being prompted by including the new date on the command line.

The *actual_date* parameter specifies the month, day, and year. The exact syntax depends on the country code set in the CONFIG.SYS file. Country code settings are discussed in Chapter 16. The syntax for *actual_date* can be in one of three forms:

> *mm-dd-yy* or *mm-dd-yyyy* for North America

> *dd-mm-yy* or *dd-mm-yyyy* for Europe

> *yy-mm-dd* or *yyyy-mm-dd* for East Asia

mm is the month; *dd* is the day; and *yy* and *yyyy* are the year.

Understanding the Operation of DATE

To enter the date December 23, 1991 on a machine configured for North America, type the following:

DATE 12-23-91

The year also can be typed in its full form as 1991. If you use two digits, the 19 is assumed. Instead of the hyphen, you can use periods or slashes as separators. Leading digits are not required. For example, if the month is January, you can type 1, instead of 01, for the month.

Letting DOS prompt you for the date is a better way to use this command, because the current date is displayed in the correct format, and you can copy the syntax rather than having to remember it. A typical DOS sequence may be as follows:

```
C:\>DATE

Current date is Mon 09-18-1991

Enter new date (mm-dd-yy): 12-23-1991
```

Pressing Enter when prompted for a new date retains the current setting. If you don't enter the date correctly or if you select a date out of the DOS range, the error message `Invalid date` is displayed, and DOS again displays the `Enter new date` prompt.

Cue:
Use the DATE command to determine the day of the week for any date.

Notice that DOS displays the day of the week along with the other date information. You can use the DATE command to determine the day of the week for a particular date by changing the date, issuing the DATE command to see the new setting, and then changing the date back again.

DOS 3.3 and later versions actually change the battery-backed clock as well as the system clock setting when you execute the DATE command. Versions of DOS prior to 3.3 do not update the date permanently in the battery-backed clock; those versions keep the date entered only for the current DOS session. When the power to the computer is turned off, the date value is the one stored in the battery-backed clock. To change the clock permanently for earlier versions of DOS, use the SETUP program supplied with your computer.

Issuing the TIME Command

The syntax for the internal TIME command is as follows:

TIME *actual_time* or **TIME**

As with DATE, if you type only **TIME** and press Enter at the command prompt, you are shown the current setting and are prompted for a new setting. You can avoid the prompt by typing the desired time as a command-line parameter.

The syntax for *actual_time* varies with the COUNTRY setting in the CONFIG.SYS file. A 12-hour or 24-hour clock is possible. The following shows the syntax for the 24-hour clock:

hrs:mins:secs.1/100secs

hrs is the hour, a number from 0 to 23; *mins* is the minutes, a number from 0 to 59; *secs* is the seconds, a number from 0 to 59; and *1/100secs* is the number of one-hundredth seconds, a number from 0 to 99.

Understanding the Operation of TIME

The DOS 4 12-hour clock uses the same syntax except that *hrs* can be a number from 1 to 12, and an *a* or *p* is added to signify a.m. or p.m. You can enter a 24-hour time, and DOS displays the time in the 12-hour format.

In either form, no spaces belong between parameters. Also, in the case of the 12-hour version, no space belongs between the end of the time elements and the *a* or *p*. You can use a period instead of the colon when separating the hours, minutes, and seconds or a comma in place of the period when separating the seconds from the hundredths of a second.

You do not have to specify all the parts of the time. Any missing elements are set to zero (using the 24-hour clock notation). To set the time to 8:25 p.m., type one of the following lines:

TIME 20:25 or **TIME 8:25p**

Either command sets the time exactly to 8:25 p.m. The seconds and hundredths of a second are set to zero. To set the clock to 12:30 a.m. type the following:

TIME :30

This command is easy to use if you have DOS prompt you for the time, because DOS shows you the syntax. A typical sequence may be as follows:

```
C:\>TIME
Current time is 2:35:07.23p
Enter  new  time: 2:40p
```

Cue:

If you enter a 24-hour time, DOS displays the time in the 12-hour format.

You can use the COUNTRY command to change the format DOS uses to display the time, as described in Chapter 16.

As with the DATE command, DOS 3.3 and 4 actually change the system clock setting when you execute the TIME command, and earlier DOS versions do not update the TIME in the battery-backed clock. You need to use the SETUP program supplied with your computer to change the clock permanently with these earlier versions.

Displaying the Version with VER

Cue:
Use VER if you troubleshoot someone else's computer.

DOS includes an internal command that displays the DOS version. The VER command is invaluable if you need to troubleshoot an unfamiliar computer. Other commands, such as DISKCOMP, FORMAT, and XCOPY, work differently or are not available with different DOS versions. New users probably do not know what version of DOS they are using, and the VER command eliminates many possible dilemmas.

Caution:
If a computer with a hard disk is booted from a floppy disk, you may be running a different version of DOS.

After you issue the VER command, DOS displays a message showing the version of DOS used to boot the computer. If a computer with a hard disk is booted from a floppy disk, you may have access to a different version of DOS than you expected. Suppose that your hard disk is formatted for DOS 5, but you use a Version 3.3 floppy disk to boot the computer. The Version 5 commands that reside on the hard disk are not available. The DOS message Incorrect DOS version is displayed when you try to use one of the Version 5 commands.

The message displayed by DOS when you use the VER command is similar to the following:

```
MS-DOS Version 4.01
```

or

```
MS-DOS Version 5.00
```

Other manufacturers supply different implementations of DOS, and consequently, you can see a different message if you use a different product. For example, COMPAQ Computer Corporation's version of DOS includes COMPAQ's name along with the version number. Because of the differences between these versions and implementations, you may be able to track down problems on a different machine more easily if you first determine the exact version number and manufacturer.

Setting the Version with SETVER

When a new version of DOS is introduced, some time passes before popular applications programs are upgraded to take full advantage of DOS's new features. Many programs query the operating system to determine which version of DOS is loaded. If an unsupported version of DOS is in memory, these programs may refuse to run. Therefore, one or more of your applications programs may refuse to run because they have not been certified by the manufacturer to run properly with DOS 5.

You can get a reluctant program to run in DOS 5 in two ways:

- Contact the software manufacturer or your vendor to determine whether you need to obtain an upgrade.

- Use the SETVER command to add the name of the applications program to DOS 5's *version table*, a list of applications programs with a corresponding DOS version number. When a program listed in the version table loads into memory and queries DOS for its version number, DOS reports the version number listed in the version table rather than reporting the actual version number— 5.0. The application is fooled into running in DOS 5.

The first option is preferable. By checking with the manufacturer, you can determine whether the applications program has been tested in DOS 5. If you use the second option, you run the risk, however slight, that data may be corrupted if the program turns out to be incompatible with DOS 5. Assuming that you choose to throw caution to the wind and modify the version table, follow the procedure set out in this section.

The SETVER command operates as a device driver and an executable command. Before DOS can use the version table, you must load SETVER.EXE as a device driver. Use the following syntax:

DEVICE=*d:path***\SETVER.EXE**

The parameters *d:* and *path* are the disk and directory that contain the SETVER.EXE external program file. The default CONFIG.SYS file, for example, created by DOS 5's installation program includes the following command:

DEVICE=\DOS\SETVER.EXE\

After the device driver SETVER.EXE is loaded into memory, DOS uses the version table to report the DOS version to listed applications programs.

You can use SETVER from the command line to display the current version table as well as to add or to delete program names. The syntax for using SETVER at the command line is as follows:

SETVER *d:path\filename.ext n.nn* */DELETE /QUIET*

To display the version table, use SETVER with no switches or parameters. DOS displays a two-column listing with applications program names in the first column and the DOS version number in the second column. Microsoft already has tested the programs listed in the initial version table and determined that they operate properly in DOS 5. The version list that displays on your screen should look similar to the following:

```
WIN200.BIN          3.40
WIN100.BIN          3.40
WINWORD.EXE         4.10
EXCEL.EXE           4.10
HITACHI.SYS         4.00
MSCDEX.EXE          4.00
REDIR4.EXE          4.00
NET.EXE             4.00
NET.COM             3.30
NETWKSTA.EXE        4.00
DXMA0MOD.SYS        3.30
BAN.EXE             4.00
BAN.COM             4.00
MSREDIR.EXE         4.00
METRO.EXE           3.31
IBMCACHE.SYS        3.40
REDIR40.EXE         4.00
DD.EXE              4.01
DD.BIN              4.01
LL3.EXE             4.01
REDIR.EXE           4.00
SYQ55.SYS           4.00
SSTDRIVE.SYS        4.00
ZDRV.SYS            4.01
ZFMT.SYS            4.01
TOPSCR.EXE          4.00
```

When you run one of the programs listed in the first column of the version table, DOS reports to the program the DOS Version number listed in the second column.

If you have trouble running a program and the application displays an error message indicating that you are trying to execute the program with an incompatible version of DOS, you may want to try adding the program to the version table. Type the SETVER command as follows:

SETVER *c:path***filename.ext n.nn**

The *c:path* parameter indicates the disk and drive where the SETVER.EXE file is located on your system.

The **filename.ext** parameter is the name and extension of the command that starts the applications program in question.

The **n.nn** parameter is a DOS version number recognized by the applications program. Consult the program's documentation to determine the versions of DOS supported.

For example, assume that you want to run the program KILLERAP.EXE, but the program supports only DOS Versions 3.0 to 3.3. To add KILLERAP.EXE to the version table, type the following command at the command prompt, and press Enter:

SETVER KILLERAP.EXE 3.30

DOS displays the following series of messages, including an initial warning:

```
WARNING - The application you are adding to the MS-DOS
version table may not have been verified by Microsoft
on this version of MS-DOS. Please contact your software
vendor for information on whether this application will
operate properly under this version of MS-DOS. If you
execute this application by instructing MS-DOS to
report a different MS-DOS version number, you may lose
or corrupt data, or cause system instabilities. In that
circumstance, Microsoft is not responsible for any loss
or damage.

Version table successfully updated

The version change will take effect the next time you
restart your system
```

To verify that the application has been added to the version table, execute SETVER again without switches or parameters. The added application is listed at the end of the list. The modified table takes effect, however, only after you restart or reboot your computer.

If you later decide to delete a program from the version list, use the /DELETE (/D) switch and the *filename* parameter. For example, to delete KILLERAP.EXE from the version table, type one of the following commands at the command line and press Enter:

>   **SETVER KILLERAP.EXE /DELETE**

or

>   **SETVER KILLERAP.EXE /D**

DOS deletes the application name from the version table and displays the following message:

```
Version table successfully updated

The version change will take effect the next time you
restart your system.
```

If you are using a batch file to delete an applications program name from the version table, you may want to suppress the preceding message. To prevent this message from displaying to screen, add the /QUIET switch in addition to the /DELETE switch.

Displaying the Amount of Free and Used Memory

Cue:
Use the MEM command to repeat the free and used memory on the system.

DOS 4 and 5 include the external MEM command, which can be used to provide system information. The command repeats the free and used memory on the system and can show which programs and devices are loaded in the system.

Issuing the MEM Command

The following line shows the syntax for the MEM command:

>   **MEM** */PROGRAM /DEBUG /CLASSIFY*

All switches are optional. You can abbreviate each switch by typing just the first letter (/P, /D, /C).

The */PROGRAM* switch gives a list of all programs currently loaded in the computer's memory.

The */DEBUG* switch gives a list of all the programs and the device drivers loaded. This listing includes the name, size, position, and type of each item.

```
0C9170   MOUSE          0031F0   Program
0CC370   DOSKEY         001020   Program
0CD3A0   MSDOS          002C50   -- Free --
      655360 bytes total   conventional memory
      655360 bytes available to MD-DOS
      582928 largest executable program size

      655360 bytes  total  EMS  memory
      262144 bytes free EMS memory

     3145728 bytes total contiguous extended memory
           0 bytes available contiguous extended memory
     2424832 bytes  available  XMS  memory
          MS-DOS resident in High Memory Area
```

The first column shows the starting address of each item that MEM found. The addresses are listed in hexadecimal (base 16). The second column shows the name of the program or device driver loaded into memory. The third column shows the amount of memory occupied by each program or driver in hexadecimal. The final column includes the type of item listed. The types include the system files IO.SYS and MSDOS.SYS, programs, installed device drivers, environment, and any data areas the programs may need.

The /DEBUG switch extends this listing further to include all the system device drivers loaded into memory.

To see a listing of programs, drivers, and free space in conventional and upper memory, type the following command and press Enter:

   MEM /C

DOS scrolls a report similar to the following down the screen:

```
Conventional Memory :

   Name         Size in Decimal              Size in Hex
   ---------    -------------------          -------------

   MSDOS        12016  ( 11.7K)                 2EF0
   HIMEM         1184  (  1.2K)                  4A0
   EMM386        8208  (  8.0K)                 2010
   SETVER         384  (  0.4K)                  180
   COMMAND       2624  (  2.6K)                  A40
   MIRROR        6528  (  6.4K)                 1980
   FREE            64  (  0.1K)                   40
   FREE           144  (  0.1K)                   90
   FREE        623968  (609.3K)                 8560

  Total   FREE  :     624176      (609.5K)
```

```
Upper Memory :

  Name        Size in Decimal              Size in Hex
  ----------  --------------------         -------------

  SYSTEM      163840  ( 160.0K)                28000
  ANSI          4192  (   4.1K)                 1060
  MOUSE        12784  (  12.5K)                 31F0
  DOSKEY        4160  (   4.1K)                 1040
  FREE           144  (   0.1K)                   90
  FREE         11376  (  11.1K)                 2C70

Total   FREE :            11520          (  11.3K)

Total bytes available to programs (Conventional+Upper):635696
(620.8K)
Largest executable program size:          623776   (609.2K)
Largest available upper memory block :     11376   ( 11.1K)

   655360 bytes total EMS memory
   262144 bytes free EMS memory
  3145728 bytes total contiguous extended memory
        0 bytes available contiguous extended memory
  2686976 bytes available XMS memory
          MS-DOS resident in High Memory Area
```

Because some of the report scrolls off the screen before you can read it, you may want to use the following variation of the same command:

MEM /C | MORE

DOS pipes the report through the MORE filter and displays the first screen of the report followed by the message `--MORE--`. Press any key when you are ready to display the next screen.

You also can send the MEM report to your printer by using the following command:

MEM /C > PRN

This command redirects the report to the DOS device PRN, your computer's first printer port.

The top portion of the report, titled `Conventional Memory`, shows you how much memory is allocated to any particular driver or program. Use the section of the report titled `Upper Memory` to determine whether any drivers or programs are loaded in upper memory and how much upper memory is still free.

Before attempting to move a driver or program from conventional to upper memory (using DEVICEHIGH or LOADHIGH), compare the driver/ program's size (in the Conventional Memory Size column) to the available upper memory block (UMB) sizes (indicated by `FREE` in the Upper Memory Name column). The available UMB must be at least as big as the driver or program before you can load the driver or program into upper memory.

After you identify a driver or memory-resident program that appears to be the right size to fit in the available UMB, edit CONFIG.SYS or AUTOEXEC.BAT to add DEVICEHIGH or LOADHIGH to the appropriate command. Reboot your computer and issue the MEM /C command again to see whether the driver or program loaded.

Arriving at the optimal combination of device drivers and memory-resident programs loaded into upper memory may require some experimentation. DOS loads programs in the largest available UMB first, so try loading the largest drivers and programs first by placing their start-up commands earliest in CONFIG.SYS or AUTOEXEC.BAT.

Listing Files with DIR

The DIR command is one of the first commands most DOS users learn. The command quickly gives a list of files, along with the date and time of creation, and the file sizes. If you type only **DIR**, you are not using the command to its full power.

Cue:
Use DIR to display a list of files, the date and time of creation, and the file sizes.

Issuing the DIR Command

The syntax of the DIR internal directory command is as follows:

DIR *d:path\filename /P /W /A:attributes /O:order /S /B /L*

d: is the drive; *path* is the path name; and *filename* is the name of the file to be displayed. The switches are used to control the file. These switches are shown in table 9.1.

Table 9.1
DIR Switches

Switch	Action
/P	Displays one screen full of information and then pauses. Pressing any key causes DIR to continue the listing.
/W	Displays only the names of files (without showing the size or modification time of each file). Files are listed in columns across the screen, rather than one per line.

continues

Table 9.1 *(continued)*

Switch	Action
/A:attributes	Displays only files that have, or lack, file attributes you specify (DOS 5 only)
/O:order	Lists files in a different sorted order (DOS 5 only)
/S	Lists the contents of subdirectories (DOS 5 only)
/B	Lists only file names, one per line (DOS 5 only)
/L	Lists file names in lowercase (DOS 5 only)

If any of the parameters are missing, the current status is assumed. For example, if you omit the path name, DOS assumes the current subdirectory. Omitting the drive causes DOS to assume the current drive.

Understanding the Operation of DIR

Hard disks are now much more prevalent on computers than they were even a couple of years ago. A hard disk holds many times the quantity of files that can be stored on a disk. You can end up with directory listings that fill the screen many times over unless you instill organization into the hard disk. Using hierarchical directories alleviates many of these problems but also can effectively hide files. The DIR command, coupled with a logical hard disk directory organization, makes all files easily accessible.

Consider the simplest form of the DIR command. Typing **DIR** at the DOS prompt when C:\DOS is the current directory gives you the full listing of the directory.

The volume label and serial number are displayed first. Then each file in the directory is listed in the following fashion:

```
EGA      SYS      4885     6-10-91      5:00a
```

The information displayed is most of the information stored in the directory table. The file attributes are not indicated but are used by DOS to determine whether a file should be displayed. Hidden files are not included in this list. The location of the first cluster in the file allocation table (FAT) for the file also is not displayed because the file's starting cluster is not of use to you.

At the end of the listing, DOS indicates the total number of files in the directory, the total number of bytes used by the listed files, and the total number of bytes free on the current disk. For example, the DIR report for C:\DOS may show the following information:

```
87 files    2105291 bytes
            8935424 bytes free
```

If you add up the size of each listed file on the disk and subtract the size from the total disk capacity, that number and the number of free bytes shown in the directory listing probably do not match. However, the directory listing is correct. Remember that hidden files are not shown, and more important, the size of the file is not necessarily the same as the amount of disk space occupied by the file.

When a file is created, no matter how small, DOS allocates a whole number of clusters on the disk for the file. The directory listing shows the file length in bytes and calculates the free space, based on the number of free clusters on the disk. These free clusters are remaining positions on the disk not yet allocated to another file. (See Chapter 2 for more information about the file storage system.)

Cue:
Free clusters are the positions remaining on the disk not allocated to another file.

The free space reported by DIR is the number of unallocated clusters (also called allocation units) multiplied times the size of a cluster (1,024 bytes on most hard disks). You also can use CHKDSK to obtain a report of the total number of allocation units available on the disk.

Displaying a Screen Full of Information with DIR

Adding the /P switch to the DIR command causes DOS to pause the scrolling of the screen at the end of each screen full of information. Pressing any key displays the next page of information. This switch works in a similar fashion to the MORE filter, discussed in Chapter 9. For the DIR command, however, the /P switch is convenient because it is built into the DIR command and does not require MORE to be in the search path.

To see more file names, use the /W switch. Figure 9.1 shows a directory listing using the /W switch.

With hierarchical directories, your directory listing includes subdirectory names and files. In the wide listing, directory names are enclosed in brackets ([ ]).

Cue:
With /W, directory names are in brackets.

Because the names are grouped so closely together, a wide listing can be useful when you want to see the types of files in a directory.

```
Volume Serial Number is 48A6-0000
Directory of C:\DOS

[.]              [..]            EGA.SYS        FORMAT.COM      NLSFUNC.EXE
COUNTRY.SYS      DISPLAY.SYS     EGA.CPI        HIMEM.SYS       KEYB.COM
KEYBOARD.SYS     MODE.COM        SETVER.EXE     ANSI.SYS        DEBUG.EXE
DOSKEY.COM       EDLIN.EXE       EMM386.EXE     FASTOPEN.EXE    FDISK.EXE
MEM.EXE          MIRROR.COM      RAMDRIVE.SYS   SHARE.EXE       SMARTDRV.SYS
SYS.COM          UNDELETE.EXE    UNFORMAT.COM   XCOPY.EXE       DOSSHELL.VID
DOSSHELL.INI     DOSSHELL.COM    DOSSHELL.EXE   DOSSHELL.GRB    DOSSWAP.EXE
PACKING.LST      PRINT.EXE       DOSHELP.HLP    DOSSHELL.HLP    HELP.EXE
RECOVER.EXE      EDIT.HLP        QBASIC.HLP     EDIT.COM        MSHERC.COM
QBASIC.EXE       GORILLA.BAS     MONEY.BAS      NIBBLES.BAS     REMLINE.BAS
APPEND.EXE       ATTRIB.EXE      BACKUP.EXE     CHKDSK.EXE      COMP.EXE
DISKCOMP.COM     DISKCOPY.COM    FC.EXE         FIND.EXE        LABEL.EXE
MORE.COM         RESTORE.EXE     SORT.EXE       4201.CPI        4208.CPI
5202.CPI         ASSIGN.COM      DRIVER.SYS     GRAFTABL.COM    GRAPHICS.COM
GRAPHICS.PRO     JOIN.EXE        LCD.CPI        PRINTER.SYS     EXE2BIN.EXE
REPLACE.EXE      TREE.COM        SUBST.EXE      LOADFIX.COM     README.TXT
APPNOTES.TXT     EXPAND.EXE      DELOLDOS.EXE   COMMAND.COM     MONEY.DAT
QBASIC.INI       [TEMP]
        87 file(s)     2105291 bytes
                       8935424 bytes free

C:\DOS>
```

Fig. 9.1. The file name, displayed in a wide format with the /W switch.

Using DIR To Control the File List Display

Chapter 6 introduces you to the DIR command and two of its switches, /P and /W. Beginning with DOS 5, the DIR command has five additional switches that enable you to control the list of files displayed at the command line by the DIR command.

By default, DIR lists file names of all files except those with the hidden attribute or system attribute. Files are listed in no particular order. By adding certain switches to the DIR command, you can cause DOS to list only file names that have specified attributes, and you can cause DOS to list file names in a specific sorted order.

The complete syntax of the DIR command is as follows:

DIR *d:path\filename* /P/W/A:*attributes*/O:*sortorder*/S/B/L

Refer to Chapter 6 for a discussion of the *d:*, *path*, and *filename* parameters and the /P and /W switches.

The /A:*attributes* switch enables you to list only the files that have at least one specific file attribute set. Substitute one or more of the following codes for the *attributes* parameter:

D	Directory attribute
R	Read-only attribute
H	Hidden attribute
A	Archive attribute
S	System attribute

For example, to see a listing of all hidden files in the current directory, type the following command and press Enter:

DIR /A:H

DOS lists all files that have the hidden attribute.

Attribute codes can be included in any combination and in any order. For example, you can list all file names with the read-only attribute and the archive attribute by issuing the following command:

DIR /A:RA

DOS lists file names that have both attributes.

To list only file names that do not have a certain attribute, insert a minus sign (–) before the attribute code. For example, to see all files that are not directories and that don't have the archive bit, type the following command at the command line and press Enter:

DIR /A:–A–D

If you include in a DIR command the /A switch with no attributes parameter, DOS lists all file names, regardless of file attribute—even the file names of hidden and system files.

The */O:sortorder* switch enables you to determine the order in which DOS lists file names. To cause DOS to sort the file list in a particular order, substitute for the *sortorder* parameter one of the following sort codes:

Reminder:
Use /O to control
the order in which
files are listed.

N	Sorts alphabetically by name
S	Sorts numerically by file size
E	Sorts alphabetically by file extension
D	Sorts chronologically by date and time
G	Groups directories first

You can include sort codes in any combination. The order of the sort codes in the DIR command denotes the priority of each sort criterion. The command DIR /O:NE sorts the file names first by name and then by extension. The command DIR /O:EN sorts files by extension (for example, grouping all COM files together and all EXE files together) and then sorts the files by name. If you include the /O switch in a DIR command without specifying a sort code, DOS sorts the files in alphabetic order by name.

By default, all sorting is in ascending order—A through Z, smallest to largest, earliest to latest. Precede a sort code with a minus sign (–) to reverse the sorted order—Z through A, largest to smallest, latest to earliest.

Use the /B switch to display a "bare" file list—a list of just file names. The default file list generated by the DIR command shows the name of each file in the directory, the file name extension, the file size, and the date and time the file was last changed. Occasionally, you may want to see just the file name of each file. Perhaps you want to print a list of the files on a floppy disk. Place the disk in drive A and issue the following command:

DIR A: /B

DOS lists on-screen all file names of files in the current directory of the disk in drive A. DOS does not list file size or file date and time. To send this list to the printer, issue the following command:

DIR A: /B >PRN

The /L switch, when used with the DIR command, causes file names to appear in lowercase letters.

Searching for Files with the DIR Command

To find a file on your disk from the command line, you can use the /S switch with the DIR command. If you want to search a specific directory, first use the CHDIR command to change to that directory. To search the entire disk, change to the root directory.

At the DOS prompt, type **DIR**, followed by the search criterion. The search criterion can be a specific file name or can contain wild-card characters (* and ?). To complete the command, add the /S switch and press Enter. The /S switch causes DOS to search the current directory and all directories lower than the current directory.

For example, to search the current disk for your budget spreadsheet (as in the example in the preceding section), change to the root directory and then type the following command:

DIR BUDG*.W?1 /S

When you press Enter, DOS displays a listing similar to the following:

```
            Volume in drive C is QUE BRUCE
            Volume Serial Number is 1628-BA9A

        Directory of C:\SPREADSH\QPRO2DAT

        BUDGET        WQ1         4037        10-05-90
    2:00A

                    1 files(s)  4037 bytes

            Directory of C:\WORD_PRO\ENDATA

        BUDGET        WK1         5120        04-07-90
    8:51p

                1 files(s)  5120 bytes

    Total files listed:

                    2 files(s)              9157 bytes
                                        9400320 bytes
    free
```

Customizing the DIR Command

If you find that you continually use one or more of the seven switches available for use with the DIR command, record the switch(es) as an environment variable named DIR

> **SET DIRCMD=***switches*

Substitute for *switches* the switch or switches you want DOS to use by default. For example, if you want DOS to sort file names alphabetically and to pause scrolling after each screen full of information, include the following command in AUTOEXEC.BAT:

> **SET DIRCMD=/O/P**

Reboot the computer. DOS creates the environment variable DIRCMD and gives it the value /O/P. Each time you issue the DIR command, DOS adds these two switches.

You can override a switch that is recorded in the DIRCMD by preceding the switch with a minus sign (–). For example, to override the /P switch that currently is recorded in DIRCMD, issue the DIR command as follows:

> **DIR /–P**

DOS lists all file names without pausing at the end of each screen full of information.

Using DOSSHELL

With Version 4 and later, DOS includes an optional graphical user interface. This interface enables you to select items from a list of options, rather than forcing you to learn each of the individual commands. If you are a new user, the interface is advantageous because you can perform basic DOS functions without extensive training.

This user interface is actually a program, the DOS Shell. You can run the program from the DOS prompt, or you can have DOS run the Shell at boot time from the AUTOEXEC.BAT file. Chapter 5 describes the various features of the Shell program.

Changing the Command Prompt with PROMPT

The default command prompt shows the current drive and a greater-than sign. The PROMPT command enables you to change from this display to a more informative and friendly prompt.

Typing **PROMPT pg** at the command prompt changes the prompt to give you the full path on the disk. This new prompt enables you to see the current directory at all times. If you use a hard disk, this display is the minimum prompt setting recommended. Navigating subdirectories is difficult if you don't know your current position.

The PROMPT command supports many more features. In its most extensive form, the command requires the ANSI.SYS device driver. ANSI.SYS is discussed in Chapter 13. However, even without using the ANSI.SYS device driver, you can choose from many different command prompts.

Issuing the PROMPT Command

The syntax for the PROMPT command is as follows:

PROMPT *string*

The *string* consists of text, a series of character pairs, or both. Each character pair, called a *meta-string*, consists of a dollar sign, followed by one of the following characters:

t d p v n g l b q h e _

The string can contain any text or any number of meta-strings in any order. Table 9.4 lists the different meta-strings.

Table 9.4
Meta-Strings for Use with the PROMPT Command

Meta-string	Displayed information or result
$_	Carriage return/line feed (moves the cursor to the beginning of the next line)
$b	Vertical bar character (|)
$d	Date
$e	Esc character
$g	Greater-than sign (>)
$h	Backspace (moves the cursor one space to the left)
$l	Less-than sign (<)
$n	Current drive
$p	Current path
$q	Equal sign (=)
$t	Time
$v	DOS version

Understanding the Operation of PROMPT

The **PROMPT pg** command shows the current path followed by the greater-than sign. Consider the following command:

PROMPT Date: $d Time: t_pg

This command displays the following prompt:

```
Date:  Mon  09-16-1991  Time:  2:35:07.23
C:\WP\MEMOS>
```

Two of the meta-strings require further explanation. The Esc character (**$e**) is used in association with the ANSI.SYS driver (explained in Chapter 12). In the same way that the dollar sign is used to indicate to DOS that the next character is a meta-string, the Esc character is used to signal ANSI.SYS that the next few characters are an ANSI.SYS command.

You can use the Backspace character (**$h**) to remove characters from the prompt. For example, in the preceding PROMPT example, the seconds and hundredths of a second in the displayed prompt are more of a distraction than they are helpful. You may, therefore, alter the command as follows:

PROMPT Date: $d Time: thhhhhh_pg

The result is the following improved prompt:

```
Date:  Mon  09-16-1991  Time:   2:35
C:\WP\MEMOS>
```

If you don't like the current prompt, type **PROMPT** at the command line, and DOS resets the prompt to the current drive letter and a greater-than sign (for example, C>). Remember if you use subdirectories, the best practice is to use **PROMPT pg** as the minimum prompt.

Altering the Look of the Screen with MODE

Cue:
Use the MODE command to change the display.

The external MODE command is used extensively with DOS to customize the standard configuration. This command sets the modes of printers, the code page switching, and the display.

You can attach two types of displays to the same computer: a monochrome display adapter and display; and a color graphics adapter and display. You switch between the displays by using the MODE command. Switching displays is particularly handy when you use graphics-based programs, such as a drawing program. MODE enables you to use the color display to show graphics programs and drawings and the monochrome display to show text-based programs.

When you type at the keyboard on a two-display system, you see the keystrokes only on one of the displays. This display is the *active display*. The keyboard and active display constitute the console. DOS uses the device name CON for the console.

Selecting the Display Type

Two forms of the MODE command can be used with any version of DOS to change the display characteristics. Additional forms are available with DOS 4 and later versions.

The following syntax, which works with any version of DOS, can be used for the simplest form of the MODE command:

MODE *dt*

dt is the display type and mode. Available options are 40, 80, BW40, BW80, CO40, CO80, or MONO.

The 40 and 80 refer to the number of columns of text to be displayed. BW stands for black and white; CO stands for color; and MONO refers to the monochrome display adapter.

To set the number of columns displayed on the active display to 40 or 80, respectively, type either of the following:

MODE 40 or **MODE 80**

To select the display attached to the monochrome display adapter as the active display, type the following:

MODE MONO

The monochrome display always displays 80 columns.

To select the color graphics display as the active display, you use one of the following commands:

MODE CO40

MODE CO80

MODE BW40

MODE BW80

The first two options select the color mode of the color display with 40 or 80 columns. The last two options select the color display but use the black-and-white display modes with 40 or 80 columns.

Shifting the Screen on a Color Graphics Adapter

The second MODE command form, available in all versions of DOS, is for use on a Color Graphics Adapter only. This form does not work on an Enhanced Graphics Adapter (EGA) or a Video Graphics Array (VGA). This MODE command form, originally developed to enable you to configure the PC to work with a television instead of a specially designed computer monitor, moves the horizontal position of the displayed image on-screen. If you cannot see the leftmost or rightmost character on-screen, the following command corrects the problem.

> **MODE** *dt,s,T*

The *dt* parameter indicates the display type (described in the preceding section). The *S* parameter can have the value *R* to move the image to the right or an *L* to move the image to the left. If the display is in 80-column mode, the image is moved two characters right or left. If in 40-column mode, the image is moved one character. The optional *T* parameter, when used, causes a test pattern to be displayed, which you can use to align the display.

If you type **MODE CO80,R,T**, you see a line of 80 characters displayed across the screen, along with the following prompt:

```
Do you see the leftmost 0? (y/n)
```

This image is moved two positions to the right of its preceding position. If you respond no to the prompt, the screen is moved farther to the right. Using the **L** option works in the same way but moves the image to the left.

Cue:
If you operate your system with the displayed image in a shifted position, you have less memory available.

If you operate your system with the displayed image in a shifted position, you have somewhat less memory available for your application. (The MODE command uses less than 1K of memory.) To display the image in a nonstandard position, DOS places a small program into memory. This program intercepts everything displayed, adjusts it, and then sends the image to the display. The program left in memory is the *memory-resident portion* of the MODE command. Other versions of the MODE command also leave a portion resident.

Using MODE To Adjust the Number of Columns or Lines On-Screen

Cue:
Use the MODE command in DOS 4 and 5 to adjust the number of columns or lines displayed.

DOS 4 introduced two additional MODE command options, which are used to alter the display modes. You can adjust the number of columns or the number of lines displayed on-screen. The ANSI.SYS device driver must be installed for both of these forms to adjust the display.

The syntax for the first form of the MODE command that can be used only in DOS 4 is as follows:

> **MODE CON COLS=*a* LINES=*b***

COLS= sets the number of columns displayed on the console to *a*, and **LINES=** sets the number of lines displayed on the console to *b*. If you omit a setting for the number of columns or the number of lines, the current setting is preserved.

Valid numbers for *a* are 40 or 80. Valid numbers for *b* on a VGA are 25, 43, or 50; valid numbers for *b* on an EGA are 25 or 43.

If ANSI.SYS is loaded via the CONFIG.SYS file, typing the following command results in a display mode 80 columns wide and 43 lines high on a computer with an EGA or VGA adapter and monitor:

MODE CON COLS=80 LINES=43

After you set the display mode, you can start your application program. The display mode, unless reset by the application, remains. For example, using the preceding MODE example on an EGA-based computer enables you to use WordPerfect in 43-line mode without adjusting the settings in WordPerfect.

Not all applications can sense that the extra lines are available. You can try some MODE CON commands to see whether you can use the extra lines. Using MODE CON to set 43 or 50 lines makes viewing long DIR listings more convenient than using the standard 25 lines.

Another MODE command option, added in DOS 4, enables you to alter the number of lines displayed on-screen without specifying that the screen is the console. This form, which is really a variation on the MODE CON theme, is handy when you use an auxiliary console instead of CON. Chapter 9 introduces the CTTY command used to establish another device as the standard input and output device.

The syntax for this form of the MODE command is as follows:

*d:path***MODE** *dt,b*

dt is the display type, and *b* is the number of lines to be displayed. The acceptable values for *dt* and *b* are as previously described. Note that not all combinations of values for *dt* and *b* are possible. For example, you cannot adjust the number of lines on a monochrome monitor or the CGA.

On a VGA system, you alter the display type to color with 40 columns and 50 lines by typing the following command:

MODE CO40,50

All the forms of the MODE command that adjust the display are similar in syntax and purpose. An incorrect command damages nothing. DOS provides reasonably clear error messages. For example, if the ANSI.SYS driver is required and not installed, the following error message is displayed:

```
ANSI.SYS must be installed to perform requested function
```

Changing the Environment

The SET command enables you to adjust the DOS environment. This command shows the current settings in the environment, or the command can add or change environment variables.

Issuing the SET Command

The syntax for the SET command is as follows:

SET *name=string*

SET can be typed at the command prompt without any variables. The command then lists all the current settings for environment variables.

name= is the name of the environment variable. The most frequently used environment variables are COMSPEC, PROMPT, and PATH. However, you can choose your own variable names in addition to these three.

string is the value to which you want to set the variable. In the case of PATH, *string* can be the list of directories that you want DOS to search through to find program files.

If you use the *name=* parameter without a value for *string*, the variable specified is a null value (contains nothing).

Changing the Environment Variables with SET

Suppose that you want to use the SET command to change the environment variables. The following three commands change the COMSPEC, PROMPT, and PATH:

```
SET   COMSPEC=C:\SYS
SET   PROMPT=$p$g
SET   PATH=C:\;C:\DOS;C:\SYS;
```

The first command tells DOS that the command processor, COMMAND.COM, is located in the SYS subdirectory of drive C. The second command sets the prompt to include the current path and a greater-than sign. The third command places the root directory, the DOS directory, and the SYS directory of drive C onto the path.

The prompt and path can be set by using the specific commands. If your command processor is not located in the root directory of the boot drive, you must include an appropriate SHELL directive in CONFIG.SYS and add the **SET COMSPEC=** command to the AUTOEXEC.BAT file that points to the command processor, or your system can fail when you leave an application program that needs to reload the command processor or when you boot the computer. This failure occurs because the system cannot find the command processor. Refer to Chapters 7 and 15 for information on how to use the SHELL directive in CONFIG.SYS to inform the system of the location of the command processor.

Reminder:
*Use SHELL to
specify the
location of the
command
processor if it is
not in the root
directory.*

Setting Your Own Environment Variables with SET

The SET command also is used to set custom variables in the environment. These variables usually are the names of directories or switches used by programs. The programs know to look for a particular variable in the environment and to take the values and use them in the program.

For example, a word processing program may look for a dictionary file called DICT in the current directory. If you use the SET command, however, a different directory can contain the dictionary file. During installation, the program probably will insert a SET command into the batch file that invokes the program. This command can use the following form:

SET DICT=C:\WP\DICT

This command enables the program to look in the WP directory for the dictionary file, instead of looking in the current directory. Remember that setting a variable in the environment is useful only to programs that know to look for that variable.

Each variable stored in the environment occupies space. Programs that need a large variables set can require that you increase the area of memory set aside for the environment when DOS is booted. You take this action through the **SHELL** command in CONFIG.SYS (see Chapter 15).

Chapter Summary

This chapter introduced the commands you use to see and alter the DOS system information. The following key points were covered in this chapter:

- The DATE and TIME commands are used to alter the date and time used by DOS when you save files to disk.

- The VER command displays the current booted version of DOS.

- The MEM command provides extensive information about the memory, programs, and devices currently running.

- The DIR command, one of the most commonly used DOS commands, provides a list of the files in a directory or on a disk.

- The PROMPT command alters the command prompt presented for you to enter commands. On systems that use hierarchical directories, changing the prompt setting to **PROMPT pg** is advisable. The current path always is displayed.

- The MODE command can be used to alter the appearance of the screen. You can alter the number of lines, number of columns, and current display.

- The SET command enables you to change individual environment variables. These variables include PROMPT, PATH, and COMSPEC.

Chapter 10 covers the commands that you use when you work with devices. You learn how to control input and output devices. Chapter 10 also completes the coverage of the DOS core commands.

10

Gaining Control
of Devices

Chapter 4 introduces the concept of peripheral devices, as you use them with a personal computer. Devices can supply input to the computer, receive output from the computer, or both accept and receive information. Examples of devices include the hard disk drive, printer, video display, keyboard, and modem.

This chapter covers the commands that control the devices you connect to your computer. You use these commands to perform functions, such as redirection, selection of alternate keyboards, or alteration of the names assigned to parts of your hard disk.

The commands covered in this chapter include the following:

- CLS
- GRAPHICS
- PRINT
- ASSIGN
- JOIN
- SUBST
- CTTY
- MODE
- MORE
- FIND
- SORT

379

Clearing the Screen with CLS

The internal command CLS clears the screen. The command causes all text that is visible on-screen to be removed. The prompt is then displayed so that you can continue to issue DOS commands.

Use the following syntax for CLS:

CLS

No switches are available with CLS.

CLS clears only the display on the standard output device. If your system uses two displays, CLS clears only the active display and not both screens.

Clearing the screen does not, however, change the mode of the display. If, for example, you operate in 40-column mode (if you issue the command **MODE CO40**), the screen clears when you type **CLS**; the DOS prompt then is redisplayed in 40-column mode. You also retain all attributes previously set—for example, if you defined a background color and foreground color by using ANSI.SYS escape sequences, these colors are retained.

You use the CLS command frequently in batch files. By inserting a CLS command at the end of the AUTOEXEC.BAT file, for example, you can remove all the messages that memory-resident programs may display as they load into memory.

Printing Graphics Screens with GRAPHICS

You use the Print Screen (PrtSc on some keyboards) key to print the contents of the display on a printer. This method, however, works only when the screen is in text mode. If you execute the external command GRAPHICS, you can use the Print Screen key to print graphics screens as well. When you execute GRAPHICS, a portion of the program remains memory-resident. Then, when you press Print Screen (or Shift-PrtSc), all necessary converting is performed before the information is sent to the printer.

Issuing the GRAPHICS Command

The following line shows the syntax for GRAPHICS with DOS Version 3.3 and previous versions:

> **GRAPHICS** *printer d:path\filename /R /B /LCD /PRINTBOX:name*

printer is the type of printer to be used.

The */R* switch forces the printout to print black as black and white as white.

The */B* switch prints the background color.

/LCD causes the printbox size to be set for liquid crystal display (LCD) aspect ratio.

/PRINTBOX:name sets the printbox size to STD when you specify **/PRINTBOX:STD**; the switch sets the printbox size to the smaller liquid crystal display size when you specify **/PRINTBOX:LCD**. You can abbreviate PRINTBOX as PB.

d:path\filename is the drive, path, and file name of a printer profile file (DOS 4 and 5 only).

Understanding the Operation of GRAPHICS

Table 10.1 lists the values that you can use for the *printer* parameter. Your printer, if not listed, may be compatible with one of these products. Refer to the printer instruction manual for details.

Table 10.1
Product Names and Printer Settings

Printer Type	Model Name
COLOR1	IBM Personal Computer Color Printer with black ribbon which prints in gray scales
COLOR4	IBM Personal Computer Color Printer with RGB (red, green, blue) ribbon which produces four colors

continues

Table 10.1 *(continued)*

Printer Type	Model Name
COLOR8	IBM Personal Computer Color Printer with CMY (cyan, magenta, yellow, and black) ribbon, which produces eight colors
DESKJET	Hewlett-Packard Deskjet printer (DOS Version 5 only)
GRAPHICS	IBM Personal Computer Graphics Printer, IBM ProPrinter, or IBM Quietwriter printer
GRAPHICSWIDE	IBM Personal Computer Graphics Printer with an 11" carriage, IBM ProPrinters II and III
HPDEFAULT	Any Hewlett-Packard PCL printer (DOS Version 5 only)
LASERJET	Hewlett-Packard LaserJet (DOS Version 5 only)
LASERJETII	Hewlett-Packard LaserJet II (DOS Version 5 only)
PAINTJET	Hewlett-Packard PaintJet printer (DOS Version 5 only)
QUIETJET	Hewlett-Packard QuietJet printer (DOS Version 5 only)
QUIETJETPLUS	Hewlett-Packard QuietJet printer (DOS 5 only)
RUGGEDWRITER	Hewlett-Packard RuggedWriter printer (DOS Version 5 only)
RUGGEDWRITERWIDE	Hewlett-Packard RuggedWriter wide printer (DOS Version 5 only)
THERMAL	IBM PC-Convertible thermal printer
THINKJET	Hewlett-Packard ThinkJet printer

If you do not specify a printer, DOS assumes the GRAPHICS printer type.

When you include the /R switch, the printed image is *reversed*—black on the screen is printed as black on the paper. On a monochrome monitor, where the text is green in color, DOS treats the green as white.

Cue:
The GRAPHICS printer type is the default with the GRAPHICS command.

If you do not use the /R switch, all on-screen information that is white prints as black, and all black on-screen information (usually the background) prints as white. The paper color in the printer is assumed to be white.

Use the /B switch when you specify the COLOR4 or COLOR8 printer type. This switch causes the *background* color to be printed. If you omit the /B switch, the background color does not print.

The liquid crystal display on many laptop computers is smaller than the display on a full-sized monitor. With such a machine, use one of the following two switches: /LCD or /PRINTBOX:LCD (or /PB:LCD).

The /PRINTBOX:STD (or /PB:STD) switch causes the printbox size to match the image on a full-sized (standard) display.

The *filename* parameter specifies a file that contains information about a printer. This file, known as a *profile*, supports the printers of other manufacturers. If your printer doesn't fit into one of the categories supported by GRAPHICS, you can create a custom printer *profile* for use with GRAPHICS.

Cue:
You can select the name of a printer profile file.

The profile file is an ASCII text file that consists of two sections for each printer in the file. A profile can include information about how the printer is controlled—selecting printer colors or adjusting the darkness of the printing. The second section lists the translation from the screen to the printer.

GRAPHICS.PRO is the profile file supplied with DOS. If you want to create a custom profile file for your printer, make a copy of the supplied GRAPHICS.PRO file and try modifying where necessary. If you are interested in the programming aspects of DOS, try this exercise. Modifying the GRAPHICS.PRO file is not necessary for most printers.

Understanding the General Rules of GRAPHICS

- After GRAPHICS is loaded, pressing the Print Screen (Shift-PrtSc) key prints graphics screens on supported graphics printers.

- If you omit /PB and /LCD switches, GRAPHICS uses the previous printbox setting.

- You can print up to 8 colors on a color printer.

- You can print up to 19 shades of gray on a black-and-white printer.

Using GRAPHICS To Print a Screen Image

Suppose that you have an IBM ProPrinter printer. If you use a monochrome system and want to print a screen image with the background as black and the text as white, type the following command:

GRAPHICS /R

After GRAPHICS loads into memory, you can create the screen of interest and press Print Screen to print to the printer.

To print eight-color images (including the background color) on an IBM Personal Computer Color Printer with a CMY ribbon installed, use the following command:

GRAPHICS COLOR8 /B

On the PC Convertible with an attached full-sized monitor, you can send the screen image to the IBM PC-Convertible thermal printer by installing GRAPHICS with the following options:

GRAPHICS THERMAL /PB:STD

Changing the command to **GRAPHICS THERMAL /PB:LCD** or **GRAPHICS THERMAL /LCD** prints the image as it normally appears on the liquid crystal display.

Printing in the Background with PRINT

In Chapter 4, you learned that the COPY command can transfer information from one device to another. For example, the command **COPY LETTER.TXT PRN** copies the file named LETTER.TXT to the device PRN, the printer. During this copying process, the computer is not available for other use.

The external command PRINT enables you to print in the background, so that you can do other work while printing is being performed. The printing occurs during the idle times—for example, when the computer waits for you to type at the keyboard. More than one file at a time can be queued for printing.

Cue:

Use the PRINT command to print in the background.

Issuing the PRINT Command

The following line shows the syntax for the external PRINT command:

> **PRINT** */D:device /B:bufsiz /M:maxtick /Q:maxfiles*
> */S:timeslice /U:busytick d1:path1\filename1 /P /T /C*
> *d2:path2\filename2 /P /C /T ...*

d1:path1\filename1 is the first drive, path, and file name of a file to be printed. *d2:path2\filename2* is the second drive, path, and file name of a file to be printed. The ellipsis (...) signifies that you can specify more files.

Wild cards are permitted in the file names.

The optional switches are listed in table 10.2.

Table 10.2
PRINT Switches

Switch	Action
/D:device	Specifies the *device* name for the output device
/B:bufsiz	Specifies the size of *buffer* used in the printing process
/M:maxtick	Specifies the *maximum* number of system clock *ticks* that the PRINT command can use at a time
/Q:maxfiles	Specifies the *maximum* number of files that can be *queued* at a time
/S:timeslice	Specifies the proportion of *time* allocated to the background printing
/U:busytick	Determines how many ticks the PRINT command waits for the printer to be not *busy*
/P	Places the file in the line for printing; places the command in *print* mode
/C	*Cancels* the background printing of the file specified
/T	*Terminates* all printing and clears the print queue

Understanding the Operation of PRINT

Like GRAPHICS, PRINT leaves a portion of itself in memory after the command is activated. These parameters alter how PRINT works. After installation, you cannot change PRINT's method of operation. You can specify the */D:device*, */Q:maxfiles*, */B:bufsiz*, */S:timeslice*, */U:busytick*, and */M:maxtick* optional switches the first time you issue the PRINT command.

The optional switches available with PRINT can change the command's operation.

/D:device specifies the device name for the output device. Acceptable values include all DOS output devices, such as LPT1, LPT2, LPT3, PRN, COM1, COM2, COM3, COM4, or AUX.

/Q:maxfiles specifies the maximum number of files—from 4 to 32—that can be queued at a time. If the switch is omitted, 10 files is the default queue size.

/B:bufsiz specifies the size of buffer used in the printing process. The data for printing is taken from the disk in chunks that are the size of this buffer. Increasing the size causes more data to be taken from the disk at a time. The minimum buffer size is 512 bytes—the maximum is 16K. If the switch is omitted, 512 bytes are set aside for the buffer. Remember that the larger the buffer, the less RAM is available for applications programs.

/S:timeslice determines the number of clock ticks allocated to the background printing. Too high a value for this switch causes the computer to respond sluggishly to other commands that you execute while printing is occurring in the background. A low value slows the printing process. The range of values is 1 to 255; the default value is 8.

/M:maxtick specifies the number of system clock ticks that the PRINT command waits for the printer to print a character. *maxtick* can be set to any value between 1 and 255; the default value is 2.

/U:busytick determines how long the PRINT command waits for the printer to be available. In most cases, the PRINT command sends data to the printer faster than the printer can actually print. The printer can store some of this information in built-in memory. When this memory fills, the printer sends a "busy" signal to the computer. The command is actually transferring the data in memory to the print head and printing on the page. When some room becomes available in the printer's memory, the printer stops sending a busy signal, and PRINT can send more data.

The /U:busytick switch can change the number of clock ticks that PRINT waits before sending data to the printer. The default setting is 1, but the setting can be altered up to as high as 255. If the printer is busy, PRINT first tries to send the data and then waits the number of clock ticks set by this switch. If the printer is still busy, PRINT immediately transfers control back to DOS for other tasks without claiming the full time allocation that is set by the */s:timeslice* setting.

Typing just **PRINT** at the prompt displays a list of all files in the queue. This list includes the name of the file that is currently printing and the order of files yet to print. Error messages also are displayed. If, for example, you forget to turn on the printer, the following error message appears:

```
Errors on list device indicate that it may be
off-line. Please check it.
```

The /P switch *places* a file in PRINT's queue. The preceding file and all subsequent files on the command line are printed.

The /C switch changes the mode to *cancel*. The file name issued before the /C, and all files after the /C on the same command line, are removed from the print queue. You must issue the /P switch to start adding files to the queue again.

If you enter file names without a /P, /C, or /T switch, DOS uses the /P switch as a default. The files are all placed in the queue for printing.

The /T switch *terminates* printing. All files are removed from the queue, including the one currently being printed. The printer alarm sounds, a file cancellation message prints, and the paper advances to the next page. This alarm also sounds if you cancel the currently printing file with the /C switch.

Understanding the General Rules of PRINT

- You can specify the /D:device, /Q:maxfiles, /B:bufsiz, /S:timeslice, /U:busytick, and /M:maxtick optional switches only the first time that you issue the PRINT command.

- If you specify /D:device, you must type this switch first, before all other switches.

- If you issue /P, the preceding file and all subsequent files entered on the command line by the PRINT command are printed until a /T or /C is issued.

- If you issue /C, the preceding file and all subsequent files are canceled from the queue of files.

- The files print in the order that you enter them at the command line.

- A page-eject sequence is sent to the printer at the end of a file.

- You cannot use the printer for other purposes while PRINT is in operation. You cannot, for example, use Print Screen when PRINT is in effect.

- The files to be printed must remain in the same disk drive and unaltered while they are in the print queue and while they are being printed.

- Specifying a nonexistent device causes unpredictable behavior by the computer.

- Tab characters in the printed file are converted to blanks, up to the next 8-column boundary.

Using PRINT To Print Several Files

Reminder:
You can specify
parameters with
PRINT only when
the command is
first issued.

You don't have to enter the names of all the files to print at one time. You can issue the PRINT command several times to add or remove files from the print queue. When you first issue the command, however, you can specify only the various parameters that affect the way PRINT operates. After activaton, you use the PRINT command to enter file names for printing.

If you enter the PRINT command for the first time without defining a device, PRINT prompts you for a device name, which is the first parallel port (LPT1) on your computer. PRN is the default offered. Pressing Enter at the DOS prompt accepts PRN.

Suppose that you want to print five files called LETTER1.TXT, MEMO1.TXT, REPORT1.TXT, REPORT2.TXT, and REPORT10.TXT. In a standard configuration, accepting PRINT's default setting, type the following on the command line:

PRINT /D:PRN LETTER1.TXT /P MEMO1.TXT REPORT1.TXT REPORT2.TXT REPORT10.TXT

If you then decide that you want to print REPORT10.TXT before REPORT2.TXT, type the following:

PRINT REPORT2.TXT /C REPORT2.TXT /P

This command first removes REPORT2.TXT from the print queue and then adds the file to the end of the queue.

You can cancel all files to be printed by typing the following command:

PRINT /T

By using a combination of the /P, /T, and /C switches, you can adjust the order in which the files print.

If you are in no hurry to collect the printed output of files and want to use the computer while the printer prints your files, you can readjust the default installation settings for PRINT. These settings can give your computer better response time.

Cue:
Adjust the default installation settings for PRINT to achieve better response time on your computer.

You can try adjusting the /M:maxtick or /S:timeslice settings. /M:maxtick alters the maximum length of time that can elapse while the printer prints a character before DOS displays an error message, and /S:timeslice determines the number of timeslices that DOS allocates for background printing. Try the following when you invoke the PRINT command for the first time:

PRINT /D:PRN /M:1 /S:25

If you are unconcerned about the sluggishness of the keyboard, you can improve the speed of the background printing by altering the buffer size, as well as adjusting /M:maxtick and /S:timeslice. Consider the following setting:

PRINT /D:PRN /B:16384 /M:1 /S:25

Experiment with these variables until you find a setting that is acceptable. A sluggish keyboard is not always tolerable. If the response time is too slow, you can make errors—for example, you may assume that a program didn't accept your keystrokes and try to retype the command. The program was only waiting to regain control.

Redirecting File I/O with ASSIGN

The external command ASSIGN is used to redirect all DOS read and write (input and output) requests from one drive to another. Each drive is a DOS device; by using the ASSIGN command, DOS can interrogate a different disk than the one actually specified on a command line.

Cue:
Use the ASSIGN command to redirect I/O requests from one drive to another.

You can find the ASSIGN command most useful with older software that expects associated programs and data on a specific drive. For example, software written for DOS Version 1, when hard disks were not available for PCs, often insists on looking for data on drive A. The ASSIGN command enables you to tell DOS to use your hard drive, even if the software attempts to use drive A.

Issuing the ASSIGN Command

Use the following syntax for the ASSIGN command:

ASSIGN d1=d2 .../STATUS

d1 is the drive letter for the original disk drive; **d2** is the drive letter for the reassignment.

The ellipsis (...) indicates that more than one drive can be reassigned on a single command line.

Use the /STATUS switch (DOS 5.0 only) with no other parameters to display a listing of current drive assignments.

Understanding the Operation of ASSIGN

When you issue the ASSIGN command, DOS redirects all read and write requests for **d1** to **d2**. If you assign drive A to drive C, all commands that refer to drive A are actually sent to drive C.

You should use the ASSIGN command sparingly. Don't use ASSIGN if you do not require the command for a particular purpose. Certain programs may require disk information unavailable from the reassigned drive.

Understanding the General Rules of ASSIGN

- You can use an optional colon after the drive letter only with DOS Version 4 and later versions.

- Remove all ASSIGN settings before running FDISK, PRINT, FORMAT, BACKUP, or RESTORE.

- Do not use ASSIGN if either JOIN or SUBST are being used.

- Do not use ASSIGN prior to using the APPEND command.

- Beware of using CHDIR, MKDIR, RMDIR, LABEL, APPEND, and PATH with any drives reassigned.

- DISKCOPY and DISKCOMP cannot recognize drive reassignments.

- **d1** and **d2** must both physically exist in the computer.

Using ASSIGN To Reassign Drives

Some early versions of programs cannot use drives other than drive A or B. In many cases, if you reassign drives A and B to drive C, you can run an otherwise uncooperative program on a hard disk.

In some cases, by reassigning a drive, you can avoid having to use a floppy disk to run a program. Certain programs assume that their program floppy disk is located in drive A. Reassignment of drive A to the hard disk results in the program being directed by DOS to the hard disk instead of to the floppy drive.

To use the ASSIGN command to assign drive A to drive C, type the following:

ASSIGN A=C

If you now issue a directory command to drive A or drive C, you will get a directory listing for drive C.

If you cannot remember which disk assignment you made, issue the following command (DOS 5.0 only):

ASSIGN /STATUS

DOS displays the following message:

```
Original A: set to C:
```

Typing only **ASSIGN** at the DOS prompt removes all previous reassignments.

Joining Two Disk Drives with JOIN

Cue:
*Use the JOIN
command to add
a disk drive to the
directory structure
of another disk.*

The ASSIGN command makes an entire disk drive appear to have a different drive letter than the actual drive letter. You can use the JOIN command to add a disk drive to the directory structure of another disk.

The external command JOIN enables you to use a floppy disk that appears to be part of a hard disk. The directory structure on the floppy disk is added to the directory structure of the hard disk. You also can use JOIN if you have two hard disks—drive C and drive D. JOIN can, for example, attach drive D to a subdirectory on drive C.

Issuing the JOIN Command

The syntax for JOIN is as follows:

JOIN d1: *d2:\path/D*

d1: is the disk drive to be connected. DOS calls this drive the *guest disk drive*.

d2: is the disk drive to which d1: is to be connected. DOS calls *d2:* the *host disk drive*.

\path is a subdirectory in the root directory of *d2:*, the host drive. DOS calls **\dirname** the *host subdirectory*. **\dirname** holds the connection to **d1:**, the guest drive.

The */D* switch disconnects the specified guest disk drive from the host disk drive.

To show currently connected drives, use the following form:

JOIN

Understanding the Operation of JOIN

Hierarchical directories and associated commands were discussed in Chapters 2 and 7. The JOIN command connects or joins a guest drive to a subdirectory position on a host drive. Any directory hierarchy on the guest disk becomes a part of the host disk's drive hierarchical structure.

Think of the JOIN command as grafting a second tree onto your directory tree. The second tree is positioned at least one level down the structure. The grafting point must be assigned a name so that DOS can locate the point. In this way, you give the root directory of the guest disk a new name. All directories below the root directory on this reassigned drive use the new name as part of their path.

DOS internally converts all I/O requests to this new subdirectory—and all layers below the subdirectory—into a drive assignment with the appropriate path.

Understanding the General Rules of JOIN

- **dirname** must either be empty or not exist.
- You cannot join a directory to the current directory.
- You cannot join to the root directory of a drive.
- When you join one drive to another, you cannot access **d1:**.
- The entire drive is joined with the JOIN command.
- You cannot specify a networked drive either as **d1:** or *d2:*.
- Do not use the JOIN command with ASSIGN or SUBST.
- The following commands do not recognize drives entered with the JOIN command: CHKDSK, SYS, LABEL, RECOVER, DISKCOPY, DISKCOMP, FDDISK, PRINT, FORMAT, BACKUP, and RESTORE.
- Beware of using CHDIR, MKDIR, RMDIR, APPEND, and PATH with any reassigned drives.

Using JOIN To Connect Drives

To JOIN drive B to drive C as a subdirectory called DRIVEB, type the following command:

JOIN B: C:\DRIVEB

Typing just **JOIN** at the prompt displays any drive reassignments. In this example, the following message appears:

```
B: => C:\DRIVEB
```

To remove a joined drive, type the following command:

JOIN B: /D

You can use the JOIN command to overcome some of the limitations of DOS. The command is not, however, an ideal solution in all cases. Certain commands must not be used when JOIN is in effect. Joining two logical partitions on a single drive overcomes the 32M partition barrier. Choosing to use the JOIN command is a compromise between full DOS functionality and the benefit of a larger partition.

Substituting a Drive Name for a Path with SUBST

Cue:
The SUBST command splits a disk's directory structure in two.

The external command SUBST is the inverse of the JOIN command. Instead of grafting a second disk onto the tree structure of another disk, the SUBST command splits a disk's directory structure in two. In effect, the SUBST command creates an alias disk drive name for a subdirectory.

Issuing the SUBST Command

The syntax for the SUBST command is as follows:

To establish an alias, use the following form:

SUBST d1: d2:pathname

To delete an alias, use this form:

SUBST d1: /D

To see the current aliases, use this form:

SUBST

d1: is a valid disk drive name that becomes the alias or nickname. **d1:** may be a nonexistent disk drive.

*d2:***pathname** is the valid disk drive name and directory path that will be nicknamed **d1:**.

Understanding the Operation of SUBST

The SUBST command replaces a path name for a subdirectory with a drive letter. After a SUBST command is in effect, DOS translates all I/O requests to a particular drive letter back to the correct path name.

As the default, DOS assigns the LASTDRIVE= parameter a value of E. Higher drive designators, however, can be made by inserting a LASTDRIVE= parameter into the CONFIG.SYS file. DOS then establishes each of the drive letters up to and including the specified LASTDRIVE as DOS devices. When you use the SUBST command, DOS understands that you are referring to a device.

The alias drive "created" by the SUBST command inherits the directory tree structure of the subdirectory reassigned to a drive letter.

Understanding the General Rules of SUBST

The SUBST command is subject to certain rules and limitations, as shown in the following list:

- **d1:** and *d2:* must be different.

- You cannot specify a networked drive either as **d1:** or *d2:*.

- **d1:** cannot be the current drive.

- **d1:** must have a designator less than the value in the LASTDRIVE statement of CONFIG.SYS. (See Chapter 14 for more information on CONFIG.SYS.)

- Do not use SUBST with ASSIGN or JOIN.

- Remove all SUBST settings before you run DISKCOPY, DISKCOMP, FDISK, PRINT, FORMAT, LABEL, BACKUP, MIRROR, RECOVER, SYS, or RESTORE.

- Beware of using CHDIR, MKDIR, RMDIR, APPEND, and PATH with any drives reassigned.

Using SUBST To Reference a Path with a Drive Letter

SUBST is commonly used in two different situations. If you want to run a program that does not support path names, you can use the SUBST command to assign a drive letter to a directory. The program then refers to the drive letter, and DOS translates the request into a path. If, for example, the data for a program is stored in C:\WORDPROC, you can type the following:

SUBST E: C:\WORDPROC

You tell the program that the data is stored in drive E.

After the substitution is made, you can issue the following command:

SUBST

The following message appears:

```
E: => C:\WORDPROC
```

To disconnect the substitution of drive E for the C:\WORDPROC directory, type the following command:

SUBST E: /D

The other use for SUBST is to reduce typing long path names. Path names can grow quite long when a PC is used by more than one person. Each user may use a separate section of the hard disk to store data files and common areas of the disk to store programs. If the paths \USER1\WORDDATA and \USER1\SPREDATA exist on drive C, the typing needed to reach files in the directories can be reduced by entering the following command:

SUBST E: C:\USER1

Issuing a directory command on drive E produces the following listing:

```
Volume in drive E is HARD DISK C
Volume Serial Number is 1573-0241
Directory of  E:\
    .           <DIR>        06-02-88    2:07p
    ..          <DIR>        06-02-88    2:07p
WORDDATA        <DIR>        05-01-89   11:59a
SPREDATA        <DIR>        06-02-88    2:08p
        4 File(s)                0 bytes
                            77824 bytes free
```

The volume label given is the label from drive C, but the directory itself is the contents of C:\USER1.

As with JOIN and ASSIGN, you can use the SUBST command to fool stubborn software that insists on using an otherwise unusable drive. For example, a friend, who has a drive D, may have written an application program. You can fool your friend's program by using SUBST to attach drive D to a subdirectory on your drive C.

Do not use the following DOS commands in conjunction with drives that you create with the SUBST command: BACKUP, CHKDSK, DISKCOMP, DISKCOPY, FDISK, FORMAT, LABEL, MIRROR, RECOVER, RESTORE, and SYS. MIRROR is new with DOS 5.

Selecting a Different Console with CTTY

DOS usually uses the keyboard and screen as the standard input and standard output devices. Together, these two elements comprise the console, known to DOS as the CON device. The internal command CTTY enables you to select a different device as the console and restore the keyboard and screen as the console.

Cue:
The CTTY command enables you to select a different console.

Issuing the CTTY command

Use the following syntax for the internal command, CTTY:

CTTY device

or

CTTY CON

device is the name of a DOS device.

Understanding the Operation of CTTY

CTTY causes DOS to intercept the I/O request calls that normally come from the keyboard and go to the screen; the command redirects these calls to an alternate device.

Understanding the General Rules of CTTY

- The character-based devices AUX, COM1, COM2, COM3, or COM4 can be used as the alternate console.

- The physical device attached to the relevant AUX, COM1, COM2, COM3, or COM4 must be able to accept input and provide output.

- Programs that do not use DOS function calls will not make use of the alternate console.

- If you load BASIC, which does not use DOS function calls, the standard input and output are restored.

Making the Serial Port the Console with CTTY

Typing the command **CTTY COM1** designates COM1 as the device that sends and receives standard input and output. This command is used in association with specialized programs that need input from a different source to the keyboard.

Another use for CTTY is possible if the computer is attached to an intelligent bar code reader that collects information from packages. This reader, in association with a specialized program, may not need to use the display or keyboard.

Typically, you probably will not use the CTTY command. Information can be gathered through these devices without altering the standard input and output devices. Certain applications, however, benefit from this feature.

Typing **CTTY CON** from the auxiliary device restores the console to the keyboard and display.

Controlling Device Operations with MODE

Cue:
Use MODE to adjust the settings for a variety of devices.

MODE is one of the more versatile external commands supplied with DOS. DOS Versions 4 and 5 extended this versatility still further. MODE is used to set the operational modes of serial ports and parallel ports, and to redirect information from a parallel port to a serial port. Other functions include setting display modes (see Chapter 8) and use with code pages (see Chapter 15).

In this chapter, the MODE functions that relate to devices are introduced. The Command Reference section details all MODE functions. You can use MODE to set a variety of devices—the serial ports and parallel ports.

Using MODE To Change Parallel Port Settings

As you learned in Chapter 4, a parallel port transmits data by transferring (usually to a printer) the entire byte at one time. The MODE command adjusts the number of lines per inch, the number of columns per line, and the retry feature.

Issuing MODE To Change Parallel Port Settings

The following line shows the syntax for the external MODE command that changes the parallel printer characteristics:

MODE LPT*x:cpl,lpi, P*

LPT*x:* is the parallel port name; *cpl* is the number of characters per line; *lpi* is the number of lines per inch; and *P* specifies continuous retries on time-out errors.

The default value of *cpl* is 80; the default value of *lpi* is 6.

An additional command mode is available with DOS Versions 4 and 5, as shown in the following syntax:

MODE LPT*x: COLS=wid, LINES=lpi, RETRY=action*

wid is the number of columns per line; *lpi* is the number of lines per inch; and *action* is the message you want DOS to return when the printer port is busy. Available actions and their results are shown in the following list:

E   Returns an *error* when the printer port is busy

B   Returns a *busy* signal when the printer port is busy

R   Returns a *ready* signal when the printer port is busy

    P   Continuous *retry* until *printer* is ready

    N   Takes no retry action (default)

Understanding the General Rules of MODE To Change Parallel Port Settings

- The default values of the port are reset if the printer is reset or initialized.

- A parameter omitted from the command line is not changed.

- Do not use the P option when printers are being shared on an IBM PC network.

Understanding the Operation of MODE with Parallel Ports

The MODE command used to adjust the parallel port alters only two items seen on the printout itself—the characters per line and the lines per inch. In general, printing is performed directly from an applications program, which is able to set many more parameters for a particular printer. The program operates by sending Escape sequences to the printer that can adjust the printed output accordingly.

The retry setting is more significant. On versions of DOS prior to Version 4, the retry option either performs no retry when a time-out error is returned, or performs continuous retries when the P option is included. When data is sent to the printer, the port expects to see signals from the printer indicating that the data was received. If no signals are received within a particular period of time, a time-out error is generated. By default, DOS does not retry to send information to the printer and returns an error message to the screen.

Including the P option prevents this error message from being displayed as DOS continuously retries to send the data. The Ctrl-Break key combination will stop this retrying process.

Cue:
DOS Versions 4 and 5 forms of MODE offer additional retry features.

In DOS Versions 4 and 5, more retry options are available. With no retry specified, DOS does not continue to try to send data when a time-out error occurs.

When the retry feature is specified, you can select from four options in DOS Version 4 or five options in DOS Version 5. The B setting returns a busy signal to the device driver when the port is busy. The R setting causes a ready signal to be returned from the port even if the port is really busy. Then, when the printer does become ready, the data is ready to send and an error message does not appear on-screen. The E option is most commonly used when the printing is being done in the background (by PRINT or a network print queue). The data is not transferred to the printer until the port is not busy. The N setting (NONE in DOS 4.0) means to take no retry action. In DOS 5, the P option also is available, which causes DOS to try the printer continuously until the busy state ends.

Using MODE To Print a Large File

In certain cases, the P option is necessary to enable a file to be printed. Consider a large DOS file that you want to copy to the printer. If the file is larger than the storage capacity of the printer, the printer port will be busy at some point during the data transfer. If the printer remains busy for too long a period of time, an error message appears on-screen; DOS thinks the printer is defective and the printing process aborts.

Cue:
Use the P option with MODE to print a large file.

Specifying **P** in DOS Version 3.3 and previous versions, or **RETRY=B** in DOS Versions 4 and 5, causes DOS to wait until the printer is ready to receive data. Use the following command for LPT1 in DOS Version 3.3:

    MODE LPT1:,,P

For DOS Versions 4 and 5, use the following command:

    MODE LPT1 RETRY=B

If the file is large, you may find printing the file with a higher number of lines per inch (8 instead of 6) more convenient, so that more lines of text can fit on a page. Also, you can specify 132 columns per line instead of 80. This setting is not a problem for a wide-carriage printer, which accepts wide paper. You need to set a printer that accepts 8 1/2-inch paper to print in a condensed character mode. This mode can fit 132 columns on a line with printers that accept 8 1/2-inch paper.

Use the following command to fit as much information as possible on a page, when the printer is attached to LPT2:

    MODE LPT2:132,8

Using MODE To Change the Serial Port

Cue:
Use MODE to alter the functions of the serial ports.

Another option of the MODE command is used to alter the functions of the serial ports. This command works in a way similar to the parallel port adjustments. DOS changes the parameters that are sent to and from the device driver.

Issuing MODE To Adjust Serial Ports

The following line shows the syntax for the MODE command that changes the serial port:

MODE COMy: *baud,parity,databits,stopbits,P*

COMy: is the name of the serial port device; *baud* is the baud rate; *parity* is the parity; *databits* is the number of data bits; *stopbits* is the number of stop bits; and *P* specifies continuous retries on time-out errors.

The baud rate for the serial port must be specified.

The default number of data bits is 7. The default number of stop bits is 1 for all baud rates except 110, when 2 stop bits are set as the default.

With DOS Versions 4 and 5, the following syntax is possible:

MODE COMy: *BAUD=baud PARITY=parity DATA=databits STOP=stopbits RETRY=action*

action is the message you want DOS to return when the port is busy.

The following list describes the available actions:

E   Returns an *error* when the printer port is busy

B   Returns a *busy* signal when the printer port is busy

R   Returns a *ready* signal when the printer port is busy

P   *Retry* continuously until the *port* is ready

Understanding the General Rules of MODE with Serial Ports

- If a retry option is set, a portion of MODE remains resident unless the **RETRY=none** option of DOS Version 4 is used.

- The retry option slows the performance of foreground tasks when computers are being shared on an IBM PC network.

- The parity settings in DOS Version 4.0 and later versions can include Mark or Space parity. All versions of DOS support *none*, *odd*, and *even* parity settings.

Understanding the Operation of MODE with Serial Ports

The acceptable serial ports are COM1, COM2, COM3, and COM4. As explained in Chapter 4, the serial port can receive and transmit data one bit at a time. The signaling rate (the number of times per second that data is transmitted) is the *baud rate*. The amount of data transferred in a second is referred to as the *bps* (bits per second). With the MODE command, the baud settings adjust the amount of data sent in a fixed time. Although referred to as a baud setting, the numbers used are actually the bits per second. Baud settings are 110, 150, 300, 600, 1200, 2400, 4800, 9600, and 19200. You need to use only the first two digits of the number to set the baud rate.

Cue:
The baud rate refers to the number of times per second that data is transmitted.

The most common peripherals that are attached to a serial port and need setting from DOS are serial printers and plotters. Although modems are serial devices, they are not usually adjusted from DOS. Communications programs, however, use the DOS functions to make adjustments to the serial ports.

Reminder:
Modems are not usually adjusted from the DOS level.

With versions of DOS prior to Version 4, the retry feature provided two choices—no retry when a time-out error is returned, or continuous retries when the P option is included. When data is sent to the printer, the port expects to see signals from the printer indicating that the data was received. If no signals are received within a particular period of time, a time-out error is generated. By default, DOS does not retry to send information to the printer and returns an error message to the screen.

Including the P option prevents the error message from being displayed, as DOS continuously retries to send the data. The Ctrl-Break key combination stops this retrying process.

With DOS Versions 4 and later, more retry options are available. With no retry specified, DOS does not retry to send data when a time-out error occurs.

When the retry feature is specified, you can select from three options. The B setting returns a busy signal to the device driver when the port is busy. The R setting causes a ready signal to be returned from the port even if the port is really busy. Then, when the printer does become ready, the data is ready to send and an error message does not appear on-screen. The

E option is most commonly used when the printing is being done in the background (by PRINT or a network print queue). The data is not transferred to the printer until the port is not busy. In DOS Version 5, the P action also is available to specify continuous retry.

Using MODE To Set the Serial Port

To set the first serial port to communicate at 2400 bps, with 8 data bits, 1 stop bit, and no parity, you type the following:

MODE COM1 2400, N, 8, 1

or

MODE COM1 24, N, 8, 1

With DOS Version 3.3 and later versions, type the following to get the same settings:

MODE COM1 BAUD=24 DATA=8 STOP=1 PARITY=NONE

Note that the printer or plotter needs to be set to receive data in the same format in which the serial port is sending the data—that is, the same baud rate, parity, and so on.

Using MODE To Redirect a Parallel Port to a Serial Port

The final MODE setting used with ports is the command to redirect a parallel port to a serial port.

Issuing the MODE Command To Redirect Ports

The following line shows the syntax for the MODE command that changes the parallel printer to a serial printer:

MODE LPT*x:* =COM*y:*

LPT*x:* is the name of the parallel printer port; **COM*y:*** is the name of the serial port.

Understanding the Operation of MODE To Redirect Ports

After you use MODE, DOS channels to the serial port all I/O requests that a program sends to the parallel port. The conversion of data from byte-wide to bit-wide is handled automatically by the electronics associated with the port.

Understanding the General Rules of MODE To Redirect Ports

- Any parallel port can be redirected to any serial port.

- The serial port must be initialized with both speed and data characteristics before the parallel port is redirected (see the preceding section on MODE).

- The initialization of the serial port must include the retry option if the attached device is a printer.

Reminder:
You can use
MODE to redirect
any parallel port
to any serial port.

Using MODE To Redirect Ports

Some early programs do not directly support serial printers. To use such a serial printer, you can set a serial port and redirect a parallel port to that serial port. This process enables you to print when you use a serial printer and a program that doesn't directly support the printer.

The serial port is initialized with DOS Version 3.3 by using a command similar to the following:

MODE COM2 2400, E, 7, 2

With DOS 4 and 5, type the following command:

MODE COM2 BAUD=96 DATA=7 STOP=2 PARITY=EVEN

You then can follow the initialization command by typing the following command:

MODE LPT1=COM2

All data that normally goes to LPT1 is transmitted from COM2 at 9600 bps, with 7 data bits, 2 stop bits, and even parity.

Using MODE To Change the Typematic Rate

When you press a key on the PC keyboard, a character appears on the display. If you hold the same key down for a short period, nothing more happens. If you continue to hold the key down, the character that is pressed repeats on-screen. The number of times a second the key is repeated is known as the *typematic rate*.

With versions of DOS prior to Version 4, you need an add-on utility program to alter the keyboard typematic rate. You now can make this setting from DOS.

Issuing the MODE Command To Set the Typematic Rate

The following line shows the syntax for the external command MODE that changes the typematic rate:

MODE CON RATE=*rate* **DELAY=***delay*

rate is the number of repetitions per second; *delay* is the time delay before DOS starts repeating a key.

Understanding the Operation of MODE To Set the Typematic Rate

Two adjustments are possible: how long you must hold down a key before the key character or action starts repeating (the *delay*) and the number of times per second the character is generated (the *rate*).

The delay is specified in 1/4-second intervals. The range for the delay is 1 through 4, making a total possible delay of 1 second.

The rate parameter can have value in the range 1 through 32. These values represent a repeat rate of from 2 to 30 characters per second (the higher the value, the faster the repeat rate). The default value is 20 for an IBM AT and 21 for an IBM PS/2, which is equivalent to approximately 10 characters per second.

Using MODE To Set a Delay

To set the keyboard so that the delay before the key repeats is 0.75 seconds, and the rate value is 24, type the following:

MODE CON RATE=24 DELAY=3

Redirecting Input and Output to Other Devices with Redirection

As explained in Chapter 4, DOS uses three standard devices: one for input, one for output, and one for errors. Usually, the console receives and accepts data. The keyboard is the standard input source. The display is the standard output and standard error device.

You type commands at the keyboard. The commands are displayed on-screen. DOS executes a command and supplies output to the screen. When an error occurs (perhaps you specify a directory command on a drive that doesn't exist), the error message is displayed on-screen.

DOS enables you to redirect the standard input and standard output information, but standard errors are always sent to the screen.

Reminder:
Standard errors always are sent as output to the screen.

Issuing the Redirection Commands

The following line shows the syntax for redirecting a program's input:

function < *inputdevice*

The syntax for redirecting a program's output is as follows:

function > *outputdevice*

The syntax for redirecting and appending to an existing file is as follows:

function >> *outputdevice*

inputdevice is the source of the input for the function. The output is sent to *outputdevice*. **function** can specify almost all DOS commands.

All DOS output devices can be used as an *outputdevice*. All DOS input devices can be used as an *inputdevice*.

Understanding the General Rules of Redirection

- Do not use redirection on a DOS command line that includes CALL, FOR, or IF.

- Using > and referring to an existing file causes the existing file to be overwritten with the new standard output.

- Using >> appends the standard output to an existing file, or creates one if the file does not exist.

Understanding the Operation of Redirection

When you use a redirection symbol, DOS either looks at a different device to receive input, or supplies the output to a different device.

Normally, redirected input comes from a file. Some devices, however, such as mice or bar code readers, can be used as a source of data. For example, a file can consist of the keystrokes used to operate a program. Alternatively, the information sent from the mouse can be used as the input to a program.

Most DOS users redirect output more often than they redirect input. The **DIR > PRN** command, which redirects the output of a directory to the printer, is a common example of redirection. When you issue this command, DOS redirects the output (the listing itself) to the PRN device instead of sending the listing to the screen. This command produces a hard copy listing of the directory.

Another common use is redirecting output to a file. For example, to review the statistics of the **MEM /DEBUG** command, type the following command:

MEM /DEBUG > DEBUG.MEM

When used in association with pipes and filters, which are discussed in a following section in this chapter, redirection becomes even more powerful.

Using Redirection To Print the Output of Commands

To redirect to the printer a copy of the directory structure on your disk, as well as a list of the files on your hard disk, type the following:

TREE C:\ /F >PRN

The TREE command does not supply a directory listing that includes file sizes, however. You can create a full listing of all the directories on your hard disk by using redirection to append the output of the command. You specify that each directory be listed and then specify that the output be appended to a file. You then can print the full list. Each directory command would have the following form:

DIR C:\NEXTPATH >> FULLLIST.DIR

You substitute the name of each directory in turn for C:\NEXTPATH.

If you are testing programs that require a large amount of user input, the following redirection method is useful. For example, you can type the following:

PROGRAM < C:TESTPAT

This command results in the file TESTPAT supplying the input to PROGRAM. The redirection process enables you to construct a file that contains the correct keystrokes needed to operate a program. You then can test the program's basic operation before all the error-trapping sequences are included. These sequences handle situations when the incorrect key is typed on the keyboard.

Introducing Filters (MORE, FIND, SORT) and Piping (¦)

DOS supplies additional functions to help you interact with devices. With three elements called filters, DOS is responsible for channeling information between devices. You can use these filters to modify information as it passes from files to the screen. Filters work only on ASCII text files.

The MORE filter acts like a screen buffer. Instead of information being sent directly to a device, MORE collects information in a temporary file on disk and displays a screen at a time. The FIND filter finds specific text within a file, and the SORT filter sorts lines of text in a file.

Cue:
You can use DOS filters to modify information as it passes from files to the screen.

These filters are often used in association with the redirection symbols so that the input can come from a different source than the keyboard or be sent to a different device than the screen.

Another feature used with these commands is piping. You use the pipe symbol (¦) to send output information that normally goes to the screen as input to another program. Piping, a form of redirection, diverts information destined for a device, but then makes the information become the input from a "device" to another program.

Buffering with the MORE Filter

The MORE filter buffers information from the standard input and only sends the data to the monitor one screen at a time.

Issuing the MORE Filter

The syntax for the MORE filter is as follows:

MORE

MORE is commonly used in two different ways:

1. **MORE** < *filename*
   filename is the input file.

2. *command* ¦ **MORE**
   command is any command or program.

Understanding the Operation of MORE

Cue:
The MORE filter stores in a temporary file information that would normally go to the screen.

MORE, a filter command, collects—and saves in a temporary disk file—information that normally goes to the screen. When a screen of input is obtained, MORE sends that information to the standard output device all at the same time. The text is channeled through the MORE filter until the end of the file. Pressing any key at the -- More -- prompt displays the next screen. After all the information is displayed on-screen, the temporary file created by MORE is erased.

Understanding the General Rules of MORE

- MORE appears to do nothing when issued alone. MORE requires input to be redirected or piped.

- To view further screens full of information, press any key at the prompt `-- More --`.

- Ctrl-Break terminates the command without displaying further screens.

Using MORE To Pause the Screen

When you use MORE to pause directory listings, the filter serves a function similar to the /P switch that is available with the DIR command.

The most common use of MORE, however, is to pause the TYPE command. To read the contents of a README.DOC file one page at a time, you type the following:

TYPE README ¦ MORE

or

MORE <README

Both methods function identically. To see the contents of a file, you can use the TYPE command. If the output of the file flows off the screen, reissue the command by using the DOS editing keys. Press F3 and add the pipe character (¦) and **MORE**.

Finding Strings of Text with FIND

The FIND filter can find strings of ASCII text in files. This filter is often used in association with redirection and piping.

Cue:
Use the FIND filter to find strings of ASCII text in files.

Issuing the FIND Filter

Use the following syntax for the FIND Filter:

>   *FIND /C /N /V /I "string" d:path\filename ...*

"string" specifies the ASCII characters for which you are searching. *d:path\filename* is the drive, path, and file name of the file to be searched. The ellipsis (...) indicates that you can specify more than one file to search.

The */C* switch changes the listing to a *count* of all lines that contain *"string"*.

The */N* switch changes the listing to include line *numbers* of the lines that contain *"string"*.

The */V* switch changes the listing to include all lines that do not contain *"string"*.

/C and */V* can be used together. The count displayed is the number of lines that do not contain *"string"*.

/V and */N* can be used together. The lines that do not contain "string" are displayed with their appropriate line numbers.

The */I* switch (Version 5 only) causes the search to be insensitive to case—upper- and lowercase letters are considered equivalent.

Understanding the General Rules of FIND

Reminder:
*Use the MORE,
FIND, and SORT
filters only with
ASCII text files.*

- Use FIND only on ASCII text files.

- The string parameter is normally case-sensitive. The string *LOOK* is not the same as the string *look*. In DOS Version 5 you can use the */I* switch to make the search *case-insensitive*.

- The string is enclosed in quotes. To include a quote in a string, you type two quotes together (" "). FIND then searches for occurrences of ".

- The standard input device is used if *filename* is not specified.

- Wild cards are not allowed in *filename*.

Understanding the Operation of FIND

If used without options, the FIND filter reads each of the specified files and displays all lines that contain a particular ASCII string. DOS takes and filters the information that normally goes to the standard output. All lines that include the ASCII string are displayed on-screen.

If you use the /V switch, lines that include the ASCII string are not passed on to the standard output. The /C switch is used as a *counter*; the text itself is not passed to the screen. Use the /N switch to locate the line *numbers* within the text file. The line numbers assigned are the line numbers in the original text file, not just sequential numbers. For example, if the third, fifth, and sixth lines in the text file contain the string, the line numbers displayed are 3, 5, and 6, not 1, 2, and 3.

Like the other filter commands, FIND often is used with redirection and piping. If you search a text file for lines that include specific information, a more useful technique may be to redirect the output to a file. You then can use the list as a reference while you look at the whole of the original file.

Using FIND To Find Files On-Disk

You can use the FIND command to find on-disk all files that have a certain extension. To find all files that have the extension LET, type the following command:

> **CHKDSK C: /V ¦ FIND ".LET"**

Because the /V switch is used with CHKDSK, all files with the extension LET are listed, including the directory in which the file is contained.

The CHKDSK command with the /V option lists all the files on a disk. The output from CHKDSK that normally goes to the display is supplied as input to the FIND command. The output from FIND is displayed on-screen.

The FIND filter also can be used with text files as a word-search utility. Consider the situation in which you forget the name of the memo you sent to your boss. You know that the file is either MEMO1, MEMO2, or MEMO3. You always use your boss's title, *Supervisor*, in memos. Type the following:

Cue:
Use the FIND filter as a word-search utility with text files.

> **FIND "Supervisor" MEMO1 MEMO2 MEMO3**

Each line in the files that contain *Supervisor* is listed. The listing appears in the following form:

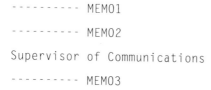

```
---------- MEMO1

---------- MEMO2

Supervisor of Communications

---------- MEMO3
```

Sorting Information with SORT

Cue:
The SORT filter sorts the information in an ASCII file before displaying the file.

The third DOS filter is SORT. SORT takes and sorts the information from an ASCII file before displaying the result on-screen. Like FIND and MORE, SORT often is used with redirection and piping.

Issuing the SORT Filter

Use the following syntax for the SORT filter:

SORT */R /+n*

/R reverses the sort order.

n is the offset column for the sorting process.

Understanding the General Rules of SORT

- If n is not specified, column 1 is assumed.
- Lines are sorted according to their ASCII binary values with two exceptions:
    1. SORT is not case-sensitive. For example, *A* and *a* are sorted as they occur in the source file.
    2. Characters with values over 127 are sorted in the order determined by the current COUNTRY code setting. (See Chapter 15 for more information.)
- The output file name must be different from the input file name when you use redirection.

Understanding the Operation of SORT

The SORT filter processes information that normally goes to the standard output device. The text from the input is analyzed on a line-by-line basis and sorted according to the ASCII binary values of the characters. This order is alphabetical, but no discrimination is made between upper- and lowercase letters.

When used with redirection or piping, sophisticated sorting occurs. The most common use of SORT is to sort a directory listing into a text file, which then can be printed.

The offset option in the command indicates the leftmost column to be sorted. With a directory listing, you can sort by date or file size rather than just by root name. Table 9.5 lists the offset values for a directory listing.

Table 9.5
Offset Values for SORT

Offset value	Sorting by
1	Root name
10	File extension
14	File size
24	File date
34	File time

Note that the sorted output is a file or text on-screen, which is not the same as altering the directory listing itself. The system directory remains unchanged.

Using SORT To Sort Subdirectories

Redirection and piping, as well as the FIND and SORT filters, can be used in many ways. In DOS Version 4 or 5, for example, you can create a sorted list of the subdirectories in the root directory by using the process outlined in the next paragraphs.

To create a sorted list of subdirectories in the root directory, type the following command:

    TREE C:\ /A ¦ FIND "—" ¦ SORT /+2 >TEMP.LST

When issued with the /A switch, the TREE command produces a listing that includes the nongraphics character set. The FIND filter then removes all lines that are not subdirectory names. The output from FIND is sorted by SORT on column 2, and the output is redirected to a temporary file.

Next, you use the temporary file as the input to the FIND filter, which removes all directories that are not in the root.

> **FIND /V "¦" <TEMP.LST**

The result is an alphabetical list of all subdirectories in the root directory.

Note that although the preceding commands work in DOS Version 5, the DIR command can perform essentially the same work in a simpler manner by combining switches /D (directories only), /S (include subdirectories), and /O (sort alphabetically by name):

> **DIR /A:D /S /O**

Chapter Summary

This chapter discussed the commands associated with changing the way DOS interacts with devices. These commands range from basic commands that clear a screen to advanced filtering and redirection commands. The following important points were covered:

- Use the CLS command to clear the currently active display.

- Use the GRAPHICS command to print graphics screens on supported printers.

- The PRINT command is a background printing program.

- The ASSIGN, JOIN, and SUBST commands are used to change the device names assigned to disk drives and directories.

- Use the CTTY command to redirect standard input and output devices.

- Use the options available with the MODE command to adjust settings for serial and parallel ports.

- You can use MODE with DOS Versions 4 and 5 to alter the keyboard typematic rate.

- The MORE, FIND, and SORT filters are used with text files. The filters are frequently used with redirection and piping.

The next chapter, which begins Part III of this book, discusses using the DOS Editor.

Part III

Expanding Your Use of DOS

Includes

Using the DOS Editor

Understanding Batch File Basics

Understanding ANSI.SYS

Learning Advanced Batch File Techniques

11

Using the DOS Editor

The DOS Editor—new with DOS 5.0—is a *text processor*, a kind of mini-word processor. The Editor is the perfect tool for creating short text documents and editing text files. The Editor is so simple and intuitive to use that you likely will become a regular user.

This chapter explains how to use the basic features of the DOS Editor, including how to use its menus and shortcut commands and how to create, edit, save, and print text.

Understanding the DOS Editor

The DOS Editor falls into a class of programs known as text editors. As the name implies, a *text editor* works with files that contain pure text (as opposed to *binary* files that contain programming instructions).

The following are some of the typical tasks for which the Editor is ideally suited:

- Creating, editing, and printing memos (and other text documents)

- Viewing text files whose contents are unknown

- Creating or modifying various system configuration files, such as AUTOEXEC.BAT and CONFIG.SYS

- Writing and modifying batch files (Batch files are discussed in Chapter 13.)

- Writing and saving README files. Many computer users place a README file in a hard disk subdirectory (or on a floppy disk) to explain the contents of other files in the subdirectory or disk.

- Creating and viewing files uploaded to or downloaded from electronic bulletin boards, such as CompuServe

- Writing programs for programming-language environments that do not include a resident editor

Document files produced by some word processors are not pure text files. The files may contain special formatting or printer-control characters. Most word processors can import the pure text files created with the DOS Editor. The Editor, however, may not successfully import word processor document files that contain certain formatting characters.

Files Required To Run the DOS Editor

The DOS Editor is part of the DOS 5.0 package. The Editor is invoked by the external command **EDIT**, which runs the program EDIT.COM. When you run the Editor, EDIT.COM calls on two other files: QBASIC.EXE and EDIT.HLP. Only QBASIC.EXE is required. EDIT.HLP contains the text of the help messages, but the Editor works without this file.

Starting the DOS Editor

You can start the DOS Editor from the DOS Shell or from the command line.

If you are running the DOS Shell, select Editor from the main program group in the program list area (see Chapter 5 for more about starting a program from the DOS Shell). After you select Editor from the DOS Shell menu, a box labeled File to Edit pops open. A message inside the box prompts you to supply a file name. To start the Editor without loading a specific file, press Enter. To load a text file into the Editor, type the file's name, including the path if the file is not located in the default directory. Then press Enter to start the Editor with your designated file loaded and ready for editing.

If you are running from the command line, type **EDIT** at the DOS prompt and press Enter.

Regardless of which method you chose for starting it, the Editor now initializes. A preliminary screen appears (see fig. 11.1).

Fig. 11.1. The preliminary DOS Editor screen.

Press Enter or Esc.

- Enter activates the Survival Guide. (The Survival Guide provides help about using the Editor.)

- Esc clears the box in the center of the screen and prepares the Editor for working on a text file.

Press Esc. Now the DOS Editor screen is blank, and you can begin writing a text file. Your screen should look like figure 11.2.

Getting Acquainted with the Initial Editor Screen

Take a moment to look at your screen (or at fig. 11.2). The screen is composed of several elements.

The *menu bar* at the top of the screen lists the available menus: File, Edit, Search, Options, and Help.

The *title bar* is a short, centered bar, immediately beneath the menu bar that contains the name of the text file being edited (the current file is Untitled).

The *status bar* is the line, across the bottom of the screen, that describes the current process and shows certain shortcut key options.

Scroll bars are a vertical strip along the right edge and a horizontal strip just above the status bar. The scroll bars are used with a mouse to move through the file. (Mouse techniques are described later in this chapter.)

The *Editor window* is the large area in which the text of your file appears.

The *cursor* is the flashing underscore character that indicates where typed text will appear.

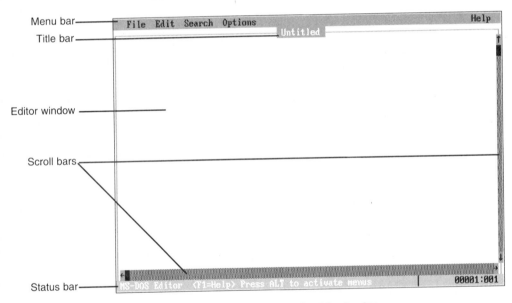

Fig. 11.2. The initial Editor screen with a blank editing area.

Navigating the DOS Editor

The DOS Editor provides several ways to perform most commands. The Editor has a user-friendly set of menus from which you can select options. Many of these options require you to enter further information in an on-screen dialog box.

The Editor also enables you to execute many commands by pressing shortcut keys. Whether you prefer shortcut commands or menus, the Editor also enables you to use a mouse input device.

The sections that follow describe how to use menus, dialog boxes, shortcut keys, and a mouse in the DOS Editor.

Understanding the Menu System

The DOS Editor menu system provides many editing commands. The menu bar contains the following options: File, Edit, Search, and Options. Selecting any of these options displays a pull-down menu. The File option displays a menu that enables you to load, save, and print files. The Edit menu is used to cut and paste text. The Search menu is used for finding and replacing specified text. The Options menu can be used to reconfigure environment options. The Help menu provides access to on-line help.

To activate the menu bar, press Alt. The first letter of each menu name is highlighted. Then press the first letter of the menu name. For example, press Alt and then **F** to activate the File menu (or just press Alt-F). Similarly, press Alt-E to activate the Edit menu, Alt-S to activate the Search menu, or Alt-O to display the Options menu.

After a menu opens, you can move from one menu to another by pressing the left- or right-arrow key. Every time you open a main menu, the first command on the submenu is highlighted. You can move this highlight to the other commands by pressing the up- or down-arrow key. As you move the highlight, notice that the information bar displays a brief description of the highlighted command.

On a menu, one letter of each command is highlighted. On most systems, the highlighted letter appears in high-intensity white. To execute a command, move the highlight to that command and press Enter or press the key that corresponds to the highlighted letter.

Depending on which editing commands you have previously executed, some commands in a menu may not be available. In such a case, the menu shows the command name in a dull color (usually gray), and no highlighted letter appears in the name. If you try to execute an unavailable command, the Editor sounds a beep and refuses to execute the command.

Pressing Esc closes the menu system and returns you to the Editor.

In the pull-down menus, an ellipsis (...) following the name of a submenu command indicates that a dialog box opens when you issue that command. (Sometimes, depending on the circumstances, a command without the ellipsis also opens a dialog box.)

Understanding Dialog Boxes

A menu command may execute immediately or, depending on the command and the current context, a dialog box may pop up. A dialog box means that the Editor needs more information before the command can be completed. For example, if you execute the command to save a new file, the Editor first needs to know what name to give the file. A dialog box prompts you for the necessary information.

For example, if you activate the Search menu and then select Change, the Editor displays the Change dialog box shown in figure 11.3.

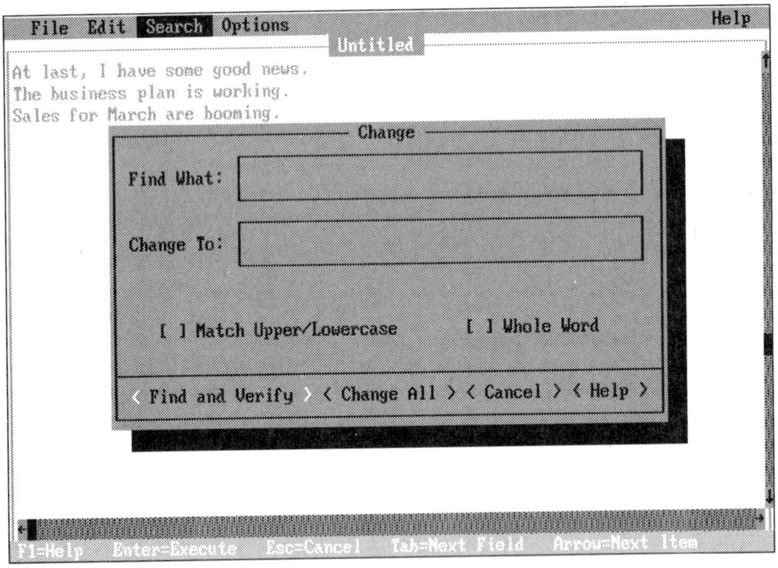

Fig. 11.3. *The Change dialog box.*

The DOS Editor uses dialog boxes to get a variety of information. Sometimes you must type something, such as a file name or a search string in a text box. At other times, you must choose from a list of options or select from a series of command buttons.

When a DOS Editor dialog box opens, the following three keys have special significance:

- Tab—Moves the cursor from one area of the dialog box to the next area. After you specify information in one area, use Tab to move to the next area.

- Esc—Pressing this key aborts the menu option and returns you to the Editor. Use Esc when you change your mind and decide against issuing a particular command.

- Enter—Press this key when all options in the dialog box are as you want them, and you are ready to execute the command. You press Enter only once while you are working inside a dialog box. Use Tab, not Enter, to move the input focus from one area of the dialog box to the next area.

In every dialog box, one command button is enclosed in highlighted angle brackets. The highlighted brackets identify the action that takes place when you press Enter. Recall that you press Enter when all the dialog box options are set the way you want.

To highlight the angle brackets of the command you want, press Tab repeatedly. Be sure not to press Enter until you have specified everything satisfactorily.

When you are working with a dialog box, pressing Alt and a highlighted letter activates an option even if the cursor is in another area.

Using Shortcut Keys

Many commonly used DOS Editor menu commands have an associated *shortcut key*. Pressing this shortcut key while you are working with the DOS Editor executes the command directly, bypassing the menu system. Table 11.1 contains a complete list of shortcut keys.

Using a Mouse

A mouse is an excellent pointing device for computer applications. The DOS Editor supports a mouse. You can execute menu commands and many editing tasks with a mouse. If your system is mouseless, you can get along fine; if you have a mouse, try it and see what you think.

Note: The DOS Editor works with any Microsoft-compatible mouse and driver. If you have a mouse, you probably know how to install and activate your mouse driver. Microsoft supplies a mouse driver as part of the DOS 5.0 package.

When the mouse is active, you see a special mouse cursor on-screen. The mouse cursor is a small rectangle, about the size of one text character, that moves as you move the mouse. Notice that the regular blinking cursor remains active. You can continue to use all the keyboard commands and features.

Table 11.1 also contains a comprehensive list of mouse techniques.

Table 11.1
DOS Editor Keyboard and Mouse Shortcuts

Shortcut Key	Effect	Mouse
F1	View help on menu or command	Click right button on desired item
Shift-F1	View help on getting started	Click on Getting Started (Help menu)
Ctrl-F1	View next help topic	Click on <Next> (status bar)
Alt-F1	Review most recent help screen	Click on <Back> (status bar)
Shift-Ctrl-F1	View preceding help topic	None
F3	Repeat the last find	Click on Repeat Last Find (Search menu)
F6	Cycle between help and editing	Click inside desired window
Shift-F6	Make preceding window active	Click inside window
Shift-Del	Cut selected text	Click on Cut (Edit menu)
Ctrl-Ins	Copy selected text	Click on Copy (Edit menu)
Shift-Ins	Paste text from clipboard	Click on Paste (Edit menu)
Del	Erase selected text	Click on Clear (Edit menu)
Ctrl-Q-A	Change text	Click on Change... (Search menu)

Shortcut Key	Effect	Mouse
Ctrl-Q-F	Search for text string	Click on Find... (Search menu)
Esc	Terminate Help system	Click on <Cancel> (status bar)
Alt	Enter menu-selection mode	None
Alt-Plus	Enlarge active window	Drag title bar up
Alt-Minus	Shrink active window down	Drag title bar

The following are some additional mouse pointers:

- To open a menu, click on the menu name in the menu bar.

- To execute a menu command, click on the command name in the menu.

- To set an option in a dialog box, click on that option.

- To abort a menu, click on a location outside the menu.

- To move the cursor in the file, click on the location you want.

- To select text, *drag* the mouse over the text. Move the mouse pointer to one end of the text to be selected and then press and hold down the mouse button while you move the mouse across the text to be selected.

- To activate the Editor window while a help screen is visible, click anywhere inside the Editor window.

- To expand or shrink the Editor window while a help screen is visible, drag the title bar of the Editor window up or down.

- To scroll the screen horizontally one character, click on the left or right arrow at either end of the horizontal scroll bar.

- To scroll the screen vertically one character, click on the up or down arrow at either end of the vertical scroll bar.

- To scroll text vertically to a specific position, move the mouse cursor to the *scroll box* (the inverse-video rectangle inside the vertical scroll bar). Then drag the scroll box along the scroll bar to the desired position.

- To scroll text one page at a time, click on the vertical scroll bar somewhere between the scroll box and the top or bottom of the scroll bar.

- To scroll horizontally several positions at the same time, click on the horizontal scroll bar somewhere between the scroll box and the left or right end of the scroll bar.

- To execute a dialog-box action shown enclosed in angle brackets, click on the name between the brackets.

- To execute any keystroke action enclosed in angle brackets in the status bar at the bottom of the screen, click on the name inside the angle brackets.

Using Fundamental Editing Techniques

Editing is a skill—almost an art. Some editing techniques are simple; others are more complex. Many editing tasks can be performed in more than one way.

This section discusses the fundamental editing skills, which include moving the cursor, scrolling, inserting text, and deleting text.

Moving the Cursor

With text in the DOS Editor, you can move the cursor around the text in several ways. The DOS Editor provides two alternative cursor-movement interfaces:

- *Keypad interface:* The specialized IBM PC keys—the arrow keys, Ins, Del, and so on—govern most editing activities. To move the cursor up, for example, you use the up-arrow key.

- *Control-key interface:* Ctrl-key combinations govern most editing activities. To move the cursor up, for example, you press Ctrl-E. This interface is used in the word processing program WordStar.

The DOS Editor accommodates both camps. Most editing techniques are available with the keypad and control-key (WordStar-style) sequences. A few techniques, however, can be performed with only one style. This chapter focuses on the keypad style. The control-key combinations are mentioned only when required by a particular editing technique.

Table 11.2 summarizes the cursor-movement commands.

Table 11.2
Cursor-Movement Commands

Effect	Keypad	WordStar style
Character left	Left	Ctrl-S
Character right	Right	Ctrl-D
Word left	Ctrl-Left	Ctrl-A
Word right	Ctrl-Right	Ctrl-F
Line up	Up	Ctrl-E
Line down	Down	Ctrl-X
First indentation level	Home	None
Beginning of line	None	Ctrl-Q-S
End of line	End	Ctrl-Q-D
Beginning of next line	Ctrl-Enter	Ctrl-J
Top of window		Ctrl-Q-E
Bottom of window		Ctrl-Q-X
Beginning of text	Ctrl-Home	Ctrl-Q-R
End of text	Ctrl-End	Ctrl-Q-C
Set marker		Ctrl-K n
Move to marker		Ctrl-Q n

Look at the rightmost end of the status bar, in the lower right corner of the DOS Editor screen. You see two numbers, separated by a colon. The two numbers indicate the cursor's current location in your file. The first number is the current row; the second number is the current column.

Use the arrow keys to move the cursor and watch the numbers change. Press Num Lock; an uppercase N appears next to the location numbers to indicate that Num Lock is on. Press Num Lock a few more times to toggle the indicator on and off. Press Caps Lock; an uppercase C appears next to the location numbers, left of the N, to indicate that the Caps Lock key is on.

Scrolling

Scrolling is the wholesale movement of text inside the Editor window. When you scroll, you bring into view a portion of the file currently not visible in the Editor window. Scrolling, which can be horizontal and vertical, keeps the cursor at the same row and column number but moves the text in the window.

Table 11.3 summarizes the scrolling commands. For large-scale scrolling, you use the PgUp and PgDn keys. Try using these keys by themselves and with the Ctrl key.

Table 11.3
Scrolling Text

Effect	Keypad	Control-key style
One line up	Ctrl-Up	Ctrl-W
One line down	Ctrl-Down	Ctrl-Z
Page up	PgUp	Ctrl-R
Page down	PgDn	Ctrl-C
One window left	Ctrl-PgUp	
One window right	Ctrl-PgDn	

Inserting Text into a Line

You can insert text into an existing line. Move the cursor to the position at which you want to insert text. Type the text you want to insert. As you type, text to the right of the cursor moves right to accommodate the inserted text. You can move off the line by using any of the cursor-movement keys. Do *not* press Enter to move off the line. Pressing Enter splits the line in two.

Deleting Text from a Line

You can use one of the following two methods to delete a few characters from a line:

- Move the cursor to the character you want to delete. Press Del. To delete consecutive characters, continue pressing Del.

• Move the cursor to the character immediately to the right of the character you want to delete. Press the Backspace key.

Most people find the first method more natural. Try both methods and make your own choice.

Splitting and Joining Lines

Sometimes you have a need to split a line of text into two lines. Move the cursor to a position beneath the character that you want to begin the second line of text. Press Enter. The line splits in two, and the second half moves down to form a new line. Succeeding lines are pushed down to accommodate the new line.

Conversely, you can join two lines together to form one line. Position the cursor in the second line and press Home to move the cursor to the left end of the line. Press Backspace. The second line moves up to the right end of the first line. Lines beneath the split line move up one line.

Inserting and Deleting a Line

To insert a blank line between two lines, move the cursor to column 1 in the lower of the two lines and then press Ctrl-N. You also can press Home (to move the cursor to the left end of the current line) and press Enter. Then move the cursor up to the new blank line.

To delete an entire line, place the cursor anywhere on the line and press Ctrl-Y.

Overtyping

By default, the DOS Editor operates in *insert* mode. If you type new text while the cursor is in the middle of a line, that new text is inserted at the cursor location.

Instead, you can *overtype*. In overtype mode, the newly typed text replaces the former text.

To activate overtype mode, press Ins. The cursor changes from a blinking line to a blinking box. The larger cursor signifies overtype mode, in which any new character you type replaces the character at the cursor location.

To return to standard insert mode, press Ins again. The Ins key acts as a toggle switch that alternates between insert and overtype modes.

Using Special Editing Techniques

In addition to the basic editing techniques, the DOS Editor provides several special editing features. The sections that follow describe how to use the automatic indenting, tab, and place marker features.

Using Automatic Indent

When you type a line and press Enter, the cursor drops down one line but returns to the column where you began the preceding line. This feature is convenient when you want to type a series of indented lines.

For example, assume that you type the following line and press Enter:

This line is not indented

The cursor moves to the beginning of the next line. Then press the space bar three times to move the cursor to column 4 and type the following:

But this line is

Press Enter again. Note that the second time you press Enter, the cursor moves to the next row but remains indented at column 4. Type **So is this one** and press Enter. The cursor remains indented.

Now press the left-arrow key repeatedly until the cursor returns to column 1. Type **Back to no indentation** and press Enter.

The short text block looks like the following:

```
This line is not indented
   But this line is
   So is this one
Back  to  no  indentation
```

Using Tab

By default, tab stops are set every eight spaces. When you press the Tab key, the cursor moves to the right to the beginning of the next tab zone. All text to the right of the cursor moves right when you press Tab. Additional tabbing techniques follow.

To indent an existing line a full tab position, move the cursor to column 1 of the line and press Tab.

To remove leading spaces and move a line to the left, move the cursor anywhere on the line and then press Shift-Tab.

To indent or unindent an entire block of lines, select the target lines by using one of the Shifted keystrokes shown in table 11.4. Then press Tab to indent the entire block or Shift-Tab to unindent the entire block.

To change the number of default tab stops, first select Display... from the Options menu. Press Tab several times to move the input focus to Tab Stops, type a new value for the number of characters per tab stop, and then press Enter to close the dialog box.

Using Place Markers

A *place marker* designates a specific location—a row and column—in your text. You can set as many as four place markers. After setting a place marker, you can move the cursor instantly from anywhere in the file to that marker's location. The markers are invisible; no character displays in the text to indicate a set marker.

To set a place marker, press Ctrl-K*n*, where *n* is a number from 0 to 3. This action associates the cursor's current position with the marker numbered *n*. To move the cursor to a previously set place marker, press Ctrl-Q*n*, where *n* is marker 0–3.

Block Editing

You can edit blocks of text as one unit. Block editing requires that you understand two relevant concepts: *selecting text* (which identifies the block of text to be edited) and the *clipboard* (which temporarily stores a block of text in a reserved area of memory).

This section describes the following techniques:

- Selecting text for block operations
- Using the clipboard
- Cutting and pasting blocks of text

Selecting Text

A block of selected text always must be one continuous piece. The block may be one character, a few characters, a line, several lines, a paragraph, or even an entire file. Selected text appears in reverse video.

Follow these steps to select a block of text:

1. Move the cursor to one end of the block.

2. While you hold down the Shift key, use cursor-movement keys to highlight the block.

Table 11.4 lists the keys used for selecting text. Generally, the keys you use to select text are the same as those you use to move the cursor, but you also press Shift when using them to select text.

Table 11.4
Selecting Text

To select	Use this key combination
Character left	Shift-←
Character right	Shift-→
To beginning of line	Shift-Home
To end of line	Shift-End
Current line	Shift-↓
Line above	Shift-↑
Word left	Shift-Ctrl-←
Word right	Shift-Ctrl-→
Screen up	Shift-PgUp
Screen down	Shift-PgDn
To beginning of text	Shift-Ctrl-Home
To end of text	Shift-Ctrl-End

After you have selected (highlighted) a block, you can deselect it by pressing any arrow key. (Don't use Shift, however). The highlighting disappears, indicating that the entire block has been deselected.

Understanding the Clipboard

The clipboard is a text storage area in memory, which acts as a kind of halfway house for blocks of text. You can place a block of text into the clipboard and later retrieve the block. The clipboard has many uses. Its most common use is to *cut and paste*—to move or copy a block of text from one place in the file to another.

The clipboard stores only one block of text at a time. When you place text in the clipboard, the incoming text completely replaces the previous contents of the clipboard. Changing the block of text in the clipboard is always an all-or-nothing affair. You cannot add or subtract incrementally. Similarly, retrieval is all-or-nothing. You cannot move only part of the clipboard's contents into your file.

Working with Text Blocks

The DOS Editor supports four block-oriented editing techniques (see table 11.5). Each technique is available from the Edit menu or by using the appropriate shortcut key. (Press Alt-E to activate the Edit menu.)

For example, to select the first three lines of text in a file, Press Ctrl-Home to return the cursor to the beginning of the file. While holding down the Shift key, press the down-arrow key three times. You have selected the first three lines of the file, which now are displayed in reverse video (highlighted).

After the three lines are selected, you can use one of the block-editing commands. To activate the Edit menu, press Alt-E. The Editor displays the Edit menu shown in figure 11.4. You now can use one of the menu commands. Alternatively, you can use one of the shortcut keys to operate on the selected block, even without displaying the Edit menu.

When you perform copy operations, a copy of the selected text moves to the clipboard but is not deleted from the original location. If you perform a cut command, however, the Editor places the highlighted text into the clipboard and removes it from the original location.

Table 11.5
Block-Editing Techniques

Menu Command	Shortcut Key	Description
Cut	Shift-Del	Deletes selected text from a file and places that text in clipboard
Copy	Ctrl-Ins	Places in clipboard a copy of selected text from file; text in file remains selected
Paste	Shift-Ins	Inserts contents of clipboard into the file at cursor; clipboard contents remain intact. If file currently contains selected text, clipboard text replaces the selected text.
Clear	Del	Deletes selected text from file; contents of clipboard are not affected

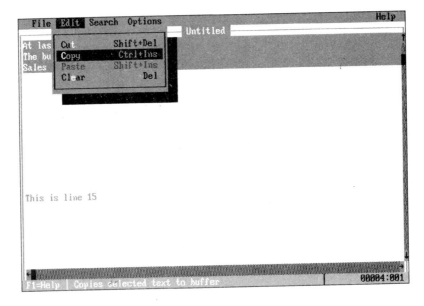

Fig. 11.4. The Edit menu.

After text has been copied or cut into the clipboard, you can use the paste operation to copy the clipboard's contents to a new location in the file. Move the cursor to the desired target location and select Paste from the Edit menu or press Shift-Ins (the shortcut key for paste). A copy of the clipboard text is inserted at the cursor's location. (The clipboard still holds a copy of the pasted text. You can insert additional copies of the clipboard text at other locations in the file.)

Pressing Del, or selecting the Clear command from the Edit menu, permanently deletes the selected text from the file, without placing a copy of the text in the clipboard.

Searching and Replacing— the Search Menu

The Search menu offers several options for searching for, finding, and replacing text. These capabilities are most useful in long files.

From the Search menu, you can perform the following actions:

- Find one or more occurrences of a designated text string.

- Replace one or more occurrences of a designated text string with a second text string.

A *text string* is a sequence of one or more consecutive text characters. These characters can be letters, digits, punctuation, special symbols—any characters you can type from the keyboard.

Finding or replacing text always involves a *search string*, which is the text string being searched for. A search string can be a single character or, more likely, a word or several consecutive characters.

You cannot search for a string that spans two or more lines. The search string is confined to a group of characters on one line. You can place some conditions on the search string. For example, you can specify that the search not discriminate between upper- and lowercase letters.

The search begins at the cursor's location and proceeds through the file. If the end of the file is reached before the search string is found, the search wraps around to the top of the file and continues until the entire file has been traversed. Table 11.6 summarizes the three commands available from the Search menu.

Table 11.6
Search Menu Commands

Command	Shortcut Key	Description
Find...	None	Opens a dialog box in which you specify the search string; finds the search string in your file
Repeat Last Find	F3	Searches for the text specified in the last Find... command
Change...	None	Replaces one text string with another

Using the Find Command

To use the Find command, first activate the Search menu by pressing Alt-S. Your screen looks similar to figure 11.5.

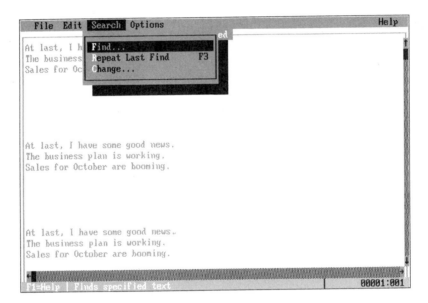

Fig. 11.5. *The Search menu.*

Select Find. The Find dialog box opens, with the cursor on the Find What text box (see fig. 11.6). The word at the cursor's current location in the file appears in the text box (or the currently selected text, if any). If you want to search for this word, press Enter. Otherwise, type the correct search string and press Enter. The Editor locates the first occurrence of the search string in your file and selects (highlights) the text found.

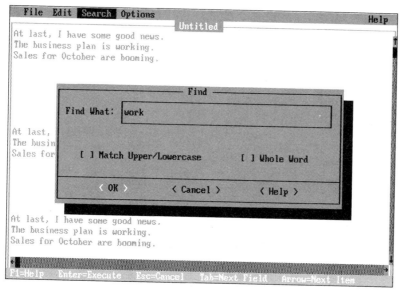

Fig. 11.6. *The Find dialog box.*

You can press F3 or select **R**epeat Last Find on the Search menu. The Editor moves to the next occurrence of the search string (if any).

As shown in figure 11.6, you can use the following check boxes in the dialog box to place conditions on the search:

- Match Upper/Lowercase. If you select this check box, a successful search only occurs when the upper- and lowercase letters in the text found exactly match those in the search string. If this option is not selected, upper- and lowercase letters are considered the same.

- Whole Word. If this option is selected, the search string must exist as an independent word that cannot be embedded inside a larger word. The character that immediately precedes and immediately follows the search string must be a blank space, a punctuation character, or one of the special characters (such as <, *, or [ ).

Using the Change Command

In addition to just searching for text, you can use the Editor to search for specific text and then replace the text with other text.

Activate the Search menu by pressing Alt-S. Select the Change command. The Editor displays the Change dialog box, shown in figure 11.7.

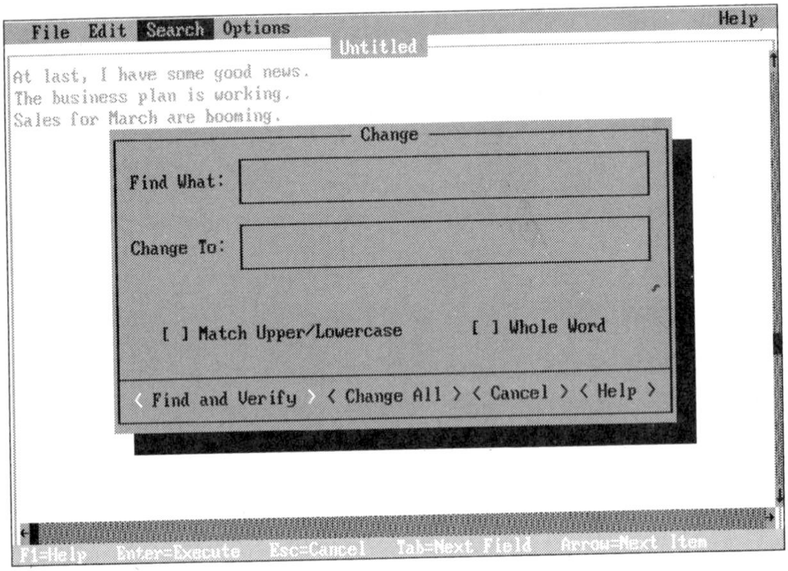

Fig. 11.7. The Change dialog box.

The first text box in the Change dialog box is labeled Find What. Type the text you want the Editor to find in this text box. The second text box is labeled Change To. A filled in Change dialog box is shown in figure 11.8.

After making the appropriate entry in the text boxes and after selecting any desired check boxes, choose from among the following four command buttons:

- Find and Verify finds each occurrence of the target string, one after another. (You specify the target string in the Find What dialog box.) As each occurrence of the target string is found, a second dialog box opens. This second box gives you the choice of making the substitution, skipping ahead to the next occurrence, or canceling the remaining searches. Find and Verify is the default option, which you select by pressing Enter.

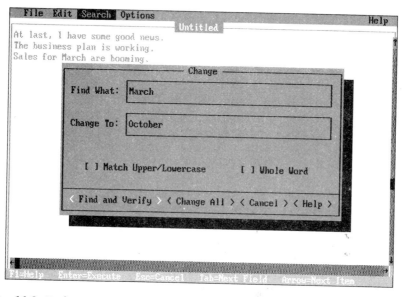

Fig. 11.8. *Performing a search-and-replace operation.*

- Change All changes all occurrences of the target string to the string specified in the Change To box. The changes occur at the same time. A dialog box informs you when the substitutions are complete.

- Cancel aborts the Change command, closing the dialog box without making any substitutions. This option is equivalent to pressing Esc.

After the Editor finishes the find-and-replace operation, it displays a second dialog box. This second box contains the message \Change complete. If no matching text can be found, the box displays the message Match not found. Select the OK command button to return to the Editor window.

Managing Files

The DOS Editor closely oversees your disk files. You can manage your directories with a complete save-and-load capability.

Using the File Menu

The File menu is your command center for loading and saving files. Six commands are available on the File menu (see fig. 11.9).

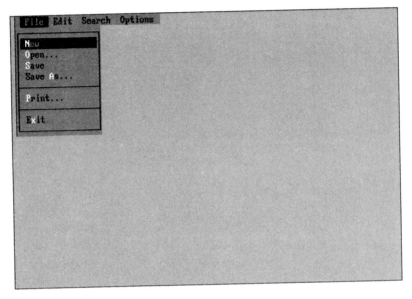

Fig. 11.9. The File menu.

The New command clears the file currently in the Editor environment. The result is a clean slate, as though you had just initialized the DOS Editor. This command does not affect other copies of the file. If the file was previously saved on disk, for example, the disk copy is not erased; only the working copy in the Editor is erased.

Open loads a file from disk into the DOS Editor environment. You also can use this command to see a list of file names in any directory.

Save saves the current file to disk.

Save As saves the current file to disk after prompting you for the file name.

Print prints all or part of the text in the DOS Editor environment.

Exit ends the editing session and returns to the DOS Shell or the command-line prompt.

The following are a few file-management maxims:

1. Until you name a file, the Editor displays the temporary name Untitled in the title bar.

2. When you save a file, the Editor adds the extension TXT to the file name if you do not specify another extension.

3. If you try to exit the Editor or open a new file without first saving a working file in the Editor, a dialog box opens to warn you.

Saving a File

When you save a file for the first time, you must specify two file attributes: the file path (the directory or disk on which to save the file) and the file name.

The DOS Editor stores files on disk in ASCII format. Such files are text files that can be manipulated by most text editors and word processors. You can view ASCII files directly from the DOS command line by using the TYPE command. For a complete list of the ASCII character set, see Appendix B.

Using the Save As Command

Follow these steps to save the current untitled file:

1. Select Save As from the File menu. In the dialog box that opens (see fig. 11.10), the current path is shown below the words File Name. A list box, below the label Dirs/Drives, lists the directories and disk drives available on your system.

2. Type the new file name in the File Name box. You may specify any file extension as part of the file name. Typical file extensions for ASCII text files are TXT and DOC.

3. Press Enter to save the file.

The DOS Editor saves the file to disk, in the directory specified by the current path.

Save As is commonly used for storing a file the first time you create it and for saving the second version of a file in a different directory or with a different name than the first version.

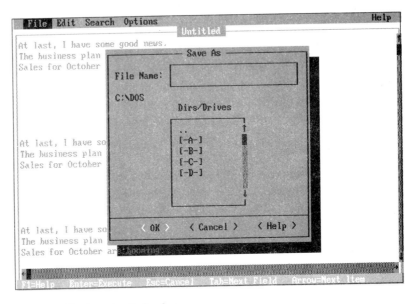

Fig. 11.10. *The Save As dialog box.*

For example, assume that you are editing an existing file named MYWORK.TXT. After making a few changes, you decide to save the new version of the file under the name MEAGAIN.TXT. Display the File menu and select Save As. The Editor displays the Save As dialog box.

The File Name text box contains the current file name, MYWORK.TXT. Type **MEAGAIN.TXT** and press Enter. The DOS Editor stores the file on disk as MEAGAIN.TXT, changing the name in the title bar accordingly. The file MYWORK.TXT remains stored on disk. Remember that if you continue editing the file on-screen, you are editing MEAGAIN.TXT (as indicated in the title bar), not MYWORK.TXT.

To store a file in a directory other than that specified by the current path, type the new directory path as part of the file name. For example, if you type the file name **\MEMOS\PLAN.BID**, the Editor stores the file with the name PLAN.BID in the directory C:\MEMOS. After saving the file, the name PLAN.BID appears in the title bar. The next time you issue the Save As... command, the default directory path is specified in the dialog box as C:\MEMOS. If you save a new file without including an explicit path, the file is saved in the C:\MEMOS directory.

You can use this technique to save files on different disk drives. To save a file named MYFILE.TXT in the root directory of the disk in the A drive, for example, type the file name as **A:\MYFILE.TXT**.

Using the Save Command

Use Save to store a file you already have named. No dialog box appears. The current version of the file in the Editor is saved to disk under the existing file name.

Using Save on an unnamed (untitled) file has nearly the same effect as using Save As; the Editor opens a dialog box similar to that shown in figure 11.10 so that you can enter a file name.

When you use the Save command while editing an existing file, the Editor does not prompt you for a file name. Instead, the Editor saves the new edited version of the file in place of the old version on disk. As you edit a file, use Save periodically to update the file on disk.

Using the Open Command
To Load a File

After text files are stored on disk, you can load a file into the DOS Editor with the Open command. Because this command lists files in any directory, you also can use Open to search your directories for specific file names. When you select Open, a dialog box pops open (see fig. 11.11).

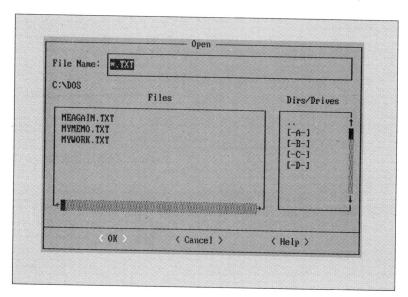

Fig. 11.11. The Open dialog box.

The Open dialog box contains the File Name text box. By default, this box contains *.TXT, the wild-card file name for all files with the extension TXT. The current directory path (C:\DOS, in fig. 11.11) is below the File Name text box. In the File Name text box, type a file name or a directory path using the * and ? wild-card characters.

To change the default path, specify a path in the File Name text box and press Enter. Otherwise, the Editor looks for files from the current directory with the extension TXT.

The Files list box contains the names of all files that satisfy the current directory-path and file-name specification. In figure 11.10, the Files box shows all files that satisfy the path and file-name specification C:\DOS*.TXT.

The Dirs/Drives list box lists available directories and disks. You can move the cursor to the Dirs/Drives list box by pressing Tab repeatedly. Then press the up- and down-arrow keys to move the highlight to one of the directories or drives listed in the box. Press Enter to change the default path.

To load a specific file into the Editor, you can use the File Name box or the Files box. To use the File Name box, type the name of the specific file, including a path (or rely on the default path shown below the box). If you do not specify an extension, the Editor assumes the TXT extension. For example, to load the file MYFILE.TXT, which is found in the current directory, type **MYFILE** and press Enter. By default, the Editor assumes the extension TXT.

You also can select a file name from the Files list box if it contains the file name you want. First, press Tab to move the cursor to the Files list box. Then use the cursor-movement keys to highlight the target file name. You also can press the first letter of the file name to move the highlight. When the name you want is highlighted, press Enter.

The Editor loads the file so that you can edit or view it.

Loading a File When You Start the DOS Editor

You can load a file when you first start the DOS Editor. The technique you use depends on whether you start the Editor from the DOS Shell or from the command line.

Use this technique if you are starting the Editor from the DOS Shell:

> After you select Editor from the DOS Shell menu, a box labeled `File to Edit` pops open. A message inside the box prompts you to supply a file name. When you type the file name, include the path if the file is not located in the default directory. Then press Enter to start the Editor with your designated file loaded and ready for editing.

When starting the Editor from the command line, use the following technique:

> At the DOS prompt, type **EDIT**, followed by a space and the file name. Include the path if the file is not in the current directory. For example, to start the Editor with the file \SALES\MYFILE.TXT loaded, type the following line:
>
> **EDIT \SALES\MYFILE.TXT**

The following notes apply when you load a file when starting the DOS Editor (whether you start the Editor from the DOS Shell or the command line):

- The Editor does not assume an extension if you don't specify one.

- The Editor initializes directly without taking the intermediate step of asking whether you want to see the help material in the on-screen Survival Guide.

- If the Editor cannot locate the specified file, it assumes that you want to create a file with that name. Accordingly, the Editor initializes with a fresh slate that includes your designated file name in the title bar. After you type the file, you can save it directly with the Save command.

Using the New Command

Use New to stop work on one file and to create another file. If you haven't saved the old file, the Editor opens a dialog box for confirmation. Otherwise, the old file clears, and the screen looks as though you had just initiated the DOS Editor. You see a blank editing area with `Untitled` in the title bar.

Printing a File

Your computer system probably includes a printer. Whether you have a dot-matrix, daisywheel, or laser printer, complete the following steps to print a copy of the file currently loaded in the Editor. You can print selected text or the complete file.

1. Activate the File option on the Main menu.

2. Select **Print**. This opens the Print dialog box (see fig. 11.12).

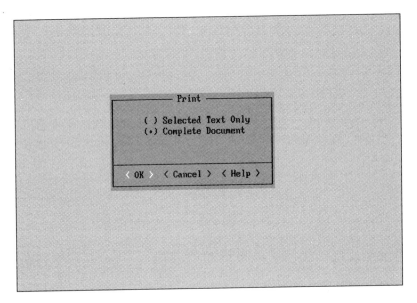

Fig. 11.12. The Print dialog box.

3. Choose from among the following option buttons:

   - `Selected Text Only` prints only selected text, which appears in reverse video in the Editor. This option is the default when a block of text is selected.

   - `Complete Document` prints the entire file. This option is the default when no text is selected.

4. Press Enter to begin printing. Make sure that your printer is turned on and is on-line.

Exiting from the DOS Editor

When you have finished editing files, you may want to quit from the Editor. Display the File menu and choose the Exit command. If the file already has been saved, the Editor returns to the DOS Shell or to the command line, depending on how you started the program.

If you try to quit without first saving the document you have been editing, the Editor opens a dialog box to ask whether you want to save the file. Select the Yes command button to save the file. Select the No command button to exit from the Editor without saving any changes to the current file.

Starting the DOS Editor with Optional Switches

When you start the DOS Editor from the command line, four special parameter switches are available. These switches are listed in table 11.7.

Table 11.7
Optional Switches for the EDIT command

Switch	Description
/B	Displays the Editor in black and white even when a color graphics adapter is present
/G	Updates editor screens as quickly as possible on systems with CGA (color graphics adapter) video. (**Note:** Some computer systems cannot support this option. If screen flicker occurs when you choose /G, your hardware is not compatible.)
/H	Displays the maximum number of lines possible with your video hardware. EGA (enhanced graphics adapter) and VGA (video graphics array) systems can produce more than the standard number of lines on-screen.
/NOHI	Effectively displays the Editor on monitors that do not support high intensity

To display the maximum number of lines when starting the Editor, for example, use the following command:

EDIT /H

A file name can be specified with one of the command options, as in the following example:

EDIT \SALES\MYFILE /H

Use the /B switch if you run the DOS Editor on a computer system with a color video adapter and a black-and-white monitor. (Many laptop computers have this configuration.) At the DOS prompt, activate the Editor as follows:

EDIT /B

Customizing the Editor Screen

Colors on the DOS Editor screen are preset. You can customize most of these colors and other attributes from the Options menu by using the Display command. If you have a color system, you may want different colors for the foreground and background text. If you do not use a mouse with the Editor, you may want to remove the scroll bars.

Changing Colors and Removing Scroll Bars

To change screen colors in the DOS Editor, display the Options menu and select Display. A dialog box similar to figure 11.13 opens.

With the cursor on the Foreground box, you can select a new foreground text color by pressing the up- and down-arrow keys. The foreground box cycles through the colors available with your particular video hardware. Note that as you press the arrow keys, the text to the left of the dialog box (Set colors for the text editor window) displays with the current foreground and background colors. Select a new foreground color by moving the highlight to the color you want. *Don't press Enter yet*. You have more selections to make before closing this dialog box.

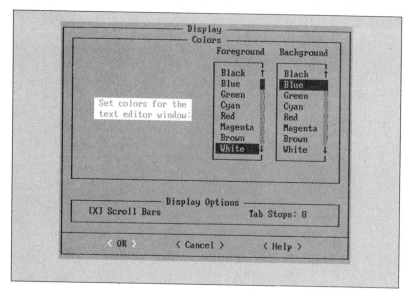

Fig. 11.13. *The Display dialog box.*

Press Tab to move the cursor to the Background box. Select a new background color; the process is similar to the one you followed to select a new foreground color.

Now press Enter to return to the Editor screen. The new colors should be in use.

If you don't use a mouse, you may want to consider removing the scroll bars from your screen. Many users think that the screen looks less cluttered without the scroll bars. To see what you prefer, try the following:

Reopen the dialog box by displaying the Options menu and selecting Display. Press Tab several times to move the cursor to the Scroll Bars check box. The X inside the brackets indicates that scroll bars currently are displayed.

Press the space bar or S to unselect the check box. Removing the X indicates that you want to deselect the display of scroll bars. Press Enter and the scroll bars are gone (see fig. 11.14).

Saving Customized Settings

If you change one or more display options, the Editor creates a file named QBASIC.INI and stores the file in the directory containing the EDIT.COM and QBASIC.EXE files. (For most systems, this directory is \DOS.)

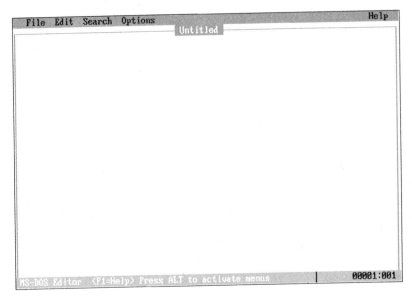

Fig. 11.14. The Editor screen with scroll bars removed.

The QBASIC.INI file contains a record of the new screen configuration. When you later restart, the Editor uses QBASIC.INI to restore the screen with your customized settings.

Every time you start the Editor, it looks for QBASIC.INI in the default directory or in the directory chain established by the PATH statements in your AUTOEXEC.BAT file. If you restart from a different directory, be sure that the Editor has access to the QBASIC.INI file.

To start the Editor with the original screen configuration, erase the QBASIC.INI file.

Note: The DOS Editor borrows the programming editor from the QBASIC.EXE file. The DOS Editor shares the editing environment found in the QBasic programming language, and the DOS Editor and QBasic share the initial configuration file (QBASIC.INI). Whether you run the DOS Editor or QBasic, the initial configuration is saved in the QBASIC.INI file.

Using the Help System

The DOS Editor provides on-line help through the Help menu (see fig. 11.15). Help screens include information about using menus and commands, using shortcut keys, interacting with dialog boxes, using keyboard actions, and using the help system.

Fig. 11.15. The Help menu.

Three categories of information are available from the Help menu:

1. Getting Started provides information about starting the Editor, using the menu and command system, and requesting help.

2. Keyboard explains the different editing keystrokes and shortcuts for moving the cursor around your text file.

3. About... shows the Editor version number and copyright information.

The following are general notes on using the Help system:

- To activate the Help system at any time, press Alt-H.

- To move the cursor to the next help topic, press Tab. When the cursor is on the topic you want, press Enter to view the help screen.

- To activate the Getting Started help menu at any time, press Shift-F1.

- To close a help window and exit the Help system, press Esc.

- A Help screen opens in a separate window. The title bar of this window shows the Help topic on display. For example, if you request help on the Save command from the File menu, the title bar of the Help window reads HELP: Save command.

- The F1 key provides express help. To get help on any menu, command, or dialog box, press F1 when the cursor or highlight is on the desired item.

- For help when an error message occurs, move the cursor to the <Help> option in the error-message box and press Enter.

- Sometime, at your leisure, consider browsing through all the help screens. To do so, press Shift-F1 and then press Ctrl-F1 repeatedly.

- To scroll any particular help screen, press PgUp or PgDn.

- When Help is active, a separate Help window opens in addition to the Editor window. You can move the cursor between the Help and the Editor windows by pressing F6 (or Shift-F6).

- When a Help window and the Editor window are open simultaneously, you can enlarge or reduce the size of the active window by pressing Alt-plus or Alt-minus. (*Plus* and *minus* refer to the gray + and – keys near the numeric keypad.)

- To cut and paste text from a Help screen into your file, first use the normal editing keys to select the text on the help screen. Copy the selected lines to the clipboard. Press F6 to activate the Editor window and then, using the normal editing keys, paste the help text into your file. Now reactivate the Help screen by pressing F6 again.

- When the Help system is active, the status bar at the bottom of the screen displays useful keystrokes. To execute a command shown enclosed in angle brackets, press the indicated keystroke or click the mouse when the mouse cursor is on the command name in the status bar.

- The Editor keeps track of the last 20 Help screens you have viewed. To cycle back through previously viewed screens, press Alt-F1.

- When you start the Editor, the initial dialog box gives you the option of seeing the Survival Guide. If you press Enter to see the Guide, the Help system is activated. A Help screen displays information about getting started with the Editor and using the Help system.

- The Editor stores the text of the help screens in a file named EDIT.HLP. To display any Help screen, the Editor must have access to this file. The Editor searches for EDIT.HLP in the current directory or in directories specified by the PATH statements of your AUTOEXEC.BAT file. Normal DOS installation places this file in the default \DOS directory. If EDIT.HLP is located outside your PATH specifications, however, you can supply the Editor with the path to EDIT.HLP by selecting the Help Path... command on the Options menu.

Chapter Summary

The DOS Editor is a text processor with which you can create, edit, and save text files. Among the Editor's features are full-screen editing, pull-down menus, shortcut keys, mouse support, and on-line help.

Although not in the same class as sophisticated word processors, the Editor is a considerable improvement from Edlin, the line-oriented editor (and the only text editor) supplied with earlier versions of DOS. The new editor is simpler to use and more powerful than Edlin.

The Editor is perfectly suited for creating short text documents such as memos, README files, and batch files.

12

Understanding
Batch File Basics

The idea of getting a computer to do work in convenient, manageable batches predates the personal computer by several years. The first computers were large and expensive, and they could do only one task at a time. Even these early machines, however, were fast. Making them wait to be told what to do next was inefficient.

Batch processing was developed to make computers more productive. Collections of tasks to be carried out consecutively were put together off-line, without using the computer's resources. The groups of tasks then were fed to the computer at a rate that kept the computer busy and productive.

Today, computers are less expensive than precious human resources. Batch processing still is used to get the computer to carry out a series of tasks without wasting a great deal of personnel time typing often-used or complex commands.

DOS has a host of special commands, *subcommands*, used most often in batch files. Although you can type these commands at the DOS prompt, their primary purpose is to enable you to carry out other DOS functions in a more useful way.

This chapter discusses the following batch subcommands:

- ECHO
- PAUSE
- REM

457

- GOTO

- CLS

Using Batch Files

A batch file is a simple ASCII file (a file made up of ASCII text) containing a series of DOS commands. Many of the commands appear in the batch file as if you typed them at the DOS prompt. A simple batch file, for example, can consist of the following three lines:

```
DIR A:
DIR B:
DIR C:
```

When executing this batch file, DOS displays first the directory of drive A, then of drive B, and then of drive C. You can call the file DIRALL.BAT; the BAT extension indicates that the file is a batch file. When you type **DIRALL** at the DOS prompt, the directories of drives A, B, and C are displayed. The three separate DOS commands are collected into one batch file and executed with the DIRALL command.

Cue:
Use batch files to perform one command or hundreds of commands.

Batch files have several advantages. After you place correctly phrased commands in a batch file, you can direct DOS to execute the commands by typing the batch file's name (without the BAT extension). You can use a batch file to direct DOS to perform one or hundreds of commands.

After a batch file is invoked, DOS does not need your attention until the batch file is finished running. This capability comes in handy for programs that take a long time to run. For example, to copy all the files from the WP to the WPBAK directory and from the DATA to the DATABAK directory on another hard drive, you can include the following commands in a batch file:

XCOPY C:\WP D:\WPBAK

XCOPY C:\DATA D:\DATABAK

Cue:
Create a batch file that does several tasks sequentially while you do something else.

The actual copying process may take a few minutes for each command. If you issue three separate XCOPY commands from the DOS prompt, you must wait until the first copy is finished before starting the second. If you put these three commands in a batch file, however, typing the batch file name invokes all three commands when appropriate; you don't have to do anything else. While the batch file is running, you can have a snack, make a phone call, or do something else useful.

If the operation you want to perform requires your input to change disks, however, a batch file cannot perform the task. You must make allowances, by using batch subcommands, for providing the correct disk if you want to use the batch file of XCOPY commands.

Understanding the Basic Rules of Batch Files

Batch files must follow certain rules. A complete list of these rules is at the end of the chapter. This section discusses some of the more prominent ones.

Because a batch file contains only ASCII text, you can use the DOS COPY CON command, the DOS EDLIN line editor, the DOS EDIT command, or another text editor to create a batch file. If you use a word processing program, make sure that the program is in a mode that enables the creation of ASCII files (sometimes called nondocument or text files) rather than word processing documents.

Cue:
You can use EDIT, EDLIN, COPY CON, or your word processor in text mode to create a batch file.

Batch file names conform to normal DOS naming rules. The root name of a batch file can be from one to eight characters long and must conform to the rules for file names. The batch file name must have the extension BAT.

When interpreting a command you type, DOS disassembles, or parses, the line to look for recognizable commands. DOS finds internal commands, such as DIR and COPY, if the commands are typed with the correct syntax. If the line includes an external command, DOS searches for a system file with a root name matching the command. If you type **FORMAT**, DOS looks for FORMAT.COM or FORMAT.EXE (the extension varies with DOS versions) in the current directory and the directory defined by the PATH statement. DOS looks for COM files first and then EXE files. If DOS does not find a COM or an EXE file matching the command, DOS looks for a system file with the BAT extension.

Reminder:
DOS searches for command files in this order: internal, external COM, external EXE, and external BAT.

Because of the order of this search, you cannot easily give a batch file the same root name as a DOS internal or external command. Nor can you give the batch file the same name as another COM or EXE file found in the current path. (You can, however, invoke a batch file named FORMAT.BAT by typing the full path name explicitly: for example, **C:\BATCH \FORMAT.BAT**.)

Creating Simple Batch Files

For practice, create a couple of simple batch files to see what they can do. In each of the following examples, use EDIT (DOS 5.0) EDLIN, COPY CON, or your word processor to create the files in plain ASCII text.

Creating a Batch File To Format Floppy Disks

The first example demonstrates how batch files can keep you from having to learn seldom-used syntax. Assume that your computer is equipped with a 3 1/2-inch, 1.44M high-density floppy disk drive. Occasionally, you want to format a 720K double-density disk so that you can exchange files with a co-worker who has a computer that cannot read high-density disks.

Caution:
Don't format double-density disks with high-density format, or you may lose data.

Some computer systems can format a 3 1/2-inch double-density disk for 720K. These computers have a sensor that detects the extra hole in 1.44M high-density disks and does not use the denser format unless the hole is found. IBM PS/2 computers don't have this sensor; you can format any 3 1/2-inch disk for 1.44M. Double-density disks almost always take a high-density format, and you can store 1.44M of data on disks formatted in this way. Weeks or months later, however, when you want to retrieve that information, you may find that reading the disk is a problem. An alarmingly high percentage of double-density disks lose data when formatted for higher density. Don't do it, unless saving a few dollars is more important than your data.

The reverse technology, however, is perfectly safe. With DOS, you can format high-density 1.44M disks for double-density 720K use. Versions of DOS after 3.3 enable you to specify track density (and other factors). With DOS 3.3, you can enter the number of sectors per track and the number of tracks. DOS ignores inappropriate parameters, however; you cannot, for example, specify 13 sectors or 43 tracks. DOS Versions 4.x and 5.0 simplify this procedure by enabling you to enter a size parameter, such as 720, 720K, 1.44, and so on.

Because you may not remember the syntax when you want to format a disk, you can create a batch file to do the job for you. Create an ASCII file called 720.BAT. Type each of the following lines on a separate line in the file:

ECHO OFF

ECHO Insert floppy disk to be formatted for 720K in drive A

ECHO Press Enter when ready

PAUSE > NUL

FORMAT A: /N:9 /T:80

This first batch file is relatively simple so that you can understand the function of each command more easily. Each of the lines in the batch file is described in the following paragraphs.

ECHO OFF

The first line of the batch file is ECHO OFF. By default, before each command in a batch file is executed, DOS displays the command. This feature is helpful if you want to know what a batch file is doing step-by-step, but the display often can be confusing or distracting. ECHO OFF tells DOS to execute each command without printing the command.

Cue:
Use ECHO OFF to turn off the display of commands in the batch file.

Because ECHO is ON when you start 720.BAT, however, you see the first command, ECHO OFF, displayed on-screen. If you have DOS Version 3.3 or later, you can eliminate that display by placing the @ symbol before the command:

@ECHO OFF

The @ tells DOS not to display the command that follows. The next two lines of the batch file are an example of a regular ECHO command:

Cue:
The @ symbol turns off the display of the command that follows.

ECHO Insert floppy disk to be formatted for 720K in drive A

ECHO Press Enter when ready

The ECHO command is used to display a short line of text. The text that follows the word ECHO is displayed on-screen. ECHO is used almost exclusively in batch files.

The text is a message to the user, explaining what is about to take place and requesting the user to press Enter when the disk is ready. You can use ECHO for prompts or to display other information in your batch files.

Reminder:
ECHO prints on-screen the characters that follow it.

PAUSE > NUL

PAUSE is another batch file subcommand. PAUSE causes the batch file to suspend execution and displays the following message on-screen:

```
Strike a key when ready . . .
```

Note: DOS 5.0 PAUSE output is Press any key to continue.

This all-purpose message is less than useful for a number of reasons. First, you may want the user to do something other than press any key when ready. Although the term "a key" implies that you can press any key in response to the PAUSE command, some keys do not work. The Caps Lock, Shift, and Ctrl keys are not acceptable entries to the PAUSE command. Batch files are stopped entirely if Ctrl-C or Ctrl-Break is pressed, so you may want to provide the user with a choice of keys to press.

Instead of "strike," you may prefer to use "press," as DOS 5.0 does. You may, for example, want to tell the user to `Press a key to proceed with reformat of drive C, or press Ctrl-C to abort.`

Cue:

Use PAUSE > NUL to pause without displaying the default message.

The redirection symbol > following the PAUSE command redirects the output of PAUSE to the NUL device. Output redirected to NUL is discarded; the message produced by the PAUSE command, therefore, does not appear on-screen. The user sees only the message displayed by the preceding ECHO command: `Press Enter when ready.`

> **FORMAT A: /N:9 /T:80**

This final line of the batch file does all the work. If you include this line in the batch file, you do not have to type the drive specification **A:** or the parameters that force the 720K format when you want to format a disk. Just type **720** at the DOS prompt and press Enter.

Creating a Batch File To Mark a Directory as "Home"

The next batch file uses only the familiar DOS ECHO and PAUSE commands. This batch file also uses redirection, but in a more useful way.

To use this batch file, you should have on your hard disk a directory called C:\DOS, in which all your DOS files (such as XCOPY.EXE) reside. (You can substitute your DOS directory in place of C:\DOS in these examples.) The PATH statement in your CONFIG.SYS file should point to the directory that contains all the DOS files so that DOS can locate any needed files, no matter which directory is current.

Create an ASCII file called MARK.BAT and type the following lines in the file:

> **ECHO OFF**
>
> **CD > C:\DOS\HOME.ASC**
>
> **COPY C:\DOS\CD.ASC+HOME.ASC C:\DOS\HOME.BAT**
>
> **ERASE C:\DOS\HOME.ASC**

In this batch file, the output of the DOS CD command is redirected to a file called HOME.ASC, which is located in the C:\DOS directory. The CD command, typed at the DOS prompt, displays the name of the current directory. By redirecting that output to a file, you create a file called HOME.ASC that contains the name of the current directory.

The third line of the batch file combines the HOME.ASC file with another file called CD.ASC. The combined files are placed in a file called HOME.BAT. CD.ASC contains only the characters CD followed by a space. When you combine CD.ASC and HOME.ASC, the following line is placed in HOME.BAT:

```
CD directoryname
```

This command changes from the current directory to the *home directory* marked by the MARK.BAT file. You can use the command MARK to invoke the MARK.BAT file to specify the current directory as the home directory. Then you can change directories (perhaps using batch files) to perform other tasks. To return to the home directory, type **HOME** to invoke the HOME.BAT file created by MARK.BAT. HOME.BAT returns you to the home directory (assuming that you didn't log over to another hard disk or to a floppy disk).

Because HOME.BAT remains on disk, the file remembers the home directory even if you turn off the computer. You can use MARK.BAT to mark a home directory for a short session or for longer use.

Before you use MARK.BAT, you must create the file CD.ASC. Follow these instructions carefully to create this file:

1. At the DOS prompt, type the following and press Enter:

   COPY CON C:\DOS\CD.ASC

   If your DOS files are located in a directory other than C:\DOS, substitute the name of that directory.

2. Enter the following line:

   CD<*space*> <*F6*> <*Enter*>

> *Note:* After you type **CD**, press the space bar, the F6 key, and Enter. Do not type the characters <*space*> <*F6*> <*Enter*>; do not press Enter before you press F6.

This process creates a file containing only the characters CD and a space, with no carriage return between them. When MARK.BAT combines CD.ASC and HOME.ASC, the text in each file is combined on one line in the HOME.BAT file.

Understanding Batch File Parameters

You can create quite sophisticated batch files by using only DOS commands and the simplest batch subcommands. The batch files created so far in this chapter carry out exactly the same functions every time you use the files. You may want a batch file to perform a different operation each time, however, even though the commands in the file are fixed. You can use the same batch file to accomplish different tasks by taking advantage of batch file parameters.

Reminder:

Parameters are additional information included in the command and separated by delimiters.

A review of parameters in general helps you understand batch file parameters. In DOS, many commands accept additional information when you issue the command. COPY is an example of such a command. The name of the file you want to copy, the destination to which you want to copy the file, and any additional switches you enter are parameters. Parameters, then, are the additional information you type after you type the command name at the DOS prompt. Commands (or command programs) can use whatever information is specified in the parameters.

Consider the following command:

COPY FORMAT.COM B: /V

Every word or set of characters separated by a space, a comma, a semicolon, or another valid delimiter specified by the command is a parameter. *FORMAT.COM*, *B:*, and */V* are parameters. Each parameter controls some aspect of the COPY command. In this example, the parameters tell COPY to copy the file FORMAT.COM from the default disk to the disk in drive B and to verify that DOS has correctly made the copy.

Cue:

Use variable markers to make your batch files work with parameters.

Batch files also use parameters, but in a different way than commands do. When you type the name of the batch file at the DOS prompt, you can add up to 9 parameters. DOS assigns a variable name to each of these parameters. You can use the variable name in your batch file in the form of a variable marker numbered from 1 to 9. (Parameter number 0 is the name of the batch file command entered at the DOS prompt.) You precede the marker number with a percent sign to inform DOS that you are specifying a replaceable parameter.

Understanding Variable Markers

This section examines how you can use variable markers in a batch file. Assume that you have a batch file called DELETE.BAT. Suppose that the batch file DELETE.BAT appears as follows:

```
ECHO ON
ERASE %1
ERASE %2
ERASE %3
ERASE %4
ERASE %5
ERASE %6
ERASE %7
ERASE %8
ERASE %9
```

When you invoke DELETE, suppose that you follow the batch file name with the names of some files to be removed, as shown in the following example:

DELETE TEST.BAK OLDFILES.* C:\BAK\JUNK.DOC

This example specifies three parameters, all of which are file specifications. TEST.BAK refers to a file in the current directory; OLDFILES.* specifies all files in the current directory with the root name OLDFILES and any extension; C:\BAK\JUNK.DOC refers to the specific file JUNK.DOC in the C:\BAK subdirectory.

When the second line of the batch file is called, DOS substitutes for *%1* the first parameter you typed at the DOS prompt: *TEST.BAK*. DOS substitutes *OLDFILES.** for *%2* and *C:\BAK\JUNK.DOC* for *%3*. Because ECHO ON enables you to see the commands, the screen shows the following:

```
ERASE TEST.BAK
ERASE OLDFILES.*
ERASE C:\BAK\JUNK.DOC
```

When a batch file calls for a parameter that isn't typed as part of the command, DOS substitutes nothing. DOS tries to carry out six more ERASE commands that, because no parameters for the variable markers %4 through %9 are specified, display on-screen:

```
ERASE
ERASE
ERASE
ERASE
ERASE
ERASE
```

For these commands, DOS reports `Invalid number of parameters` (DOS 5's message is `Required parameter missing`), and the next command in the batch file is executed. You should account for all the parameters used in the batch file. Fortunately, DOS provides easy ways to do that.

Cue:
Use the %0 variable marker to use the batch file name as a parameter.

Do not start your list of variable markers with %0 unless you want DOS to substitute the first thing you type at the DOS prompt—the batch file name—for %0. In this example, the %0 variable contains DELETE.BAT. Although the %0 variable is not used in this batch file, you may want to use that variable marker in some instances (if you create a batch file that calls itself, for example). Suppose that you included the following line in the DELETE.BAT file:

ECHO This batch file is called %0

You can rename the batch file as DELETE.BAT, DELETER.BAT, or ERASER.BAT; the proper name is substituted when you use %0.

If you want further practice including parameters in a batch file, use a text editor or the COPY CON technique to create a file called TEST.BAT. Type the following line into the file:

ECHO Hello, %1

Now type **TEST**, press the space bar, type your first name, and press Enter. The results should display on-screen as follows:

```
C>TEST DAVID
C>ECHO Hello, DAVID
Hello, DAVID
C>
```

To see how DOS replaces the parameters, create another batch file called TEST1.BAT. Type the following line into this file:

ECHO %0 %1 %2 %3 %4

After you create this file, type **TEST1**, press the space bar, type your name, press the space bar again, and type your street address. Following is the screen display:

```
C>TEST1 DAVID 1234 PIONEER STREET
C>ECHO TEST1 DAVID 1234 PIONEER STREET
```

```
TEST1 DAVID 1234 PIONEER STREET
C>
```

The batch file command instructs DOS to display the parameters 0 through 4. These parameters are the following:

Parameter	Word
%0	TEST1
%1	DAVID
%2	1234
%3	PIONEER
%4	STREET

Now try to shortchange DOS again by not specifying a sufficient number of parameters to fill each expected variable marker. Run TEST1 again, but this time give only your first name. You should see something like the following:

```
C>TEST1 DAVID
C>ECHO TEST1 DAVID
TEST1 DAVID
C>
```

DOS displays the batch file name and your first name. No other information was echoed to the screen. Although not enough parameters were specified, DOS replaced the unfilled markers with nothing. Unlike the ERASE example, the empty markers did no harm.

When you use replaceable parameters in your batch files, plan for the possibility of missing parameters. Some commands ignore missing parameters (such as the TEST1.BAT file), and others need the missing parameters (such as the earlier DELETE.BAT file).

Constructing a Batch File Using Parameters

In this section, you learn how to construct a batch file that takes advantage of parameters. Suppose that you use several computers, but one of the hard disk systems is where you store the files you want to keep.

Suppose also that you use floppy disks to move information between computers. You usually delete the file from the floppy disk after you have copied the file back to a hard disk. You use the following steps to transfer data from a floppy disk to a hard disk:

1. Copy the file from the floppy disk to the hard disk.

2. Erase the file from the floppy disk.

To simplify this process, you can create a batch file called C&E.BAT (copy and erase). Type the following commands in the file:

COPY A:%1 C:%2 /V

ERASE A:%1

To use the C&E.BAT file, type the following at the DOS prompt:

C&E *oldfilename newfilename*

The first parameter, *oldfilename*, represents the name of the file you want to copy from the floppy disk to the hard disk; *newfilename* is the new name for the copied file (to change the file name as it is being copied).

Suppose that in drive A you place a floppy disk containing the file NOTES.TXT and want to copy that file to the hard disk. Type the following command at the DOS prompt:

C&E NOTES.TXT

The screen appears as follows:

```
C>COPY A:NOTES.TXT C: /V
1 file(s) copied
C>ERASE A:NOTES.TXT
C>
```

Even though you didn't type the parameter *newfilename*, DOS executed the batch file, keeping the same file name during the copy. DOS copies NOTES.TXT from drive A to the current directory on drive C and then deletes the file on the floppy disk in drive A. The *%2* parameter is dropped, and the file does not get a new name when copied.

Cue:
Use a directory name as a parameter intended for the file's new name.

One of the benefits of constructing a batch file this way is that you can use a path name as the second parameter. By specifying a path name, you can copy the file from the floppy disk to a directory other than the current directory on the hard disk. To copy NOTES.TXT to the directory called WORDS, for example, type the following:

C&E NOTES.TXT \WORDS

The screen display is as follows:

```
C>COPY A:NOTES.TXT C:\WORDS /V
1 file(s) copied
C>ERASE A:NOTES.TXT
C>
```

Because \WORDS is the name of an existing directory, DOS knows to copy the file NOTES.TXT into the directory \WORDS. DOS does not give the new file the name WORDS.

Using Additional Batch Subcommands

This section provides additional information about several other subcommands that are useful when you are working with batch files.

Introducing REM and More about ECHO

The REM ("remark") command is used most often to include information in the batch file about who wrote the file, when the file was created, and what the file does. When the batch file is executed, DOS ignores the REM and everything else on the line.

The ECHO command does two things: ECHO ON and ECHO OFF turn on and off the display of lines from batch files as the commands are executed. ECHO also is used to display messages.

As with any other command, if ECHO has not been turned OFF, DOS displays REM statements on-screen as they are encountered. REM is used sometimes in place of the ECHO command to display information on-screen if ECHO OFF is not executed. With REM, you avoid the double message seen when ECHO is used; when ECHO is used with ECHO ON, DOS first displays the ECHO command and then displays the message.

You can put ECHO and REM to good use in a batch file. When you review a batch file, you may have forgotten why you used certain commands or why you constructed the batch file in a particular way. Leave reminders in your batch file with REM statements. Comments in REM statements don't appear on-screen if you first issue the ECHO OFF command. The comments make the batch file self-documenting, which you and other users will appreciate. If you want the batch file to display particular messages, use ECHO. Messages set with ECHO appear on-screen whether or not you set ECHO to OFF.

Cue:
Use REM with ECHO OFF for comments you don't want to display on-screen; use ECHO for messages you want to display.

Cue:
Use a colon at the beginning of a line to indicate a remark or a label.

Another way to include a remark in a batch file is by using a colon (:). If the first character on a line in a batch file is a colon, DOS assumes that the line is a label and does not try to carry out any commands on that line. Lines beginning with the colon are not displayed even if ECHO is ON. Using colons, however, may confuse DOS into thinking that the "remark" is a true label. You must be certain that the first eight characters of a statement you want interpreted as a remark don't match the characters of an actual label used elsewhere in the file.

Reminder:
Use the colon to indicate a line you do not want displayed or executed.

You can use the colon to provide a second type of remark—one not displayed under any circumstances, whether or not ECHO OFF is set. You can use the colon to mark sections of the batch file where ECHO ON has been set but where you still do not want to display any REM statements. You also can use the colon to remove temporarily portions of the file you don't want DOS to execute. You may want to mark sections of a file in this way when you debug or test the file.

Controlling the Display with CLS

Cue:
Use CLS to clear the screen completely.

You can use the DOS CLS command at the DOS prompt to clear the screen. In batch files, CLS is used commonly after the ECHO OFF command because the ECHO OFF command appears on-screen. To keep the screen clear, issue the CLS command as shown:

ECHO OFF

CLS

With DOS Version 3.3 or later versions, you can use the @ feature to prevent the ECHO OFF command from appearing on-screen. Replace the preceding two command lines with the following line:

@ECHO OFF

Because @ is the first character on the line, ECHO OFF does not appear on-screen, and the ECHO OFF command stays in effect until the end of the batch file. Using the @ feature, however, does not clear the screen. To clear the screen when you start a batch file, use the CLS command in the batch file.

Branching with GOTO

The DOS GOTO batch subcommand is similar to the GOTO command in the BASIC programming language. With the DOS GOTO command, you can jump to another part of your batch file. The DOS GOTO command uses a label to specify the destination. A label is a batch file line that starts with a colon and contains a one- to eight-character name. The label name can be longer than eight characters, but only the first eight characters are significant as a label.

When encountering a GOTO command in the batch file, DOS starts at the beginning of the batch file and searches for a label matching the one specified by GOTO. DOS then jumps to the line in the batch file following the line with the label and continues executing commands from that point.

Suppose that you create the following batch file named TEST2.BAT:

```
:START
ECHO Hello, %1
PAUSE
GOTO START
```

This file is similar to the TEST.BAT batch file you created previously, with the addition of the GOTO and PAUSE subcommands. If you invoke the batch file by typing **TEST2 DAVID**, the screen shows the following:

```
C>TEST2 DAVID
C>ECHO Hello, DAVID
Hello, DAVID
C>PAUSE
Strike a key when ready... <space>
C>GOTO START
C>ECHO Hello, DAVID
Hello, DAVID
C>PAUSE
Strike a key when ready...^C
Terminate batch job (Y/N)? Y
C>
```

The batch file begins by echoing the message that includes the name DAVID. The file then pauses so that you can press a key. After you press a key (in this example, the space bar), DOS executes the GOTO START command. DOS then jumps to the line following :START and continues. When DOS pauses a second time, you press Ctrl-C to stop the batch file. DOS then asks whether you want to stop the batch file. You respond Y for yes, so DOS stops processing the batch file and returns to the system prompt. This type of batch file causes DOS to loop continuously until you press the Ctrl-C or Ctrl-Break sequence.

Cue:
GOTO can cause an infinite loop that you can break by pressing Ctrl-C or Ctrl-Break.

You can use an endless loop to repeat a group of commands in a batch file. You also can repeat the batch file a different number of times each time you invoke the file.

Suppose that you want to copy the files CHKDSK.COM, FORMAT.COM, DISKCOMP.COM, and DISKCOPY.COM to several disks. You may want to copy these files onto one, two, or a hundred disks. With a batch file, you can make DOS do the hard work.

Assume that the computer has two disk drives. The floppy disk that contains the files CHKDSK.COM, FORMAT.COM, DISKCOMP.COM, DISKCOPY.COM, and the new batch file is in drive A. The floppy disk to receive the files is in drive B.

First, create a batch file called FLOPPY.BAT. Enter the following statements in the file (remember that the @ symbol in line 1 can be used only with Versions 3.3, 4, and 5). Do not type the line numbers at the beginning of each line; these numbers are references only.

(1) **@ECHO OFF**

(2) **:START**

(3) **ECHO Place the disk to receive CHKDSK.COM, FORMAT.COM,**

(4) **ECHO DISKCOMP.COM, and DISKCOPY.COM in drive B.**

(5) **ECHO To quit, press Ctrl-C and press Y, or**

(6) **PAUSE**

(7) **COPY A:CHKDSK.COM B: /V**

(8) **COPY A:FORMAT.COM B: /V**

(9) **COPY A:DISKCOMP.COM B: /V**

(10) **COPY A:DISKCOPY.COM B: /V**

(11) **ECHO Files are copied.**

(12) **GOTO START**

In this file, the GOTO command on line 12 causes an endless loop. The file also exhibits several batch file subcommands.

Line 1 sets ECHO OFF so that the commands are not displayed. The @ sign at the beginning of the line stops the ECHO OFF line from being displayed. Lines 2 through 5 tell the user of the batch file to put a floppy disk in drive B or to press Ctrl-C and Y to quit.

The PAUSE command on line 6 displays the `Strike a key when ready...` message. If you have finished copying files when this prompt appears, press Ctrl-C and answer Y to the `Terminate batch job (Y/N)?` prompt. Otherwise, press any key to continue the copying process.

Lines 7 through 10 copy the four programs to the disk in drive B. Line 11 is the reassurance line that tells you that the files have been copied. This line is not necessary but assures you that all has gone well. Line 12 is the GOTO line that starts the process over again.

Notice the arrangement of lines 2 through 5. The on-screen result is as follows:

```
Place the disk to receive CHKDSK.COM, FORMAT.COM,
DISKCOMP.COM, and DISKCOPY.COM in drive B.
To quit, press Ctrl-C and press Y, or
Strike a key when ready...
```

Remember, the `Strike a key when ready...` message is generated by the PAUSE command. (DOS 5.0's PAUSE message is `Press any key to continue....`) Using ECHO to create your own message that duplicates the PAUSE message isn't necessary. Instead of inserting a customized message, this file depends on the PAUSE message to tell you to press any key when ready. You can, however, include the line **PAUSE > NUL** to redirect the PAUSE message to the NUL device; then you can supply your own message.

Cue:
You can incorporate the PAUSE message into a string of ECHO commands.

Reviewing Batch File Rules

This chapter explores the basics of understanding batch files. Additional batch file commands are explained in Chapter 14, but you have learned enough about batch files to be able to understand and use a brief list of rules that apply to batch files. A few of these rules require some additional explanations found in Chapter 14 before you can put the rules to work.

Rules for Batch Files

1. If you do not specify a disk drive name when starting a batch file, the current disk drive is used.

2. If you do not specify a path, the current directory is used.

3. To invoke a batch file, type the root name (the file name without the BAT extension) and press Enter. A batch file with the same root name and the extension COM or EXE in the current directory or in the PATH causes problems. DOS looks for COM files first, then for EXE files, and then for BAT files.

4. If the batch file is not in the current directory of the disk drive, and you did not specify a path name, DOS searches the directory or directories specified by the PATH statement to find the batch file.

5. DOS executes each command in the batch file one line at a time. Any specified parameters are substituted for the variable markers in the file.

6. DOS recognizes a maximum of 10 parameters, numbered %0 through %9. The %0 parameter is the name of the command file. (You may use the SHIFT subcommand to get around this limitation.)

7. If DOS encounters an incorrectly phrased command when running a batch file, you see an error message. The exact error message shown depends on the command being executed. The incorrect command is ignored, and the batch file continues with the next command.

8. You can stop a batch file by pressing Ctrl-Break or Ctrl-C. DOS displays the following message:

```
Terminate batch job (Y/N)?
```

If you answer Y, the rest of the commands in the file are ignored, and the system prompt appears. If you answer N, DOS skips the current command but continues processing the other commands in the file.

9. Most versions of DOS remember which disk drive holds the batch file, so you can change disk drives freely. DOS 3.0, however, does not remember which disk holds the batch file. If you remove the floppy disk that holds the batch file, DOS 3.0 displays an error message. Later versions of DOS request that you reinsert the disk holding the batch file and press a key to continue.

10. You can instruct one batch file to run another batch file after the first batch file is finished. When you enter the name of a second batch file as the last command in the first batch file, control of the computer passes to the second batch file. If you use the COMMAND or CALL command to call the second batch file, the second batch file is executed, and control returns to the first batch file. (For more information on COMMAND and CALL, see Chapter 14.)

Chapter Summary

Batch files can make your computer do the hard work for you. They can replace repetitive typing with commands. As you work with batch files, remember the following key points:

- You must give batch files the extension BAT.

- You invoke batch files by typing the root name of the batch file and pressing Enter. You may specify an optional disk drive name and path name in front of the batch file name.

- A batch file can contain any command you can type at the DOS prompt.

- You can use the ECHO subcommand to turn on or off the display of DOS commands being executed by the batch file.

- The PAUSE subcommand causes the batch file to suspend execution and displays a message on-screen.

- Use the REM subcommand to leave comments and reminders in your batch file; the comments do not display on-screen.

- Each word (or set of characters) separated by a delimiter in a batch command line is a parameter. When you use a batch file, DOS substitutes the appropriate parameters for the variable markers (%1 to %9) in the file.

- You can use the GOTO subcommand to create a loop in the batch file.

- Use the CLS subcommand to clear the screen.

In the next chapter, you learn more about ANSI.SYS, the device driver used to enhance your keyboard and display.

13

Understanding ANSI.SYS

Before continuing to learn about batch files, you should learn about the ANSI.SYS device driver. ANSI.SYS enables you to perform many useful tasks with batch files. This chapter explains how to use ANSI.SYS with DOS; the next chapter explains some techniques for incorporating these capabilities into batch files.

ANSI.SYS is a device driver you can use to give DOS more elaborate control over the computer's display screen. ANSI.SYS fits between the keyboard and the CPU and between the CPU and the monitor to intercept and act on special characters. If you don't use ANSI.SYS, DOS takes care of the display in a satisfactory manner. Using ANSI.SYS, however, enables you to control more directly what appears on-screen.

The ANSI.SYS driver enables you to enhance your control over the appearance of your screen by using the PROMPT command to change the look of your DOS prompt. You also can change the assignments of the keys on your keyboard. Some programs use the ANSI.SYS driver to control the screen, although most programs have their own screen controls. Many bulletin board systems and terminal emulation programs send out special control sequences to change the appearance of the displayed text, so ANSI.SYS will be used with these applications.

Installing Device Drivers

DOS can work with many different peripherals or devices, including printers, hard disks, scanners, and mice. Even your keyboard and display monitor are treated as separate devices by DOS.

DOS and the ROM-BIOS of your computer can work with this array of devices adequately. As long as your printer accepts a standard set of commands, you can, for example, connect the printer to the LPT or COM ports and issue the appropriate DOS commands. DOS also knows how to handle other common devices, such as the keyboard and display.

The operating system would be limited if it could talk with only the devices known at the time that version of DOS was issued. Requiring the programmers of the operating system to rework DOS every time a manufacturer comes out with a new nonstandard device or asking the manufacturers to provide patches for DOS would be inefficient.

Reminder:
Use device drivers to expand DOS's capabilities.

DOS enables you to specify the *device drivers* in a start-up file named CONFIG.SYS. The CONFIG.SYS file can have many different directives or commands, such as BUFFERS and FILES. This chapter concentrates on the DEVICE directive that enables you to install drivers like ANSI.SYS.

A device driver is a low-level program that interfaces between DOS and a device. DOS uses these device driver programs to control the device. For example, a portion of DOS contains a device driver that controls and accesses the information on the floppy or hard disk. Other device drivers control other parts of your system, such as monitors, keyboards, and input-output devices like the parallel or serial ports. These device drivers are built into DOS.

ANSI.SYS is a device driver supplied with DOS that works with the display and keyboard. ANSI.SYS provides additional capabilities beyond those built into DOS. For example, you can use ANSI.SYS to change the action of a key on your keyboard or to change the colors and prompts displayed on-screen. You don't actually change the ANSI.SYS file; you use directives to enable particular parts of the ANSI.SYS device driver to accomplish what you want to do. After the device driver is activated, the driver always is ready to respond to your commands.

Reminder:
If you have DOS Version 2.0 or later, you can use device drivers.

Version 2.0 was the first version of DOS to include provisions for device drivers. Version 2.0 opened the door to a whole world of new peripherals by simplifying the process of writing device drivers. Users, in turn, easily can install these prewritten drivers by including the following directive in CONFIG.SYS:

DEVICE = *<driver filename>*

Like a batch file, CONFIG.SYS is an ASCII text file containing a few commands or directives. You can create a CONFIG.SYS with COPY CON, EDLIN, or your word processor (in text mode). DOS checks CONFIG.SYS while booting up, performing the commands or directives that CONFIG.SYS specifies. After the CONFIG.SYS commands are completed, the commands in AUTOEXEC.BAT are executed. CONFIG.SYS has fewer legitimate directives than AUTOEXEC.BAT.

The CONFIG.SYS file must be located in the root directory of the disk you use to boot DOS. You already may have a CONFIG.SYS file. If so, you can display this file by typing one of the following commands at the DOS prompt: **TYPE C:\CONFIG.SYS** (on a hard disk-based system) or **TYPE A:\CONFIG.SYS** (for a floppy-based system). Look at the display and see whether one of the lines is similar to the following:

Reminder: CONFIG.SYS must be in the root directory.

```
DEVICE=ANSI.SYS
```

(You may see a drive and directory name specified, as in `C:\DOS\ANSI.SYS`.)

If you don't have a CONFIG.SYS file, create one by typing the following at the DOS prompt:

COPY CON \CONFIG.SYS

DEVICE=ANSI.SYS<F6><Enter>

In this example, ANSI.SYS is located in the root directory with CONFIG.SYS. You can locate ANSI.SYS in a subdirectory if you specify that directory in the DEVICE statement, as shown in the following example in which the ANSI.SYS file is located in the \DOS directory of drive C:

DEVICE = C:\DOS\ANSI.SYS

In either case, CONFIG.SYS must be located in the root directory of the boot disk, usually drive A on a floppy-based system or drive C on a hard disk system. To activate the ANSI.SYS driver, you must reboot your computer. In DOS 5, ANSI.SYS requires about 4.1K of memory.

Communicating with ANSI.SYS

After ANSI.SYS is loaded by CONFIG.SYS, all input from the keyboard and output to the screen are routed through the ANSI.SYS device driver. If you don't load ANSI.SYS, DOS uses simple, input/output routines built into the DOS kernel to control the keyboard and display. You can communicate with ANSI.SYS by adding special character strings to the characters the device driver receives and sends. All ANSI.SYS commands begin with the escape character, which alerts ANSI.SYS to look for one of the special ANSI.SYS directives in the string that immediately follows.

When you press the Esc key, however, DOS's default response is to cancel the current operation and move the cursor down to the next line. You have to send the escape character to ANSI.SYS in an encoded fashion using one of two simple methods.

Embedding Escape Characters in Files

Reminder:
If you use EDLIN to edit ANSI.SYS, enter an escape character.

The first way to enter the escape character is to embed the character in a file, which you then can send to the screen by using the TYPE command. When ANSI.SYS receives the escape character and the following directive, ANSI.SYS carries out the directive as specified. Many word processors don't enable you to enter an escape character directly. For example, EDLIN doesn't, but EDLIN does enable you to type an escape character. You press Ctrl-V and the opening bracket ([). When these characters are entered, you see something like the following:

    ^V[

When you list the line, however, the V is not shown. With most versions of DOS, the line looks like the following:

    1:*^[

With DOS Versions 3.0 and 3.1, the bracket and caret are reversed:

    1:*[^

After the escape character has been entered into a file, save the file and use the DOS TYPE command to display the file on-screen. In the process of sending the characters in the file to the display, ANSI.SYS recognizes the escape character as a special character, holds that character (does not display it), and waits for another character or string of characters to complete the directive begun with the escape character. You can include the remaining characters in the file or complete the directive by typing the appropriate characters from the keyboard after ANSI.SYS has intercepted the escape character in the file. You use this procedure later in this chapter.

Using PROMPT

A second way to send an escape character to ANSI.SYS is with the DOS PROMPT command. You can use this command in a batch file or at the DOS prompt. The syntax for this command is as follows:

SET PROMPT <*string*>

or

PROMPT <*string*>

Normally, *string* is a set of characters you want to use as the DOS prompt, such as *By Your Command, Master!* However, DOS provides a group of special subcommands that PROMPT can use as arguments interpreted and acted on by ANSI.SYS. Many of these subcommands (called *metacommands*) enable you to personalize your system prompt. These metacommands are variables replaced by DOS with the current disk drive letter, the subdirectory, and so forth. The metacommands consist of the dollar sign ($) and another character, as shown in table 13.1.

Table 13.1
PROMPT Subcommands

Symbol	Meaning
$e	Escape character
$t	Time
$d	Date
$v	DOS version number
$n	Default drive name
$g	Greater-than symbol (>)
$l	Less-than symbol (<)
$p	Current drive and path
$b	Vertical bar (|)
$q	Equal sign (=)
$$	Dollar sign ($)
$h	Backspace
$_	New line (line feed and carriage return)

Reminder:
You can use the $e parameter with the PROMPT command to enter an escape character.

You must use lowercase characters for the PROMPT subcommands. If you use PROMPT to send directives to ANSI.SYS, you must make sure that the batch file has the command ECHO ON, or ANSI.SYS never sees the

Reminder:
Use lowercase letters for PROMPT subcommands.

characters you are sending. (Batch files have ECHO ON by default.) To send an escape character to ANSI.SYS by using the PROMPT command, include a line such as the following in a batch file:

PROMPT $e<*ANSI directives*>

When you run the batch file and DOS tries to display the characters specified by the PROMPT line, ANSI.SYS sees the $e and interprets the symbol as the beginning of a special directive. You can append other subcommands to this same PROMPT line.

You can alert ANSI.SYS that a command is being sent by preceding the command with an escape character. You send the escape character and command to ANSI.SYS by creating a file into which the escape character (Ctrl-V [) and command are entered and then using the DOS TYPE command with that file or by using the PROMPT command to specify the escape character ($e). The following sections present the actual ANSI.SYS commands. The commands are divided into screen commands, cursor-movement commands, and keyboard commands.

Using the Cursor-Movement Commands

When you enter the CLS command at the DOS prompt, the on-screen image is erased, and the cursor character and the current DOS prompt appear in row 1, column 1 of the upper left corner of the screen. Subsequent characters that appear on-screen are located one space farther to the right, until you reach the right side of the screen (and then the line wraps around) or until you press Enter to finish the command.

Reminder:
Cursor-movement commands begin with an escape character and [.

You also can move the cursor by using ANSI.SYS commands. The commands to move the cursor begin with the escape character (as described in the preceding section) followed by a left bracket. When you use EDLIN for text files, use Ctrl-V[[for the escape character. If you use the PROMPT command to send directives to ANSI.SYS, type *$e[*. The following instructions show the escape-left bracket sequence as ESC[.

Table 13.2 lists the ANSI.SYS commands you can use to move the cursor. Make sure that you type the commands with the capitalization given in the table. Notice that the variables <row> and <col> are used in place of the actual row or column number where you want to move the cursor; <lines> and <columns> are used in place of the number of rows or columns you want to move the cursor.

Table 13.2
ANSI.SYS Cursor-Movement Commands

Command	Description
ESC[<row>;<col>H	Moves the cursor to the specified row and column. If you do not specify the row and column, the cursor moves to the home position (row 1, column 1). To move the cursor to row 3, column 8, for example, type the following: ESC[3;8H
ESC[<row>;<col>f	Same as ESC[<row>;<col>H
ESC[<lines>A	Moves the cursor up the specified number of <lines>. The column in which the cursor appears is unchanged.
ESC[<lines>B	Moves the cursor down the specified number of <lines>. The column in which the cursor appears is unchanged.
ESC[<columns>C	Moves the cursor the specified number of <columns> to the right. If you do not specify the number of <columns>, the cursor moves one column to the right. This command is ignored if the cursor is already at the far right of the screen; you cannot wrap text around to the next line.
ESC[<columns>D	Moves the cursor the specified number of <columns> to the left. If you do not specify the number of <columns>, the cursor moves one column to the left. This command is ignored if the cursor is already at the far left of the screen; you cannot wrap text around to the preceding line.
ESC[s	Saves the current cursor position
ESC[u	Restores the cursor to the location stored by ESC[s
ESC[2J	Clears the display and places the cursor at the home position at column 0, row 0
ESC[K	Clears the rest of the current line, starting at (and including) the current column

The ESC[s and ESC[u commands enable cursor movement without destroying the current location of the cursor. These two commands report and save the current position of the cursor and restore the cursor to that position. These commands are useful if you want to move the cursor to display something in a new location and then put the cursor back in its old position. For example, you can type the following PROMPT statement:

PROMPT pg$e[s$e[1;4Hde[u

This example changes the appearance of the system prompt by using cursor-movement commands and two other PROMPT subcommands. The $p and $g represent the current default drive/directory (path) and the greater-than symbol that make up the standard system prompt (such as C>). $e[s stores the current cursor position. $e[1;4H positions the cursor at row 1, column 4. The $d causes the system date to be printed at the cursor location (row 1, column 4). $e[u restores the cursor to its former position.

Using this PROMPT command causes the standard prompt to appear on the appropriate line, but the system date always prints at the top of the screen (see fig. 13.1). DOS uses this prompt until you reboot the computer or reset the prompt.

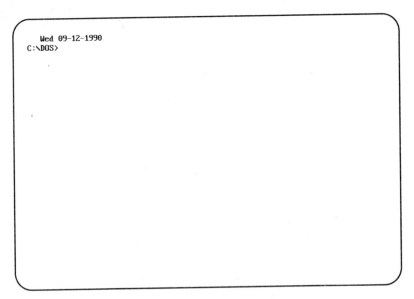

Fig. 13.1. The results of PROMPT pg$e[s$e[1;4Hde[u.

Using the Screen Commands

Other ANSI commands are available to change the attributes of the video images displayed on-screen. If you have a color monitor, you can change the foreground and background colors of the screen (or the prompt); if you have a monochrome monitor, you can alter the screen images to include reverse video, blinking, and other attributes.

The screen attribute commands all begin with ESC[followed by one or more numbers and a lowercase m. You can include several numbers in one command to set more than one attribute, as long as each number is separated with a semicolon (;). The valid attribute numbers are shown in tables 13.3 and 13.4.

Reminder:
Use screen commands to set the attributes of your monitor.

Reminder:
Screen-attribute commands begin with ESC[.

Table 13.3
ANSI.SYS Screen Commands for Monochrome and Color Monitors

Number	Result
0	Normal characters
1	High-intensity (bold) characters
4	Underlined characters (monochrome only)
5	Blinking characters
7	Reverse-video characters
8	Invisible characters

The ANSI.SYS driver also enables you to set some video modes and resolutions. The ESC[=<number>h command enables you to set the screen width or type. The ESC[=<number>l command activates Reset mode, which uses the same values as Set mode, except for mode 7, which disables line wrapping. The Set and Reset modes are different only with mode 7. Table 13.5 shows the video mode settings for each <number>.

Table 13.4
ANSI.SYS Screen Commands for Color Monitors

Number	Foreground colors
30	Black characters
31	Red characters
32	Green characters
33	Yellow characters
34	Blue characters
35	Magenta characters
36	Cyan (light blue) characters
37	White characters

Number	Background Colors
40	Black background
41	Red background
42	Green background
43	Yellow background
44	Blue background
45	Magenta background
46	Cyan (light blue) background
47	White background

Creating Colorful Screen Messages

By creating a text file with EDLIN, you can print colorful messages on-screen. For example, you can place the message WARNING! Don't Touch! in blinking red characters on a black background. Then the colors can be changed to normal (nonblinking) cyan characters on a blue background for the rest of your message.

To create this example, type the command **EDLIN WARNING.TXT**. (Remember that the Version 5 EDIT program doesn't enable you to enter escape characters.) When typing the text in EDLIN, press Ctrl-V to create the escape character. A ^V character is shown when you first enter the text, but EDLIN's List command shows only the caret (^) character. Enter the text on one line as shown and then exit EDLIN.

   <Ctrl-V>[5;40;31m WARNING! Don't Touch! <Ctrl-V>[0;36;44m

To show the warning on-screen, use the following command at the DOS prompt:

   TYPE COLOR.TXT

Table 13.5
Screen Mode Command Values

Number	Screen type
0	40 x 25 monochrome
1	40 x 25 color
2	80 x 25 monochrome
3	80 x 25 color
4	320 x 200 color
5	320 x 200 monochrome
6	640 x 200 monochrome
7	(Set mode) Wraps at the end of each line
7	(Reset mode) Disables line wrap
14	640 x 200 color
15	640 x 350 monochrome
16	640 x 360 color
17	640 x 480 monochrome
18	640 x 480 color
19	320 x 200 color

The TYPE command prints the COLOR.TXT file on-screen. When the ANSI.SYS driver sees the escape sequence, ANSI.SYS interprets the commands to change the colors and prints the warning message. The colors then are changed again. After the color sequence is interpreted by ANSI.SYS, the color changes are permanent until changed again. The text message is not permanent; this message scrolls off the screen as you type additional DOS commands.

Using Colors in Your DOS Prompt

If you want your DOS prompt to include color commands, use the PROMPT command. When you use the PROMPT command, the color and text you specify are shown on-screen as part of every DOS prompt. The following example sets your prompt to include the text Yes, Master in green characters on a black background. The current drive and path are shown in cyan characters on a blue background.

PROMPT $e[32;40mYes, Master $e[36;44m$p$g

Because you don't want to type long command sequences like this one each time you boot DOS, you can incorporate the commands into a special batch file called AUTOEXEC.BAT.

You may want to experiment with some batch files by using ANSI.SYS. Following is a commonly used ANSI.SYS sequence that places the date, time, and currently logged subdirectory in the upper right corner of your screen. ECHO ON must be set if ANSI.SYS is to interpret the PROMPT string, so don't include an ECHO OFF statement in your batch file. If you put this PROMPT line in a batch file that does other things, put an ECHO ON statement on the line preceding the following PROMPT command:

PROMPT $e[s$e[1;50Hthhhhhhd$e[u$n$g

This line creates the blinking prompt shown in figure 13.2. You also can add color commands to various parts of the command sequence.

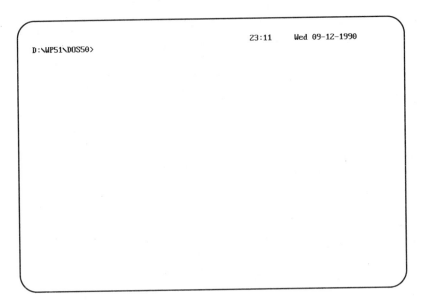

Fig. 13.2. The results of PROMPT $e[s$e[1;50Hthhhhhhd$e[u$n$g.

Using Keyboard Commands

A great deal happens when you press a key on your keyboard. Circuitry in your keyboard determines when a key has been pressed. The keyboard also can tell when a key has been released. Each time you press a key, a *scan code* is sent from the keyboard through the connecting cable to your computer system. DOS takes the scan code, compares the code to a table of assignments, and determines the character for that particular scan code.

When active, ANSI.SYS handles the scan codes. If ANSI.SYS is not active, the DOS kernel handles this input and output. Ordinarily, ANSI.SYS passes the default value for each key to DOS. When you press Shift-A, ANSI.SYS receives a scan code of 65 and sends the DOS code for A to the operating system.

Understanding Scan Codes

Nearly every key on the keyboard has a unique scan code (the exceptions are explained shortly). For example, the uppercase letters A to Z are assigned scan codes 65 to 90. Lowercase letters a to z are represented by scan codes 97 to 122. Because these codes coincide with the ASCII codes for the same characters, the scan codes are easy to remember—if you have memorized the ASCII codes.

Reminder:
Scan codes are different than, but correspond to, the ASCII codes for the characters.

You press Shift-A to produce the uppercase letter A. Scan codes also represent other shifted states, such as Ctrl-A or Alt-A. The keystrokes Ctrl-A through Ctrl-Z are represented by scan codes of 1 to 26.

Scan codes are 8-bit bytes, so only 256 scan codes are possible. Obviously, 256 numbers (0 to 255) aren't enough to represent all the possible key and shifted-key combinations. DOS gets around this limit by preceding some codes with a 0. Because no key is assigned a scan code of only 0, adding a 0 to the beginning of a scan code does not cause confusion. When ANSI.SYS receives a 0 scan code, the device driver knows that an extended scan code is being sent and interprets differently the next number it receives.

When ANSI.SYS receives a scan code of 65, for example, the device driver knows that Shift-A has been pressed. When ANSI.SYS receives 0;65, the device driver interprets that sequence as the F7 key. Several keys in the numeric keypad share the same scan code. The keypad 0 and Shift-Ins keys, for example, have the same code: 48. If you notice, the 0 is located on the Ins key, so the fact that they share a scan code should not be surprising. The Shift-Home, Shift-left arrow, Shift-right arrow, and other keys in that region share the same scan codes as the numbers on the keys. DOS checks whether the Shift or Num Lock key has been pressed to determine which value for the scan code is intended.

A few key combinations have no scan codes, such as Ctrl-up arrow and Alt-Home. DOS cannot recognize these null key combinations.

Reminder:
A few key combinations have no scan code.

Think of scan codes as values in tables that ANSI.SYS uses to look up the definitions it passes to DOS (see tables 13.6 and 13.7). You can use ANSI.SYS commands to change the definitions in the tables. When ANSI.SYS receives a scan code of 65 from the keyboard, the device driver checks the table for the definition of that scan code. If you have not redefined the scan code, key 65 is the default value of A, and A is sent to DOS. If you substitute a new definition for scan code 65, such as *Hurrah for A!!*, that new string is sent to DOS instead of the A.

Table 13.6
Scan Codes for IBM PC and Compatibles

Key	Unshift	Shift	Control	Alt
A	97	65	1	0;30
B	98	66	2	0;48
C	99	67	3	0;46
D	100	68	4	0;32
E	101	69	5	0;18
F	102	70	6	0;33
G	103	71	7	0;34
H	104	72	8	0;35
I	105	73	9	0;23
J	106	74	10	0;36
K	107	75	11	0;37
L	108	76	12	0;38
M	109	77	13	0;50
N	110	78	14	0;49
O	111	79	15	0;24
P	112	80	16	0;25
Q	113	81	17	0;16
R	114	82	18	0;19
S	115	83	19	0;31
T	116	84	20	0;20
U	117	85	21	0;22
V	118	86	22	0;47
W	119	87	23	0;17
X	120	88	24	0;45
Y	121	89	25	0;21
Z	122	90	26	0;44
1	49	33		0;120
2	50	64		0;121
3	51	35		0;122
4	52	36		0;123

Key	Unshift	Shift	Control	Alt
5	53	37		0;124
6	54	94		0;125
7	55	38		0;126
8	56	42		0;127
9	57	40		0;128
0	48	41		0;129
–	45	95		0;130
=	61	43		0;131
Tab	9	0;15		
Space	57			
Null	0;3			

Table 13.7
Extended Scan Codes for Numeric Keypad and Function Keys

Key	Unshift	Shift	Control	Alt
F1	0;59	0;84	0;94	0;104
F2	0;60	0;85	0;95	0;105
F3	0;61	0;86	0;96	0;106
F4	0;62	0;87	0;97	0;107
F5	0;63	0;88	0;98	0;108
F6	0;64	0;89	0;99	0;109
F7	0;65	0;90	0;100	0;110
F8	0;66	0;91	0;101	0;111
F9	0;67	0;92	0;102	0;112
F10	0;68	0;93	0;103	0;113
F11	0;133	0;135	0;137	0;139
F12	0;134	0;136	0;138	0;140
Home	0;71	55	0;119	0;155
↑	0;72	56	0;141	0;152
PgUp	0;73	57	0;132	0;153
←	0;75	52	0;115	0;155
→	0;77	54	0;116	0;157
End	0;79	49	0;117	0;159
↓	0;80	50	0;145	0;160
PgDn	0;81	51	0;118	0;161
Ins	0;82	48	0;146	0;162
Del	0;83	46	0;147	0;163
PrtSc		0;114		

Reminder: Don't redefine keys you use with DOS or other programs.

You can assign the definition Z to the scan code for the letter A or define the scan code for A as an entire sentence, such as *Hurrah for A!!* Generally, you do not redefine keys you need to use DOS (such as the alphanumeric keys). If you redefine the A key as *Hurrah for A!!* and then type the command *DIR A:*, DOS understands that as `DIR Hurrah for A!!:`. (This command is difficult to use!) Generally, you should redefine only the function keys not used for DOS or EDLIN editing and Alt-key and Ctrl-key combinations not used by any program that uses ANSI.SYS for keyboard interpretation. You can assign a different definition to each key combination, for example, so that you can have separate definitions for F10, Shift-F10, Alt-F10, and Ctrl-F10.

Caution: Use only 200 bytes to redefine keys or your computer will lock up.

The only limiting factor you have when defining scan codes is the amount of space DOS sets aside for these definitions. ANSI.SYS allows about 200 bytes for your new key definitions. If you use more than 200 bytes, the COMMAND.COM file is overwritten, and your computer locks up.

Creating a More Complex Prompt

The following DOS prompt is a bit fancier than most. Because this prompt is so complex, you may get an `Out of environment space` error when you try to execute the PROMPT command. The environment is an area of memory used to store system settings, such as your PROMPT command, PATH settings, and any variables specified with the SET command. The environment also contains information about where to look for the command processor (COMMAND.COM) when it needs to be reloaded. The default size of the environment is 256 bytes in the later versions of DOS.

To make the DOS environment larger, add the following command to the beginning of your CONFIG.SYS file:

SHELL = C:\COMMAND.COM C:\ /P /E:384

If you have DOS 3.1 or earlier, use the following command:

SHELL = C:\COMMAND.COM C:\ /P /E:20

(The SHELL command is discussed in Chapter 15.)

After you have made the change to the CONFIG.SYS file, reboot your computer so that the increased environment is enabled. Then create a batch file called MYPROMPT.BAT that contains two lines. You can use EDIT, EDLIN, or your word processor in ASCII format. (Some word processors call the ASCII format *text mode*; with others, you must open a nondocument file.) For the first line, type **@ECHO OFF**. The second line is as follows:

prompt $e[s$e[H$e[K$e[41;1;37m$e[0;0H$p$e[1;57H$e[44;1;36m

THHHHH$H de[u$e[44;36m Enter Command —

Ge[0m$e[32m<F6>

The entire command should be on one line (it is split here so that it will fit on the page). Two spaces are between the $H and $d, and the <F6> code means that you should press the F6 function key. Enter the line carefully, checking for accuracy. When you are sure that this line is correct, save the file.

The following lines tell you what each part of the PROMPT command does.

The PROMPT command

$e[s	Saves the current cursor position
$e[H	Moves to the top left corner of the screen
$e[K	Erases the text on the current line from the current cursor position
$e[e41;1;37m	Sets the colors for a red background with bold characters and white text
$e[0;0H	Moves the cursor back to top left corner of the screen
$p	Prints the current drive/path
$e[1;57H	Moves over to row 1, column 57
$e[44;1;36m	Sets the colors for a blue background with bold characters and cyan text
$T	Prints the current time (HH:MM:SS.hh)
HHHHHH	Backspaces six times to get rid of the seconds and hundredth seconds—the last six characters of the time
$d	Prints the current date (after printing the two space characters)
$e[u	Places the cursor back in the saved position
$e[44;36m	Sets the colors for a blue background with cyan text (Characters are still bold because they haven't been reset.)

continues

The PROMPT command (continued)

Enter Command	Prints the text "Enter Command —"
$G	Prints the greater-than symbol (>)
$e[0m	Sets normal characters (turns bold off)
$e[32m	Sets colors for green text
<F6>	The F6 key makes sure that you don't get an extra prompt on-screen.

Enter the command *MYPROMPT* to see the results of your work. If the results are not quite right, you probably have an error in the second line. Type the command *PROMPT pg* to set the prompt back to normal and then edit the file and make the corrections.

Redefining Scan Codes

To redefine the ANSI.SYS scan codes, you use escape sequences. You can use the PROMPT command or EDLIN to create the line that communicates with ANSI.SYS. (Remember that you cannot use EDIT because you have no way to type the escape character; <Ctrl-V> means to hold down the Ctrl key and press V.) The syntax of the PROMPT command you use to redefine a scan code is as follows:

PROMPT $e[*<scan code>*;"*<new definition>*"p

If you use EDLIN, the following syntax works:

<Ctrl-V>[[*<scan code>*;"*<new definition>*"p

Cue:
To include a carriage return with the new definition, use 13p instead of p in the redefinition command.

If you want the new key definition to end with a carriage return, substitute 13p for p in the command. In these commands, *<scan code>* is the scan code of the key you want to redefine (refer to tables 13.6 and 13.7); *<new definition>* is the new character or characters you want the scan code to return. To define the scan code with a string of characters, enclose the string in quotation marks, as shown in the following example:

PROMPT $e[*65;"Hey I pressed A!"p*

With EDLIN, the command is as follows:

^V[[*65;"Hey I pressed A!"p*

Then use the TYPE command as you did in the preceding section. If you defined the A key in this way, every time you press Shift-A, ANSI.SYS sends the string *Hey I pressed A!* (instead of the uppercase letter A) to DOS.

To define a scan code with another scan code (suppose that you want to substitute scan code 97 for 65 so that when you press Shift-A, a lowercase a appears), you can drop the quotation marks and use the second scan code, as shown in the following example:

PROMPT $e[65;97p

You also can make this same assignment with the following command:

PROMPT $e[65;"a"p

If you use EDLIN, the command is as follows:

^V[[65;97p

To return the 65 scan code to its original definition, you can reboot the computer to return all scan codes to their default values or issue the following statement, placing the original scan code in the second position:

PROMPT $e[65;65p

With EDLIN, the command is as follows:

^V[[65;65p

When you use extended scan codes, separate the 0 and the second number of the scan code with a semicolon and separate the entire scan code from the new definition with another semicolon, as shown in the following examples:

PROMPT $e[0;59;"Hey I pressed F1!"p

^V[[0;59;"Hey I pressed F1!"p

The redefinition procedure is made a bit clearer with some examples. The scan codes 0;59 through 0;68 have the default definitions F1 through F10. You can change the definitions of these scan codes to produce `DIR A:<Enter>`, `DIR B:<Enter>`, and `DIR C: /P<Enter>` when you press F8, F9, or F10 with the following commands:

PROMPT $e[0;66;"DIR A:";13p

PROMPT $e[0;67;"DIR B:";13p

PROMPT $e[0;68;"DIR C: /P";13p

With EDLIN, the commands are the following:

^V[[0;66;"DIR A:";13p

^V[[0;67;"DIR B:";13p

^V[[0;68;"DIR C: /P";13p

Cue:
To reset scan codes to their default values, reboot the computer.

The values 0;66, 0;67, and 0;68 are the scan codes for F8, F9, and F10. The characters in quotation marks are the new definitions for these function keys. The *13p* is used to tell ANSI.SYS to press the Enter key.

A number of programs enable you to redefine keys by creating macros that are even more sophisticated than these simple redefinitions. To redefine keys quickly with short strings, however, the ANSI.SYS method is fun and easy to use.

Chapter Summary

In this chapter, you learned how to use ANSI.SYS to move the cursor, change keyboard definitions, and control the attributes that appear on-screen. Following are the key points to remember from this chapter:

- DOS works with other devices through the use of installable driver files such as ANSI.SYS.

- ANSI.SYS extends the capabilities of ROM-BIOS and DOS for screen and keyboard control.

- You can communicate with ANSI.SYS by sending sequences of characters that start with the escape character.

- You can generate an escape character with the PROMPT command or by using EDLIN (not EDIT) to create a text file.

- You can control where the cursor moves on-screen by using the PROMPT command with ANSI.SYS.

- You can set screen attributes and colors by using the PROMPT command with ANSI.SYS.

- Key redefinition involves the use of scan codes to change the strings DOS receives when a key is pressed.

Chapter 14 explains more about batch files and shows you how to integrate the things you have learned about ANSI.SYS into a batch file.

14

Learning Advanced
Batch File Techniques

Chapter 12 discussed how batch files work and showed you some examples of how you can put them to work for you. This chapter explains batch file techniques in more detail.

This chapter discusses the following batch commands:

- IF

- FOR..IN..DO

- SHIFT

- CALL

- COMMAND /C

Reviewing Batch File Subcommands

Table 14.1 is a complete list of batch subcommands for DOS Versions 3 through 5.

Table 14.1
Batch File Subcommands for DOS Versions 3 and 4

Subcommand	Function
@	Suppresses the display of a line on-screen (DOS Versions 3.3 and later)
CALL	Runs another batch file and returns to the original batch file (DOS Versions 3.3 and later)
CLS	Clears the screen and returns the cursor to the upper left corner of the screen
COMMAND	Invokes a second copy of the command processor, COMMAND.COM, to call another batch file. Available for versions prior to 3.3; the CALL command of Version 3.3 and above is preferable.
ECHO	Turns on or off the display of batch commands as they execute; also can display a message on-screen
FOR..IN..DO	Enables the use of the same command for a group of files
GOTO	Jumps to the line following the specified label in a batch file
IF	Enables conditional execution of a command
PAUSE	Halts processing until a key is pressed; displays the message `Press any key to continue.`
REM	Allows for comments or unexecuted batch commands
SHIFT	Shifts the command-line parameters one parameter to the left

Reminder:
Most batch-file subcommands have limited use at the operating-system level.

Any subcommand from table 14.1 can be used in a batch file. Most of them also can be used at the DOS system level. For example, you can type **ECHO** at the DOS prompt, with or without an argument. DOS displays the string you type after the ECHO command or, if you provide no argument, tells you whether ECHO is ON or OFF. You can type **PAUSE** at the DOS prompt, and DOS pauses, displaying the `Press any key to continue...` message on-screen. Neither of these commands is of much use at the operating-system level. The FOR..IN..DO command structure, however, can be quite useful at the operating-system level to carry out repetitive commands.

This chapter explains the four batch subcommands you didn't learn in Chapter 12: IF, FOR..IN..DO, SHIFT, and CALL. Examples of how each subcommand can be used also are provided.

Using IF

The IF subcommand is a conditional command. When the condition is true, IF executes the command on the same line. When the condition is false, IF ignores the line. The DOS IF subcommand works like the IF statement in BASIC. The subcommand can be used to test one of the following three conditions:

- The ERRORLEVEL of a program
- Whether a string is equal to another string
- Whether a file exists

Using IF To Test ERRORLEVEL

An ERRORLEVEL is the numerical value that a program may leave for DOS when the program is exited. ERRORLEVEL often is referred to as *exit level*. In DOS Version 5, many of the DOS commands leave an exit code when they complete. The error levels are detailed in the DOS reference manual.

Reminder:
You can use the IF command to test ERRORLEVEL.

An exit code of zero (0) usually means that the program functioned properly. Any number greater than 0 usually indicates that something went wrong: no files were found; the program encountered an error; or the operator aborted the program. By including an IF command in a batch file, you can test ERRORLEVEL to see whether a program worked properly.

If the exit code you test for is equal to or greater than the number you specify in the batch file, the ERRORLEVEL condition is true. Think of this condition as a BASIC-like statement:

```
IF ERRORLEVEL > number THEN do this
```

When you use the IF ERRORLEVEL command, remember to test for the highest ERRORLEVEL value first. For example, if you need to test for ERRORLEVELs 1 through 4, place the commands in the following order:

IF ERRORLEVEL 4 THEN GOTO ERROR4

IF ERRORLEVEL 3 THEN GOTO ERROR3

IF ERRORLEVEL 2 THEN GOTO ERROR2

IF ERRORLEVEL 1 THEN GOTO ERROR1

Your batch file then would have labels of ERROR4, ERROR3, ERROR2, and ERROR1 to handle the instances of the ERRORLEVELS of 1 to 4. Note that if the program returns an errorlevel of 5, the ERROR4 routine will be used, because the IF ERRORLEVEL command tests for an ERRORLEVEL equal to or higher than the value used. The first command in the preceding list causes the batch file to jump to the ERROR4 routine if the ERRORLEVEL is 4 or higher. If the ERRORLEVEL is less than 4, the next command is executed.

The IF ERRORLEVEL command also is useful with any of the noncopyrighted public-domain utilities (INPUT.COM and ASK.COM, for example). A batch file using these utilities can pause and wait for keyboard input. The utility records a value in ERRORLEVEL related to the scan code of the key you press. You can make your batch file branch or perform some other task based on the pressed key. A batch file accepts keyboard input only when provided on a batch-file command line.

Using IF To Compare Strings

Reminder:
You can use the IF command to test whether two strings are equal.

The second condition that the IF command can be used to test is whether two strings are equal. The *IF <string1> == <string2>* condition usually is used with replaceable parameters and variable markers. (Replaceable parameters are discussed in Chapter 12.) Create a batch file called ISIBM.BAT and type the following:

IF %1 == IBM ECHO I'm an IBM computer

If you type **ISIBM IBM** at the DOS prompt, you see the following:

```
I'm an IBM computer
```

If you type something other than IBM as the first parameter, such as **ISIBM APPLE**, no message appears on-screen.

If you don't provide enough parameters with the IF command, DOS replaces the parameter marker with nothing, displays the message Syntax error, and aborts the batch file.

To avoid a syntax error, first test whether a parameter is empty before trying another test. You can see the general technique in this revised version of ISIBM.BAT:

```
IF "%1" == "" GOTO NOANSWER
IF %1 == IBM GOTO IBM
ECHO What computer are you?
GOTO END
:IBM
ECHO I'm an IBM computer GOTO END
:NOANSWER
ECHO Pardon me, I could not hear you.
:END
```

> **Note:** :END often is used as a convenient GOTO label when none of the IF conditions are met. In this batch file, when the IF statements do not branch to NOANSWER or IBM, the message What computer are you? appears, and the batch file branches to END. Because no commands follow the END label, the batch file quits.

The first line of the revised ISIBM.BAT places quotation marks around %1 and tests to see whether %1 is empty. If %1 is null (meaning ISIBM was called with no parameters), the line effectively reads as follows:

```
IF "" == "" GOTO NOANSWER
```

This line traps the error condition of too few batch-file parameters. If you need to check for a nonexistent parameter, use this format.

Cue:
Use quotation marks to test whether a parameter has been provided for a variable marker.

The quotation marks around the variable marker are used in this example because quotation marks are easy to understand, especially for BASIC programmers. A comparison with any letter, number, or symbol can do the job. One common procedure is to use a period instead of the quotation marks, as shown in the following example:

```
IF %1. == . GOTO NOANSWER
```

If no parameter is entered for %1, DOS interprets the line as follows:

```
IF . == . GOTO NOANSWER
```

Cue:
Use a period instead of quotation marks in the IF statement.

If %1 equals blank characters, DOS branches to the line following the label NOANSWER, and the message Pardon me, I could not hear you appears on-screen.

If %1 equals something other than blank characters, DOS executes the second line in the batch file. The second line tests to see whether **IBM** was entered. Notice that GOTO statements are used to jump around the parts of the batch file that should not be executed. If %1 equals IBM, the message I'm an IBM computer appears. If the parameter is not empty and is not IBM, the message What computer are you? appears.

Cue:
Use GOTO statements to jump around in the batch file.

DOS compares strings literally. Uppercase characters are different than lowercase characters. If you invoke ISIBM.BAT, DOS compares the lower-case "ibm" to the uppercase "IBM" and decides that the two strings are not the same. The IF test fails, and I'm an IBM computer does not appear. You can use the FOR..IN..DO command to check for all possible answers.

Using IF To Look for Files

The third condition you can use the IF subcommand to test is *IF EXIST <filename>*. This IF condition tests whether the file is on-disk. To test for a file on a drive other than the current drive, place the disk drive name in front of *<filename>* (for example, B:CHKDSK.COM).

You also can test for the opposite of these three IF conditions. You can test whether a condition is false by adding the word NOT. For example, you can use the statement IF NOT EXIST <filename> to check whether a file does not exist on the disk. If the result of the statement is true (the file does not exist), the command following the IF statement is executed. You can use this command in a batch file to make sure that a program file exists before trying to start the program.

Using FOR..IN..DO

FOR..IN..DO is an unusual and extremely powerful batch subcommand. This command enables you to use one command line that repeats a command for a group of files or drives. For example, one command line can perform a CHKDSK command for several different drives, rather than entering a separate CHKDSK command for each drive. The subcommand's syntax is as follows:

**FOR %%*<variable>* IN *(<set>)* DO *<command>*

<variable> is a one-letter name that takes on the value of each item in the set. The double percent sign in front of the variable is important. If you use one percent sign, DOS confuses the symbol with the parameter marker and does not work properly.

<set> is the list of the items, commands, or disk files you want *<variable>* to take the value of. You can use wild-card filenames with this parameter. You also can use drive names and paths with any filenames you specify. If you have more than one filename or other item in the set, use a space or comma between the names. Notice that the *<set>* must be enclosed by parentheses.

<command> is any valid DOS command that you want to perform for each item in *<set>*.

Using FOR..IN..DO at the DOS Prompt

When necessary, you may want to issue commands like the ones in CHECKIT at the DOS prompt. Instead of using the batch file for the preceding example, you can change subdirectories and then type the FOR..IN..DO line (the line that does all the work in the batch file) at the DOS prompt. If you do use FOR..IN..DO outside a batch file, enter only one of the percent signs.

Reminder:
If you use FOR..IN..DO at the DOS prompt, enter only one percent sign.

For example, to run a program called OPTIMIZE on drives C through F, you can type this command at the DOS prompt:

FOR %1 IN *(C: D: E: F:)* **DO OPTIMIZE %1**

To use this command in a batch file, use the command **FOR %%1 IN (C: D: E: F:) DO OPTIMIZE %1**.

If you copy files from a disk to the wrong subdirectory on a hard disk, you can delete the files from the hard disk using FOR..IN..DO.

Using a FOR..IN..DO Batch File

An interesting example of the use of FOR..IN..DO is a simple batch file that compares file names on a floppy disk with file names on another disk or in a hard disk subdirectory. To see how this batch file works, copy some files to a disk, from another disk, or from a hard disk subdirectory. Create the batch file CHECKIT.BAT and type the following in the file:

```
@ECHO OFF

IF "%1"=="" GOTO END

FOR %%a IN (B: C: D: E: b: c: d: e:) DO
IF "%%a"=="%1" GOTO COMPARE

GOTO END

:COMPARE

%1

CD \%2

FOR %%a IN (*.*) DO IF EXIST A:%%a
ECHO %%a is on this disk also.

:END
```

Place the disk you want to compare in drive A. Type the following:

CHECKIT A: *.*

The directory you want to compare is optional, but if you specify a directory, you must separate the directory from the drive name with a space. This convention is followed because two batch-file parameters (%1 and %2) are used to store the letter of the drive and the directory name. If you don't specify a directory name, the root directory of the drive you specify is used. If you type **CHECKIT B:\GAMES**, for example, the file searches drive A for the B:\GAMES directory.

When the CHECKIT batch file is called, DOS first checks whether %1 is empty (%1 is empty if no parameters were provided when the command was issued). If %1 is empty, DOS branches to the end of the file. Otherwise, DOS goes to the third line and checks whether a valid drive letter was entered (the valid drive letters are B, C, D, E, b, c, d, and e; if your system has more or fewer drives, change this line to reflect your configuration). If an invalid drive letter is found, DOS branches to the end of the batch file. Invoke this batch file with the drive name and the colon, separated by no space, or the comparison fails.

If the specified drive is valid, CHECKIT accesses the COMPARE section of the file. The first thing COMPARE does is change the currently logged drive to the drive specified by %1. COMPARE then changes to the subdirectory specified by %2. If %2 is empty, the root directory of the disk is used. If %2 is a valid subdirectory name for that disk, the default directory is changed to %2. The CD\ command is valid even when %2 is null; no syntax error appears in this instance. A syntax error appears only when a null parameter makes the statement invalid.

The eighth line looks at all the files in the current directory to see whether a file with the same name as the one you specified in CHECKIT exists on drive A. If a match is found, the message `<filename> is on this disk also` appears on-screen.

Using FOR..IN..DO with Wild Cards

FOR..IN..DO also enables you to use wild-card file names with certain commands. The TYPE command, for example, does not accept wild-card file names; you must use a specific file name. If you make a batch file, however, you can use FOR..IN..DO to type a series of files. If you create the batch file TYPER.BAT to do this operation, the file may consist of the following statement:

```
@FOR %%d IN (%1 %2 %3 %4 %5) DO TYPE %%d
```

This statement substitutes up to five specific file names for the wild-card parameter you supplied when you invoked TYPER.BAT and then executes the TYPE command for each file. If you type **$$ TYPER *.BAT $$**, the batch file will TYPE all the BAT files found in the root directory of the current drive. They may scroll by too fast for you to read, however. You can send the output of the TYPE command to the printer by changing your batch file to the following:

> **FOR %%D IN (%A %2 %3 %4 %5) DO TYPE %%D > LPT1:**

> `C:\>TYPE AUTOEXEC.BAT`

(AUTOEXEC.BAT's contents are displayed)

> `C:\>TYPE TYPER.BAT`

(TYPER.BAT's contents are displayed)

> `C:\>TYPE STARTUP.BAT`

(STARTUP.BAT's contents are displayed)

> `C:\>$$`

Another example of the use of FOR..IN..DO is a batch file that stops you from inadvertently formatting drive C. To use this batch file, rename the DOS file FORMAT.COM to FORMATR.COM. When you create the batch file FORMAT.BAT, store the file in a directory specified by the current PATH or in the current directory. When FORMAT.BAT is created, type the following into the file:

> **@ECHO OFF**

> **IF %1. == . GOTO WHATDRIVE**

> **FOR %%d IN** *(A:,a:,B:,b:)* **DO IF %1 == %%d GOTO FORMAT**

> **GOTO BADDRIVE**

> **:FORMAT**

> **C:\DOS\FORMATR %1 %2 %3 %4 %5**

> **GOTO END**

> **:BADDRIVE**

> **ECHO You cannot format %1!**

> **ECHO %1 is not a floppy disk drive**

> **:WHATDRIVE**

> **ECHO Please try again and specify the disk drive you**
>
> **ECHO want to use, such as FORMAT A: or FORMAT B:**
>
> **:END**

The working line in FORMAT.BAT is the FOR..IN..DO command on line 6. This command tests whether the first parameter (which should be the disk drive name) is A, a, B, or b. If a match is found, DOS jumps to the FORMAT part of the file. If no match is found, DOS jumps to the BADDRIVE part of the file. (Notice that if you type **C:**, no match is found; this file does not enable you to format drive C.) Also notice that the second line of the file checks for a missing parameter.

If a matching drive name is found, DOS executes the FORMATR program (the renamed FORMAT.COM program found in the C:\DOS directory) for the drive specified by %1. The additional variable markers (%2, %3, %4, and %5) are included in case you want to type some switches for FORMAT. If you don't type any switches, DOS fills these variable markers with nothing, and the blank variables do not interfere with FORMAT.

The error messages in this file are a little vague: both error conditions (no parameter and the wrong drive name) use the same error message. If the specified drive is incorrect, the batch file goes to :BADDRIVE and displays that message. The batch file then continues with the :WHATDRIVE message.

Redirecting FOR..IN..DO

Before continuing, you should become familiar with one limitation of the FOR..IN..DO subcommand and redirection. The FOR..IN..DO variable is not expanded by DOS. Like TYPE, MORE does not accept wild-card file names. In fact, MORE does not accept any file name (you must redirect the input of MORE). You may think that a batch file like TYPER is perfect for MORE. To test this theory, include the following line in a batch file called MORER.BAT:

> **@FOR %%d IN (*%1 %2 %3 %4 %5*) DO MORE < %%d**

Note: MORE is a DOS filter that displays a text file on-screen, one screen at a time, with the message `-- MORE --` at the bottom of the screen. When you press the space bar, the next screen appears, with the message `-- MORE --`, until the entire file has been displayed.

If you run MORER.BAT, the result is the `File not found` error message. Remove the @ from the batch file so that you can see the commands after DOS replaces the %1 through %5 parameters. Rerun the file, and the following appears on-screen:

```
C:\>MORER *.BAT
C:\>FOR %d IN (*.BAT   ) DO MORE < %d
File not found
C:\>
```

The spaces following `*.BAT` in parentheses show that DOS expanded %1 through %5. Instead of expanding %%d to the appropriate file names, DOS tries to open the file called %d because MORE's input comes from %d. You cannot use the FOR..IN..DO variable with redirection for input or output. If you attempt to use `>> %%d` with a command within a batch file, the output of the command is placed in a file called %d. If you use %%d instead, the output from the command running is placed in the %d file. (Each time the %d symbol is encountered, the earlier version of the %d file is destroyed.) For more information about redirection, refer to your DOS manual.

Using FOR..IN..DO with Other Commands

FOR..IN..DO works equally well with commands and file names.

Instead of naming a set of files, you can name a series of commands you want DOS to carry out. Consider the following example:

```
FOR %%a IN (COPY ERASE) DO %%a C:*.* C:\SAVEFILE
```

In a batch file, this line first copies all the files from the current directory on drive C to the C:\SAVEFILE directory and then erases the files from the current directory on drive C. (Make sure that you aren't in the C:\ directory when you do this, or you cannot reboot the computer.) You can place a replaceable parameter in the line instead of explicitly naming the drive and file specifications, as in the following example:

**FOR %%a IN (COPY ERASE) DO %%a *%1*

To use this batch file, you first must change to the destination directory (for example, D:\BAK). When you invoke this version of the batch file, you type the files you want copied and removed. If you name the batch file MOVER.BAT, you can type the following to invoke the file:

MOVER C:\WP

MOVER.BAT copies all the files in the subdirectory C:\WP to D:\BAK and then erases the files in C:\WP. This file works much like the C&E.BAT file created in Chapter 12.

Moving Parameters with SHIFT

Cue:

Use SHIFT to trick DOS into accepting more than 10 replaceable parameters.

The SHIFT subcommand moves the parameters in the command one parameter to the left. SHIFT tricks DOS into accepting more than 10 parameters. The diagram of SHIFT is as follows:

```
%0 → %1 → %2 → %3 → %4 → %5 . . .
↓
bit bucket
```

In this diagram, the SHIFT command causes parameter %0 to be dropped in the bit bucket. The old parameter %1 becomes parameter %0. The old parameter %2 becomes parameter %1; parameter %3 becomes %2; parameter %4 becomes %3; and so on.

The SHIFTIT.BAT batch file is a simple example of the use of the SHIFT command:

```
:START
ECHO %0 %1 %2 %3 %4 %5 %6 %7 %8 %9
SHIFT
PAUSE
GOTO START
```

Suppose that you type the following:

SHIFTIT A B C D E F G H I J K L M N O P Q R S T U V W X Y Z

The screen shows the following:

```
SHIFTIT A B C D E F G H I
Press any key to continue. . .
```

The batch filename is displayed because %0 holds the name of the batch file before the first shift. Press a key to continue; ECHO now shows the following:

```
A B C D E F G H I J
Press any key to continue. . .
```

In this case, the filename has been dropped into the bit bucket. %0 now equals A. All the parameters have shifted one to the left. Press a key to continue; SHIFT continues moving down the list of parameters you initially typed. Press Ctrl-C to stop.

SHIFT has many uses. You can use this command to build a new version of the C&E.BAT file created in Chapter 12. The following modified version of the copy-and-erase batch file, MOVE.BAT, shows a use for SHIFT:

```
:LOOP
COPY %1 C: /V
ERASE %1
SHIFT
IF NOT %1. == . GOTO LOOP
```

This batch file copies and erases the specified file or files. This batch file assumes nothing about the files to be copied; you can specify a disk drive, a path, and a file name. The batch file copies the files to the current directory on drive C and then erases the files from the original disk or directory.

The last two lines shift the parameters to the left, test whether any parameters remain, and then repeat the operation if necessary.

Running Batch Files from Other Batch Files

You may want to run a batch file from another batch file. One method is a one-way transfer of control. The other two ways show you how to run a second batch file and return control to the first batch file. These techniques are useful for building menus with batch files or using one batch file to set up and start another batch file.

Calling a Batch File at the End of Another

The first method of calling a second batch file is simple. Include the root name of the second batch file as the final line of the first batch file. The first batch file runs the second batch file as if you had typed the second batch file's root name at the DOS prompt. To run BATCH2.BAT, for example, the final line of BATCH1.BAT is as follows:

Reminder:
Call a second batch file from the last line of the first batch file for a one-way transfer of control.

```
BATCH2
```

DOS loads and executes the lines from BATCH2.BAT. Control passes in one direction: from the first batch file to the second. When BATCH2.BAT finishes executing, DOS displays the system prompt. You can consider this technique an interbatch-file GOTO. Control goes to the second file but doesn't come back to the first file.

Calling a Batch File with CALL

Reminder:
Call a second
batch file and
return to the first
using COMMAND
or CALL.

In all versions of DOS, you can call a second batch file from the first, execute the second batch file, return to the first batch file, and continue processing the first. With DOS Version 3.0 through 3.2, use COMMAND, the DOS command processor. Starting with Version 3.3, you can use the COMMAND or the CALL subcommand.

The syntax of the CALL subcommand is as follows:

> **CALL** *<d:path\filename> <parameters>*

d:path is the optional disk drive and path name of the second batch file you want to execute. The *filename* variable is the file name of the second batch file. You can place the CALL subcommand anywhere in the first batch file. DOS executes the batch file named by the CALL subcommand, returns to the first batch file, and executes the remainder of the first batch file. When you use the CALL subcommand, you can specify any parameters you want to pass to the batch file you are calling.

Understanding CALL Batch Files

If you use Version 3.3 or later, type the following files. The BATCH3.BAT file uses the MEM command available with Version 4 and above; if you are using a prior version of DOS, substitute the CHKDSK command.

BATCH1.BAT:

```
@ECHO OFF
REM This file does the setup work for demonstrating
REM the CALL subcommand or COMMAND /C.
ECHO This is the STARTUP batch file
ECHO The command parameters are %%0-%0 %%1-%1
```

```
CALL batch2 second
ECHO MEM from %0
MEM
ECHO Done!
```

BATCH2.BAT:

```
ECHO This is the SECOND batch file
ECHO The command parameters are %%0-%0 %%1-%1
CALL batch3 third
ECHO MEM from %0
MEM
```

BATCH3.BAT:

```
ECHO This is the THIRD batch file
ECHO The command parameters are %%0-%0 %%1-%1
ECHO MEM from %0
MEM
```

The first line of BATCH1.BAT sets ECHO OFF. When you set ECHO OFF in Version 3 and above, it stays off. With Version 2, ECHO turns back ON each time a new batch file starts. The next two lines in BATCH1 are REM comments. Because ECHO is OFF, the REM statements do not display when the batch file runs.

Reminder:
Starting with DOS Version 3, ECHO OFF stays off for all the batch files.

The next two ECHO lines are similar for all three batch files. The first of the two lines identifies the batch file being used. The second of the two lines shows the zero parameter (the name by which the batch file was invoked) and the first parameter (the first argument) for the batch file. To display the strings *%0* and *%1*, you must use two percent signs (%%0 and %%1). If you use one percent sign, DOS interprets the string as a replaceable parameter and does not display the actual % symbol.

Cue:
Use two percent signs in an ECHO statement to display %.

The CALL statement in the first and second batch files invokes another batch file. In the first batch file, BATCH2.BAT is invoked. In the second batch file, BATCH3.BAT is invoked. In each case, one argument is passed to the batch file being called: the word *second* to BATCH2.BAT and the word *third* to BATCH3.BAT.

Each batch file then displays its name (by using the *%0* variable) as the file invoking the MEM command and then invokes MEM. When DOS encounters the end of the batch file, DOS returns to the invoking batch file.

Analyzing Results of CALL Batch Files

Cue:
Use Ctrl-PrtSc to make the printer print what is echoed to the screen.

After you type the batch files explained in the preceding section, make sure that your printer is ready. Press Ctrl-PrtSc to start the printer. Type **BATCH1 FIRST**. When the printer is finished, toggle off the printer's capability to print echoed lines by pressing Ctrl-PrtSc again. If you do not have a printer to record the information displayed on-screen, press Ctrl-S to pause the screen as needed. When you have viewed the screen, press Ctrl-S again to unpause the screen display.

Check the printout or the screen display for the number of bytes of available RAM each time MEM runs. The following abbreviated screen output is the result of typing **BATCH1 FIRST** on a 386SX computer with expanded memory using DOS 5.0. The values you see on your computer may be different:

```
This is the STARTUP batch file
The command line parameters are %0-BATCH1 %1-FIRST
This is the SECOND batch file
The command line parameters are %0-batch2 %1-second
This is the THIRD batch file
The command line parameters are %0-batch3 %1-third
```

Output of MEM from BATCH3.BAT:

```
 655360 bytes total conventional memory
 655360 bytes available to MS-DOS
 142320 largest executable program size

 655360 bytes total EMS memory
  98304 bytes free EMS memory

3145728 bytes total contiguous extended memory
      0 bytes available contiguous extended memory
2719744 bytes available XMS memory
        MS-DOS resident in High Memory Area
```

Output of MEM from BATCH2.BAT:

```
 655360 bytes total conventional memory
 655360 bytes available to MS-DOS
 142416 largest executable program size

 655360 bytes total EMS memory
  98304 bytes free EMS memory

3145728 bytes total contiguous extended memory
      0 bytes available contiguous extended memory
2719744 bytes available XMS memory
        MS-DOS resident in High Memory Area
```

Output of MEM from BATCH1.BAT:

```
 655360  bytes  total  conventional  memory
 655360  bytes available to MS-DOS
 142512  largest executable program size

 655360  bytes total EMS memory
  98304  bytes free EMS memory

3145728  bytes total contiguous extended memory
      0  bytes available contiguous extended memory
2719744  bytes available XMS memory
         MS-DOS resident in High Memory Area
DONE!
C:\>
```

Each time you use the CALL command, DOS temporarily uses 96 bytes of RAM until the called batch file finishes running. Because DOS uses free memory, you can run out of memory if you use many batch-file CALL commands. Not many people create long, *nested* calls. The accumulated memory-usage problem occurs only when batch files continue to call other batch files. One batch file can use the CALL command as many times as desired and only use the same 96 bytes of RAM for each call.

Reminder:
DOS uses 96 bytes of memory each time you use the CALL command.

You can use batch files like the ones described in this section with versions of DOS before 3.3 by making three changes. First, delete the @ character in the first line of BATCH1.BAT. The @ feature is not available in versions of DOS before 3.3. Second, change the reference to CALL in BATCH1.BAT and BATCH2.BAT to COMMAND /C. Third, replace the MEM command with CHKDSK. You then can run the batch files.

Calling a Batch File with COMMAND /C

If you use a version of DOS before 3.3, you can use the command interpreter to call other batch files. If you use Version 3.3 or later versions, you can use CALL or COMMAND to call other batch files. The syntax of the COMMAND subcommand is as follows:

Reminder:
Use COMMAND /C with DOS versions before 3.3 to call other batch files.

COMMAND /C d:path\filename string

One difference between the syntax of CALL and COMMAND is that you must use COMMAND's /C switch. The /C switch accepts one string (*d:path\filename string*) that can include spaces and any other information. COMMAND.COM is a program that loads and executes string. When

COMMAND.COM executes string, two copies of COMMAND.COM are in memory: the original and the one executing string. When string is finished executing, the second copy of COMMAND.COM leaves memory, and the original copy regains control.

If you use COMMAND /C in the example batch files, the results are almost identical to results when CALL is used. Each copy of COMMAND.COM, however, uses more memory than the CALL subcommand. The amount of memory used by COMMAND.COM varies among versions of DOS but is less than 4K.

Caution:
If you make changes to the system environment when you use COMMAND /C, the changes are temporary.

Another difference between CALL and COMMAND /C is worth noting. Because COMMAND /C loads a new version of COMMAND.COM, any changes you make to the environment are lost when you return to the batch file that invoked COMMAND. If you invoke another batch file with CALL and then change the environment, the changes are made to the copy of the environment currently used by that batch file. This distinction can be important if you write batch files that make changes to the environment as a way of *flagging* processes you carry out. With COMMAND /C, the current batch file does not know what happened; any batch files you run later also do not inherit the changed environment. If you use CALL, the environment changes are permanent and are available to the current batch file later on, as well as to other programs run by the same command processor.

To understand this process better, look at the following example. Because these batch files use the CALL command, they work with DOS 3.3 or later versions.

TEST1.BAT:

```
ECHO OFF
SET VAR1=VAR1
COMMAND /C TEST2
CALL TEST3
```

TEST2.BAT:

```
SET VAR2=VAR2
```

TEST3.BAT:

```
SET VAR3=VAR3
```

Run the files by typing **TEST1** and pressing Enter. When the files are finished running, type **SET** (the DOS command that displays the environment) to see something like the following:

```
PATH=C:\BATCH;C:\DOS;C:$\UTILS;C:\
COMSPEC=C:\DOS\COMMAND.COM
VAR1=VAR1
VAR3=VAR3
```

Look at the last two lines. If the SET command lists the variables currently in memory, what happened to VAR2? This variable was set when TEST1.BAT used COMMAND /C to invoke TEST2.BAT. Because DOS loaded a new copy of COMMAND.COM to run TEST2.BAT, the variable VAR2 was lost when DOS returned to the original copy of COMMAND.COM to continue processing TEST1.BAT. Because CALL was used to invoke TEST3.BAT, however, VAR3 is not lost when DOS returns to TEST1.BAT.

Using AUTOEXEC.BAT

AUTOEXEC.BAT is a batch file that DOS executes when the computer is booted, if the file is located in the root directory of your boot disk. You can include in AUTOEXEC.BAT a list of commands you want DOS to carry out at the beginning of each session.

Reminder:
AUTOEXEC.BAT
executes when
the computer is
booted.

The AUTOEXEC.BAT file also can be run at any time, as if you wanted to reset your PATH. This procedure is not recommended, however, if your batch file runs any memory resident programs, because running the AUTOEXEC.BAT file again loads two copies of the memory resident program. The two copies of the program probably would cause erratic operation of your system. You can create a separate batch file that contains commands to reset your system path to the defaults. A quick way to create this batch file is with the following command:

PATH > C:\PATHSET.BAT

If you place this command directly after the PATH command in your AUTOEXEC.BAT file, you then can run the PATHSET.BAT file at any time to reset your PATH to the values set in the AUTOEXEC.BAT file.

Remember the following when you use AUTOEXEC.BAT:

1. The contents of AUTOEXEC.BAT must conform to the rules for creating batch files.

2. The date and time are not requested when AUTOEXEC.BAT is executed after DOS is booted. To get the current date and time, place the DATE and TIME commands into AUTOEXEC.BAT. (Because PCs and XTs normally do not have a battery-backed clock, you must reset the clock each time you start the computer.

Including the DATE and TIME commands in AUTOEXEC.BAT is a good idea for these computers. AT and 386/486 computers have an internal clock loaded when the computer is started.)

Viewing a Sample AUTOEXEC.BAT File

To better understand AUTOEXEC.BAT, look at the following example of a typical AUTOEXEC.BAT file. The line numbers are used only for reference.

Caution: Do not use the following file as your AUTOEXEC.BAT file. The file is given for explanatory purposes only and probably will not work on your computer.

```
(1) @ECHO ON
(2) PROMPT $e[36;44m
(3) PROMPT $e[s$e[2;53H$p$e[1;53H$t$h$h$h$h$h$h $d$e[u$n$g
(4) @ECHO OFF
(5) SET COMSPEC=C:\DOS\COMMAND.COM
(6) C:\KWIK\SUPERPCK /EM
(7) CLS
(8) PATH H:\;C:\BATCH;C:\WINDOWS;C:\BATCH;C:\DOS;C:\UTILITY
(9) C:\UTILS\FASTATKB 00 NUL
(10)C:\MOUSE\PCMOUSE2 /A0
(11) ECHO ATS0=0 > COM1:
(12) CALL C:\BATCH\RAMDISK
(13) CALL C:\BATCH\KEYWORKS
(14) CALL C:\BATCH\SIDEKICK
(15) SUBST E: D:\EDRIVE
(16) SUBST F: D:\FDRIVE
(17) SUBST G: D:\GDRIVE
(18) MENU
```

Understanding the Sample AUTOEXEC.BAT File

This section provides a line-by-line description of the AUTOEXEC.BAT file listed in the preceding section.

Because ECHO ON must be set for the PROMPT commands in the lines that follow, line 1 turns on echoing of screen commands. DOS normally begins batch files with ECHO ON. Setting ECHO ON here ensures that ECHO is on, even in the unlikely event that AUTOEXEC.BAT is called by another batch file.

The PROMPT $e[36;44m statement in line 2 sets the screen characters to cyan on a blue background for the color monitor used with this particular computer system.

The PROMPT $e[s$e[2;53Hpe[1;53Hthhhhh$h de[ung statement in line 3 customizes the system prompt with the time, date, and current directory name (refer to Chapter 13 for an example of how this command works).

ECHO ON had to be set for the PROMPT lines but is no longer required, so ECHO is turned off in line 4.

If you use more than one operating system on your computer, such as OS/2 and DOS 5.0, you can boot only one from the hard disk. The others boot from a floppy disk. The SET COMSPEC=C:\DOS\COMMAND.COM statement in line 5 boots DOS 5.0 from drive C. This statement should be different for each AUTOEXEC.BAT file from which you boot. The purpose of this statement is to tell DOS or OS/2 where to look for its command interpreter.

The C:\KWIK\SUPERPCK /EM statement in line 6 loads a disk-caching program (disk-caching programs are explained in Chapter 15).

Because the screen may be cluttered at this point, the CLS command in line 7 clears the screen.

The PATH H:\;C:\BATCH;C:\WINDOWS;C:\BATCH;C:\DOS;C:\UTILITY statement in line 8 sets up the PATH for this version of DOS. All DOS programs in this system, such as FORMAT, are kept in separate subdirectories named \DOS. This PATH command ensures that each version of DOS accesses only its own files. This line varies depending on the AUTOEXEC.BAT file you are booting from (see line 5).

Line 9, C:\UTILS\FASTATKB 00 NUL, loads an optional, public-domain keyboard speedup utility.

The C:\MOUSE\PCMOUSE2 /A0 statement in line 10 loads the software for a particular mouse. Some systems put the mouse driver file in the CONFIG.SYS file instead. Check the documentation that came with your mouse to determine the correct command.

The modem connected to this system and initialized with this AUTOEXEC.BAT file is connected to COM1. The modem is used for dialing calls with the SideKick program. Line 11, `ECHO ATS0=0 > COM1:`, tells the modem not to answer the phone.

This computer system has a RAM disk installed as drive H. The `CALL C:\BATCH\RAMDISK` statement in line 12 invokes a batch file called RAMDISK to copy frequently used files to drive H. (RAM disks are described in Chapter 15.)

Line 13, `CALL C:\BATCH\KEYWORKS`, calls a batch file that loads Keyworks, a keyboard-macro program. The batch file uses a utility to mark the memory the program uses so that Keyworks can be uninstalled when using memory-hungry software like Ventura Publisher.

SideKick Plus is another terminate-and-stay-resident (TSR) program used on this computer system. SideKick Plus is loaded and unloaded in the same way as Keyworks. Line 14, `CALL C:\BATCH\SIDEKICK`, loads the program.

Line 15, `SUBST E: D:\EDRIVE`; line 16, `SUBST F: D:\FDRIVE`; and line 17, `SUBST G: D:\GDRIVE`, have the same function. They enable a computer with one 80M hard disk (divided into drives C and D) to mimic a computer with a 44M and an 80M hard disk (divided into drives E, F, and G). The `SUBST E: D:\EDRIVE` command fools DOS into thinking that the D:\EDRIVE directory is actually drive E. By placing software from drive E, F, or G on drive C or D, you can use the same batch files and other techniques on both computers. DOS thinks you have the same directory structure on both machines.

The last line in this batch file, `MENU`, calls an all-purpose menu batch file. Menus are described in the following section.

Building Menus

Cue:
Use DOS menus to make starting programs from your computer easy.

Self-written menus like the one in this section are a convenient way to load individual programs without resorting to a complex shell. Following is a sample menu batch file, called MENU.BAT, that you can customize and enhance for your own use. When you understand how a basic menu works, you can jazz up the menu with ANSI.SYS commands, as described in the last section of this chapter.

```
@ECHO OFF
CLS
ECHO Enter the following to run these programs:
ECHO 1.) Word Processing
```

```
ECHO 2.) Spreadsheet
ECHO  3.)  DataBase  Program
ECHO 4.) BASIC
ECHO 5.) Communications
ECHO -- ENTER CHOICE AND PRESS ENTER --
```

Substitute your favorite programs for those in the sample batch file. Then create batch files that call up those programs and name these batch files 1.BAT, 2.BAT, 3.BAT, and so on, to correspond with the menu entries. If you use DOS 3.0 or later versions, your batch files can call programs by using path names. For example, the following 1.BAT file calls the WordPerfect program located in the C:\WP51 directory:

Reminder:
If you use DOS 3.0 or later, your menu batch files can specify drives and directories.

```
@ECHO OFF
CALL C:\WP51\WP %1 %2 %3
MENU
```

When you press 1 at the menu displayed by MENU.BAT, 1.BAT is invoked to access the WordPerfect program. The replaceable parameters are passed to the WP program.

You can create dummy batch files with the names of other numbers that are called if the user of the menu types an incorrect number. These batch files can display error messages. For example, you can create the file 6.BAT to work with the sample MENU.BAT file:

```
ECHO OFF
ECHO No such menu choice! Try again!
PAUSE
CLS
MENU
```

If you select 6 from the menu, the message No such menu choice! Try again! appears and the PAUSE message Press any key to continue. . . appears. The file waits for you to press a key, clears the screen, and calls MENU.BAT to display the menu again.

Dressing Up the Menu with ANSI.SYS

Now that you understand the basic concept behind MENU.BAT, you can spice the menu up with a few of the ANSI.SYS techniques presented in Chapter 13. Examine the new menu batch file. This file may be slightly hard to decipher because of the embedded escape sequences. This listing shows the ^V[[escape codes you would see if you entered the batch file with EDLIN. If you use another editor that enables you to enter escape codes, replace ^V[[with the appropriate escape sequence and a left bracket ([).

```
@ECHO OFF
CLS
ECHO ^V[[31m^V[[1mEnter the following to run these programs:
ECHO ^V[[1m^V[[32m1.) ^V[[0m^V[[32mWord Processing
ECHO ^V[[1m^V[[33m2.) ^V[[0m^V[[33mSpreadsheet
ECHO ^V[[1m^V[[34m3.) ^V[[0m^V[[34mDataBase Program
ECHO ^V[[1m^V[[35m4.) ^V[[0m^V[[35mBASIC
ECHO ^V[[1m^V[[36m5.) ^V[[0m^V[[36mCommunications
ECHO ^V[[7m^V[[5m-- TYPE CHOICE AND PRESS ENTER --^
V[[0m
```

To use this batch file, load ANSI.SYS through your CONFIG.SYS file. For best results, use a color monitor. You still can see the effects of this menu if you have a monochrome monitor, but only the reverse video and high-intensity characters are shown differently on-screen.

The fourth line in this file uses the ESC[31m code to change the screen foreground display color to red. The ESC[1m code changes the text to high intensity. As a result, the message Enter the following to run these programs: is displayed in high-intensity red characters on a color monitor or in high-intensity characters on a monochrome monitor.

The next five lines display the options available on the menu, each in a different color. The number choice next to the option is displayed in high intensity, and the choice is shown in regular intensity. Each line begins with an *ESC[1m* code (high intensity) followed by an *ESC[3<x>m* code. The <x> in ESC[3<x>m is replaced by a number from 2 to 6, representing the color green, yellow, blue, magenta, or cyan. Recall that 32 through 36 are the numbers that represent these colors when using the foreground-color ANSI.SYS command.

The colors are switched from high intensity to regular intensity with the ESC[0ESC[3x command that follows on each line.

Finally, the message -- TYPE CHOICE AND PRESS ENTER -- is displayed in reverse, blinking video with the ESC[7m and ESC[5m commands. Reverse, blinking characters draw attention to the message.

Enhancing the Batch files

The batch file in the preceding section uses a series of ECHO statements to show messages on-screen. When you run the menu batch file, each line from the batch file must be read by DOS. This process can slow down the execution of the batch file.

To speed things up, you can place the menu screen in a text file and use a TYPE command to display the menu screen. Each command in the menu then calls its own batch file.

Copy the MENU.BAT file to a file called MENU.TXT. Then Edit MENU.TXT and remove the CLS line and the ECHO words. Save the MENU.TXT file and create a MENU.BAT batch file that contains the following lines:

```
@ECHO OFF
CLS
TYPE C:\BATCH\MENU.TXT
```

The TYPE command displays the menu faster than using ECHO statements in the batch file. You can use the control characters and ANSI.SYS statements in your MENU.TXT file as shown in the preceding section.

Chapter Summary

In this chapter, you learned the following about batch files:

- Several advanced subcommands can be used in batch files: IF tests for a condition or for the opposite condition; SHIFT shifts command parameters to the left; FOR..IN..DO can repeat a batch-file command for one or more files or commands.

- The @ character suppresses the display of a line from a batch file.

- COMMAND /C and CALL can be used to invoke a second batch file and return control of the computer to the first batch file.

- You can use ANSI.SYS directives to dress up a menu with color and different intensities.

Chapter 15 provides information about the CONFIG.SYS directives you can use to configure and customize your computer.

Part IV

Advancing Your DOS Capabilities

Includes

Configuring Your Computer

Understanding the International Features of DOS

Understanding QBasic

Programming with QBasic

15

Configuring Your Computer

A great deal of flexibility is built into DOS. The default configuration of DOS may be fine for millions of users, but you also can make some changes to better suit your needs or to fine-tune your computer system.

DOS's flexibility translates into more choices for you to make. To make intelligent choices, you must understand exactly how DOS is configured. You don't need to learn arcane techniques or undergo painful *sysgen* (system generation) procedures. Customizing DOS is as easy as collecting a few commands in a plain ASCII file and rebooting. All the information you need to configure your computer is in this chapter.

This chapter covers the following CONFIG.SYS directives:

- BREAK
- BUFFERS
- DEVICE
- DEVICEHIGH (Version 5)
- DOS (Version 5)
- DRIVEPARM
- FCBS
- FILES
- INSTALL
- LASTDRIVE

- REM
- SHELL
- STACKS
- SWITCHES (Version 4 only)

The COUNTRY directive for CONFIG.SYS is discussed in Chapter 16.

Understanding CONFIG.SYS

Perhaps you don't have a CONFIG.SYS file or have never examined the CONFIG.SYS file placed on your hard disk by the person who installed your computer. Perhaps you only know that CONFIG.SYS has the BUFFERS = 15 and FILES = 10 lines someone said you needed. The CONFIG.SYS file can contain commands that enable you to have a more efficient computer system. Because you should be using these enhancements, this section provides an explanation of the commands available for use in the CONFIG.SYS file.

Reminder:
CONFIG.SYS is an ASCII text file in the root directory of the boot disk.

After DOS starts, but before the AUTOEXEC.BAT file is invoked, DOS looks in the root directory of the boot disk for the CONFIG.SYS file. If DOS finds CONFIG.SYS, the operating system attempts to carry out the commands in that file before proceeding with the AUTOEXEC.BAT file. You cannot abort the CONFIG.SYS file by pressing Ctrl-C or Ctrl-Break as you can the AUTOEXEC.BAT file.

Like AUTOEXEC.BAT, CONFIG.SYS is a plain ASCII text file that lists special commands, called directives. Only 13 sets of directives are available as legal commands in CONFIG.SYS. You can, however, accomplish a great deal with these 13 commands.

Reminder:
Create CONFIG.SYS using COPY CON, EDLIN, EDIT (DOS 5), or a word processor.

If you don't have a CONFIG.SYS file, you can create one with the COPY CON \CONFIG.SYS command. You also can create the file or edit the existing file, using the DOS Editor or a word processor that can output plain ASCII text. (EDIT is explained in Chapter 10.) Use the EDLIN command for DOS Version 4 and earlier versions.

The CONFIG.SYS file contains the directives that alter some of DOS's functions and features. Table 15.1 lists the directives you can use in your CONFIG.SYS file and describes the functions these directives control. Some of the directives are available only in DOS Versions 4 and 5.

Table 15.1
CONFIG.SYS Directives

Directive	Action
BREAK	Determines when DOS recognizes the Ctrl-Break sequence
BUFFERS	Sets the number of buffers DOS uses
COUNTRY	Sets country-dependent information
DEVICE	Allows different devices to be used with DOS
DEVICEHIGH	Allows different devices to be used with DOS and loads the device drivers in high memory (Version 5)
DOS	Allows DOS to be loaded in high memory (Version 5)
DRIVEPARM	Adds support for additional disk and tape drives
FCBS	Controls file-handling for DOS 1
FILES	Sets the maximum number of open files that can be used by DOS
INSTALL	Installs memory-resident programs (Version 4 and above)
LASTDRIVE	Specifies the highest disk drive on the computer
REM	Flags a line as a remarks line (Version 4 and above)
SHELL	Informs DOS what command processor should be used and where that processor is located
STACKS	Sets the number of stacks that DOS uses
SWITCHES	Disables extended keyboard functions (Version 4 and above)

This chapter discusses the CONFIG.SYS directives in the order they are listed in table 15.1. The directives you probably use most are FILES, BUFFERS, and DEVICE; you probably want to pay special attention to the discussions of these directives. With Version 5, the DOS and DEVICEHIGH directives enable you to use your system's memory even more efficiently.

Telling DOS When To Check for a Ctrl-Break

Early in your computing career, you probably learned that Ctrl-Break and Ctrl-C are helpful—but not foolproof—panic buttons. Who hasn't pounded frantically on the keyboard, using one of these sequences in an attempt to unfreeze a locked-up or bombed applications program?

Only a second may have passed from the time you pressed the panic button until DOS responded, but you still had time to wonder why DOS took so long to respond. The answer is that DOS is busy doing other things most of the time and only looks for Ctrl-Break at intervals. The BREAK directive (identical to the DOS BREAK command) tells DOS when to check for this key sequence. BREAK does not enable or disable this feature.

If you set BREAK ON in CONFIG.SYS, DOS checks to see whether you have pressed Ctrl-Break when a program requests some activity from DOS (performs a DOS function call). If you set BREAK OFF (the default), DOS checks for a Ctrl-Break only when DOS is working with the video display, keyboard, printer, or asynchronous serial adapters (the ports in the back of the computer).

If you use programs that do a great deal of disk accessing but little keyboard or screen work, you may want to set BREAK ON. This setting enables you to break out of the program if something goes wrong.

If BREAK is set on, DOS spends more time looking for the Ctrl-Break keystroke, which can slow down operations somewhat. Also, some programs can disable or change how the Ctrl-Break keystroke is used. For those programs, the BREAK setting is ignored. Other programs may work erratically with BREAK ON; check the program's documentation for this potential problem.

The syntax structures for the BREAK directive are as follows:

```
BREAK ON
BREAK OFF
```

The default setting for the BREAK directive is BREAK OFF.

Using BUFFERS To Increase Disk Performance

The BUFFERS directive tells DOS how many disk buffers to use. Before the introduction of disk-caching programs (which also keep disk information in memory), BUFFERS had the potential for the greatest impact on disk performance. This directive was changed significantly in DOS Version 4.

RAM access speed is rated in nanoseconds (billionths of a second); hard disks access data in as little as 18 to 28 milliseconds (thousandths of a second).

Reminder:
RAM access is much faster than hard disk access.

A *buffer* is a reserved area of RAM set up by DOS to store information read from disk. If you have configured your system with enough buffers, DOS frequently finds the information it needs in buffered memory.

A buffer is about 512 bytes long (plus 16 bytes for overhead). The BUFFERS directive controls how many disk buffers your computer uses. The syntax for this directive is as follows:

BUFFERS = number

In this syntax, *number* is the number of disk buffers you want. Table 15.2 lists the different buffer configurations.

Reminder:
A buffer is 528 bytes long; you can specify up to 99 buffers with DOS versions before 4.

Table 15.2
Default Number of Disk BUFFERS

DOS Version	Number of BUFFERS	Hardware
pre-Version 3	2	Floppy disk drives
	3	Hard disk
Versions 3.3 and above	2	360K floppy disk drive
	3	Any other hard or floppy disk drive
	5	More than 128K of RAM
	10	More than 256K of RAM
	15	More than 512K of RAM

You can use fewer BUFFERS than the default numbers shown in table 15.2.

Understanding How DOS Uses Disk Buffers

Reminder:
DOS reads and writes to the disk in full sectors and uses buffers as a holding area.

When DOS is asked to get information from a disk, DOS reads information in increments of whole sectors. The size of the sector varies among disk types and sizes. Excess data not required from that sector is left in the buffer. If this data is needed later, DOS doesn't have to perform another disk access to retrieve the data. Similarly, DOS tries to reduce disk activity when the operating system writes information to the disk. If less than a full sector is to be written to the disk, DOS accumulates the information in a disk buffer. When the buffer is full, DOS writes the information to the disk. This action is called *flushing the buffer*. To make sure that all pertinent information is placed into a file, DOS also flushes the buffers when a program closes a disk file.

When a disk buffer becomes full or empty, DOS marks the buffer to indicate that the buffer has been used recently. When DOS needs to reuse the buffers for new information, the operating system takes the buffer that hasn't been used for the longest time.

Cue:
Set a higher number of buffers if you do a great deal of random disk work.

If your program does much random disk work (reading and writing information in different parts of a file), you may want to specify a higher number of buffers. The more buffers you have, the better the chance that the information DOS wants is already in memory (the disk buffer).

Fine-Tuning with Buffers

The number of disk buffers you should have depends on the programs you run on your computer and how much memory you have. If your day-to-day use of the computer does not involve accounting or database work (which use files with small groups of data), the right number of buffers is from 10 to 20. If you do accounting or database work, you should have between 20 and 40 buffers (more, if you use expanded memory with Versions 4 and 5). If you use many subdirectories or have subdirectories with a large number of files, using more disk buffers can increase your computer's performance.

Caution:
If you use too many buffers, you may not be able to use some programs and utilities.

Because each disk buffer takes 528 bytes of memory, every two disk buffers you use costs just over 1K of RAM. If you use many memory-hungry programs and terminate-and-stay-resident (TSR) utilities, you may need to use a minimal number of buffers to preserve precious RAM.

DOS Version 5 slows slightly if you specify more than about 50 disk buffers because DOS spends more time searching the buffers for information than reading or writing the disk.

If you use a floppy disk system, start with 10 disk buffers; start with 20 buffers for hard disk systems. Fine-tune the number by increasing or decreasing the number by 1 to 5 buffers every few hours or once a day. Reboot DOS and examine its performance. Keep doing this until you think you have the best performance.

Cue:
Change the number of buffers until you think you have the best performance.

Understanding DOS BUFFERS Options

DOS Version 4 added important options to the BUFFERS directive. The numbers of buffers you can set with Version 4 was increased to 10,000— if you have expanded memory. In addition, you now can use a *look-ahead* buffer to increase disk efficiency.

Reminder:
If you have expanded memory, Version 4 enables you to use up to 10,000 buffers and 8 look-ahead buffers.

DOS Version 4 introduced support for expanded memory, and BUFFERS is one of the features that can use that memory. If you add the /X switch to the BUFFERS directive in your CONFIG.SYS file, DOS uses expanded memory to store buffered information.

DOS uses Look-ahead buffers to store sectors ahead of the sector requested by a DOS read operation. A look-ahead buffer requires 512 bytes of memory. You can specify from 0 to 8 look-ahead buffers. If your application or DOS needs one of the sectors already read, DOS finds the sectors in the look-ahead buffer and does not have to make another disk access. Look-ahead buffers can be powerful performance enhancers.

The BUFFERS command is different in DOS 5.0. Because DOS now can be loaded into the high memory area, the buffers are loaded into high memory with DOS. The /X switch, therefore, is no longer available in DOS 5.0.

The default number of look-ahead buffers is 1. The default number of buffers depends on the amount of conventional memory you have (see table 15.3).

Table 15.3
Number of Default Buffers with Conventional Memory

Memory	Buffers	Bytes used
< 255K	5	2672
256K to 511K	10	5328
512K to 640K	15	7984

Although you can specify any number of buffers, too many buffers can slow you down. The maximum value depends on the size of your hard disk (see table 15.4).

Table 15.4
Maximum Number of Buffers with Hard Disk

Hard disk size	Max buffers
< 40M	20
40 to 79M	30
80 to 119	40
120M or more	50

Installing Device Drivers with DEVICE

Reminder:
Device drivers are interfaces between the operating system and the device.

You learned about device drivers in the discussion of ANSI.SYS in Chapter 13. DOS is supplied with a wealth of other device drivers that you can use to make better use of your current—and future—computer hardware equipment. To make DOS aware of the device drivers you want to use, include the DEVICE directive in the CONFIG.SYS file. The syntax for the DEVICE directive is as follows:

DEVICE=_d:path_**filename.**_ext /switches_

Note: You do not have to include spaces on either side of the equal sign in this syntax.

In this syntax, _d:_ is the disk drive where the device-driver file resides, _path_ is the directory path to the device-driver file, and _filename.ext_ is the name of the device-driver file. The _/switches_ are any switches needed by the device-driver software.

You can load as many device drivers as you need, but you have to use a separate DEVICE line for each driver you install. As each device driver is loaded, DOS extends its control to that device. Remember that the device driver must be accessible when DOS starts. For convenience, floppy disk users should place device-driver files in the root directory. Hard disk users can make a special subdirectory called \DRIVERS or \SYS and place the driver files in this directory, out of the way of daily files. If you place the driver files in a separate subdirectory, add the directory path name to the device-driver file name, as in the following examples:

DEVICE = C:\DRIVERS\ANSI.SYS
DEVICE = C:\SYS\ANSI.SYS

The preceding sections in this chapter began showing you how to use memory efficiently with the BUFFERS directive. The following sections show you how to gain extra horsepower from your system with some device drivers. Some of these drivers are supplied with DOS; others are supplied with the mouse, printer, or other software.

Understanding Disk Caches

Strictly speaking, the device-driver file is not part of DOS. Some versions of DOS come with the SMARTDRV.SYS file; other versions of DOS don't have this file; if your version of DOS doesn't come with the file, you have to purchase Windows to get SMARTDRV.SYS. DOS 5.0 does include SMARTDRV.SYS. No discussion of device drivers is complete without an understanding of disk-cache systems. The concepts discussed in this section apply to both of these programs and other caching programs. Make sure that the version of SMARTDRV and the version of DOS are compatible or performance may suffer.

You can think of SMARTDRV.SYS as a large, smart buffer. Like a buffer, a disk cache operates from a section of RAM you request from DOS. A disk cache and a disk buffer accumulate information going to the disk or coming from the disk. When information is read from the disk, the information is placed in a buffer or cache; the information requested by the program is sent to the program. Like a buffer, a disk cache can read more information than requested by the program. When information is written to the disk, the information may be stored in the buffer or cache until the buffer or cache is full and then written to the disk. (Most caches have a *write-through* feature: the cache writes information to disk frequently to avoid data loss if the system is turned off or loses power. Smart caches eliminate redundant writes by placing information on disk only when the data is different from what is already there.) If you use a cache or buffers, your program performance improves because slow disk accesses are replaced by higher speed memory-to-memory transfers.

Reminder:
A disk cache is an intelligent buffer.

Although a DOS disk buffer is a form of a disk cache, a good caching program outperforms a buffer. Disk caches are better performers because they have more intelligence than buffers. You may find that the performance of a disk cache is hampered if you make the cache too large or too small. Test different applications that you use and vary the size of the cache to find the optimum performance.

A disk cache remembers what sections of the disk have been used most frequently. When the cache must be recycled, the program keeps the more frequently used areas and discards those less frequently used. Buffers, as you recall, are recycled based on how old the buffer is, regardless of how frequently the buffer is used.

In an absolutely random disk access, in which program and data files are scattered uniformly across the disk, the cache method of recycling the least-frequently used area is more efficient than the buffer method of recycling the oldest area. A cache tends to keep in memory the most heavily used areas of the disk.

Like Versions 4 and 5 BUFFERS directives, many disk caches have look-ahead capabilities, a technique in which the cache reads more sectors than the program requests.

In many cases, using a disk cache to help with disk activity is preferable to using a RAM disk program like RAMDRIVE.SYS (discussed later in this chapter). A RAM disk helps only with files copied to the RAM disk (loading a program with overlays into a RAM disk may be better than using a cache to speed up a slow disk). The cache's activity is effortless and transparent to the user; a RAM disk requires separate directives to access the needed files.

A disk cache also is preferable to a RAM disk because the danger of losing information with a cache can be less. You have a greater probability of losing information when files are written to a RAM disk than when files are written to the cache. The cache, like a DOS buffer, holds the information for only a few seconds before writing it to the disk. During this brief period, the information is at risk. If power is lost to the RAM disk, however, all files on the RAM disk are destroyed. You have to issue commands to copy the information in the RAM disk to the safety of a hard disk; the RAM disk does not perform this action automatically.

In two situations, however, a RAM disk is preferred to a disk cache. When you need to copy files between disks on a computer with one floppy disk drive, copying to and from the RAM disk is convenient. You first copy the files to the RAM disk, change disks, and then copy the files from the RAM disk to the second disk. A disk cache cannot help you copy files between disks. (The XCOPY command in Versions 4 and greater makes copying a group of files much easier.)

You also may prefer to use a RAM disk if you frequently use nonchanging files that can be placed completely on the RAM disk. A good example is Turbo Lightning; you can place its dictionary and thesaurus files on a RAM disk. Because you access these files frequently—but rarely the same spots in the files—having the files on a RAM disk provides better performance than having the files in a disk cache.

You also should be careful about installing multiple disk codes. For example, dBASE IV and Windows 3.0 use their own disk-caching programs. Running two disk-caching programs can cause data loss.

Installing SMARTDRV.SYS

With MS-DOS comes a disk-cache program called SMARTDRV.SYS. (SMARTDRV.SYS also comes with Microsoft Windows.) You can use SMARTDRV.SYS instead of IBMCACHE.SYS. This section explains how to install and use SMARTDRV.SYS.

No installation program is necessary for SMARTDRV.SYS, although the Windows 3.0 installation process installs SMARTDRV.SYS. To install this program, place a correctly worded directive in CONFIG.SYS. The syntax for installing SMARTDRV.SYS in Version 4 is as follows:

> **DEVICE** = *d:path***SMARTDRV.SYS** *size /A*

In this syntax, *d:path* is the optional disk drive and path name for the SMARTDRV.SYS program, and *size* is an optional parameter that specifies how much memory you want SMARTDRV to use. The default size is 256K. If you don't have expanded or extended memory, you may want to specify a smaller size than 256K to limit the cache size. Unless you limit the size of the cache, you may not have enough memory to run large programs.

The */A* parameter tells SMARTDRV to use expanded memory, if it is available, or to use extended memory as expanded memory. If this switch is not used, SMARTDRV uses extended memory.

For DOS Version 5, the syntax was changed slightly:

> **DEVICE** = *d:path***SMARTDRV.SYS** *initial size min. size /A*

As before, you should specify the complete drive/path of the SMARTDRV.SYS file. The *initial size* is the amount of memory to set aside for the cache, with a default of 256 and a range of 128 to 8192. The *min. size* is the minimum cache size; some programs can reduce the size of the cache. In both cases, the values are rounded to the nearest multiple of 16. The amount of memory to specify should be between 256K and 2048K. Smaller values

Cue:
If you do not have expanded or extended memory, you cannot use the SMARTDRV.SYS program.

don't cache enough information; larger values cache too much information. Your value depends on the amount of extended and expanded memory you have available.

The /A parameter tells SMARTDRV to use expanded memory; otherwise it uses extended memory. If you specify the /A parameter, the expanded memory device driver (DOS's EMM386.SYS, Quarterdeck's QEMM386.SYS, AST's REMM.SYS, and so on) must be loaded before the SMARTDRV.SYS file. If you don't specify the /A parameter, the extended memory driver (DOS's HIMEM.SYS) must be loaded before SMARTDRV.SYS. If you have a 286 or 386 computer, you probably get better performance if you use extended memory for the SMARTDRV.SYS file. Using extended memory also enables you to use the expanded memory more efficiently.

After you insert the SMARTDRV.SYS directive in CONFIG.SYS and boot the computer, you see something like the following message:

```
Microsoft SMARTDrive RAM Cache version x.xx
Cache Size: 256K in 80286 Extended Memory
```

The version number and size of the cache vary depending on how SMARTDRV was set up.

Using RAMDRIVE To Make a RAM Disk

Another device driver you can install is RAMDRIVE.SYS (also called VDISK.SYS in some implementations of DOS). This program enables you to install an imaginary disk in memory. Like buffers and disk caches, a RAM disk is much faster than ordinary disk access.

RAM disks are given a drive allocation such as D: or E:. You can use RAM disks just like an ordinary drive, but you lose the contents of the drive when you turn off the computer.

To install RAMDRIVE and create an imaginary (or virtual) disk, just insert a line in CONFIG.SYS. The syntax is slightly different for DOS Versions 4 and 5. For Version 4, invoke RAMDRIVE from CONFIG.SYS with the following syntax:

> **DEVICE =** d:path**RAMDRIVE.SYS** disk size sector size
> # of entries /E:max or /X

For Version 5, the command syntax is as follows:

> **DEVICE =** d:path**RAMDRIVE.SYS** disk size sector size
> # of entries /E /A

In this syntax, *d:* is the disk drive, and *path* is the directory path for RAMDRIVE.SYS.

Note that although the */E* and */A* parameters are not required (and should not be used simultaneously), you should specify one of the parameters. If you don't, the RAMDRIVE is created in conventional memory, which reduces the amount of memory available for your programs. The */E* parameter requires an extended memory driver. The */A* parameter requires an expanded memory driver. Both parameters require that expanded or extended memory is installed in your computer.

The options for RAMDRIVE are listed in table 15.5 and are described in the following section.

Table 15.5
RAMDRIVE Command Options

Option	Description
disk size	The size (in K) of the RAM disk: the default is 64; the range is from 16 to 4096.
sector size	The size (in bytes) of the RAM-disk sectors: default is 512; valid values are 128, 256, and 512. Specifying *sector size* requires the use of *disk size*.
# of entries	The number of directory entries (files) for the RAM disk: default is 64; range is from 2 to 1024.
/E	The switch for extended memory
/A	The switch for expanded memory

Some programs create temporary files. These files normally are stored in the current directory but can be stored in the directory specified by the TEMP environment variable. Relocating temporary files can be done by placing the line **SET TEMP=***RAM disk drive* in your CONFIG.SYS file after the RAMDRIVE.SYS line. The drive letter to specify is the drive letter of your RAM disk. The drive letter depends on the order of the RAMDRIVE.SYS and any other disk device drivers you have specified in the CONFIG.SYS file. DOS assigns drive letters as the device drivers are loaded. Drive A and B are the first two floppy drives. Drive C is the hard disk. If the hard disk has been partitioned with DOS FDISK, the additional logical drives are assigned the next letters. Then any drive device drivers, whether floppy or hard, are assigned the following drive letters in the order that they are loaded.

See table 15.6 for an example of a CONFIG.SYS file that loads two floppy drives, one hard disk partitioned with FDISK as drives C and D, and several device drivers.

Table 15.6
Devices and Assigned Drive Letters

Device\drive	Assigned drive letter
Floppy drives	A, B
Hard disk	C, D
RAMDRIVE.SYS	E
DRIVER.SYS	F
RAMDRIVE.SYS	G

If you have enough extended memory, you can set up several RAM disks. Just specify additional **DEVICE = RAMDRIVE.SYS** statements in CONFIG.SYS. Each statement installs an additional RAM disk.

To use a RAM disk with the features of a 360K, double-sided disk, for example, use the following command line:

DEVICE = RAMDRIVE.SYS 360 512 112

If you want a RAM disk that uses all the extended memory on a computer with 1M of RAM, use the following command line:

DEVICE = RAMDRIVE.SYS 384 512 112 /E

This statement creates a RAM disk of 384K (384K is the difference between 1M of RAM and 640K of conventional memory), with 512-byte sectors, and 112 directory entries. (*Note:* This command works only if you have config- ured the 384K of memory as extended memory—not all PCs provide this capability.) The /E:8 (Version 4) or /E (Version 5) switch tells DOS to install the RAM disk in extended memory and transfer 8 sectors to and from the RAM disk at a time. If you omit the /E switch, DOS installs the RAM disk in the 640K of DOS memory.

Cue:
If you have DOS
Version 4, you
can put RAM
disks in expanded
memory instead
of extended
memory.

The /A switch enables you to use expanded memory (instead of extended memory) for the RAM disk. To use expanded memory, you must load the expanded-memory driver (such as DOS 5's EMM386.EXE) before loading RAMDRIVE.SYS. You cannot use the /A and /E switches for the same RAM disk. You may create different RAM disks, however—some using extended memory and others using expanded memory. Insert multiple DEVICE statements in CONFIG.SYS.

Learning More about RAM Disks

The amount of RAM in your computer, the programs you use, and the convenience of a RAM disk play a part in determining the size of RAM disk you use—or whether you even should use a RAM disk. This section helps you determine whether you should bother using a RAM disk, and if so, what size may help you the most.

A RAM Disk in 640K of Memory

Although all computers can accommodate a RAM disk, your computer may not be able to accommodate a RAM disk while using other programs.

When DOS Version 4.01 is loaded on a computer with 640K of memory, for example, 581K is left for programs to use (640K is actually 655,360 bytes). DOS Version 4.01, using the CONFIG.SYS FILES and BUFFERS directives and the ANSI.SYS device driver, uses about 74K of RAM. IF DOS Version 5 is loaded into high memory, as much as 628K of memory is left for programs to use.

The bottom line is that if you have only conventional memory, you may find that a RAM disk does not optimize your use of memory. If the program you use does not take up a great deal of memory, however, you may be able to use a RAM disk, but you should probably limit its size to no more than 100K.

If you set up a 100K RAM disk, you cannot store a large quantity of information on the disk. You probably can use the RAM disk only for temporary storage of rather small files. To create a 100K RAM disk with 128-byte sectors and 64 directory entries, type the following directive in your CONFIG.SYS file:

> **DEVICE = C:\RAMDRIVE.SYS 100 128 64**

Because the RAM disk uses some of the allocated space for the directory and file-allocation table (FAT), only 98.9K is actually usable.

The small sector size of 128 bytes is assigned in this example to maximize the performance of the RAM disk. If you set up the disk with 128-byte sectors and the disk contains 10 files of 600 bytes each, 92.5K is available for further storage. If you set up the RAM disk with 512-byte sectors and have the same files, only 89K is available.

Because one file does not share a sector with another file, one 600-byte file uses five 128-byte sectors, wasting 40 bytes. The same 600-byte file uses only two 512-byte sectors; however, 497 bytes are wasted.

Reminder:
Although any computer can accept a RAM disk, you may not have enough memory for a RAM disk and an active program.

Cue:
If you have 640K of RAM, you may want to specify a RAM disk of only 100K.

If you plan to store only one or two larger files on the 100K RAM disk, however, you may be better off setting a larger sector size. You realize a time savings when fewer, larger sectors are read or written rather than more, smaller sectors.

The size of the directory also influences the usable size of the RAM disk; the larger the directory, the more room is needed to track files. A 100K RAM disk set up to store 64 files has 98.9K available for storage. The same 100K RAM disk with a directory size of 192 files has only 94.9K for storage. You get a 4-percent larger disk by using the smaller directory size. You rarely store more than 64 files on a 100K RAM disk.

A RAM Disk in Expanded or Extended Memory

If your computer has extended or expanded memory, you may find that a RAM disk is worthwhile. With expanded or extended memory, the actual memory used by the RAM disk is located outside the conventional memory used by programs. You can create a RAM disk without giving up program memory. If you decide to use a RAM disk on a computer with expanded or extended memory, the issues are how large the RAM disk should be and what settings you should use.

If you have expanded memory and use a program like 1-2-3 Release 2.01 or 2.2, you have to decide how much expanded memory to dedicate to a RAM disk, because 1-2-3 can store data in expanded memory. Creating a RAM disk in expanded memory decreases the amount of expanded memory that 1-2-3 can use. If you have 2M of expanded memory, for example, you may find you can set aside as much as 512K for a RAM disk without affecting programs that use expanded memory.

If your computer has extended memory, you must decide how much extended memory to use as a RAM disk, if any. Programs such as 1-2-3 Release 3 use a DOS extender to make extended memory available to the program for data storage. Creating a RAM disk in extended memory decreases the amount of memory available to programs that use DOS extenders.

Reminder:
You may want to use some extended or expanded memory for disk caches instead of a RAM disk.

Whether you have extended or expanded memory, you also must decide what you can use that memory for in addition to programs. You may want to use some of that memory for SMARTDRV.SYS or IBMCACHE.SYS, for example. If the programs you use are disk oriented rather than RAM oriented (dBASE is disk oriented; 1-2-3 is RAM oriented), you can use expanded or extended memory for a large disk cache. The use of a large disk cache may make a RAM disk an obsolete option, because the disk cache speeds access to your data files.

If you create a RAM disk in expanded or extended memory, you may create a disk larger than one created in conventional memory. When you create a larger RAM disk, you can vary the settings for sector size and directory size. The values you give for these settings, however, still depend on the quantity and size of the files to be stored on the RAM disk.

If you create a 512K RAM disk, for example, you may find that a sector size of 512 bytes is adequate, even if you store small files on the RAM disk. You also may find that a directory size of 64 is adequate because you seldom store more than 64 files on a RAM disk. If, however, you plan to use the RAM disk to aid you in copying files from one disk to another, change the directory value to 112. Only 112 files can be stored on a 360K disk.

Cue:
If you use a RAM disk to help copy files between disks, set the directory size to 112.

To create a 512K RAM disk with 512-byte sectors and 112 directory entries in expanded memory, include the following directive in CONFIG.SYS:

DEVICE = C:\RAMDRIVE.SYS 512 512 112 /A

To create the same RAM disk in extended memory, include the following directive in CONFIG.SYS:

DEVICE = C:\RAMDRIVE.SYS 512 512 112 /E

These directives create a RAM disk adequate for temporary storage. Remember the word temporary; when the power goes out, you lose what is on the RAM disk. Frequently back up important files on the RAM disk to your hard or floppy disk.

Controlling Additional Disk Drives with DRIVER.SYS

DRIVER.SYS is a device driver for disk drives. Although DRIVER.SYS is optional on most systems, it is required on some systems that use an external floppy disk drive. DRIVER.SYS also may be required for older systems that don't support the newer 3 1/2-inch disk drives.

> **Note:** Many older systems also require a ROM upgrade to use 1.44M 3 1/2-inch disk drives.

When you have only one floppy disk drive, DOS establishes two logical disk drives, A and B, from the physical disk drive. You can perform the same kind of trick on any disk drive with DRIVER.SYS.

Cue:
Use DRIVER.SYS to create two logical drives from one physical drive.

DRIVER.SYS can be used if you have an external floppy disk drive, a nonsupported floppy disk, or a nonstandard hard drive. You must inform DOS that the additional disk drive is attached to your system. When you invoke DRIVER.SYS for these disk drives, DOS makes them integral parts of the system.

You also can load an additional copy of DRIVER.SYS so that DOS makes two logical disk drives out of any physical disk drive. If drive A is 1.2M and drive B is 360K, for example, you can use DRIVER.SYS to make drive A work as a 360K drive D.

Before you use DRIVER.SYS, read the information and explanations on the directive's switches, particularly the /D switch. If you do not provide DOS with the needed information, DRIVER.SYS does not work properly.

The syntax for invoking DRIVER.SYS is as follows:

DEVICE = *d:path***DRIVER.SYS** */D:ddd* */F:f* */T:ttt* */S:ss* */H:hh* */C* */N* *(Version 4)*

DEVICE = *d:path***DRIVER.SYS** */D:ddd* */F:f* */T:ttt* */S:ss* */H:hh* */C* *(Version 5)*

The DRIVER.SYS Switches

In the syntax given in the preceding section, *d:* is the disk drive, and *path* is the directory path to DRIVER.SYS. Both directives are optional but usually are given. DRIVER.SYS has seven switches which are described in the rest of this section.

The */D:ddd* switch is mandatory and lists the physical disk drive number. The allowable numbers for *ddd* are 0 to 255. You use the numbers 0 to 127 for floppy disk drives. The first physical floppy disk drive, drive A, is 0; the second, drive B, is 1; and the third is 2 (the drive name of the third floppy disk drive varies based on the number of hard drives installed). The values 3 to 127 for floppy disks are possible in theory, but most computers do not support these additional drives. You use the numbers 128 to 255 for hard disk drives. The first hard disk, drive C, is 128, and the second is 129. As with floppy disks, the rest of the numbers (130 to 255) are theoretically available for additional hard disk drives, but in reality, they cannot be used.

If you have an external floppy disk drive for a PS/2 computer with one internal floppy disk drive, the external drive is the second physical disk drive. Use a 1 for the external disk drive.

If you give a number that corresponds to a nonexistent disk drive, DRIVER.SYS is installed with no indication that anything is wrong. When you attempt to use the disk drive with its logical drive name, however, DOS displays a general failure error. To correct the problem, you must edit the incorrect DRIVER.SYS entry and reboot the computer.

The */F:f* switch identifies the type of disk drive used. */F:f* is the form-factor switch. The *f* portion of the switch is a single digit taken from table 15.7. Table 15.7 also shows the default number of sectors used with each form-factor switch.

Table 15.7
Values for the Form Factors and Sectors Switches

f value	s value	Type of disk drive
0	9	160K to 360K floppy disk drive—5 1/4"
1	15	1.2M floppy disk drive—5 1/4"
2	9	720K floppy disk drive—3 1/2"
3	n/a	8-inch single-density disk drive (Version 3.3 and below)
4	n/a	8-inch double-density disk drive (Version 3.3 and below)
5	n/a	Hard drive (Version 3.3 and below)
6	n/a	Tape drive (Version 3.3 and below)
7	18	1.44M floppy disk drive—3 1/2"
9	36	2.88M floppy disk drive—3 1/2"

If you do not use the /F:f switch, DOS assumes a form factor of 2. If you use the /F:f switch and the number of heads, sectors, and tracks are normal for that type of drive, you don't need to specify the /h, /s, and /t parameters.

The */T:ttt* switch indicates the number of tracks per side (or cylinder) for the disk drive. The *ttt* portion of the switch can range from 1 to 999. If you do not specify the switch, a value of 80 tracks is assumed (1.2M, 720K, 1.44M, and 2.88M floppy disk drives use 80 tracks; other floppy disk drives use 40 tracks) unless you use the /f:0 switch, in which case DOS assumes 40 tracks. Refer to the documentation that came with your disk drive for the number of tracks used by the drive.

The */S:ss* switch indicates the number of sectors per track. The *ss* portion of the switch can range from 1 to 99. If you do not specify the switch, a value of 9 sectors per track is assumed (360K and 720K floppy disk drives use 9 sectors per track) unless you have specified a form-factor using the /f switch (see table 15.7). Refer to the documentation that came with your disk drive for the number of sectors used by the drive.

The /H:*hh* switch indicates the maximum number of recording heads per disk drive. The range of *hh* is from 1 to 99. If you do not specify the switch, two heads per disk drive are assumed. (Older, single-sided, floppy disk drives use a value of 1; most other floppy disk drives use 2; hard disks use values higher than 2.)

The /C switch indicates that the disk drive supports a changeline. A changeline tells the disk drive when the floppy disk has been ejected or when the floppy disk drive door has been opened. This switch is used with 1.2M, 720K, and 1.44M disk drives on PS/2, AT, and compatibles.

The Version 4 /N switch indicates that the disk drive is nonremovable—that the drive is a hard drive. This switch should not be used with floppy disk drives or with external hard drives.

Sample DRIVER.SYS Directives

This section presents some examples of using DRIVER.SYS. Most newer 286 and 386 systems with standard internal disk drives installed support the various drive types without using DRIVER.SYS. You normally set the drive A and B types in the setup of your system. You need the DRIVER.SYS device driver on many XTs or if you are adding a third or fourth internal or external disk drive.

If you have a PS/2 computer with two internal disk drives, use the following syntax for an external 60K floppy disk drive:

DEVICE = DRIVER.SYS /D:2 /F:0

/D:2 designates the third disk drive. The /F:0 switch denotes the 360K form factor. By default, DOS assumes 2 heads, 40 tracks per side, and 9 sectors per track.

To use the external physical disk drive as two logical disk drives, load the device driver twice. The syntax for this setup is as follows:

DEVICE = DRIVER.SYS /D:2 /F:0

DEVICE = DRIVER.SYS /D:2 /F:0

Each time you load the driver, DOS assigns the physical disk drive an additional valid drive letter—D the first time and E the second time, for example. You then may refer to the drive by either of the two new designations.

To use an external 1.2M disk drive on a PS/2 computer, load the driver with the following syntax line:

DEVICE = DRIVER.SYS /D:2 /F:1 /C

Because the form factor for this disk drive is different from the default, you must provide the /F switch (the default value is 2). Notice the use of the /C switch, the changeline-support switch. Because PS/2s, ATs, and 286-XTs can recognize and use the changeline of floppy disk drives, DOS specifies the /C switch.

Changeline support is the reason this directive is used for an external 720K floppy on an AT or 286-XT; the syntax is as follows:

DEVICE = DRIVER.SYS /D:2 /C

Use the following DRIVER.SYS syntax for an external 720K floppy disk drive on a PC or XT:

DEVICE = DRIVER.SYS /D:2

The PC and XT do not recognize disk drive changelines, so the syntax does not use a /C switch. None of the other switches are given because DRIVER.SYS's default settings fit the 720K disk drive.

If the 720K disk drive used in the preceding examples is the second drive, you use 1 for the value of the /D switch. For example, to use an external 720K floppy disk drive in an AT, type the following:

DEVICE = DRIVER.SYS /D:1 /C

Regardless of drive type, /D:1 designates the second floppy disk drive.

You also can load a copy of DRIVER.SYS for use with established disk drives. The copy of DRIVER.SYS, with the appropriate switches, establishes a second logical disk drive for the physical disk.

You do not need this technique if you have a one floppy disk drive computer. DOS always enables you to refer to a floppy disk as drive A and B. You can, however, use the technique when you have two disk drives. Suppose that you have an AT with 1.2M and 360K internal floppy disk drives. To use drive A as two logical disk drives, issue the following directive in CONFIG.SYS:

DEVICE = DRIVER.SYS /D:0 /F:1 /C

To use drive B, the 360K drive, as two logical disk drives, type the following directive:

DEVICE = DRIVER.SYS /D:1 /T:40 /F:0

You can use both directives to create four logical drives from the two physical disk drives. If you have one hard disk drive, the second 1.2M drive is drive D, and the second 360K drive is drive E. By setting up your system in this way, you can use either disk drive to perform the DISKCOPY command.

Naming Disk Drives

Cue:
*Understand how
DOS names your
disk drives.*

The logical disk drive names that DOS assigns to disks created by DRIVER.SYS and RAMDRIVE.SYS depend on the placement of the directives in the CONFIG.SYS file. You may try to use the wrong disk drive name if you do not know how DOS assigns drive names. Normally, CONFIG.SYS directives are order independent. You can give the directives in any order, and the computer does not change how the directive operates.

RAMDRIVE.SYS and DRIVER.SYS do not have the same independence, however. You can load RAMDRIVE.SYS and DRIVER.SYS in any order, and the device drivers work, but the disk drive names change. When DOS encounters a block-device driver (any device that transfers data in blocks, rather than in bytes), DOS assigns the next highest drive letter to the device. The order is first come, first assigned.

If you load a copy of RAMDRIVE.SYS on a system with a hard disk, for example, DOS assigns the name D to the RAM disk. If you load a second copy of RAMDRIVE.SYS, DOS assigns the name E to the second RAM disk. Even if the system has only one floppy disk drive, the first RAM disk is assigned the name A; the letter B is reserved for a second floppy disk drive.

If you load a copy of DRIVER.SYS for the external floppy disk drive instead of RAMDRIVE on the same computer, DOS assigns the external disk drive the name D. If you load another copy of DRIVER.SYS for the same external drive, DOS assigns the logical name E to this disk drive.

Reminder:
*Additional
partitions of the
hard disk are
named before
drives created by
CONFIG.SYS.*

Remember that additional hard disks or additional logical disks add to the starting letter of drives created by CONFIG.SYS. Suppose that the hard drive on a 44M system has the drive names C and D. DOS assigns additional partitions of the hard disk the next available drive letters before drives created by CONFIG.SYS directives are named. (The FDISK command partitions hard disks, which are assigned driver letters whether or not you use DRIVER.SYS.) DOS names the second partition of the hard disk D. RAMDRIVE, if used, is assigned the drive name E. DOS assigns DRIVER.SYS, if used instead of RAMDRIVE, the drive name E.

The potential for further confusion comes when several block-device drivers are loaded. The order of loading, determined by the order of the directives in the CONFIG.SYS file, determines the names assigned by DOS.

If you load RAMDRIVE.SYS first and DRIVER.SYS second, the RAM disk may be named D, and the DRIVER.SYS disk is one letter higher (E). If you switch the lines so that DRIVER.SYS is loaded first, the disk drive names also are switched. The DRIVER.SYS disk is named D, and the RAM disk is named E.

Optimizing Memory Resources

A requirement for running most applications software is to have sufficient memory resources in your computer system. Often, a program refuses to run if sufficient memory is not available. At other times, you may be able to run the program, but you may not be able to access all its features.

The most pervasive limitation to the memory available to a program traditionally has been imposed by DOS. Even though PCs with 80286, 80386, or 808486 CPUs can have megabytes of memory chips physically installed—usually referred to as *extended memory*—DOS enables software to access no more than 640K of memory. PC manufacturers and programmers have come up with several different approaches to getting around this 640K barrier erected by DOS. The most popular approach—*EMS*, or *expanded memory*—can supply up to 32M of memory to applications but normally requires special hardware and software.

Versions of DOS before 5.0 do not address directly the issue of providing more memory for applications programs. DOS 5.0, however, provides several techniques that usually can free up some of the first 640K of memory; in some cases, these techniques provide access to your computer's extended memory by converting that memory to expanded memory. The following sections explain how you can take advantage of these DOS 5.0 enhancements.

Using Extended Memory and HIMEM.SYS

The most significant improvement offered by DOS 5.0 is the capacity to load most of the operating system software into extended memory. *Extended memory* is the portion of your computer's random-access memory (RAM) above the 1 megabyte (1,024K) mark. Only PCs based on an 80286, 80386 (DX or SX), or 80486 CPU can have extended memory. Not all PCs in this category have extended memory installed.

Most currently available applications programs don't use extended memory, but they often do need as much *conventional* (below 640K) memory as they can get. By loading most of the operating system software into extended memory, DOS 5.0 provides more conventional memory for applications, ultimately improving the performance of your system.

Before DOS or applications software can use extended memory, you must add to your CONFIG.SYS file an *extended memory manager*—a driver that provides a standard way for applications to address extended memory so that no two programs use the same portion of extended memory at the same time. DOS 4.0 and later versions include the extended memory manager HIMEM.SYS.

HIMEM.SYS manages memory according to the rules set out in the Extended Memory Specification (XMS) Version 2.0. According to this specification, three areas of memory above the conventional 640K barrier can be made available for programs to use:

- *Upper Memory Area*—also known as *upper memory, upper memory blocks,* or *reserved memory*—consists of the memory between 640K and 1,024K. The PC's video adapter uses a portion of this area of memory; upper memory also may be used to place a copy of the computer's ROM (read-only memory) into RAM (random-access memory). DOS 5.0 can load device drivers and memory-resident programs into the upper memory area. Upper memory sometimes is referred to as *high memory*.

- *High Memory Area (HMA)* is the first 64K of memory above 1,024K. DOS 5.0 can load a portion of the operating system into the HMA.

- *Extended Memory Blocks (XMS memory)* include all memory above 1,024K. When extended memory is managed by an extended memory manager, the memory is called XMS memory.

When used on an 80286, 80386, or 80486 PC, HIMEM.SYS provides HMA and XMS memory to programs that know how to use it. To access upper memory, however, the PC must contain an 80386 or 80486 CPU, and you must include one of the following device driver commands in CONFIG.SYS:

DEVICE=EMM386.EXE RAM
DEVICE=EMM386.EXE NOEMS

The syntax for using HIMEM.SYS is as follows:

DEVICE=*d:path***HIMEM.SYS** */HMAMIN=m /NUMHANDLES=n /INT15=xxxx /MACHINE:xx /SHADOWRAM:ON|OFF /CPUCLOCK:ON|OFF*

d: is the disk drive where the HIMEM.SYS resides, and *path* is the directory containing the device driver file.

For example, if HIMEM.SYS is contained in the \DOS directory on your C drive, include the following command in CONFIG.SYS:

DEVICE=C:\DOS\HIMEM.SYS

In most cases, you need only this command to activate the extended memory manager. In special cases, however, you may need to use one of the available switches described in the following paragraphs. The next section continues the discussion of loading DOS into upper memory.

According to the XMS specification, only one program at a time can use the high memory area. The switch */HMAMIN=n* sets the minimum amount of memory that must be requested by an application before the application is permitted to use HMA. If you load DOS into HMA, you can omit this switch (see discussion of the DOS=HIGH command later in this chapter).

When the extended memory manager assigns memory to a particular program, the extended memory manager assigns one or more *extended memory block handles* to the program. The */numhandles=n* switch indicates the maximum number of handles available. The number *n* must be from 1 to 128. The default is 32 handles, usually a sufficient number. Each reserved handle requires an additional 6 bytes of memory.

Most current versions of commercial software support the XMS specification for addressing extended memory. Some older versions of programs, however, use a different method of addressing extended memory, known as the *Interrupt 15h* (*INT15h*) interface. Add the */INT15=xxxx* switch if you want to load DOS into HMA and work with software that uses the INT15h interface. The number *xxxx* indicates the amount of extended memory you want HIMEM.SYS to assign to the INT15h interface; this number must be from 64 to 65,535 (kilobytes). The default is 0. This memory is not available to programs that expect XMS memory.

DOS uses the A20 memory address line to access the high memory area. Not all brands of PCs, however, handle the A20 line in the same way. Normally, HIMEM.SYS can detect your computer's A20 handler. If not, HIMEM.SYS displays the following error message:

```
Unable to control A20
```

If you see this message, use the */MACHINE:xx* switch in the HIMEM.SYS command to specify which type of A20 handler is being used. Insert the code that matches your computer for *xx* in the */MACHINE* switch. You will find the text codes in the Code column and the number codes in the Number column in table 15.8. If you see the error message but your computer is not listed in table 15.8, try the switch */MACHINE:1*.

You may have listed in CONFIG.SYS before DEVICE=HIMEM.SYS a device driver that also uses the A20 line. By default, HIMEM.SYS takes control of A20 even though the line is turned on when HIMEM.SYS loads. HIMEM.SYS warns you when this condition occurs by displaying the following message:

```
Warning: The A20 Line was already enabled!
```

Table 15.8
A20 Handler Codes

Code	Number	Computer
at	1	IBM PC/AT
ps2	2	IBM PS/2
pt1cascade	3	Phoenix Cascade BIOS
hpvectra	4	HP Vectra (A and A+)
att6300plus	5	AT&T 6300 Plus
acer1100	6	Acer 1100
toshiba	7	Toshiba 1600 and 1200XE
wyse	8	Wyse 12.5 MHz 286
tulip	9	Tulip SX
zenith	10	Zenith ZBIOS
at1	11	IBM PC/AT
at2	12	IBM PC/AT (alternative delay)
css	12	CSS Labs
at3	13	IBM PC/AT (alternative delay)
philips	13	Philips
fasthp	14	HP Vectra

Determine whether you really intend to have both drivers installed at once. If so, you can prevent HIMEM.SYS from taking control of A20 by adding the switch */A20CONTROL:OFF* (the default setting is */A20CONTROL:ON*).

Many 80386 computers offer a feature known as *shadow RAM*, which places a copy of the system's read-only memory (ROM) into the computer's upper memory (RAM). The purpose of this trick is to make the software stored in ROM more responsive, increasing the computer's overall performance. If you prefer to increase the amount of upper memory available for device drivers and memory-resident programs, use the */SHADOWRAM:OFF* switch. As HIMEM.SYS loads, it displays the message `Shadow RAM disabled`.

In some cases, DOS cannot turn off shadow RAM. Instead, DOS displays the message `Shadow RAM disable not supported on this system` **or**

Shadow RAM is in use and can't be disabled. (*Note:* Check your hardware documentation for other methods of disabling shadow RAM.)

The */CPUCLOCK:ON* switch ensures that HIMEM.SYS does not slow your computer's *clock speed*, the speed at which your computer processes instructions. (Any change in clock speed does not affect your computer's real-time clock, which keeps the time of day.) Many PCs have on the front panel an LED or other indicator that indicates the current clock speed. To prevent the clock speed from slowing, add the */CPUCLOCK:ON* switch to the DEVICE=HIMEM.SYS command in CONFIG.SYS.

Loading DOS into High Memory

As mentioned earlier in this chapter, DOS 5.0 enables you to load most of the operating system into an area of extended memory known as the high memory area (HMA), or just high memory (the first 64K of extended memory). After the device driver HIMEM.SYS is loaded into the computer's memory, the following command in CONFIG.SYS loads DOS into high memory:

DOS=HIGH

The next time you boot the computer, DOS uses about 14K of space in conventional memory and loads the remainder of the operating system in upper memory. If you don't use this command in CONFIG.SYS, however, or don't have extended memory installed in your computer, DOS 5.0 occupies more than 62K of conventional memory. By loading the operating system into high memory, DOS 5.0 can free up about 48K of conventional memory.

Using Expanded Memory and EMM386.EXE

Expanded memory is memory that meets a published specification known as the Lotus-Intel-Microsoft Expanded Memory Specification, LIM/EMS, or just EMS. The purpose of the EMS specification is to enable DOS applications to access memory above the 640K limit.

The first version of the EMS specification, published in 1985, was numbered EMS Version 3.0 because it was compatible with DOS 3.0. The second revision was numbered EMS Version 3.2. Both EMS 3.0 and EMS 3.2 provided up to 8 megabytes of additional memory to applications written to take advantage of this specification. The most recent EMS revision, Version 4.0, announced in August 1987, can address up to 32 megabytes of expanded memory.

Even though many PCs can contain megabytes of extended memory—memory above 1,024K—most DOS applications software cannot use extended memory. A large number of applications programs are available, however, that can use expanded memory.

The EMS specification normally requires special hardware and software to operate. EMS does not use the generally less expensive extended memory; EMS requires memory boards designed specifically for use as expanded memory. The EMS standard also requires a special device driver called an *expanded memory manager*.

DOS does not provide an expanded memory manager per se because each expanded memory board manufacturer supplies a driver. DOS 5.0 does, however, provide the device driver EMM386.EXE, which can be used in 80386 and 80486 PCs to take the place of an expanded memory manager. EMM386.EXE uses extended memory to *emulate* (act like) expanded memory. EMM386.EXE therefore most accurately can be called an expanded memory *emulator*, even though EMM386.EXE fills the role of an expanded memory manager.

> *Note:* The device driver HIMEM.SYS, discussed in this section, must be loaded before EMM386.EXE. In other words, list DEVICE=HIMEM.SYS before DEVICE=EMM386.EXE in the CONFIG.SYS file.
>
> Do not use EMM386.EXE as an expanded memory emulator if you are already using another driver as an expanded memory manager.

In addition to its role as an expanded memory emulator, EMM386.EXE also is a *UMB provider*, working with HIMEM.SYS to provide upper memory blocks (UMBs) into which you can load device drivers and memory-resident programs. Refer to the next section for further discussion of providing UMBs.

The syntax of the command for EMM386.EXE, used as a device driver, is as follows:

DEVICE=c:\path**EMM386.EXE** ON|OFF|AUTO MEMORY W=ON|OFF
MIX|FRAME=address /Pmmmm Pn=adress X=mmmm-nnn
I=mmmm-nnn B=address L=minxms A=altregs H=handles
D=nnn RAM NOEMS

In many cases, the following command is sufficient:

DEVICE=EMM386.EXE RAM

This command loads the expanded memory emulator and allocates 256K of EMS memory. The *RAM* switch enables upper memory. The remaining switches for the EMM386.EXE device driver are sometimes needed to customize your computer for use with particularly demanding software or hardware.

You can specify *ON*, *OFF*, or *AUTO* in the EMM386.EXE device driver command to indicate whether your computer starts in the EMM386.EXE active, inactive, or automatic mode. By default, the device driver is active, and EMM386.EXE makes extended memory available. However, some applications programs may not run properly when EMM386.EXE is active because EMM386.EXE places the computer in a mode known as virtual 8086 mode. When you use EMM386.EXE as a device driver, the driver loads in memory and remains active (ON) unless you specify otherwise with the *OFF* switch.

The *OFF* switch starts the computer with EMM386.EXE loaded in memory but inactive. The XMS memory allocated as EMS memory is unavailable for any purpose. You can activate the driver with the following command at the DOS command prompt:

EMM386 ON

The *OFF* switch is not compatible, however, with the *RAM* or *NOEMS* switches, discussed later in this section.

Use *AUTO* if you want EMM386.EXE to activate only when an application requests EMS memory. This setting provides maximum compatibility with software that may not work properly in virtual 8086 mode. Like the *OFF* switch, *AUTO* is not compatible with the *RAM* or *NOEMS* switches.

> *Note:* Even though EMM386.EXE activates when an applications program requests EMS memory, the driver does not automatically deactivate when the applications program terminates. To turn off the driver, you have to issue the following command at the command prompt:
>
> **EMM386 OFF**

The *memory* parameter enables you to specify the amount of XMS memory you want EMM386.EXE to allocate as EMS memory. Type the number of kilobytes in the range 16 to 32,768. EMM386.EXE rounds any number you type down to the nearest multiple of 16. All unallocated memory remains available as XMS memory. The default EMS memory allocated is 256K. In other words, if you leave this parameter blank, DOS allocates 256K of EMS memory.

> *Tip:* As a general rule, allocate only as much EMS memory as is required by your applications programs. Any memory allocated as EMS memory is no longer available as XMS memory. Some of the most powerful applications programs currently available, such as Microsoft Windows 3.0, work best with the maximum amount of XMS memory available.

Use the *L=minxms* switch, in which *minxms* is the number of kilobytes, to indicate the minimum XMS memory that EMM386.EXE should allocate. This parameter overrides the *memory* parameter.

If you have installed a Weitek *math coprocessor* chip—a special computer chip that improves the performance of computation-intensive software such as computer-aided design (CAD) software—use the *W=ON* switch. By default, the device driver does not support this type of coprocessor. You also can turn on or off support for the Weitek coprocessor with one of the following commands at the DOS prompt:

```
EMM386 W=ON
EMM386 W=OFF
```

In some circumstances, you may want to use upper memory for device drivers and memory-resident programs, but you don't need EMS memory. Use the *NOEMS* switch with the EMM386.EXE driver to free the maximum amount of upper memory and to provide no EMS memory. For example, you may intend to run Windows 3.0 on your computer. Windows can use all your XMS memory, so this software doesn't need EMS memory.

The *NOEMS* switch has two disadvantages:

- Windows 3.0 cannot provide EMS to an application running in a DOS session.

- Applications that support the Virtual Control Program Interface (VCPI) for use of XMS memory in protected mode do not run in protected mode when the NOEMS switch is used with EMM386.EXE.

Use the *RAM* switch instead of *NOEMS* if you want to have access to upper memory and you intend to run a program that requires EMS memory in a Windows 3.0 DOS session, or if you expect to use a program that requires VCPI support.

The remaining switches available for use with EMM386.EXE are highly technical and therefore beyond the scope of this book. Refer to Que's *DOS Programmer's Reference*, 3rd Edition, or to your DOS User's Guide or Technical Reference Manual for more information.

Loading Device Drivers and TSRs into Upper Memory

In addition to enabling you to run DOS in high memory, DOS 5.0 provides the capability of loading memory-resident programs and device drivers into an area of memory between 640K and 1,024K, freeing more conventional memory for other applications programs. DOS can access this area of memory—called the *upper memory area*, *upper memory*, *upper memory blocks*, or *reserved memory*—in 80386 and 80486 PCs that have 1M or more of memory.

The PC's video adapter uses a portion of upper memory. Sometimes, upper memory also is used to store a copy of the computer's ROM—a technique often called *shadow RAM*.

> *Note:* The upper memory area is sometimes also referred to as *high memory*, but DOS 5.0 uses the term high memory to refer to the first 64K of extended memory.

To load device drivers or memory-resident programs, or *terminate-and-stay-resident (TSR) programs*, into upper memory, all the following conditions must be met:

- Your computer has an 80386 or 80486 CPU.

- HIMEM.SYS is loaded as a device driver.

- EMM386.EXE is loaded as a device driver with the RAM or NOEMS switch.

- The following command appears in the CONFIG.SYS file:

      DOS=UMB

If you also want to use the command DOS=HIGH to load DOS into high memory, combine the two commands as follows:

      DOS=HIGH, UMB

You can load two types of programs into upper memory: device drivers and memory-resident programs (TSRs). You already know that device drivers normally are loaded using the DEVICE command. When you want to load a device driver into upper memory, use the DEVICEHIGH command. The syntax for this configuration command is as follows:

DEVICEHIGH=c:path**filename.ext** /switches

For example, to load into upper memory the screen driver ANSI.SYS, type the following command in CONFIG.SYS:

DEVICEHIGH=C:\DOS\ANSI.SYS

The next time you boot the computer, DOS attempts to load ANSI.SYS into the upper memory area.

To load a memory-resident program into upper memory, precede the program's start-up command with LOADHIGH. (**Note:** You can use LH in place of LOADHIGH.) The syntax for the command for LOADHIGH is as follows:

LOADHIGH *c:path***programname** */switches*

For example, to load DOSKey (discussed in Chapter 13) into upper memory each time you start your computer, add the following command to your AUTOEXEC.BAT file:

LOADHIGH DOSKEY

The next time you reboot the computer, DOS attempts to load DOSKey into upper memory.

DOS does not load a program into upper memory if the program requests that DOS allocate more memory during initialization than is available in the largest available upper memory block. If DOS is not successful when it tries to load device drivers or TSRs into the upper memory area, DOS loads the program into conventional memory instead.

DOS may successfully load a device driver into upper memory only to have the driver allocate more memory some time after initialization, potentially causing the system to "lock up." To prevent this occurrence, insert the following parameter in place of the equal sign in the DEVICEHIGH command:

SIZE=*hhhh*

For *hhhh*, insert a hexadecimal (base 16) number that denotes the maximum amount of upper memory required to run the program. (You can use DOS 5.0's MEM command, discussed in the next section, to determine the amount of memory allocated by a program.) If DOS cannot find the amount of upper memory indicated by the SIZE parameter, DOS loads the driver into conventional memory.

Use the MEM command to determine whether a driver or program has loaded into upper memory.

Displaying the Amount of Free and Used Memory

To enable you to make the most efficient use of DOS 5.0's memory management utilities, discussed in the preceding sections, DOS also enables you to display the amount of free and used memory at any point during a DOS session. Use DOS 5.0's MEM command for this purpose.

The syntax for the MEM command is as follows:

MEM */PROGRAM /DEBUG /CLASSIFY*

You can abbreviate each switch by typing just the first letter (/P, /D, or /C).

To see a "short" version of the memory report that indicates the amount of free conventional memory, EMS memory, and XMS memory, type **MEM** with no switch. DOS displays a report similar to the following:

```
 655360    bytes total conventional memory
 655360    bytes available to MS-DOS
 623776    largest executable program size

 655360    bytes EMS memory
 262144    free EMS memory

3145728    bytes total contiguous extended memory
       0    bytes available contiguous extended memory
2686976    bytes available XMS memory
           MS-DOS resident in High Memory Area
```

This report tells you the following information about the conventional memory: the total amount of conventional memory (640K where 1K = 1,024 bytes); the amount of conventional memory available to DOS (usually the same as the preceding number); and the largest program you can run in conventional memory. In this example, 623,776 bytes of the original 655,360 bytes are available to any applications program you may decide to run.

The MEM report then shows the total amount of EMS memory and the amount free for use by an applications program. The first number includes the 384K reserved (upper) memory area between 640K and 1,024K. In the example, 262,144 bytes (256K) of EMS memory are free.

Next, MEM tells you the total amount of extended memory installed in your computer and the amount of extended memory that has been mapped (converted) to XMS memory and is available for use. In the example, 2,686,976 bytes of XMS memory of the original 3,145,728 bytes (3,072K or 3M) are available.

If you are not using an extended memory manager (such as HIMEM.SYS), MEM also indicates the amount of available extended (non-XMS) memory; otherwise, this number is 0.

Finally, MEM indicates whether MS-DOS is currently loaded in the high memory area.

Sometimes, MEM's short report doesn't provide enough information to meet your needs. The three available switches produce longer versions of the report. Because these reports do not fit on a single DOS screen, you usually use the pipe feature with the MORE command to display one screen of the report at a time.

The reports generated by MEM's */PROGRAM* (/P) and */DEBUG* (/D) switches are highly technical in content and therefore are not discussed here. However, the report produced by */CLASSIFY* (/C) is useful in determining whether device drivers and TSRs can be loaded into upper memory.

To see a listing of programs, drivers, and free space in conventional and upper memory, type the following command and press Enter:

MEM /C

DOS scrolls a report similar to the following on the screen:

```
Conventional Memory :

    Name    Size in Decimal          Size in Hex
----------  ----------------       --------------
    MSDOS    12016  ( 11.7K)            2EF0
    HIMEM     1184  (  1.2K)             4A0
    EMM386    8208  (  8.0K)            2010
    SETVER     384  (  0.4K)             180
    COMMAND   2624  (  2.6K)             A40
    MIRROR    6528  (  6.4K)            1980
    FREE        64  (  0.1K)              40
    FREE       144  (  0.1K)              90
    FREE    623968  (609.3K)            8560

Total  FREE :     624176          (609.5K)

Upper Memory:

    Name    Size in Decimal          Size in Hex
----------  ----------------       --------------
   SYSTEM  163840  (160.0K)            28000
   ANSI      4192  (  4.1K)             1060
   MOUSE    12784  ( 12.5K)             31F0
```

```
DOSKEY      4160  (   4.1K)            1040
FREE         144  (   0.1K)              90
FREE       11376  (  11.1K)            2C70

Total FREE :        11520        (  11.3K)

Total bytes available to programs (Conventional+Upper) : 635696    (620.8K)
Largest executable program size:                         623776    (609.2K)
Largest available upper memoryblock :                     11376    ( 11.1K)

    655360   bytes total EMS memory
    262144   bytes free EMS memory
   3145728   bytes total contiguous extended memory
         0   bytes available contiguous extended memory
   2686976   bytes available XMS memory
            MS-DOS resident in High Memory Area
```

Because some of the report scrolls off the screen before you can read it, you may want to use the following variation of the same command:

MEM /C ¦ MORE

DOS pipes the report through the MORE filter and displays the first screen of the report followed by the message - - MORE - -. Press any key when you are ready to display the next screen.

You also can send the MEM report to your printer by using the following command:

MEM /C > PRN

This command redirects the report to the DOS device PRN, your computer's first printer port.

The top portion of the report, titled Conventional Memory, shows you how much memory is allocated to any particular driver or program. Use the section of the report titled Upper Memory to determine whether any drivers or programs are loaded in upper memory and how much upper memory is still free.

Before attempting to move a driver or program from conventional to upper memory (using DEVICEHIGH or LOADHIGH), compare the driver or program's size (in the conventional memory Size column) to the available upper memory block (UMB) sizes (indicated by FREE in the upper memory Name column). The available UMB must be at least as big as the driver or program before you can load the driver or program into upper memory.

After you identify a driver or memory-resident program that appears to be the right size to fit in the available UMB, edit CONFIG.SYS or AUTOEXEC.BAT to add DEVICEHIGH or LOADHIGH to the appropriate command. Reboot your computer and issue the MEM /C command again to see if it worked.

> ***Tip:*** Arriving at the optimal combination of device drivers and memory-resident programs loaded into upper memory may require some experimentation. DOS loads programs in the largest available UMB first, so try loading the largest drivers and programs first by placing these start-up commands earliest in CONFIG.SYS or AUTOEXEC.BAT.

Displaying and Printing Different Languages

To display more than one code page or print non-English-language characters, you must use the DISPLAY.SYS and PRINTER.SYS device drivers. (Code pages are described fully in Chapter 16.)

Reminder:
Use
DISPLAY.SYS
and
PRINTER.SYS to
display and print
foreign-language
characters.

Using DISPLAY.SYS in your CONFIG.SYS file enables you to switch code pages without restarting DOS. Using PRINTER.SYS enables you to download a font table to certain printers so that they can print non-English-language and graphic characters.

DOS's support of different languages depends not only on these two device drivers but also on the NLSFUNC program and on the CHCP, MODE PREPARE, MODE SELECT, MODE REFRESH, and KEYB commands. These commands are discussed in Chapter 16.

Displaying International Characters with DISPLAY.SYS

The DISPLAY.SYS driver enables the switching of code pages on most video adapters. DISPLAY.SYS is ineffective with a monochrome or color-graphics adapter: the code pages of these adapters are fixed and cannot be switched. If you have a monochrome or color-graphics adapter, DISPLAY.SYS is not recommended for your use. With DOS Version 4, DISPLAY.SYS was enhanced to check your hardware to determine the type of display you have if you don't specify the adapter type.

You can use DISPLAY.SYS effectively with the following adapters: PC Convertible LCD, EGA, and VGA.

The syntax of the line you add to the CONFIG.SYS file to invoke the DISPLAY.SYS driver is as follows:

DEVICE = d:path\DISPLAY.SYS CON: =
(type, hw_codepage, added_codepages, subfonts)

Code pages are discussed more completely in Chapter 16 and are beyond the scope of this brief device-driver overview. The following paragraphs, however, review the parameters shown in the directive.

The *d:path* parameter is the drive name and path to the DISPLAY.SYS file. If DISPLAY.SYS is not in the root directory of your starting disk, supply the drive and path name.

CON: is the DOS device name for the console—the keyboard and display. The colon after the device name is optional.

Following CON is an equal sign and the parameters to be passed to DISPLAY.SYS enclosed in parentheses. The equal sign and enclosing parentheses must be specified. The *type* parameter can be any of the following:

Parameter	Meaning
MONO	Monochrome adapter
CGA	Color-graphics adapter
EGA	Enhanced color-graphics adapter (EGA) and video graphics array (VGA) or PS/2
LCD	Convertible LCD

The second parameter passed to DISPLAY.SYS is *hw_codepage*, which stands for the hardware code-page built into your adapter (437, 850, 860, 863, or 865). DISPLAY.SYS uses the code page given to the COUNTRY directive. (COUNTRY is discussed in Chapter 16.)

The *added_codepages* parameter is the maximum number of additional code pages that the adapter can use. This parameter actually refers to the number of code pages that can be prepared and used with the MODE command. Refer to Chapter 16 for a full description of changing the code pages with MODE.

The subfonts parameter refers to the dot resolution of the character displayed. Characters can be formed from a box of 9-by-14 dots, 9-by-16 dots, or 8-by-8dots. The subfonts value can range from 0 to 2, depending on the adapter you use. If you use a monochrome or CGA adapter, set subfonts to 0 (the value DOS assumes if you do not specify a subfonts value). If you use a convertible LCD display, set subfonts to 1 (the value DOS assumes if you don't specify subfonts for the LCD display). If you use an EGA or VGA adapter, set subfonts to 1 or 2. (DOS defaults to 2 if you use an EGA adapter and don't specify this parameter.)

If you use an EGA or VGA monitor and want to specify 437 as the hardware code page, include the following command in CONFIG.SYS:

DEVICE = C:\SYS\DISPLAY.SYS CON = (EGA,437,1)

This command specifies an EGA or VGA display (you specify EGA if you have an EGA or a VGA display), 437 for the starting code page, and 1 additional code page. You don't have to use additional code pages, but if you plan to, specify a value for added codepages.

The following command specifies an EGA display and a code page of 863 (French Canadian):

DEVICE = C:\SYS\DISPLAY.SYS CON = (EGA,863,2)

Notice that the existing code page is 863 but that the specified code page is 850. If your existing code page is not 437, always use 850 as the new code page and 2 as the value for added code pages.

Reminder:
Include the
ANSI.SYS
directive in
CONFIG.SYS
before the
DISPLAY.SYS
directive.
If you use ANSI.SYS and DISPLAY.SYS in your CONFIG.SYS file, the ANSI.SYS directive must appear before the DISPLAY.SYS directive. If the order is reversed, you lose ANSI.SYS capability. Remember that you do not have to include DISPLAY.SYS if you do not use code-page switching. If you are new to DOS and do not use a font different from the one built into your display, you do not have to include the DISPLAY.SYS driver in your CONFIG.SYS file.

Printing International Characters with PRINTER.SYS

PRINTER.SYS is the device driver that enables the characters shown in the code page to be printed on certain printers. DOS Version 3.3 supports code pages on only two printers:

> IBM ProPrinter Model 4201
>
> IBM Quietwriter III Model 5202

DOS Versions 4 and 5 add support for the following printers:

> IBM Proprinter Model 4202
>
> IBM Proprinter Model 4207
>
> IBM Proprinter Model 4208

These printers are the only printers on which DOS can control the printing of foreign-language characters; other printers are controlled in other ways.

To use code-page switching with other printers, you must add **PRINTER.SYS** to your CONFIG.SYS file. The syntax for PRINTER.SYS is similar to that for DISPLAY.SYS:

> **DEVICE = d:path\PRINTER.SYS LPTx: =**
> **(type, hw_codepage, added_codepages) . . .**

or

> **DEVICE = d:path\PRINTER.SYS LPTx: =**
> **(type, hw_codepage1,hw_codepage2, added_codepages) . . .**

Notice that on one line, you must specify code pages for printers on multiple parallel ports (designated by the three-dot ellipsis). This section explains each element in the directive and then gives sample lines to show how the directive varies for each printer.

The *d:path* parameter is the drive name and path to the PRINTER.SYS file. If PRINTER.SYS is not in the root directory of your starting disk, give the disk drive and path name.

The *LPTx:* parameter is the DOS device name for the line printer. The *x* is the number of the parallel printer port: 1, 2, or 3 (DOS does not support serial printers when printing international characters); the colon after the device name is optional. Because you can have up to three parallel printers, you must specify the parallel port to which the printer is connected by including up to three **DEVICE = PRINTER.SYS** lines in CONFIG.SYS.

Reminder:
You can specify up to three parallel printers.

Following the LPTx parameter is an equal sign and the parameters passed to PRINTER.SYS enclosed in parentheses. The equal sign and enclosing parentheses must be given. The printer type is the model number for the printer: 4201 for the ProPrinter (with DOS Version 3.3); 4202, 4207, or 4208 (with DOS Version 4); or 5202 for the Quietwriter III (DOS Version 3.3 or 4). Use 4201, 4208, or 5202 with DOS Version 5.

The *hw_codepage* parameter stands for the hardware code-page built into your printer. (Code pages are explained fully in Chapter 16.)

The *added_codepages* parameter is the maximum number of additional code pages that the printer can use. The value for this parameter can range from 0 to 12.

Following is an example of the directive to use with a ProPrinter:

> **DEVICE = C:\SYS\PRINTER.SYS LPT1 = (4201,437,1)**

This directive specifies a ProPrinter 4201 connected to the first parallel port (LPT1), 437 as the starting code page, and 1 as the additional code page. You don't have to use additional code pages, but if you plan to, specify a value for *added_codepages*.

This example shows that the PRINTER.SYS file is in a subdirectory on drive C called \SYS. If PRINTER.SYS is in a different directory, change the disk drive and path information but leave all other information the same.

Remember that you do not have to include PRINTER.SYS in CONFIG.SYS if you do not use code-page switching with the DOS-supported printers. You also can ignore the PRINTER.SYS device driver if you do not use a font different from the one built into your printer or if you do not use one of the supported printers.

DOS Versions 3.3, 4, and 5 users receive two additional SYS files: COUNTRY.SYS and KEYBOARD.SYS. These files are not device drivers. Do not attempt to use them with the DEVICE directive. These files are discussed in Chapter 16.

Accessing Files through FCBS

Cue:
FCBS enables you to use programs written for DOS Version 1 with new versions of DOS.

Some DOS users find the FCBS directive indispensable. This directive enables you to use useful, but antiquated, programs written for DOS Version 1 with later versions of DOS. Most applications don't require this command in the CONFIG.SYS file.

FCB is an acronym for File Control Block. FCBs are one way a program can access a file. This method of file access was used by DOS Version 1 to communicate with programs. Later versions of DOS borrow a UNIX-like method for controlling files, called *handles* (discussed later in this chapter). Although FCBs can be used with any version of DOS, handles can be used only with DOS Version 2 and above.

To use the FCBS directive in the CONFIG.SYS file, use the following syntax:

FCBS = *maxopen, neverclose*   *(Version 4)*

FCBS = *maxopen*   *(Version 5)*

In this syntax, *maxopen* is the maximum number of unique FCBs that programs can open at one time, and *neverclose* is the number of FCBs that DOS cannot reuse automatically. (The *neverclose* parameter is only available with Version 4.) You must specify *maxopen*, which can be a number from 1 to 255; the default value is 4. The optional *neverclose* parameter must be a number less than or equal to *maxopen*. If you don't specify *neverclose*, the default value is 0. Set these values by trial and error; if you set values, run the program, and the program cannot open all the required files (a message to this effect appears), set the FCBS parameters to higher values.

Although the IBM documentation states that FCBs are closed only when you use the SHARE command for a local area network, this situation is not true with DOS Versions 3.0 and 3.1. If you use an older program that doesn't support path names, the program uses FCBs, and you should set the FCBS directive.

You pay a small price in RAM to use the FCBS directive. For each number above 4 that *maxopen* exceeds, DOS uses about 40 bytes. Considering that most people have 256K or more of RAM in their computers, the use of this extra RAM should not be a problem.

Using the FILES Directive

As the FCBS directive decreases in importance with the later versions of DOS, the FILES directive increases. FILES is the DOS Versions 2 through 5 directive used to enable UNIX-like or XENIX-like file handling. UNIX and XENIX—and later versions of DOS—use a file handle (a number corresponding to the filename) instead of file-control blocks to access files. Your program gives the operating system the name of the file or device you want to use. The operating system gives back to your program a handle—a two-byte number. From that point on, your programs use the handle, rather than the FCB, to manipulate the file or device.

To include the FILES directive in CONFIG.SYS, use the following syntax:

FILES = nn

In this syntax, *nn* is the number of files you want opened at any time. The maximum is 255, and the minimum is 8. If you give a FILES directive with a number less than 8, or if you omit this directive, DOS makes the number 8. Each additional file over 8 increases the size of DOS by 39 bytes.

The name FILES is somewhat deceiving because handles are used by files and devices. For example, standard devices such as the display, keyboard, or printer receive one file handle each. If you do not specify the FILES directive, DOS starts with eight file handles and immediately takes five handles for the standard devices, leaving only three handles for your programs. Including the following directive in your CONFIG.SYS file is a good idea:

Cue:
Set FILES to at least 10.

FILES = 20

This directive establishes 20 file handles, which should be enough for most programs. If a program displays an error message about file handles, edit CONFIG.SYS and increase the number of handles to 25 or 30. These higher numbers are sufficient for most existing programs. Some programs may need higher values: for example, Windows 3.0 may work better with **FILES = 60**.

Using LASTDRIVE To Change the Number of Disk Drives

The LASTDRIVE directive informs DOS of the maximum number of disk drives on your system. Generally, LASTDRIVE is a directive used with networked computers or with the pretender commands (such as SUBST).

If you don't use the LASTDRIVE directive, DOS assumes that the last disk drive on your system is E. If you give DOS a letter corresponding to fewer drives than are attached to your computer, DOS ignores the directive. The LASTDRIVE directive enables you to tell DOS how many disk drives, real or apparent, are on your system. Suppose that you have a system with two floppy disk drives and a hard disk partitioned into three drives (C, D, and E). If you issue the directive **LASTDRIVE = D**, DOS ignores the directive because the operating system knows the last drive is E.

To use the LASTDRIVE directive in CONFIG.SYS, use the following syntax:

LASTDRIVE = drive letter

drive letter is the alphabetical character for the last disk drive on your system. The letters A through Z, in uppercase or lowercase, are acceptable.

You want to use the LASTDRIVE directive so that you can use multiple RAM disks. Suppose that you have a system with two floppy disk drives (drives A and B) and a hard drive (drive C). You create two RAM drives (drives D and E). To create a third RAM drive, you must issue the directive **LASTDRIVE = F** so that you can control the third RAM drive as drive F.

Another reason you may want to use LASTDRIVE is to establish logical disk drives. A logical disk drive can be a nickname for another disk drive (see the SUBST command). A logical disk drive also may be another partition of the hard disk. A logical disk drive is just a name, but DOS thinks that the drive is real.

Using the SHELL Command

The SHELL command was originally implemented to enable programmers to replace the DOS command interpreter (COMMAND.COM) with other command interpreters. The SHELL command is more commonly used, however, to perform two other functions:

- Inform DOS that the command interpreter is in another directory, not in the boot disk's root directory.

- Expand the size of the *environment*—an area of RAM that stores named variables used by DOS and applications programs. Commands such as PATH and PROMPT store their current settings as environment variables. To display the contents of the environment, type **SET** at the command prompt and press Enter.

> ***Warning:*** SHELL is a tricky command that you should use cautiously. Used incorrectly, the SHELL command can lock up your system. Keep a bootable floppy disk handy for restarting your computer should you run into a problem.

The syntax for the SHELL command is as follows:

SHELL = *d:path***filename.ext** *parameters*

The *d:path* parameter specifies the disk drive and path that contain the command processor you want to use. **filename.ext** is the name of the command processor.

The SHELL command itself doesn't take any other parameters or switches, but you can add command-line parameters or switches available for use with the command processor.

When used from the command line, the COMMAND command loads a copy of the command processor into memory. A common use of COMMAND is as a parameter of the SHELL command.

The syntax for COMMAND is as follows:

COMMAND *d:path\ device /E:size /P /C string /MSG*

The *d:path* parameter specifies the disk drive and path that contain the command processor if it is not located in the root directory. Always use this parameter when including COMMAND in the SHELL configuration command. This parameter has the additional effect of setting an environment variable named *COMSPEC*, which informs DOS and other programs of the location and name of the current command processor.

/E:size is an optional switch that sets the environment space. The *size* parameter is a number from 160 to 32,768 that denotes the amount of memory reserved for the environment. (If you do not specify a multiple of 16, DOS rounds the *size* parameter up to the next highest multiple of 16). By default, DOS 5.0 reserves 256 bytes for the environment (160 bytes in DOS 3.2 through 4.0).

The /P switch instructs DOS to load the command processor permanently. Without the /P switch, DOS loads COMMAND.COM only temporarily into memory. When you are using COMMAND with the SHELL command in CONFIG.SYS, be sure to use the /P switch. Otherwise, you cannot access the command line until you reboot the system using a disk that doesn't contain the inappropriate SHELL command.

The /C switch and *string* parameter work together. This combination causes DOS to load the command processor, execute any command represented by *string*, and then unload the command processor. Chapter 13 discusses how to use COMMAND with /C *string* to call a batch file from within a batch file. Don't use this switch-parameter combination with SHELL.

The /MSG switch tells DOS to store all its error messages into memory rather than reading them from the disk. This feature can speed operation somewhat. More important, when you are running a floppy disk system, you sometimes remove from the disk drive the disk that contains COMMAND.COM. Without the /MSG switch, DOS cannot access error messages contained on disk within the COMMAND.COM file itself. You normally should use this switch only if running DOS from floppy disks. You also must use the /P switch any time you use the /MSG switch.

The DOS 5.0 Setup program adds the following command to the default CONFIG.SYS file, listed earlier in the chapter:

SHELL=C:\DOS\COMMAND.COM C:\DOS\ /P

This configuration command tells DOS that COMMAND.COM is the command interpreter and that it is located in the \DOS directory on the C drive. The /P switch causes the command interpreter to be loaded permanently, not temporarily, in memory.

The preceding SHELL command enables you to place a copy of COMMAND.COM in C:\DOS and delete the copy in the root directory. This practice helps you maintain a clean root directory (discussed in Chapter 9) and protects COMMAND.COM from being replaced by an older version that may be on a floppy disk you are copying. If you accidentally copy the disk to the root directory, you don't overwrite the current version of COMMAND.COM.

Sometimes you create such a long PATH command in AUTOEXEC.BAT that you fill the available environment space, causing DOS to display the message `Out of environment space`. If you see this message, use COMMAND with the SHELL command and the /E switch to specify a larger environment space. For example, the following command, used in CONFIG.SYS, increases the environment to 384 bytes:

> **SHELL**=C:\DOS\COMMAND.COM /E:384

If you already have a SHELL command in CONFIG.SYS, you can add the /E switch. For example, combining the two preceding SHELL commands, you can include the following command in CONFIG.SYS:

> **SHELL**=C:\DOS\COMMAND.COM C:\DOS\ /P /E:384

Note: The SHELL command itself doesn't use any memory, but by increasing the environment space, you are reducing the amount of free conventional memory by an equal amount. In other words, increasing the environment space from 256 bytes to 384 bytes reduces free memory by 128 bytes.

Using the STACKS Command

The STACKS directive was added in DOS Version 3.2 and was changed slightly with Version 3.3. If you do not have an Enhanced Keyboard, this directive may be of little use to you. If you have a PS/2, AT, or 286-XT, you may find this directive very useful. To understand why, you need to know a few things about your computer's internal operation.

A *stack* is an area of RAM. The CPU (*central processing unit*, or brain of your computer) uses this area to temporarily hold information. High-speed instructions place items onto the stack and remove items from the stack. The IBM's CPU can use a stack anywhere in memory, and each program you use can have its own stack.

Reminder:
The CPU uses stacks to store information it needs to return to when it is interrupted.

The CPU often receives *hardware interrupts* (messages sent by the keyboard, mouse, disk drive, or the like that demand the computer's attention). When a hardware interrupt causes the computer to stop what it was doing to respond to the interrupt, the CPU stores the information that was being acted on (before the interrupt) in a stack.

Unfortunately, it's possible to interrupt an interrupt, so the stack can be filled quickly. Versions of DOS before 3.2 used a single-stack method to handle interrupts. When too many interrupts occurred and the stack overflowed, the system would mysteriously lock up, and no error message would be given.

DOS Version 3.2 and later versions use a pool of stacks. When a hardware interrupt occurs, DOS draws another stack from the pool. When DOS has successfully answered the interrupt, the operating system returns the stack to the pool for use later when another interrupt occurs. Overall, the lock-up problems have been reduced considerably.

Today, most stack problems surface when you use an Enhanced Keyboard and certain programs, such as dBASE III Plus. Holding down a key can trigger stack failure. The electronics in an Enhanced Keyboard send signals more quickly than does a standard keyboard, making the stack fill up too quickly. To prevent the problem of stack overflows, DOS provides the STACKS directive. The syntax for this directive is as follows:

STACKS = *number, size*

Cue:
Use STACKS to specify how many stacks DOS is to use.

In this syntax, *number* is the number of stacks that DOS is to establish to handle the interrupts. The value of *number* should be from 8 to 64. The *size* parameter is the size in bytes of each stack. This value can be from 32 to 512.

The default value of the STACKS directive varies by machine. For DOS Versions 3.2 through 5 on a PS/2, AT, XT, and 286-XT (with an Enhanced Keyboard), as well as the PC Convertible, DOS starts with 9 stacks of 128 bytes each (equivalent to giving the directive STACKS = 9, 128). On the PC, XT, and PC Portable, DOS allocates no stacks by default.

To revert to the *no-stacks-fits-all* approach for handling interrupts, use the following directive:

STACKS = **0,0**

Using this directive conserves valuable memory for use by applications. The DOS 5.0 installation program adds this directive to your CONFIG.SYS file.

Generally, you don't have to worry about the STACKS directive. If you get a stack error, however, you are using a program that triggers the hardware problem. Immediately change the CONFIG.SYS file to increase the number of stacks without altering the size of the stacks. A comfortable line to use is one that establishes 12 stacks of 128 bytes each:

STACKS = **12, 128**

Understanding the REM, SWITCHES, and INSTALL Commands

In addition to the new device drivers, DOS provides three additional CONFIG.SYS commands: REM, SWITCHES, and INSTALL.

Using the REM Command

REM enables you to insert remarks in your CONFIG.SYS file. You can leave notes to yourself (or others) explaining what particular lines do. This kind of documentation in a CONFIG.SYS file is especially helpful if you use non-DOS device drivers for your hardware. You also can remove temporarily a CONFIG.SYS statement by prefacing the statement with a REM directive. When you test a new configuration, you can enable only those features you want by removing REM.

To use the REM directive, use the following syntax:

REM remarks

Cue:
Use REM to insert remarks or to keep the processor from executing other directives.

Using the SWITCHES Command

SWITCHES turns off Extended Keyboard functions. This command works like the ANSI.SYS /K switch (described in Chapter 13). The syntax for this directive is as follows:

SWITCHES = /K

Some software cannot work with the Extended Keyboard. If you use this directive to disable the Extended Keyboard for that software, the software should function properly.

Using the INSTALL Command

INSTALL enables you to load from the CONFIG.SYS file certain utility programs that remain in memory. In versions of DOS before 4, you had to load these programs from the DOS prompt or through a batch file such as

AUTOEXEC.BAT. Versions 4 and 5 support loading any of the following programs using INSTALL:

> FASTOPEN.EXE
> KEYB.COM
> NLSFUNC.EXE
> SHARE.EXE

The command reference section of this book can provide more information about these programs. Loading these programs from CONFIG.SYS instead of from AUTOEXEC.BAT can result in a memory savings of several kilobytes per program.

The syntax for using INSTALL in CONFIG.SYS is as follows:

> **INSTALL** = *d:path***program**

In this syntax, *d:path* is the disk and path information, and *program* is the name of the utility you want to load. You may be able to use INSTALL with some non-DOS utilities, such as SideKick and Keyworks. The program you install with this directive must have the extension COM or EXE.

You can use the LOADHIGH command in Version 5 to load TSR programs into upper memory.

Gaining More Speed with FASTOPEN

Cue:
Use FASTOPEN
if BUFFERS
doesn't make your
hard drive act fast
enough.

Although FASTOPEN is not a CONFIG.SYS directive, it is appropriate to discuss the directive after discussing the INSTALL directive. FASTOPEN, introduced with DOS Version 3.3, can be used only with hard drives. Where buffers store information moved from disk to user memory, FASTOPEN allocates memory to store directory information. FASTOPEN partially solves a performance problem not resolved by the CONFIG.SYS BUFFERS directive. BUFFERS helps when your computer reads or writes information to several files; BUFFERS helps most when disk activity is isolated to a file's few key portions.

If you use many of the same files during the day, however, (particularly small files that DOS can read or write in one cluster) BUFFERS is not a major benefit. The time DOS spends traversing the subdirectory system and opening the files may take more time than actually reading or writing the files.

FASTOPEN caches directory information, holding in memory the locations of frequently used files and directories. Directories are a type of file, not accessible by users, that DOS reads and writes in a manner similar to other files. A part of the directory entry for a file or subdirectory holds the starting point for the file in the file allocation table (FAT). Because DOS typically holds the FAT in the disk buffers, FASTOPEN was developed to hold directory entries in memory.

FASTOPEN is not a complex command, but you must do a little work before you can use FASTOPEN effectively. FASTOPEN's syntax is as follows:

INSTALL *d:path*\ **FASTOPEN.EXE** **d: = nnn**

or

d:path\ **FASTOPEN.EXE** *d:* **= nnn**

You use INSTALL and the EXE extension only if you use this line in CONFIG.SYS. If you issue this command at the DOS prompt, omit these items and type the rest of the command.

The *d:path* parameter is the disk drive and path to the FASTOPEN.EXE file. The *d:* following the file name is the name of the hard drive you want FASTOPEN to act on and is a mandatory part of the command. The *nnn* parameter is the number of directory entries that FASTOPEN should cache. Each file or subdirectory requires one directory entry, and you can enter a value from 10 to 999. If you do not specify a value for *nnn*, DOS defaults to 34.

If you use DOS Version 4 or 5, you can use several additional parameters with this command, as shown in the following syntax line:

INSTALL d:path\FASTOPEN.EXE d: = (nnn,mmm) /X

or

d:path\FASTOPEN.EXE d: = (nnn,mmm) /X

The new *mmm* parameter refers to the number of fragmented entries (the DOS manual calls them *continuous space buffers*) for the drive. Using this parameter improves performance when files on your hard disk become fragmented. The values you can use for *mmm* range from 1 to 999. DOS has no default value for fragmented entries. If a value is not given, the feature is not active.

The */X* switch is similar to the /X switches of other commands. This switch enables FASTOPEN information to reside in expanded memory.

You can use FASTOPEN on as many disks as you want. Note, however, that the total number of directory entries or fragment entries FASTOPEN can handle is 999. If you issue the command for several disk drives, the sum of *nnn* values or the sum of *mmm* values cannot exceed 999. This limit is FASTOPEN's physical limit.

Cue:
Use FASTOPEN to speed performance on as many hard disks as you have on your computer.

The practical limit of *nnn* is between 100 and 200 per disk. If you specify a value much higher, DOS wades through the internal directory entries slower than it reads information from the disk. Additionally, each directory entry stored in memory takes 35 bytes. Considering the speed-and-memory trade-off, the limit of 100 to 200 entry yields adequate performance.

Using too small a number for *nnn* can be a disadvantage as well. When directory entries are recycled, the least recently used entry is discarded if a new entry is needed. If the *nnn* value is too small, DOS discards entries it may still need. The object is to have enough entries in memory so that FASTOPEN operates efficiently but not so many that FASTOPEN wastes time wading through directory entries.

At the very least, *nnn* must exceed the number of subdirectories you travel to get to the deepest subdirectory. The minimum value for *nnn* is 10; this value often exceeds the number of levels in your directory organization. Suppose that you have a directory structure like \DOS\BASIC\TEST. The deepest level is 3 down from the root, much less than DOS's default of 10. Try beginning with 100 and fine-tune up or down by 5 until you feel the right performance.

The value you specify for *mmm* depends on how fragmented your files are. Use the **CHKDSK *.*** command in subdirectories where you store data files to get a report of fragmentation. The more fragmentation, the larger the value you should assign to *mmm*. A general rule is to use a value for *mmm* that is twice the number of *nnn*s as your *mmm* entry.

Reminder:
Install FASTOPEN after you define all disk drives.

You should observe three restrictions about using FASTOPEN. First, the disk drive you name cannot be one on which you use JOIN, SUBST, or ASSIGN, because these commands do not create real drives. Second, if you load a disk drive device driver through AUTOEXEC.BAT rather than through CONFIG.SYS (some manufacturers provide a driver that must be started from a batch file or from the DOS prompt rather than from CONFIG.SYS), you must use FASTOPEN after you have defined all disk drives. FASTOPEN can become confused if you add additional disk drives after you have invoked FASTOPEN. Third, using FASTOPEN with a disk-caching program may slow down disk access.

Making a CONFIG.SYS File

The following is a sample CONFIG.SYS file:

```
DEVICE = C:\SYS\SJDRIVER.SYS /M
DEVICE = C:\SYS\HPSCANER.SYS
DEVICE = C:\SYS\HIMEM.SYS
```

```
DEVICE = C:\SYS\EMM386.EXE RAM
DEVICE = C:\SYS\SMARTDRV.SYS
LASTDRIVE = G
BUFFERS = 10
COUNTRY = 001,,C:\SYS\COUNTRY.SYS
DEVICE = C:\SYS\DISPLAY.SYS CON = (,437,1)
SHELL = C:\DOS\COMMAND.COM C:\DOS /P /MSG
DEVICE = C:\SYS\ANSI.SYS /L
REM DEVICE = C:\SYS\RAMDRIVE.SYS 360 /E
INSTALL C:\DOS\FASTOPEN.EXE C: = 100 /X
FILES = 30
```

By examining this specialized file you can learn some useful tips for building a customized CONFIG.SYS file of your own. This sample file assumes that you have a subdirectory called \SYS on your hard disk and that device drivers are in this subdirectory.

The first two lines load special third-party device drivers needed to operate an HP ScanJet scanner. Consult the syntax recommendations of your software or hardware vendors to see exactly how to phrase your own DEVICE directives when installing such drivers.

The LASTDRIVE and BUFFERS commands were explained earlier in this chapter. Only 10 buffers are used because the SMARTDRV.SYS driver reduces the need for a larger number of buffers.

Several other directives are in the CONFIG.SYS file for various reasons. For example, the COUNTRY directive and DEVICE = DISPLAY.SYS statement are given to use codepages. The SHELL directive tells DOS where the command processor is located, passes the directory of the command processor to COMSPEC, and makes memory-resident the messages COMMAND.COM uses. ANSI.SYS is loaded as a device driver so that ANSI-compatible programs can use ANSI.SYS to control the screen. FILES is set to 30 to allow up to 30 files to be open at the same time.

In the listing shown, notice that the line where RAMDRIVE.SYS is loaded has been commented out with the REM directive. DOS sees REM and then ignores the rest of the line. When you don't need a directive you have written into your CONFIG.SYS file, you may find it convenient to precede that directive with REM. When you need that directive again, edit the CONFIG.SYS file and remove REM from the line. Using REM is much faster than typing the complete directive when you need it and erasing the directive completely when you don't need it.

Chapter Summary

In this chapter, you learned the following important points:

- DOS can alter system settings through instructions in the CONFIG.SYS file.

- The CONFIG.SYS file must be in the root directory of the boot disk. When you alter CONFIG.SYS, the changes do not occur until DOS is rebooted.

- You can tell DOS when to look for the Ctrl-Break key sequence.

- Disk buffers make DOS work faster by placing requested information in RAM.

- Disk caches like the DOS IBMCACHE program can speed up certain disk operations.

- RAMDRIVE, the DOS RAM disk software, can speed disk operations if your computer has sufficient random-access memory.

- DRIVER.SYS, the device driver for disk drives, must be used for external or non-IBM hard disk drives. DRIVER also can be used to make additional logical disk drives from a physical disk drive.

- DOS Versions 4 and 5 enable the use of expanded memory.

- DISPLAY.SYS and PRINTER.SYS are used to display and print foreign-language characters.

- DOS Version 1 used a different method of accessing files; this method can be reproduced with later versions of DOS by using the FCBS directive.

- The FILES directive sets the number of files DOS can open at any one time.

- The LASTDRIVE directive specifies the letter of the last disk drive installed in your system.

- You can replace the command processor DOS uses by invoking the SHELL directive.

- You can specify the number of stacks available to the processor during an interrupt with the STACKS directive.

In Chapter 16, you learn about the files and commands you need to use for the international features of DOS.

16

Understanding the International Features of DOS

The Personal Computer, PS/2 computers, and DOS are American inventions. DOS, however, is an international operating system. Vast changes in DOS Version 2.11 made the program easier to use in countries outside the United States. Additional changes occurred in each revision of DOS Version 3. Versions 4 and 5 added some minor enhancements. If you use your computer in a country other than the United States, these changes make your computer more natural to operate.

DOS versions since 3.3 have several international features seldom noticed by users in the United States. One feature is that the date and time can be displayed in three different formats. In addition, DOS can tell a program, on request, which characters to use for the decimal point, the thousand separator, and the currency symbol. DOS even can tell the program whether the currency symbol precedes or follows the amount and whether a space should separate the symbol from the amount.

Cue:
With DOS
Version 3 and
above, the date
and time can be
displayed in one
of three formats.

Furthermore, the displays and keyboards of Personal Computers and PS/2s can be changed to produce characters appropriate for countries other than the United States. Although users outside the United States have had these programs since DOS Version 1.1, IBM now distributes the programs as part of Versions 3 and above in the United States.

To make DOS go international, you must alter your CONFIG.SYS and AUTOEXEC.BAT files. These changes are recommended only for those who need international capability. If you do not need such capability, you can skip this chapter until you do.

To customize DOS for international use, you may need to perform several actions:

1. Add the following items to your CONFIG.SYS file:

    a. The **COUNTRY** directive

    b. The **DEVICE = DISPLAY.SYS** directive

    c. The **DEVICE = PRINTER.SYS** directive

2. Add the **NLSFUNC**, **MODE**, **CHCP**, and/or **KEYB** commands to your AUTOEXEC.BAT file.

To understand how international-character support works in DOS, you first need to understand the concept of code pages.

Understanding Code Pages

Code pages enable the computer to use, display, and print non-English characters with minimal effort on your part.

Your computer uses ASCII to communicate to the peripherals. Internally, your computer works with patterns of numeric values. These ASCII values are the numeric representation of letters, numbers, and characters.

Each character that can be displayed on-screen is represented by an ASCII value from 0 to 255. For example, the ACII value of the letter A is 65.

Cue:
A font is a particular shape of characters.

The common name for the shape of characters is *font*. Depending on the adapter in use, the fonts are switchable, meaning that different character sets can be displayed.

Cue:
A code page is a font set.

Basically, a code page is a font set. You may recognize names for typewriter and typesetting faces, such as Courier, Elite, and Times Roman. Similarly, code pages allow for different typefaces of English and international language characters.

Five video adapters are available: the Monochrome Display Adapter (MDA), the Color Graphics Adapter (CGA), the Enhanced Graphics Adapter (EGA), the Liquid Crystal Display (LCD) of the PC-convertible laptop, and the Video Graphics Array (VGA) of the PS/2 and other systems. (LCDs and VGAs are not necessarily adapters; some LCDs and VGAs are integrated circuitry built into the computers and are responsible for the display of information.)

The VGA, EGA, and LCD adapters can use the five international font sets listed in table 16.1. Depending on the code page used, you can display various language characters, as indicated in the table. Monochrome and CGA adapters cannot support switchable code pages.

Table 16.1
Code Page Numbers

Font	Code Page Number
United States (English)	437
Multilingual	850
Portuguese	860
Canada (French)	863
Nordic	865

Suppose that you want to display the ASCII character 236. Each font set except the multilingual code page displays the infinity character. The multilingual code page displays an accented Y. For ASCII character 157, the North American set displays a double-bar Y. If you use the multilingual or Norwegian-Danish set, you get an empty-set symbol. The Portuguese and French Canadian sets display a back-accented U as ASCII character 157. Many characters are identical in all five fonts sets, but some are customized for various localities.

The major difference among the code pages used by PCs and PS/2 computers is the characters whose values are in the range 128 through 255 (columns 9 through F on the charts). No widely used, prevailing standard exists for these characters. DOS sacrifices some of the scientific and graphics characters in this range when the program substitutes the needed language characters.

Printers also use code pages; what can be displayed on-screen, therefore, can be reproduced on the printed page. DOS Version 3.3 includes code pages for IBM ProPrinter Model 4201 and Quietwriter III 5202. DOS Versions 4 and 5 support those printers along with IBM ProPrinter Models 4202, 4207, and 4208. You can expect other printer manufacturers to follow the lead of Microsoft and IBM in building code-page support into

Reminder:
Because printers use code pages, what you can display on-screen can be reproduced on paper.

DOS and to provide code pages for their printers in the near future. Many printers now emulate to some degree one of these IBM printers. Check your printer manual to determine the printer's code-page compatibility.

Reminder:
Select a starting
code page to use
a particular
language font.

To use a particular language font, you select a starting code page; you can change code pages freely. You may find, however, that code page switching is completely unnecessary if your video adapter and printer start with the right code page. Most North American users find the built-in DOS code pages adequate and probably never use code-page switching.

Switching code pages may be important for international users, however, including those who have files established in early versions of DOS. In addition, the ability to change fonts on the fly can be valuable. International users find that code pages provide a logical and powerful way to handle languages.

Using the International Directives of DOS

DOS uses directives and device drivers to set up your computer so that it uses a particular character set. The directives are COUNTRY, NLSFUNC, KEYB, MODE (in three forms), and CHCP. The device drivers are KEYBOARD.SYS, PRINTER.SYS, and DRIVER.SYS. Some directives and device drivers are included in the CONFIG.SYS file. Other commands required for international support can be included in your AUTOEXEC.BAT file, enabling them to run each time you boot your system.

Changing the CONFIG.SYS File

You include in your CONFIG.SYS file the **COUNTRY** directive and two drivers that control devices attached to your system: **DISPLAY.SYS** for the display and **PRINTER.SYS** for the printer. The following sections discuss these changes to CONFIG.SYS.

Adding the COUNTRY Directive

The first step in making DOS go international is to issue the **COUNTRY** directive, which informs DOS how to customize itself for your location.

When you issue the COUNTRY directive, DOS changes the date and time formats to conform to the practice in the country specified. In addition, DOS can tell inquiring programs which characters to use for lists, currency symbols, the thousand separator, and decimal fractions.

The syntax for COUNTRY differs according to which version of DOS you use. For DOS Versions 3 through 3.2, you use the following syntax:

> **COUNTRY = <nnn>**

<nnn> is a three-digit country code.

For DOS Version 3.3 and above, you use the following:

> **COUNTRY = <*countrycode*>, <*codepage*>
> <*d:path\filename.ext*>**

<countrycode> is the mandatory three-digit code for the country. The default country code is that of the United States—001.

<codepage> is the code page number (see table 16.2). North American users of English should use the United States code page number (437). If you cannot find a code page number for your country, the multilingual code page number (850) is probably your best choice.

<d:path\filename.ext> is the path and file name for the file that contains country information. If you use the COUNTRY directive but do not provide a file name, DOS assumes that the information is in the COUNTRY.SYS file (which is supplied on the DOS Startup/Operating or Startup disk). COUNTRY.SYS is the only DOS-supplied file that you can specify as *<filename.ext>*.

The code page and the country information file do not need to be specified. To skip the code page, use two commas between the country code and the COUNTRY.SYS file:

> **COUNTRY = 001,,C:\COUNTRY.SYS**

The two commas instruct DOS to use the default code page. You also can omit the file name and supply the country code or the country code and code page, as in the following examples:

> **COUNTRY = 001**

> **COUNTRY = 001 437**

Cue:
To skip the code page, insert two commas between the country code and COUNTRY.SYS file.

Table 16.2
Country Codes

Country/Language	Country Code	Keyboard Code	Existing Code Page	New Code Page
Arabic	785	None	None	None
Australia	061	US	437	850
Belgium	032	BE	437	850
Canada (English)	001	US	437	850
Canada (French)	002	CF	863	850
Denmark	045	DK	865	850
Finland	358	SU	437	850
France	033	FR	437	850
Germany	049	GR	437	850
Israel	972	None	437	850
Italy	039	IT	437	850
Japan*	081	None	437	932
Korea*	082	None	437	934
Latin America	003	LA	437	850
Netherlands	031	NL	437	850
Norway	047	NO	865	850
PRC*	088	None	437	938
Portugal	351	PO	860	850
Spain	034	SP	437	850
Sweden	046	SV	437	850
Switzerland (French)	041	SF	437	850
Switzerland (German)	041	SG	437	850
Taiwan*	086	None	437	936
United Kingdom	044	UK	437	850
United States	001	US	437	850

*Added in DOS Version 4. Supported only on versions sold in Asia.

Note that if you use the COUNTRY directive, DOS searches for the file COUNTRY.SYS in the root directory of the boot disk. If DOS cannot find the file, the operating system displays the following message:

```
Bad or missing \COUNTRY.SYS
```

Although the full path name for your COUNTRY.SYS is not required, you always should supply the full name. Doing so ensures that DOS can locate the correct file.

Reminder:
Always supply the full path name for COUNTRY.SYS.

Table 16.3 shows how DOS changes the display when you use various COUNTRY codes.

Table 16.3
Effects of COUNTRY Codes on Display

	US-English	UK	Sweden
Country code	1	44	46
Code page*	437	437	437
Currency symbol	$	£	Skr
Digits after decimal separator in currency	2	2	2
Thousand separator	,	,	.
Decimal separator	.	.	.
Data list separator	,	,	;
Date separator	-	-	-
Time separator	:	:	.
Time format	24-hour	24-hour	24-hour
Current date	Mon 11-25-1991	Mon 25-11-1991	Mon 1991-11-25
Current time	16:24:39.01	16:24:39.01	16.24.39,01

*Although the country code currently supports 19 countries (23 with DOS Version 4), only five code pages are available.

Additional information about a country is made available to programs with DOS Version 3.3 and above—including information about switching lower- and uppercase letters and sorting characters' equivalents. DOS uses the country code and code page, both of which affect the sorting order, to maintain information on sorting characters.

COUNTRY does have some limitations: DOS does not automatically display prompts in languages other than English. For that refinement, DOS messages must be rewritten.

Adding DISPLAY.SYS

Reminder:
*Using
DISPLAY.SYS,
you can switch
code pages
without restarting
DOS.*

To display more than one code page or to print non-English language characters, you must use DISPLAY.SYS and PRINTER.SYS. Using DISPLAY.SYS in your CONFIG.SYS file enables you to switch code pages without restarting DOS. Using PRINTER.SYS enables you to download a font table to certain printers so that they can print non-English language and graphics characters.

The DISPLAY.SYS driver enables you to switch code pages on video adapters other than the monochrome display adapter or the color graphics adapter. The adapters that can be used effectively with DISPLAY.SYS are the PC Convertible LCD, the EGA, and the VGA. In DOS Versions 4 and 5, if you do not specify the adapter type, DISPLAY.SYS checks your hardware to determine the type of active display.

To add DISPLAY.SYS to the CONFIG.SYS file, you use the following syntax:

DEVICE = *d:path***DISPLAY.SYS CON:** =
(**<type>**, *<hw_codepage>*, *<added_codepages>*)

d:path is the drive name and path to DISPLAY.SYS. If DISPLAY.SYS is not in the root directory of your boot disk, give the disk drive and path name.

CON: is the DOS device name for the console—the keyboard and display. The colon is optional.

The parameters of DISPLAY.SYS are enclosed in one set of parentheses. The first parameter, the display type, can be any of the following:

MONO	Monochrome Display Adapter
CGA	Color Graphics Adapter
EGA	Enhanced Graphics Adapter, PS/2, or VGA
LCD	Convertible LCD

The second parameter is *<hw_codepage>*, which stands for the hardware code page built into your adapter. The possible values follow:

437	United States
850	Multilingual
860	Portugal
863	Canada (French)
865	Norway

If you do not supply the *hw_codepage*, DISPLAY.SYS uses the code page given to the COUNTRY directive.

<added_codepages> is the maximum number of additional code pages the adapter can use; the range is from 0 to 12. Use 0 for MONO and CGA displays because they do not support code-page switching. Use 1 for LCD and 2 for EGA and VGA displays, including the PS/2. *<added_codepages>* actually refers to the number of code pages you can prepare and use with the MODE command, which is discussed later in this chapter.

The following is a sample DISPLAY.SYS directive for those who use an EGA or VGA and 437 as the hardware code page:

DEVICE = C:\DOS\DISPLAY.SYS CON = (EGA,437,1)

This command specifies an EGA adapter (EGA is used for the EGA and VGA displays), 437 as the starting code page, and one additional code page. This example assumes that the DISPLAY.SYS file is placed in a subdirectory called \DOS on drive C. The following command line assumes that an EGA adapter is used and that the existing code page (the default code page for the country where the computer is sold) is 863, for French-speaking Canada:

DEVICE = C:\DOS\DISPLAY.SYS CON = (EGA,850,2)

Notice that the existing code page is 863 but that the specified code page is 850. If your existing code page is not 437, always use 850 as the new code page and 2 as the value for additional code pages.

> *Note:* If you use ANSI.SYS and DISPLAY.SYS in your CONFIG.SYS file, the ANSI.SYS directive must appear before the DISPLAY.SYS directive. If the order is reversed, you lose the capability of ANSI.SYS.

Adding PRINTER.SYS

PRINTER.SYS enables the characters shown in the code page sets to be printed on certain printers. DOS Version 3.3 supports code pages on the following printers:

IBM ProPrinter Model 4201

IBM Quietwriter III Model 5202

DOS Versions 4 and 5 adds support for the following printers:

Reminder:
With PRINTER.SYS, certain printers can print those characters shown in the code page sets.

IBM ProPrinter Model 4202

IBM ProPrinter Model 4207

IBM ProPrinter Model 4208

To use code-page switching with these printers, you must add the **DEVICE = PRINTER.SYS** line to your CONFIG.SYS file. The syntax for adding PRINTER.SYS is similar to that for adding DISPLAY.SYS:

DEVICE = *d:path***PRINTER.SYS LPTx:** =
(**<type>**, *<hw_codepage>*, *<added_codepages>*) ...

d:path is the drive name and path to PRINTER.SYS. If PRINTER.SYS is not in the root directory of your starting disk, supply the disk drive and path name.

LPTx: is the DOS device name for the line printer. The *x* is the number of the parallel printer: 1, 2, or 3. The colon is optional.

The parameters of PRINTER.SYS are enclosed in parentheses. The printer *<type>* is the printer's model number: for the ProPrinter, 4201 (with DOS Version 3.3) or 4201 and 4208 (with Version 4); for the Quietwriter III, 5202. For DOS Versions 4 and 5, the 4201 parameter is for the 4201 or 4202 ProPrinter; the 4208 parameter is for the 4207 or 4208 ProPrinter.

The second parameter, *<hw_codepage>*, stands for the hardware code page built into your printer. As with DISPLAY.SYS, the possible values are 437, 850, 860, 863, and 865.

There is a difference between the possible *<hw_codepage>* values for the two kinds of printers. ProPrinters have one font built into the device. This font is moved to the printer's RAM. When you change the code page for this printer, DOS overwrites the font in memory.

The Quietwriter III, however, uses hardware font cartridges. Each cartridge holds several code pages in the same type style. To use a particular code page, you must select the appropriate cartridge. The Quietwriter III cannot inform DOS when a cartridge has been changed; DOS must assume that the appropriate cartridge is in the printer.

The result is that you can specify one hardware code page for ProPrinters and two for the Quietwriter III. If, however, you specify two code pages for the Quietwriter III, you cannot prepare any code pages for the printer— DOS assumes that both code pages are fixed in hardware.

For ProPrinters, the value for *<hw_codepage>* follows the same guidelines as for DISPLAY.SYS. For the Quietwriter III, the value follows the same guidelines, with one exception: you may specify two hardware code pages, in which case DOS assumes that no code pages should be prepared for the Quietwriter III.

<added_codepages> is the maximum number of additional code pages that the printer can use. *<added_codepages>* can range from 0 to 12.

For ProPrinters, if you specify 0 or omit *<added_codepages>*, you get the ProPrinter's built-in font. If you specify a number other than 0, the number is the maximum number of additional code pages the ProPrinter can use. Generally, use 1 if your hardware code page is 437; otherwise, use 2.

For the Quietwriter III, if you have specified two code pages, you must omit *<added_codepages>* or specify a value of 0. No code pages can be prepared if you have specified two hardware code pages.

An example of the directive to use with a ProPrinter is the following:

DEVICE = C:\DOS\PRINTER.SYS LPT1 = (4201, 437,1)

This directive calls for a ProPrinter connected to the first parallel port (LPT1), for 437 as the starting code page, and for one additional code page. As with DISPLAY.SYS, this example assumes that the PRINTER.SYS file is placed in a subdirectory called \DOS on drive C. If PRINTER.SYS is in a different directory, change the disk drive and path information but leave all other information the same.

The following command assumes that a ProPrinter is used and that the existing code page is 863 (French-speaking Canada):

DEVICE = C:\DOS\PRINTER.SYS LPT1 = (4201,850,2)

Notice that the existing code page is 863 but that the specified code page is 850. Again, if your existing code page is not 437, always use 850 as the new code page and use 2 as the value for additional code pages.

Now look at an example for the Quietwriter III, using a cartridge that holds a 437 code page and an 850 code page:

DEVICE = C:\DOS\PRINTER.SYS LPT1 = (5202,(437,850),0)

Reminder:
If you specify two code pages, surround them with parentheses.

This directive follows the general form of the ProPrinter directive but includes the model number of the Quietwriter III (5202). Notice the parentheses that enclose the two code pages; if you give two code pages, you must surround them with parentheses. In addition, the number of added code pages is set to 0.

If you have more than one of these printers attached to your system, you can include that information on one directive line. For example, if the ProPrinter is connected to LPT1 and the Quietwriter III is connected to LPT2, you can use the following command:

DEVICE = C:\DOS\PRINTER.SYS LPT1 =
(4201,437,2) LPT2 = (5202,(437,850),0)

You use a space after the information for LPT1 and before LPT2. DOS loads PRINTER.SYS and sets up both printers at the same time.

Changing the AUTOEXEC.BAT File

DOS Versions 3.3 and above international language support depends not only on the COUNTRY directive and the two device drivers but also on the following additional directives to set up and switch code pages for your display, printer, and keyboard:

NLSFUNC	Enables the CHCP command
CHCP	Activates (changes) code pages
KEYB	Loads and activates code pages for the keyboard
MODE	Loads and activates code pages for the display and printer

Reminder:
You can include CHCP, NLSFUNC, KEYB, and MODE in the AUTOEXEC.BAT file.

You can include these directives in the AUTOEXEC.BAT file. (With Versions 4 and 5, you can use the INSTALL command in the CONFIG.SYS file to install the NLSFUNC and KEYB programs; just specify them after the COUNTRY command.) Table 16.4 summarizes the effects that these directives have on DOS, the console (the CON: device, including the display and the keyboard), and the printer. You may want to refer to this table as you read the rest of the chapter.

Table 16.4
Effects of Commands and Device Drivers on DOS,
the Console, and the Printer

Command/ Device Driver	CON DOS	Display	Keyboard	Printer
DISPLAY.SYS	X	X	O	-
PRINTER.SYS	-	-	-	X
NLSFUNC	X	-	-	-
CHCP	X	X	X	X
MODE CODEPAGE PREPARE	-	X	O	X
MODE CODEPAGE SELECT	-	X	O	X
MODE CODEPAGE REFRESH	-	X	O	X
KEYB	-	O	X	-

Key: X   Sets or changes
O   Affects but does not set or change
-    No effect

CHCP, NLSFUNC, KEYB, and MODE are closely linked. CHCP depends on NLSFUNC, and KEYB depends on MODE and CHCP. The following sections present these commands, explain briefly what each command does, how to use the command, and what steps must be performed before and after you use the command.

Supporting National Languages with NLSFUNC

NLSFUNC, the National Language Support FUNCtion, is a device driver that was first available with DOS Version 3.3. This driver performs two tasks: first, the driver hooks into DOS and provides programs with extended information about the specified country; and second, the program enables you to use the CHCP (change code page) command. If you will be switching code pages for any device except the keyboard, you need the NLSFUNC command. Fortunately, NLSFUNC is one of the easiest commands to use.

You use the following syntax for NLSFUNC:

*dc:pathc***NLSFUNC** *d:path\\COUNTRY.SYS*

dc: is the name of the disk drive that holds the NLSFUNC command, and *pathc* is the directory path to the command. The parameter to NLSFUNC is the full file name to the COUNTRY.SYS file. To simplify the use of NLSFUNC, use the COUNTRY directive in your CONFIG.SYS file and give the full file name for the country information file. Also, place the NLSFUNC command in your AUTOEXEC.BAT file. Certain applications programs may require that you run NLSFUNC. These programs use the new extended country information provided by DOS Version 3.3. Your program's documentation should state whether the program requires NLSFUNC.

Because NLSFUNC becomes part of DOS, using NLSFUNC increases DOS's use of RAM by almost 2,700 bytes. NLSFUNC remains in memory until you turn off the computer or restart DOS. You need to run NLSFUNC only once after you have started DOS. Running NLSFUNC a second time produces an error message.

Reminder: Using NLSFUNC increases Versions 4's and 5's use of RAM.

Changing the Code Page with CHCP

CHCP, or CHange Code Page, was introduced with DOS Version 3.3 and is the simplest method of changing code pages. Because the CHCP command also can affect the keyboard, users of the KEYB program should be familiar with CHCP.

The syntax for CHCP is the following:

CHCP *<codepage>*

<codepage>—the new code page for DOS and all the devices to use—can be 437, 850, 860, 863, or 865.

Using CHCP sets the code page for DOS and establishes information about sorting and about switching lower- and uppercase letters. CHCP also sets the code page for devices. If you have included DISPLAY.SYS in your CONFIG.SYS file, CHCP sets the code page for the display. If you have included PRINTER.SYS in CONFIG.SYS, CHCP sets the code page for the printer. If you have used the KEYB program, CHCP also sets the keyboard's code page. Because of these capabilities, CHCP is a system-wide program. If you set up any device to use code-page switching, CHCP sets the device.

Before you use CHCP, you first must be sure that you have performed the following actions:

- Issued the NLSFUNC command

- Given the COUNTRY directive in the CONFIG.SYS file

- Issued the necessary MODE CODEPAGE PREPARE commands (MODE is covered later in this chapter.)

You use the following command to set the code pages for DOS and all the devices to 437:

CHCP 437

You can determine the current code page that DOS is using by issuing the CHCP command without a code page number:

CHCP

Interestingly, CHCP can report the current code page for DOS even if you have not used NLSFUNC. CHCP does not increase the size of DOS and can be issued as often as you want.

Selecting a Language for the Keyboard

Reminder:
KEYB makes
certain keyboards
multilingual.

The KEYB command is a program (or programs) that makes the keyboards of the PS/2, Personal Computer, and compatible systems multilingual. KEYB determines which characters can be typed on the keyboard.

KEYB for DOS Version 3.3 and above is quite different from KEYB for versions of DOS prior to Version 3.3. KEYB programs for DOS Version 3.2

and earlier versions should not be used with Version 3.3 and above. Each version is discussed separately in the following sections.

KEYB for Version 3.2 and Earlier

You use the following syntax for the KEYB command for DOS Version 3.2 and earlier:

> *d:path***KEYB<xx>**

d:path is the optional disk drive and path name to the KEYB programs. The *<xx>*, which can be any one of the keyboard codes in table 16.5, adapts the keyboard and the display to the character set of a particular language.

Table 16.5
Keyboard Codes for KEYBxx for Versions 3.0 through 3.2

Country	Code
France	FR
Germany	GR
Italy	IT
Spain	SP
United Kingdom	UK
United States	US

The KEYBxx program takes about 2K of memory and becomes a resident program. KEYBxx remains in memory until you reboot DOS or turn off the computer. After the program is loaded, the native language character set for the KEYBxx program becomes active.

Reminder:
KEYBxx remains in memory until you reboot DOS.

KEYB for Version 3.3 and above

The KEYB command for Versions 3.3 and 4 has a different syntax and set of requirements. KEYB alters the code page of the console (CON:, which includes the display and keyboard). If you will be using keyboard layouts that need different code pages, you must prepare the console; you must use the MODE CON CODEPAGE PREPARE command before you use KEYB.

Use the following syntax for KEYB Version 3.3:

>   *d:path***KEYB** *<keyboardcode>, <codepage>, d:path\filename.ext*

DOS Version 4 added one more parameter:

>   */ID: <zzz>*

DOS Version 5 added the */e* parameter.

<keyboardcode> is the two-character keyboard code for your country (see table 16.5). If your country is not listed in table 16.5, use the keyboard code that comes close to meeting your needs. To set the keyboard to use a different language, give a keyboard code.

<codepage> is the optional code page that you want to use with the keyboard. If you do not specify a code page, KEYB uses the default code page. With DOS Version 4, you may use the */ID:<zzz>* parameter to select a specific keyboard layout for those countries that have available more than one Enhanced Keyboard. These countries are France (189, 120), Italy (141, 142), and the United Kingdom (166, 168). Replace *<zzz>* with the keyboard ID code for the Enhanced Keyboard. The manual that came with your computer tells you the layouts of the various Enhanced Keyboards so that you can select the one you want.

With DOS Version 5, the */e* parameter enables KEYB to assume that an Enhanced Keyboard is installed. This parameter most often is used on an XT (8086/8088) system, because DOS cannot display the keyboard type on those computers.

d:path\filename.ext is the optional full disk drive, path, and file name for KEYBOARD.SYS, the file that holds the information KEYB uses to build the various translation tables. KEYB places one restriction on keyboard codes and code pages: the keyboard code, the code page given to KEYB, and the console code page (as well as the keyboard ID number, if used) must all be compatible. Table 16.6 shows the allowable combinations for the first three parameters.

Table 16.6
Compatible Code Page and Keyboard Code Combinations for KEYB

Code Page	Keyboard Codes
437	FR, GR, IT, LA, NL, SP, SU, SV, UK, US
850	All
860	PO
863	CF
865	DK, NO

Basically, KEYB translates into ASCII characters the raw on-and-off codes produced by the keyboard hardware. The ASCII characters built by KEYB are determined by the keyboard code and code page used by KEYB and by the code page used by the console. KEYB builds a table of keystroke codes to character translations for each prepared console code page. The different combinations substitute the correct characters for each language. With each set of substitutions, some characters disappear, and other characters appear.

KEYB, however, can build these translation tables only for certain keyboard/code-page combinations. Occasionally, graphics characters must be sacrificed for language characters. The characters to type for these languages appear in certain code pages but not others. Using a keyboard layout with the wrong console code page means that you get the wrong characters on-screen. You type the right character, but you see the wrong character. For this reason, the keyboard code and code page that KEYB uses must agree with the console code page. The appendix of your DOS manual contains information about the various keyboard and code page layouts.

Reminder:
The keyboard code and code page used by KEYB must agree with the console code page.

Avoiding the following traps helps you use keyboard codes and code pages effectively:

- Do not give a keyboard code and code page that don't agree.

- If you are switching code pages, do not give a code page not on the list of code pages given to a MODE CON CODEPAGE PREPARE command.

- Do not give a keyboard code that does not agree with the console (CON) code page used in a CHCP command or a MODE CON CODEPAGE PREPARE SELECT command.

- Do not use KEYB with a keyboard code or a code page that conflicts with the current console code page. Use MODE CON CODEPAGE SELECT or CHCP to switch the console code page before you use KEYB for a different code page. If you do not, KEYB issues a warning about incompatible combinations.

The manual for your computer and the DOS reference manual have a set of templates showing the different keyboard layouts. If you want to experiment, you can load the KEYB programs and try typing some characters.

When any version of KEYB is loaded, you can switch easily between the U.S. character set and another language set. The key combination Ctrl-Alt-F1 switches to the U.S. character set. Ctrl-Alt-F2 switches back to the other language set. Version 5 adds Ctrl-Alt-F7 to switch to typewriter mode, the standard for some countries.

The KEYB program stays in memory until you reboot DOS or turn off the computer. You can use the KEYB program for DOS Version 3.3 and above as many times as you want. The first time you use KEYB, the program increases the size of DOS by about 7,800 bytes. Using KEYB again does not increase the size of DOS. If you use KEYB without any parameters, DOS reports on the current keyboard code and its related code page; DOS also shows you the code page being used by the console screen (CON). The following is an example of the output of the KEYB command without parameters:

```
Current keyboard code: FR code page: 437
Current CON code page: 437
```

If you have the KEYB program for DOS Version 3.2 or an earlier version, load only one KEYBxx program. In DOS Version 3.2, KEYB consumes about 2K of RAM. If you load a second KEYBxx, the program assumes control, and the first KEYBxx program is deactivated. The first program, however, is trapped in memory and continues to eat its 2K of space until you reboot DOS or turn off the computer.

Some computers are manufactured specifically for non-U.S. use. These computers have a different ROM BIOS and multilingual character set. Loading KEYB has no effect on such computers.

Changing the Code Page with MODE

To use different code pages with your computer, prepare each code page for each device and then activate the code page. The MODE command prepares and selects code pages for each device.

Reminder:
The MODE command controls devices.

MODE is the command that controls devices. Before DOS Version 3.3, MODE consisted of four subcommands. Version 3.3 added four more. The four additional subcommands handle code page switching. Fortunately, you do not need to use every MODE subcommand each time you start DOS. To switch code pages on a device, assemble the code pages for use. The MODE CODEPAGE PREPARE command loads code pages into the computer's memory. The MODE CODEPAGE SELECT command downloads any needed code page to the device and tells that device which code page to use. MODE CODEPAGE SELECT also can tell the device to forget a software font and switch back to the font built into the device.

Because some fonts are placed in the device's RAM, you may turn the device off and lose the information. A stray program also may wipe out the code page information. For these reasons, the MODE command can remind the device of the font in use. This activity is the function of MODE CODEPAGE REFRESH.

The MODE CODEPAGE/STATUS command rounds out MODE, displaying the number of the available code pages for a device and indicating which code page is active.

DOS provides some abbreviations for parts of the command. You can use the abbreviations listed in table 16.7 when you use the MODE CODEPAGE command.

Table 16.7
MODE CODEPAGE Abbreviations

Word	Shorthand
CODEPAGE	CP
PREPARE	PREP
SELECT	SEL
REFRESH	REF
STATUS	STA

Defining Code Pages
with MODE CODEPAGE PREPARE

The first step in using switchable code pages is to use the MODE CODEPAGE PREPARE command to load the disk-based code pages into the computer's memory. The syntax for MODE CODEPAGE PREPARE is the most complex of any MODE subcommand, but the command can be tamed. The command syntax follows:

*dc:pathc***MODE <device> CODEPAGE PREPARE =**
((<code page>, ...)*d:path***filename.ext)**

dc:pathc is the optional disk drive and directory path to the MODE command. *device* is the name of the device that MODE uses. You must specify the device, which can be any of the following:

CON: Console

LPT1: First parallel printer

LPT2: Second parallel printer

LPT3: Third parallel printer

PRN: The current system printer, usually a synonym for LPT1:

Reminder:
Use MODE CODEPAGE PREPARE to load disk-based code pages into memory.

As with all device names, the colon is optional. For each specified device, a driver must have been loaded through the CONFIG.SYS file. To use CON in this command, you must include DISPLAY.SYS in CONFIG.SYS; to use the remaining devices, you must include PRINTER.SYS in CONFIG.SYS.

The *<code page>* numbers must be enclosed within a set of parentheses. If you need more than one code page, separate the code page numbers with a comma. The ellipsis (...) represents the other optional code pages. Remember to give a closing parenthesis after the final code page.

For example, to use 850 as a code page, you use the following form:

$$= (850)$$

To use the 437 and 850 code pages, you use the following form:

$$= (437, 850)$$

Spaces are optional.

Reminder:
Do not give a
hardware code
page number to
MODE
CODEPAGE
PREPARE.

Avoid giving a hardware code page number to MODE CODEPAGE PREPARE. Remember the code page that you gave to DISPLAY.SYS or PRINTER.SYS. Do not give MODE CODEPAGE PREPARE the same code page number. If, for example, you used the following line in your CONFIG.SYS file, do not give 437 to MODE CODEPAGE PREPARE:

DEVICE = C:\DOS\DISPLAY.SYS CON = (EGA, 437, 2, 2)

The driver already knows that the 437 code page is built into the adapter. Giving 437 to MODE causes MODE to reload the 437 code page, wasting memory that other fonts could use. You also force the computer to download the font each time the 437 code page is selected—a minor, but avoidable, waste of time.

The final information you must give to MODE CODEPAGE PREPARE is the drive name, path name, and file name for the file that holds the font information for the device. The general form of the file name is **<devicename>.CPI**. The *<devicename>* can be any of the following:

EGA   EGA and VGA display adapters

LCD   PC Convertible LCD display

4201   IBM ProPrinter

5202   IBM Quietwriter III

The CPI extension is for code-page information.

The EGA.CPI and LCD.CPI files, of course, are used with the CON device. The 4201.CPI and 5202.CPI files are used with the PRN or LPT devices.

If the code page information file is not on the current disk or in the current directory, provide the needed information. The full file name is mandatory. Because all DOS-included code page files have an extension of CPI, you usually give the root name and the extension.

Note that you cannot prepare more code pages than the number you gave to DISPLAY.SYS or PRINTER.SYS for *<added_codepages>*. If you need more code pages, edit the DISPLAY.SYS or PRINTER.SYS line in your CONFIG.SYS file and then restart DOS. Excessive code page commands are ignored by DOS.

Remember that if you give two hardware code pages for the Quietwriter III, you must give a value of 0 for *<added_codepages>*. DOS assumes that the two code pages are in the printer. In this case, you do not need to use MODE CODEPAGE PREPARE on the Quietwriter III.

If you issue the MODE CODEPAGE PREPARE command more than once, you can skip the code pages that you do not want to change. For example, you use the following MODE command to load the 850, 860, and 863 code pages:

MODE CON CODEPAGE PREPARE = ((850, 860, 863) C:\EGA.CPI)

If you later want to use the 850 and 863 code pages, but you want the 865 code page instead of the 860 code page, you drop the number and insert a comma for the unchanged code pages. To change the 860 code page to the 865, you use the following command:

MODE CON CODEPAGE PREPARE = ((,865,) C:\EGA.CPI)

A more common example would be first using this command to load into memory the multilingual code page:

MODE CON CODEPAGE PREPARE = ((850) C:\EGA.CPI)

Later, you may want to add another code page to the list. For example, to add the 860 code page, you use the following command:

MODE CON CODEPAGE PREPARE = ((,860) C:\EGA.CPI)

Now the 850 or 860 code page can be used. Remember that the value for *<added_codepages>* given to DISPLAY.SYS must be at least 2 for this example to work and 3 for the preceding example to work.

Suppose that you give an incorrect code page number or give the name of an existing file that is not a code page information file. DOS displays the message `Font file contents invalid`. The code page at that position in the syntax line is removed from the list. Using the preceding example (which has the 850 and 860 code pages prepared), assume that you issue the following command:

> **MODE CON CODEPAGE PREPARE = ((,836) C:\EGA.CPI)**

DOS tells you that the code page file does not have the given font. The code page 836 cannot replace the code page in the second position, which was 860. However, 860 is removed from memory. To use 860, you must reload it with the MODE CODEPAGE PREPARE command.

Remember that the commands can be abbreviated, as in the following examples:

> **MODE CON CP PREP = (850, 863) C:\EGA.CPI**

> **MODE LPT1 CP PREP = (860, 863) C:\4201.CPI**

Activating Code Pages with MODE CODEPAGE SELECT

After code pages are prepared, they can be used. One command to activate the code pages is MODE CODEPAGE SELECT (the other is CHCP).

Cue:
If you do not want the same code page active on all devices, use MODE CODEPAGE SELECT.

CHCP is the preferred command for activating code pages. You can use CHCP to activate the code pages for DOS and all the devices at one time. CHCP also is easier to use than MODE CODEPAGE SELECT. Occasionally, however, you may not want the same code page active on all devices. Then you must use MODE CODEPAGE SELECT.

Suppose that you have edited a document with code page 437 and have started printing the document in the background. Now you want to edit another document. That document was created with the 850 code page. You need to use the 860 code page for the console (the display and keyboard).

If you use CHCP in this situation, you affect the display and the printer. Because you do not want that, your only choice is to use MODE CODEPAGE SELECT to switch fonts on the display.

You use the following syntax for MODE CODEPAGE SELECT:

> *dc:pathc***MODE** <device> **CODEPAGE SELECT** = <codepage>

dc:pathc is the optional drive and directory path to the MODE command. *<device>* is the name of the device whose code page is activated by MODE; device can be CON, LPTx, or PRN. *<codepage>* is the code page the device uses. *<codepage>* must be the hardware code page given to the appropriate device driver or one of the code pages given to the MODE CODEPAGE PREPARE command. One, and only one, code page can be given.

Using the MODE CODEPAGE SELECT command downloads the appropriate font to the device and activates the font. The device uses that font until you issue another MODE CODEPAGE SELECT or CHCP command, or until you turn off the device or restart DOS.

Ordinarily, you use one of the following forms for MODE CODEPAGE SELECT:

MODE CON CP SEL = <codepage>

MODE LPT1 CP SEL = <codepage>

For example, you enter the following:

MODE CON CP SEL = 860

Refreshing a Device's Memory with MODE CODEPAGE REFRESH

MODE CODEPAGE REFRESH reminds the device which font the device should be using. Generally, the command is not needed on the display unless a program has affected the screen in an undesirable manner. The command is used more frequently for the printer. If you turn the printer off and on again, the software code page is lost. DOS can lose track of the code page that the printer is using. The printer and DOS then must be resynchronized.

Reminder: MODE CODEPAGE REFRESH reminds the device which font it should use.

The MODE CODEPAGE REFRESH command reloads and activates any needed font. You use the following syntax for MODE CODEPAGE REFRESH:

*dc:pathc***MODE <device> CODEPAGE REFRESH**

<device> is the name of the device whose code page should be reestablished. Do not give a code page number. MODE uses the last code page used in the MODE CODEPAGE SELECT command.

To use MODE CODEPAGE REFRESH, you must have used MODE CODEPAGE PREPARE and MODE CODEPAGE SELECT for the device or the CHCP command. You can issue MODE CODEPAGE REFRESH as often as needed. The following are examples of the shorthand form of MODE CODEPAGE REFRESH:

MODE LPT1 CP REF

MODE CON CP REF

Checking Code Pages with MODE /STATUS

You can use the MODE /STATUS command to display code page information about a device. MODE /STATUS lists the following information:

- The number of the active code page, if any
- The number of the hardware code page
- The numbers of any prepared code pages

You use the following syntax for MODE /STATUS:

dc:pathc**MODE <device> CODEPAGE /STATUS**

<device> is the name of the device whose code page information you want displayed. Notice that this command is a switch. You must give the switch character (the slash), followed by the word **STATUS**.

The next examples display the output of the MODE/STATUS command for the console. DOS was started with the following command in the CONFIG.SYS file:

DEVICE = C:\DOS\DISPLAY.SYS CON = (EGA, 437, 4)

The DISPLAY.SYS file has been set up for an EGA or VGA display (EGA), a hardware code page of 437, and four additional code pages. The first two of the following commands establish two of the four code pages. The third command requests the code page status from DOS.

C>**MODE CON CODEPAGE PREP = (850, 860) C:\EGA.CPI**

C>**MODE CON CODEPAGE SELECT = 850**

C>**MODE CON CODEPAGE /STATUS**

DOS issues the following status report:

```
hardware codepages:
    Codepage 437
prepared codepages:
    Codepage 850
    Codepage 860
    Codepage not prepared
    Codepage not prepared
MODE Status Codepage function completed
```

The first MODE command sets up the console to use the 850 and 860 code pages, in addition to the 437 code page built into the display adapter. The second MODE command activates the 850 code page.

The first line of the MODE/STATUS command's report shows the active code page. The next two lines give the hardware code page based on the DISPLAY.SYS or PRINTER.SYS line in the CONFIG.SYS file. The lines that follow show the software code pages; the number of lines is based on the *added_codepages* number given to DISPLAY.SYS or PRINTER.SYS. If a code page is prepared, you see the number listed. The message Codepage not prepared indicates that additional areas for code pages are available.

You can use MODE/STATUS at any time. You get an error message, however, if the appropriate device driver has not been installed for the device. For the console, you can use the following abbreviated form for MODE/STATUS:

MODE CON CP /STA

For the first line printer, you can use the following form:

MODE LPT1 CP /STA

Solving Display Problems with GRAFTABL

A minor problem occurs in displaying non-English characters on the IBM Color Graphics Adapter (CGA). When you attempt to display characters in the ASCII range of 128 to 255 while in graphics mode, the characters are almost unreadable. Unfortunately, the non-English language characters are in the range of 128 to 255. This problem affects only the CGA. The problem occurs only in medium-resolution, 320-by-200, 4-color mode—not in normal alphanumeric text mode or in high-resolution, 640-by-200, 2-color mode.

To get a legible display in medium-resolution graphics mode, use the GRAFTABL command. GRAFTABL loads the alternative character set into the computer's memory and then directs the CGA to use this set when in graphics mode. The ASCII characters in the range of 128 to 255, therefore, are displayed legibly.

Reminder:
GRAFTABL provides a legible display in medium-resolution graphics mode.

You use the following syntax for GRAFTABL:

*dc:pathc***GRAFTABL**

The GRAFTABL command uses about 1,200 bytes of RAM. This memory remains trapped until you restart DOS or turn off the computer. Running GRAFTABL more than once wastes 1,200 bytes of memory each time you run the command. If a program that you frequently run requires GRAFTABL, add the command to your AUTOEXEC.BAT file.

With DOS Version 4, GRAFTABL was enhanced to support code page 850, the multilingual code page.

Using SELECT To Set Country Information

The utility program SELECT was extended in DOS 4.0 to enable you to install DOS 4.0 on a floppy disk or on your hard disk (the installation program for DOS 5.0 is named SETUP). Before Version 4, however, SELECT existed as a program with more limited capabilities.

In Version 3.x, SELECT is used solely to automate the selection of the country code and keyboard program. SELECT for versions of DOS before 3.2 destroys any previously established CONFIG.SYS and AUTOEXEC.BAT files. SELECT for Versions 3.2 and 3.3 runs FORMAT and destroys all the files on the disk. If you already have set up your disk, you should edit your existing CONFIG.SYS and AUTOEXEC.BAT files instead of running SELECT.

A Sample COUNTRY Setup

In the examples presented here, assume that you have a hard disk and that all the DOS program files are copied to a subdirectory called C:\DOS. Also assume that all SYS-extension files have been copied to C:\DOS. You can change the disk drive and path name to match your system. Floppy disk users should omit the path name and use A in place of C.

The examples are for DOS Version 3.3 and above only. Consult your DOS manual for the correct setup if you are using an earlier version of DOS.

Adding International Directives to CONFIG.SYS

To use the international features of DOS, start by adding the following line to your CONFIG.SYS file:

COUNTRY = 001, 437, C:\DOS\SYS\COUNTRY.SYS

If you have a PC Convertible LCD display, an EGA, or a VGA, use the following DEVICE = DISPLAY.SYS line:

DEVICE = C:\DOS\SYS\DISPLAY.SYS CON = (EGA, 437, 1)

This line sets up the display for the 437 code page and one additional code page.

For a monochrome display adapter, use the following line:

DEVICE = C:\DOS\SYS\DISPLAY.SYS CON = (MONO, 437, 0)

Remember that the number of additional code pages for a monochrome display adapter is always 0.

If you use ANSI.SYS, the DRIVER.SYS line must appear after the ANSI.SYS line. Reversing this order causes you to lose the features that ANSI.SYS offers.

If you have the IBM ProPrinter or the Quietwriter III, use PRINTER.SYS. For the ProPrinter, use the following line:

DEVICE = C:\DOS\SYS\PRINTER.SYS LPT1 = (4201, 437, 1)

This line sets up the ProPrinter for the first parallel port (LPT1), the 437 code page, and one additional code page.

In the preceding lines, if 437 is not your existing code page, use the existing code page and specify 2 instead of 1 for the additional code pages to be used. For example, the DISPLAY.SYS line appears as follows:

DEVICE = C:\DOS\SYS\DISPLAY.SYS CON = (EGA, 863, 2)

The code page 863 for French-speaking Canada is built into the adapter, and two additional code pages are to be used.

Remember that the CONFIG.SYS file must be in the root directory of the boot floppy disk or hard disk and that you must restart DOS before the change takes place.

Adding International Directives to AUTOEXEC.BAT

Add the following lines to the AUTOEXEC.BAT file of your start-up disk. If the start-up disk is a hard disk, place these additional commands after the line that holds your PATH command. When the commands occur after PATH, DOS finds the commands.

NLSFUNC

The INSTALL command also can be used to load NLSFUNC, KEYB, and other memory resident programs. See Chapter 14 for more information on the INSTALL command.

The next step is to use MODE CODEPAGE PREPARE on each device. If DISPLAY.SYS is installed, use the MODE CON CODEPAGE PREPARE command (abbreviated here):

MODE CON CP PREP = (850) C:\DOS\EGA.CPI

This command prepares the 850 code page for use with EGA/VGA-type displays. If your hardware code page is 437, use 850 as the prepared code page. If your hardware code page is not 437, use 850 and the existing code page:

MODE CON CP PREP = (850, 863) C:\DOS\EGA.CPI

This command adds the code page for French-speaking Canada to the multilingual code page.

If PRINTER.SYS is installed, use the MODE LPTx CODEPAGE PREPARE command. The line for the ProPrinter is the following:

MODE LPT1 CP PREP = (850) C:\DOS\4201.CPI

This line prepares the 850 code page for use with the ProPrinter Model 4201. If the hardware code page is not 437, you prepare the 850 but add another code page:

MODE LPT1 CP PREP = (850, 863) C:\DOS\4201.CPI

This line adds the code page for French-speaking Canada to the multilingual code page.

If you gave two hardware code pages for the Quietwriter III, you do not need to issue the MODE CODEPAGE PREPARE command for this printer. Otherwise, follow the same form for the ProPrinter but use 5202.CPI for the code page information file name.

After you add the commands to prepare the code pages, use the CHCP command to activate the pages. The CHCP command has the following syntax:

CHCP <codepage>

The command you type into your AUTOEXEC.BAT, therefore, is as follows:

CHCP 437

437 is the existing code page.

Finally, add a line to enable the switching of your keyboard. For this example, use the following line:

KEYB US,,C:\DOS\SYS\KEYBOARD.SYS

If you use KEYB frequently on the hard disk and follow the suggestion to copy the file to the root directory, add the following command to the AUTOEXEC.BAT file instead:

KEYB US,,C:\KEYBOARD.SYS

If you have a color graphics adapter and use medium-resolution graphics mode frequently, add the following line:

GRAFTABL

Now restart DOS and watch your display. If you see any error messages, check the lines in your CONFIG.SYS and AUTOEXEC.BAT files. You may have misspelled a command or forgotten to give the correct file name. Correct the mistake and try restarting DOS.

Chapter Summary

In this chapter, the following important points wre discussed:

- Code pages are font sets. Some code pages are built into hardware, and some are loadable from a file.

- You use the CONFIG.SYS COUNTRY directive to tell DOS which international country code and which code page to use.

- DOS adapts the format for the date and time depending on the country code.

- The DISPLAY.SYS device driver enables code page switching on some video displays.

- The PRINTER.SYS device driver enables code page switching on some printers.

- The NLSFUNC command provides additional functions that make DOS go international and enables the CHCP command to be used.

- The CHCP command switches code pages for DOS and all devices at one time.

- The MODE CODEPAGE subcommands load, activate, reselect, and display selected code pages.

- The KEYB command alters the keyboard for different languages.

- The GRAFTABL command enables you to display legibly non-English language characters and certain graphics characters when you use the color graphics adapter in medium-resolution mode.

17

Understanding QBasic

DOS 5 marks the debut of QBasic—a modern, feature-laden version of the popular programming language known as BASIC. Through the years, BASIC has enjoyed widespread use on large and small computers. Today, more people program with BASIC than with any other computer language.

The next two chapters introduce QBasic. This chapter has three principal objectives:

- To give you a perspective on what programming is all about

- To acquaint you with the QBasic programming environment

- To introduce you to a few short program examples

Chapter 18, "Programming with QBasic," explores the QBasic language in more depth.

If you have never programmed, try the introductory tutorials in the next two chapters. Programming is easier and more enjoyable than you may think. QBasic is an ideal language for beginners.

If you already have dabbled with another version of BASIC, learning QBasic will be a snap. QBasic builds on the features of earlier BASIC versions. In fact, most programs written in another version of BASIC run fine with QBasic.

Programming and BASIC

Before delving into the QBasic language, this section quickly reviews programming basics and the origins of BASIC. The chapter then explains where QBasic fits into BASIC's evolution.

Learning How To Program

Programmers have power—the power to make a computer do exactly what they want. By learning QBasic, you can write programs that perform an endless variety of useful tasks. The following are just a few programming tasks you may want to tackle:

- Track a hobby collection, such as a coin collection.

- Analyze sales for a business; plot graphs of trends.

- Design and play a computer game. The game may include music and color graphics.

- Compute solutions to mathematical and scientific problems.

Programming is creative, fun (most of the time), and challenging—a unique blend of art and skill. When your programs run properly, you enjoy a satisfying feeling of accomplishment.

QBasic is a modern version of BASIC, which was designed for novice programmers. In fact, the *B* in BASIC stands for *Beginners*. (BASIC is an acronym for Beginners All-purpose Symbolic Instruction Code.) QBasic retains the qualities that have always made BASIC an ideal first programming language.

QBasic is easy to learn for the following reasons:

- QBasic instructions are descriptive and English-like, making QBasic programs understandable and easy to read.

- QBasic provides immediate feedback. When you run a program, the computer executes your instructions and produces results.

- QBasic is interactive, providing built-in help. When an error occurs, QBasic immediately reports the error with an informative message. Often, you can quickly correct the problem and resume your program.

Defining a Program

A *program* is a series of instructions written according to the rules of a programming language. A QBasic program, therefore, is a series of instructions written in the QBasic language.

A program is a series of instructions written for a computer to perform. The computer executes the instructions, and if all goes well, you end up with a successful and useful program.

QBasic *runs* a program when you have QBasic execute the instructions that comprise the program. Essentially, QBasic is a translator. QBasic translates the instructions of your program into machine-level instructions that the computer understands. After your program is translated, the processor chip in your computer executes the machine-level instructions.

Understanding the Evolution of QBasic

The original BASIC was developed in the mid-1960s at Dartmouth College by professors John Kemeny and Thomas Kurtz. Kemeny and Kurtz designed BASIC to be a vehicle for teaching programming. BASIC, therefore, has English-like commands, is easy to use, and requires no specialized hardware knowledge.

BASIC always has been popular on microcomputers. On IBM computers, earlier versions of DOS (1, 2, 3, and 4) included a form of BASIC called *BASICA* or *GW-BASIC*. (BASICA and GW-BASIC are identical. BASICA runs on true IBM computers; GW-BASIC runs on compatibles.)

BASICA and GW-BASIC were not suited for large programming tasks. Many professional programmers turned to more contemporary, structured programming languages such as C and Pascal.

In the late 1980s, Microsoft introduced QuickBASIC. This new version of BASIC is sold as a separate product. QuickBASIC is built from the core language of BASICA and GW-BASIC, but QuickBASIC adds modern structured-language enhancements. QuickBASIC also contains a sleek user interface with full-screen editing and pull-down menus. QuickBASIC again made BASIC a state-of-the-art language.

With the arrival of DOS 5, Microsoft abandoned BASICA and GW-BASIC in favor of QBasic. QBasic is a slightly stripped down version of QuickBASIC.

QBasic and QuickBASIC, although similar, are not identical. If you become a serious QBasic programmer, you may consider purchasing QuickBASIC. The end of the Chapter 18 provides more information about QuickBASIC.

Understanding the Features of QBasic

QBasic provides a complete BASIC programming environment. The major features of the QBasic environment are as follows:

- Compatibility with IBM BASICA and Microsoft's GW-BASIC

- A smoothly integrated environment boasting a full-screen editor, a file manager, and debugging tools—all accessible through pull-down menus

- Fast execution time for programs

- Modern language enhancements, such as user-defined procedures, local variables, and block structures, which bring structured programming to BASIC

- A smart editor that finds syntax errors as you type and reformats instructions into a standardized appearance

- Built-in help

- Support for most hardware peripherals, including a mouse, math coprocessor, and color video (CGA, EGA, and VGA)

Using QBasic

Even if you have no programming experience, you can become a QBasic programmer within a few minutes.

In this section, you learn to do the following:

- Start QBasic

- Type and edit a short program

- Run the program

- Use the QBasic editor

- Save the program to disk

Invoking QBasic

QBasic comes bundled with DOS 5 in a file named QBASIC.EXE. By installing DOS 5 on your computer system, you automatically install QBasic. You can start QBasic from the DOS Shell or from the command line.

If you are running the DOS Shell, you select QBasic from the main menu as follows:

1. Use the Tab key to move the highlight to the main window at the bottom of the screen.

2. Highlight MS-DOS QBasic by moving the cursor with the up- and down-arrow keys. Press Enter.

3. Press Enter again when the QBasic File window appears in the center of the screen. (For now, don't type a file name to retrieve or create a file.)

If you are working from the command line, type **QBASIC** at the DOS prompt. (The DOS prompt is typically C> on hard drive systems.)

If you have DOS installed in a directory not included in a PATH statement of your AUTOEXEC.BAT file, you first need to make that directory the current directory. Use a CD command such as the following:

> **CD \DOS**

If you have DOS installed in a directory with a name other than DOS, use your directory name (and path) instead of DOS as shown here.

> *Note:* If you run QBasic on a computer system with a color video adapter and a black-and-white monitor (many laptop computers have this configuration), you invoke QBasic from the DOS command line by using the /B parameter as follows to get a readable display:
>
> C>**QBASIC /B**

No matter which method you choose, QBasic now initializes. A preliminary screen appears as shown in figure 17.1.

You now have two choices: you can press Enter or Esc.

- Pressing Enter invokes the QBasic Survival Guide, which provides help with using QBasic. (Refer to the discussion of the Help system later in this chapter.)

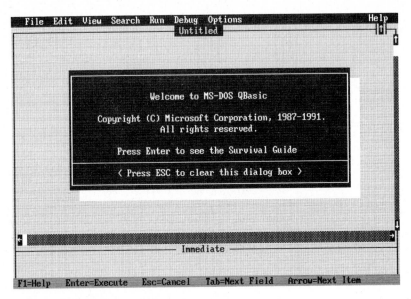

Fig. 17.1. *The preliminary QBasic screen.*

- Pressing Esc clears the box in the center of the screen and prepares the editor for working on a QBasic program.

Press Esc. You now have a blank editor screen and can begin QBasic programming. Your screen should look like figure 17.2.

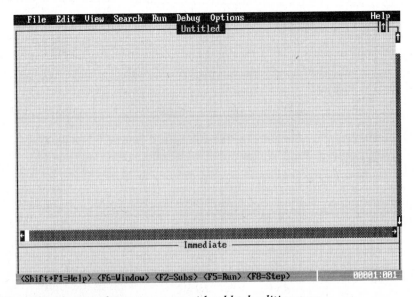

Fig. 17.2. *The initial QBasic screen with a blank editing area.*

Getting Acquainted with the QBasic Editor

If you already know the DOS Editor, you will have no trouble learning the QBasic editor. The QBasic editor and the DOS Editor share the same look and feel. Both editors use the same operating environment, with full-screen editing and similar pull-down menus. Editing techniques, mouse commands, and shortcut keys are the same.

This chapter assumes that you have a working familiarity with the DOS Editor. You should know the fundamental techniques of using the menu system, performing full-screen editing, and saving and loading files. If you do not, please review Chapter 11, "Using the DOS Editor," before continuing with this chapter.

The major difference between the QBasic and DOS editors is that the QBasic editor is adapted for working with programs, but the DOS Editor is designed for generic text documents. The QBasic menu system adds commands for running a program, viewing output, and debugging errors. In addition, the QBasic editor checks what you type for conformity with proper QBasic syntax.

> *Note:* In essence, the QBASIC and DOS editors are similar because they share the same QBASIC.EXE file. DOS 5 furnishes QBasic in QBASIC.EXE, which includes the QBasic programming language and the QBasic editor.
>
> The DOS Editor is actually a stripped-down version of the QBasic editor. When you run the DOS Editor, the computer activates the QBASIC.EXE file, extracts the editor from the file, and discards the part of the editor that applies only to QBasic programming.

The QBasic editor has many features available through pull-down menus. Take a moment to look at figure 17.2. Table 17.1 explains the main items that you see.

Entering Your First Program

When you initialize QBasic, the full-screen editor is in control, enabling you to type a program immediately. With the editor, you enter and modify QBasic programs directly from the keyboard.

Table 17.1
Components of the QBasic Editor Screen

Item	Description
Menu bar	The line along the top of the screen that displays the available menus: File, Edit, View, and so on
Title bar	The short centered bar just below the menu bar, that contains the name of the current program
Status bar	The line along the bottom of the screen that describes information about the process at hand and shows certain shortcut key options
Scroll bars	The two strips—a vertical strip along the right edge and a horizontal strip just above the word Immediate—with a matte-like appearance; used with a mouse (see the description later in this chapter)
View window	The large boxed area where the text of your program appears
Immediate window	The boxed area bounded on the top by the word Immediate and on the bottom by the information bar; directly executes QBasic instructions, as explained in Chapter 18
Cursor	The flashing underscore character that indicates where the next character you type will be displayed

Note the blinking cursor near the upper left corner of the View window. Type the following one-line program, substituting your name for *John Doe*. Don't forget the two quotation marks.

PRINT "This program was written by John Doe"

You don't have to press Enter at the end of this line, but you can.

If you make any typing errors, you can edit the line just as you edit with the DOS Editor. (Use the cursor-movement keys to move the cursor to the error; then insert new characters or delete characters with the Del key.)

Running a Program and Viewing Output

You have just typed a complete QBasic program, even though it is just one line. This short program consists of a single PRINT instruction. A PRINT instruction commands QBasic to display on-screen the message contained between the two quotation marks.

To run the program, you need to invoke the Run menu. Follow these steps:

1. Press Alt-R to open the Run menu (see fig. 17.3).

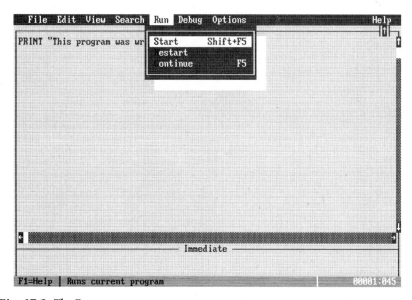

***Fig. 17.3.** The Run menu.*

2. Note that the highlight bar is on Start when the Run menu opens. Press Enter to select Start. The program begins execution.

   The screen clears and then shows the output of your program. Your screen should look similar to the screen shown in figure 17.4. When a program runs, QBasic clears the editor screen and switches the display to the output screen.

   QBasic displays the text message contained between the quotation marks of your PRINT instruction. You have successfully run a QBasic program.

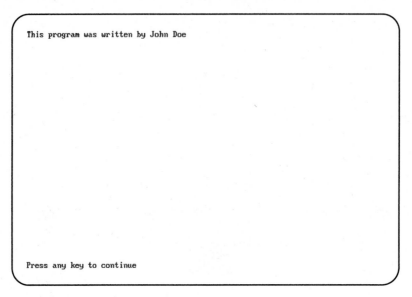

Fig. 17.4. Output from the one-line program.

3. Look along the bottom edge of your screen. After running a program, QBasic displays the following message at the bottom of the output screen:

   ```
   Press any key to continue
   ```

   Press a key, and the editor screen is back in control.

4. Press F4.

   The screen display switches back to the output screen. When you are in the editor, you can view the output screen by selecting the Output Screen command from the View menu or by pressing the F4 shortcut key.

5. Press any key to return to the editor.

6. Press Shift-F5.

   This shortcut key is equivalent to selecting Start from the Run menu. By pressing Shift-F5, you run your program a second time. Note that a second copy of your output appears on the output window below the first copy. QBasic does not blank the output screen between successive runs of a program. (As the next chapter explains, you can blank the output screen with a CLS program instruction.)

To run a program, you can press the Shift-F5 shortcut key or select Start from the Run menu.

7. Press any key to return to the editor.

Saving a Program

You save a program file with the QBasic editor in the same way you save a text file with the DOS Editor. Follow these steps:

1. Invoke the File menu by pressing Alt-F.

2. Move the highlight to Save As.

3. Press Enter. A dialog box opens for you to type the name of the file.

4. Type **myname**. You can type the file name in lower- or uppercase letters. The dialog box indicates the path to the directory where the file is to be saved. You can change this path by including a new path when you type the file name.

5. Press Enter to save the program on disk.

Your screen now should look like figure 17.5. The program name appears as MYNAME.BAS in the title bar.

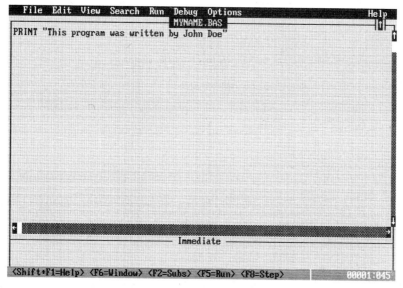

Fig. 17.5. The program is saved to disk.

If you don't specify an extension, QBasic adds the BAS extension to the file name. This default extension indicates that the file is a QBasic program.

An Overview of the Menu Commands

You use the QBasic editor when you type or run a program. This editor features a pull-down menu system from which various editing commands are available. Table 17.2 presents an overview of the editor's main menus.

Table 17.2
Overview of the Main Menu

Menu option	Major features
File	Loads and saves program files; prints a program listing
Edit	Cuts and pastes text; creates user-defined procedures
View	Displays pieces of a program and program output
Search	Finds and replaces specified text
Run	Executes a program
Debug	Debugs a program
Options	Reconfigures environment options
Help	Displays on-line help

You should be familiar with most of these menus because the DOS Editor has several identical menus (see Chapter 11). A few of the menus in table 17.2 are new to QBasic, however, and some menus contain new features. The following list gives you a quick look at each QBasic menu, comparing that menu's features to the same menu of the DOS Editor:

- File. Same features.

- Edit. Same cutting and pasting features but adds features for editing user-defined subprograms and functions. See the next chapter for a brief discussion of subprograms and functions.

- View. A new menu that enables you to control what the editor screen displays. You can view subprograms and functions, display program output, or split the screen into two windows.

- Search. Same features.

- Run. A new menu from which you can run your program or restart a program that has been temporarily interrupted.

- Debug. A new menu that contains special features for tracking down programming errors.

- Options. Same features but adds an option to control whether the editor checks the syntax of typed program lines.

- Help. Similar on-line help features but adds the capability to display context-sensitive help on individual keywords in the QBasic language.

Navigating the Menu System

You navigate the QBasic menu system as you navigate the DOS Editor menu system. The Alt key, dialog boxes, shortcut keys, mouse, Esc key, and other features work in the same way.

The DOS Editor's shortcut keys and mouse commands work in QBasic. However, the QBasic editor includes additional shortcut keys that invoke features unique to the QBasic editor. Table 17.3 presents the complete list of QBasic shortcut keys.

Table 17.3
Shortcut Keys and Mouse Commands

Shortcut key	Effect	Mouse
F1	Show help on keyword or topic	Click right button on keyword in program
Shift-F1	Show help on using help	Click Using Help (Help menu)
Ctrl-F1	View next topic in help file	Click <Next> (status bar)
Alt-F1	Review most recently viewed help screen	Click <Back> (status bar)

continues

Table 17.3 *(continued)*

Shortcut key	*Effect*	*Mouse*
Shift-Ctrl-F1	View preceding topic in help file	None
F2	Display loaded procedures	Click SUBs (View menu)
Shift-F2	Display next procedure	None
Ctrl-F2	Display preceding procedure	None
F3	Repeat the last Find	Click Repeat Last Find (Search menu)
F4	View the output screen	Click Output Screen (View menu)
F5	Continue program execution	Click Continue (Run menu)
Shift-F5	Start program execution	Click Start (Run menu)
F6	Make next window active	Click inside desired window
Shift-F6	Make preceding window active	Click inside desired window
F7	Execute program up to cursor position	None
F8	Execute next instruction (single step)	Click Step (Debug menu)
F9	Toggle breakpoint on/off	Click Toggle Breakpoint (Debug menu)
F10	Execute next instruction (procedure step)	Click Procedure Step (Debug menu)
Ctrl-F10	Enlarge active window/ Restore split screen	Double-click title bar/click maximize icon
Shift-Del	Cut selected text	Click Cut (Edit menu)

Shortcut key	Effect	Mouse
Ctrl-Ins	Copy selected text	Click Copy (Edit menu)
Shift-Ins	Paste text from clipboard	Click Paste (Edit menu)
Del	Erase selected text	Click Clear (Edit menu)
Ctrl-Q-A	Change text	Click Change (Search menu)
Ctrl-Q-F	Search for text string	Click Find (Search menu)
Esc	Terminate Help system	Click <Cancel> (status bar)
Alt	Enter menu-selection mode	None
Alt-+	Enlarge active window	Drag title bar up
Alt-–	Shrink active window	Drag title bar down
Up	Scroll line up	Click up arrow
Down	Scroll line down	Click down arrow
PgUp	Scroll page up	None
PgDn	Scroll page down	None
Ctrl-Home	Scroll to top of window	None
Ctrl-End	Scroll to bottom of window	None

Using Shortcut Keys and Mouse Commands

Table 17.3 lists the shortcut keys and mouse techniques available from the QBasic editor. Most of these shortcut keys are the same as those used with the DOS Editor. Shortcuts new to QBasic use the F2, F4, F5, F7, F8, F9, and F10 keys. The F2 shortcut key manipulates procedures, user-defined sub-programs, and functions. (Procedures are discussed briefly in the next chapter.) The F4 shortcut key switches the video display between the editor screen and the program output screen. The F5 shortcut key runs a program. The F7 through F10 shortcut keys invoke special debugging techniques found on the Debug menu. Space restrictions prohibit a detailed description of the Debug menu, but the shortcut keys are listed here for reference.

Understanding QBasic Fundamentals

The following program is only a little more complicated than the simple one-line program you ran earlier:

```
10 PRINT "HELLO"
20 END
```

You probably already have guessed that this program displays the message HELLO and then ends. Note the following differences between this program and the similar one-line program you tried earlier:

- Each line begins with a number.

- An END instruction appears.

Using Line Numbers

This two-line sample program has a *line number* at the start of each line. Older versions of BASIC (such as BASICA and GW-BASIC) require a line number on every line. With newer BASICs, such as QBasic, line numbers are optional. When you write programs, you can omit line numbers; you can number only the lines that need numbers; or for compatibility with older BASIC programs, you can number every line.

Using END

The program's second line ends the program. Actually, the END instruction is not required by QBasic, so you can leave it off. (Recall that the first one-line program did not have an END instruction.)

QBasic is smart enough to realize that your program ends after the final line. Sometimes the structure of a program requires an internal END instruction to terminate the program before the last instruction executes.

The next chapter gives some examples of programs that use an END instruction.

Understanding Reserved Words (Keywords)

PRINT and END are two examples of QBasic's *reserved words*. The vocabulary of QBasic includes approximately two hundred reserved words. Each reserved word causes QBasic to take a particular action. You construct meaningful program instructions by using reserved words (along with other program components). Another term for a reserved word is *keyword*.

Understanding the Smart Editor

To get to know the QBasic editor better, try typing the two-line program. Follow these steps:

1. If you have an old program in the editor, you first must erase the old program by using the New command from the File menu.

2. Type the first line of the program as follows, with all uppercase letters:

   10 PRINT "HELLO"

   Don't forget the quotation marks around *HELLO*. (If you make any typing mistakes, move to the error using the arrow keys and retype. You can delete characters with the Del key.) After typing the line, press Enter. The cursor moves down a row and back to the leftmost column in anticipation of your next typed line.

3. Type the second line of the program, this time with lowercase letters:

   20 end

4. Press Enter. Notice that *end* changes to uppercase letters.

The QBasic editor reformats your typed program instructions according to a set style, capitalizing all keywords. You can type keywords such as END and PRINT in uppercase, lowercase, or even mixed (*PRinT*, for example), and the editor converts them all into uppercase letters.

Text between quotation marks, however, is preserved exactly the way you type it. This distinction means that you can display HELLO, Hello, hello, or even HeLLO. This book shows QBasic's reserved words in uppercase for compatibility with the editor's formatting.

This smart editor is one of the major differences between the QBasic editor and the DOS Editor. In QBasic, the editor assumes that you are creating a program. Every time you type a line, the editor checks for legal QBasic syntax and corrects minor errors. Many other syntax errors result in a diagnostic message when you press Enter. Usually the message tells you exactly what is wrong, indicating a missing keyword or punctuation symbol, for example. Some errors, however, are not caught until you try to run the program.

The editor also manipulates your typed instructions into a standardized format: keywords in uppercase, one space between operators, and so on. You become more familiar with this formatting as you follow the exercises in the next section and the program examples in the next chapter. The editor is superbly adapted to the creation of QBasic programs.

Typing a Program

When you type a line and press Enter (or move the cursor off a line with an arrow key), QBasic examines the line you just typed for the following characteristics:

- Syntax. *Syntax* refers to the way the various language components are put together to form a program instruction. QBasic has set syntax rules so that each program instruction must conform to this syntax.

- Format. Each line of your program must conform to a standard format—keywords in uppercase, one space between operators, and so on.

- Consistency. The editor checks for consistency and makes corrections. All occurrences of the same variable name, for example, are adjusted to a consistent upper- and lowercase lettering.

Try the following exercise to get better acquainted with the smart editor:

1. Type **print"Hello** exactly as shown and press Enter.

    QBasic converts the line to PRINT "Hello".

The keyword PRINT is capitalized. Standard format requires a space after PRINT. The editor also caught and corrected the missing trailing quotation mark, a minor syntax error.

2. Type **PRINT 0.3** and press Enter.

   QBasic converts the line to `PRINT .3`.

   QBasic has a standard format for displaying numbers. The editor automatically converts numbers you type to the standard format.

3. Type **MYAGE=32** and press Enter.

   The editor adds a space before and after the equal sign so that the line reads `MYAGE = 32`. Standard format requires a space on each side of an equal sign or any other operator symbol.

   In this instruction, *MYAGE* is a variable assigned the value 32. Don't worry if you don't understand what a variable is. Variables are explained in the next chapter. The purpose here is only to demonstrate how the editor works.

4. Type **PRINT MyAge** and press Enter. Note the combination of upper- and lowercase letters in the variable name MyAge. Nothing happens to this line, but look at the preceding line, which now reads `MyAge = 32`.

   For consistency, when you type a variable name in a program line, QBasic adjusts all other occurrences of the same variable name to conform with the new upper- and lowercase form.

5. Type **PRINT SQR(25(** and press Enter. Note that both parentheses are left parentheses. (SQR is the square-root function, explained in the next chapter with other functions.)

   A dialog box opens with a message warning you of a syntax error (see fig. 17.6). QBasic expects the second parenthesis to be a right parenthesis; instead, you typed a left parenthesis. In your program, notice that the editor has highlighted the incorrect left parenthesis.

6. Press Enter to close the dialog box. The cursor returns to your program at the location of the error.

7. To correct the error, press Del and then type). Then press Enter.

When an error-message dialog box opens, you do not have to correct the error. After you close the dialog box, you can move the cursor off the questioned line. If you don't correct the error, you get an error message when you try to run the program.

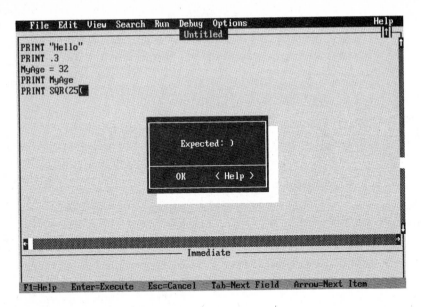

Fig. 17.6. *A diagnostic dialog box.*

Printing a Program Listing

Your computer system probably includes a printer—perhaps a dot-matrix, daisywheel, or laser printer. Hardcopy program listings provide a convenient way to study programs, mark changes, and discuss your programs with others.

Follow these steps to generate a printed listing while working with a program in the editor. You can print selected text or the complete program.

1. Select the File option from the Main menu (Alt-F).

2. Select Print (use cursor keys or press P) to open the Print dialog box (see fig. 17.7).

3. Choose one of the three available options. (Use cursor keys or the highlighted shortcut key.)

   The Selected Text Only option prints only the selected text in the active window. (Chapter 11 explains how to select text.)

   The Current Window option prints the entire contents of the active window, not just what appears on-screen. The active window can be the main program, a help screen, or a SUB or FUNCTION procedure.

The Entire Program option prints the entire program (the main program, subprograms, and user-defined functions). This option is the default (when no text is selected).

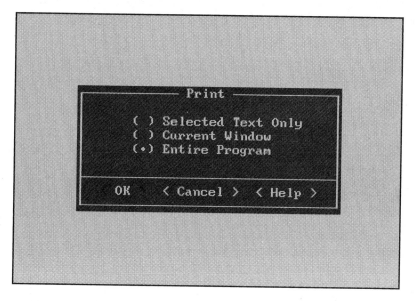

Fig. 17.7. The Print dialog box.

4. Press Enter to begin printing. Be sure that your printer is turned on and is on-line.

Loading a Program When Starting QBasic

You can load a previously saved program into the editor at the same time that you invoke QBasic. The technique depends on whether you are starting QBasic from the DOS Shell or from the command line.

When starting QBasic from the DOS Shell, first select MS-DOS QBasic from the DOS Shell menu. The QBASIC File dialog box opens with the message QBasic File? prompting you to supply a file name. Type your desired file name, including the path if the file is not located in the default directory. Then press Enter; you invoke QBasic with your designated file loaded into the editor.

When starting QBasic from the command line, type **qbasic** followed by the desired file name at the DOS prompt, leaving a blank space between **qbasic** and the file name. Include the path if the file is not in the current directory. For example, type the following line to invoke QBasic with the file \SALES\MYPROG.BAS loaded into the editor:

C>**qbasic \sales\myprog**

The following notes apply whether you try this technique from the DOS Shell or from the command line:

- QBasic assumes the extension BAS if you don't specify an explicit extension as part of your file name.

- QBasic initializes directly without taking the intermediate step of asking whether you want to see the help material in the on-screen Survival Guide.

- If QBasic cannot find the specified file, the program assumes that you want to create a program with that name. Accordingly, QBasic initializes with a fresh editing slate that includes your designated file name in the title bar. After typing the program, you can save the file directly with the Save command. (You don't need to use Save As and specify the file name a second time.)

> *Note:* You can load a BASICA or GW-BASIC program into the QBasic environment only if the program is stored in ASCII format. QBasic cannot read the standard files saved with BASICA or GW-BASIC. To save a BASICA or GW-BASIC file in ASCII format, use the A parameter with the SAVE command in BASICA or GW-BASIC, for example:
>
> **SAVE "MYPROG.BAS", A**
>
> Consult your BASICA or GW-BASIC documentation for details.

Using the Help System

QBasic provides extensive on-line help through the Help menu (see fig. 17.8). Help screens include information on QBasic keywords, shortcut keys, editing techniques, programming topics, error handling, and even on using the Help system.

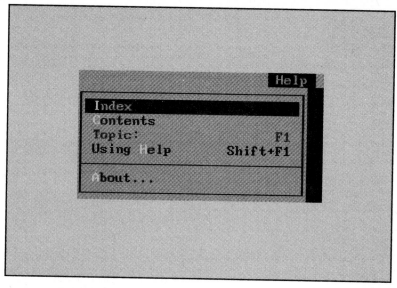

Fig. 17.8. The Help menu.

Five options for help are available from the Help menu:

- Index provides an alphabetical list of QBasic keywords about which you can request help.

- Contents has a functionally grouped collection of help information, including an orientation, a shortcut key list, tips on using QBasic, and a Quick Reference.

- Topic provides context-sensitive help for the keyword at the current cursor location. Alternatively, while editing, you can place the cursor on any keyword and then press F1 to get help for that keyword.

- Using Help has information about how to use the Help system.

- About shows the QBasic version number and copyright information.

The following are some general notes on using the Help system:

- Help screens open in a separate window. The title bar of this window shows the Help topic on display.

- To get help on a specific QBasic keyword, select the Index option from the Help menu. Type the first letter of the keyword for which you want help. The screen shows a list of all keywords beginning with that letter. Move the cursor to the keyword for which you want help and press Enter or F1.

- The F1 key provides express help about any keyword while you are programming. To get help on a keyword, place the cursor on the keyword anywhere in your program. Then press F1 (or select Topic from the Help menu).

- To get help about a general programming subject, select Contents from the Help menu. Press Tab to move the cursor to the topic for which you want help. Press Enter or F1.

- To get help about an error when an error message occurs, move the cursor to the <Help> option in the error message box and press Enter.

- To start the Help system at any time, press Shift-F1. This shortcut key provides help on using Help. Alternatively, you can select Using Help from the Help menu.

- To browse through all the help screens, press Shift-F1 and then press Ctrl-F1 repeatedly.

- To scroll any particular help screen, press PgUp or PgDn.

- When Help is active, the help screens open in a separate window. You can move the cursor between the Help, View, and Immediate windows by pressing F6 (or Shift-F6).

- Help screens for individual keywords often include sample program fragments demonstrating typical uses of that keyword. You can cut and paste these program lines directly from a help screen into your own program. Select the program lines on the help screen using the normal editing keys. Copy the selected lines to the clipboard. Then press F6 repeatedly until your program window becomes active. Paste the lines into your program using the normal editing keys. You now can reactivate the help screen by pressing F6 as many times as necessary.

- When the Help system is active, as in all QBasic contexts, the status bar at the bottom of the screen shows useful keystrokes. If a command on the status bar is enclosed by angle brackets, you can select that command by pressing the indicated keystroke or by clicking the mouse with the mouse cursor on the command name in the status bar.

- When you invoke QBasic, a dialog box opens, giving you the option of seeing the Survival Guide. Press Enter to see the guide. This action activates the Help system and shows a help screen displaying information about using QBasic and the Help system.

- QBasic stores the help screen information in QBASIC.HLP. To use the Help system, QBasic must have access to this file. QBasic searches for this help file in the current directory or in directories specified by the PATH statements of your AUTOEXEC.BAT file. If the help file is located outside your PATH specifications, you can supply QBasic with the path to the QBASIC.HLP file by selecting the Help Path command on the Options menu.

- To close the Help window and exit the Help system, press Esc.

Chapter Summary

QBasic is a full-featured version of the BASIC programming language. QBasic is ideal for beginning programmers because the language combines descriptive, English-like syntax with a highly interactive programming environment. In this chapter, you learned the following concepts:

- How to start QBasic

- How to write simple QBasic programs

- How to write programs that create customized software

- How to interact with the editor

- How the editor reformats your typed program lines to conform with a set style

- How to print a program listing

The next chapter explores QBasic programming topics in considerably more depth.

18

Programming with QBasic

You are no longer a QBasic novice. If you tried the short exercises in the preceding chapter, you already understand the essentials of creating and running a program. You know that a PRINT instruction can make QBasic display a message on the video screen. You are familiar with PRINT and END, two keywords used to construct QBasic programs.

PRINT and END, however, are only two of approximately 200 available QBasic keywords. This chapter introduces several other keywords and explores various topics of QBasic programming.

This chapter is designed to provide a sound introduction to QBasic programming, with an emphasis on the fundamental topics. This chapter examines several keywords and teaches you the important rules of constructing programs.

The following topics are introduced in this chapter:

- On-screen displays

- Strings

- Variables and arrays

- Loops

- Logic flow

- Error correction

- Graphics

- Functions

- Subroutines

Like all computer languages, QBasic is designed so that programmers can tell computers what to do. In its original form, BASIC is one of the simplest computer languages. The addition of many features over the years has caused many BASIC versions, such as QBasic, to become relatively sophisticated. Fortunately, QBasic's core of instructions remains simple, and that core is primarily what this chapter covers.

> *Note:* Some people are convinced before they start that they never will understand how to program a computer—that they cannot learn to write simple programs. If you are one of these people, don't be afraid. You don't need to be a technical genius, or even mathematically inclined, to use QBasic.

Understanding Fundamentals

To begin, type the following program into the QBasic editor. (If you already have a program in the editor, use the New command from the Run menu to erase the existing program.)

```
PRINT "Please enter your name"
INPUT YourName$
PRINT "Hello, "; YourName$
```

You may notice immediately that this program contains no line numbers. Line numbers are optional. When running a program, unless you specify otherwise, QBasic executes the lines of a program one after another in top-to-bottom sequence.

A new keyword in the preceding program is *INPUT*. INPUT instructions request that the user provide some input while the program is running.

Introducing Variables

The INPUT instruction in the preceding example contains a *variable* named *YourName$*. A variable is a name you give to a memory location where data is stored. The value of the data can (and usually does) change while the program is running. By referencing a variable, you are saying to the computer, "Use whatever value I currently have stored in the memory location reserved for that variable." Some QBasic instructions change the value of a variable; other instructions only retrieve and use the value.

A variable enables a program to perform a different task each time the program is run, depending on the value assigned to the variable. The variable in the preceding program asks for the user's name, which may be almost anything.

The dollar sign in the *YourName$* variable is important. The dollar sign indicates the variable type. QBasic categorizes data into two fundamentally different types: numeric data and string, or text, data. Accordingly, QBasic variables fall into the following two fundamental categories, depending on which kind of data the variable can store:

- *Numeric variables* store numeric data, values such as 14, 33.8, and so on. You can change the value stored in a numeric variable, but the value always must be a number.

- *String variables* store text data, words, or phrases such as "Hello," "Indiana Jones," or "76 trombones." You can change the value stored in a string variable, but the value always must be text data.

Every variable is a numeric or a string variable. A dollar sign at the end of a variable name indicates that the variable is a string variable. Data stored in a string variable is alphanumeric pieces of data (letters, numbers, and other characters) strung together in any desired length. The data in a string variable is treated as a sequence of text characters, whether those characters are letters, digits, or symbols.

A variable name that does not end with a dollar sign is a numeric variable. *YourName* is a numeric variable. Consequently, *YourName* stores a numeric quantity. *YourName* and *YourName$* can coexist in the same program, but they are two distinct variables, each storing different information.

Reminder:
A variable is the name of a memory location.

Reminder:
Variable names without a $ are numeric.

Note: Variable names must follow certain rules, which have evolved over the years. Old BASIC versions allow only one- or two-character names, but newer versions allow much longer, descriptive names.

QBasic permits variable names of up to 40 characters. The first character of each variable name must be a letter. Subsequent characters, if any, can be letters, numbers, and certain special characters.

Most versions of BASIC, including QBasic, treat upper- and lower-case letters of variable names as if they were identical. For example, *YOURNAME$*, *YourName$*, and *yourname$* are treated as the same variable, not as three different variables.

Introducing Literals

Reminder:
A literal is any data value expressed explicitly.

In QBasic, a *literal* is any data value expressed explicitly (as opposed to a data value expressed by the value stored in a variable). Two types of literals exist: numeric and string. A *numeric literal* is a number written with numeric digits in the conventional manner, such as 321 or 13.65. A *string literal* is a sequence of text characters, such as "Elvis" or "Hello out there."

In QBasic, you place quotation marks around a string literal. The quotation marks signify that the enclosed text constitutes a string literal and not a variable name, reserved word, or other construct. In the preceding chapter, you used string literals in PRINT instructions to display messages on-screen.

Using INPUT

Again consider the following program:

```
PRINT "Please enter your name"
INPUT YourName$
PRINT "Hello, "; YourName$
```

The contents of the variable *YourName$* depend on what you type when you are prompted by the INPUT instruction. When you run the preceding program and type your name as a response, the following output appears on-screen (if your name is Michael, that is):

```
Please enter your name
? Michael
Hello, Michael
```

The first line of the program is no mystery. The PRINT instruction directs QBasic to display on-screen the message Please enter your name.

The computer then displays a question mark at the beginning of the next output line. This question mark is a prompt character produced by the INPUT instruction in the second line of the program. The program is prompting the user for input. INPUT, like PRINT and END, is a QBasic keyword.

In the preceding example, the user typed **Michael** and pressed Enter. The INPUT instruction then stores the text string *Michael* into the string variable *YourName$*.

Displaying the Value of String Variables

The PRINT instruction in the third line of the program directs QBasic to display the message Hello, Michael. The PRINT instruction in this example demonstrates PRINT's flexibility. The instruction displays the string literal ("Hello, ") and the value of the variable *YourName$*—Michael.

Using Spaces and Semicolon Separators

Look back at the third line of the program. Did you notice the space after the comma that follows Hello? If you don't type a space after the comma, no space appears between the comma and the user's name in the output.

In the third program line, a semicolon separates the items to be printed. A semicolon tells QBasic to leave no additional spaces in the output. Try changing the number of spaces after the comma to see how the output's spacing changes. You may try rerunning the program and typing other names.

Cue:
A semicolon tells QBasic not to leave spaces.

Assigning Values to Variables

QBasic provides many ways of assigning a value to a variable. The preceding program demonstrates one way: an INPUT instruction that assigns a string value to a string variable. (In the preceding program, *YourName$* is a string variable, and the user types the string value to be assigned to *YourName$*.)

The most straightforward assignment method, however, uses the equal sign to assign a value to a variable. You place the variable name on the left of the equal sign and the value to be assigned on the right.

For example, try the following program:

```
MyName$ = "Jack Benny"
MyAge = 39
PRINT MyName$
PRINT "is"
PRINT MyAge
```

Running this program produces the following output:

```
Jack Benny
is
39
```

The first two lines assign values to the variables *MyName$* and *MyAge*, respectively. Instructions that directly assign values to variables are *assignment instructions*. Assignment instructions work equally well for string and numeric variables.

Caution:
Assign numeric values to numeric variables.

You must be careful, however, to assign only numeric values to numeric variables and only string values to string variables. The following two instructions are improper:

```
MyName$ = 25
MyAge = "Teenager"
```

The first line of instruction attempts to assign a numeric value to a string variable, and the second line does the reverse.

Note: What happens if you run a program containing an illegal assignment instruction? When running the program, QBasic catches the error, returns to the editor, and displays an informative error message. Press Enter to remove the message box so that you can correct the incorrect instruction.

Assignment instructions occur frequently in QBasic programs. The right side of assignment instructions can be simple (as in the preceding examples) or elaborate. Sometimes the right side of the equal sign contains expressions involving several terms.

By default, QBasic assigns an initial value of 0 to each numeric variable. If you display (with PRINT) the value of a numeric variable that has not been assigned a value, you get 0 as the result. For example, the following program prints the values of the numeric variables A, B, and C:

```
A = 1
C = 3
PRINT A
PRINT B
PRINT C
```

The result is

```
1
0
3
```

The value of B prints as 0 (the default value) because the program assigns no other value to the variable.

Clearing the Screen with CLS

QBasic does not automatically clear the output screen when you run a new program. As you run programs, the output screen can become cluttered. For example, if you run the one-line program PRINT "Hello" repeatedly, the output screen becomes full of Hello messages.

A CLS instruction clears the output screen. A PRINT instruction that follows a CLS instruction displays output in the upper left corner of a blank screen. Try running the following program a few times:

```
CLS
PRINT "Hello"
```

The screen clears at the beginning of each run. As a result, only one Hello message appears on-screen with each run.

The letters CLS stand for CLear Screen. A CLS instruction does not erase anything in the computer's memory. Many programmers place CLS at the beginning of each program.

Performing Simple Arithmetic

Suppose that you want a program to ask the user to supply two numbers and then calculate the sum and product of the two numbers.

A previous program contains a PRINT instruction that prompts the user to enter certain information, followed by an INPUT instruction for the data entry. The following program uses another form of the INPUT instruction—a form that accomplishes both tasks.

```
PRINT "This program makes calculations using two numbers"
INPUT "First number"; Num1
INPUT "Second number"; Num2
PRINT "The sum is"; Num1 + Num2
PRINT "The product is"; Num1 * Num2
```

If you run this program and enter the numbers 7 and 5, the following output is displayed:

```
This program makes calculations using two numbers
First number? 7
Second number? 5
The sum is 12
The product is 35
```

The variables in this program, *Num1* and *Num2*, do not end with dollar signs. The absence of trailing dollar signs means that *Num1* and *Num2* are numeric variables. According to QBasic's rules, you can name the variables almost anything—Fred, TheFirstNumber, or XB47JQX35R, for example. By choosing simple but descriptive variable names, you create more understandable programs.

Cue:
*An * indicates multiplication.*

QBasic uses the asterisk (*) to indicate multiplication. The plus and minus signs indicate addition and subtraction, respectively. A slash (/) denotes division.

Each INPUT instruction contains a string literal separated from the variable name by a semicolon. When QBasic prompts the user on-screen, it prints the string literal (from the INPUT instruction) followed by a question mark. In this way, one INPUT instruction replaces the PRINT and INPUT combination used previously.

Altering Logic Flow

Suppose that you want to make the same calculations shown in the preceding program but for many pairs of numbers. You do not have to run the program from the beginning each time. You can insert instructions that alter the *logic flow*. Logic flow is the order in which your program instructions execute.

Reminder:
Logic Flow is
the order in
which program
instructions
execute.

Instead of allowing the preceding program to end after its final instruction, you can add a new instruction that tells QBasic to go back to the beginning of the program or to any other point in the program. By telling QBasic to return to preceding lines, you cause some instructions to repeat.

To specify the line to which the program should jump, you need a way to identify program lines. Here is where line numbers and QBasic's new alternative to line numbers, alphanumeric labels, come into play. Alphanumeric labels make programs more understandable than line numbers can.

Modify the preceding program as follows:

```
PRINT "This program makes calculations using two numbers"
GetMoreNumbers:
    INPUT "First number"; Num1
    INPUT "Second number"; Num2
    PRINT "The sum is"; Num1 + Num2
    PRINT "The product is"; Num1 * Num2
GOTO GetMoreNumbers
```

> *Note:* Four lines in the preceding program are indented from the others. Indentation is entirely optional. You can put as many spaces as you want at the beginning of a line. Indentation provides a useful way to visually set off a block of related instructions. Indenting an instruction does not affect the way the instruction performs when you run a program.

In early versions of BASIC, every line begins with a line number, and GOTO instructions reference line numbers. For example, the last line of this program may have read `GOTO 20` if it were programmed in an early version of BASIC.

Notice the final program line. The GOTO instruction directly transfers program flow back to the line containing the alphanumeric label *GetMoreNumbers*. After QBasic executes the program's final line, QBasic goes back and re-executes the first INPUT instruction. From there, QBasic continues through the program, re-executing the second INPUT instruction and subsequent PRINT instructions. When QBasic again executes the last line, program control returns to the GetMoreNumbers label.

In the line containing the alphanumeric label, you must use a colon after the label; however, in a GOTO instruction, you do not use a colon after the name of the label.

Looping

The preceding modified program has a problem. The final line of the program always tells QBasic to go back and get two more numbers, creating an *endless loop*, or *infinite loop*. A *loop* is any group of instructions executed repeatedly. Looping is a powerful programming technique. Many kinds of loops exist.

Endless loops, as the name suggests, repeat endlessly. The indented lines of the preceding program (the INPUT and PRINT instructions) constitute an endless loop because these lines repeat with no way of stopping. If you are stuck in the preceding program's loop, press Ctrl-Break instead of entering a number to interrupt the endless loop.

What the preceding program needs is a *conditional loop*. Such a loop repeats until a certain condition occurs. The following revised program solves the problem:

```
PRINT "This program makes calculations using two numbers"
GetMoreNumbers:
    INPUT "First number"; Num1
    INPUT "Second number"; Num2
    IF Num1 = 0 AND Num2 = 0 THEN PRINT "All Done": END
    PRINT "The sum is"; Num1 + Num2
    PRINT "The product is"; Num1 * Num2
GOTO GetMoreNumbers
```

An IF instruction now appears in the middle of the loop. This IF instruction causes the program to end when certain conditions are satisfied. The conditions in this program are that *Num1* and *Num2* must equal zero, which occurs if you type **0** in response to both prompts. When these conditions are met, the program displays the All Done message and ends.

Placing Multiple Instructions on One Program Line

Note the use of the colon (:) in the IF instruction in the preceding program. The colon enables you to combine two or more instructions in one program line. Don't confuse the colon with the semicolon; their uses are entirely different.

Caution:
A colon and a semicolon have different uses.

> *Note:* Punctuation characters are critical to QBasic programs. Simple but hard-to-notice typing errors involving punctuation can cause annoying error messages and incorrect program results.

Using Expressions and Operators

An *expression* specifies a single data value. Expressions occur frequently in QBasic instructions.

Expressions can vary. For example, an expression may consist of a single literal (such as 38.66 or "No thank you"), a variable (such as MyAge), or a combination of these elements formed with a suitable operator (such as MyAge + 10).

Every valid expression, simple or complex, evaluates to one value. The value may be numeric or string. For example, if the variable X has the value 2, and Y has the value 5, the expression X + Y has the value 7.

Cue:
All valid expressions evaluate to one value.

When an expression contains two or more parts, some sort of *operator* combines the parts to create a value. In programming terminology, an operator manipulates one or more *operands* to create a value. In the preceding example, X and Y are operands, and the plus sign (+) is an operator.

Wherever QBasic expects a value, you can substitute an expression. Composite expressions often occur on the right-hand side of assignment instructions.

For example, look at the following instructions, which illustrate the fundamental arithmetic operators. (Recall that the operators +, −, *, and /, specify addition, subtraction, multiplication, and division, respectively.)

```
MyAge = YourAge - 5
Area = Length * Height
TotalCost = 122.76 + 43.18 + 12.95
UnitCost = TotalCost / NumItems
```

String Operators

Cue:
A + merges two
strings into a
composite string.

Instead of adding the strings in an arithmetical sense, the plus sign merges the text of two strings into one composite string. This process has the fancy name of *concatenation*. The text of one string is juxtaposed with the text of a second string to create one string. The following program demonstrates the technique:

```
FirstPart$ = "Coca"
LastPart$ = "Cola"
FullName$ = FirstPart$ + LastPart$
PRINT FullName$
```

The output is as follows:

```
CocaCola
```

In the third program line, the plus sign performs concatenation. The instruction concatenates the value of *FirstPart$* (namely Coca) with the value of *LastPart$* (namely Cola) to form the result (CocaCola) and then assigns the result to the variable *FullName$*.

Operator Precedence

So far, most of the sample expressions in this chapter have two operands and one operator. What happens when an expression contains more than one operator?

Consider the following instruction:

```
PRINT 4 + 3 * 2
```

Is the result 14 or 10? The answer is 14 if you add 4 and 3 before multiplying by 2 (4 plus 3 is 7, and 7 times 2 is 14), but the answer is 10 if you add 4 to the product of 3 times 2 (3 times 2 is 6, and 4 plus 6 is 10).

When multiple operators occur in an expression, certain operations are performed before others. QBasic has rules for *operator precedence*; some operators have precedence over others.

Of the fundamental arithmetic operators, multiplication and division have precedence over addition and subtraction. The expression *4 + 3 * 2* evaluates to 10 because multiplication has higher precedence than addition. Three is first multiplied by 2 to yield 6. Then 4 is added to 6 to produce 10.

Reminder:
Multiplication and division have precedence.

When multiple operators of the same level of precedence occur in an expression, resolution proceeds from left to right. The expression *9 - 4 - 2* yields 3 because 4 is first subtracted from 9 to yield 5, and then 2 is subtracted from 5 to produce 3 as the final answer. (The result would be 7 if the second subtraction were done first.)

Expressions Containing Parentheses

Suppose that in the following instruction, you want the addition to occur before the multiplication:

```
PRINT 4 + 3 * 2
```

Use parentheses to override the standard operator precedence. When an expression contains parentheses, QBasic evaluates the terms inside the parentheses before evaluating terms outside the parentheses. The following instruction is written so that the addition is done first:

Cue:
Use parentheses to override operator precedence.

```
PRINT (4 + 3) * 2
```

Now the result is 14. The parentheses force QBasic to evaluate 4 + 3 before multiplying the product by 2.

For more complicated expressions, parentheses can be nested inside each other. When an expression contains parentheses within parentheses, QBasic evaluates terms inside the inner parentheses before terms in the outer parentheses.

The following instruction, for example, contains parentheses within parentheses:

```
PRINT (24 - (3 * 5)) / 2
```

The result is 4.5. In this example, QBasic first evaluates the expression in the deeper nested parentheses. The first calculation, therefore, is 3 times 5, yielding 15. Then 15 is subtracted from 24, which yields 9. Finally 9 is divided by 2 to yield the answer 4.5.

Right-Hand Sides of Assignment Instructions

The right-hand side of an assignment instruction can consist of any expression (a literal, a variable, or a more complex expression containing operators). The following two examples of right-hand sides contain general expressions:

```
Tax = Cost * .06
Volume = Depth * Height * Length / 9
```

Two things occur when an assignment instruction executes:

1. The expression on the right-hand side is evaluated to produce a value.

2. This value is assigned to the variable on the left-hand side.

The equal sign in an assignment instruction means "is now assigned the value of." Therefore, the instruction *NumItems = 29* means "the variable NumItems is now assigned the value of 29."

Study the following instruction:

```
X = X + 1
```

Does the instruction make sense to you? When the preceding instruction is viewed as a reassignment of the variable X, the instruction makes perfect sense. The instruction says "the new value of the variable X is now assigned the value of X plus 1."

In other words, first add 1 to the value of X. Then store this updated value back in the variable named X. The effect is that X now contains a value 1 greater than its preceding value. This kind of instruction occurs frequently in practical programs.

Using IF for Making Decisions

IF is one of QBasic's most important instructions because IF enables you to program decisions.

Just as decision making is a significant and frequent part of your everyday life, decision making is a perpetual programming theme. Programs make decisions by evaluating test conditions and then taking various actions, depending on the results of the evaluations. Like a fork in the road, a *logic juncture* is a place in your program where the subsequent logic flow can go one of two or more different ways.

When you program a logic juncture, your thoughts are as follows: "If such and such is true, I want this to happen. If not, then this should happen instead."

You choose the program path based on the evaluation of a test condition. Your foremost tool is the IF...THEN instruction, which tests whether a condition is true or false and then directs logic flow depending on the result.

The Basic Form of IF...THEN

The following program demonstrates the basic form of the IF...THEN instruction:

```
INPUT "What is the temperature outside"; Temp
IF Temp > 100 THEN PRINT "It's hot"
PRINT "So long for now"
```

Following are two different runs of this program:

```
What is the temperature outside? 106
It's hot
So long for now

What is the temperature outside? 84
So long for now
```

The second line of the program is an IF...THEN instruction. If the value of the variable *Temp* is greater than 100, the program displays the message It's hot. (The > character is a relational operator meaning greater than.)

Study the preceding two sample runs. The first time, the user entered 106 as the temperature. Because 106 is greater than 100, the program dutifully displays the It's hot message.

The second time, however, the user supplied 84 as the temperature. When the test condition of an IF...THEN instruction is false, QBasic disregards the part of the instruction that follows THEN. The program moves to the next program line. In the second run, the value of *Temp* is 84. The test condition is false because 84 is not greater than 100. As a result, QBasic ignores the part of the instruction following THEN (that is, the PRINT clause) and moves to the next program line. The next line displays the So long for now message.

Reminder:
When the test condition is false, the instruction following THEN is ignored.

The ELSE Clause

To perform one action if a test condition is true but another action if the test condition is false, you can use a second form of IF...THEN that adds an ELSE clause for this purpose.

Change the second program line so that the new program looks like the following:

```
INPUT "What is the temperature outside"; Temp
IF Temp > 100 THEN PRINT "It's hot" ELSE PRINT "Not too bad"
PRINT "So long for now"
```

Now try the two runs again:

```
What is the temperature outside? 106
It's hot
So long for now
```

```
What is the temperature outside? 84
Not too bad
So long for now
```

When the temperature is given as 106, the result is the same as before; but now when you give the temperature as 84, the computer displays the Not too bad message.

By adding an ELSE clause to an IF...THEN instruction, you specify what happens when the testing condition is false (the ELSE part) and what happens when the testing condition is true (the THEN part).

The Relational Operators

Cue:
The testing expression evaluates to true or false.

In an IF instruction, the testing expression must evaluate to true or false. Such expressions are called *relational expressions*. QBasic provides six *relational operators* for forming relational expressions (see table 18.1).

Each example in the last column of the table is true.

Note that the relational operators work with strings and numbers:

```
IF Animal$ = "Dog" THEN PRINT "It's a pooch"
```

Two strings are equal only if both strings contain exactly the same sequence of characters, including upper- and lowercase distinctions. If *Animal$* has the value DOG (all caps), the result is false. *DOG* and *Dog* are not identical strings.

Table 18.1
Relational operators

Symbol	Name	Example
=	Is equal to	4 = (3 + 1)
<>	Is not equal to	"Dog" <> "Cat"
>	Is greater than	8 > 5
<	Is less than	3 < 6
>=	Is greater than or equal to	9 >= 9
<=	Is less than or equal to	1 <= 7

Creating Simple Sounds

You can write program instructions that play sound effects or music through the computer's speaker. QBasic includes several keywords for constructing such instructions. The simplest of these keywords is BEEP, which is a legal instruction.

BEEP creates a short (approximately a quarter second) tone. Use BEEP to get your user's attention. Typical occasions are when your program requests input or displays an error message.

For example, a checkbook-balancing program may include the following two lines:

```
PRINT "Sorry, your checkbook is out of balance."
BEEP
```

To see (hear) the effect, try running the preceding two lines as an entire program.

Interrupting a Program with Ctrl-Break

When testing a new program, you may discover that your program unfortunately goes into an endless loop. Endless looping happens when a section of your program executes over and over continuously. You may realize your programming error, but meanwhile, your program keeps running with no end in sight.

Reminder:

The F5 key is equivalent to issuing the Continue command.

While pressing the Ctrl key, press the Break key. QBasic terminates your program and returns to the editor. After interrupting a program with Ctrl-Break, you can resume execution with the Continue command from the Run menu. The F5 shortcut key is equivalent to issuing the Continue command. F5 and Shift-F5 are not the same. Shift-F5 starts a program from the beginning; F5 resumes an interrupted program.

Try the following short program to acquaint yourself with Ctrl-Break:

```
StartLoop:
     BEEP
 GOTO StartLoop
```

This program creates an endless loop. The BEEP instruction executes continuously. The result is a constant drone from your speaker. (The individual beeps blend into one continuous sound.) Press Ctrl-Break to get out of the loop.

Dealing with Program Errors

Errors are a fact of programming life. All programmers make mistakes, so don't feel bad when errors occur. Recognize that errors are bound to happen—learn from them and forge ahead.

Errors that you don't discover until you run a program are *run-time errors*. The three fundamental types of run-time errors are as follows:

- *Syntax errors.* A syntax error occurs when an instruction does not follow the rules of QBasic. For example, you may spell a keyword incorrectly, use improper punctuation, or combine keywords in an illegal way. In such a case, the instruction is meaningless. As a result, QBasic cannot attempt to execute the instruction. The editor catches some syntax errors as you type (when you move the cursor off the line containing the error). Other syntax errors are not caught until you actually run the program.

- *Execution errors.* An execution error occurs when an instruction requests an action that QBasic cannot perform. For example, you may instruct QBasic to divide a number by zero. In such a case, no syntax error is present. (The instruction is legally constructed according to the rules of QBasic.) In the context of the whole program, however, the instruction attempts something illegal. QBasic understands the instruction but cannot perform the requested action.

- *Logic errors*. A logic error occurs when a program runs to completion but produces incorrect results. Somehow the program works incorrectly. In programming jargon, your program contains a *bug*. You (the programmer) must *debug* the program, which means finding and correcting the error.

Correcting Syntax Errors

When a syntax error occurs, QBasic stops running your program and informs you of the incorrect line.

Try the following experiment. Type the second line exactly as shown, with PRINT incorrectly spelled PRNT.

```
PRINT "Hello"
PRNT "Goodbye"
```

Nothing special happens when you type the incorrect line. QBasic does not catch most syntax errors in program instructions until you actually try to run the program.

Now run the program. QBasic finds the syntax error. The screen shifts back to the editor, and a message box opens. Inside the box is a message indicating that a syntax error is present. The incorrect line is highlighted in your program. Press Enter to close the message box. The cursor is on the incorrect word *PRNT*. You now can edit *PRNT* to read *PRINT*.

Caution: Syntax errors usually aren't caught until the program runs.

When you run a program, QBasic's first action is to examine all your program instructions for syntax errors. In the preceding program, QBasic finds your misspelled keyword and cannot make any sense out of *PRNT*.

Correcting Execution Errors

When an execution error occurs, QBasic stops your program and displays an explanatory error message. Try the following experiment:

```
FindBatAve:
    INPUT "Number of hits"; NumHits
    INPUT "Number of times at bat"; NumAB
    PRINT "Batting average is"
    PRINT NumHits / NumAB
    PRINT
    GOTO FindBatAve
```

This program computes baseball batting averages. The program consists of a loop so that multiple batting averages can be computed.

Suppose that you want to calculate the following three batting averages with this program. First, in one season, a player had 128 hits from 523 times at bat. Second, in one month, a player had 27 hits from 79 times at bat. Third, in one week, a player had 8 hits from 30 times at bat.

When running this program, suppose that you make a mistake by inadvertently entering 0 as the number of times at bat for the third calculation. The output is as follows:

```
Number of hits? 128
Number of times at bat? 523
Batting average is
 .2447419

Number of hits? 27
Number of times at bat? 79
Batting average is
 .3417721

Number of hits? 8
Number of times at bat? 0
Batting average is
```

The first calculation displays a batting average of .2447419. Batting averages are rounded to three digits, making 0.245 the first batting average.

Before asking for the input for the second calculation, QBasic displays a blank line on the screen because PRINT creates a blank line when placed on a line by itself.

The second batting average is .3417721, or 0.342 when rounded to three digits. For the number of times at bat, you inadvertently entered **0** instead of **30**. The value of the variable *NumAB* becomes 0, and in the fifth program line, QBasic tries to divide by 0. Division by 0 is an illegal mathematical operation.

QBasic switches your screen back to the editor, displays a `Division by zero` error message, and highlights the line in your program that caused the error. You now can press Enter to clear the error message box and retry the program. After computing the correct result, press Ctrl-Break to exit from the program.

Debugging a Program— Correcting Logic Errors

Logic errors are the hardest errors to debug. Your program runs to completion, but the results are not right. All your instructions have legal syntax, and QBasic executes all of them. As far as QBasic is concerned, everything is fine; however, the program doesn't work correctly. Often a logic error results in program output that is clearly wrong. Although space restrictions prohibit a detailed discussion of QBasic's built-in debugging tools (from the Debug menu), QBasic has a number of these tools that are helpful.

Caution:
Logic errors are the hardest errors to debug.

Logic errors usually result from typing mistakes that don't result in syntax or execution errors. When you find that a program has a logic error, first carefully check your typing. Make sure that your program reads as you intended.

Cue:
Logic errors often result from typos.

Study the following short program, which contains a simple logic error resulting from a typing mistake:

```
NumItems = 50
UnitCost = 2.25
PRINT "Total cost is"
PRINT UnitsCost * NumItems
```

The output is as follows:

```
Total cost is
 0
```

The result cannot be right. The bottom program line contains the variable UnitsCost, but UnitCost was intended. Because they have different names, *UnitCost* and *UnitsCost* are two different variables.

When a numeric variable is not assigned a value, QBasic uses the default value of 0; therefore, the value of *UnitsCost* is 0 when the last line executes. The program displays the product of *UnitsCost* (0) and *NumItems* (50), which produces the result of 0.

In the last line, change the variable name *UnitsCost* to *UnitCost* to make the program work.

Understanding How PRINT Displays Results

Programs frequently use PRINT instructions to display results. PRINT works for strings and numbers.

String PRINT Formats

When PRINT displays a string value, each character from the string occupies one character position on-screen. PRINT can display a string literal or a string variable. Study the following example:

```
Message$ = "There is no"
PRINT Message$
PRINT "place like home."
```

The output is as follows:

```
There is no
place like home.
```

Cue:
A string literal must be enclosed in quotation marks.

Remember that in a PRINT instruction a string literal must be enclosed in quotation marks. Without the quotation marks, QBasic attempts to interpret the text that follows PRINT as a variable name or numeric quantity.

Numeric PRINT Formats

When you display numbers, PRINT uses the following formats:

- Every number prints with a trailing space.

- Negative numbers have a leading minus sign (–).

- Positive numbers (and zero) have a leading space.

If the number is a whole number, PRINT displays the number without using a decimal point. If the number contains a fractional component, a decimal point appears. The following examples should make this distinction clear:

```
Example1 = 2.5 * 4
Example2 = 1 / 1000
Example3 = -1 / 3
```

```
Example4 = 100000 / 3
Example5 = 123 + .456
PRINT Example1
PRINT Example2
PRINT Example3
PRINT Example4
PRINT Example5
PRINT 1 / 7
```

The output is as follows:

```
 10
 .001
-.3333333
 33333.33
 123.456
 .1428571
```

Note that the positive numbers print with a leading space. PRINT displays numbers with up to seven digits of precision. The largest possible value is 9999999, and the smallest possible (positive) value is .0000001.

To display values beyond these limits, PRINT resorts to exponential format. Again, the maximum degree of precision is seven digits. The exponential indicator, E, sets the decimal points through the number range from approximately $-1.0E-38$ to $1.0E+38$.

> **Note:** When numbers become extremely large or extremely small, a specialized notation is necessary. Writing numbers such as .000000000000389 or 4589100000 is awkward.
>
> To express such numbers, QBasic uses *exponential notation*, also called *scientific notation*. For example, $3.89E-14$ and $4.5891E+09$ specify the two numbers given in the preceding paragraph.
>
> To interpret exponential notation, move the decimal point the number of places indicated by the exponent after the E. Move the decimal point to the right for positive exponents, left for negative exponents. You may have to pad the number with zeros to complete the alignment. For example, $2.89E+05$ is 289,000 and $-1.67E-06$ is -0.00000167.

The following program fragment demonstrates exponential format:

```
Example1 = 10000000 * 10
Example2 = 1 / Example1 / 3
```

```
PRINT Example1
PRINT Example2
```

The output is as follows:

```
1E+08
3.333333E-09
```

> *Note:* Occasionally, you need to compute numeric quantities with a precision greater than seven digits. For such occasions, QBasic has a numeric data type known as *double-precision*. To create a double-precision variable, place a pound sign (#) at the end of the variable name. For example, *MyDebt#* is a double-precision variable.
>
> Double-precision variables are accurate to, at least, 16 digits. PRINT displays the full 16 digits when you print the value of a double-precision variable.

PRINT Formats with Multiple Expressions

Reminder:
A PRINT instruction can display two or more values on one screen line.

A PRINT instruction can display two or more values on one screen line. All you need to do is place multiple values in the expression list that follows the PRINT keyword. Use a semicolon or a comma to separate the individual items in your list. When displaying the output, QBasic inserts spaces between the displayed items. The number of inserted spaces depends on whether you choose a semicolon or comma for the delimiter.

The Semicolon Delimiter

If a semicolon separates the two items, no spaces are inserted in the output, and the items are juxtaposed:

```
MyString$ = "This is a note"
PRINT MyString$; "worthy achievement"
```

The PRINT instruction produces the following output:

```
This is a noteworthy achievement
```

The PRINT instruction displays the value of *MyString$* and the string literal "worthy achievement." The text output displays a line with no spaces between the two items. The result is a meaningful sentence.

You must be careful with numeric output. Recall that PRINT displays numbers with one trailing space. Positive numbers and zero display with a leading space; negative numbers display a leading minus sign but no space before the minus sign.

The following program demonstrates how this automatic formatting of numbers can be helpful or annoying when you display multiple expressions with one PRINT instruction.

```
HighTemp = 47
LowTemp = -12
PRINT "The high today was"; HighTemp; "degrees"
PRINT "and the low was"; LowTemp; "degrees."
```

The output is as follows:

```
The high today was 47 degrees
and the low was-12 degrees.
```

Note that the first line of output looks good. A space appears before and after 47. In the second line, however, no space appears before –12.

The Comma Delimiter and PRINT Zones

If you separate the items in your expression list with commas, a PRINT instruction aligns output into predefined fields or zones.

To understand this zoning, picture each 80-character line of screen output divided into five zones. Each zone, except the last, is 14 characters wide. The zones begin in column positions 1, 15, 29, 43, and 57.

When you place a comma between items in your expression list, you request tabbing to successive zones. Consider the following one-line program:

```
PRINT "Zone1", "Zone2", "Zone3"
```

The result is zoned output as follows:

```
Zone1      Zone2      Zone3
```

Numbers still display inside the print zones with the usual leading and trailing spaces. One convenient use of comma separators is to display simple tables neatly:

```
PRINT , "Position", "Batting Avg"
PRINT
PRINT "Rose", "First Base", .347
PRINT "DiMaggio", "Center", .287
PRINT "Ruth", "Right Field", .301
PRINT "Uecker", "Catcher", .106
```

This program results in the following aligned table:

```
            Position    Batting Avg

Rose        First Base    .347
DiMaggio    Center        .287
Ruth        Right Field   .301
Uecker      Catcher       .106
```

Note how the beginning comma in the first PRINT instruction forces *Position* to align in the second print zone.

Introducing FOR...NEXT Loops

Recall the previous examples of loops. An endless loop executes forever (or until your electricity shuts off, your computer breaks down, or you press Ctrl-Break). Useful programming loops must have a way to end naturally.

Reminder:
A controlled loop has an end.

A loop that has an ending mechanism is a *controlled loop*. A controlled loop executes until some predetermined condition is satisfied. Some form of controlled loop occurs in most practical programs.

QBasic provides special structures and several keywords for the programming of controlled loops. The most common structure is the FOR...NEXT loop.

A FOR...NEXT loop uses a numeric variable to control the number of repetitions. This special variable is called a *counter variable*, or *control variable*.

The easiest way to explain a FOR...NEXT loop is with an example. The following program displays a table of the squares of the numbers from 0 to 6. (The square of a number is the number multiplied by itself.) This kind of task is perfect for a FOR...NEXT loop.

```
PRINT "Number", "Square"
FOR Number = 0 TO 6
   Square = Number * Number
```

```
      PRINT Number, Square
   NEXT Number
   PRINT "End of table"
```

The output is as follows:

```
   Number          Square
      0             0
      1             1
      2             4
      3             9
      4             16
      5             25
      6             36
   End of table
```

The first line of the program displays the titles of the two columns of the table. The comma in the PRINT instruction aligns the output into the two print zones.

The loop starts with the FOR instruction in the next line. FOR signifies that a loop is beginning. In this example, the counter variable is *Number*. The value of *Number* changes each time through the loop. This FOR instruction specifies that the first value of *Number* should be 0, and the final value should be 6.

Cue:
FOR signifies
the beginning
of a loop.

In the fifth line, the NEXT instruction marks the end of the loop. FOR and NEXT are like a pair of bookends that surround a loop. In a FOR...NEXT loop, all the instructions between the FOR and NEXT are called the *body* of the loop.

The body of a loop can contain any number of instructions. Occasionally, program loops have more than 100 instructions. The body of the loop in the preceding program modestly consists of the two indented instructions between FOR and NEXT.

Do you understand how the loop works? The body of the loop executes repetitively. In succession, *Number* takes on the values 0, 1, 2, 3, 4, 5, and 6. The PRINT instruction, just above NEXT, displays every one of the numeric lines in the table. Again, the comma aligns the output into columns.

The first time through the loop, *Number* is 0. The assignment instruction (the instruction below FOR) computes the square of *Number*, making *Square* 0. The ensuing PRINT instruction then displays the first line of the table.

In effect, the NEXT instruction says, "I now have reached the bottom of the loop, which means that it is time to increase the value of *Number* and go back through the loop."

By default, the value of a counter variable increases by one each time through a FOR...NEXT loop. The new value of *Number*, therefore, becomes 1 (0 + 1 equals 1).

The program then returns to the beginning of the loop, to the line just below the FOR instruction. Here the new value of *Number* (1) is compared against the final value of the loop (6). Because the final value is not yet exceeded, the body of the loop executes again. *Number* is 1, and *Square* also becomes 1 (1 times 1 is 1). The next line then prints the second line of the table.

This looping process continues, with *Number* continually increasing by one. Eventually, *Number* reaches 6. The body of the loop still executes because *Number* equals—but does not exceed—the final value of the loop.

The NEXT instruction then increases the value of *Number* to 7. When control returns to the FOR instruction at the top of the loop, the value of *Number* is greater than the maximum loop value of 6, signaling that the loop is over. The program then proceeds with the first line after the NEXT instruction. In this case, control passes to the PRINT instruction at the end of the program, which prints the closing message.

The STEP Clause

Sometimes you want the increment in the counter variable to be a number other than one. You can alter the increment by adding a STEP clause to the end of the FOR instruction. Using the squares program, try changing the FOR instruction to the following:

```
FOR Number = 0 TO 6 STEP 2
```

The output now is as follows:

```
Number          Square
  0               0
  2               4
  4               16
  6               36
End of table
```

The STEP clause specifies an increment of 2 each time through the loop. As a result, *Number* becomes successively 0, 2, 4, and 6.

More about FOR...NEXT Loops

The FOR...NEXT loop is a flexible program structure. The following list presents some additional features and capabilities of FOR...NEXT.

- STEP clauses can specify negative increments. When the increment is negative, the counter variable decreases each time through the loop. For example, you can write

```
FOR Number = 8 TO -2 STEP -1
```

- QBasic bypasses a FOR...NEXT loop if the starting loop value is greater than the final loop value when the STEP increment is positive or if the starting loop value is smaller than the final loop value when the increment is negative. In such cases, the loop doesn't execute. The program continues with the line that follows the NEXT instruction.

- In a FOR instruction, you can use variables to specify the loop limits, the STEP increment, or both. For example, the following instruction is acceptable:

```
FOR Number = 1 TO FinalValue STEP Increment
```

FinalValue and *Increment* are numeric variables.

- FOR...NEXT loops can be nested. In such a case, a second FOR...NEXT loop opens inside the body of the original loop. Each loop uses a distinct counter variable. Loops can be nested to several levels. The innermost loops execute first.

- In a NEXT instruction, the counter variable is optional. The NEXT instruction of the squares program can be as follows:

```
NEXT
```

QBasic pairs any bare NEXT instruction with the most recently unmatched FOR instruction. The recommended technique, however, is to include the counter variable in NEXT instructions. This practice is especially necessary in nested loop situations.

Manipulating Strings

Many QBasic programs manipulate text data. You have studied several QBasic programs in this chapter. Text data is stored in strings, and QBasic has an entire group of string manipulation instructions that operate on text data.

The following program illustrates several facets of string manipulation:

```
REM - STRING1.BAS - This program manipulates strings
INPUT "What is your name"; YourName$
FOR Pointer = 1 to LEN(YourName$)
    PRINT Pointer, MID$(YourName$, Pointer, 1)
NEXT Pointer
```

This program introduces several new QBasic keywords, which are explained in the ensuing discussion. Before learning about the new keywords, try running the preceding program, supplying *John* as the answer to What is your name?. The output you see is as follows:

```
What is your name? John
 1                  J
 2                  o
 3                  h
 4                  n
```

Including Comments in a Program

Reminder:
REM is not an active program instruction.

The first line in the preceding program is a REM instruction. REM stands for remark and causes the remainder of a line to be treated as a programmer's comment instead of as an active program instruction. When REM occurs, QBasic ignores the remainder of the line and proceeds directly to the next line.

With REM instructions, programmers self-document their programs by inserting comments and explanations. When someone else reads the program, these remarks tell the person what the program is all about and how it works.

In the preceding program, the REM instruction shows the program name (STRING1.BAS), along with a short description of what the program does. The hyphens around the program name are arbitrary, just a way to separate the program name from the description.

Note: Using many comments is a good idea. You will be amazed how much help a few comments can provide when you resume work on a program after a few months.

Besides REM, another way to indicate a comment is by using an apostrophe (']). Many programmers get into the habit of using the one-keystroke apostrophe rather than the three-keystroke REM instruction.

The second line of the preceding program is nothing new, just an INPUT instruction that prompts the user for his or her name. The third, fourth, and fifth lines constitute a FOR...NEXT loop that introduces some new concepts.

Introducing Functions

A *function* operates on one or more arguments and produces one value. Depending on the particular function, the arguments can be numeric or string, and the value returned can be numeric or string. QBasic provides a number of built-in functions, and each function is specified by a reserved keyword.

LEN is a string function that determines the length of any string given in parentheses. In the preceding program, the string in parentheses consists solely of the variable *YourName$*. The length does not refer to the length of the variable name but instead to the length of the string data stored in that variable. If you type **John**, *LEN(YourName$)* is 4. The third program line, therefore, is equivalent to the following:

```
FOR Pointer = 1 TO 4
```

The programmer, however, does not know how long the entered names will be. LEN enables the program to do its job for any name, not just a four-character name.

Notice the PRINT instruction in the fourth line. The comma causes the output to align into two printing zones. The first output on each line is the value of the counter variable, named *Pointer* in this case. In this loop, *Pointer* identifies, or points to, the character being processed in each repetition of the loop.

MID$ is another example of a QBasic string function. MID$ extracts a portion (a *substring*) of a target string. MID$ can have two or three parameters. In the three-parameter form used here, the parameters specify in order: the string to operate on, the extraction starting position, and the length of the extracted string. The first time the PRINT instruction executes, Pointer points at the first character, and MID$ extracts only that one character (the *J* in *John*). The second time, Pointer points to the second character (the *o* in *John*), and MID$ again extracts only that one character, and so on.

QBasic contains many built-in functions, string and numeric. Some examples of mathematical functions are trigonometric functions (SIN and COS), logarithmic functions (EXP and LOG), and arithmetic functions (ABS for absolute value and SQR for square roots).

Understanding the QBasic Editor's Windows

The lower part of your editor screen contains the Immediate window. This section describes the QBasic editor's windowing system, including techniques for manipulating multiple windows. Chapter 17 contains additional information about the QBasic editor's windows.

The screen for the QBasic editing environment is partitioned into windows. When you invoke QBasic, two windows are visible: the View window and the Immediate window.

Manipulating Windows

In certain contexts, QBasic can open additional windows. Help screens open in a separate window, and the View window can be split into two separate windows.

Open windows can be activated and resized with the following techniques:

- To activate an alternate window, press F6 (or Shift-F6). Either key cycles the cursor through the opened windows. The window that contains the cursor is the *active* window. When a window is active, the title bar for that window appears highlighted.

- To enlarge the active window one line, press Alt-+, where + is the + key on your numeric keypad.

- To reduce the active window one line, press Alt-minus (–), where – is the – key on your numeric keypad.

- To make the active window fill the entire screen, press Ctrl-F10.

- To return to a multiple-window screen after making the active window fill the entire screen, press Ctrl-F10. This keystroke is a toggle switch. Repeatedly pressing Ctrl-F10 alternates between a multiple-window view and a full-screen view of the active window.

Using the Immediate Window

The Immediate window executes QBasic instructions instantly. When you type a QBasic instruction in the Immediate window, the instruction runs when you press Enter. The following list contains some of the tasks you can perform with the Immediate window:

Reminder:
The Immediate window immediately executes instructions.

- Calculate and display the value of any numeric or string expression

- Display the value of a program variable after running or interrupting a program

- Change the value of a variable and then resume execution of an interrupted program

- Test a small group of QBasic instructions before you add it to your program

The Immediate window is similar to BASICA's direct mode. With BASICA, any instruction you type without a line number executes immediately. With QBasic, any instruction you type in the Immediate window executes immediately.

The following short exercise acquaints you with the Immediate window:

1. Activate the Immediate window by pressing F6 or Shift-F6 until the cursor moves inside the Immediate window. Note that Immediate is highlighted.

2. Type **beep** and press Enter (see fig. 18.1). You should hear a beep from your speaker. Remember that BEEP is a QBasic instruction that sounds your speaker.

3. Type the following instruction and press Enter:

      PRINT 25 / 16

   QBasic calculates the value of 25 divided by 16 and displays the result on the output screen.

4. Press any key to return to the Immediate window.

5. Type the following instruction, and press Enter:

      A = 5

   You just assigned the value of 5 to a variable named *A*.

6. Type the following line, and press Enter.

      FOR Index = 1 TO A: PRINT "OK": NEXT Index

You should see OK displayed five times on your screen. By separating the individual instructions with a colon, you cause the program to place a complete FOR...NEXT loop on one line. Note that QBasic remembers and uses the current value of *A* as the maximum value of the counter variable Index.

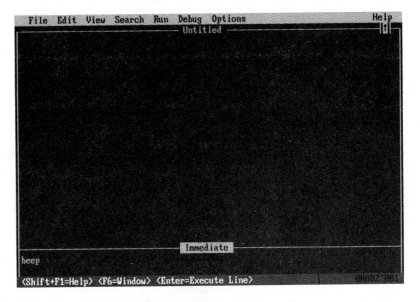

Fig. 18.1. *Typing an instruction in the Immediate window.*

7. Press any key to return to the Immediate window.

8. Use the up- and down-arrow keys to scroll through the lines you have typed already.

9. Place the cursor on the line that reads beep.

10. Press Enter. The speaker beeps. Notice that you can re-execute a line by placing the cursor on a previously typed line and then pressing Enter.

11. Expand the Immediate window to fill the entire screen by pressing Ctrl-F10. If you don't see all the lines you typed, press the up-arrow key until you do.

12. Shrink the Immediate window to its former size by pressing Ctrl-F10.

13. Press F6 to reactivate the View window.

The Immediate window can hold only 10 lines at one time. Typing an additional line scrolls the first line off the screen. You can, however, type a new line over an existing line.

Programming Graphics

So far, the sample programs have worked with numbers and text. You now venture into the stimulating world of another kind of data—graphics. With QBasic, you can create many interesting pictures on-screen.

Suppose that you want to write a short program that draws three nested rectangles. In the middle of the innermost rectangle, you want to draw a circle. Finally, between two of the rectangles, you want to display a short text title. The output should look like figure 18.2.

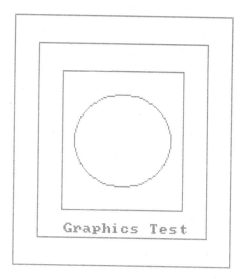

Fig. 18.2. *Desired output from a graphics program.*

QBasic includes a number of graphics keywords that simplify drawing certain shapes. In particular, LINE draws lines and rectangles (boxes), and CIRCLE draws circles.

The following program uses LINE and CIRCLE instructions to create the graphics display. Graphics output is possible only if your video hardware supports graphics; the IBM Monochrome Display Adapter (MDA) does not support graphics, but the Color Graphics Adapter (CGA), Enhanced Graphics Adapter (EGA), and Video Graphics Array (VGA) do.

```
REM - GRTEST.BAS - draw circle and three nested boxes
SCREEN 1
XCent = 160: YCent = 100
LINE (XCent - 50, YCent - 50)-(XCent + 50, YCent + 50), 3, B
LINE (XCent - 70, YCent - 70)-(XCent + 70, YCent + 70), 3, B
LINE (XCent - 90, YCent - 90)-(XCent + 90, YCent + 90), 3, B
CIRCLE (XCent, YCent), 40
LOCATE 21, 15
PRINT "Graphics Test"
```

For the rest of this section, you are taken through this program line-by-line to get a feeling for what each instruction does. Keep in mind the graphics display shown in figure 18.2. Please be aware that graphics instructions provide many options. Rather than provide detailed explanations of all the options, the intent here is to give you a general understanding of how the graphics work.

The first program line is a familiar REM instruction—a comment providing the program name and a description of what the program does. Line 2 is a SCREEN instruction. Depending on your hardware, your computer can use many different graphics screen modes. SCREEN 1 is the simplest graphics mode: 320 dots horizontally (0-319) and 200 vertically (0-199) in black and white.

Line 3 sets up the dot coordinates of the center of the screen, 160 dots horizontally and 100 dots vertically. In QBasic, the screen dots are referenced a bit differently from conventional x- and y-coordinates. The upper left corner is dot coordinate (0, 0) and the lower right corner is (319, 199). The center of the screen, therefore, is approximately 160 points to the right of the upper left corner and 100 points down from the top—(160, 100). Line 3 doesn't actually do anything with this center point. All the line does is establish two variables (*XCent* and *YCent*) that the program uses to represent the x- and y-coordinates of the center.

Note: Note that the third line of the program contains two assignment instructions separated by a colon. Recall that by using a colon to separate instructions, you can place two or more instructions on the same program line.

Line 4 is a LINE instruction that draws the innermost rectangle. With LINE, you can draw a straight line between two specified points or draw a rectangle defined by two points on opposite corners.

The B parameter at the end of the LINE instruction indicates that in this case, a rectangle is desired. (The *B* stands for Box.) If you omit the *B*, QBasic draws a straight diagonal line instead of the rectangle.

The 3 in each LINE instruction specifies the color of the rectangle, which is white in this case.

The three LINE instructions in the program are all the same, except for a constant number (50, 70, or 90) added or subtracted from the coordinates of the screen's center. This technique (adding or subtracting from the same starting position) centers the rectangles without forcing the programmer to figure out each set of coordinates—arithmetical drudgery.

The first rectangle extends from 50 points left of center to 50 points right of center, and from 50 points above center to 50 points below center, making each side 100 units long.

The other two rectangles are 140 and 180 units per side. All squares are rectangles, so calling them rectangles is accurate. The horizontal and vertical dot spacings also are not exactly the same, causing the rectangle not to look like a square.

After the three rectangles are drawn, the CIRCLE instruction in line 7 draws a circle, the center of which matches the rectangles' center and which has a radius of 40 units.

The program's last two lines combine to display a short text title on the same screen with the graphics output. The LOCATE instruction moves the invisible text cursor to the spot where subsequent text is to be displayed. That is, LOCATE indicates where text from the PRINT instruction is to be displayed. In this case, the text starts on the 21st line (the top line is line 1, not 0) in the 15th column position on that line.

Just how were these particular LOCATE numbers picked? In truth, a rough guess was first made of how the text characters would map onto the graphics screen. Then the numbers were adjusted after a few trial-and-error attempts.

This discussion has skimmed over the complete syntax available for LINE and CIRCLE instructions. The syntax for LINE and CIRCLE instructions permits other parameters that create more intricate effects. Space limitations prevent a more detailed explanation, but the purpose here is to give you a taste of how QBasic graphics work.

Now that you have reviewed the entire program, go back and make a few changes in the preceding program to see how the output is affected. Make the radius of the circle 50 or 99. Change the LOCATE parameters to move the text to another part of the screen. Change *XCent* in line 3 to 100 or 200.

Introducing Subroutines

As an introduction to subroutines—a critical programming concept—modify the preceding program.

The preceding graphics program, GRTEST.BAS, contains three consecutive LINE instructions. These three instructions are almost identical; the only difference is the numbers added to or subtracted from the coordinates of the screen's center. Most programs have many such similar sections of repetitive instructions—sometimes just one or two instructions and sometimes hundreds of instructions.

Rather than force programmers to rewrite the same (or similar) instructions, most languages have one or more ways to create a block of instructions that can be called when needed. Such a block of instructions is a *subroutine* or *subprogram*. The two terms actually have slightly different meanings. (Subprograms are discussed briefly at the end of this chapter in "Introducing Advanced Features of QBasic.")

The following program, GRTEST2.BAS, is GRTEST.BAS rewritten to use a subroutine instead of three separate LINE instructions.

```
REM - GRTEST2.BAS - draw circle and three nested boxes
SCREEN 1
XCent = 160: YCent = 100
HS = 50: GOSUB DrawBox        'HS is length of half a side
HS = 70: GOSUB DrawBox
HS = 90: GOSUB DrawBox
CIRCLE (XCent, YCent), 40
LOCATE 21, 15
PRINT "Graphics Test"
END
DrawBox:
LINE (XCent - HS, YCent - HS)-(XCent + HS, YCent + HS), 3, B
RETURN
```

This program produces the same output as the preceding program (again see fig. 18.2).

A Simple Subroutine?

Look at the last three lines of this program. These three lines make up the new box-drawing subroutine. Line 11 creates a label, which has the effect of naming the subroutine, DrawBox. Because the label is defined, the subroutine can be referenced from other points in the program (the label designates where the subroutine begins).

After the label, the next program line is a LINE instruction, which actually does the subroutine's work. This LINE instruction is similar to the three LINE instructions in the GRTEST.BAS program. The difference is that in line 12, the variable name *HS* appears where formerly a number appeared. You now can assign *HS* whatever value you need (50, 70, or 90) and then use the subroutine to draw a box of the appropriate size.

The final line, RETURN, tells QBasic that the subroutine is finished (subroutines can include many more instructions than one instruction) and that control should return to the place in the program where the subroutine was called.

Refer to lines 4, 5, and 6 of the program, which have been changed to use the subroutine. Each of these three lines is two instructions separated by a colon. These separator colons have a different meaning from the colon after the name DrawBox.

> *Note:* The colon is used as a separator so that you can put multiple QBasic instructions on the same line. The colon also is required as the last character in a subroutine name. In QBasic, just as in English, a punctuation symbol may have more than one meaning.

Caution:
A colon is required to end a subroutine name.

Each first instruction on lines 4, 5, and 6 assigns to *HS* the number needed to draw the proper box. The second instruction on each line, GOSUB DrawBox, tells QBasic to go find the subroutine named DrawBox, perform the instructions given there, and then come back to continue the program.

Line 4 contains an apostrophe followed by a textual comment. Remember, an apostrophe means that the rest of the line is a comment and, therefore, is not to be treated as an active QBasic instruction.

The program has one other instruction, END (line 10), just before the DrawBox subroutine. For the program to terminate properly, this END instruction is necessary. Without this END, after the program performs the PRINT instruction, the next sequential instructions are those in the DrawBox subroutine. The program would fall into the subroutine and begin executing the instructions found in the subroutine. Subroutines should execute only when properly invoked by a GOSUB instruction; otherwise, the results can be unpredictable and erroneous.

Benefits of Using Subroutines

In a comparison of small programs such as GRTEST2.BAS and GRTEST.BAS, the benefits are not as obvious as would be the case for large programs. The fundamental benefits of subroutines are the following:

- Avoid repetitious programming

- Reduce program size

- Simplify program logic

- Facilitate future program changes

- Segment a big problem into little ones

These benefits are all important, but perhaps the most important is the last. The human mind cannot keep track of hundreds of details at the same time. When using subroutines (and subprograms), you can think of a program in terms of functional units instead of endless details. You should be concentrating on what the program is supposed to accomplish, not worrying about the details of programming one particular instruction.

> *Note:* Deciding which parts of a program should be subroutines (or subprograms) and which parts should not is a complex issue that separates advanced programmers from novices. One rule of thumb is that program sections that do not fit on one printed page (about 50 lines) need to be broken into subroutines (or subprograms) to create smaller, more understandable program chunks.

This section completes the introduction to QBasic programming. Using the keywords and techniques covered in the last two chapters, you can write many useful programs. Of course, two chapters cannot fully explain the many features and details of the language. For comprehensive coverage of QBasic programming, read *Using QBasic* by Phil Feldman and Tom Rugg, also published by Que Corporation.

Introducing Advanced Features of QBasic

In addition to the topics covered in the last two chapters, QBasic has many other commands and features. To get a taste of what lies on the horizon should you pursue QBasic further, read the following list of some QBasic features not covered in this book.

- Other variable types. *Integer* variables provide increased mathematical flexibility. (Integer variables assume only whole number values; these variable names end with a percent sign %.) An *array* is like a super variable. An array stores multiple values in one variable name. With a data structure called a *record*, you can custom design individual data types for a particular application.

- Additional operators. QBasic supports several operators, including logical operators (such as NOT, AND, and OR) for constructing compound relational expressions.

- An extensive collection of built-in functions for mathematical work, string manipulation, and the handling of dates and times

- Special format instructions for displaying results on-screen

- Advanced graphic commands and functions, including VGA support, animation, and shading

- File processing commands that read and write disk files

- Support for hardware devices such as a line printer, mouse, joystick, keyboard, and light pen

- Support for independent modules called *subprograms*. A subprogram is like a secondary program that your main program can invoke. Unlike a subroutine, variables in a subprogram are defined only within the subprogram; you can combine two different subprograms that use the same variable name without worrying about conflicts in the values of the variables. You can pass values to a subprogram, and the subprogram can return values to your main program. In the editor environment, QBasic maintains subprograms in separate windows, which you can manipulate from the View menu. You may use the same subprogram in several different main programs. By using subprograms, you can break a large programming task into isolated chunks. This concept is one of the foundations behind the modern concept of structured programming.

- User-defined functions. You can create your own special functions that you can invoke throughout a program.

- Advanced debugging tools. The Debug menu provides special features for debugging troublesome programs. These features include program tracing and breakpoint setting. With these tools, you can execute a program line-by-line and track down intermediate results.

- Event handling. Your program can monitor external devices and branch to a specified subroutine when a particular event occurs. You can monitor events such as keystrokes, joystick manipulation, data arriving at a serial port, or the elapsing of a particular time period.

Creating Programs for Other Users

A QBasic program easily can be saved on disk and given to somebody else. After you start programming, you may find many occasions for distributing programs. Perhaps coworkers, friends, or family can benefit from your programming efforts. You may even try selling your software.

Anyone who wants to run one of your programs, however, must have QBasic. When you give a program to someone, he or she first must start QBasic and then load your program.

Reminder:
QBasic cannot create executable files.

QBasic cannot create *executable files*. An executable file is a stand-alone program that can be run directly from the DOS command line. Such a file has the EXE or COM extension on its file name.

To turn a QBasic program into an executable file, consider purchasing Microsoft's QuickBASIC. Remember that QBasic and QuickBASIC are closely related and quite similar. If you know how to program with one, you know how to program with the other; however, QuickBASIC does have a few features not found in QBasic.

Probably the most significant of these differences is that QuickBASIC can create a stand-alone EXE file from a program. After you create and distribute an EXE version of your program, anyone can run the program directly from the DOS command line (without needing QBasic).

Chapter Summary

QBasic is a modern version of the venerable programming language known as BASIC. QBasic is new with DOS 5.0 and effectively replaces the BASICA and GW-BASIC languages that came with previous versions of DOS. Compared to BASICA and GW-BASIC, QBasic offers a full-screen editing environment and many important language enhancements.

By learning QBasic, you can custom design programs specifically for your needs or for the needs of others. With an understanding of the material covered in the last two chapters of this book, you are well on your way to writing useful programs.

Part V

Command Reference

Introduction to the Command Reference

This command reference includes all DOS commands. The commands are presented with the command name appearing first, followed by the versions of DOS to which the command applies.

Next, the terms *internal* and *external* indicate whether the command is built into DOS or is disk-resident. A brief description of the command's purpose immediately follows the title line. Each command entry illustrates the syntax in one or more syntax lines, showing how to invoke the command. Occasionally, a command may have a long and a short form, equally valid as command terms in a syntactical structure. In these instances, both forms are illustrated.

When switches can be used in the command line, these are listed and defined. You may get syntax help for each command in DOS 5 by adding the /? switch to the command line or by using the HELP command. If you enter only **HELP**, a list of commands with an accompanying one line description is displayed on-screen.

Notes give further information about the command, amplifying the purpose, giving insight into its efficient use, or otherwise acquainting you with the scope of the command. As appropriate, cautionary notes are included to help you avoid particular pitfalls associated with a command. A reference may be given, directing you to a chapter within the body of the book that treats the command at greater length. When necessary for clarity, examples of how to use the command are given.

The messages section is an alphabetical listing of the messages produced by the command. The following three types of messages are indicated:

- INFORMATION — This message informs the operator that the activity is taking place—or the message may prompt the operator for a response.

- WARNING — This message warns the operator of a possible problem. The command continues to function.

- ERROR — This message indicates that an error has occurred. The error may be a command error caused by the way the information on the command line was entered. The error message may occur during an operation, indicating a disk or other hardware error. The command terminates after an error message.

Command Reference Conventions

Great effort has been taken to make the command reference as easy as possible to use. Yet to understand fully the syntax lines discussed you must be familiar with a few conventions. These conventions signal key properties of the terms shown in the command line, indicating what is mandatory or merely optional and what components of the syntax line are variable.

Expressing File Names

The following syntax line shows how a file name is represented:

*d:path***filename.ext**

The *d:* represents a drive designation and can be any valid drive letter available on your computer.

path represents a subdirectory or a path of subdirectories on a valid drive.

filename.ext represents the full file name and its extension. When specifying a file name, you must give the extension if one exists. When a file has no extension, omit this portion of the file name specification.

When the syntax specifies an external command, you see a command line that resembles the following:

*dc:pathc***command_name**

The *dc:* represents the *drive* that contains the command. This value can be any valid drive letter on your computer.

pathc represents the subdirectory or *path* of subdirectories that leads to the command.

command_name is any valid DOS command. **FORMAT**, for example, may replace **command_name** in an actual line. When entering the command name, you do not need to specify the extension.

Using Upper- and Lowercase Letters

In any syntax line, not all elements of the syntax can be represented in a literal manner. For example, *filename.ext* can represent any file name with any extension. In this command reference, any literal text that you can type in a syntax line is shown in uppercase letters. Any text that you can replace with other text (variable text) is shown in lowercase letters.

For example, the following syntax line

FORMAT d:

means that you must type **FORMAT** to format a disk. The **d** can be replaced by any valid disk drive letter.

Recognizing Mandatory and Optional Syntax

Not all parts of a syntax line are essential when you type the command. Any mandatory portions of a syntax line are shown in **boldface**; what you see in *italic* is optional.

Typing the drive and path that contains a command is not always mandatory. For example, if FORMAT.COM is in the \DOS directory on drive C, and your current directory is C:\DOS, you do not have to type the drive and path to start FORMAT.COM. In this instance, the syntax form can omit this information:

*C:\DOS***FORMAT**

If you have FORMAT.COM residing on a drive and directory other than those shown in this example, the syntax is represented as follows:

*dc:pathc***FORMAT**

dc:pathc is variable text and optional, and **FORMAT** is literal text and mandatory.

DOS Messages

DOS messages fall into two groups: *general* and *device error* messages. The larger group, general DOS messages, is listed first.

The wording of error messages for your version of DOS may differ from those shown here. If you see a message that you cannot locate in this guide, refer to the DOS manual for your computer.

General DOS Messages

The following messages may appear when you are starting DOS or using your computer. Messages that occur only when you are starting DOS are marked "start-up." With most start-up errors, DOS did not start; you must reboot the system. Other error messages occur when DOS aborts a program and returns to the system prompt, such as A> or C>. Messages that apply to specific commands are listed in the "Messages" sections of each command entry in the command reference.

```
Abort edit (Y/N)?
```

You ended an edit session in Edlin with Q (Quit). This message gives you one last chance to cancel the command before leaving without saving any changes. To cancel and return to Edlin, press N. Otherwise, press Y to quit.

```
Allocation error, size adjusted
```

The contents of a file have been truncated because the size indicated in the directory is not consistent with the amount of data allocated to the file. Use CHKDSK /F to correct the discrepancy.

```
All specified files are contiguous
```

All files are written sequentially to disk. When you are using CHKDSK, this message may display. ANSI.SYS must be installed to perform requested functions.

While using MODE, you requested a screen function that cannot be performed until you load ANSI.SYS.

`Bad command or filename`

ERROR: You entered an invalid name for invoking a command, program, or batch file. The most frequent causes are the following: you misspelled a name, you omitted a required disk drive or path name, or you omitted the command name when giving parameters (for example, omitting the WordStar command, **ws**, by typing **myfile** instead of **ws myfile**).

Check the spelling on the command line and make sure that the command, program, or batch file is in the location specified. Then try the command again.

`Bad or Missing Command Interpreter`

ERROR (start-up): DOS does not start because it cannot find COMMAND.COM, the command interpreter.

If this message appears during start-up, COMMAND.COM is not on the start-up disk, or a COMMAND.COM file from a previous version of DOS is on the disk. If you have used the SHELL directive in CONFIG.SYS, the message means that the SHELL directive is improperly phrased or that COMMAND.COM is not where you specified. Place another disk that contains the operating system (IBMBIO.COM, IBMDOS.COM, and COMMAND.COM) in the floppy disk drive and reset the system. After DOS has started, copy COMMAND.COM to the original start-up disk so that you can boot DOS in the future.

If this message appears while you are running DOS, several explanations are possible. COMMAND.COM has been erased from the disk and directory you used when starting DOS; a version of COMMAND.COM from a previous version of DOS has overwritten the good version; or the COMSPEC entry in the environment has been changed. You must restart DOS by resetting the system.

If resetting the system does not solve your problem, restart the computer from a copy of your DOS master disk. Copy COMMAND.COM from this disk to the offending disk.

`Bad or missing filename`

WARNING (start-up): This message means that the device driver file name was not found, that an error occurred when the device driver was loaded, that a break address for the device driver was beyond the RAM available to the computer, or that DOS detected an error while loading the driver into memory. DOS continues booting without the device driver file name.

If DOS loads, check your CONFIG.SYS file for the line `DEVICE=filename`. Make sure that the line is typed correctly and that the device driver is at the specified location; then reboot the system. If the message reappears, copy the file from its original disk to the boot disk and try starting DOS again. If the error persists, the device driver is bad, and you should contact the dealer or publisher who sold the driver to you.

Batch file missing

DOS could not find the batch file it was processing. The batch file may have been erased or renamed. With DOS 3.0, the disk containing the batch file may have been changed, causing DOS to abort processing the batch file.

If you are using DOS 3.0 and you changed the disk that contains the batch file, restart the batch file without changing the disk. You may need to edit the batch file so that you do not need to change disks. This procedure applies only to DOS 3.0.

If the batch file includes a RENAME command that causes the originating batch file name to change, edit the batch file to prevent renaming when it is processed again. If the file was erased, re-create the batch file from its backup file if possible. Edit the file to ensure that the batch file does not erase itself.

Cannot find file QBASIC.EXE

ERROR: DOS 5.0 could not find the QBASIC program because QBASIC.EXE is in another subdirectory or not on the path; QBASIC.EXE is on a disk in another drive; or the program is otherwise unavailable. Insert a disk containing QBASIC.EXE into a floppy disk drive to continue.

Cannot find GRAPHICS profile

ERROR: You did not give the path of the GRAPHICS.PRO file; DOS cannot find the file in the current directory.

Cannot load COMMAND, system halted

ERROR: DOS attempted to reload COMMAND.COM, but the area where DOS tracks the memory was destroyed, or the command processor was not found in the directory specified by the COMSPEC= entry. The system halts.

This message may indicate that COMMAND.COM was erased from the disk and directory you used when starting DOS or that the COMSPEC= entry in the environment has been changed. Restart DOS from your usual start-up disk. If DOS does not start, the copy of COMMAND.COM has been erased. Restart DOS from the DOS start-up or master disk and copy COMMAND.COM onto your usual start-up disk.

`Cannot read file allocation table`

ERROR: The file allocation table (FAT) resides in a bad sector of a defective disk. Recovering your data from the bad sectors may be impossible.

`Cannot setup expanded memory`

ERROR: Your expanded memory (EMS) card is not functioning properly and should be serviced.

`Cannot specify default drive`

ERROR: You entered identical drive letters with SYS (for example, SYS A: A:). You must enter different letters.

`Cannot start COMMAND, exiting`

ERROR: You or one of your programs directed DOS to load another copy of COMMAND.COM, but DOS could not. Your CONFIG.SYS FILES directive is set too low, or you do not have enough free memory for another copy of COMMAND.COM.

If your system has 256K or more and FILES is less than 10, edit the CONFIG.SYS file on your start-up disk, using **FILES = 15** or **FILES = 20**. Then restart DOS.

If the problem recurs, you do not have enough memory in your computer, or you have too many resident or background programs competing for memory space. Restart DOS, loading only the essential programs. If necessary, eliminate unneeded device drivers or RAM disk software. You also can obtain additional RAM for your system.

`xxxxxxx code page cannot be initialized`

ERROR (start-up): PRINTER.SYS or DISPLAY.SYS did not start. Check your CONFIG.SYS file's DEVICE command line and look for illegal parameters.

`Code page operation not supported on this device`

ERROR: While using MODE, you selected a device and code page combination not recognized by DOS. Make sure that you specified a valid device and code page and that the code page you selected is supported on the device.

`Code page specified has not been designated`

ERROR: You issued the KEYB command with an unrecognized code page. Prepare the code page for your CON (your console screen device) using the MODE prepare command; then retry KEYB.

`Code page xxx`

INFORMATION: This message displays the code page currently in use by the specified device. For example, if you type **MODE CON**, the message returns the code page in use for your screen.

`Code pages cannot be prepared`

ERROR: You attempted to use a duplicate code page for the specified device; or with MODE prepare, you specified more code pages than DOS supports for that device. Check CONFIG.SYS to see how many prepared code pages your device command line allows or issue MODE /status at the command line (for example, MODE /STATUS CON) to view the code pages already prepared for the device.

`Configuration too large`

ERROR (start-up): DOS could not load because you set too many FILES or BUFFERS in your CONFIG.SYS file or specified too large an environment area (/E) with the SHELL command. This problem should occur only on systems with less than 256K.

Restart DOS with a different disk. Edit the CONFIG.SYS file on your boot disk, lowering the number of FILES, BUFFERS, or both. You also can edit CONFIG.SYS to reduce the size of the environment in addition to lowering the number of FILES and BUFFERS. Restart DOS with the edited disk.

Another alternative is to increase the RAM in your system.

`Current drive is no longer valid`

WARNING: At the DOS system level, DOS attempted to read the current directory for the disk drive and found the drive no longer valid.

If the current disk drive is set for a floppy disk, this warning appears when you do not have a disk in the disk drive. Insert a floppy disk into the disk drive or type another drive designation.

The invalid drive error also occurs when a current networked or SUBST disk drive is deleted or disconnected. Change the current drive to a valid disk drive.

```
Disk boot failure
```

ERROR (start-up): An error occurred when DOS tried to load into memory. The disk contained IBMBIO.COM and IBMDOS.COM, but one of the two files could not be loaded.

Try starting DOS from the disk again. If the error recurs, try starting DOS from a disk you know is good, such as a copy of your DOS start-up or master disk. If DOS still fails to boot, you have a disk drive problem. Contact your dealer.

```
Disk full. Edits lost.
```

ERROR: Edlin cannot save your work to disk because the designated disk is full. Always make sure that you have a disk with plenty of room to save your files.

```
DOS memory-arena error
```

ERROR: When using the DOS Editor, this message indicates a serious memory error. If possible, save your work to a different file and reboot your computer.

```
Error in EXE file
```

ERROR: DOS detected an error while attempting to load a program stored in an EXE file. The problem, which is in the relocation information DOS needs to load the program, may occur if the EXE file has been altered.

Restart DOS and try the program again, this time using a backup copy of the program. If the message appears again, the program is flawed. If you are using a purchased program, contact the dealer or publisher. If you wrote the program, issue LINK to produce another copy of the program.

```
Error loading operating system
```

ERROR (start-up): A disk error occurred when DOS was loading from the hard disk. DOS does not start.

Restart the computer. If the error occurs after several tries, restart DOS from the floppy disk drive. If the hard disk does not respond (you cannot run DIR or CHKDSK without getting an error), you have a problem with the hard disk. Contact your dealer. If the hard disk does respond, place another copy of DOS onto your hard disk using SYS. You also may need to copy COMMAND.COM to the hard disk.

```
Error reading directory
```

ERROR: During a FORMAT procedure, DOS was unable to read the directory; bad sectors may have developed in the file allocation table (FAT) structure.

If the message occurs when DOS is reading a floppy disk, the disk is unusable and should be thrown away. If DOS cannot read your hard disk, however, the problem is more serious, and you may have to reformat your disk. Remember to back up your data files on a regular basis to prevent major losses.

```
Error reading (or writing) partition table
```

ERROR: DOS could not read from (or write to) the disk's partition table during the FORMAT operation because the partition table is corrupted. Run FDISK on the disk and reformat the disk.

```
File allocation table bad, drive d
Abort, Retry, Fail?
```

WARNING: DOS encountered a problem in the file allocation table of the disk in drive d. Press R to retry several times; if the message recurs, press A to abort.

If you are using a floppy disk, try to copy all the files to another disk, and then reformat or discard the original disk. If you are using a hard disk, back up files on the disk and then reformat it. You cannot use the disk until you have reformatted it.

```
filename device driver cannot be initialized
```

WARNING (start-up): In CONFIG.SYS, the parameters in the device driver file name or the syntax of the DEVICE line is incorrect. Check for incorrect parameters and phrasing errors in the DEVICE line. Edit the DEVICE line in the CONFIG.SYS file, save the file, and restart DOS.

```
Incorrect DOS Version
```

ERROR: The copy of the file holding the command you just entered is from a different version of DOS.

Get a copy of the command from the correct version of DOS (usually from your copy of the DOS start-up or master disk), and try the command again. If the disk you are using has been updated to hold new versions of DOS, copy the new versions over the old ones.

```
Insert disk with batch file
and press any key when ready
```

PROMPT: DOS attempted to execute the next command from a batch file, but the disk holding the batch file is not in the disk drive. This message occurs for DOS 3.1 and later versions. DOS 3.0 gives a fatal error when the disk is changed.

Insert the disk with the batch file into the disk drive and press a key to continue.

```
Insert disk with \COMMAND.COM in drive d
and strike any key when ready
```

PROMPT: DOS needs to reload COMMAND.COM but cannot find it on the start-up disk. If you are using floppy disks, the disk in drive d (usually A) has most likely been changed. Place a disk with a good copy of COMMAND.COM in drive d and press a key.

```
Insert diskette for drive x and strike
any key when ready
```

PROMPT: On a system with one floppy disk drive or a system in which DRIVER.SYS creates more than one logical disk drive from a physical disk drive, you or one of your programs specified a tandem disk drive x (such as A or B) that is different from the current disk drive.

If the correct disk is in the disk drive, press a key. Otherwise, insert the correct disk into the floppy disk drive and then press a key.

```
Intermediate file error during pipe
```

ERROR: DOS is unable to create or write to one or both of the intermediate files it uses when piping information between programs because the disk is full, the root directory of the current disk is full, or DOS cannot find the files. The most frequent cause is insufficient disk space.

Run DIR on the root directory of the current disk drive to make sure that you have enough room in the root directory for two additional files. If you do not have enough room, create room by deleting or copying and deleting files. You also may copy the necessary files to a different disk with sufficient room.

This error also may occur if a program is deleting files, including the temporary files DOS creates. In this case, you should correct the program, contact the dealer or program publisher, or avoid using the program with piping.

```
Internal stack overflow
System halted
```

ERROR: Your programs and DOS have exhausted the stack, the memory space reserved for temporary use. This problem is usually caused by a rapid succession of hardware devices demanding attention. DOS stops, and the system must be turned off and on again to restart DOS.

The circumstances that cause this message are generally infrequent and erratic, and they may not recur. If you want to prevent this error from occurring, add the STACKS directive to your CONFIG.SYS file. If the directive is already in your CONFIG.SYS file, increase the number of stacks specified. Chapter 17 provides information on the STACKS directive.

```
Invalid COMMAND.COM in drive d:
```

WARNING: DOS tried to reload COMMAND.COM from the disk in drive *d* and found that the file was from a different version of DOS. Follow the instructions for inserting a disk with the correct version.

If you frequently use the disk that generated this warning message, copy the correct version of COMMAND.COM to that disk.

```
Invalid COMMAND.COM, system halted
```

ERROR: DOS could not find COMMAND.COM on the hard disk. DOS halts and must be restarted.

COMMAND.COM may have been erased, or the COMSPEC variable in the environment may have been changed. Restart the computer from the hard disk. If a message indicates that COMMAND.COM is missing, the file was erased. Restart DOS from a floppy disk and copy COMMAND.COM to the root directory of the hard disk, or to the location your SHELL directive indicates, if you have placed this command in your CONFIG.SYS file.

If you restart DOS and this message appears again, a program or batch file is erasing COMMAND.COM or altering the COMSPEC variable. If a program is erasing COMMAND.COM, contact the dealer or publisher who sold you the program. If a batch file is erasing COMMAND.COM, edit the batch file. If COMSPEC is being altered, edit the offending batch file or program or place COMMAND.COM in the subdirectory your program or batch file expects.

```
Invalid disk change
```

WARNING: The disk in the 720K, 1.2M, or 1.44M disk drive was changed while a program had open files to be written to the disk. You see the message `Abort, Retry, Fail.` Place the correct disk in the disk drive and press R to retry.

`Invalid environment size specified`

WARNING: You gave an invalid SHELL directive in CONFIG.SYS. The environment-size switch (</E:*size*) contains nonnumeric characters or a number less than 160 or greater than 32,768.

Check the form of your CONFIG.SYS SHELL directive; it must be exact. You need a colon (:) between /E and *size*, no comma or space should occur, and *size* should be from 160 to 32768.

`Invalid partition table`

ERROR (start-up): DOS detected a problem in the hard disk's partition information. Restart DOS from a floppy disk. Back up all files from the hard disk, if possible, and run FDISK to correct the problem. If you change the partition information, you must reformat the hard disk and restore all its files.

`Invalid STACK parameter`

WARNING (start-up): One of the following problems exists with the STACKS directive in your CONFIG.SYS file: a comma is missing between the number of stacks and the size of the stack, the number of stack frames is not in the range of 8 to 64, the stack size is not in the range of 32 to 512, you have omitted the number of stack frames or the stack size, or the stack frame or the stack size (but not both) is 0. DOS continues to start but ignores the STACKS directive.

Check the STACKS directive in your CONFIG.SYS file. Edit and save the file; then restart DOS.

`Invalid switch character`

WARNING: DOS loaded VDISK, located in your CONFIG.SYS file, attempting to install it in low (nonextended) memory, but encountered a switch other than the /E extended memory switch. You misspelled the /E switch, or you left a space between the / and the E. Edit and save your CONFIG.SYS file, and then restart DOS.

`Memory allocation error`
`Cannot load COMMAND, system halted`

ERROR: A program destroyed the area where DOS keeps track of memory. You must restart DOS. If this error occurs again with the same program, the program has a flaw. Try a backup copy of the program. If the problem persists, contact the dealer or program publisher.

Missing operating system

ERROR (start-up): The DOS hard disk partition entry is marked as bootable (able to start DOS), but the DOS partition does not contain a copy of DOS. DOS does not start.

Start DOS from a floppy disk. Issue the SYS C: command to place DOS on the hard disk, and then copy COMMAND.COM to the disk. If this command fails to solve the problem, you must back up the existing files, if any, from the hard disk; then issue FORMAT /S to place a copy of the operating system on the hard disk. If necessary, restore the files you backed up.

Must enter both /T and /N parameters

ERROR: You must specify /T (number of tracks per side) and /N (number of sectors per disk) on the same command line.

No free file handles
Cannot start COMMAND, exiting

ERROR: DOS could not load an additional copy of COMMAND.COM because no file handles were available. Edit the CONFIG.SYS file on your start-up disk to increase the number of file handles (using the FILES directive) by five. Restart DOS and try the command again.

Non-System disk or disk error
Replace and strike any key when ready

ERROR (start-up): Your disk does not contain IBMBIO.COM and IBMDOS.COM, or IO.SYS and MSDOS.SYS for Microsoft DOS, or a read error occurred when you started the system. DOS does not start.

If you are using a floppy disk system, insert a bootable disk in drive A and press a key. The most frequent cause of this message on hard disk systems is leaving a nonbootable disk in drive A with the door closed. Open the door to disk drive A and press a key. DOS boots from the hard disk.

No system on default drive

ERROR: SYS cannot find the system files. Insert a disk containing the system files, such as the DOS disk, and type the command again.

Not enough memory

or

Insufficient memory

ERROR: The computer does not have enough free RAM memory to execute the program or command. If you loaded a resident program such as PRINT, GRAPHICS, SideKick, or ProKey, restart DOS and try the command again before loading any resident program. If this method fails to solve the problem, remove any nonessential device drivers or RAMdisk software from CONFIG.SYS and restart DOS. If this option also fails, your computer does not have enough memory for this command. You must increase your RAM memory to run the command.

```
Out of environment space
```

WARNING: DOS cannot add additional strings to the environment from the SET command because the environment cannot be expanded. This error occurs when loading a resident program such as MODE, PRINT, GRAPHICS, SideKick, or ProKey.

If you are running DOS 3.1 or a later version, refer to the SHELL directive in Chapter 15 (on customizing DOS) for information about expanding the default space for the environment. DOS 3.0 has no method for expanding the environment.

```
Parameters not supported
```

or

```
Parameters not supported on drive
```

ERROR: You entered parameters that do not exist, that are not supported by the DOS version you are running, or that are incompatible with the specified disk drive. Run VER to determine whether the current DOS version supports the parameters (or switches) you specified.

```
Program too big to fit in memory
```

ERROR: The computer does not have enough memory to load the program or the command you invoked. If you have any resident programs loaded (such as PRINT, GRAPHICS, or SideKick), restart DOS and try the command again without loading the resident programs. If this message appears again, reduce the number of buffers (BUFFERS) in the CONFIG.SYS file, eliminate nonessential device drivers or RAMdisk software, and restart DOS. If the problem persists, your computer does not have enough RAM memory for the program or command. You must increase the amount of RAM memory in your computer to run the program.

```
Same parameter entered twice
```

ERROR: You duplicated a switch when you typed a command. Retype the command using a parameter only once.

Sector size too large in file *filename*

WARNING: The device driver filename is inconsistent. The device driver defined a particular sector size for DOS but attempted to use a different size. The copy of the device driver is bad, or the device driver is incorrect. Make a backup copy of the device driver on the boot disk and then reboot DOS. If the message appears again, the device driver is incorrect. If you wrote the driver, correct the error. If you purchased the program, contact the dealer or software publisher.

Syntax error

ERROR: You phrased a command improperly by omitting needed information, giving extraneous information, inserting an extra space in a file or path name, or using an incorrect switch. Check the command line for these possibilities and try the command again.

TARGET media has lower capacity than SOURCE
Continue anyway (Y/N)?

WARNING: The target disk can hold fewer bytes of data than the source disk. The most likely cause is bad sectors on the target disk. If you press Y, some data on the source disk may not fit onto the target disk.

To avoid the possibility of an incomplete transfer of data, type N and insert a disk with the same capacity as the source disk. If you are not copying "hidden" files, you also can issue the COPY *.* command to transfer files.

Too many block devices

WARNING (start-up): Your CONFIG.SYS file contains too many DEVICE directives. DOS continues to start but does not install additional device drivers.

DOS can handle only 26 block devices. The block devices created by the DEVICE directives, plus the number of block devices automatically created by DOS, exceed this number. Remove any unnecessary DEVICE directives in your CONFIG.SYS file and restart DOS.

Top level process aborted, cannot continue

ERROR (start-up): COMMAND.COM or another DOS command detected a disk error, and you chose the A (Abort) option. DOS cannot finish starting, and the system halts.

Try to start DOS again. If the error recurs, start DOS from a floppy disk (if starting from the hard disk) or from a different floppy disk (if starting from a floppy disk). After DOS has started, issue the SYS command to place another copy of the operating system on the disk, and copy COMMAND.COM to the disk. If DOS reports an error while copying, the disk is bad. Reformat or discard the floppy disk, or back up and reformat the hard disk.

```
There is not enough room to create a restore file
You will not be able to use the unformat utility
Proceed with Format (Y/N)?
```

WARNING: The disk lacks sufficient room to create a restore file. Without this file, you cannot use UNFORMAT to reverse the format you are attempting.

```
Unable to create directory
```

ERROR: A directory could not be created for one of the following reasons: a directory by the same name already exists; a file by the same name already exists; you are adding a directory to the root directory, and the root directory is full; or the directory name has illegal characters or is a device name.

Issue DIR to make sure that no file or directory already exists with the same name. If you are adding the directory to the root directory, remove or move (copy, then erase) any nonessential files or directories. Check the spelling of the directory name and make sure that the command is properly phrased.

```
Unable to load MS-DOS Shell, Retry (y/n)?
```

ERROR, PROMPT: DOS could not load the Shell. You may be using a DOS command line feature of a program, and the Shell does not fit into memory. The DOS Shell program also may be corrupted.

Exit the program and try to load the Shell. If the Shell still doesn't load, it is probably corrupt. Reboot your system and load the Shell. If the same error message appears, copy Shell from a backup disk to your hard disk.

```
Unrecognized command in CONFIG.SYS
```

WARNING (start-up): DOS detected an improperly phrased directive in CONFIG.SYS. The directive is ignored, and DOS continues to start, but DOS does not indicate the incorrect line. Examine the CONFIG.SYS file, looking for improperly phrased or incorrect directives. Edit the line, save the file, and restart DOS.

```
Write failure, diskette unusable
```

ERROR: DOS found bad sectors in the boot or FAT areas of the target disk. Discard the disk and use another to create a System disk.

```
Wrong DOS
```

ERROR: The version of DOS is incompatible with UNFORMAT.

DOS Device Error Messages

When DOS detects an error while reading or writing to disk drives or other devices, one of the following messages appears:

```
type error reading device

type error writing device
```

type is the type of error, and *device* is the device at fault. If the device is a floppy disk drive, do not remove the disk from the drive. Refer to the possible causes and corrective actions described in this section, which lists the types of error messages that may appear.

```
Bad call format
```

A device driver was given a requested header with an incorrect length. The problem is that the application software is making the call.

```
Bad command
```

The device driver issued an invalid or unsupported command to the device. The problem may be with the device driver software or with other software trying to use the device driver. If you wrote the program, correct it. For a purchased program, contact the dealer or publisher who sold you the program.

```
Bad format call
```

The device driver at fault passed an incorrect header length to DOS. If you wrote this device driver, you must rewrite it to correct the problem. For a purchased program, contact the dealer or publisher who sold you the driver.

```
Bad unit
```

An invalid subunit number was passed to the device driver. The problem may be with the device driver software or with other software trying to use the device driver. Contact the dealer who sold you the device driver.

```
Data
```

DOS could not correctly read or write the data. The disk most likely has developed a defective spot.

Drive not ready

An error occurred when DOS tried to read or write to the disk drive. For floppy disk drives, the drive door may be open, the floppy disk may not have been inserted, or the disk may not be formatted. For hard disk drives, the drive may not be properly prepared; that is, you may have a hardware problem.

FCB unavailable

With the file-sharing program (SHARE.EXE) loaded, a program using the DOS 1 method of file handling attempted to open concurrently more file control blocks than were specified with the FCBS directive.

Select the Abort option (see the end of this section). Increase the value of the FCBS CONFIG.SYS directive (usually by four), and reboot the system. If the message appears again, increase the value again and reboot.

General failure

This message is a catchall for errors not covered elsewhere. The error usually occurs for one of the following reasons: you are using an unformatted disk; the disk drive door is open; the floppy disk is not seated properly; or you are using the wrong type of disk in a disk drive, such as a 1.2M disk in a 360K disk drive.

Lock violation

With the file-sharing program (SHARE.EXE) or the network software loaded, a program attempted to access a locked file. Your best choice is Retry. Then try Abort. If you press A, however, any data in memory is lost.

Must specify COM1, COM2, COM3 or COM4

You must specify the COM port in the MODE command.

No paper

The printer is out of paper or not turned on.

Non-DOS disk

The FAT has invalid information, making the disk unusable. You can abort and run CHKDSK to determine whether corrective action is possible. If CHKDSK fails, you can reformat the disk. Reformatting, however, destroys any remaining information on the disk.

If you use more than one operating system, the disk has probably been formatted under the other operating system and should not be reformatted.

Not ready

The device is not ready and cannot receive or transmit data. Check the connections, making sure that the power is on and the device is ready. For floppy disk drives, make sure that the disk is formatted and properly seated in the disk drive.

Read fault

DOS was unable to read the data, probably from a disk. Check the disk drive doors to make sure that the disk is inserted properly.

Sector not found

The disk drive was unable to find the sector on the disk. This error is usually the result of a defective spot on the disk or of defective drive electronics. Some copy-protection schemes also use a defective spot to prevent unauthorized duplication of the disk.

Seek

The disk drive could not find the proper track on the disk. This error is usually the result of a defective spot on the disk, an unformatted disk, or problems with the drive electronics problems.

Write fault

DOS could not write the data to this device. You may have inserted the disk improperly or left the disk drive door open. Another possibility is an electronics failure in the floppy or hard disk drive. The most frequent cause is a bad spot on the disk.

Write protect

The disk is write-protected.

> *Note:* One of the previously listed messages (usually Data, Read fault, or Write fault) appears when you are using a double-sided disk in a single-sided disk drive or a 9-sector disk (DOS 2 and later) with a version of DOS 1.
>
> DOS displays one of these error messages and the Abort,Retry,Fail? prompt for DOS 3.3, 4.x, and 5.0 or Abort,Retry,Ignore? for versions of DOS before 3.3.

If you press A for Abort, DOS ends the program that requested the read or write condition. Pressing R for Retry causes DOS to try the operation again. If you press F for Fail or I for Ignore, DOS skips the operation, and the program continues. Some data may be lost, however, when you select Fail or Ignore.

The order of preference, unless stated differently under the message, is R, A, and F or I. You should retry the operation at least twice. If the condition persists, you must decide whether to abort the program or ignore the error. If you ignore the error, data may be lost. If you abort, data still being processed by the program and not yet written to the disk is lost.

Command Reference

APPEND

V3.3, V4, V5—External

Instructs DOS to search the specified directories on the specified disks for nonprogram and nonbatch files.

Syntax

To establish the data-file search path the first time, use the following form:

*dc:pathc***APPEND** *d1:path1;d2:path2;d3:path3; . . .*

dc: is the name of the disk drive that holds the command.

pathc is the path to the command.

d1:, d2:, d3: are valid disk drive names.

path1, path2, path3 are valid paths to the directories you want DOS to search for nonprogram/nonbatch files. The three periods (. . .) represent additional disk drive and path names.

To use either of the APPEND switches, use the following:

*dc:pathc***APPEND** */X /E*

With DOS 4 and 5, you also can use the following syntax for the */X* switch:

*dc:pathc***APPEND/X:OFF**
*dc:pathc***APPEND /X:ON**

701

To change the data-file search path, use the following:

> **APPEND** *d1:path1,d2:path2;d3:path3;* . . .

With DOS 4 and 5, the default state for a search for files that have the drive or path specified is as follows:

> **APPEND** */PATH:ON*

To turn off a search for files that have the drive or path specified (for DOS 4 and 5), use the following form:

> **APPEND** */PATH:OFF*

To see the search path, use the following form:

> **APPEND**

To disconnect the data-file search, use the following form:

> **APPEND;**

Switches

/X	Redirects programs that use the DOS function calls SEARCH FIRST, FIND FIRST, and EXEC.
/X:ON	Same as /X (DOS 4 and 5).
/X:OFF	Turns this feature off (DOS 4 and 5).
/E	Places the disk drive paths in the environment.
/PATH:ON	Turns on search for files that have drive or path specified (DOS 4 and 5).
/PATH:OFF	Turns off search for files that have drive or path specified (DOS 4 and 5).

Reference

See Chapter 7.

Rules

1. The first time you execute APPEND, the program loads from the disk and installs itself in DOS. APPEND then becomes an internal command and is not reloaded from the disk until you restart DOS.

2. You can give the /X and /E switches only when you first invoke APPEND. You cannot give any path names with these two switches.

3. If you specify more than one set of paths, the following rules apply:

    a. The path sets must be separated by semicolons.

    b. The search for the nonprogram files is made in the order in which you gave the path sets. First the specified directory (or current directory if none is specified) is searched. Then *d1:path1* is searched, followed by *d2:path2*, and so on, either until the file is found or when APPEND exhausts the list of directory paths.

4. The length of the paths given for APPEND cannot exceed 127 characters; this limit includes the APPEND command name.

5. If an invalid path is encountered, such as a misspelled path or a path that no longer exists, DOS skips the path and does not display a message.

6. If you use the /X switch, APPEND processes the DOS function calls SEARCH FIRST, FIND FIRST, and EXEC.

7. With DOS 4 and 5, you can disable the /X switch by using **/X:OFF**.

8. Do not use RESTORE while you are using the /X switch.

9. To disable APPEND, give the command followed by a semicolon. APPEND remains resident but inactive until you issue another APPEND command with path names.

10. If you use the /E switch, DOS establishes an environmental variable named APPEND. The variable holds the current paths that APPEND uses.

11. The file found by APPEND can be safely read by the program. However, any changes to the file are saved in a copy of the file placed in the current directory. The original file remains intact.

12. If you are using the ASSIGN command with APPEND, you must issue the APPEND command before you use ASSIGN.

Examples

1. **APPEND /X /E**

    Loads the APPEND command and establishes APPEND to intercept the DOS function calls SEARCH FIRST, FIND FIRST, and EXEC (the /X switch). DOS places in the environment the paths you give to APPEND (the /E switch). This example assumes that APPEND is in the current directory or on the PATH.

2. **APPEND C:\BIN;C:\BIN\OVR**

   Instructs APPEND to search the specified or current directory for nonprogram files and then to search the directories C:\BIN and C:\BIN\OVR.

3. **APPEND /PATH:ON**

   Instructs APPEND to ignore invalid drive or path designations and search the APPEND path for the file. If you enter **TYPE C:\TEMP\DOCUMENT.TXT**, but the directory C:\TEMP does not exist, the APPEND paths are searched for DOCUMENT.TXT.

4. **APPEND;**

   Disables the APPEND command. The APPEND command stays in memory until you restart DOS. To reactivate APPEND, simply give a set of path names to the command.

Notes

APPEND is the counterpart of the PATH command, which works with program files. APPEND is the PATH command for data and other nonprogram files. The command is especially useful if you run programs that do not support hierarchical directories. With the APPEND command, you can place additional program files (such as those used with WordStar Release 3) or data files in any directory.

You can use APPEND /X to trick programs at three levels. First, when a program attempts to open a file to read, APPEND enables the program to find the file to be opened. Second, when a program simply searches for a file name, APPEND enables the program to find the file name. Third, when a program attempts to execute another program, APPEND helps to find and then to execute the program.

The /E switch places the paths fed to APPEND in the environment, under the variable named APPEND. If you use /E, programs can examine the environment for the APPEND variable and use the contents to find their files. However, do not use APPEND from within a program if you use /E. The changes that APPEND makes to the environment are temporary—the copy of COMMAND.COM used to run APPEND is temporary. When you return to the program, changes made by APPEND are lost.

Be cautious if you write to files that APPEND finds. APPEND tricks programs into reading files from any location. APPEND does not trick programs when the programs write files. DOS saves changes you make to a file in a copy of that file, which DOS then places in the current directory. The original file in the directory on which you used APPEND remains unchanged. This file duplication can be confusing when you use a file in one directory and save the new version, and then move to another directory and attempt to reuse the file. You are working with the original file without the changes, while the altered file remains in the directory from which you made the changes.

If used with the ASSIGN command, APPEND is an *open-me-first* command. You must start APPEND before you use the ASSIGN command. Reversing the order causes APPEND to deliver an error message, and the command does not load.

For more information, see the PATH command in this Command Reference.

Messages

1. `APPEND/ASSIGN Conflict`
   `APPEND/TopView Conflict`

   ERROR: You tried to use APPEND after you loaded ASSIGN, TopView, or DESQview. If you are using TopView or DESQview, exit the program, give the APPEND command, and then restart your program. If you are using ASSIGN, break the assignment, issue the APPEND command, and reissue ASSIGN.

2. `APPEND already installed`

   WARNING: You attempted to load APPEND again by giving a disk drive or path name for a command. You need to load APPEND only once. Give the command again without the command's drive or path name.

3. `Incorrect APPEND Version`

   ERROR: You used a version of APPEND from a different version of DOS. Make sure that you do not use an APPEND version from the IBM Local Area Network (LAN) program. The problem can be that the wrong version of APPEND is loading first from a PATHed directory.

4. `No Append`

   INFORMATION: You typed APPEND to see the current path, and APPEND is currently inactive.

ASSIGN

Instructs DOS to use a disk drive other than the one specified by a program or command.

Syntax

To reroute drive activity, use the following form:

*dc:pathc***ASSIGN d1=d2** . . . */STATUS /?*

dc: is the name of the disk drive that holds the command.

pathc is the path to the command.

d1 is the letter of the disk drive the program or DOS normally uses.

d2 is the letter of the disk drive that you want the program or DOS to use instead of the usual drive.

The three periods (. . .) represent additional disk drive assignments.

To clear the reassignment, use the following form:

*dc:pathc***ASSIGN**

Switch

/STATUS   Displays all current drive assignments.

Reference

See Chapter 10.

Rules

1. You can reassign any valid DOS drive to any other drive, but not to itself.

2. Do not use a colon after the disk drive letter for **d1** or **d2**. You can use a space on either side of the equal sign.

3. You can give more than one assignment on the same line. Use a space between each set of assignments, as in the following example:

    ASSIGN B=C A=C

4. Use ASSIGN only when necessary.

5. Do not ASSIGN a disk drive to a drive that is not on your system. If you make this mistake, DOS returns the error message:

    ```
    Invalid parameter
    ```

Examples

1. **ASSIGN A = C** or **ASSIGN A=C**

   DOS reroutes to drive C any activity for drive A. You can use a
   space on either side of the equals sign.

2. **ASSIGN A=C B=C**

   DOS reroutes to drive C any activity for drives A and B.

3. **ASSIGN** /*STATUS*

   or

   ASSIGN /*S*

   Displays the current drive assignments.

4. **ASSIGN**

   Clears any previous drive reassignment.

Note

With DOS 3.1 and more recent versions, an alternative to ASSIGN is
SUBST, which assigns a disk drive letter to a subdirectory (see the
SUBST command). For compatibility with future versions of DOS,
consider using SUBST rather than ASSIGN.

ATTRIB   V3, V4, V5—External

Displays, sets, or clears a file's read-only or archive attributes.

Syntax

To set the file's attributes on, use the following form:

*dc:pathc***ATTRIB** +*R* +*A* +*S* + *H d:path***filename.ext**/*s*

To clear the file's attributes, use the following form:

*dc:pathc***ATTRIB** –*R* –*A* –*S* –*H d:path***filename.ext**/*s*

To display a file's attribute status, use the following form:

*dc:pathc***ATTRIB** *d:path***filename.ext**/*s*

dc: is the name of the disk drive that holds the command.

pathc is the path to the command.

+*R*/–*R* sets a file's read-only attribute on and off.

+*A*/–*A* sets a file's archive attribute on and off.

+*S*/–*S* sets the file's system attribute on and off (Version 5 only).

+*H*/–*H* sets a file's hidden attribute on and off (Version 5 only).

d: is the name of the disk drive that holds the files for which the read-only attribute are displayed or changed.

path\ is the path to the files for which the read-only attribute will be displayed or changed.

filename.ext is the name of the file(s) for which the read-only attribute will be displayed or changed. Wild cards are permitted.

Switch

/*S*   Sets or clears the attributes of the specified files in the specified directory and all subdirectories to that directory.

Reference

See Chapter 8.

Rules

1. If you do not give an file name (**filename.ext**), DOS displays the following error message:

```
Invalid path or filename not found
```

If you give an incorrect file name, DOS displays the error message:

```
Invalid parameters
```

2. You can use **R, A, S,** and **H** characters together or individually in the command. You can mix the plus and minus attributes of the commands (for example, **+R –A**), but you cannot use plus and minus for the same character in the command (for example, **+R –R**).

Message

```
Access denied
```

ERROR: You are attempting to delete a read-only file. To delete the file, use ATTRIB with the –R parameter to remove the read-only attribute. Then use DEL to delete the file.

Backup c:\ B: /s.

BACKUP

V2, V3, V4, V5—External

Backs up one or more files from a hard disk or a floppy disk to another disk.

Syntax

*dc:pathc***BACKUP d1:***path\filename.ext* **d2:** */S /M /A*

/D:date /T:time /F /L:dl:filenamel:extl

dc: is the disk drive that holds the command.

pathc is the path to the command.

d1: is the hard disk or floppy disk drive to be backed up.

path is the starting directory path for backup.

filename.ext specifies the name(s) of the file(s) you want to back up. Wild cards are allowed.

d2: is the hard disk or floppy disk drive that receives the backup files.

Switches

/S	Backs up all *subdirectories*, starting with the specified or current directory on the source disk and working downward.
/M	Backs up all files *modified* since the last backup.
/A	*Adds* the file(s) to be backed up to the files already on the specified floppy disk drive.
/D:date	Backs up any file that you create or change on or after the specified *date*.
/T:time	Backs up any file that you create or change on or after the specified *time* on the specified date (given with the /D switch).
/F	*Formats* the destination floppy disk if the disk is not formatted. DOS 4 and 5 formats the target floppy disks automatically without the use of this switch.
/F:size	With DOS 4 and 5, *formats* the destination floppy disk according to the *size* specified. If you have a 1.2M disk drive, but only 360K disks, you can specify **/F:360** to format the 360K disk in the 1.2M drive.
/L:dl:pathl\filenamel.ext	Creates a *log* file.

Exit Codes

0 Successful backup

1 No files found to be backed up

2 Some files not backed up because of sharing problems

3 Aborted by the user (Ctrl-Break or Ctrl-C)

4 Aborted because of an error

Reference

See Chapter 8.

Rules

1. Give both a source and a destination for BACKUP. Neither disk can be a networked disk, and neither disk can be used in an ASSIGN, SUBST, or JOIN command.

2. The source name must specify the valid name of the disk drive to be backed up. The source name also can include either or both of the following:

   a. A valid directory path that contains the files to be backed up.

   b. A file name with appropriate extensions, if desired. Wild cards are allowed.

3. The destination is any valid name for a floppy or hard disk drive.

4. To keep the files on a previously backed-up disk, use the /A option. If you do not use this switch, all files previously stored on the receiving disk are destroyed, or all files in the \BACKUP subdirectory of the hard disk are destroyed.

   To use the /A option with floppy disks, you must start with a disk that contains the special files created by BACKUP, named CONTROL.xxx and BACKUP.xxx (xxx is the number of the disk). Otherwise, BACKUP displays the message `Last backup diskette not inserted` and aborts the process.

5. If you back up onto floppy disks, all files are placed in the root directory. If you back up onto another hard disk, the files are stored in the subdirectory \BACKUP.

6. To create a log of the files that BACKUP processed, give the /L switch. If you do not specify a full file name, BACKUP creates

the log file under the name BACKUP.LOG in the source disk's root directory.

7. If you do not specify a file name (*filenamel.extl*) for the log file, BACKUP displays an error message and aborts.

If you give a log file name, you must use a colon between the **L** and the first character in the name. Do not use spaces from the beginning of the switch to the end of the log file name. If you do not give a log file name, do not use a colon after the **L**.

If a log file already exists, BACKUP adds to the log file. If a file does not exist, a new file is created. You cannot place the log file on the destination disk (the disk used to store the backup files).

Examples

For the following examples, assume that the hard disk is C and that the following subdirectories exist:

```
C:\
C:\DOS
C:\WP
C:\DATA
C:\DATA\LETTERS
C:\DATA\MEMOS
```

1. Backing Up the Entire Hard Disk

   BACKUP C:\ A: /S

   Here, the source to back up is specified as **C:**. The /S switch instructs BACKUP to backup all subdirectories of the source—that is, all subdirectories of the root directory.

2. Backing Up a Specific Subdirectory

   BACKUP C:\DATA\LETTERS A:

   This example shows how to back up only a single subdirectory. In this case, the subdirectory **LETTERS** are backed up. You do not need to use any switches.

3. Backing Up Several Subdirectories

   BACKUP C:\DATA A: /S

   In this example, **DATA** is the source to back up. Because of the /S switch, all subdirectories of \DATA are backed up.

4. Backing Up All Files as of a Specified Date

   BACKUP C:\ A: /S /D:08/21/89

   In this example, all files that were created or modified on or after August 21, 1989, are backed up. Note that the root directory is the source and that the /S switch is given to back up all subdirectories of the source directory.

5. Backing Up Modified Files Only

   BACKUP C:\ A: /S /M

   The /M switch tells BACKUP to back up all files with the archive bit set on. When you create or modify a file, the archive bit is set on. When you back up a file, BACKUP turns off the archive bit.

6. Adding Modified Files to the Current Backup Disks

   BACKUP C:\ A: /S /M /A

   As with the previous example, only modified files are backed up. But, here, BACKUP does not overwrite files on the backup disk. Instead, you see the following message:

   ```
   Insert last backup diskette in drive A:
   Press any key to continue ...
   ```

   BACKUP begins to add modified files to the backup disks, because of the /A switch.

Notes

Depending on the DOS version, the features of BACKUP vary. Prior to DOS 3.3, BACKUP creates a heading file called *BACKUPID.@@@* on each floppy disk. This file holds the date, time, and disk number of the backup. BACKUP stores each backed-up file individually on the disk. Each file contains a 128-byte heading that identifies the path, file name, the file's original directory attributes, and whether the file is complete or partial.

With 3.3 and more recent versions, BACKUP uses a different approach for the floppy disk that holds the backup files. A file called *CONTROL.nnn* holds the directory, file names, and other housekeeping information. All backed-up files are placed in one large file called *BACKUP.nnn*. (For both files, the *nnn* represents the number of the backup disk.) The two files are marked as read-only, so that you do not inadvertently erase or alter them.

BACKUP 3.3 and more recent versions places all the files into a larger file and thereby gains speed over its predecessors. The backup process is reduced to less than half the time required by previous versions. You cannot, however, determine which disk holds a given file. The log file is the only method for locating a file with DOS 3.3 and more recent versions.

Messages

1. `Cannot find FORMAT.EXE`

   ERROR: While running BACKUP, you provided an unformatted floppy disk, and BACKUP could not find the FORMAT command.

2. `Cannot FORMAT nonremovable drive d:`

   ERROR: The destination disk is a hard disk or networked disk drive, and you used the /F switch to request formatting.

   When you see this message, BACKUP aborts. To recover from this error, issue the BACKUP command again without the /F switch or use a floppy disk drive as the destination.

3. `Insert backup diskette nn in drive d:`

   ```
   Warning! Files in the target drive
   d:\  root directory will be erased
   Press any key to continue
   ```

   INFORMATION and WARNING: This message appears during the backup process when you back up to floppy disks. When you use the /A switch, the message does not appear for the first target disk, but does appear for subsequent disks. This message appears for all disks when you do not use /A.

   The message instructs you to put the first or next backup disk (disk number nn in the series) into drive d: and press any key to continue. The message also warns that BACKUP deletes all existing files in the root directory of the receiving disk before files are transferred. Make sure that the proper disk is in the disk drive and press any key to start.

4. `Insert last backup diskette in drive d:`
   `Strike any key when ready`

   INFORMATION: This message appears only when you use the /A switch and invoke BACKUP without placing the final disk for the backup set in the correct disk drive. Put the proper disk into the disk drive and press any key to start.

5. Insert backup source diskette in drive d:
   Strike any key when ready

   INFORMATION: You specified a floppy disk drive as the
   source for BACKUP. BACKUP is instructing you to insert the
   source disk and press any key when you are ready to begin
   the backup process.

6. Last backup diskette not inserted

   WARNING or ERROR: This message appears when you use the
   /A switch and when the disk in the disk drive is not the last
   disk of a previous series. If you used a disk previously processed by BACKUP, this message appears with the Insert
   last backup disk in drive d: message. If the disk was
   not previously processed by BACKUP, BACKUP aborts.

Batch Command   V1, V2, V3, V4, V5—Internal

Executes one or more commands contained in an ASCII disk file that
has a BAT extension.

Syntax

   *dc:pathc***filename** *parameters*

   dc: is the disk drive that holds the batch file.

   pathc is the path to the batch file.

   filename is the root name of the batch file.

   parameters are the parameters to be used by the batch file.

Reference

   See Chapter 12.

Rules for Batch Files

   1. A batch file must use the extension BAT.

   2. To invoke a batch file, simply type the root name. For ex-
      ample, to invoke the batch file OFTEN.BAT, type **OFTEN** and
      press Enter.

   3. DOS executes each command one line at a time. The specified
      parameters are substituted for the markers when the com-
      mand is used.

4. DOS recognizes a maximum of ten parameters. You can use the SHIFT subcommand to get around this limitation.

5. You can stop a running batch file by pressing Ctrl-Break. DOS displays the following message:

```
Terminate batch job (Y/N)?
```

If you press Y for yes, all subsequent commands are ignored and the system prompt appears. If you press N for no, DOS skips the current command, but continues to process the other commands in the file.

6. You can make DOS execute a second batch file immediately after the first is finished. Enter the name of the second batch file as the last command in the first file. You also can execute a second batch file within the first and return to the first file by using the CALL subcommand.

Rules for the AUTOEXEC.BAT File

1. AUTOEXEC.BAT must reside in the boot disk directory.

2. DOS, when booted, automatically executes the AUTOEXEC.BAT file.

3. When DOS executes the AUTOEXEC.BAT file after the computer boots, the system does not automatically request date and time. You must place DATE and TIME commands in the AUTOEXEC.BAT file to change the system date and time.

Rules for Creating Batch Files

1. A batch file contains ASCII text.

2. You can include any valid DOS system-level command in a batch file.

3. You can enter any valid batch subcommand. (The batch subcommands are included in this Command Reference.) You also can use replaceable parameters (%0–%9). You can use environmental variables by enclosing the name of the variable in percent signs (such as %COMSPEC%).

4. To designate a file name that contains a percent symbol as part of the file name, enter the percent symbol twice. For example, to use a file called A100%.TXT, you enter **A100%%.TXT**. This rule differs from the one for parameter markers, where percent symbols precede the parameter markers, and for environmental variables, which are enclosed in percent symbols.

5. Beginning with DOS 3.3, you can prevent the display of any line from the batch file if an @ is the first character on the line.

Batch Command
CALL   V3.3, V4, V5

Runs a second batch file and returns control to the first batch file.

Syntax

CALL *dc:pathc***filename** *parameters*

dc: is the disk drive that holds the called batch file.

pathc is the path to the called batch file.

filename is the root name of the called batch file.

parameters are the parameters to be used by the batch file.

Reference

See Chapter 14.

Rule

The named batch file is run as if invoked from the keyboard. Parameters are passed to the called batch file just as if the file were invoked from the keyboard.

Notes

You can duplicate this procedure in versions of DOS prior to 3.3 by using COMMAND in the following form:

COMMAND /C *dc:pathc***filename** *parameters*

filename is the root name of the second batch file.

Batch Command
ECHO   V2, V3, V4, V5

Displays a message and enables or prevents the display of batch commands and other messages as DOS executes batch subcommands.

Syntax

To display a message, use the following form:

ECHO *message*

To turn off the display of commands and other batch command messages, use the form:

ECHO OFF

To turn on the display of commands and messages, use the form:

ECHO ON

To see the status of ECHO, use the form:

ECHO

message is the text of the message to be displayed on the screen.

Reference

See Chapter 14.

Rules

1. For unconditional display of a message on the screen, use the command **ECHO MESSAGE**. The **MESSAGE** you designate is displayed whether ECHO is on or off.

2. When ECHO is on, the batch file displays commands as DOS executes each line. The batch file also displays any messages from the batch subcommands.

3. When ECHO is off, the batch file does not display the commands as DOS executes them. Additionally, the batch file displays no messages produced by other batch subcommands. Exceptions to this rule are the `Strike a key when ready` message generated by the PAUSE subcommand and any ECHO message command.

4. DOS starts the system with ECHO on.

5. An ECHO OFF command is active until batch processing is complete or until an ECHO ON command is encountered. If one batch file invokes another, ECHO OFF remains in effect until the final batch file is processed.

6. ECHO affects messages produced only by batch subcommands. The command does not affect messages from other DOS commands or programs.

Notes

You can suppress the display of a single batch file line by using the @ as the first character in a line. When you use the line @ECHO OFF, the command ECHO OFF is not displayed.

To suppress the output of a command, use I/O redirection to the null device (NUL). For example, to suppress a copied file message when you are using COPY, use the following form:

COPY file1.ext file2.ext >NUL

The command output is sent to the null device and is not displayed on the screen.

Batch Command
FOR..IN..DO   V2, V3, V4, V5

Enables iterative (repeated) processing of a DOS command.

Syntax

FOR %%*variable* IN (*set*) **DO** *command*

variable is a single letter.

set is one or more words or file specifications. The file specification is in the form *d:path\filename.ext*. Wild cards are allowed.

command is the DOS command to be performed for each word or file in the set.

Reference

See Chapter 14.

Rules

1. You can use more than one word or a full file specification in the set. You must separate words or file specifications by spaces or by commas.

2. %%*variable* becomes each literal word or full file specification in the set. If you use wild-card characters, FOR..IN..DO executes once for each file that matches the wild-card file specification.

3. You can use path names with FOR..IN..DO.

4. You cannot nest FOR..IN..DO subcommands (put two of these commands on the same line). You can use other batch subcommands with FOR..IN..DO.

Batch Command
GOTO

Jumps (transfers control) to the line following the label in the batch file and continues batch file execution from that line.

Syntax

GOTO label

label is the name used for one or more characters, preceded by a colon. Only the first eight characters of the label name are significant.

Reference

See Chapter 12.

Rules

1. The label must be the first item on a line in a batch file and must start with a colon (:).

2. When the command **GOTO label** is executed, DOS jumps to the line following **label** and continues execution of the batch file.

Batch Command
IF

Enables conditional execution of a DOS command.

Syntax

IF *NOT* **condition command**

NOT tests for the opposite of the condition (executes the command if the condition is false).

condition is what is being tested. Condition can be one of the following:

ERRORLEVEL number	DOS tests the exit code (0 to 255) of the program. If the exit code is greater than or equal to the number, the condition is true.
string1 = = string2	DOS compares these two alphanumeric strings to find whether they are identical.
EXIST *d:path***filename.***ext*	DOS tests whether *d:path***filename.***ext* is in the specified drive or path (if you give a drive name or path name) or is on the current disk drive and directory.

command is any valid DOS batch file command.

Reference

See Chapter 14.

Rules

1. For the IF subcommand, if **condition** is true, **command** is executed. If **condition** is false, **command** is skipped and the next line of the batch file is immediately executed.

2. For the IF NOT subcommand, if **condition** is false, the command is executed. If **condition** is true, **command** is skipped, and the next line of the batch file is immediately executed.

3. The only DOS programs that produce exit codes are BACKUP, FORMAT, GRAFTABL, KEYB, REPLACE, and RESTORE. Using an ERRORLEVEL condition with a program that does not leave an exit code is meaningless.

4. For **string1 = = string2**, DOS makes a literal, character-by-character comparison of the two strings. The comparison is based on the ASCII character set, and upper- and lowercase letters are distinguished.

5. When you are using **string1 = = string2** with the parameter markers (%0–%9), neither string can be null (empty, or nonexistent). If either string is null, DOS displays a Syntax error message and aborts the batch file.

Batch Command
PAUSE
V1, V2, V3, V4, V5

Suspends batch file processing until a key is pressed and optionally displays a message.

Syntax

PAUSE *message*

message is a string of up to 121 characters.

Reference

See Chapter 14.

Rules

1. The message, a series of up to 121 characters, must be on the same batch file line with the word PAUSE.

2. When DOS encounters a PAUSE subcommand in a batch file, DOS displays the optional message only if ECHO is on.

3. Regardless of the ECHO setting, DOS displays the following message:

```
Strike a key when ready
```

Batch Command
REM
V1, V2, V3, V4, V5

Places a comment within a batch file or within the CONFIG.SYS file.

Syntax

REM *message*

message is a string of up to 123 characters.

Reference

See Chapters 12 and 14.

Rules

1. REM must be the last batch file command on the line when used with the subcommands IF or FOR..IN..DO.

2. The optional message can contain up to 123 characters and must immediately follow the word REM.

3. When DOS encounters a REM subcommand in a batch file, DOS displays the message if ECHO is on. If ECHO is off, DOS does not display the message.

Batch Command
SHIFT
V2, V3, V4, V5

Shifts command line parameters one position to the left when a batch file is invoked.

Syntax

SHIFT

Reference

See Chapter 14.

Rules

1. When you use SHIFT, DOS moves the command line parameters one position to the left.

2. DOS discards the former first parameter (%0).

BREAK
V2, V3, V4, V5—Internal

Determines when DOS looks for a Ctrl-Break sequence to stop a program.

Syntax

To turn on BREAK, use the following form:

BREAK ON

To turn off BREAK, use the following form:

BREAK OFF

To determine whether BREAK is on or off, use the following form:

BREAK

Reference

See Chapter 14.

CHCP

V3.3, V4, V5—Internal

Changes or displays the code page (font) used by DOS.

Syntax

To change the current code page, use the following form:

CHCP codepage

To display the current code page, use the following form:

CHCP

codepage is a valid three-digit code page number.

Codepage	Country
437	United States
850	Multilingual
860	Portuguese
863	Canadian-French
865	Nordic

Reference

See Chapter 16.

Rule

You must use NLSFUNC prior to issuing this command.

Notes

CHCP is a system-wide code page (font) changer. CHCP simultaneously resets all affected devices to the changed font. MODE works similarly but changes only one device at a time.

When you successfully select a code page, the new code page becomes the specified code. If you include CONFIG.SYS directives for devices that use code pages, such as DEVICE=PRINTER.SYS or DEVICE=DISPLAY.SYS, CHCP loads the correct code pages for the devices.

You can access the COUNTRY.SYS file to get new country information. If you do not specify the location of COUNTRY.SYS when you invoke NLSFUNC, COUNTRY.SYS must exist in the current disk's root directory or DOS will return a File not found message.

Messages

1. Code page *nnn* not prepared for all devices

   ERROR: CHCP could not select the code page *nnn* because of one of the following errors: (1) you did not use MODE to prepare a code page for this device, (2) an I/O error occurred while DOS was sending the new font information to the device, (3) the device is busy (for example, a printer is in use or off-line), or (4) the device does not support code-page switching.

   Check to make sure that the command **MODE CODEPAGE PREPARE** was issued for the appropriate devices and that the devices are on-line and ready. Then try CHCP again.

2. Code page *nnn* not prepared for system

   ERROR: CHCP could not select the code page nnn because of one of the following errors: (1) you did not run NLSFUNC, (2) you specified an invalid code page (*nnn*) for your country, or (3) you did not prepare a code page using the MODE command. Be sure that you run NLSFUNC and that you use the command **MODE CODEPAGE PREPARE** to prepare the code page for the appropriate devices.

3. NLSFUNC not installed

   ERROR: You attempted to change the code page but did not initiate NLSFUNC prior to using CHCP. If you plan to use code pages, and you have the correct directives in CONFIG.SYS, add NLSFUNC to your AUTOEXEC.BAT file so that the command is executed when you boot the computer.

CHDIR or CD V2, V3, V4, V5—Internal

Changes or shows the path of the current directory.

Syntax

To change the current directory, use either of the following forms:

> **CHDIR** *d:***path**

or

> **CD** *d:***path**

To show the current directory path on a disk drive, use either of these forms:

> **CHDIR** *d:*

or

> **CD** *d:*

d: is a valid disk drive name.

path is a valid directory path.

Reference

See Chapter 7.

Rule

To start the move with the disk's root directory, use the backslash (\) as the path's first character. Otherwise, DOS assumes that the path starts with the current directory.

Notes

To move through more than one directory at a time, separate each directory name with the path character (\). You can chain together as many directories as you want, provided that the total number of characters for the path does not exceed 63.

You are not restricted to changing directories on the current disk. For example, if the current drive is drive A and the disk with the sample directory is in drive B, you can type **B:** before each path name, and your commands work the same way.

CHDSK   V1, V2, V3, V4, V5—External

Checks the directory and the file allocation table (FAT) of the disk and reports disk and memory status. CHKDSK also can repair errors in the directories or the FAT.

Syntax

*dc:pathc***CHKDSK** *d:path\\filename.ext /F/V*

dc: is the disk drive holding the command.

pathc is the path to the command.

d: is the disk drive to be analyzed.

path is the directory path to the files to be analyzed.

filename.ext is a valid DOS file name. Wild cards are permitted.

Switches

/F   Fixes the file allocation table and other problems if errors are found.

/V   Shows CHKDSK's progress and displays more detailed information about the errors the program finds. (This switch is known as the verbose switch.)

Reference

See Chapter 6.

Rules

1. You must direct CHKDSK to make repairs to the disk by giving the /F switch. CHKDSK asks you to confirm that you want the repairs made before the program proceeds.

2. CHKDSK cannot process a directory on which you used the JOIN command—that is, a second disk joined to a subdirectory.

3. CHKDSK does not process a disk on which you used a SUBST command.

4. CHKDSK cannot process a disk drive on which you used the ASSIGN command.

5. CHKDSK cannot process a networked (shared) disk.

Notes

CHKDSK shows you the following items of information:

1. Volume name and creation date (only disks with volume labels)

2. Total disk space

3. Number of files and bytes used for hidden or system files

4. Number of files and bytes used for directories

5. Number of files and bytes used for user (normal) files

6. Bytes used by bad sectors (flawed disk space)

7. Bytes available (free space) on disk

8. Bytes of total memory (RAM)

9. Bytes of free memory

With DOS 4, CHKDSK also reports the following:

1. Total bytes in each allocation unit

2. Total allocation units on the disk

3. The available allocation units on the disk

An allocation unit equates to a cluster.

CHKDSK checks a disk's directories and the FAT. The command also checks the amount of memory in the system and determines how much of that memory is free. If errors are found, CHKDSK reports them on-screen before making a status report.

If lost clusters are found, CHKDSK asks whether you want to repair them. You must answer Y or N. If you answer Y, CHKDSK shows a report on-screen as if the lost clusters are repaired. This report is only a simulation, however. To actually reclaim the lost clusters, you must issue **CHKDSK /F**; the /F switch actually starts the repair.

The command **CHKDSK filename** checks to see if the specified files are stored contiguously on the disk. DOS reports any noncontiguously stored programs and how many different sections store the file(s). If CHKDSK reports many noncontiguous files on a floppy disk, format a new disk. Use the command **COPY *.*** (not DISKCOPY) to consolidate files from the old to the new disk.

Messages

1. `All specified file(s) are contiguous`

   INFORMATION: The files you specified are stored in contiguous sectors on the disk, and the performance from this disk or disk subdirectory is optimal.

2. `filename contains n non-contiguous blocks`

   INFORMATION and WARNING: The file is written nonsequentially on the disk, which leads to less than optimal disk performance.

3. `filename`
   `Allocation error for file, size adjusted`

   WARNING: The file name has an invalid sector number in the file allocation table (FAT). The file was truncated by CHKDSK at the end of the last valid sector.

   Check this file to verify that all information in the file is correct. If you find a problem, use your backup copy of the file. This message is usually displayed when the problem is in the FAT, not in the file. Your file probably is still good.

4. `filename`
   `Contains invalid cluster, file truncated`

   WARNING: `filename` has a bad pointer to a section in the FAT on the disk. If you give the /F switch, DOS truncates the file at the last valid sector. Otherwise, no action is taken.

   Check this file to see whether all information is intact. If the file is intact, CHKDSK usually can correct the problem with no loss of file information.

5. `filename`
   `Contains xxx noncontiguous blocks`

   INFORMATION: filename is not stored contiguously on the floppy disk or hard disk but is stored in *xxx* number of pieces. If you find that many files on a floppy disk are stored in noncontiguous pieces, copy the files to another disk to increase performance. If use a hard disk, back up, format, and then restore the hard disk. (Use the COPY, BACKUP, FORMAT, and RESTORE commands.)

6. `directoryname`
   `Convert directory to file (Y/N)?`

   WARNING: `directoryname` contains so much bad information that the directory is no longer usable. If you press Y, CHKDSK converts the directory into a file so that you can use DEBUG or another tool to repair the directory. If you press N, no action is taken.

   Respond with N the first time you see this message. Try to copy any files you can from this directory to another disk. Check the copied files to see whether they are usable. Then rerun CHKDSK to convert the directory into a file and try to recover the rest of the files.

7. `directoryname`
   `is joined,`
   `tree past this point not processed`

   WARNING: CHKDSK encountered a directory that is actually a disk joined to the currently processed disk. CHKDSK does not process this subdirectory but will continue to process the remaining portion of the real disk.

8. `Errors found, F parameter not specified`
   `Corrections will not be written to the disk`

   INFORMATION: An error was found by CHKDSK. This message tells you that CHKDSK will go through the motions to repair the disk but does not actually change the file because you did not give the /F switch.

9. `filename`
   `First cluster number is invalid,`
   `entry truncated`

   WARNING: filename's first entry in the FAT refers to a nonexistent portion of the disk. If you gave the /F switch, the file becomes a zero-length file (truncated).

   Try to copy this file to another floppy disk before CHKDSK truncates the file. You may not get a useful copy, however, and the original file will be lost.

10. `. or ..`

    `Entry has a bad attribute`
    `or Entry has a bad size or`
    `Entry has a bad link`

    WARNING: The link to the parent directory (..) or the current directory (.) has a problem. If you gave the /F switch, CHKDSK attempts to repair the problem. Normally, this procedure is safe, and you do not risk losing files.

11. `filename`
    `has invalid cluster, file truncated`

    INFORMATION and WARNING: Part of the chain of FAT entries for `filename` points to a nonexistent part of the disk. The /F switch truncates the file at its last valid sector. If you did not give /F, DOS takes no corrective action. Try to copy this file to a different disk, and rerun CHKDSK with the /F switch. Part of the file may be lost.

12. *filename1*
    Is cross linked on cluster x
    filename2
    Is cross linked on cluster x

    WARNING: Two files—*filename1* and *filename2*—had an
    entry in the FAT that points to the same area (cluster) of the
    disk. In other words, the two files believe they own the same
    piece of the disk.

    CHKDSK takes no action. To handle the problem, complete
    the following steps: (1) copy both files to another floppy disk,
    (2) delete the files from the original disk, and (3) edit the files
    as necessary. The files may contain garbage.

13. Insufficient room in root directory
    Erase files from root and repeat CHKDSK

    ERROR: CHKDSK recovered so many "lost" clusters from the
    disk that the root directory is full. CHKDSK aborts at this
    point.

    Examine the FILE*xxxx*.CHK files. If you find nothing useful,
    delete them. Rerun **CHKDSK** with the **/F** switch to continue
    recovering lost clusters.

14. *xxxxxxxxx* bytes disk space freed

    INFORMATION: CHKDSK regained some disk space that was
    improperly marked as "in use." *xxxxxxxxx* tells you how
    many additional bytes are now available. To free this disk
    space, review and delete any FILE*xxxx*.CHK file that does not
    contain useful information.

15. *xxx* lost clusters found in *yyy* chains
    Convert lost chains to files (Y/N)?

    INFORMATION: Although CHKDSK found *xxx* blocks of data
    allocated in the FAT, no file on the disk is using these blocks.
    They are lost clusters, which normally can be freed by
    CHKDSK if no other error or warning message appears.

    If you gave the /F switch and answer Y, CHKDSK joins each set
    of lost chains into a file placed in the root directory of the
    disk, called FILE*xxxx*.CHK, in which *xxxx* is a consecutive
    number between 0000 and 9999. Examine, and delete those
    files that contain no useful information.

    If you answer N and you used the /F switch, CHKDSK simply
    frees the lost chains so that the disk space can be reused by

other files. No files are created. If you answer Y and omitted /F, CHKDSK displays the actions you can take, but does not take any action.

CLS
(Clear screen)   V2, V3, V4, V5—Internal

Erases the display screen.

Syntax

CLS

Reference

See Chapters 12 and 14.

Notes

This command clears all information on the screen and places the cursor at the home position in the upper left corner.

This command affects only the active video display, not memory.

If you used the ANSI control codes to set the foreground and background, the color settings remain in effect.

If you did not set the foreground/background color, the screen reverts to light characters on a dark background.

COMMAND   V2, V3, V4, V5—External

Invokes another copy of COMMAND.COM, the command processor.

Syntax

*dc:pathc***COMMAND** *d:path\ cttydevice /E:size /P /C string*

dc: is the drive where DOS can find a copy of COMMAND.COM.

pathc is the DOS path to the copy of COMMAND.COM.

d:path is the drive and directory location of COMMAND.COM. This path is assigned to the COMSPEC environment table.

cttydevice is the device used for input and output. The default is CON:.

string is the set of characters you pass to the new copy of the command interpreter.

Switches

/E:*size*	Sets the *size* of the *environment*. Size is a decimal number from 160 to 32,768 bytes, rounded up to the nearest multiple of 16 (refer to the SHELL command).
/P	Keeps this copy permanently in memory (until the next system reset).
/C	Passes the string of commands (the string) to the new copy of COMMAND.COM and returns to primary processor.
/MSG	Loads all error messages into memory. Must be used with /P.

Reference

See Chapter 9.

Rules

1. The string in the /C option is interpreted by the additional copy of COMMAND.COM, just as though you had typed the string at the system level. The /C must be the last switch used on the line. Do not use the form **COMMAND**/C *string* /P.

2. You can exit from the second copy of the command processor by issuing the command EXIT unless you used the /P option (permanent).

3. If you issue the /P and /C switches together, /P is ignored.

Notes

COMMAND is often used with the SHELL directive. This combination enables you to relocate COMMAND.COM from the root directory of a disk to a subdirectory.

You can use COMMAND with all versions of DOS to call a second batch file from an originating batch file. For example, suppose that a batch file called BATCH1.BAT contains the following line:

```
COMMAND /C BATCH2
```

BATCH1 calls BATCH2.BAT. BATCH2.BAT executes and, after completing the last line of the batch file, returns to BATCH1 to complete the originating batch file. This method of calling a batch file is similar to the CALL batch subcommand in available DOS 3.3 and more recent versions.

If you use DOS 5 with a floppy disk only system, you can specify the /MSG switch in the SHELL directive of CONFIG.SYS. This switch loads all error messages in memory. If an error occurs, you do not need a disk with COMMAND.COM in the drive. The switch uses an additional 1K of RAM.

COMP   V1, V2, V3, V4, V5—External

Compares two sets of disk files of the same name and length. This command is not available with some DOS versions. If COMP is not available on your version of DOS, see the FC command.

Syntax

*dc:pathc***COMP** *d1:path1\\filename1.ext1*
    d2:path2\\filename2.ext2

Version 5 Only

*dc:pathc***COMP** *d1:path1\\filename1.ext1*
    d2:path2\\filename2.ext2 */D/A/L/N=x/C*

dc: is the disk drive that holds the command.

pathc is the path to the command.

d1: is the drive that contains the first set of files to be compared.

path1 is the path to the first set of files.

filename1.ext1 is the file name for the first set of files. Wild cards are allowed.

d2: is the drive that contains the second set of files to be compared.

path2 is the path to the second set of files.

filename2.ext2 is the file name for the second set of files. Wild cards are allowed.

d1 and *d2* may be the same.

path1 and *path2* may be the same.

filename1.ext and *filename2.ext2* may be the same.

Special Terms:

d1:path1\\filename1.ext1 is the *primary* file set.

d2:path2\\filename2.ext2 is the *secondary* file set.

Switches

Available with Version 5 only:

/D	Displays differences in hex format.
/A	Displays differences as characters.
/L	Displays number of the line in which difference occurred.
/N=x	Compares the first x number of lines of a file.
/C	Does a comparison of files that is not case-sensitive.

Reference

See Chapter 8.

Rules

1. If you do not enter a file name, all files for that set, whether primary or secondary, are compared, which is the same as entering *.*. However, only the files in the secondary set with names that match file names in the primary set are compared.

2. If you do not enter a drive, path, or file name, COMP prompts you for the primary and secondary file sets to compare. Otherwise, the correct disks must be in the correct drive if you are comparing files on disks. COMP does not wait for you to insert disks if you give both primary and secondary file names.

3. After 10 mismatches (unequal comparisons) between the contents of two compared files, COMP ends the comparison and aborts.

Note

A more versatile utility for file comparison is FC, also discussed in this command reference.

Messages

1. `Compare error at offset xxxxxxxx`

    INFORMATION: The files you are comparing are not the same. The difference occurs at *xxxxxxxx* bytes from the start of the file. The number given is in hexadecimal format, base 16. The values for the differing bytes in the files also are displayed in hexadecimal format.

2. `Files are different sizes`

   WARNING: You asked COMP to compare two files of different lengths. Because COMP compares only files of the same size, COMP skips the comparison.

3. `10 Mismatches - ending compare`

   WARNING: COMP found ten mismatches between the two files you compared. COMP therefore assumes that no reason exists to continue, and the comparison is aborted.

Configuration Command
BREAK
V3, V4, V5—Internal

Determines when DOS looks for a Ctrl-Break or Ctrl-C to stop a program.

Syntax

To turn on BREAK, use the following form:

BREAK = ON

To turn off BREAK, use the following form:

BREAK = OFF

Reference

See Chapter 15.

Note

The setting for BREAK in the CONFIG.SYS file works in the same manner as setting BREAK from the DOS prompt.

Configuration Command
BUFFERS
V2, V3, V4, V5—Internal

Sets the number of disk buffers set aside by DOS in memory.

Syntax

BUFFERS = nn

If you have DOS 4, use the following form:

BUFFERS = nn,*mm* /X

If you have DOS 5, use the following form:

BUFFERS = nn,*mm*

nn is the number of buffers to set, in the range of 1 to 99. If you have DOS 4, you can set a maximum of 10,000 buffers by using the /X switch.

mm is the number of sectors, from 1 to 8, that can be read or written at a time. The default is one.

Switch

/X Uses expanded memory for buffer storage (DOS 4 only).

Reference

See Chapter 15.

Note

Do not set more buffers than you need. One buffer occupies 528 bytes, so that the setting of 50 buffers takes over 26K of RAM. You may find that a setting of 15 to 25 is adequate. Many software programs recommend specific buffer settings; set the buffers accordingly.

Configuration Command COUNTRY
V3, V4, V5—Internal

Instructs DOS to modify the input and display of date, time, and field divider information to match the time and date formats of other countries.

Syntax

COUNTRY = nnn

If you have DOS 3.3 or more recent, use the following form:

COUNTRY = nnn,*mmm,d:path\filenamef.extf*

nnn is the country code.

mmm is the code page.

d: is the drive that contains *filenamef.extf*

path is the path that contains *filenamef.extf*

filenamef.extf is the file that contains the country information—for example, COUNTRY.SYS.

Country	keycode	codepage	code
Australia	us	850, 437	(none)
Belgium	be	850, 437	(none)
Brazil	br	850, 437	(none)
Canadian-French	cf	850, 863	(none)
Denmark	dk	850, 865	(none)
Finland	su	850, 437	(none)
France	fr	850, 437	129, 189
Germany	gr	850, 437	(none)
Italy	it	850, 437	141, 142
Latin America	la	850, 437	(none)
Netherlands	nl	850, 437	(none)
Norway	no	850, 865	(none)
Portugal	po	850, 860	(none)
Spain	sp	850, 437	(none)
Sweden	sv	850, 437	(none)
Swiss-French	sf	850, 437	(none)
Swiss-German	sg	850, 437	(none)
United Kingdom	uk	850, 437	166, 168
United States	us	850, 437	(none)

Reference

See Chapter 16.

Rule

You cannot mix page codes with country codes. If you use the country code 001 (United States), you cannot use the code page code 863 (Canadian-French).

Configuration Command
DEVICE
V2, V3, V4, V5—Internal

Instructs DOS to load, link, and use a special device driver.

Syntax

DEVICE = *d:path***filename.ext** *options*

d: is the drive where DOS can find the device driver to be used.

path is the DOS path to the device driver.

filename.ext is the root file name and optional extension of the device driver.

options are any parameters or switches that may be used with a device driver.

Reference

See Chapter 15.

Configuration Command DEVICEHIGH   V5—Internal

Loads device drivers into reserved memory.

Syntax

DEVICEHIGH *SIZE* = *hexbyte d:path***filename.ext** *options*

d: is the drive where DOS can find the device driver to be used.

path is the DOS path to the device driver.

filename.ext is the root file name and optional extension of the device driver.

options are any parameters or switches that may be used with a device driver.

SIZE = *hexbyte* is the amount of reserved memory that must be available for the device driver to be loaded into memory. *hexbyte* is the size in bytes, expressed as a hexadecimal value.

Reference

See Chapter 15

Notes

To use the DEVICEHIGH command, you must include the DOS=UMB command line in your CONFIG.SYS file. For more information, see DOS command.

You can not load a device driver into reserved memory until the EMM386.EXE driver is installed. Use the DEVICE command to install EMM386.EXE.

Configuration Command
DOS

V5—External

Frees up conventional memory; accomplished by loading a portion of DOS into high memory area (HMA) or extended memory.

Syntax

DOS = *UMB│NOUMB, HIGH│LOW*

Switches

UMB   Tells DOS to maintain a link between conventional memory and reserved memory (upper memory blocks), enabling you to load some device drivers and memory-resident programs into reserved memory.

NOUMB   Disconnects the link established by *umb*.

HIGH   Loads part of DOS into the first 64K of extended memory—the *high memory area* (HMA).

LOW   Keeps all of DOS in conventional memory.

Reference

See Chapter 15.

Rules

1. HIMEM memory manager must be loaded before DOS can run in extended memory (HMA).

2. For DOS=UMB to be effective, your computer must have an 80386 or 80486 CPU, and EMM 386.EXE must be loaded as a device driver with the RAM or the NOEMS switch.

3. If you attempt to load DOS into extended memory, the DOS command must come after the DEVICE = HIMEM.SYS command in the CONFIG.SYS file.

Notes

If you are using DOS 5 on an 80286, 80386sx, 80386, or 80486 computer with at least 1M of RAM (including at least 64K extended memory), DOS=High enables DOS to relocate a portion into the high-memory area (HMA). Doing so frees up conventional memory for your programs' use.

If you are using an 80386sx, 80386, or 80486 computer with at least 1M of RAM, you can enable DOS to remap memory into the reserved area between 640K and 1M using HIMEM.SYS, EMM386.EXE, and the DOS=UMB command. Doing so enables DOS to load device drivers and memory-resident programs into the reserved area, freeing up conventional memory for programs.

Message

```
HMA not available: loading DOS low
```

Your CONFIG.SYS contains the line DOS = high, but DOS cannot load into high memory because no memory is available. This error can because no **DEVICE = HIMEM.SYS** command is in your CONFIG.SYS file.

Configuration Command
DRIVPARM   V3, V4, V5—Internal

Defines or changes the parameters of a block device, such as a disk drive.

Syntax

DRIVPARM = /D:num /C /F:type /H:bds /I /N /S:sec /T:trk

Switches

/D:num   Specifies the drive number, *num*, ranging from 0 to 255, where drive A=0, drive B=1, drive C=2, etc.

/C   Specifies that the drive supports *change-line*, meaning that the drive has sensor support to determine when the drive door is open. When the drive door is open, the drive is sensed as empty.

/F:type   Determines the type of drive. *type* is one of the following:

Type	Drive specification
0	160K/320K/180K/360K
1	1.2M
2	720K
3	Single-density 8" disk (not available in Version 5, see SETVER)
4	Double-density 8" disk (not available in Version 5, see SETVER)
5	Hard disk
6	Tape drive
7	1.44M
8	Read/write optical disk
9	2.88M

Type 2 is the default if you do not specify /F.

/H:hds   Specifies the total number of drive heads, where *hds* is a number from 1 to 99. The default for *hds* is 2.

/I   Used if you have a 3 1/2-inch drive connected internally to your floppy drive controller, but your ROM BIOS does not support a 3 1/2-inch drive.

/N   Specifies that your drive or other block device is not removable, in other words, a hard disk.

/S:sec   Specifies the total number of sectors per side on the drive. *sec* can be a number from 1 to 999.

/T:trk   Specifies the number of tracks per side of a disk or the total number of tracks per tape. *trk* can be a number from 1 to 99.

Reference

See Chapter 15.

Configuration Command
FCBS

Specifies the number of DOS file control blocks that can be open simultaneously and how many are always kept open.

Syntax

FCBS = maxopen, *neverclose*

maxopen is the number of File Control Blocks, or FCBs, that can be open at any given time. The default is 4.

neverclose is the number of FCBs that are always open. The default value is 0. This variable is not used in DOS 5.

Reference

See Chapter 15.

Note

FCBS is rarely used. DOS began to use file handles rather than File Control Blocks, starting with Version 2.0. The number of programs available that use FCBs is diminishing. All major commercial programs available as of this printing use file handles. However, you may find a DOS 1 program using FCBs that you find helpful, and, in this case, use the FCBS setting.

Configuration Command
FILES

Specifies the number of file handles that can be open at any given time.

Syntax

FILES = nnn

nnn is the number of file handles that can be open at any given time. The default value is 8.

Reference

See Chapter 15.

Rule

If you use several programs that require FILES settings, set your FILES statement to the maximum required value.

Configuration Command
INSTALL
V4, V5—Internal

Starts memory-resident program from CONFIG.SYS. Valid programs to start with INSTALL are FASTOPEN, KEYB, NLSFUNC, and SHARE.

Syntax

INSTALL = *dc:pathc***filename.ext** *options*

dc: is the drive that contains *filename.ext*.

pathc is the subdirectory where the *filename.ext* is located.

filename.ext is the name of the file, e.g., FASTOPEN, KEYB, NLSFUNC, or SHARE.

options is any parameter(s) that *filename.ext* command requires to function.

Reference

See Chapter 15.

Configuration Command
LASTDRIVE
V3, V4, V5—Internal

Sets the last valid drive letter acceptable to DOS.

Syntax

LASTDRIVE = x

x is the alphabetical character for the highest system drive. The highest default drive letter is E.

Reference

See Chapter 15.

Note

If you use the SUBST command to assign drive letters to subdirectories, use the LASTDRIVE statement to increase the usable drive letters. Also, if you use a local area network, you can use the LASTDRIVE statement to identify the highest letter that can be assigned as a drive letter to a subdirectory.

Configuration Command
REM   V4, V5—Internal

Places remarks or hide statements in the CONFIG.SYS file.

Syntax

REM *remark*

Reference

See Chapter 12.

Configuration Command
SHELL   V3, V4, V5—Internal

Changes the default DOS command processor. Can be used with COMMAND to increase the size of the DOS environment.

Syntax

SHELL = *d:path***filename.ext** *parameters*

d: is the name of the drive where DOS can find the command processor to be used.

path is the DOS path to the command processor.

filename.ext is the root file name and optional extension of the command processor.

parameters is the optional parameters that the command processor uses.

Reference

See Chapter 15. Also see COMMAND in this Command Reference.

Configuration Command
STACKS   V3.2, V3.3, V4.0, V4.01, V5—Internal

Allots memory used to store information when a hardware interrupt occurs.

Syntax

STACKS = n,m

n is the number of stacks to allot. The default for computers that use the 8088/8086 microprocessor is 0; the default for those computers that use the 80286, 80386sx and 80386 is 9.

m is the size in bytes of each stack. The default for computers that use the 8088/8086 microprocessor is 0; the default for computers that use the 80286, 80386sx and 80386 is 128.

Reference

See Chapter 15.

Note

You may find that the default stacks are adequate for normal usage. However, if you regularly receive the message `Fatal: Internal Stack Failure, System Halted`, increase the stacks. First, increase the number of stacks. If the error persists, increase the size of each stack.

COPY   V1, V2, V3, V4, V5—Internal

Copies files between disk drives or between drives and devices, and enables you to either keep or change the file names.

Syntax

To copy a file, use the following form:

COPY/*A/B d1:path1***filename1.ext1**/*A/B*

d0:path2**filename0.ext0**/*A/B/V*

or

COPY /*A/B d1:path1***filename1.ext1**/*A/B/V*

To join several files into one, use the following form:

COPY /A/B *d1:path1***filename1.ext1**/A/B
+ *d2:path2***filename2.ext2**/A/B +. . .

d1:, *d2:*, and *d0:* are valid disk drive names.

path1 and *path2* are valid path names.

filename1.ext1 and **filename2.ext2** are valid file names. Wild cards are allowed.

The three periods (. . .) represent additional files in the form *dx:pathx/***filenamex.extx**.

Special Terms:

The file copied *from* is the *source file*. The names that contain 1 and 2 are the source files.

The file copied *to* is the *destination file*. This file is represented by a 0.

Switches

/V   Verifies that the copy was recorded correctly.

The following switches create different effects on the source and the destination:

For the source file:

/A   Treats the file as an ASCII (text) file. The command copies all the information in the file up to, but not including, the end-of-file marker (Ctrl-Z). Data after the end-of-file marker is ignored.

/B   Copies the entire file (based on size, as listed in the directory) as if the file were a program file *(binary1)*. All end-of-file markers (Ctrl-Z) are treated as normal characters, and EOF characters are copied.

For the destination file:

/A   Adds an end-of-file marker (Ctrl-Z) to the end of the ASCII text file at the end of the copying process.

/B   Does not add the end-of-file marker to this binary file.

References

See Chapters 2, 4, and 8.

Rules

To copy files with both source and destination given:

1. The following rules apply to the file name:

    a. You must give either a path name or a file name. Wild cards are allowed in the source file name. If you do not give a file name but give a path name for the source, DOS assumes *.*.

    b. If you do not give a destination file name, the copied file has the same name as the source file.

2. You can substitute a device name for the complete source or destination name.

3. When you copy between disk drives, COPY assumes that binary files are copied (as though the /B switch were given).

4. When you copy to or from a device other than a disk drive, COPY assumes that ASCII files are copied (as though the /A switch were given).

5. An /A or /B switch overrides the default settings for COPY (Rules 6 and 7).

To copy files with only one file specified:

1. The file specification you give *(d1:path1***filename1.ext1***)* is the source. This specification needs one or both of the following:

    a. A valid file name. Wild cards are allowed.

    b. A drive name, a path name, or both. If you give only one name, that name must differ from the current drive name or path name. If both names are given, at least one name must differ from the current drive name or path name.

2. The source cannot be a device name.

3. The destination is the current drive and current directory.

4. The copied file(s) use the same name as the source file(s).

5. COPY assumes that binary files are copied (as though a /B switch is given).

To concatenate files:

1. The destination file is the last file in the list unless you add a plus sign (+) before that file name. If you do not specify a destination file name, the first source name becomes the destination name.

2. If you do not give a drive name, the current drive is used.

3. If you do not give a path, the current directory is used.

4. The following rules apply to source files:

    a. You must give a valid file name. Wild cards are allowed, but their use can be dangerous. If you do not give a destination file name, the first file name is used as the destination file name.

    b. After the first file name, any additional source file specifications must be preceded by a plus sign (+).

5. The following rules apply to the destination file:

    a. You can have only one destination file specification. If you give a destination without wild cards, only one destination file is used. If you give a destination file name with wild cards, one or more destination files are used.

    b. If you do not give a destination, the first source file also is used as the destination, with the following results: (1) the first file that matches the wild-card file name is used as the destination file if you gave a wild card as part of the first source file name; and (2) the files to be joined are appended to the first source file.

Notes

The meanings of the /A and /B switches depend on their positions in the line. The /A or the /B switch affects the file that immediately precedes the switch and all files that follow the switch until another /A or /B is encountered. When you use one of these switches before a file name, the switch affects all following files until contradicted by another /A or /B.

1. Content of destination lost before copy

    WARNING: A destination file was not the first source file. The previous contents were destroyed. COPY continues to concatenate any remaining files.

2. File cannot be copied onto itself

    ERROR: You attempted to COPY a file back to the same disk and directory that contains the same file name. This error usually occurs when you misspell or when you omit parts of the source or destination drive, path, or file name. Check your spelling and the source and destination names. Try the command again.

CTTY

V2, V3, V4, V5—Internal

Changes the standard input and output device to an auxiliary console, or changes the input and output device back from an auxiliary console to the keyboard and video display.

Syntax

CTTY device

device is the device you want to use as the new standard input and output device. This name must be a valid DOS device name.

Reference

See Chapter 10.

Rules

1. The device must be a character-oriented device capable of both input and output.

2. Typing a colon (:) after the device name is optional.

3. CTTY does not affect any other form of redirected I/O or piping. For example, the < (redirect from), the > (redirect to), and the | (pipe between programs) work as usual.

Note

The CTTY command is designed so that a terminal or teleprinter, rather than the normal keyboard and video display, can be used for console input and output. This versatility has little effect on most personal computer users.

DATE

V1, V2, V3, V4, V5—Internal

Displays and/or changes the system date.

Syntax

DATE *date_string*

date_string is in one of the following forms:

mmddyy or *mmddyyyy* for North America

dd-mm-yy or *dd-mm-yyyy* for Europe

yy-mm-dd or *yyyy-mm-dd* for East Asia

mm is a one- or two-digit number for the month (1 to 12).

dd is a one- or two-digit number for the day (1 to 31).

yy is a one- or two-digit number for the year (80 to 99). The 19 is assumed.

yyyy is a four-digit number for the year (1980 to 2099).

The delimiters between the day, month, and year can be hyphens, periods, or slashes. The result that can be displayed varies, depending on the country code set in the CONFIG.SYS file.

Reference

See Chapter 9.

Rule

Date entry and display correspond to the country setting in your CONFIG.SYS file.

Notes

When you boot the computer, DOS issues the DATE and TIME commands to set the system clock. If you placed an AUTOEXEC.BAT file on the boot disk, DOS does not display a prompt for the date or time. You can include the DATE or TIME commands in the AUTOEXEC.BAT file to have these functions set when DOS boots.

Some computers, such as the IBM Personal Computer AT and compatibles, use battery-operated clocks. After you set the clock when you first install the system, you need not enter the date or time until the battery wears out.

DOS uses the date and time. When you create or update a file, DOS updates the directory with the date you entered. This date shows which copy is the latest revision of the file. The DOS BACKUP command uses the date in selecting files to back up.

The day-of-year calendar uses the time-of-day clock. If you leave your system on overnight, the day advances by one at midnight. DOS also makes appropriate calendar adjustments for leap years. However, you must access this clock once each day in order for DOS to advance the date properly. If your computer is left on but not used during the weekend, DOS will be one day behind when you return on Monday.

DEBUG

A utility to test and edit programs. DEBUG also assembles the machine code from assembly language mnemonics, unassembles bytes into source statements, and allocates EMS.

Syntax

*dc:pathc***DEBUG** *de:pathe\filenamee.exte*

dc:pathc are the disk drive and directory that hold the command.

de:pathe are the disk drive and directory that hold the file to edit.

filenamee.exte is the file to load into memory for editing.

Reference

See Chapter 3.

Rules

1. If DEBUG.EXE is not in the search path, you must specify the drive and directory where DEBUG is located.

2. You can create small assembly language programs with DEBUG, using 8088/8086 op codes only.

3. You must specify the complete filename, including location to debug, if you specify the filename.

Examples

1. **DEBUG**

   Starts DEBUG.

2. **DEBUG C:\UTILS\PROGRAM.EXE**

   Starts DEBUG loading PROGRAM.EXE from C:\UTILS for editing.

Note

DEBUG is a utility that enables you to load a program in memory and then edit, test, and save the edited program back to the disk. Also, with debug, you can create small machine language programs. You also can use assembly language to create small programs.

DEL   V1, V2, V3, V4, V5—Internal

Deletes files from the disk.

DEL is an alternative command for ERASE and performs the same functions. See ERASE for a complete description.

DELOLDOS   V5—External

Removes all DOS files of the pre-DOS 5 version of DOS from the hard disk.

Syntax

*dc:pathc***DELOLDOS** */B*

dc:pathc are the disk drive and directory that hold the command.

Switch

/B Forces black-and-white screen mode.

Reference

See Appendixes A and D.

Rules

1. After you start DELOLDOS, you can exit without deleting the old version of DOS by pressing any key except Y.

2. Be sure that all your programs are compatible with DOS 5 before you delete the old version of DOS.

Note

When you upgrade to DOS 5, the old version of DOS is preserved on your hard disk and on the Recover disks that the DOS 5 Setup program creates. After you are sure that the upgrade works correctly and that you find no incompatibility with programs that you normally use, you can delete the old DOS from the hard disk, which frees additional storage room.

DIR   V1, V2, V3, V4, V5—Internal

Lists any or all files and subdirectories in a disk directory.

Syntax

> **DIR** *d:path\filename.ext* */P/W*

For DOS 5. only:

> **DIR** *d:path\filename.ext* */P/W/A:attributes/O:sortorder/S/B/L*

d: is the drive holding the disk you want to examine.

path is the path to the directory you want to examine.

filename.ext is a valid file name. Wild cards are permitted.

Switches

/P	Pauses when the screen is full and waits for you to press any key.
/W	Gives a wide (80-column) display of the file names. Information about file size, date, and time is not displayed.

The following switches are valid for DOS 5 only.

/A:*attributes*	Displays only files with the attributes you specify. The colon (:) is optional.
no switch	Displays all files except system and hidden files.
H	Displays hidden files.
–H	Displays all files that are not hidden.
S	Displays only system files.
–S	Displays all files except system files.
D	Displays only directories (no files).
–D	Displays files only (no directories).
A	Displays files ready for archiving.
–A	Displays files that are archived.
R	Displays read-only files.
–R	Displays files that are not read-only.
/O:*sortorder*	Controls the order in which DOS sorts and displays files. If you omit this switch DIR displays files in the order they occur in the directory. The colon (:) is optional.
no switch	Directories before names, sorted alphabetically by name.
N	Sorts alphabetically by name.
–N	Sorts by name in reverse order (Z to A).
E	Sorts alphabetically by extension.
–E	Sorts by extension in reverse order (Z to A).

D	Sorts by date and time (earliest to latest).
D	Sorts by date and time in reverse order.
S	Sorts by size (smallest first).
–S	Sorts by size (largest first).
G	Groups directories before files.
–G	Groups directories after files.
/S	Lists all occurrences, in the specified directory and all lower-level subdirectories, of the specified filename.
/B	Lists only file names with no header or trailer information.
/L	Displays all information in lowercase.

Reference

See Chapter 9.

Rule

You cannot use the DIR command on a disk drive on which you used the ASSIGN or JOIN command. You must break the assignment before you view the directory on a drive on which you used ASSIGN. Use the path name of the disk that you used in the JOIN command. You can use the DIR command on the host disk drive involved in a JOIN command.

Notes

DIR does not report statistics for disk drives on which you used the ASSIGN or JOIN commands. For disk drives on which you used JOIN, DIR reports the free space of the host disk drive (the disk drive to which the second disk drive is joined). DIR does not, however, report the total of the two disk drives on which you use JOIN. First remove ASSIGN from the drive to find its amount of free space.

For DOS 5, you can set DIR switches in the AUTOEXEC.BAT file with **SET DIRCMD**. If you want DIR to always display files and directories a page at a time, enter the following into your AUTOEXEC.BAT file:

SET DIRCMD=/P

To override the preset switch use:

DIR/–P

To view the options set with the **DIRCMD** variable, enter:

SET

DISKCOMP

V1, V2, V3, V4, V5—External

Compares two floppy disks on a track-for-track, sector-for-sector basis to see whether their contents are identical.

Syntax

*dc:pathc***DISKCOMP** *d1: d2: /1 /8*

dc: is the disk drive that holds the command.

pathc is the path to the command.

d1: and *d2:* are the disk drives that hold the disks to be compared. These drives can be the same or different.

Switches

/1 Compares only the first side of the floppy disk, even if the disk or disk drive is double-sided.

/8 Compares only 8 sectors per track, even if the first disk has a different number of sectors per track.

Exit Codes

0 Compared OK.

1 Did not compare.

2 CTRL +C error.

3 Hard error.

4 Initialization error.

Reference

See Chapter 6.

Rules

1. If you give only one valid floppy disk drive name, that drive is used for the comparison.

2. Only compatible floppy disks should be compared. The two disks must be formatted with the same number of tracks, sectors, and sides.

3. Do not use DISKCOMP with a disk drive on which you used the ASSIGN, JOIN, or SUBST command.

Note

Remember: compare only floppy disks that were duplicated with DISKCOPY.

Messages

1. ```
   Compare error(s) on
   Track tt, side s
   ```

   WARNING: The disks you are comparing are different at track number tt, side s. DISKCOMP does not specify which sectors are different, only that one or more sectors differ. If you just used DISKCOPY on these disks and no problem was reported, the second disk probably has a flaw. Reformat the disk and try DISKCOPY again. Otherwise, assume that the disks are different.

2. ```
   Diskettes compare OK
   ```

   INFORMATION: DISKCOMP compared the two floppy disks and found that they match.

3. ```
   Drive or diskette types not compatible
   ```

   or

   ```
   Incompatible disks
   ```

   ERROR: The disk drives or floppy disks are different. The first disk was successfully read on both sides. However, the second disk or disk drive is not identical to the first disk or drive.

4. ```
   Unrecoverable read error on drive x
   Track tt, side s
   ```

   WARNING: Four attempts were made to read the data from the floppy disk in the specified drive. The error is at track number tt, side s. If drive x is the disk that holds the destination (copied) disk, the copy is probably bad. (The disk has a "hard" read error.) If drive x holds the original disk, a flaw existed when the disk was formatted or a flaw developed during use.

   Run CHKDSK on the original disk and look for the line bytes in bad sectors. If this line is displayed, the original disk and the copy may be good. When you format a disk, FORMAT detects bad sectors and "hides" them. However, DISKCOMP does not check for bad sectors and attempts to compare the tracks, even if bad sectors are present. Although CHKDSK shows that the original disk has bad sectors, the destination disk may be good. Either way, retire the original disk soon.

DISKCOPY V1, V2, V3, V4, V5—External

Copies the entire contents of one floppy disk to another on a track-for-track basis, making a "carbon copy." DISKCOPY works only with floppy disks.

Syntax

*dc:pathc***DISKCOPY** *d1: d2: /1 /V*

dc: is the disk drive that holds the command.

pathc is the path to the command.

d1: is the floppy disk drive that holds the source (original) disk.

d2: is the floppy disk drive that holds the destination disk (disk to be copied to).

Switches

/1 Copies only the first side of the disk. This switch is not available on the Epson Equity version of DOS.

/V Verifies that the copy is correct. This switch slows the copy process (Versions 4 and 5).

Special Terms:

The floppy disk you are copying *from* is the *source* or first floppy disk.

The floppy disk you are copying *to* is the *destination* or second disk.

Exit Codes

0 Successful Copy.

1 Nonfatal error, read/write error.

2 CTRL +C error.

3 Fatal hard error.

4 Initialization error.

Reference

See Chapter 6.

Rules

1. The source and destination disk drives must be real floppy disk drives. They cannot be hard or networked disk drives, RAM disks, or disk drives on which you used the JOIN or SUBST command. Defaulting to or giving a nonreal source or destination disk drive causes DOS to return an error message and abort the disk copy.

2. If you do not give a source disk drive name, DISKCOPY uses the default disk drive. If you give an improper source disk drive, DISKCOPY issues an error message and aborts. In other instances, DISKCOPY uses the current disk drive as the source disk drive.

3. If your system has a single floppy disk drive and if you give only one valid floppy disk drive name, the name is used as both the source and destination disk drives for the copy. If your system uses two floppy disk drives, giving only one valid disk drive name results in the message `Invalid drive specification error`.

4. DISKCOPY destroys any information recorded previously on the destination disk. Do not use as the destination disk one that contains information you want to keep.

5. To ensure that the copy is correct, run DISKCOMP on the two disks.

6. DISKCOPY ignores the effects of an ASSIGN command.

Notes

Write-protecting the source disk is important when you use only one floppy disk drive to make a copy of a disk. DOS periodically prompts you to change the disk. A write-protected source disk cannot be damaged by inadvertently inserting the disk when DOS asks for the destination disk.

When you use DISKCOPY, DOS reads into memory as much information as possible from the source disk. DOS then copies this information to the destination disk and reads the next batch of information from the source disk. The more free memory available, the less time you need to copy a disk.

Messages

1. `Drive types or diskette types not compatible`

ERROR: The message indicates that the drive types or disk capacities you tried to use are different and cannot handle the operation or that the destination disk is the wrong capacity. The first disk was successfully read, but the drive specified to make the copy (destination) disk is not the right type. You cannot DISKCOPY HC disks on non-HC disk drives or copy double-sided disks on single-sided disk drives. See the identical message under DISKCOMP for remedial action.

2. `Read error on drive d:`
   `Write error on drive d:`

   WARNING: DISKCOPY cannot accurately read or write the disk in drive `d:`. The disk is not properly inserted, the source disk is not formatted or is a non-DOS disk, or the drive door is open. Check these possibilities.

3. `SOURCE diskette bad or incompatible TARGET diskette bad or incompatible`

   WARNING: DISKCOPY detected errors while reading the source disk (first message) or writing the destination (target) disk (second message). The cause can be bad sectors on either disk, or the disk can be in the wrong type of disk drive.

   Determine whether either floppy disk has bad sectors. If so, do not use either disk with DISKCOPY. If the source disk is bad, use COPY *. to copy files from the source disk. If the destination disk is bad, try a different disk or try to reformat the disk and use DISKCOPY.

DOSKEY

V5—External

Enables you to repeat DOS commands and create macros.

Syntax

DOSKEY */REINSTALL /BUFSIZE=SIZE /MACROS /HISTORY /INSERT /OVERSTRIKE MACRO=TEXT*

Switches

/REINSTALL	Installs a new copy of DOSKEY even if a copy is already installed.
/BUFSIZE=SIZE	Specifies the buffer size in hexidecimal. The default is 1024.

/MACROS	Displays a listing of DOSKEY-created macros. You can redirect output by using the redirection symbol.
/HISTORY	Displays a list of all commands stored by DOSKEY. You can redirect output by using the redirection symbol.
/INSERT	Inserts new text into the file (as if the insert key was always pressed).
/OVERSTRIKE	New text overwrites old text (as if the type over key was always pressed).

Notes

Ordinarily, DOS remembers the last command typed at the command line. With DOSKEY, however, a history of commands can be stored in memory. The number of commands retained in memory depends on the size of the buffer (normally 512 bytes of memory). When the buffer is full, the oldest command is eliminated to make room for the new command. The buffer contains macros and history of commands.

Several keys are used to recall a command in the history. The keys and their functions are as follows:

Key	Function
↑	Displays last command in history
↓	Displays next command in history; when last command is reached, the first command is redisplayed
PgUp	Displays first command in history
PgDn	Displays last command in history

In addition to the standard DOS editing keys, you can use several other keys and key combinations to edit a command on the command line. These additional keys are as follows:

Key	Function
←	Moves cursor one character to the left
Ctrl-←	Moves cursor one word to the left
→	Moves cursor one character to the right
Ctrl-→	Moves cursor one word to the right
Home	Moves cursor to first character in command line

Key	Function
End	Moves cursor to final position in command line
Esc	Erases current command line
F7	Numbers and lists all commands in history and indicates which is current command
Alt-F7	Erases all commands from history
F9	Enables you to specify, by number, which command in history to make current (To see command numbers, press F7.)
F10	Lists all macros in memory
Alt-F10	Erases all macros from memory

DOSKEY enables you to create macros. A macro, like a batch file, is used to perform one or more DOS commands assigned to a specific name. After you type the name of a macro and press Enter, the macro executes the commands assigned to the macro name. When you create a macro, a few special symbols cannot be used; however, you can use the $ character equivalents as follows:

Code	Description
$g or $G	Used for redirecting output; use instead of >
$l or $L	Used for redirecting input; use instead of <
$b or $B	Used for piping; use instead of |
$t or $T	Separates macro commands
$$	Uses the dollar sign in the command line
$1 through $9	Replaceable parameters; same as %1 through %9 in a batch file
$*	A replaceable parameter that represents everything typed on the command line after the macro name

When you create a macro, you can include any valid DOS command, including the name of a batch file. You can start a batch file from a macro, but you cannot start a macro from a batch file.

Reference

See Chapter 3 and Appendix A.

Examples

DOSKEY /HISTORY > MYHIST.BAT

Copies the most recent DOS commands to the batch file MYHIST.BAT. DOSKEY enables you to permanently save DOS commands that then can be executed at any time.

Messages

1. `Cannot change BUFSIZE`

   ERROR: You cannot change the DOSKEY buffer.

2. `Insufficent memory to store macro. Use the DOSKEY command with the /BUFSIZE switch to increase available memory.`

   WARNING: Your DOSKEY macros have filled the total space set aside for them. You must enlarge the memory area for macros (the default is 512 bytes) by using the BUFSIZE switch before you can enter any new macros.

3. `Invalid macro definition`

   ERROR: You entered an illegal character or command with DOSKEY or attempted to create a DOSKEY macro with an illegal definition. For example, this message displays if you use a GOTO command in a DOSKEY macro. Correct any errors and carefully retype the macro.

DOSSHELL   V4, V5—External

Start the Shell (a graphical user interface) that accompanies DOS.

Syntax

To start DOS Shell in text mode, use the form:

*dc:pathc***DOSSHELL** */T:screen /B*

To start DOS Shell in graphics mode, use the form:

*dc:pathc***DOSSHELL** */G:screen /B*

To start DOS Shell in the default screen mode, type the form:

*dc:pathc***DOSSHELL**

dc:pathc is the disk drive and subdirectory where DOSSHELL is located.

Switches

/T:screen	Displays DOS Shell in text mode, using the resolution described by *screen*.
/G:screen	Displays DOS Shell in graphics mode, using the resolution described by *screen*.

Switch	Monochome/CGA	EGA	VGA
/T:L	25 lines	25 lines	25 lines
/T:M	x	43 lines	43 lines
/T:M1	x	43 lines	43 lines
/T:M2	x	43 lines	50 lines
/T:H	x	43 lines	43 lines
/T:H1	x	43 lines	43 lines
/T:H2	x	43 lines	50 lines
/G:L	25 lines	25 lines	25 lines
/G:M	x	43 lines	30 lines
/G:M1	x	43 lines	30 lines
/G:M2	x	43 lines	34 lines
/G:H	x	43 lines	43 lines
/G:H1	x	43 lines	43 lines
/G:H2	x	43 lines	60 lines

/B	Starts DOS Shell in black-and-white rather than in color.

Reference

See Chapter 5.

Rules

1. When you start the DOS Shell without switches, the display is based on the default display and color settings.

2. To start the DOS Shell with a screen display other than the default, you must use the /G or /T switch.

3. Each time you start the DOS Shell, the disk is searched for directories and files.

Examples

1. **DOSSHELL**

   Starts the DOS Shell in the default screen mode.

2. **DOSSHELL /B**

   DOSSHELL starts in black-and-white mode. Use this command if you use a black-and-white monitor or if you use a laptop or notebook computer with an LCD screen.

Note

DOSSHELL was improved between DOS 4 and 5. In Version 4, DOSSHELL was a batch file that started the shell and held all the switches needed to start the shell in the correct configuration for your computer. However, DOSSHELL in Version 5 is a COM file. When installing DOS, DOSSHELL is configured for your computer system.

Messages

1. `Not enough memory to run DOSSHELL`

   Not enough conventional memory is available to start DOSSHELL. You may have too many TSRs loaded into memory, or you may be trying to start DOSSHELL while you jumped to DOS from a program without first exiting the program. Remove TSRs from memory, or exit the program loaded in memory and try to restart DOSSHELL.

2. `Not enough free conventional memory to run program`

   or

   `Not enough free extended memory to run program`

   Either of these messages can appear when you try to start a program from the DOS Shell, but not enough memory is available to start the program from DOS Shell. You may need to adjust the memory settings for the program item by using File, Properties and select Advanced. Change the Conventional Memory KB Required setting or the XMS Memory KB Required setting. Or, if you loaded TSRs before you loaded DOSSHELL, remove the TSRs from memory to free conventional memory.

3. `Unable to run specified program.`
   `Too many tasks running.`

   You opened to many tasks, and you switched to open another task. You can open and switch thirteen tasks. Attempting to open the fourteenth task causes this message in a dialog box. Close one or more of the tasks that are open.

4. `Unable to run specified program.`

   The program that you tried to start cannot be started correctly. You may have specified the program name incorrectly.

5. `You cannot quit MS-DOS Shell with programs in the Active Task List; quit those programs first.`

You tried to exit the DOS Shell while at least one program was switched. Exit the switched program and then quit DOS Shell.

EMM386.EXE

Enables a 80386sx, 80386, or 80486 computer to convert extended memory into EMS 4.0 expanded memory and to control that expanded memory; also remaps extended memory to reserved memory

Syntax

As a device driver:

DEVICE = *dc:pathc***EMM386.EXE** *ramval W=ON|OFF*
  Ms FRAME=xxxx   /Pn=xxxx X=xxxx-xxxx B=xxxx
  L=xms A=regs H=hhh RAM|NOEMS

ramval is the amount of RAM in 1K bytes to assign as EMS 4.0 memory. Enter a value (from 16 to 32768) as a multiple of 16. Any number you enter is rounded to the nearest 16. The default is 256.

W=ON|OFF enables or disables support for the Weitek Coprocessor. The default is *W=OFF*.

Ms is used to specify the segment base address. *s* is a number used to represent the address. The segment base address is the beginning address of the EMS page frame. The numbers and associated addresses (listed in hexidecimal) are as follows:

s	Address
1	C000
2	C400
3	C800
4	CC00
5	D000
6	D400
7	D800
8	DC00
9	E000
10	8000
11	8400
12	8800
13	8C00
14	9000

FRAME=xxxx specifies the beginning address of the EMS page frame. *xxxx* may be one of the addresses listed under *Ms.*

/Pxxxx specifies the beginning address.

Pn=xxxx defines an address for a page segment. *n* represents the numbers 0, 1, 2, 3, 254, and 255. To remain compatible with EMS 3.2, P0 through P3 must be contiguous addresses. You may not use this option if you use *Ms, FRAME=xxxx,* or */Pxxxx.*

X=xxxx-xxxx specifies that a range of memory should not be used for the EMS page frame. *xxxx-xxxx* are the ranges to keep free.

B=xxxx specifies the lowest address to use for bank switching. The default is 4000.

L=xmsmem specifies the number of 1K bytes that remain as extended memory instead of being converted to EMS memory. *xmsmem* is the value of 1K of memory. For 1M to remain as extended memory, use the parameters L=1024.

A=regs is used to allocate the number of alternative registers EMM386 may use. Although the default number is 7, you can specify a number from 0 to 254 for *regs*.

H=hhh enables you to change the number of handles (EMM386 uses a default number of 64). *hhh* may be a number from 2 to 255.

RAM|NOEMS is used to allocate reserved memory (to place some extended memory in open areas in the 640K to 1M address space). RAM leaves room in the reserved area for an EMS page frame; whereas *NOEMS* does not leave room for the EMS page frame.

As a command:

   *dc:pathc***EMM386** *ON | OFF | AUTO W=ON | OFF*

dc:pathc are the disk drive and directory that hold EMM386.EXE.

ON enables expanded memory.

OFF disables expanded memory.

AUTO enables expanded Weitek Coprocessor support when a program requests it.

W=ON | OFF enables (or disables) Weitek Coprocessor support.

Reference

See Chapter 15.

Rules

1. Works only on 80386sx, 80386 and 80486 systems.

2. HIMEM.SYS must be installed as a device driver in CONFIG.SYS before EMM386.EXE.

3. To create UMBs, you must include the *RAM* or *NOEMS* parameters, and you must include at least DOS=UMB in CONFIG.SYS.

4. Before you can use EMM386.EXE from the command line, you must install EMM386 as a device driver in CONFIG.SYS.

5. Any DEVICEHIGH commands in CONFIG.SYS must come after the DEVICE=HIMEM.SYS, DEVICE=EMM386.EXE RAM (or NOEMS) and DOS=HIGH,UMB commands.

Note

Used from the DOS command line, EMM386 enables or disables expanded memory or sets expanded memory in auto mode. In auto mode, expanded memory is enabled only when requested. EMM386 also enables or disables support for a Weitek math coprocessor.

ERASE

V1, V2, V3, V4, V5—Internal

Removes one or more files from the directory.

Syntax

ERASE *d:path***filename.ext**

or

DEL *d:path***filename.ext**

With DOS 4 and 5, you can add the /P switch, as in the following examples:

ERASE *d:path***filename.ext** */P*

or

DEL *d:path***filename.ext** */P*

d: is the name of the disk drive that holds the file(s) to be erased.

path is the directory of the file(s) to be erased.

filename.ext is the name of the file(s) to be erased. Wild cards are allowed.

Switch

/P   With DOS 4 and 5, prompts you before erasing the file with the message `filename.ext, Delete (Y/N)?`

Reference

See Chapter 8.

Rules

1. If you do not give a disk drive name, the current disk drive is used.

2. If you do not give a path name, the current directory is used.

3. If you give a disk drive name or path name, or both, but no file name, DOS assumes that the file name is *.* (all files).

4. If you specify *.*, or no name for the file name (when you give a disk drive name and/or path name), DOS displays the following prompt:

```
All files in directory will be deleted
Are you sure (Y/N)?
```

If you answer Y, all files in the specified directory are erased. If you answer N, no files are erased.

Note

As long as you do not place more information on the floppy disk, you can recover the erased file with the special DOS 5.0 utility program UNDELETE. DOS's RECOVER does not recover erased files, as you might expect. RECOVER is designed only to repair a file that contains bad sectors or has a bad directory entry.

Message

```
Access denied
```

ERROR: You attempted to erase a file that is marked as read-only or is in use by another program or computer and is temporarily marked as read-only.

If the file you intend to erase has the read-only attribute set, use the ATTRIB command to turn off the read-only flag.

EXE2BIN

V1.1. V2, V3, V5—External

Changes suitably formatted EXE files into BIN or COM files.

Syntax

*dc:pathc***EXE2BIN** *d1:path1/***filename1.ext1**
d2:path2/filename2.ext2

dc: is the disk drive that holds the command.

pathc is the path to the command.

d1: is the disk drive that holds the file to be converted.

path1/ is the directory of the file to be converted.

filename1 is the root name of the file to be converted.

d2: is the disk drive for the output file.

path2/ is the directory of the output file.

filename2 is the root name of the output file.

Special Terms:

The file to be converted is the *source* file.

The output file is the *destination* file.

·Rules

1. You must specify a name for the source file (the file to be converted).

2. If you do not specify a name for the destination file, EXE2BIN uses the name of the source file.

3. If you do not specify an extension for the source file, EXE2BIN uses the extension EXE.

4. If you do not specify an extension for the destination file, EXE2BIN uses the extension BIN.

5. The EXE file must be in the correct format (following the Microsoft conventions).

Note

EXE2BIN is a programming utility that converts EXE (executable) program files to COM or BIN (binary image) files. The resulting program takes less disk space and loads faster. Unless you use a compiler-based programming language, you probably won't use this command.

EXIT   V2, V3, V4, V5—Internal

Quits COMMAND.COM and returns to the program that started COMMAND.COM.

Syntax

EXIT

Reference

See Chapter 9; also see the description for COMMAND in this Command Reference.

Rule

This command has no effect if COMMAND.COM is loaded with the /P switch.

EXPAND   V5—External

Copies a compressed, unusable file from the original DOS disks to an uncompressed, usable form.

Syntax

*dc:pathc***EXPAND** *d1:path1***filename.ext** . . .
    dd:*pathd\filenamed.extd*

dc:pathc are the disk drive and directory that hold the command.

d1:path1 is the letter of the disk drive and path where the compressed file is located.

filename.ext is the name of the compressed file.

The three periods (. . .) represent additional compressed file specifications.

dd:*pathd\filenamed.extd* is the drive or path or new file name to which the compressed file is expanded.

Reference

See Appendix A.

Rule

You can use EXPAND only to decompress files from the original DOS disks.

Example

EXPAND A:FORMAT.CO_ C:\DOS\FORMAT.COM

Expands FORMAT.COM from DOS 5.0 DISK 1 to C:\DOS\.

Notes

Files stored on the original DOS 5 disks are compressed files. This compression enables more data to be stored on fewer disks than files that are not compressed. However, before you can use a file on these disks, you must first decompress the file.

When you use SETUP to install DOS, the files are decompressed as they are transferred to the correct disks. However, suppose that you delete a file accidentally, or for some reason a file gets corrupted. You must transfer the file from the original DOS disk. EXPAND transfers and decompresses the file as it transfers. Consider EXPAND as a form of COPY—however, EXPAND is a "one-way" copy.

Messages

1. `Input file 'filename' already in expanded format`

   You attempted to expand a file that is not compressed. Verify that you specified the correct compressed file.

2. `Error in compressed input file format: filename`

   The compressed file was corrupted. Use a copy of the compressed file to expand.

FASTOPEN
V3.3, V4, V5—External

Keeps directory information in memory so that DOS can quickly find and use frequently needed files.

Syntax

*dc:pathc***FASTOPEN d:**=*nnn . . .*

The following syntax is available in DOS 4:

*dc:pathc***FASTOPEN d:**=*(nnn,mmm)* . . . */X*

In DOS 5, use the following syntax:

*dc:pathc***FASTOPEN d:***nnn* . . . */x*

dc: is the name of the disk drive that holds the command.

pathc is the path to the command.

d: is the name of the disk drive whose directory information should be held in memory.

nnn is the number of directory entries to be held in memory (10 to 999).

mmm is the number of fragmented entries for the drive (1 to 999).

Switch

/X   Tells DOS to use expanded memory to store the information buffered by FASTOPEN.

Reference

See Chapters 3 and 15.

Rules

1. You must specify the name of the disk drive whose entries are in memory. The drive cannot be a floppy disk drive.

2. You can use FASTOPEN on an unlimited number of nonfloppy disk drives. Simply give the additional disk drives, separated by a space, on the same command line or repeat the command for each disk drive.

3. If you do not specify *nnn*, FASTOPEN uses the value of 34.

4. If you give *nnn*, the value must be between 10 and 999, inclusive. FASTOPEN's minimum value is the maximum level of your deepest directory plus 1, or 10, whichever is greater.

5. The sum of *nnn* for all successful FASTOPEN commands cannot exceed 999.

Notes

FASTOPEN works by keeping directory information in memory. Because disk buffers already hold the file allocation table information, FASTOPEN enables DOS to search memory for a file or a subdirectory entry, to locate quickly the corresponding FAT entry, and to open the file. If you have many files and use FASTOPEN effectively, you can increase DOS's performance.

As with BUFFERS, no predetermined best number exists. The default value of 34 works well with many installations. If your subdirectories run many levels deep or if you use many files, specifying a larger number can improve performance. However, using too large a value for *nnn* (greater than 200) slows the system. DOS spends more time examining in-memory directory entries than rereading the entries from the disk.

FC

V2, V3, V4, V5—External

Compares two sets of disk files.

Syntax

> *dc:pathc***FC** */A /B /C /L /LBx /N /T /W /x*
>   *d1:path1***filename1.ext1** *d2:path2***filename2.ext2**

dc: is the disk drive that holds the command.

pathc is the path to the command.

d1: is the drive that holds the first set of files to compare.

path1 is the path to the first set of files.

filename1.ext1 is the file name for the first set of files. Wild cards are allowed.

d2: is the drive that contains the second set of files to compare.

path2 is the path to the second set of files.

filename2.ext2 is the file name for the second set of files. Wild cards are allowed.

Special Terms

d1:path1\filename1.ext1 is the *primary* file set.

d2:path2\filename2.ext2 is the *secondary file* set.

Switches

/A	Abbreviates ASCII comparison displays.
/B	Forces a binary file comparison.

/C	Causes DOS to ignore the case of letters.
/L	Compares files in ASCII mode.
/LB *n*	Sets internal buffer to *n* lines.
/N	Displays line numbers for ASCII comparisons.
/T	Suppresses expansion of tabs to spaces.
/W	Compresses tabs and spaces.
/*x*	Sets the number of lines (1–9) to match (the default is 2).

Reference

See Chapter 8.

Note

FC is a file comparison program similar to COMP, but more powerful (see COMP in this Command Reference). With FC, in addition to comparing binary files byte by byte, you can compare ASCII files of different lengths.

FDISK   V2, V3, V4, V5—External

Readies a hard disk to accept an operating system such as DOS.

Syntax

*dc:pathc***FDISK**

dc:pathc are the disk drive and directory that hold the command.

Rules

1. You must use FDISK to create a partition on a hard disk before you can use FORMAT to format the hard disk.

2. You may change the size of a partition only by removing existing partitions, causing loss of all data on the hard disk.

Example

To start FDISK from a floppy disk in drive A, with drive A as the current drive, use the following format:

FDISK

Notes

In versions of DOS earlier than 4, DOS can recognize only a hard disk of 32M or less. Starting with DOS 3.3, DOS can create multiple logical partitions. A 40M hard disk can be partitioned into two drives—C and D, for example. Starting with DOS 4, however, FDISK can partition a disk larger than 32M into one drive.

If you plan to use more than one operating system, use FDISK to partition part of the hard disk for DOS and another part of the hard disk for the other operating system.

Caution: Do not use FDISK to remove or change a partition unless you have all data on the partition safely backed up. Removing or changing a partition causes all data on that partition to be lost.

FIND   V2, V3, V4, V5—External

Displays from the designated files all the lines that match (or do not match, depending on the switches used) the specified string. This command also can display the line numbers.

Syntax

*dc:pathc***FIND***/V/C/N/I* **"string"***d:path***filename.ext...**

dc: is the disk drive that holds the FIND command.

pathc is the path to the command.

string is the set of characters you want to find. As indicated in the syntax line, string must be enclosed in quotation marks.

d: is the disk drive for the file.

path is the directory that holds the file.

filename.ext is the file you want to search.

Switches

/V   Displays lines that do not contain **string**.

/C   Displays total number of lines that contains **string**.

/N   Displays lines that contain **string**, preceded by file line number.

/I   Specifies that the search is case-insensitive (DOS 5 only).

Reference

See Chapter 10.

Rules

1. You can use more than one file specification. All file specifications must appear after the string and be separated by spaces.

2. If you do not give any file specifications, FIND expects information from the keyboard (standard input).

3. If you use switches with FIND, you must place them between the word FIND and the string. Most DOS commands require that you place switches at the end of the command line.

4. You must enclose the string in double-quotes. To use the double-quote character in the string, use two double-quote characters in a row.

Notes

FIND is one of several filters provided with DOS 3 and more recent versions. The command can find lines that contain strings and those that do not. FIND also can number and count—rather than simply display—lines of text.

This filter is useful when combined with DOS I/O redirection. You can redirect FIND's output to a file by using the **>** redirection symbol. Because FIND accepts a sequence of files to search, you do not need to redirect the input to FIND.

FORMAT   V1, V2, V3, V4, V5—External

Initializes a disk to accept DOS information and files. FORMAT also checks the disk for defective tracks and optionally places DOS on the floppy disk or hard disk.

Syntax

*dc:pathc***FORMAT d:** */S/1/8/V/B/4/N:ss/T:tt*

With DOS 4 and 5, you also can add the */V:label* and */F:size* switches:

*dc:pathc***FORMAT d:** */S/1/8/V/B/4/N:ss/T:tt /V:label/F:size*

With DOS 5, you also can add the /U and /Q switches:

*dc:pathc***FORMAT d:** */S/1/8/V/B/4/N:ss/T:tt /V:label/F:size/U/Q*

dc: is the disk drive that holds the command.

pathc is the path to the command.

d: is a valid disk drive name.

Switches

/S	Places a copy of the operating system on a disk so that DOS can boot from the disk.
/1	Formats only the first side of the floppy disk.
/8	Formats an eight-sector floppy disk (Version 1).
/V	Writes a volume label on the disk.
/B	Formats an eight-sector floppy disk, leaving the proper places in the directory for any operating system version, but does not place the operating system on the disk.
/4	Formats a floppy disk in a 1.2M disk drive for double-density (320K/360K) use.
/N:ss	Formats the disk with *ss* number of sectors—*ss* ranges from 1 to 99.
T:ttt	Formats the disk with *ttt* number of tracks per side—*ttt* ranges from 1 to 999.
/F:size	Formats the disk to less than the disk drive's maximum capacity, with size designating one of the following values:

Drive	*Allowable Values for size*
160K, 180K	160, 160K, 160KB, 180, 180K, 180KB
320K, 360K	All of above, plus 320, 320K, 320KB, 360, 360K, 360KB
1.2M	All of above, plus 1200, 1200K, 1200KB, 1.2, 1.2M, 1.2MB
720K	720, 720K, 720KB
1.44M	All for 720K, plus 1440, 1440K, 1440KB, 1.44, 1.44M, 1.44MB
2.88M	All for 1.44M plus 2880, 2880K, 2880KB, 2.88, 2.88M, 2.88MB

/V:label	Transfers *volume* label to formatted disk. Replaces label with 11-character name for new disk.

/U   Specifies an *unconditional* format for a floppy disk. Unconditional formatting destroys all data on a floppy disk, which prevents you from unformatting the disk. For information on unformatting see the UNFORMAT command.

/Q   FORMAT performs a *quick* format by clearing only the file allocation table and root directory on the disk, but does not check the disk for bad sectors.

Exit Codes

0   Successful completion of last format

1   Not defined

2   Not defined

3   Aborted by user (Ctrl-Break)

4   Aborted due to error

5   Aborted due to N response on a hard disk format

Reference

See Chapter 6.

Rules

1. If you do not give a disk drive name, the current disk drive is used.

2. Unless otherwise directed through a switch, DOS formats the disk to the DOS maximum capacity for the drive.

3. Some switches do not work together. For example, you cannot use the following switch combinations:

   a. /V or /S with /B

   b. /V with /8

   c. /N or /T with a 320/360K or hard disk drive

   d. /1, /4, /8, or /B with the hard disk

   e. /F with /N and /T

   f. /Q with /V

4. If you do not specify any switches other than /B, /S, or /V, format performs a "safe" format. When you perform a safe format, FORMAT creates a file containing file information and

saves the file to a safe place on disk where the UNFORMAT command can find it if you need to unformat the disk. FORMAT then clears the file allocation table and root directory of the disk, but does not erase any data. Therefore, the UNFORMAT command enables you to restore a disk if you did not intend to format the disk.

5. If you are formatting a hard disk, FORMAT displays the following message:

```
WARNING, ALL DATA ON NON_REMOVABLE DISK
DRIVE d: WILL BE LOST!
Proceed with Format (Y/N)?
```

Press Y for yes to format the hard disk; N for no to abort formatting the hard disk.

Notes

Do not try to format any type of virtual disk; on a disk that is part of an ASSIGN, SUBST, or JOIN command; or on a networked disk. FORMAT usually gives an error message and aborts the operation.

Never try to format a RAM disk. Under some circumstances, FORMAT acts erratically when formatting a RAM disk, particularly RAMDRIVE (the DOS RAM disk program). The responses can range from a DOS display of a `Divide overflow` message to a lockup of your computer. If the computer locks up, first turn the system off, then on again. Obviously, you lose the RAM disk's contents, but no hard or floppy disks are damaged.

With versions of DOS earlier than 5, FORMAT destroys information previously recorded on a floppy or hard disk; do not use the command on a disk—floppy or hard—that contains useful information.

With DOS 5, however, FORMAT performs a safe format. When you use the command to format a previously formatted disk, the file allocation table and root directory are copied before they are cleared, and the disk is checked. The existing data is not cleared. If you accidentally format a safely formatted disk, you can unformat the disk. To erase all data from a previously used floppy disk, issue the /U switch. An unconditional format takes about 27 percent longer than the default safe format.

The /Q switch, another feature of DOS 5, enables you to format a disk quickly. The /Q switch clears the file allocation table and root directory, but does not check the disk for bad sectors. To reuse a disk that you know is good, use the /Q switch. The quick format is nearly 80 percent faster than the default safe format.

Messages

1. Checking existing disk format.

   INFORMATION: FORMAT is checking the disk to see whether it has been formatted previously.

2. Saving UNFORMAT information.

   INFORMATION: If the disk has been formatted, the directory and FAT are saved on the disk, and a safe format is performed. A safely formatted disk can be unformatted.

3. Drive A error. Insufficient space for the MIRROR image file.
   There was an error creating the format recovery file.

   WARNING: The previously formatted disk doesn't have room for the mirror-image file, the file that contains a copy of the FAT and root directory. The disk doesn't have enough room to save a copy of the root directory and FAT. Be sure that you want to format the disk located in the drive.

4. This disk cannot be unformatted.

   WARNING: You cannot unformat this disk after it has been formatted. There is not enough room to save a copy of the root directory and FAT, or you are changing the contents of the disk, using the /B, /S switches.

5. Invalid media or track 0 bad
   disk unusable

   WARNING: Track 0 holds the boot record, the FAT, and the directory. This track is bad, and the floppy disk is unusable. Try reformatting the floppy disk. If the error recurs, the floppy disk cannot be used.

   This error can occur when you format 720K floppy disks as 1.44M floppy disks (if you forget to give the /N:9 switch when you formatted on a 1.44M disk drive), or when you format 360K floppy disks as 1.2M floppy disks (if you forget the /4 switch).

   This error also can occur when you format 1.2M floppy disks at lower capacities, such as 360K, and give the /4 switch. In this case, try using a floppy disk rated for double-sided, double-density use.

6. WARNING! ALL DATA ON NONREMOVABLE
   DISK DRIVE *d:* WILL BE LOST
   Proceed with Format (Y/N)?

   WARNING: FORMAT is warning that you are about to format a
   hard disk. Answer Y and press Enter to format the hard disk. If
   you do not want to format the hard disk, press N and press
   Enter.

GRAFTABL   V3, V4, V5—External

Loads into memory the tables of additional character sets to be
displayed on the Color/Graphics Adapter (CGA).

Syntax

To install or change the table used by the CGA, use the following form:

   *dc:pathc***GRAFTABL** *codepage*

To display the number of the current table, use the form:

   *dc:pathc***GRAFTABL** **/STATUS**

dc: is the disk drive that holds the command.

pathc is the path to the command.

codepage is the three-digit number of the code page for the display.

Exit Codes

0 GRAFTABL installed successfully for the first time.

1 The code page used for GRAFTABL was successfully changed,
   or, if no new code page was specified, an existing code page
   exists.

2 GRAFTABL is installed, no previous code page was installed or is
   installed.

3 Incorrect parameter, no change in GRAFTABL.

4 Incorrect version of DOS.

Reference

See Chapter 16.

Rules

1. To display legible characters in the ASCII range of 128 to 255 when you are in APA (all-points-addressable) mode on the Color/Graphics Adapter, load GRAFTABL.

2. GRAFTABL increases the size of DOS by 1,360 bytes.

3. *codepage* is the appropriate code page; codepage can be any of the following:

   437   United States

   850   Multilingual

   852   Slavic

   860   Portugal

   863   Canadian-French

   865   Norway and Denmark

   If no page is specified, the code 437 is assumed.

4. After you invoke GRAFTABL, the only way to deactivate the command is to restart DOS.

Notes

The IBM Color/Graphics Adapter in graphics mode produces low-quality ASCII characters in the 128-to-255 range.

GRAFTABL is useful only when your system is equipped with the Color/Graphics Adapter and when you use the Adapter in medium- or high-resolution graphics mode.

GRAPHICS   V2, V3, V4, V5—External

Prints the graphics-screen contents on a suitable printer.

Syntax

*dc:pathc***GRAPHICS** *printer* /R /B /LCD

With DOS 4 and 5, you can add the name of a file that contains printer information:

*dc:pathc***GRAPHICS** *printer d:path\\filename.ext* /R /B /LCD
/PRINTBOX:x

dc: is the disk drive that holds the command.

pathc is the path to the command.

printer is the type of IBM Personal Computer printer you are using. The printer can be one of the following:

COLOR1	Color printer with a black ribbon
COLOR4	Color printer with an RGB (red, green, blue, and black) ribbon, which produces four colors
COLOR8	Color printer with a CMY (cyan, magenta, yellow, and black) ribbon, which produces eight colors
COMPACT	Compact printer (not an option with DOS 4 and more recent versions)
GRAPHICS	Graphics printer and IBM ProPrinter
THERMALPC	Convertible Printer

With DOS 4 and 5, you also can specify the following printer:

GRAPHICSWIDE	Graphics Printer and IBM ProPrinter with 11-inch wide carriage

Using DOS 5, you also can specify the following printers:

HPDEFAULT	Any Hewlett-Packard PCL printer
LASERJET	A Hewlett-Packard PCL printer
DESKJET	A Hewlett-Packard DeskJet printer
QUIETJETPLUS	A Hewlett-Packard QuietJet Plus printer
LASERJETII	A Hewlett-Packard LaserJet II printer
PAINTJET	A Hewlett-Packard PaintJet printer
QUIETJET	A Hewlett-Packard printer
RUGGEDWRITER	A Hewlett-Packard RuggedWriter printer
RUGGEDWRITERWIDE	A Hewlett-Packard RuggedWriterwide printer
THINKJET	A Hewlett-Packard ThinkJet printer

filename is the file name that contains printer information (DOS 4 and 5). If no file name is specified, DOS uses the name GRAPHICS.PRO.

Switches

/R	Reverses colors so that the image on the paper matches the screen—a white image on black background.
/B	Prints the background color of the screen. You can use this switch only when the printer type is COLOR4 or COLOR8.
/LCD	Prints the image as displayed on the PC Convertible's LCD display.
/PRINTBOX:x	Prints the image and uses the print box size *id* represented by *x*. This value must match the first entry of a Printbox statement in the printer profile (DOS 4 and 5), such as *lcd* or *std*.

Reference

See Chapter 10.

HELP   V5—External

Displays syntax help for a DOS command.

Syntax

> *dc:pathc***HELP** *command*

or

> *command* /?

dc: is the drive that contains HELP.EXE.

pathc is the directory where HELP.EXE is located.

Rules

1. If you do not type a command with help, a list of commands with a one line description is displayed.

2. Help is not displayed for CONFIG.SYS commands.

3. If *command* is not available on the disk and is not located in the search path, help is not displayed.

Notes

You may get syntax help for each command in DOS 5. The following information is displayed with HELP:

1. A one-line description of the command

2. The correct syntax to use the command

3. Switches that may be used with the command

You may get help for any command at the DOS prompt. If you enter only HELP, a list of commands with an accompanying one-line description is displayed on-screen.

JOIN   V3.1, V3.2, V3.3, V4, V5—External

Produces a directory structure by connecting one disk drive to a subdirectory of another disk drive.

Syntax

To connect disk drives, use the following form:

   *dc:pathc***JOIN d1:** *d2:***\dirname**

To disconnect disk drives, use this form of the command:

   *dc:pathc***JOIN d1:** **/D**

To show currently connected drives, use the following form:

   *dc:pathc***JOIN**

dc: is the disk drive that holds the command.

pathc is the path to the command.

d1: is the disk drive to be connected. DOS calls **1:d** the *guest disk drive*.

d2: is the disk drive to which **d1:** is to be connected. DOS calls *d2:* the *host disk drive*.

\dirname is a subdirectory in the root directory of *d2:*, the host drive. DOS calls **\dirname** the *host subdirectory*. **\dirname** holds the connection to **d1:**, the guest drive.

Switch

/D   Disconnects the specified guest disk drive from the host drive.

Reference

See Chapter 10.

Rules

1. You must specify the guest disk drive name.

2. If you do not name a host disk drive, DOS uses the current disk drive.

3. You must specify the host subdirectory name. This subdirectory must be a level-one subdirectory.

4. With DOS 3.1 and 3.2, you cannot use the host disk drive's current directory as the host subdirectory.

5. The host and guest disk drives must not be networked disk drives.

6. The host and guest disk drives must not be part of a SUBST or ASSIGN command.

7. You cannot use the current disk drive as the guest disk drive.

8. If the host subdirectory does not exist, JOIN creates one. The subdirectory, if it exists, must be empty (DIR must show only the . and .. entries).

9. When the disk drives are joined, the guest drive's root directory and entire directory tree are added to the host subdirectory. All subdirectories of the guest's root directory become subdirectories of the host subdirectory.

10. A guest disk drive, when joined, appears to be part of the host subdirectory. You can access this disk drive only through the host disk drive and subdirectory.

11. To break the connection, specify the guest drive's normal name with the /D switch. You can use the guest drive's normal name only when you disconnect the drives.

12. To see all the current disk drive connections, type **JOIN** with no parameters. If no connections exist, JOIN does not display any message, and the system prompt appears.

13. Do not use the BACKUP, CHKDSK, DISKCOMP, DISKCOPY, FDISK, RESTORE, or FORMAT commands on the guest or host disk drive.

14. When JOIN is in effect, the DIR command works normally but reports the bytes free only for the host disk drive.

15. While JOIN is in effect, CHKDSK processes the host disk drive but does not process or report information on the guest

portion of the drive. To run CHKDSK on the guest disk drive, you first must disconnect the guest drive from the host drive.

Notes

You can use JOIN to connect a RAM disk to a real disk, enabling the RAM disk to be used as though it were part of a floppy disk or hard disk drive. You also can use JOIN to connect two hard disk drives.

Some programs allow only one disk drive to hold data or certain parts of the program. Programs written for DOS 2 and more recent versions, however, enable you to specify subdirectory names. If you use such a program, you can invoke the JOIN command to trick the program into using multiple disk drives as though they were one large disk drive.

JOIN does not affect the guest disk drive. Rather, JOIN affects only the way you access the files on that disk drive. You cannot exceed the maximum number of files in the guest disk's root directory. In the host subdirectory, a file's size cannot exceed the guest disk's size.

Message

```
Directory not empty
```

ERROR: You tried to use a host subdirectory that is not empty; that is, the subdirectory contains files other than the . and .. entries. You can either: (1) delete all files in the host subdirectory; (2) specify an empty subdirectory; (3) create a new subdirectory; or (4) name a nonexistent host subdirectory. Then try the command again.

KEYB
V2, V3, V4, V5—External

Changes the keyboard layout and characters to one of five languages other than American English.

Syntax

To change the current keyboard layout, use the following form:

 *dc:pathc***KEYB** *keycode, codepage, d:path***KEYBOARD.SYS**

To specify a particular keyboard identification code, use the following form:

 *dc:pathc***KEYB** *keycode, codepage, d:path***KEYBOARD.SYS**
  /ID:*code*

In DOS 5, you can use the following form:

> *dc:pathc***KEYB** *keycode, codepage, d:path***KEYBOARD.SYS**
> */ID:code /E*

To display the current values for KEYB, use the following form:

> *dc:pathc***KEYB**

dc: is the disk drive that holds the command.

pathc is the path to the command.

keycode is the two-character keyboard code for your location.

codepage is the three-digit code page that you want to use.

*d:path***KEYBOARD.SYS** is the drive and path to the KEYBOARD.SYS file.

Switches

DOS 5 only

/E Directs the **keyb** command to assume that an enhanced is installed.

/ID:code Specifies the type of Enhanced Keyboard that you want to use.

Country	Keycode	Codepage	Code
Australia	us	850, 437	(none)
Belgium	be	850, 437	(none)
Brazil	br	850, 437	(none)
Canadian-French	cf	850, 863	(none)
Denmark	dk	850, 865	(none)
Finland	su	850, 437	(none)
France	fr	850, 437	129, 189
Germany	gr	850, 437	(none)
Italy	it	850, 437	141, 142
Latin America	la	850, 437	(none)
Netherlands	nl	850, 437	(none)
Norway	no	850, 865	(none)
Portugal	po	850, 860	(none)
Spain	sp	850, 437	(none)
Sweden	sv	850, 437	(none)
Swiss-French	sf	850, 437	(none)
Swiss-German	sg	850, 437	(none)
United Kingdom	uk	850, 437	166, 168
United States	us	850, 437	(none)

Exit Codes

0 KEYB ran successfully.

1 Invalid keycode type, code page, or other syntax error.

2 Bad or missing KEYBOARD.SYS file.

3 KEYB could not create a keyboard table in memory (not available in DOS 5).

4 KEYB could not communicate successfully with CON (the console).

5 The specified code page was not prepared.

6 The internal translation table for the selected code page could not be found; the *keycode* and *codepage* are incompatible (not available in DOS 5).

DOS 4 features the following exit code:

7 Incorrect version of DOS (not available in DOS 5).

Reference

See Chapter 16.

Rules

1. To use one of the foreign-language character sets, load the **KEYB** program and type the appropriate two-letter code for your country.

2. If you do not specify a *codepage*, DOS uses the default code page for your country. The default code page is established by the COUNTRY directive in CONFIG.SYS or, if the COUNTRY directive is not used, the DOS default code page.

3. You must specify a code page compatible with your keyboard code selection.

4. If you do not specify the keyboard definition file (KEYBOARD.SYS), DOS looks for this file in the current disk's root directory. Otherwise, DOS uses the full file name to search for the file. If you do not specify a disk drive, DOS searches the current disk drive. If you do not specify a path, DOS searches the current directory. The file name (KEYBOARD.SYS) must be included.

5. After loading, the program reconfigures the keyboard into the appropriate layout for the specified language.

6. To use the American English layout after you issue the KEYB command, press Ctrl-Alt-F1. To return to the foreign-language layout, press Ctrl-Alt-F2.

7. When used the first time, the KEYB command increases the size of DOS by approximately 2K. After that, you can use KEYB as often as you want without further enlarging DOS.

8. To display the active keyboard and the code pages, type **KEYB** without any parameters.

Messages

1. Active code page not available from CON device

   INFORMATION: You issued the KEYB command to display the current setting, but the command could not determine what code page is in use. The DEVICE=DISPLAY.SYS directive was not given in CONFIG.SYS, or no currently loaded CON code page is active.

   If the DISPLAY.SYS line was included in your CONFIG.SYS file, you must give the MODE CON CODEPAGE PREPARE command to load the font files into memory.

2. Bad or missing Keyboard Definition File

   ERROR: The keyboard definition file (usually KEYBOARD.SYS) is corrupted, or KEYB can not find the file. If you did not specify a disk drive and path name, KEYB looks for the file in the current disk drive's root directory.

   Copy the file to the root directory or give the full disk drive and path name for the file to KEYB.

3. Code page requested (codepage) is not valid for given keyboard code

   ERROR: You gave a keyboard code to KEYB, but you did not give a code page. The specified keyboard code does not match the currently active code page for the console. KEYB does not alter the current keyboard or code page. Choose a new console code page that matches the keyboard code (by using the MODE CON CODEPAGE SELECT command), or specify the appropriate matching code page when you reissue the KEYB command.

4. Code page specified is inconsistent with the selected code page

WARNING: You specified a keyboard code and a code page to KEYB, but a different code page was active for the console (CON). The code page specified to KEYB is now active for the keyboard but not for the video display.

Use the MODE CON CODEPAGE SELECT command to activate the correct code page (the one specified to KEYB) for the video screen.

5. `Code page specified has not been prepared`

ERROR: The DEVICE=DISPLAY.SYS directive was included in your CONFIG.SYS file, but your KEYB command specified a keyboard code that needs a code page that is not prepared. Use the MODE CON CODEPAGE PREPARE command to prepare the code page for the keyboard code you want to use.

6. `Current CON code page:` *codepage*

INFORMATION: The console's current code page is designated by the number codepage.

7. `Current keyboard code:` *keycode*
   `code page:` *codepage*

INFORMATION: The current keyboard code is a two-character keycode, and the code page used by the keyboard is a three-digit codepage.

8. `One or more CON code pages invalid for given keyboard code`

WARNING: You used the MODE command to prepare several code pages for the console (CON), but you gave a keyboard code not compatible with one or more console code pages. KEYB creates the necessary information to work with those keyboard and code pages that are compatible. DOS ignores the incompatible keyboard and code page combinations.

LABEL   V3, V4, V5—External

Creates, changes, or deletes a volume label for a disk.

Syntax

*dc:pathc***LABEL** *d:volume_label*

dc: is the disk drive that holds the command.

pathc is the path to the command.

d: is the disk drive whose label you want to change.

volume_label is the disk's new volume label.

Reference

See Chapter 6.

Rules

1. When given, a valid volume label immediately becomes the volume label for the specified disk drive.

2. If you do not specify a volume label, DOS prompts you to enter a new volume label. You can do one of the following:

    a. Enter a valid volume name and press Enter. DOS makes this name the new volume label. If a volume label already exists, DOS replaces the old volume label with the new.

    b. Press Enter to delete the current label without specifying a replacement label. DOS asks you to confirm the deletion.

3. If you enter an invalid volume label, DOS responds with a warning message and asks again for the new volume label.

4. Do not use LABEL on a networked disk drive (one that belongs to another computer). If you try to label a networked drive, DOS displays an error message and ignores the command.

5. Do not use LABEL on a disk in any drive that is affected by the SUBST or ASSIGN commands because DOS labels the "real" disk in the disk drive instead. Suppose that you used the command **ASSIGN A=C**. If you then enter the command **LABEL A:**, DOS actually changes the volume label of the disk in drive C.

Notes

When you format a disk with DOS 4 and 5, you are prompted to enter a volume label. Whether or not you assign a label, DOS gives the disk a serial number. The serial number is not part of the volume label. Remember that a space is a valid character in a volume label.

Spaces and underscores can increase the readability of a volume label. LABEL 3.0 and 3.1, however, reject a space in a volume name when the name is given on the command line, such as **LABEL MY DISK**. To put a space in a volume label, type **LABEL**, a space, and the disk drive name, if needed, and press Enter. Do not enter a volume label on the command line. When LABEL asks for a new volume label, you can enter the label with spaces.

Message

```
Delete current volume label (Y/N)?
```

INFORMATION and WARNING: You did not enter a volume label when requested. DOS is asking whether to delete, or to leave the current label unaltered. You can delete the current label by pressing Y or keep the label intact by pressing N.

LOADFIX   V5—External

Loads and executes a program that gives `Packed file corrupt` error message when the file is executed.

Syntax

   *dc:pathc***LOADFIX** *d:path***filename.ext**

   dc:pathc are the disk drive and directory that hold the command.

   filename.ext is the name of the file to execute.

Rule

Use LOADFIX only to start a program when you receive the message `Packed file corrupted`.

Note

When loaded into memory, some files expand. Such files are sometimes referred to as *protected files*. If you are using DOS 5.0's capability to load DOS into the High Memory Area (HMA), a packed file may be loaded into the first 64K of RAM. You may see the error message `Packed file corrupted` and the computer return to the DOS prompt. If this message appears, use LOADFIX to load the packed file above the first 64K of RAM.

LOADHIGH   V5—Internal

Load device drivers or memory-resident programs into high memory, beyond conventional memory.

Syntax

> **LOADHIGH** *d:pathc***filename.ext** *prog_options*

or

> **LH** *d:path***filename.ext** *prog_options*

d:path is the location of the device driver or memory-resident program to load high.

filename.ext is the name of the device driver or memory-resident program to load high.

prog_options are any options that are required by **filename.ext.**

Reference

See Chapter 15.

Rules

1. You must use a computer equipped with an Intel 80386sx, 80386, or 80486 microprocessor and at least 1M of RAM.

2. Your CONFIG.SYS file must contain at least the following statements:

   ```
   DEVICE=HIMEM.SYS
   DEVICE=EMM386.EXE RAM
   DOS=UMB
   ```

3. You must have sufficient reserved memory available. Determine available memory by using MEM /CLASSIFY.

4. If not enough reserved memory is available to accommodate the program, the program is loaded in conventional memory without warning.

Note

Before you can use LOADHIGH, you must install HIMEM.SYS and EMM386.EXE (using the RAM or NOEMS parameter) as device drivers in CONFIG.SYS. Also, you must include in CONFIG.SYS the statement DOS=UMB.

MEM   V4, V5—External

Displays the amount of used and unused memory, allocated and open memory areas, and all programs currently in the system.

Syntax

*dc:pathc***MEM** */PROGRAM /DEBUG /CLASSIFY*

dc: is the optional drive that contains MEM.

pathc is the optional subdirectory where MEM is located.

Switches

/PROGRAM	Displays programs that reside in memory, including the address, name, size, and type of each file for every program. Also shows current free memory. You can use the short form */P*.
/DEBUG	Displays programs that are in memory, including the address, name, size, and type of each file for every program. Also displays system device drivers and installed device drivers, as well as all unused memory. You can use the short form */D*.
/CLASSIFY	Displays programs that are in memory, including program name, size in bytes shown in decimal and hexidecimal. Programs are shown loaded in conventional memory and, if available, reserved memory (upper memory blocks). Displays the total bytes free (conventional memory plus reserved memory) and the largest executable program size. You can use the short form */C*.

Reference

See Chapter 8.

Rule

You cannot specify /PROGRAM and /DEBUG and /CLASSIFY at the same time.

Notes

You can use MEM to display information on how memory is used. MEM displays statistics for conventional memory and for upper (reserved) extended and expanded memory if the latter three are available. You cannot specify /PROGRAM, /DEBUG, and /CLASSIFY at the same time.

If you use a 80386-based PC, you can use MEM /CLASSIFY extensively as you begin loading device drivers and TSRs in reserved memory. MEM gives the location and size of each program in memory. This information can help you determine the order that device drivers and TSRs load to best use the reserved memory space.

MKDIR or MD V2, V3, V4, V5—Internal

Creates a subdirectory.

Syntax

MKDIR *d:path***dirname**

or

MD *d:path***dirname**

d: is the disk drive for the subdirectory.

path indicates the path to the directory to hold the subdirectory.

dirname is the subdirectory you are creating.

Reference

See Chapter 7.

Rules

1. If you do not specify a path name but give a disk drive name, the subdirectory is established in the current directory of the specified drive. If you do not specify a path name or a disk drive name, the subdirectory is established in the current directory of the current disk drive.

2. If you use a path name, separate the path name from the directory name with the path character, the backslash (\\).

3. You must specify the new subdirectory name, which uses from one to eight characters, and an optional extension. The name must conform to the rules for creating directory names.

4. You cannot use a directory name that is identical to a file name in the parent directory. For example, if you have a file named MYFILE in the current directory, you cannot create the subdirectory MYFILE in this directory. If the file is named MYFILE.TXT, however, the names do not conflict, and you can create the MYFILE subdirectory.

Note

You are not restricted to creating subdirectories in the current directory. If you add a path name, DOS establishes a new subdirectory in the directory you specify.

Message

```
Unable to create directory
```

ERROR: One of the following errors occurred: (1) you tried to create a directory that already exists; (2) you gave an incorrect path name; (3) the disk's root directory is full; (4) the disk is full; or (5) a file by the same name already exists.

Check the directory in which the new subdirectory was to be created. If a conflicting name exists, either change the file name or use a new directory name. If the disk or the root directory is full, delete some files, create the subdirectory in a different directory, or use a different disk.

MIRROR   V5—External

Records information about the file allocation table (FAT) and the root-directory to enable you to use the UNFORMAT and UNDELETE commands.

Syntax

> *dc:pathc***MIRROR** *d1 d2 dn: /Tdrive-entries /1*

To save information about a drive partition, use the following form:

> *dc:pathc***MIRROR** *d1: d2: dn:* /**PARTN**

To quit tracking deleted files, use the form:

> *dc:pathc***MIRROR**/*u*

dc:pathc is the optional disk drive and subdirectory where MIRROR is located.

d1:, *d2:*, and *dn:* are the disk drives that you track with MIRROR.

Switches

/Tdrive-entries	Loads a memory resident tracking program that records information about deleted files. The drive specifies the drive where **MIRROR** saves information about deleted files. The *-entries* are an optional value from 1 to 999 that specifies the maximum number of deleted files to track.
/1	Keeps MIRROR from creating a backup of the mirror file when the file is updated.

/PARTN   Makes a copy of the drive's partition table.

/U   Removes the tracking program from the part of memory that keeps track of deleted files.

Reference

See Chapter 6.

Rules

1. Do not use the /U switch on drives that use JOIN or SUBST.

2. If you use ASSIGN, you must place this command before the MIRROR command.

3. Information about deleted files is saved in the file PCTRACKR.DEL. This file is used by the UNDELETE command.

4. System information, file allocation table and root-directory, are saved in the file MIRROR.FIL, which is used by the UNFORMAT command.

5. Information about the hard drive partition is saved in the file PARTNSAV.FIL. This file is used by UNFORMAT.

Notes

When you track deleted files, you can specify how many files are contained in the PCTRACKR.DEL file. You can specify from 1 to 999. The default values, however, probably are satisfactory. The values are as follows:

Size of Disk	Entries Stored
360K	25
720K	50
1.2M/1.44M	75
20M	101
32M	202
Over 32M	303

Using the /PARTN switch with MIRROR creates the file PARTNSAV.FIL. This file contains information from the drives partition table. The partition is initially created with FDISK. Rather than saving PARTNSAV.FIL on the hard disk, however, you are instructed to place a floppy disk in drive A. The file is saved on the disk. Label and store the disk in a safe place.

UNFORMAT, a companion of MIRROR, uses these files. If you lose information, if you accidentally format a disk, or if the partition table is in some way damaged, you may recover by using UNFORMAT, if you previously used MIRROR.

Caution: The MIRROR and UNFORMAT commands are not a replacement for proper backups of your hard disk!

Messages

1. ```
Creates an image of the system area.
Drive C being processed.
The MIRROR process was successful.
```

   These messages appear when you issue the command **MIRROR** while drive C is the current drive. The messages indicate that MIRROR performed successfully.

2. ```
Deletion-tracking software being installed.
The following drives are supported:

Drive C - Default files saved.
Installation complete.
```

   These messages appear when you install MIRROR with delete tracking. The messages indicate that delete tracking for drive C is installed correctly.

3. ```
WARNING! Unrecognized DOS INT 25h/26h handler.
Some other TSR programs may behave erratically
while deletion-tracking software is resident!
```

   Try installing the MIRROR program before other resident programs.

   Some other TSR conflicted with delete tracking. Experiment with loading TSRs and delete tracking in a different order. When you find the correct order, modify AUTOEXEC.BAT so that the TSRs and delete tracking are loaded in the correct sequence.
```

MODE
CODE PAGE PREP V3.3, V4.0, V4.01, V5—External

Prepares (chooses) the code pages to be used with a device.

Syntax

*dc:pathc***MODE device CODEPAGE PREPARE =**
((**codepage***,** *codepage,* . . .*)dp:pathp***pagefile.***ext)*

or

*dc:pathc***MODE device CP PREP =** *((***codepage***,* *codepage,* . . .*)*
*dc:pathp***pagefile.***ext)*

dc: is the disk drive that holds the command.

pathc is the path to the command.

device is the device for which code page(s) is chosen. You can select one of the following devices:

CON:	The console
PRN:	The first parallel printer
LPTx:	The first, second, or third parallel printer (**x** is 1, 2, or 3)

codepage is the number of the code page(s) to be used with the device. The ellipsis (. . .) represents additional code pages.

dp: is the disk drive that holds the code page (font) information.

pathp is the path to the file that holds the code page (font) information.

pagefile.*ext* is the file that holds the code page (font) information.

pagefile.ext	Description
EGA.CPI	Enhanced Graphics Adapter (EGA)
4201.CPI	IBM ProPrinter, ProPrinter XL, and compatibles
4208.CPI	IBM ProPrinter X24, ProPrinter XL24, and compatibles
5202.CPI	IBM QuietWriter III
LCD.CPI	IBM PC-convertible screen

Reference

See Chapter 16.

Rules

1. You must specify a valid device. The options are CON:, PRN:, LPT1:, LPT2:, or LPT3:. The colon after the device name is optional.

2. You must use the word **CODEPAGE** or **CP**, and **PREPARE** or **PREP**.

3. You must specify one or more code pages. You must separate each number with a comma if you give more than one code page. You must enclose the entire list of code pages in parentheses.

4. When you add or replace code pages, enter a comma for any code page that you do not want to change.

5. Do not use a hardware code page (the code page given to DISPLAY.SYS for the console or to PRINTER.SYS for printers).

Note

MODE CODEPAGE PREPARE is used to prepare code pages (fonts) for the console (keyboard and display) and the printers. Issue this subcommand before issuing the MODE CODEPAGE SELECT subcommand, unless you use the IBM QuietWriter III printer, whose font information is held in cartridges. If the needed code page is in a cartridge and the code page was specified to the PRINTER.SYS driver, no PREPARE command is needed.

MODE
CODE PAGE REFRESH

V3.3, V4.0, V4.01, V5—External

Reloads and reactivates the code page used with a device.

Syntax

*dc:pathc***MODE device CODEPAGE REFRESH**

or

*dc:pathc***MODE device CP REF**

dc: is the disk drive that holds the command.

pathc is the path to the command.

device is the device for which you choose The code page(s). You can select one of the following devices:

CON:	The console
PRN:	The first parallel printer
LPTx:	The first, second, or third parallel printer (**x** is 1, 2, or 3)

Reference

See Chapter 16.

Rules

1. You must specify a valid device. The options are CON:, PRN:, LPT1:, LPT2:, or LPT3:. The colon after the device name is optional.

2. You must use the word **CODEPAGE** or **CP**, and **REFRESH** or **REF**.

Note

MODE CODEPAGE REFRESH downloads, if necessary, and reactivates the currently selected code page on a device. Use this command after you turn on your printer, or after a program messes up the video display and leaves the console code page in ruins.

MODE CODE PAGE SELECT
V3.3, V4.0, V4.01, V5—External

Activates the code page used with a device.

Syntax

*dc:pathc***MODE device CODEPAGE SELECT = codepage**

or

*dc:pathc***MODE device CP SEL = codepage**

dc: is the disk drive that holds the command.

pathc is the path to the command.

device is the device for which code page(s) is chosen. You can select one of the following devices:

CON:	The console
PRN:	The first parallel printer
LPTx:	The first, second, or third parallel printer (**x** is 1, 2, or 3)

codepage is the number of the code page(s) to be used with the device.

Reference

See Chapter 16.

Rules

1. You must specify a valid device. The options are CON:, PRN:, LPT1:, LPT2:, or LPT3:. The colon after the device name is optional.

2. You must use the word **CODEPAGE** or **CP**, and **SELECT** or **SEL**.

3. You must specify a code page **CODEPAGE**. The code page must be either part of a MODE CODEPAGE PREPARE command for the device or the hardware code page specified to the appropriate device driver.

Notes

MODE CODEPAGE SELECT activates a currently prepared code page or reactivates a hardware code page. You can use MODE CODEPAGE SELECT only on these two types of code pages.

MODE CODEPAGE SELECT usually completes a downloading of any software font to the device, except for the QuietWriter III printer, which uses cartridges.

MODE CODEPAGE SELECT activates code pages for individual devices. You can use the CHCP command to activate the code pages for all available devices.

Reference

See Chapter 16.

MODE
CODE PAGE STATUS

V3.3, V4.0, V4.01, V5—External

Displays a device's code page status.

Syntax

*dc:pathc***MODE device CODEPAGE** */STATUS*

or

*dc:pathc***MODE device CP** */STA*

dc: is the disk drive that holds the command.

pathc is the path to the command.

device is the device for which code page(s) is chosen. You can select one of the following devices:

CON:	The console
PRN:	The first parallel printer
LPTx:	The first, second, or third parallel printer (**x** is 1, 2, or 3)

Switch

/STATUS
or */STA*   Displays the status of the device's code pages.

Reference

See Chapter 16.

Rules

1. You must specify a valid device. The options are CON:, PRN:, LPT1:, LPT2:, or LPT3:. The colon after the device name is optional.

2. You must use the word **CODEPAGE** or **CP**.

3. You can use the /STATUS or /STA switch. If you omit all other MODE keywords and the switch (that is, if you type only **MODE** and press Enter), MODE assumes that you want the STATUS subcommand.

4. MODE /STATUS displays the following information about the device:

   a. The selected (active) code page, if one is selected.

   b. The hardware code page(s).

   c. Any prepared code page(s).

   d. Any available positions for additional prepared code pages.

Note

MODE CODEPAGE /STATUS shows the device's current code page status.

MODE
COM PORT   V1.1, V2, V3, V3.3, V4, V5—External

Controls the protocol characteristics of the Asynchronous Communications Adapter.

Syntax

*dc:pathc***MODE COMy:** **baud**, *parity, databits, stopbits, P*

If you have DOS 4 or 5, you can use the following form:

*dc:pathc***MODE COMy:** *BAUD=baud PARITY=parity DATA=databits STOP=stopbits RETRY=ret*

y: is the adapter number (1, 2, 3, or 4); the colon after the number is optional.

baud is the baud rate (110, 150, 300, 600, 1200, 2400, 4800, 9600, or 19200).

parity is the parity checking (None, Odd, or Even; in versions of DOS before 4.0, use N, O, or E).

databits is the number of data bits (7 or 8).

stopbits is the number of stop bits (1 or 2).

P represents continuous retries on time-out errors.

ret tells DOS what to do when a time-out error occurs. You can choose from the following options:

ret	Action
E	Return the error when port is busy (default).
B	Return busy when port is busy.
P	Retry until output is accepted
R	Return ready when port is busy (infinite retry).
NONE	Take no action.

Reference

See Chapter 10.

Rules

1. You must enter the adapter's number, followed by a space and a baud rate. If you type the optional colon, you must immediately follow it with the adapter number. All other parameters are optional.

2. If you do not want to change a parameter, enter a comma for that value.

3. If you enter an invalid parameter, DOS responds with an invalid parameter message and takes no further action.

4. You can enter only the first two digits of the baud rate (for example, 11 for 110 baud and 96 for 9600 baud).

5. The 19200 baud rate is valid only for PS/2 computers. If you try to use the 19200 baud rate on a PC or compatible, DOS displays an `Invalid parameter` message and takes no further action.

6. If you want continuous retries after a time-out, you must enter the **P** or **RETRY=B** whenever you use the MODE COMn: command.

7. If the adapter is set for continuous retries (*P* or **RETRY=B**) and the device is not ready, the computer appears to be locked up. You can abort this loop by pressing Ctrl-Break.

MODE DISPLAY

V2, V3, V4—External

Switches the active display adapter between the monochrome display and a graphics adapter/array (Color Graphics Adapter, Enhanced

Color Graphics Adapater, or Video Graphics Array) on a two-display system, and sets the graphics adapter/array's characteristics.

Syntax

*dc:pathc***MODE dt**

*dc:pathc***MODE** *dt,* **s**, *T*

If you are using DOS 4.0 or 4.01, you can use the following forms:

*dc:pathc***MODE CON: COLS=***x* **LINES=***y*

or

*dc:pathc***MODE dt,***y*

dc: is the name of the disk drive holding the command.

pathc is the path to the command.

dt is the display type, which may be one of the following:

40	Sets the display to 40 characters per line for the graphics display
80	Sets the display to 80 character per line for the graphics display
BW40	Makes the graphics display the active display and sets the mode to 40 characters per line, black-and-white (color disabled)
BW80	Makes the graphics display the active display and sets the mode to 80 characters per line, black-and-white (color disabled)
CO40	Makes the graphics display the active display and sets the mode to 40 characters per line (color enabled)
CO80	Makes the graphics display the active display and sets the mode to 80 characters per line (color enabled)
MONO	Makes the monochrome display the active display

s shifts the display right (**R**) or left (**L**) one character.

T requests alignment of the graphics display screen with a one-line test pattern.

x specifies the number of columns to display; 40 or 80 columns are possible.

y specifies the number of lines on the display and can have the value 25, 43, or 50. (Your display adapter may not support all three values.)

Reference

See Chapter 9.

Rules

1. For the first form of the command, you must enter the dispslay type (dt); all other parameters are optional.

2. For the second form of the command, you must enter the shift parameter s (which is an **R** or **L** for shifting right or left); the display type (dt) and test pattern (**T**) are optional.

3. The s (R or L) parameter works only with the Color Graphics Adapter; the display does not shift if you use this command with any other adapter. The T parameter displays the test pattern only on a Color Graphics Adapter.

MODE
KEY REPEAT   V4, V5—External

Adjusts the rate at which the keyboard repeats a character.

Syntax

*dc:pathc***MODE CON RATE** = *x* **DELAY** = *y*

dc is the drive containing the MODE command.

pathc is the optional path containing the MODE command.

x is a value that specifies the character-repeat rate. You can select a value between 1 and 32.

y is a value that specifies the length of delay between the initial pressing of the key and the start of automatic character repetition. This value can be 1, 2, 3, or 4, which represent delays of 1/4 second, 1/2 second, 3/4 second, and one full second, respectively.

Reference

See Chapter 10.

MODE
Printer Port   V1, V2, V3, V4, V5—External

Sets the parallel printer characteristics.

Syntax

> *dc:pathc***MODE LPTx:***cpl,lpi,P*

If you have DOS 4 or 5, you can use the following form:

> *dc:pathc***MODE LPTx:** *COLS=cpl LINES=lpi RETRY=ret*

dc: is the disk drive that holds the command.

pathc is the path to the command.

x: is the printer number (1, 2, or 3). The colon is optional.

cpl is the number of characters per line (80, 132).

lpi is the number of lines per inch (six or eight).

P specifies continuous retries on time-out errors.

ret tells DOS what to do when a time-out error occurs. You can choose from the following options:

ret	Action
E	Return the error when port is busy (default).
B	Return busy when port is busy.
P	Retry until printer is not busy.
R	Return ready when port is busy (infinite retry).
NONE	Take no action.

Reference

See Chapter 10.

Rules

1. You must specify a printer number, but all other parameters are optional, including the colon after the printer number.

2. If you do not want to change a parameter, enter a comma for that parameter.

3. This command cancels the effect of **MODE LPTx: = COMy:**.

4. A parameter does not change if you skip that parameter or instead use an invalid parameter. This is not true of the printer number, however, which must be entered correctly.

5. With versions through DOS 3.3, if you specify a *P* for continuous retries, you can cancel the *P* only by reentering the MODE

command without the *P*. With DOS 4 and 5, RETRY=B option has the same effect as the *P* option of previous DOS versions.

6. If you use a networked printer, do not use the *P* option of DOS Version 3.3 and earlier with the retry options of 4 and 5.

7. The characters-per-line and lines-per-inch portions of the command affect only IBM printers, Epson printers, and other printers that use Epson-compatible control codes.

Notes

This command controls the IBM Matrix and Graphics Printers, all Epson printers, and Epson-compatible printers. The command may work partially or not at all on other printers.

When you change the column width, MODE sends the special printer-control code that specifies the normal font (80) or the condensed font (132). When you change the lines-per-inch setting, MODE sends the correct printer-control code for printing six or eight lines per inch. MODE also sets the printer to 88 lines per page for an eight lines-per-inch setting and to 66 lines per page for a six lines-per-inch setting.

If you give the option *P* in versions of DOS through DOS 3.3 or the *B* retry option of 4 or 5 and attempt to print on a deselected printer, the computer does not issue a time-out error. Rather, the computer internally loops until the printer is ready (turned on, connected to the PC, and selected). For about a minute, the computer appears to be locked up. To abort the continuous retry, press Ctrl-Break.

MODE
REDIRECTION   V2, V3, V4, V5—External

Forces DOS to print to a serial printer rather than a parallel printer.

Syntax

*dc:pathc***MODE LPTx:** = **COMy:**

dc: is the disk drive that holds the command.

pathc is the path to the command.

x: is the parallel printer number (1, 2, or 3). The colon is optional.

y: is the Asynchronous Communications Adapter number (1, 2, 3, or 4).

Reference

See Chapter 10.

Rules

1. You must give a valid number for both the parallel printer and the serial printer.

2. After you give the command, all printing that normally goes to the parallel printer goes to the designated serial printer.

3. This command can be canceled by the MODE LPTx: command.

Notes

This form of MODE is useful for systems connected to a serial printer. When you type the following command, the serial printer receives all the output that usually is sent to the system printer (assuming that the serial printer is connected to the first Asynchronous Communications Adapter):

MODE LPT1: = COM1:

This output includes the print-screen (Shift-PrtSc) function. Before you issue the MODE LPT=COMy command, use the MODE COMn: command to set up the serial adapter used for the serial printer.

MODE
STATUS
                                            V4, V5—External

Displays the status of a specified device or of all devices that can be set by MODE.

Syntax

*dc:pathc***MODE** *device* **/STATUS**

dc: is the disk drive that holds the command.

pathc is the path to the command.

device is the optional device to be checked by MODE.

Switch

/STATUS   Checks the status of a device or devices. If you prefer, you can enter just **/STA** rather than the complete **/STATUS**.

Reference

See Chapter 16.

Note

This command enables you to see the status of any device that you normally set with MODE. Typing **MODE LPT1 /STA**, for example, displays the status of the first parallel port.

MORE   V2, V3, V4, V5—External

Displays one screen of information from the standard input device and pauses and displays the message —More—. When you press any key, MORE displays the next screen of information.

Syntax

  *dc:pathc***MORE**

dc: is the disk drive that holds the command.

pathc is the path to the command.

Reference

See Chapter 10.

Rules

1. MORE displays one screen of information on the standard output (display).

2. After displaying a screen of information, MORE waits for a keystroke before filling the screen with new information. This process repeats until all output is displayed.

3. MORE is useful with I/O redirection and piping.

Notes

MORE is a DOS filter that enables you to display information without manually pausing the screen.

MORE, when used with redirection or piping, is similar to the TYPE command, but MORE pauses after each screen of information.

One screen of information is based on 40 or 80 characters per line and 23 lines per screen. MORE, however, does not always display 23 lines from the file. Rather, the command acts intelligently with long lines, wrapping those that exceed the display width (40 or 80 characters). If one of the file's lines takes 3 lines to display, MORE displays a maximum of 21 lines from the file, pauses, and shows the next screenful of lines.

NLSFUNC
V3.3, V4, V5—External

Supports extended country information in DOS and enables use of the CHCP command.

Syntax

*dc:pathc***NLSFUNC** *d:path\\filename.ext*

dc: is the disk drive that holds the command.

pathc is the path to the command.

d: is the disk drive that holds the country information file.

path is the path to the country information file.

filename.ext is the country information file. This information is contained in the file COUNTRY.SYS.

Reference

See Chapter 16.

Rules

1. If you give a drive or path name, you also must give the name of the information file, which usually is COUNTRY.SYS.

2. If you omit the full file name, DOS searches for the file COUNTRY.SYS in the current disk's root directory.

3. Once loaded, NLSFUNC remains active until you restart DOS.

Notes

You can use INSTALL command in DOS 4 and 5 to activate the NLSFUNC command from CONFIG.SYS. After specifying the COUNTRY line in CONFIG.SYS, use the following form:

INSTALL=*dc:path***NLSFUNC** *d:path\\filename.ext*

This method uses less memory than starting NLSFUNC from the DOS prompt.

PATH

Tells DOS to search specific directories on the specified drives if a program or batch file is not found in the current directory.

Syntax

PATH *d1:path1;d2:path2;d3:path3;* . . .

d1:, *d2:*, and *d3:* are valid disk drive names.

path1, *path2*, and *path3* are valid path names to the commands you want to run while in any directory.

The ellipsis (. . .) represents additional disk drives and path names.

Reference

See Chapter 7.

Rule

If you specify more than one set of paths, the following rules apply:

a. The path sets must be separated by semicolons.

b. The search for the programs or batch files is made in the order in which you give the path sets. First, the current directory is searched. First, d1:path1 is searched, then d2:path2, d3:path3, and so on, until the command or batch file is found.

Notes

The PATH command establishes the value of an environment variable named PATH. To view the current value of PATH, use the PATH or the SET command with no arguments.

When you type the name of a program or batch file, the current directory is searched. If the program or batch file is not found, DOS searches through each path in sequence. If the program or batch file is not found in any of the paths, DOS displays the `Bad command or filename` error message.

Message

`Invalid drive in search path`

WARNING: You specified a nonexistent disk drive name in one of the paths. This message appears when DOS searches for a program or batch file, not when you give the PATH command.

Use PATH or SET to see the current path. If the disk drive is temporarily invalid because of a JOIN or SUBST command, you can ignore this message. If you specified the wrong disk drive, issue the PATH command again and give the complete set of directory paths you want to use.

PRINT

V2, V3, V4, V5—External

Causes the printer to print a list of files while the computer performs other tasks.

Syntax

*dc:pathc***PRINT** */D:device /B:bufsiz /M:maxtick /Q:maxfiles /S:timeslice /U:busytick d1:path1\\filename1.ext1 /P/T/C d2:path2\\filename2.ext2/P/T/C . . .*

d1: and *d2:* are valid disk drive names.

path1 and *path2* are valid path names to the files for printing.

filename1.ext1 and *filename2.ext2* are the files you want to print. Wild cards are allowed.

The ellipsis (...) represents additional file names in the form *dx:pathx\\filenamex.extx.*

Switches

You can specify any one of the following switches, but only the first time you start PRINT:

/D:device	Specifies the device to be used for printing. *device* is any valid DOS device name. (You must list this switch first whenever you use /D:device.)
/B:bufsiz	Specifies the size of the memory buffer to be used while the files are printing. *bufsiz* can be any number from 1 to 16,386. The default is 512 bytes.
/M:maxtick	Specifies in clock ticks the maximum amount of time that PRINT uses to send characters to the printer every time PRINT gets a turn. (A tick is the smallest measure of time used on PCs. A tick happens every 1/18.2 [0.0549]seconds.) *maxtick* can be any number from 1 to 255. Default is 2.

/Q:maxfiles	Specifies the number of files that can be in the queue (line) for printing. *maxfiles* can be any number from 4 to 32. Default is 10.
/S:timeslice	Specifies the number of slices in each second. *timeslice* can be a number from 1 to 255. Default is 8.
/U:busytick	Specifies in clock ticks the maximum amount of time for the program to wait for a busy or unavailable printer. *busytick* can be any number from 1 to 255. The default value is 1.

You can specify any one of the following switches whenever you use PRINT:

/P	Queues up the file(s) (*places* the file[s] in the line) for printing.
/T	*Terminates* the background printing of all files, including any file currently printing.
/C	*Cancels* the background printing of the file(s).

Reference

See Chapter 10.

Rules

1. If you do not give a file name, the background printing status is displayed.

2. You can specify any of the switches from first set (/D, /B, /M, /Q, /S, and /U) only when you first use PRINT. If you give the /D switch, you must type this switch first on the line. You can give the group's remaining five switches in any order before you specify a file name.

3. The /D switch specifies the print device that you want to use. If you omit /D the first time you use PRINT, DOS displays the following prompt:

   ```
   Name of list device [PRN]:
   ```

   You can respond in one of two ways:

   a. Press Enter to send the files to PRN (normally LPT1:). If LPT1: is redirected (see the MODE command), the files are rerouted.

b. Enter a valid DOS device name. Printing is directed to this device. If you enter a device that is not connected to your system, PRINT will accept files in the queue. The files are not processed, however, and you lose processing speed.

You cannot change the assignment for background printing until you restart DOS.

4. If you name a file with no switch, DOS assumes that the /P (print) switch is given.

5. Files print in the order in which you give their names. If wild cards are used, the files are printed in the order in which they are listed in the directory.

6. The command **PRINT** /C has no effect if no file name is specified.

7. The first time you invoke PRINT, DOS increases in size by approximately 5,500 bytes. When you increase or decrease certain default settings, you proportionally change the size of DOS. To regain this memory space, however, you must restart DOS.

Notes

The /B switch acts as a disk buffer. PRINT reads into memory a portion of the document to print. As you increase the value of *bufsiz*, you decrease the number of times that PRINT must read the file from the disk, and thereby increase printing throughput. Always use a multiple of 512, such as 1,024, 2,048, and so on, as the value of *bufsiz*. The default size (512 bytes) is adequate for most uses, but using **/B:4096** increases performance for most documents of two pages or less.

For the /M or /S switch, the following formula shows how much CPU time PRINT gets per second:

$$\text{PRINT's \% of CPU time} = \frac{maxtick}{(1 + timeslice)} * 100$$

When the default values are assumed, PRINT gets 22 percent of the computer's time. Increasing *maxtick* gives PRINT more time; increasing *timeslice* gives PRINT less time. Because the keyboard action becomes sluggish as PRINT uses more time, the default values for PRINT usually work well.

The position of the /P, /C, and /T switches on the command line is important. Each switch affects the immediately preceding file, and all following files, until DOS encounters another switch. For example, the following command places the files LETTER.TXT and PROGRAM.DOC in the queue to be background-printed:

PRINT LETTER.TXT /P PROGRAM.DOC MYFILE.TXT /C TEST.DOC

The /C switch, however, cancels the background printing of MYFILE.TXT and TEST.DOC.

In this example, the /P switch affects the preceding file (LETTER.TXT) and the following file (PROGRAM.DOC). Similarly, the /C switch affects the preceding file (MYFILE.TXT) and the following file (TEXT.DOC).

If you use the /T switch, background printing is canceled for all files in the queue, including the file currently printing. You do not need to give /T with a file name because the switch terminates printing for all files, including file names given on the command line.

If a disk error occurs during background printing, DOS cancels the current file and places a disk-error message on the printout. The printer then performs a form feed, the bell rings, and DOS prints all remaining files in the queue.

Messages

1. `filename is currently being printed`
   `filename is in queue`

   INFORMATION: This message tells you which file is printing and names the files that are in line to be printed. The message appears when you use PRINT with no parameters or when you queue additional files.

2. `PRINT queue is empty`

   INFORMATION: No files are in line to be printed by PRINT.

3. `PRINT queue is full`

   WARNING: You attempted to place too many files in the PRINT queue. The request to add more files fails for each file past the limit. You must wait until PRINT processes a file before you can add another file to the queue.

4. `Resident part of PRINT installed`

   INFORMATION: The first time you use PRINT, this message indicates that PRINT installed itself in DOS and increased the size of DOS by about 5,500 bytes.

PROMPT

V2, V3, V4, V5—Internal

Customizes the DOS system prompt (A>, the A prompt).

Syntax

> **PROMPT** *promptstring*

promptstring is the text to be used for the new system prompt.

Reference

See Chapters 7 and 9.

Rules

1. If you do not enter the *promptstring*, the standard system prompt reappears (A>).

2. Any text entered for *promptstring* becomes the new system prompt. You can enter special characters by using the meta-strings.

3. The new system prompt stays in effect until you restart DOS or reissue the PROMPT command.

4. The PROMPT command creates an environment variable named PROMPT. You can use the SET command to see the value of the PROMPT variable.

Meta-Strings

A *meta-string* is a group of characters that is transformed into another character or group of characters. All meta-strings begin with the dollar sign ($) and have two characters, including the $. The following list contains meta-string characters and their meanings:

Metastring	What the character produces
$$	$, the dollar sign
_(underscore)	New line, (moves to the first position of the next line)
$b	|, the vertical *bar*
$e	The *E*scape character, CHR$(27)
$d	The *d*ate, like the DATE command
$h	The backspace character, CHR$(8), which erases the previous character

$g	>, the greater-than character
$l	<, the less-than character
$n	The current disk drive
$p	The current disk drive and path, including the current directory
$q	=, the equal sign
$t	The time, like the TIME command
$v	The DOS version number
$(Any other)	Nothing or null; the character is ignored

QBASIC   V5—External

Loads the BASIC interpreter into memory for BASIC programming.

Syntax

> *dc:pathc***QBASIC** *d:path\filename.ext* */H /NOHI /B /EDITOR /G /MBF /RUN d:pathc\filename.ext*

dc:pathc is the drive and subdirectory where QBASIC is located.

d:path is optional location of the BASIC program to load into memory.

filename.ext is the name of the BASIC program.

Switches

/H	Changes the display mode to view QBASIC with the maximum number of lines on the screen.
/NOHI	Enables QBASIC to work with monitors that do not support the high intensity video.
/B	Switches QBASIC to black-and-white mode.
/EDITOR	Starts the editor in nonprogramming mode.
/G	Enables CGA monitors to quickly update. Do not use this switch if "snow" appears on the screen.

/MBF	Enables the QBASIC statements CVS, CVD, MKS$, and MKD$ to use the Microsoft Binary Format for numbers.
/RUN d:path\filename.ext	Loads *filename.ext* in memory and starts execution.

Reference

See Chapters 17 and 18.

Rule

The file that you specify when starting QBasic is loaded into memory for editing. You must start execution manually unless you specify the /RUN switch.

Note

QBASIC is a comprehensive development environment for interpreted BASIC and a subset of Microsoft QuickBASIC. BASIC and BASICA are provided with IBM DOS 5.0 but may not be provided with future versions. GWBASIC is no longer provided.

RECOVER   V2, V3, V4, V5—External

Recovers a file with bad sectors or a file from a disk with a damaged directory.

Syntax

To recover a file, use the following form:

> *dc:pathc***RECOVER** *d:path\\filename.ext*

To recover a disk with a damaged directory, use this form:

> *dc:pathc***RECOVER d:**

dc: is the disk drive that holds the command.

pathc is the path to the command.

d: is the disk drive that holds the damaged file or floppy disk.

path is the path to the directory that holds the file to be recovered.

filename.ext is the file that you want to recover.

Reference

See Chapter 6.

Rules

1. If you give only a drive name, DOS attempts to recover the disk's directory. (This rule applies to the second syntax line shown earlier.)

2. RECOVER does not restore erased files.

3. Do not use RECOVER with ASSIGN, SUBST, or JOIN command. The results are unpredictable.

Notes

RECOVER attempts to recover either a file with a bad sector or a disk with a directory that contains a bad sector. To recover a file that holds one or more bad sectors, type **RECOVER d:filename.ext**. (DOS tells you if a file has bad sectors, by displaying a disk-error message when you try to use the file.)

When RECOVER works on a file, DOS attempts to read the file's sectors one at a time. After RECOVER successfully reads a sector, the information is placed in a temporary file. RECOVER skips any sectors that cannot successfully be read, but the FAT is marked so that no other program can use the bad sector. This process continues until the entire file is read. RECOVER then erases the old file and gives the old file's name to the temporary file, which becomes a new replacement file. This new file is placed in the directory where the old file resided.

If the damaged file is a program file, the program probably cannot be used. If the file is a data or text file, some information can be recovered. Because RECOVER reads the entire file, make sure that you use a text editor or word processor to eliminate any garbage at the end of the file.

Do not use RECOVER to recover an entire disk. DOS creates a new root directory and recovers each file and subdirectory. The system names the recovered files FILE *nnnn*.REC (*nnnn* is a four-digit number). Even good files are placed in FILE *nnnn*.REC files. To determine which original file corresponds to a FILE *nnnn*.REC file, you must either use the TYPE command to view each file, or print each file and use the last printed directory of the disk, or have a good memory.

RECOVER does not recover erased files. Use the UNDELETE command to recover erased files.

RENAME or REN   V1, V2, V3, V4, V5—Internal

Changes the name of the disk file(s).

Syntax

> **RENAME** *d:path***filename1**.*ext1* **filename2**.*ext2*

or

> **REN** *d:path***filename1**.*ext1* **filename2**.*ext2*

d: is the disk drive that holds the file(s) to be renamed.

path\\ is the path to the file(s) to be renamed.

filename1.*ext1* is the file's current name. Wild cards are allowed.

filename2.*ext2* is the file's new name. Wild cards are allowed.

Reference

See Chapter 8.

Rules

1. You can give a disk name and path name only for the first file name.

2. You must give both the old and the new file names and all appropriate extensions. Wild-card characters are permitted in the file names.

Notes

RENAME, or the short form REN, changes the name of a file on the disk.

Because you are renaming an established disk file, the file's drive or path designation goes with the old name so that DOS knows which file to rename.

Wild-card characters are acceptable in either the old or the new name.

Message

```
Duplicate filename or File not found
```

ERROR: You attempted to change a file name to a name that already exists, or you asked DOS to rename a file that does not exist in the directory. Check the directory for conflicting names. Make sure that the file name exists and that you spelled the name correctly. Reissue the command.

REPLACE

Selectively replaces files on one disk with files of the same name from another disk; selectively adds files to a disk by copying the files from another disk.

Syntax

*dc:pathc***REPLACE** *ds:paths***filename***.ext dd:pathd /A/P/R/S/W*

With DOS 4 and 5, you can add a /U switch:

*dc:pathc***REPLACE** *ds:paths***filename***.ext dd:pathd /A/P/R/S/W/U*

dc: is the disk drive that holds the command.

pathc is the path to the command.

ds: is the disk drive that holds the replacement file(s).

paths is the path to the replacement file(s).

filenames*.exts* is the name of the replacement file(s). Wild cards are permitted.

dd: is the disk drive whose file(s) you want to replace.

pathd is the directory to receive the replacement file(s).

Switches

/A   *Adds* files from the source disk that do not exist on the destination disk.

/P   Displays a *prompt* that asks if you want the file replaced or added to the destination.

/R   Replaces files on the destination disk, although the files' *read-only* attribute is on.

/S   Replaces all files with matching names in the current directory and the subordinate *subdirectories*. /S does not work with the /A switch.

/W   Causes REPLACE to prompt and *wait* for the source floppy disk to be inserted.

/U   Replaces only files whose date and time are earlier than the source file's date and time (DOS 4 and 5).

Exit Codes

REPLACE returns the DOS exit codes. A zero exit code indicates successful completion, and nonzero exit codes indicate various types of errors. Common exit levels are these:

0 Successful operation

2 No source files were found.

3 Source or target path is invalid.

5 Access denied to the file or directory.

8 Out of memory

11 Invalid parameter or incorrect number of parameters

15 Invalid disk drive (not in DOS 5)

22 Incorrect version of DOS (not in DOS 5)

Reference

See Chapter 6.

Rules

1. If you do not name the source disk drive, DOS uses the current disk drive.

2. If you do not name the source path, DOS uses the current directory.

3. You must specify a source file name. Wild cards are allowed.

4. If you do not name the destination disk drive, DOS adds files to—or replaces files on—the current drive.

5. If you do not name the destination path, DOS adds files to— or replaces files in—the current directory.

Notes

If you do not use REPLACE with caution, this command's speedy "find and replace" capability can have the effect of an unrelenting "search and destroy" mission on your data. Be careful when you unleash REPLACE on several subdirectories at a time, particularly when you use REPLACE /S on the entire disk. You could replace a file that you want to save somewhere on the disk, because REPLACE updates the file based on file name alone.

To prevent such unwanted replacements, limit the destination path name to cover only the directories that hold the files you want replaced. Check the source and destination directories for matching file names. If you find conflicts or have doubts, use the /P switch; REPLACE asks for approval before replacing files.

If you use DOS 4.0 or 5.0, the /U switch can help you avoid replacing wrong files. /U compares the files' date and time stamp. The destination file is replaced only if the file is older than the source file.

Messages

1. `File cannot be copied onto itself` *filename*

   WARNING: The source and destination disk and directories are identical. You probably did not specify a destination, so the source disk and directory are the current disk and directory. Otherwise, you specified the same disk drive and directory twice. REPLACE does not process *filename*.

   Check the command line to ensure that you specified the correct source and destination for REPLACE and try the command again.

2. *nnn* `file(s) added`

   or

   nnn `file(s) replaced`

   INFORMATION: REPLACE indicates how many files are successfully added or replaced. The first message appears when you use the /A switch; the second message appears if /A is not used. The message does not indicate that potential files are added or replaced successfully. Rather, the message appears when at least one file is added or replaced successfully, regardless of errors that occur later.

3. `No files found` *filename*

   ERROR: REPLACE could not find any files that matched the source file name *filename*. One of the following errors probably occurred: (1) you misspelled the source file name; (2) you gave the disk drive and directory name but omitted the file name; (3) you gave the wrong disk drive or directory name for the source; or (4) you put the wrong floppy disk in the disk drive. Check the command line to ensure that the correct disk is in the disk drive and retry the command.

4. Parameters not compatible

ERROR: You gave both the /A and /S switches, which cannot be used together in the same REPLACE command. To replace files, omit /A. Remember that, because you cannot add files to more than one directory at a time, you cannot give /S along with /A. To add files to more than one directory, issue separate REPLACE commands, each time specifying a different directory to which files are to be added.

RESTORE   V2, V3, V4, V5—External

Restores one or more backup files from one disk onto another disk. This command complements the BACKUP command.

Syntax

*dc:pathc***RESTORE d1:** *d2:path***/filename.ext** */S* /P /M /N

/B:date /A:*date* /L:*time* /E:*time* /D /?

dc: is the disk drive that holds the command.

pathc is the path to the command.

d1: is the disk drive that holds the backup files.

d2: is the disk drive to receive the restored files.

path is the path to the directory to receive the restored files.

filename.ext is the file that you want to restore. Wild cards are allowed.

Switches

/S   Restores files in the current directory and all subordinate *subdirectories*. When this switch is given, RESTORE re-creates all necessary subdirectories that were removed, then restores the files in the re-created subdirectories.

/P   Causes RESTORE to *prompt* for your approval before restoring a file that was changed since the last backup, or before restoring a file marked as read-only.

/M   Restores all files that were *modified* or deleted since the backup set was made.

/N   Restores all files that *no longer* exist on the destination.

/B:*date*	Restores all files that were created or modified on or *before* the *date* you specify.
/A:*date*	Restores all files that were created or modified on or *after* the *date* you specify.
/L:*time*	Restores all files that were created or modified at or *later* than the *time* you specify.
/E:*time*	Restores all files that were created or modified at or *earlier* than the *time* you specify.
/D	Lists files to be restored without actually performing the restoration (DOS 5 only).

Exit Codes

0 Normal completion

1 No files were found to restore.

3 Terminated by the operator (through a Ctrl-Break or Esc)

4 Terminated by an encountered error

Reference

See Chapter 8.

Rules

1. You must give the name of the drive that holds the backup files. If the current disk is the disk to receive the restored files, you do not need to specify the destination disk drive.

2. If you do not name a path, RESTORE uses the current directory of the receiving disk.

3. If you do not give a file name, RESTORE restores all backup files from the directory. Giving no file name is the same as using *.*.

4. RESTORE prompts you to insert the backup disks in order. If you insert a disk out of order, RESTORE prompts you to insert the correct disk.

5. Do not combine the /B, /A, and /N switches in the same RESTORE command.

6. Be cautious when you restore files that were backed up while an ASSIGN, SUBST, or JOIN command was in effect. When you use RESTORE, clear any existing APPEND, ASSIGN, SUBST, or JOIN commands. Do not use RESTORE /M or

RESTORE /N while APPEND /X is in effect. RESTORE attempts to search the directories for modified or missing files. APPEND tricks RESTORE into finding files in the paths specified to the APPEND command. RESTORE then may restore files that should not be restored, and not restore files that should be restored. Give the **APPEND;** command to disable APPEND.

Notes

BACKUP and RESTORE 3.3, 4.0, 4.01, and 5.0 are radically different from previous versions. BACKUP 3.3 and more recent versions place all backed-up files in one larger file and maintain a separate information file on the same disk. In DOS 3.3 and more recent versions, RESTORE handles the new and old backup file formats, which means that these newer versions of RESTORE can restore backups created by any version of BACKUP.

DOS 5.0's RESTORE command can restore files created by any previous version of the DOS BACKUP command.

Messages

1. `Insert backup diskette` *nn* `in drive` *d:*
   `Strike any key when ready`

   INFORMATION: RESTORE wants the next disk in sequence. This message appears when you are restoring files that were backed up onto floppy disks. Insert the next floppy disk (in the proper sequence) in drive `d:` and press any key.

2. `Insert restore target in drive` *d:*
   `Strike any key when ready`

   RESTORE is asking you to insert the floppy disk to receive the restored files. This message appears only when you restore files onto floppy disks. Insert the target disk in drive `d:` and press any key.

3. `*** Listing files on drive A: ***`

   You used the /D switch with RESTORE, and the files that *would be* restored are listed. The files listed follow the file specification that you used for restoration.

4. `Source does not contain backup files`

   ERROR: RESTORE found no files that were backed up with the BACKUP command. BACKUP may have malfunctioned when backing up files, or you inserted the wrong disk.

5. Source and target drives are the same

ERROR: RESTORE determined that the disk drive that holds the backup files is the same as the drive that you designated to receive the restored files. You may have forgotten to specify the disk drive that holds the backup files or the target disk. If your system has one floppy disk drive and you tried to restore files onto a floppy disk, specify drives A and B.

6. System files restored
   Target disk may not be bootable

WARNING: You restored the three system files (IO.SYS, MSDOS.SYS, and COMMAND.COM) from the backup floppy disks. These files may not have been restored to the proper location on the disk, and they cannot be used to start (or boot) DOS.

7. Warning! Diskette is out of sequence
   Replace the diskette or continue if okay
   Strike any key when ready

WARNING: You inserted a backup floppy disk out of order. Place the correct disk in the drive and continue.

8. Warning! File *filename*
   was changed after it was backed up
   or is a read-only file
   Replace the file (Y/N)?

WARNING: This message appears when you use the /P switch. The file *filename* already exists on the hard disk and is marked as read-only, or the date of the file on the target disk is later than that of the backup copy, which may mean that the backup copy is obsolete. Answer Y to replace the existing file with the backup copy or N to skip the file.

RMDIR or RD   V2, V3, V4, V5—Internal

Removes a directory or subdirectory.

Syntax

RMDIR *d:***path**

or

RD *d:***path**

d: is the drive that holds the subdirectory.

path is the path to the subdirectory. The last path name is the subdirectory you want to delete.

Reference

See Chapter 7.

Rules

1. You must name the subdirectory to be deleted.

2. The subdirectory to be deleted must be empty, including hidden files.

3. You cannot delete the current directory.

Message

```
Invalid path, not directory
or directory not empty
```

RMDIR did not remove the specified directory because one of the following errors occurred: (1) you gave an invalid directory in the path; (2) files other than the . and .. entries still exist; or (3) you misspelled the path or directory name to be removed. Check each possibility and try again.

SELECT   V3, V4—External

Prepares a disk with the DOS files and configures the CONFIG.SYS and AUTOEXEC.BAT files for your country. For DOS 4, SELECT was expanded to a full-featured, menu-oriented DOS installation utility. SELECT is not included in DOS 5.0.

Syntax

For DOS 3.0 through 3.3, use the following form:

*dc:pathc***SELECT** *ds: dd:pathd* **countrycode keycode**

dc: is the disk drive that holds the command.

pathc is the path to the command.

ds: is the source disk.

dd:pathd is the destination disk and subdirectory.

Reference

See Chapter 16.

SET

V2, V3, V4, V5—Internal

Sets or shows the system environment.

Syntax

To display the environment, use the following form:

SET

To add to or alter the environment, use this form:

SET name=string

name is the string you want to add to the environment.

string is the information you want to store in the environment.

The *environment* is the portion of RAM reserved for alphanumeric information that can be examined and used by DOS commands or user programs. For example, the environment usually contains COMSPEC, which is the location of COMMAND.COM; PATH, the additional paths for finding programs and batch files; and PROMPT, the string defining the DOS system prompt.

Reference

See Chapter 9.

Rules

1. To delete a name, use **SET name=** without specifying a *string*.

2. Any lowercase letters in **name** are changed to uppercase letters when placed in the environment. The characters in *string* are not changed.

3. You can use the SET command rather than PROMPT or PATH to set the system prompt and the information for the PATH command.

SETVER.EXE

V5—External

When used as a device driver, SETVER.EXE loads into memory the DOS version table, which reports the DOS version number to applications listed in the table.

When used from the command line, SETVER.EXE enables DOS 5.0 to report a different DOS version number to a particular applications program by adding an entry to the DOS version table.

Syntax

To load the DOS version table into memory, in CONFIG.SYS use the form:

> **DEVICE=***dc:pathc***SETVER.EXE**

To add a program to the version table, use the form:

> *dc:pathc***SETVER** *d:* **filename.ext dosver**

To remove a program from the version table, use the form:

> *dc:pathc***SETVER filename.ext** */DELETE /QUIET*

To view the version table, from the command line use the form:

> *dc:pathc***SETVER**

dc:pathc is the drive and subdirectory path where SETVER is located.

d: is the drive that contains the DOS system files.

Wild cards are not permitted.

Switches

N.NN   The DOS version required by your executable file.

/DELETE Deletes the entry for the specified program.

/QUIET   Displays no messages, works only with DELETE.

Exit Codes

0   Successful completion.

1   Invalid command switch.

2   Invalid file name specified.

3   Insufficient memory.

4   Invalid version number format.

5   Specified entry was not found in table.

6   DOS system files not found.

7   Invalid drive specifier.

8   Too many command line parameters.

9   Missing parameters.

10   Error reading DOS system files.

11   Version table is corrupt in system files.

12   Specified DOS system files do not support a version table.

13   Insufficient space in version table for new entry.

14   Error writing DOS systems files.

Reference

See Chapter 9.

Rules

1. You must include SETVER.EXE in CONFIG.SYS as a device driver to load the version table into memory.

2. You must reboot the computer to affect any changes made to the version table.

3. If you specify a program already in the version table, the new entry overwrites the old one.

Notes

SETVER enables programs that have not been certified by their manufacturers as compatible with DOS 5.0 to operate with DOS 5. To enable SETVER capabilities, you must first install SETVER.EXE as a device through CONFIG.SYS.

Warning: When possible, contact your software dealer or the software manufacturer to verify compatibility with DOS 5.0. Fooling an application program into running under DOS 5.0 may result in corruption or loss of data.

When you use SETVER, the current version table is affected. If you specify SETVER with no parameters, then the current version table is displayed to the screen. You can use SETVER with redirection to print the contents of the version table.

Message

```
Version table successfully updated
The version change will take effect the next time you
restart your system
```

You successfully updated the version table. However, you are reminded that you must restart the computer system for the changes to take place.

SHARE   V3, V4, V5—External

Enables DOS support for file and record locking. For DOS 4, also used to support large disk partitions. This command is not available in the Epson Equity implementation of DOS.

Syntax

*dc:pathc***SHARE** */F:name_space /L:numlocks*

dc: is the disk drive holding the command.

pathc is the path to the command.

Switches

/F:name_space   Sets the amount of memory space (*name_space* bytes large) used for file sharing. Default is 2,048.

/L:numlocks   Sets the maximum number (*numlocks*) of file/record locks to use. Default is 20.

Reference

See Chapter 15.

Rules

1. When SHARE is loaded, DOS checks for file and record locks as each file is opened, read, and written.

2. SHARE normally enlarges DOS by approximately 6,192 bytes (DOS 5.0). If the number of locks (/L switch) or memory space (/F switch) is increased or decreased, DOS also increases or decreases proportionately in size.

3. The only way to remove SHARE is to restart DOS.

4. For DOS 4.0, you should use SHARE if your hard disk is formatted with partitions larger than 32M. SHARE is not required to use large partitions in DOS 5.0.

5. You can load SHARE with INSTALL in your CONFIG.SYS file (DOS 4.0 and 5.0).

Notes

You use SHARE when two or more programs or processes share a single computer's files. After SHARE is loaded, DOS checks each file for locks whenever the file is opened, read, or written. If a file is open for exclusive use, an error message results from subsequent attempts to open the file. If one program locks a portion of a file, an error message results if another program tries to read or write the locked portion.

SHARE is most effective when all file-sharing programs can handle the DOS 3, 4, and 5 functions for locking files and records. SHARE is either partially or completely ineffective with programs that do not use the DOS file and record-locking features.

SHARE affects two or more programs running on the same computer—not two or more computers using the same file (networked computers). For networks, record and file locking are made possible by software provided with the network.

You must use SHARE if you use DOS 4.0 or 4.01 and your hard disk is formatted larger than 32M. For convenience, you can use INSTALL in the CONFIG.SYS file to activate SHARE. In the CONFIG.SYS file, for example, the following command activates SHARE if SHARE.EXE is found in the \DOS subdirectory on drive C:

INSTALL = C:\DOS\SHARE.EXE

SORT   V2, V3, V4, V5—External

Reads lines from the standard input device, performs an ASCII sort of the lines, then writes the lines to the standard output device. The sorting can be in ascending or descending order and can start at any column in the line.

Syntax

*dc:pathc***SORT** */R* */+c*

dc: is the disk drive holding the command.

pathc is the path to the command.

Switches

/R   Sorts in reverse order. Thus, the letter Z comes first, and the letter A comes last. The default sort order is ascending.

/+c Starts sorting with column number *c*. *c* is a positive integer.

Reference

See Chapter 10.

Rules

1. If you do not specify the /+c switch, sorting starts with the first column (first character on the line).

2. If you do not redirect the input or output, all input is from the keyboard (standard input) and all output is to the video display (standard output). If you redirect input and output, use different names for the input and output files.

3. Sort can handle a maximum file size of 63K (64,512 characters).

4. SORT sorts text files and discards any information after—and including—the end-of-file marker.

Examples

1. **SORT <WORDS.TXT**

   SORT sorts the lines in the file WORDS.TXT and displays the sorted lines on the video screen.

2. **SORT <WORDS.TXT /R**

   SORT sorts in reverse order the lines in the file WORDS.TXT and displays the lines on the video screen.

3. **SORT /+8 <WORDS.TXT**

   SORT starts sorting at the eighth character of each line in WORDS.TXT and displays the output on the video screen.

4. **DIR | SORT /+14**

   SORT displays the directory information sorted by file size. (The file size starts in the fourteenth column.) Unfortunately, other lines, such as the volume label, also are sorted starting at the fourteenth column.

SUBST

V3.1, V3.2, V3.3, V4, V5—External

Creates an alias disk drive name for a subdirectory; used principally with programs that do not use path names. This command is not available in the Epson Equity implementation of DOS.

Syntax

To establish an alias, use the following form:

*dc:pathc***SUBST d1:** *d2:***pathname**

To delete an alias, use this form:

*dc:pathc***SUBST d1: /D**

To see the current aliases, use this form:

*dc:pathc***SUBST**

dc: is the disk drive holding the command.

pathc is the path to the command.

d1: is a valid disk drive name that becomes the alias or nickname. **d1:** may be a nonexistent disk drive.

*d2:***pathname** is the valid disk drive name and directory path that will be nicknamed **d1:**.

Switch

/D   Deletes the alias.

Reference

See Chapter 10.

Notes

While SUBST is in effect, CHKDSK works only on the real disk drive name and path name.

Avoid using ASSIGN and JOIN and LABEL.

Do not use BACKUP, DISKCOPY, DISKCOMP, FDISK, FORMAT, or RESTORE with the SUBST disk drive name.

Messages

1. `Cannot SUBST a network drive`

   ERROR: You tried to use another computer's disk drive (that is, a networked disk drive) as the alias or nicknamed disk drive. You cannot use a networked disk drive with SUBST, nor can you "cover" a network disk drive with a SUBST command.

2. `Invalid parameter`

SYS

V1, V2, V3, V4, V5—External

Places a copy of DOS (IO.SYS, MSDOS.SYS, and COMMAND.COM for MS-DOS; IBMBIO.COM, IBMDOS.COM, and COMMAND.COM for IBM DOS) on the specified disk.

Syntax

*dc:pathc***SYS d:**

dc: is the disk drive holding the command.

pathc is the path to the command.

d2: is the disk drive to receive the copy of DOS.

For DOS 4 and 5 you also may specify a source drive for the system files by using the following line:

*dc:pathc***SYS d1: d2:**

d1: is the source drive for the system files.

Reference

See Chapter 6.

Rules

1. You must specify the disk drive to receive a copy of DOS.

2. For versions of DOS prior to 4.0, to receive the copy of DOS, the disk must be one of the following:

   a. Formatted with the /S option.

   b. Formatted with the /B option.

   c. Formatted but empty.

   If you attempt to put the system on a disk that does not meet one of these conditions, a `No room for system on desti-nation disk` message appears, and DOS does not perform the operation.

3. DOS 4.0 and 5.0 require only that the target disk contains sufficient free space to accommodate the operating system files IO.SYS, MS-DOS.SYS (IBMBIO.COM and IBMDOS.COM in IBM DOS) and COMMAND.COM.

4. A copy of DOS (the IO.SYS and MSDOS.SYS files) should reside on the current disk. Otherwise, you are prompted to insert a floppy disk containing these files into the disk drive.

5. You cannot use SYS on a networked disk drive.

6. For versions prior to DOS 5.0, you have to copy COMMAND.COM to the target disk as a separate step.

Messages

1. ```
No system on default disk drive
Insert system disk in drive d:
and strike any key when ready
```

   INFORMATION: DOS tried to load into memory but did not find IO.SYS, MSDOS.SYS, or COMMAND.COM. You must load these files into memory before SYS can place the operating system on a disk. Put the floppy disk that holds all three programs into drive d: and press a key.

2. ```
System transferred
```

   INFORMATION: DOS successfully placed IO.SYS and MSDOS.SYS on the target disk.

TIME   V1, V2, V3, V4, V5—Internal

Sets and shows the system time.

Syntax

To enter the time, use the form:

TIME *hh:mm:ss.xx*

With DOS 4 or 5, use the form:

TIME *hh:mm:ss.xxA|P*

hh is the one- or two-digit number for hours (0 to 23).

mm is the one- or two-digit number for minutes (0 to 59).

ss is the one- or two-digit number for seconds (0 to 59).

xx is the one- or two-digit number for hundredths of a second (0 to 99).

A|*P* may be typed to designate AM or PM. If you do not use *A* or *P*, you must enter the time in military hours.

> *Note:* Depending on the country code's setting in your CONFIG.SYS file, a comma may be the separator between seconds and hundredths of seconds.

Reference

See Chapter 9.

Notes

The TIME command sets the computer's internal 24-hour clock. The time and date are recorded in the directory when you create or change a file. This information can help you find the most recent version of a file when you check your directory.

Personal computers sold in the United States use a software clock that is based on the 60 Hz power supply. This kind of clock usually loses or gains several seconds a day. The inaccuracy is not the computer's fault, but a normal problem with the AC power provided by your power company.

If you do not enter the time when starting up most PCs, the time defaults to 00:00:00.00. If you want your system to use the correct time, you must set the time manually.

Many computers retain the time of day through a battery-backed circuit. The real-time clock is read and displayed when you start the computer. Such clocks usually are accurate to within one minute a month, which is about the same accuracy as a digital watch. After you boot your computer, DOS uses the software time clock, which suffers from the same inaccuracies as the PC clock.

TREE   V2, V3, V4, V5—External

Displays all the subdirectories on a disk and optionally displays all the files in each directory.

Syntax

*dc:pathc***TREE** *d: /F /a*

dc: is the disk drive holding the command.

pathc is the path to the command.

d: is the disk drive holding the disk you want to examine.

Switches

/F   Displays all files in the directories.

/A   Graphically displays the connection of subdirectories.

Reference

See Chapter 7.

TYPE   V1, V2, V3, V4, V5—Internal

Displays a file's contents on the monitor.

Syntax

TYPE *d:path***filename.***ext*

d: is the disk drive that holds the file to be displayed on the screen.

path is the DOS path to the file.

filename.*ext* is the file to be displayed. Wild cards are not permitted.

Reference

See Chapter 8.

Notes

The TYPE command displays a file's characters on the video screen. You can use TYPE to see a file's contents.

Strange characters appear on the screen when you use TYPE on some data files and most program files because TYPE tries to display the machine-language instructions as ASCII characters.

The output of TYPE, like most other DOS commands, can be redirected to the printer by adding **>PRN** to the command line or by pressing Ctrl-PrtSc. (Don't forget to press Ctrl-PrtSc again to turn off the printing.)

UNDELETE

Recovers files that were deleted using the **DEL** command. When available, UNDELETE uses **MIRROR**'s delete-tracking file, if available, to restore a deleted file.

Syntax

*dc:pathc***UNDELETE***d:/LIST/DT/DOS/ALL*

dc: is the disk drive holding the command.

pathc is the path to the command.

d: is the disk drive where deleted file resides.

path is the directory path to the file.

Wild cards are permitted.

Switches

/LIST Provides a list of deleted files.

/DT Restores files listed in the delete tracking program produced by the MIRROR command. DOS prompts you before each file is restored.

/DOS Restores files listed as deleted by DOS. DOS prompts you before each file is restored.

/ALL Restores files without prompting. /ALL can be used with any of the other switches.

Rules

1. Undelete cannot restore deleted subdirectories.

2. Undelete cannot restore a file, if you removed the subdirectory which contained the file.

Notes

With UNDELETE, you can restore deleted files, using the delete-tracking file or the standard DOS directory.

When a file is deleted, the first character in the file name is removed. If you use UNDELETE with the \DOS switch, you are prompted for the character to replace the missing first character. If you use the /ALL switch, and a delete-tracking file does not exist, each deleted file is restored without prompts; the character # is placed as the first character in the file name. A deleted file named BETTER.TXT is undeleted as #ETTER.TXT.

If BETTER.TXT and LETTER.TXT are deleted, BETTER.TXT is restored as #ETTER.TXT, and LETTER.TXT is restored as %ETTER.TXT. UNDELETE uses the following replacement characters in the order listed:

% & - 0 1 2 3 4 5 6 7 8 9

Although UNDELETE enables you to recover files that have been deleted accidentally, do not use this command as a substitute for backing up data. Be sure to keep up-to-date backups of your data.

Examples

For the following examples, assume that the DOS commands are stored in C:\DOS.

1. **C:\DOS\UNDELETE C:/ALL**

   The preceding command restores all deleted files on drive C.

2. **UNDELETE**

   The preceding command provides a listing of all presently deleted files.

UNFORMAT   V5—External

Recovers disks that were inadvertently reformatted. When available, **UNFORMAT** uses the **MIRROR** command to restore the disk to the condition that existed prior to reformatting. The **UNFORMAT** command works on both hard disks and floppy disks.

Syntax

*dc:pathc***UNFORMAT** *d:/J/P/L/U/TEST/PARTN*

dc: is the disk drive holding the command.

pathc is the path to the command.

d: is the disk drive where deleted file resides.

path is the directory path to the file.

Wild cards are permitted.

Switches

/J Validates that the MIRROR command contains the necessary information to restore the disk. This switch does not unformat the disk.

/P ¬oes not use files created by MIRROR. Directs all output to the printer.

/L Lists all files and directory names found. If used with the PARTN switch, /L displays current partition tables.

/U Unformats without using the files created by MIRROR.

/TEST Use this switch if you do not want UNFORMAT to use files created by the MIRROR command. /TEST shows how UNFORMAT re-creates the information on the disk. Like the /J switch, this switch does not actually unformat the disk.

/PARTN Restores the partition table of a hard disk. You must use the PARTNSAV.FIL file created by the MIRROR/PARTN command.

Reference

See Chapter 6.

Rules

1. To unformat your hard disk you first must reboot from drive A.

2. If you format a floppy disk by using the /U FORMAT switch, UNFORMAT cannot restore the disk.

Note

UNFORMAT attempts to recover a formatted disk by using the mirror-image files created by MIRROR or created by the format command. If no mirror-image files created by MIRROR ɔr FORMAT exist on the drive, unformatting a hard disk still is possible, but is slower and less reliable.

To prepare for the eventuality that you may need to use UNFORMAT, format a floppy disk, using the /S switch to make the disk bootable, and transfer the UNFORMAT.EXE file to that floppy disk. Transfer any device drivers needed for the computer's operation, including the CONFIG.SYS and AUTOEXEC.BAT files. If the hard disk gets formatted accidentally, you can boot from the floppy disk and perform UNFORMAT.

Before you use UNFORMAT to recover the disk, use the command with the /J or /TEST switches to determine whether your MIRROR files are up-to-date, or whether the UNFORMAT can recover files as you expect.

VER   V2, V3, V4, V5—Internal

Shows the DOS version number on the video display.

Syntax

VER

Reference

See Chapter 9.

Note

The VER command displays a one-digit DOS version number, followed by a two-digit revision number, reminding you which DOS version (Version 2 through 5) the computer is using.

VERIFY   V2, V3, V4, V5—Internal

Sets the computer to check the accuracy of data written to a disk to ensure that information was recorded properly, then shows whether the data was checked.

Syntax

To show the verify status, use the following form:

VERIFY

To set the verify status, use this form:

VERIFY ON

or

VERIFY OFF

By default, VERIFY is off.

Reference

See Chapter 8.

Rules

1. VERIFY accepts only the parameters ON or OFF.

2. When on, VERIFY remains on until one of the following events occurs:

   a. A VERIFY OFF is issued.

   b. A SET VERIFY system call turns off the command.

   c. DOS is restarted.

Note

If VERIFY is on, data integrity is assured. If VERIFY is off, you can write to the disk faster. You are usually safe to leave VERIFY off if you are not working with critical information, such as a company's accounting figures. You are wise to turn VERIFY on, however, when backing up your hard disk or making important copies on floppy disks.

VOL   V2, V3, V4, V5—Internal

Displays the disk's volume label, if a label exists.

Syntax

VOL *d:*

d: is the disk drive whose label you want to display.

Reference

See Chapter 6.

XCOPY   V3.2, V3.3, V4, V5—External

Selectively copies groups of files from one or more subdirectories.

Syntax

*dc:pathc***XCOPY** *ds:paths\\filenames.exts*
dd:pathd\\filenamed.extd /A/D/E/M/P/S/V/W

dc: is the disk drive that holds the command.

pathc is the path to the command.

ds: is the source disk drive, which holds the files to be copied.

paths is the starting directory path to the files that you want to copy.

filenames.ext is the file to be copied. Wild cards are allowed.

dd: is the destination disk drive, which receives the copied files. DOS refers to the destination drive as the *target*.

pathd is the starting directory to receive the copied files.

filenamed.extd is the new name of the file that is copied. Wild cards are allowed.

Switches

/A	Copies files whose *archive* flag is on, but does not turn off the archive flag (similar to the /M switch).
/E	Creates parallel subdirectories on the destination disk even if the original subdirectory is *empty*.
/D:*date*	Copies files that were changed or created on or after the date you specify. The date's form depends on the setting of the COUNTRY directive in CONFIG.SYS.
/M	Copies files whose archive flag is on (*modified* files) and turns the archive flag off (similar to the /A switch).
/P	Causes XCOPY to prompt you for approval before copying a file.
/S	Copies files from this directory and all subsequent subdirectories.
/V	Verifies that the copy was recorded correctly.
/W	Causes XCOPY to prompt and wait for the correct source floppy disk to be inserted.

Reference

See Chapters 7 and 8.

Rules

1. You must specify the source drive, path, and file name first, then the destination drive, path, and file name.

2. Do not use a device name other than a disk drive for the source or destination name. For example, you cannot use LPT1:, COM1:, and so on.

3. The source file specification (*ds:paths\\filenames.exts*) must have one or both of the following:

    a. A valid file name. Wild cards are permitted.

    b. A drive name, a path name, or both.

4. If you do not specify the source drive name, DOS uses the current drive.

5. If you do not specify the source path, DOS uses the disk drive's current directory.

6. If you specify a disk drive or path for the source but do not specify a source file name (*filenames.exts*), DOS assumes *.*.

7. If you omit a new file name for the destination file, the copied file uses the same name as the source file.

8. If you do not give the destination file specification, the source file specification must have either or both of the following:

    a. A disk drive name other than the current disk drive.

    b. A path name other than the current disk's current directory.

9. Do not use the source disk in an APPEND /X command. If the source disk is part of an APPEND command, disconnect the command by using **APPEND;** before you use XCOPY.

Notes

To use XCOPY to copy more files than fit on one destination disk, make sure that the files' archive attribute is on. You can perform this step with the ATTRIB command. Then use the XCOPY command repeatedly with the /M or /M /S switches.

When the destination floppy disk is full, change floppy disks and reissue the same command. The files that were copied now have their archive attribute turned off, so XCOPY skips these files. XCOPY copies the files that were not yet copied—those files that have the archive attribute turned on.

XCOPY and APPEND /X are a troublesome combination. To use XCOPY on a disk involved in a APPEND command, disconnect APPEND before you execute the XCOPY command.

Messages

1. `Cannot perform a cyclic copy`

    ERROR: You used the /S switch, and one or more of the destination directories are subdirectories of the source directories. When /S is given, XCOPY cannot copy to destination directories that are part of the source directories. If you must copy files from more than one directory, issue individual XCOPY commands to copy the directories one at a time.

2. `Cannot XCOPY from a reserved device`

3. `Does %s specify a file name`
   `or directory name on the target`
   `(F = file, D = directory)?`

   INFORMATION: You gave a destination file name in which the final name does not exist as a directory. XCOPY does not know whether the final name in the destination is a file name or a directory.

   If the destination name is a directory, answer D for directory. XCOPY creates the needed directory and begins copying files. If the destination name is a file name, XCOPY copies files to this file.

4. `nnn File(s) copied`

   INFORMATION: XCOPY copied nnn files to the destination disk. This message appears regardless of errors that occur.

5. `Insufficient disk space`

   ERROR: The destination disk ran out of space. The file that you were copying when the error occurred was erased from the destination. Either delete any unneeded files from the destination disk or use a different disk and retry the command.

6. `Reading source file(s) . . .`

   INFORMATION: XCOPY is reading the source directories for file names.

7. `Unable to create directory`

   ERROR: XCOPY could not create a subdirectory on the destination disk due to one of the following errors: (1) part of the destination path name is wrong or misspelled; (2) the disk's root directory is full; (3) the disk is full; (4) a file by the same name as the created directory already exists; or (5) you gave a directory name that actually is a device name.

   Be sure that the destination name is correct. Check the destination disk by using the DIR command. If the disk or the root directory is full, erase files or use another destination disk. If a file exists that uses the same name as the intended directory, either rename the file or change the directory's name when you reissue the XCOPY command.

Changes between
Versions of DOS

S everal major changes occurred between DOS Version 2.x and 3.0. Additional revisions occurred between DOS 3.0 and 3.3, between DOS 3.3 and 4.0, and between DOS 4.0 and 5.0. All these changes are described briefly in this appendix.

Changes between DOS 2.x and DOS 3.0

DOS 3.0 offers several new commands, changed commands, and changed features, when compared to earlier versions of DOS.

The following configuration commands are new in DOS 3.0 for use in CONFIG.SYS:

COUNTRY   Causes DOS to change the way date, time, and other characteristics are displayed, for international use

FCBS   Controls DOS's reactions to a program's use of DOS Version 1's file handling

LASTDRIVE   Sets the last disk letter drive that DOS will use

VDISK.SYS   Provides a RAM (virtual) disk

The following command-line commands were added in DOS 3.0:

ATTRIB	Enables the user to set the read-only attribute of a file
GRAFTABL	Allows legible display of some graphics characters if you use the Color/Graphics Adapter in medium-resolution graphics mode
KEYBxx	Changes the keyboard layout for use with international character sets
LABEL	Enables a user to add, change, or delete a disk's volume label
SELECT	Enables a user to customize the start-up disk for use with international character sets other than English
SHARE	Provides file sharing (file and record locking)

The following command-line commands were changed between DOS 2.x and DOS 3.0:

BACKUP and RESTORE	Includes the backing up of floppy disks and enables backups to be placed on another hard disk
DATE and TIME	Supports international date and time formats
FORMAT	Includes the /4 switch to format 360K floppy disks on 1.2M disk drives; also warns you when you are about to format a hard disk
GRAPHICS	Enables you to print graphics screens on certain dot-matrix and color printers

With DOS 3.0 and later, a drive name and a path name can be specified before an external command or program name. Using this command format enables you to run programs that do not reside in the current directory or in a directory specified in the PATH command.

Changes between DOS 3.0 and DOS 3.1

The following commands are new with DOS 3.1:

JOIN   Enables the user to connect the directory structures of two different disk drives—creating one disk drive

SUBST   Enables a subdirectory to be used as though it were a disk drive

DOS 3.1 supports the IBM PC Network.

The following command-line commands were changed between DOS 3.0 and DOS 3.1:

LABEL   Prompts the user before deleting a volume label

TREE   Adds the /F switch, which causes file names to be displayed along with the directory tree

The following configuration commands are new in DOS 3.2:

DRIVER.SYS   Supports various-sized floppy disks, particularly 720K microfloppy drives on Personal Computers

STACKS   Sets the number and size of the DOS internal stacks

DOS 3.2 supports the IBM Token Ring.

The following command-line commands were changed in DOS 3.2:

REPLACE   Selectively updates files in one or many directories; adds missing files to a directory

XCOPY   Copies files from one or more directories to another; selectively copies files

The following commands were changed between DOS 3.1 and DOS 3.2:

AT TRIB   +A/–A switch added; controls the character attribute

COMMAND   /E switch added; supports the environment size (often used with the SHELL configuration command)

DISKCOPY/DISKCOMP	Supports 720K floppy disks
FORMAT	Supports formatting of 720K floppy disks; requests verification before formatting a nonremovable disk that has a volume label; disk drive name required
SELECT	Formats the hard disk and copies DOS files

Changes between DOS 3.2 and DOS 3.3

The following device drivers for use with the DEVICE configuration command were added in DOS 3.3:

DISPLAY.SYS	Supports code pages (multiple fonts) on EGA, VGA, and PC Convertible displays
PRINTER.SYS	Supports code pages (multiple fonts) on the IBM ProPrinter and Quietwriter III printers

DOS 3.3 supports 1.44M microfloppy disks, COM4:, 19,200 baud rates, and switchable code pages (international character fonts).

The following command-line commands are new with DOS 3.3:

APPEND	Performs PATH-like function for data files
CHCP	Provides code page changing
FASTOPEN	Provides a directory-caching program for hard disks
NLSFUNC	Provides support for additional international character sets (code pages)

The following commands were changed between DOS 3.2 and DOS 3.3:

ATTRIB	The /S switch changes the attributes of files in subdirectories.
BACKUP	The /F switch formats floppy disks; the /T switch backs up files based on their time; the /L switch produces a log file; BACKUP also places all backed-up files into one file on each backup disk.
batch files	Supports use of the environment variable (*%variable%*); @ suppresses display of a

	line; and the CALL command runs a second batch file, returning control to the first batch file
BUFFERS	Default buffers based on random-access memory in the computer
COMMAND	Default environment size changed from 128 to 160 bytes
COUNTRY	Supports code pages and a separate country information file (COUNTRY.SYS)
DATE and TIME	Set the computer's clock/calendar
DISKCOPY/DISKCOMP	Support 1.44M floppy disks
FDISK	Supports multiple logical disks on a large hard disk
FORMAT	Adds the /N switch for number of sectors and the /T switch for number of tracks
GRAFTABL	Supports code pages; also supports additional devices and higher baud rates
KEYB	Replaces the KEYBxx programs and supports additional layouts
MODE	Supports code pages; also supports additional devices and higher baud rate
RESTORE	Adds the /N switch to restore erased or modified files, the /B switch to restore files modified before a given date, and the /L and /E switches to restore files modified after or before a given time

Changes between DOS 3.3 and DOS 4.0

The following configuration commands are new with DOS 4.0:

INSTALL	Enables the loading of terminate-and-stay-resident programs that were previously loaded from the DOS command prompt or in the AUTOEXEC.BAT file; installable programs include FASTOPEN.EXE, KEYB.COM, NLSFUNC.EXE, and SHARE.EXE

REM	Enables the insertion of remarks in a CONFIG.SYS file, which DOS ignores when the computer is booted
SWITCHES	Disables Enhanced Keyboard functions for compatibility with software that does not recognize the enhanced keyboard
XMA2EMS.SYS	An expanded memory manager
XMAEM.SYS	Uses extended memory to emulate an expanded memory adapter on 80386 machines

A new user interface, the DOS Shell, enables you to run programs and manage files using a visually oriented menu system. Many error messages have been changed, and error checking is refined.

The following command-line commands were added in DOS 4.0:

MEM	Provides a report on available conventional, extended, and expanded memory and lists how much of each is unused
TRUENAME	Lists the actual name of a drive or directory affected by a JOIN or SUBST command

The following commands were changed between DOS 3.3 and DOS 4.0:

ANSI.SYS	/X redefines keys added to Enhanced Keyboards; /L tells DOS to override any applications program that resets the number of screen rows to 25; and /K turns off extended keyboard functions, for compatibility with older software
APPEND	Ignores file operations that already include a drive or path in the original specification
BACKUP	Formats target floppy disks if necessary
BUFFERS	/X tells DOS to use expanded memory; specifies up to 10,000 buffers and 1 to 8 look-ahead buffers
CHKDSK	Shows the disk's serial number and tells the size and number of allocation units
COUNTRY	Provides support for Japanese, Korean, and Chinese characters—on special Asian hardware only
DEL/ERASE	/P prompts for confirmation before each file is deleted
DIR	Shows the disk's serial number

DISPLAY.SYS	Checks hardware and chooses the most appropriate type of active display if you don't specify an adapter type
FASTOPEN	/X tells DOS to use expanded memory
FDISK	Supports larger disk partitions and has easier-to-use menus and displays
FORMAT	/V:label switch specifies the volume label; /F:size indicates the size of a floppy disk
GRAFTABL	Supports code page 850
GRAPHICS	Supports EGA and VGA adapters and can support more printers
KEYB	/ID.nnn chooses a specific keyboard for countries like France, Italy, and Great Britain that have more than one Enhanced Keyboard
MODE	Specifies the keyboard rate and number of lines displayed on-screen; has parameters for the COM ports
PRINTER.SYS	Supports additional features of the IBM ProPrinter
REPLACE	/U tells DOS to update files that have a more recent date and time
SELECT	Installs DOS
SYS	Enables specification of an optional source drive
TIME	Enables a 12-hour or 24-hour clock, depending on the country code in use
TREE	Creates a graphical depiction of the directory tree
VDISK.SYS	/X tells DOS to use expanded memory; /E tells DOS to use extended memory

Changes between DOS 4.0 and DOS 5.0

The following configuration commands are new with DOS 5.0:

DEVICEHIGH	Loads device drivers into reserved memory

DOS	Loads the operating system in the High Memory Area and supports loading of device drivers in upper memory blocks
EMM386.EXE	Provides expanded memory management; uses XMS memory to emulate expanded memory in 80386 and 80486 PCs; provides upper memory block (UMB) support in 80386 and 80486 PCs; includes VCPI and busmaster support
HIMEM.SYS	Manages extended memory in compliance with the extended memory specification (XMS)
SETVER	Enables you to control the DOS version reported to an application

The following commands are new in DOS 5.0:

DELOLDOS	Removes all pre-DOS 5.0-related files from the hard disk (upgrade version only)
DOSKEY	Stores command-line statements in memory for later editing and use
EDIT	Invokes a full-screen, mouse-compatible ASCII-file editor that has on-line documentation with hypertext links
LOADHIGH (LH)	Loads programs into upper (reserved) memory
MIRROR	Saves FAT (file allocation table) information; loads delete-tracking memory-resident program
QBASIC	Invokes an improved BASIC programming language interpreter and a full-screen programming environment
SETUP	Installs DOS 5.0
UNDELETE	Recovers a deleted file
UNFORMAT	Recovers data after you accidentally format a disk

The following commands were changed between DOS 4.0 and DOS 5.0

ATTRIB	+/–s sets and clears the system attribute; +/–h sets and clears the hidden attribute
DIR	/S searches multiple subdirectories for files; /O sorts the directory listing by file size, file name, type of

file, and by date and time of file creation; /A displays file attributes; the DIRCMD environment variable stores DIR settings; /B displays just file name; /L displays file names in lower case.

DOSSHELL	Enables you to simultaneously view the file-list area and program-list area, to rename directories, to search for files, and to switch between active programs; provides full mouse support
FDISK	Creates a partition up to 2G (gigabytes); SHARE is no longer needed to access partitions larger than 32M.
FIND	Ignores case of characters during a search for a character string
FORMAT	Runs MIRROR in anticipation of a possible need to unformat a disk; /Q quick formats a previously formatted disk; /U performs unconditional format; supports 2.88M 3 1/2-inch floppy disks.
MEM	/Program and /Debug switches enable you to see the status of programs, drivers, and other information regarding the use and availability of RAM; /Classify lists the sizes of programs, summarizes memory in use, and lists the largest blocks of RAM available in conventional memory and in upper memory
MODE	Sets typematic rate and delay
On-line help	/? after any command-line command, or HELP before any command-line command, displays a short description of the command's purpose as well as command syntax

ASCII and Extended ASCII Codes

T his appendix presents the ASCII, Extended ASCII, and Extended-Function ASCII codes. In the tables, a ^ represents the Control (Ctrl) key. For example, ^C represents Ctrl-C.

ASCII Codes

The codes for the American Standard Code for Information Interchange (ASCII) are presented in the following table:

Decimal	Hex	Octal	Binary	Graphic Character	ASCII Meaning
0	0	0	00000000		^@ NUL (null)
1	1	1	00000001	☺	^A SOH (start-of-header)
2	2	2	00000010	●	^B STX (start-of-transmission)
3	3	3	00000011	♥	^C ETX (end-of-transmission)
4	4	4	00000100	♦	^D EOT (end-of-text)
5	5	5	00000101	♣	^E ENQ (enquiry)
6	6	6	00000110	♠	^F ACK (acknowledge)
7	7	7	00000111	·	^G BEL (bell)
8	8	10	00001000	■	^H BS (backspace)
9	9	11	00001001	○	^I HT (horizontal tab)
10	A	12	00001010	■	^J LF (line feed - also ^Enter)
11	B	13	00001011	♂	^K VT (vertical tab)
12	C	14	00001100	♀	^L FF (form feed)
13	D	15	00001101	♪	^M CR (carriage return)
14	E	16	00001110	♫	^N SO

Decimal	Hex	Octal	Binary	Graphic Character	ASCII Meaning
15	F	17	00001111	☼	^O SI
16	10	20	00010000	►	^P DLE
17	11	21	00010001	◄	^Q DC1
18	12	22	00010010	↕	^R DC2
19	13	23	00010011	‼	^S DC3
20	14	24	00010100	¶	^T DC4
21	15	25	00010101	§	^U NAK
22	16	26	00010110	▬	^V SYN
23	17	27	00010111	↨	^W ETB
24	18	30	00011000	↑	^X CAN (cancel)
25	19	31	00011001	↓	^Y EM
26	1A	32	00011010	→	^Z SUB (also end-of-file)
27	1B	33	00011011	←	^[ESC (Escape)
28	1C	34	00011100	∟	^\ FS (field separator)
29	1D	35	00011101	↔	^] GS
30	1E	36	00011110	▲	^^ RS (record separator)
31	1F	37	00011111	▼	^_ US
32	20	40	00100000		Space
33	21	41	00100001	!	!
34	22	42	00100010	"	"
35	23	43	00100011	#	#
36	24	44	00100100	$	$
37	25	45	00100101	%	%
38	26	46	00100110	&	&
39	27	47	00100111	'	'
40	28	50	00101000	(	(
41	29	51	00101001	)	)
42	2A	52	00101010	*	*
43	2B	53	00101011	+	+
44	2C	54	00101100	,	,
45	2D	55	00101101	-	-
46	2E	56	00101110	.	.
47	2F	57	00101111	/	/
48	30	60	00110000	0	0
49	31	61	00110001	1	1
50	32	62	00110010	2	2
51	33	63	00110011	3	3
52	34	64	00110100	4	4
53	35	65	00110101	5	5
54	36	66	00110110	6	6
55	37	67	00110111	7	7
56	38	70	00111000	8	8
57	39	71	00111001	9	9
58	3A	72	00111010	:	:
59	3B	73	00111011	;	;
60	3C	74	00111100	<	<
61	3D	75	00111101	=	=
62	3E	76	00111110	>	>
63	3F	77	00111111	?	?
64	40	100	01000000	@	@
65	41	101	01000001	A	A
66	42	102	01000010	B	B

Decimal	Hex	Octal	Binary	Graphic Character	ASCII Meaning
67	43	103	01000011	C	C
68	44	104	01000100	D	D
69	45	105	01000101	E	E
70	46	106	01000110	F	F
71	47	107	01000111	G	G
72	48	110	01001000	H	H
73	49	111	01001001	I	I
74	4A	112	01001010	J	J
75	4B	113	01001011	K	K
76	4C	114	01001100	L	L
77	4D	115	01001101	M	M
78	4E	116	01001110	N	N
79	4F	117	01001111	O	O
80	50	120	01010000	P	P
81	51	121	01010001	Q	Q
82	52	122	01010010	R	R
83	53	123	01010011	S	S
84	54	124	01010100	T	T
85	55	125	01010101	U	U
86	56	126	01010110	V	V
87	57	127	01010111	W	W
88	58	130	01011000	X	X
89	59	131	01011001	Y	Y
90	5A	132	01011010	Z	Z
91	5B	133	01011011	[	[
92	5C	134	01011100	\	\
93	5D	135	01011101	]	]
94	5E	136	01011110	^	^
95	5F	137	01011111	—	—
96	60	140	01100000	`	`
97	61	141	01100001	a	a
98	62	142	01100010	b	b
99	63	143	01100011	c	c
100	64	144	01100100	d	d
101	65	145	01100101	e	e
102	66	146	01100110	f	f
103	67	147	01100111	g	g
104	68	150	01101000	h	h
105	69	151	01101001	i	i
106	6A	152	01101010	j	j
107	6B	153	01101011	k	k
108	6C	154	01101100	l	l
109	6D	155	01101101	m	m
110	6E	156	01101110	n	n
111	6F	157	01101111	o	o
112	70	160	01110000	p	p
113	71	161	01110001	q	q
114	72	162	01110010	r	r
115	73	163	01110011	s	s
116	74	164	01110100	t	t
117	75	165	01110101	u	u
118	76	166	01110110	v	v

Decimal	Hex	Octal	Binary	Graphic Character	
119	77	167	01110111	w	w
120	78	170	01111000	x	x
121	79	171	01111001	y	y
122	7A	172	01111010	z	z
123	7B	173	01111011	{	{
124	7C	174	01111100	|	|
125	7D	175	01111101	}	}
126	7E	176	01111110	~	~
127	7F	177	01111111	Δ	Del
128	80	200	10000000	Ç	
129	81	201	10000001	ü	
130	82	202	10000010	é	
131	83	203	10000011	â	
132	84	204	10000100	ä	
133	85	205	10000101	à	
134	86	206	10000110	å	
135	87	207	10000111	ç	
136	88	210	10001000	ê	
137	89	211	10001001	ë	
138	8A	212	10001010	è	
139	8B	213	10001011	ï	
140	8C	214	10001100	î	
141	8D	215	10001101	ì	
142	8E	216	10001110	Ä	
143	8F	217	10001111	Å	
144	90	220	10010000	É	
145	91	221	10010001	æ	
146	92	222	10010010	Æ	
147	93	223	10010011	ô	
148	94	224	10010100	ö	
149	95	225	10010101	ò	
150	96	226	10010110	û	
151	97	227	10010111	ù	
152	98	230	10011000	ÿ	
153	99	231	10011001	Ö	
154	9A	232	10011010	Ü	
155	9B	233	10011011	¢	
156	9C	234	10011100	£	
157	9D	235	10011101	¥	
158	9E	236	10011110	₧	
159	9F	237	10011111	ƒ	
160	A0	240	10100000	á	
161	A1	241	10100001	í	
162	A2	242	10100010	ó	
163	A3	243	10100011	ú	
164	A4	244	10100100	ñ	
165	A5	245	10100101	Ñ	
166	A6	246	10100110	ª	
167	A7	247	10100111	º	
168	A8	250	10101000	¿	
169	A9	251	10101001	⌐	

Decimal	Hex	Octal	Binary	Graphic Character
170	AA	252	10101010	¬
171	AB	253	10101011	½
172	AC	254	10101100	¼
173	AD	255	10101101	¡
174	AE	256	10101110	«
175	AF	257	10101111	»
176	B0	260	10110000	▒
177	B1	261	10110001	▓
178	B2	262	10110010	█
179	B3	263	10110011	│
180	B4	264	10110100	┤
181	B5	265	10110101	╡
182	B6	266	10110110	╢
183	B7	267	10110111	╖
184	B8	270	10111000	╕
185	B9	271	10111001	╣
186	BA	272	10111010	║
187	BB	273	10111011	╗
188	BC	274	10111100	╝
189	BD	275	10111101	╜
190	BE	276	10111110	╛
191	BF	277	10111111	┐
192	C0	300	11000000	└
193	C1	301	11000001	┴
194	C2	302	11000010	┬
195	C3	303	11000011	├
196	C4	304	11000100	─
197	C5	305	11000101	┼
198	C6	306	11000110	╞
199	C7	307	11000111	╟
200	C8	310	11001000	╚
201	C9	311	11001001	╔
202	CA	312	11001010	╩
203	CB	313	11001011	╦
204	CC	314	11001100	╠
205	CD	315	11001101	═
206	CE	316	11001110	╬
207	CF	317	11001111	╧
208	D0	320	11010000	╨
209	D1	321	11010001	╤
210	D2	322	11010010	╥
211	D3	323	11010011	╙
212	D4	324	11010100	╘
213	D5	325	11010101	╒
214	D6	326	11010110	╓
215	D7	327	11010111	╫
216	D8	330	11011000	╪
217	D9	331	11011001	┘
218	DA	332	11011010	┌
219	DB	333	11011011	█

Decimal	Hex	Octal	Binary	*Graphic Character*
220	DC	334	11011100	▄
221	DD	335	11011101	▌
222	DE	336	11011110	▐
223	DF	337	11011111	▀
224	E0	340	11100000	∝
225	E1	341	11100001	β
226	E2	342	11100010	Γ
227	E3	343	11100011	π
228	E4	344	11100100	Σ
229	E5	345	11100101	σ
230	E6	346	11100110	μ
231	E7	347	11100111	τ
232	E8	350	11101000	Φ
233	E9	351	11101001	Θ
234	EA	352	11101010	Ω
235	EB	353	11101011	δ
236	EC	354	11101100	∞
237	ED	355	11101101	φ
238	EE	356	11101110	∈
239	EF	357	11101111	∩
240	F0	360	11110000	≡
241	F1	361	11110001	±
242	F2	362	11110010	≥
243	F3	363	11110011	≤
244	F4	364	11110100	⌠
245	F5	365	11110101	⌡
246	F6	366	11110110	÷
247	F7	367	11110111	≈
248	F8	370	11111000	°
249	F9	371	11111001	·
250	FA	372	11111010	·
251	FB	373	11111011	√
252	FC	374	11111100	ⁿ
253	FD	375	11111101	²
254	FE	376	11111110	■
255	FF	377	11111111	

Extended ASCII Keyboard Codes

Certain keys cannot be represented by the standard ASCII codes. To represent the codes, a two-character sequence is used. The first character is always an ASCII NUL (0). The second character and its translation are listed in the following table. Some codes expand to multikeystroke characters.

If an asterisk (*) appears in the column Enhanced Only, the sequence is available only on the Enhanced Keyboards (101- and 102-key keyboards).

Enhanced Only	Decimal Meaning	Hex	Octal	Binary	Extended ASCII
*	1	01	001	00000001	Alt-Esc
	3	03	003	00000011	Null (null character)
*	14	0E	016	00001110	Alt-Backspace
	15	0F	017	00001111	Shift-Tab (back-tab)
	16	10	020	00010000	Alt-Q
	17	11	021	00010001	Alt-W
	18	12	022	00010010	Alt-E
	19	13	023	00010011	Alt-R
	20	14	024	00010100	Alt-T
	21	15	025	00010101	Alt-Y
	22	16	026	00010110	Alt-U
	23	17	027	00010111	Alt-I
	24	18	030	00011000	Alt-O
	25	19	031	00011001	Alt-P
*	26	1A	032	00011010	Alt-[
*	27	1B	033	00011011	Alt-]
*	28	1C	034	00011100	Alt-Enter
	30	1E	036	00011110	Alt-A
	31	1F	037	00011111	Alt-S
	32	20	040	00100000	Alt-D
	33	21	041	00100001	Alt-F
	34	22	042	00100010	Alt-G
	35	23	043	00100011	Alt-H
	36	24	044	00100100	Alt-J
	37	25	045	00100101	Alt-K
	38	26	046	00100110	Alt-L
*	39	27	047	00100111	Alt-;
*	40	28	050	00101000	Alt-'
*	41	29	051	00101001	Alt-'
*	43	2B	053	00101011	Alt-\
	44	2C	054	00101100	Alt-Z
	45	2D	055	00101101	Alt-X
	46	2E	056	00101110	Alt-C
	47	2F	057	00101111	Alt-V
	48	30	060	00110000	Alt-B
	49	31	061	00110001	Alt-N
	50	32	062	00110010	Alt-M
*	51	33	063	00110011	Alt-,
*	52	34	064	00110100	Alt-.

Enhanced Only	Decimal Meaning	Hex	Octal	Binary	Extended ASCII
*	53	35	065	00110101	Alt-/
*	55	37	067	00110111	Alt-* (keypad)
	57	39	071	00111001	Alt-space bar
	59	3B	073	00111011	F1
	60	3C	074	00111100	F2
	61	3D	075	00111101	F3
	62	3E	076	00111110	F4
	63	3F	077	00111111	F5
	64	40	100	01000000	F6
	65	41	101	01000001	F7
	66	42	102	01000010	F8
	67	43	103	01000011	F9
	68	44	104	01000100	F10
	71	47	107	01000111	Home
	72	48	110	01001000	↑
	73	49	111	01001001	PgUp
	74	4A	112	01001010	Alt-Ω(keypad)
	75	4B	113	01001011	←
	76	4C	114	01001100	Shift-5 (keypad)
	77	4D	115	01001101	«
	78	4E	116	01001110	Alt-+ (keypad)
	79	4F	117	01001111	End
*	80	50	120	01010000	»
*	81	51	121	01010001	PgDn
*	82	52	122	01010010	Ins (Insert)
	83	53	123	01010011	Del (Delete)
	84	54	124	01010100	Shift-F1
	85	55	125	01010101	Shift-F2
	86	56	126	01010110	Shift-F3
	87	57	127	01010111	Shift-F4
	88	58	130	01011000	Shift-F5
	89	59	131	01011001	Shift-F6
	90	5A	132	01011010	Shift-F7
	91	5B	133	01011011	Shift-F8
	92	5C	134	01011100	Shift-F9
	93	5D	135	01011101	Shift-F10
	94	5E	136	01011110	Ctrl-F1
	95	5F	137	01011111	Ctrl-F2
	96	60	140	01100000	Ctrl-F3
	97	61	141	01100001	Ctrl-F4
	98	62	142	01100010	Ctrl-F5

Enhanced Only	Decimal Meaning	Hex	Octal	Binary	Extended ASCII
	99	63	143	01100011	Ctrl-F6
	100	64	144	01100100	Ctrl-F7
	101	65	145	01100101	Ctrl-F8
	102	66	146	01100110	Ctrl-F9
	103	67	147	01100111	Ctrl-F10
	104	68	150	01101000	Alt-F1
	105	69	151	01101001	Alt-F2
	106	6A	152	01101010	Alt-F3
	107	6B	153	01101011	Alt-F4
	108	6C	154	01101100	Alt-F5
	109	6D	155	01101101	Alt-F6
	110	6E	156	01101110	Alt-F7
	111	6F	157	01101111	Alt-F8
	112	70	160	01110000	Alt-F9
	113	71	161	01110001	Alt-F10
	114	72	162	01110010	Ctrl-PrtSc
	115	73	163	01110011	Ctrl-←
	116	74	164	01110100	Ctrl-→
	117	75	165	01110101	Ctrl-End
	118	76	166	01110110	Ctrl-PgDn
	119	77	167	01110111	Ctrl-Home
	120	78	170	01111000	Alt-1 (keyboard)
	121	79	171	01111001	Alt-2 (keyboard)
	122	7A	172	01111010	Alt-3 (keyboard)
	123	7B	173	01111011	Alt-4 (keyboard)
	124	7C	174	01111100	Alt-5 (keyboard)
	125	7D	175	01111101	Alt-6 (keyboard)
	126	7E	176	01111110	Alt-7 (keyboard)
	127	7F	177	01111111	Alt-8 (keyboard)
	128	80	200	10000000	Alt-9 (keyboard)
	129	81	201	10000001	Alt-0 (keyboard)
	130	82	202	10000010	Alt--(keyboard)
	131	83	203	10000011	Alt-= (keyboard)
	132	84	204	10000100	Ctrl-PgUp
*	133	85	205	10000101	F11
*	134	86	206	10000110	F12
*	135	87	207	10000111	Shift-F11
*	136	88	210	10001000	Shift-F12
*	137	89	211	10001001	Ctrl-F11
*	138	8A	212	10001010	Ctrl-F12
*	139	8B	213	10001011	Alt-F11

Enhanced Only	Decimal Meaning	Hex	Octal	Binary	Extended ASCII
*	140	8C	214	10001100	Alt-F12
	141	8D	215	10001101	Ctrl-↑/8 (keypad)
	142	8E	216	10001110	Ctrl--(keypad)
	143	8F	217	10001111	Ctrl-5 (keypad)
	144	90	220	10010000	Ctrl-+ (keypad)
	145	91	221	10010001	Ctrl-↓/2 (keypad)
	146	92	222	10010010	Ctrl-Ins/0 (keypad)
	147	93	223	10010011	Ctrl-Del/. (keypad)
	148	94	224	10010100	Ctrl-Tab
*	149	95	225	10010101	Ctrl-/ (keypad)
*	150	96	226	10010110	Ctrl-* (keypad)
*	151	97	227	10010111	Alt-Home
*	152	98	230	10011000	Alt-↓
*	153	99	231	10011001	Alt-Page Up
*	155	9B	233	10011011	Alt-←
*	157	9D	235	10011101	Alt-→
*	159	9F	237	10011111	Alt-End
*	160	A0	240	10100000	Alt-↑
*	161	A1	241	10100001	Alt-Page Down
*	162	A2	242	10100010	Alt-Insert
*	163	A3	243	10100011	Alt-Delete
*	164	A4	244	10100100	Alt-/ (keypad)
*	165	A5	245	10100101	Alt-Tab
*	166	A6	256	10100110	Alt-Enter (keypad)

Extended Function ASCII Codes

The following extended codes are available only with the Enhanced Keyboards (101/102-key keyboards); the codes are available for key reassignment only under DOS 4.0 and later. The keys include the six-key editing pad and the four-key cursor-control pad. To reassign these keys, you must include the **DEVICE = ANSI.SYS /X** command in CONFIG.SYS or issue the enable extended function codes escape sequence (**Esc[1q**). All extended codes are prefixed by 224 decimal (E0 hex).

Decimal Meaning	Hex	Octal	Binary	Extended ASCII
71	47	107	01000111	Home
72	48	110	01001000	↑
73	49	111	01001001	Page Up
75	4B	113	01001011	←
77	4D	115	01001101	→
79	4F	117	01001111	End
80	50	120	01010000	↓
81	51	121	01010001	Page Down
82	52	122	01010010	Insert
83	53	123	01010011	Delete
115	73	163	01110011	Ctrl-←
116	74	164	01110100	Ctrl-→
117	75	165	01110101	Ctrl-End
118	76	166	01110110	Ctrl-Page Down
119	77	167	01110111	Ctrl-Home
132	84	204	10000100	Ctrl-Page Up
141	8D	215	10001101	Ctrl-↑
145	91	221	10010001	Ctrl-↓
146	92	222	10010010	Ctrl-Insert
147	93	223	10010011	Ctrl-Delete

C

DOS Control and Editing Keys

This appendix lists the usual functions of various keystrokes for control and editing when used at the command line and within the DOS Shell.

Command-Line Control Keys

Enter or ↵	Tells DOS to act on the line you just typed
←	Backs up and deletes one character from the line
Ctrl-C/Ctrl-Break	Stops a command
Ctrl-Num Lock/Ctrl-S	Freezes the video display; pressing any other key restarts the display
PrtSc/Print Screen	Prints the contents of the video display
Ctrl-PrtSc/ Ctrl-Print Screen/ Ctrl-P	Echoes lines sent to the screen to the printer; giving this sequence a second time turns off this function (printer echo feature).
Ctrl-Alt-Del	Restarts DOS (reboots)

Command-Line Editing Keys

When you type a line at the DOS prompt and press Enter, DOS copies the line into an input buffer. By using certain keys, you can use the same line repeatedly. The following keys enable you to edit the input buffer line. When you press Enter, the new line is placed into the primary input buffer, as DOS executes the line.

|← →|	Moves the cursor to the next tab stop
Esc	Cancels the current line and does not change the buffer
Ins	Enables you to insert characters in the line
Del	Deletes a character from the line
F1 or →	Copies one character from the preceding command line
F2	Copies all characters from the preceding command line up to, but not including, the next character you type
F3	Copies all remaining characters from the preceding command line
F4	Deletes all characters from the preceding command line up to, but not including, the next character you type (opposite of F2)
F5	Moves the current line into the buffer but does not enable DOS to execute the line
F6	Produces an end-of-file marker ($^\wedge$Z) when you copy from the console to a disk file

If you have DOSKEY loaded, the following keys also are available:

←	Moves the cursor one character to the left
→	Moves the cursor one character to the right
Backspace	Moves the cursor one character to the left; in insert mode, also erases the character to the left
Ctrl-←	Moves the cursor one word to the left
Ctrl-→	Moves the cursor one word to the right
Home	Moves the cursor to the left end of the command line
End	Moves the cursor to the space after the last character in the command line
Esc	Erases the contents of the command line

Del	Deletes the character positioned directly above the cursor
Ctrl-End	Removes all characters from the cursor to the end of the line
Ctrl-Home	Removes all characters from the cursor to the beginning of the line
Ins	Toggles between replace mode (the default) and insert mode
↑	Displays the preceding DOS command
↓	Displays the DOS command issued after the one currently displayed or displays a blank line when you are at the end of the list
PgUp	Displays the earliest command issued that is stored in the DOSKey command buffer
PgDn	Displays the last command stored in the DOSKey command buffer
F7	Displays contents of the command-history buffer in a numbered list
Alt-F7	Clears the command-history buffer
F8	Searches for the command(s) that most closely match characters typed at the command line
F9	Prompts for a line number, where *line number* refers to the number displayed next to a command in the command-history list generated by pressing F7. Press the number to display the corresponding command.

Keystroke Commands within the DOS Shell

DOS Version 5.0 assigns functions to the following keys on the keyboard when used within the DOS Shell:

F1	Displays context-sensitive help
F3	Exits the DOS Shell, returns to the command line, and removes the DOS Shell from memory (same as Alt-F4)

Alt-F4	Exits the DOS Shell and returns to the command line (same as F3)
F5	Refreshes the file list(s)
Shift-F5	Repaints the screen
F7	Moves selected file(s)
F8	Copies selected file(s)
Shift-F8	Toggles ADD mode for extending selection of nonconsecutive files; you select files by pressing the space bar.
F9	Enables you to view file contents
Shift-F9	Accesses the command line without removing the DOS Shell from memory
F10	Activates the menu bar (same as Alt)
Alt	Activates the menu bar (same as F10)
Del	Deletes selected file(s)
+	Expands one level of the current branch in the directory tree
*	Expands all levels of the current branch in the directory tree
Ctrl-*	Expands all branches in the directory tree
–	Collapses the current branch in the directory tree
Tab	Cycles between areas of the DOS Shell window in a clockwise direction
Shift-Tab	Cycles between areas of the DOS Shell window in a counter-clockwise direction
Alt-Tab	Switches between active task and DOS Shell
Esc	Cancels the current function
Alt-Esc	Cycles through active tasks
↑ or →	Moves selection cursor in the direction of the arrow
Shift-↑ or ↓	While in the file list area, extends selection in the direction of the arrow
PgUp	Scrolls up through the selected area one screen at a time

PgDn	Scrolls down through the selected area one screen at a time
Home	Moves to the top of the selected area
End	Moves to the bottom of the selected area
Ctrl-/	Selects all files in the selected directory
Ctrl-\	Deselects all files in the selected directory

D

Installing DOS
Version 5.0

DOS Version 5.0 comes with a Setup program to help you install the
operating system on your computer. Unlike previous versions of
DOS, Setup cannot be copied onto the hard disk. Many of the programs on
the DOS Version 5.0 distribution disks are in a compressed format. You
cannot run these programs until they have been installed on the hard disk
by using Setup. This appendix explains how to use Setup to install DOS
Version 5.0. If you need to install an older version of DOS, refer to the
documentation provided with the operating system software.

DOS Version 5.0 is distributed in two different formats. If you received
Version 5.0 with a new computer, you have the OEM format. If you
purchased Version 5.0 retail, you have the upgrade format. The two
formats differ mainly in their installation procedures. This appendix explains the installation of OEM first. To install the upgrade format, refer to
"Upgrading to DOS Version 5.0," later in this appendix.

Installing Version 5.0
on a New Computer

The Setup program in the OEM format installs the operating system on a
computer that does not already contain DOS. Setup guides you through
disk preparation and installation.

Before you use Setup to install DOS on your new computer, make sure that your system meets the following minimum requirements:

- IBM PC, PC/XT, AT, PS/1, PS/2, or compatible

- At least 256K of memory

If your system meets the minimum requirements for Version 5.0, perform the following steps:

1. Insert the distribution disk marked Disk 1 into floppy disk drive A and start the computer.

   After the computer completes any built-in test procedures, DOS starts the installation program Setup.

   When Setup begins, the following message appears on-screen:

   ```
   Please wait
   Setup is determining your system configuration.
   ```

   Setup determines what type of system you have, the current date and time settings, the country setting, whether the system has a hard disk, the display type, CPU type, and amount of memory. Setup then displays the following message:

   ```
   Welcome to Setup.
   Setup prepares MS-DOS Version 5.0 to run on
   your system. Each screen has basic instructions for
   completing a step of the installation. If you want
   additional information and instructions about a
   screen or option, press the Help key, F1.
   To continue Setup, press Enter.
   ```

2. Press Enter to continue with installation or press F3 to Exit. (If you have a black-and-white display or a monochrome LCD display [such as on a portable computer], press F5 to make the screens more readable.)

   After you press Enter at the initial screen, Setup displays a small box on-screen containing the following lines:

   - DATE/TIME: Indicates the current date and time settings of the system clock. These settings are applied to files when they are created or changed. Most new PCs have battery operated clocks that maintain the correct date and time, but your computer's clock may need to be set.

   - COUNTRY: Indicates the format the system uses to display time, date, currency, and characters. The default is USA format.

- KEYBOARD: Indicates the international keyboard setting.

- INSTALL TO: Indicates whether Setup is about to install DOS Version 5.0 to the hard disk (the default) or to floppy disks.

3. To change the date or time, use the up-arrow key to move the highlighted selection bar to the first line in the box and press Enter. Setup displays a smaller box that shows System Date on one line and System Time on another. Use the up- and down-arrow keys to move between the two lines. Use the left- and right-arrow keys, Ins, Del, number keys, and space bar to edit the date and time. After the date and time are correct, press Enter at each line to return to the preceding box.

4. If you are using DOS in a country other than the USA, use the up-arrow key to move the highlighted selection bar to the second line in the box and press Enter.

   Setup displays the following list of countries for which DOS Version 5.0 has a special character set, date-and-time format, and currency format:

   ```
   Australia
   Belgium
   Brazil
   Canada (Canadian French)
   Denmark
   Finland
   France
   Germany
   Italy
   Latin America
   Netherlands
   Norway
   Portugal
   Spain
   Sweden
   Switzerland
   United Kingdom
   USA
   ```

5. Use the arrow keys to highlight the country in which you plan to use the computer system and press Enter.

   For example, assume that you want DOS to use a character set, date-and-time format, and currency format specific to Germany. Use the arrow keys to highlight Germany and press Enter.

If you select an international character set with the preceding option, you should select a matching international keyboard setting. If you aren't sure which keyboard you have, compare your keyboard to the figures displayed in Chapter 13 of the *MS-DOS Users' Guide and Reference*, which is distributed with DOS Version 5.0.

6. To select an international keyboard setting, use the up-arrow key to highlight the line labeled KEYBOARD and press Enter.

   Setup lists the following keyboard options:

   ```
   Belgian
   Brazilian
   Canadian French
   Danish
   French
   German
   Italian
   Latin American
   Dutch
   Norwegian
   Portuguese
   Swiss (French)
   Swiss (German)
   Spanish
   Finnish
   Swedish
   UK English
   US Default
   ```

7. Use the arrow keys to highlight the keyboard setting that matches your keyboard and press Enter.

   Setup returns to the preceding screen.

8. To continue the installation of Version 5.0 to a hard disk, use the default setting in the INSTALL TO line. To install DOS to a set of floppy disks, press the up-arrow key to highlight the line labeled INSTALL TO and then press Enter.

   Setup displays the following two options:

   ```
   Floppy disks
   Hard disk
   ```

9. Use the up-arrow key to highlight Floppy disks and press Enter.

   Setup returns to the preceding screen.

10. After you are satisfied with the DATE/TIME, COUNTRY, KEY-
    BOARD, and INSTALL TO settings, press Enter to continue with
    installation.

The procedure for installing DOS varies depending on whether you are
installing the operating system to a hard disk or to floppy disks. Follow
the remaining installation procedures described in one of the following
sections.

Installing Version 5.0 on a Hard Disk

After you accept the entries in the first on-screen box—assuming that you
want to install Version 5.0 to the computer's hard disk—Setup displays
another small box on-screen. This second box lists two more options:

- `Setup to:` Determines the directory on the hard disk to which
  Setup copies DOS files. The default directory is \DOS on drive C.

- `Run Shell on startup:` Indicates whether you want the DOS
  Shell to display at startup. By default, the setting is `YES`. Setup
  installs DOS to start the Shell each time you turn on or reboot the
  computer.

To continue installing DOS Version 5.0 to the hard disk, complete the
following steps:

1. If you don't want DOS installed to drive C, or if you want DOS
   installed to a directory other than \DOS, use the up-arrow key to
   highlight the `Setup to` line and press Enter.

   Setup displays a highlighted area on-screen that shows the following path:

   `C:\DOS`

2. Use the left- and right-arrow keys, Ins, Del, number keys, and
   space bar to edit this line. Indicate the disk drive and directory to
   which you want Setup to copy DOS files and then press Enter.

   Setup returns to the preceding screen.

New DOS users may want to use the DOS Shell to perform most DOS tasks.
If you are an experienced DOS user, however, or plan to use an alternative
DOS shell, you can instruct Setup not to run the DOS Shell on startup.

3. To cause the DOS Shell to run every time you boot the computer, press the up-arrow key to highlight the `Run Shell on startup` line and then press Enter.

   Setup displays a small on-screen box containing the following options:

   ```
   Run the Shell on startup
   Do not run the Shell on startup
   ```

   When Setup displays this box, the first option is highlighted.

4. Use the down-arrow key to highlight the second option and press Enter. Setup installs DOS so that the DOS Shell does not run every time you reboot the computer.

   Setup returns to the preceding on-screen box.

5. After you have made desired changes in the on-screen box, highlight the line that indicates `The listed options are correct` and press Enter.

   Setup displays the following message:

   ```
   Your system has one or more hard disks with free space
   that can be used by MS-DOS Version 5.0. This space
   needs to be set up before MS-DOS can use it.
   ```

   Note: If you are installing DOS Version 5.0 to the hard disk for a second or subsequent time, Setup does not display the preceding message and skips over the partitioning and formatting steps described next.

   After the message, Setup displays a box containing the following options. Select one of the actions and press Enter.

   • `Partition all free space for MS-DOS.` Select this option to partition the hard disk. This option is the default and should be your choice unless you plan to install another operating system (such as OS/2 or UNIX) in a second partition on the same disk.

   • `Partition some of the free space for MS-DOS.` Use this option only if you intend to install another operating system to this disk.

- Do not partition free space for MS-DOS. If you select this
  option, you can install DOS only to floppy disks, and the hard
  disk becomes unusable by DOS or any DOS applications programs.

6. Highlight the desired selection and press Enter.

   If you choose to use all of the hard disk for the DOS partition,
   Setup creates the partition and then reboots (restarts) the computer. After the computer completes its self-testing procedures,
   Setup begins to format the hard disk and displays the following
   message:

   ```
   Formatting Hard Disk Partitions
   You have set up some or all of the disk space for use
   with MS-DOS. This space is being formatted now.
   ```

   Following this message, Setup displays an on-screen box containing another message that tells you which drive is being formatted.
   This box also indicates the percentage of the disk that has been
   formatted. After Setup completes the formatting process, Setup
   displays the following message:

   ```
   MS-DOS Version 5.0 is now being set up. Setup
   installs a basic MS-DOS system. See the 'MS-DOS
   User's Guide and Reference' to learn about
   additional features. You may want to read the
   chapter on optimizing your system. The chapter
   describes how to fine-tune MS-DOS to achieve
   maximum performance.
   ```

   Setup begins copying files to the hard disk.

7. Remove and insert disks only when prompted to do so.

   During the installation procedure, Setup indicates progress by
   displaying a number that denotes the percentage completed.
   Setup also shows a vertical bar graph that expands according to
   the number of files copied to the hard disk.

8. When Setup is finished, remove the last disk from the floppy drive
   and press Enter.

   Setup reboots the computer. If you indicated that you want the
   Shell to run at startup, the DOS Shell screen appears. Otherwise,
   you see the following prompt:

   ```
   C:\>
   ```

The installation process is complete.

Installing Version 5.0 on Floppy Disks

After you accept the entries in the first on-screen box—assuming that you want to install DOS Version 5.0 to floppy disks—Setup displays another small box on-screen. This second box lists a single setting:

`Setup to:`

This line indicates the floppy disk drive and directory to which you want Setup to copy files. The default value is `A:\`, the root directory of drive A. To use the default drive or to select an alternative drive, perform the following steps:

1. To select a different disk drive, use the up-arrow key to highlight the `Setup to` line and press Enter.

   Setup displays an on-screen box containing a list of the floppy disk drives available in the computer.

2. Use the arrow keys to highlight the disk drive you want to use and press Enter.

   Setup returns to the preceding box.

3. Make sure that the message `The listed options are correct` is highlighted and then press Enter.

   Setup next displays a message informing you that the installation procedure will create a set of working disks.

4. Obtain seven floppy disks, formatted or unformatted, and label them as follows:

   STARTUP

   SUPPORT

   SHELL

   HELP

   BASIC/EDIT

   UTILITY

   SUPPLEMENTAL

Note: If you are using 3 1/2-inch disks, you can install DOS Version 5.0 to fewer disks. Double-density 3 1/2-inch disks hold twice as much as double-density 5 1/4-inch disks. Label four 3 1/2-inch disks as follows:

STARTUP/SUPPORT

SHELL/HELP

BASIC/EDIT/UTILITY

SUPPLEMENTAL

5. When you are ready to proceed with installation, press Enter.

Setup displays the following message:

```
MS-DOS Version 5.0 is now being set up.
Setup installs a basic MS-DOS system. See the 'MS-DOS
User's Guide and Reference' to learn about additional
features. You may want to read the chapter on
optimizing your system. The chapter describes how to
fine-tune MS-DOS to achieve maximum performance.
```

Setup begins reading files into memory.

6. Remove and insert disks only when prompted to do so. Be careful to note which disk and drive Setup specifies each time you are instructed to remove and insert disks.

During the installation procedure, Setup indicates progress by displaying a number that denotes the percentage completed. Setup also shows a vertical bar graph that expands according to the number of files copied to the disks.

7. Remove the last disk from the floppy drive, replace this disk with the disk labeled Startup, and press Enter.

Setup reboots the computer. You see the following prompt:

```
A:\>
```

The installation process is complete.

Upgrading to Version 5.0

This section explains how to install the upgrade version of DOS Version 5.0. The Setup program in the upgrade version installs the operating system on a computer that already contains an earlier version of DOS. You do not have to reformat your hard disk. Existing data is untouched. Microsoft does, however, recommend that you back up the system before beginning installation. If you decide to uninstall DOS Version 5.0 and revert to the earlier version of DOS, an uninstall procedure enables you to do so.

Before you can use the Setup program, your system must meet the following minimum requirements:

- DOS Version 2.11 or later

- At least 256K of memory

- If you have a hard disk, at least 2.5M of available space

Versions of DOS before 4.0 did not recognize hard disk partitions larger than 32M. If you have been using one of these versions of DOS and have a hard disk larger than 32M, repartition and reformat the hard disk by using DOS Version 5.0 before running Setup. For more information, refer to the "Repartitioning Your Hard Disk" section at the end of this appendix.

1. If your system meets the minimum requirements for DOS Version 5.0 (and you have repartitioned and reformatted your hard disk), insert the DOS Version 5.0 distribution disk marked Disk 1 into floppy disk drive A.

2. Access the DOS prompt and change to the drive containing Disk 1. To start Setup, type **SETUP** and press Enter.

> *Caution:* The disks distributed with the DOS Version 5.0 upgrade are not bootable—they cannot be used to start the computer. To create a bootable disk, the operating system files first must be installed by Setup on a separate disk. When Setup installs DOS Version 5.0 on a hard disk, the hard disk is bootable. If you have a problem with the hard disk, you may need to boot from a floppy disk. Create a bootable DOS Version 5.0 disk as a part of the initial installation.

To force Setup to install to floppies, even if the system has a hard disk, type the following command at the DOS prompt and press Enter:

SETUP /F

Follow the procedure described in the "Upgrading DOS Version 5.0 to Floppy Disks" section of this appendix to create the set of DOS floppy disks. You may want to create a complete set of disks as a convenient backup copy. If you want to create only a bootable disk, however, you don't have to go through the entire installation process. Use Setup to create the floppy disk labeled Startup and press F3 to exit to the DOS prompt. The Startup disk is bootable. Use this disk any time you need to start the computer from a floppy drive.

Alternatively, after DOS is installed to the hard disk, you also can create a bootable disk with the SYS command. SYS is discussed in Chapter 5 and in the command reference.

When Setup begins, it briefly displays the following message:

```
Please wait.
Setup is determining your system configuration.
```

Setup attempts to determine the type of system you have, the current date and time settings, the country setting, whether the system has a hard disk, the display type, CPU type, and amount of memory.

If you have a hard disk, Setup displays the following message:

```
Welcome to Setup.
Setup installs Microsoft MS-DOS Version 5.0 on the
hard disk. During Setup, some of the current system
files will be saved on one high-density or two double-
density floppy disks that you provide and label as
follows:

  UNINSTALL #1
  UNINSTALL #2 (if needed)

The disk(s), which can be unformatted or newly
formatted, must be used in drive A. Setup copies
some files onto the UNINSTALL disk(s), and
others to a directory on the hard disk called
OLD_DOS. By using these files, you can remove MS-DOS
from the hard disk and reinstall the old DOS if
needed.
```

If the system has only floppy disks, Setup displays the following message:

```
Welcome to Setup.
Setup helps you create a set of working disks
of MS-DOS Version 5.0. During Setup, MS-DOS files
are copied onto floppy disks that you provide
```

and label as follows. These disks can be formatted
or unformatted.

```
STARTUP
SUPPORT
SHELL
HELP
BASIC/EDIT
UTILITY
SUPPLEMENTAL
```

If you want additional information or instructions
about a screen or option during Setup, press the
Help key, F1. To continue Setup, press Enter. To
exit Setup without creating a set of MS-DOS
working disks, press F3.

Note: If you are using 3 1/2-inch disks, you can install DOS Version
5.0 to fewer disks. Double-density 3 1/2-inch disks hold twice as
much as double-density 5 1/4-inch disks. Label four 3 1/2-inch disks
as follows:

STARTUP/SUPPORT

SHELL/HELP

BASIC/EDIT/UTILITY

SUPPLEMENTAL

DOS Version 5.0 upgrading procedures vary depending on whether you
are upgrading the operating system to a hard disk or to floppy disks. Follow
the upgrade procedures described in one of the following sections.

Upgrading Version 5.0 to a Hard Disk

Use the following steps to upgrade DOS Version 5.0 to a hard disk:

1. At the initial screen, press Enter to continue with installation or
   press F3 to Exit. (If you have a black-and-white display or a monochrome LCD display—such as on a portable computer—press F5
   to make the screens more readable.)

After you press Enter at the initial screen, Setup displays a small box on-screen containing a message that asks whether you are installing DOS to a computer attached to a network.

2. If you are installing DOS Version 5.0 to a networked computer, press **Y** and follow the instructions that appear on-screen. Otherwise, press **N** to continue with installation.

Next, Setup displays an on-screen box that provides the following options:

- `Back up hard disk(s)`. Backs up the hard disk by using DOS's BACKUP program.

- `Do not back up hard disk(s)`. Proceeds with installation without performing a backup.

3. Select the `Back up hard disk(s)` option to make a copy of the files on the hard disk before proceeding with the installation of DOS Version 5.0. You also can press F3 to cancel the installation procedure and use another backup program to make a copy of the existing files on the hard disk.

4. Choose the second option to continue with the installation procedure without making a copy of the files (or if you already have performed a backup operation).

Setup next displays an on-screen box that shows the following lines:

- `DOS Type`: Indicates the manufacturer of the version of DOS currently installed on your system. For example, this line may display `IBM PC-DOS`. If Setup cannot determine the manufacturer, the line displays `MS-DOS`.

- `DOS Path`: Indicates the directory in which DOS files currently are installed.

- `MS-DOS Shell`: Indicates whether you want the DOS Shell to display at startup. By default, the setting is `Do not run MS-DOS Shell on startup`. With this setting, Setup installs DOS so that the Shell does not display each time you reboot the computer.

- `Display Type`: Denotes the display type Setup expects the system to have, based on Setup's initial analysis of the system.

5. If the `DOS Type` line indicates `MS-DOS`, rather than a specific manufacturer, you need to modify this setting. Your version of DOS may have special files unique to your brand of computer. Use the up-arrow key to highlight the `DOS Type` line and then press Enter.

Setup displays an on-screen box that shows a list of companies licensed to produce the version of DOS installed on your system. The entire list does not display at the same time but can be scrolled by using the up- and down-arrow keys.

6. Use the up- and down-arrow keys to scroll through the list. Highlight the name of the company that manufactured your current DOS version. Making this selection causes Setup to maintain any files in the DOS directory that may be needed by the hardware. If you cannot determine the company that produced the DOS currently on your system, select MS-DOS or OTHER.

   After you highlight a selection and press Enter, Setup returns to the preceding on-screen box.

7. If you don't want DOS installed to the same disk and directory in which the current DOS is stored, use the up-arrow key to highlight the DOS Path line and press Enter. Setup displays a highlighted area on-screen that shows the current path.

   For example, Setup may display the following path:

   ```
   C:\DOS
   ```

8. Use the left- and right-arrow keys, Ins, Del, number keys, and space bar to edit the path. Indicate the disk drive and directory to which you want Setup to copy DOS files and press Enter. Setup returns to the preceding on-screen box.

Many DOS users may want to use the DOS Shell to perform most DOS tasks. By default, however, the upgrade version of Setup installs DOS Version 5.0 so that the Shell does not run when you start the computer.

9. If you want the DOS Shell to run every time you turn on or reboot the computer, press the up-arrow key to highlight the MS-DOS Shell line and press Enter.

   Setup displays a small on-screen box containing the following options:

   ```
   Run MS-DOS Shell on startup
   Do not run the MS-DOS Shell on startup
   ```

   When Setup displays the box that contains the preceding options, the second option is highlighted.

10. Use the up-arrow key to highlight the Run MS-DOS Shell on startup option and then press Enter.

Selecting this option tells Setup to install DOS so that the DOS
Shell runs every time you reboot the computer. After you make
the selection, Setup returns to the preceding on-screen box.

11. To change the display type, use the up-arrow key to highlight the
    `Display Type` line and then press Enter.

    Setup displays the following choices:

    ```
    Monochrome
    CGA
    EGA
    EGA Monochrome
    VGA
    VGA Monochrome
    Hercules
    MCGA
    ```

12. Use the up- and down-arrow keys to highlight the video display
    type that matches the video adapter used in the computer and
    then press Enter.

    Setup returns to the preceding on-screen box.

13. After you have selected or confirmed the DOS manufacturer, DOS
    path, whether you want the DOS Shell to run on startup, and the
    display type, highlight the line that displays the following message
    and press Enter:

    ```
    Continue Setup: The information above is correct.
    ```

    Setup displays the following message:

    ```
    Setup is ready to install MS-DOS Version 5.0. If
    you choose to continue, you may not be able to
    interrupt Setup until it has completed installing
    MS-DOS on your system. To install MS-DOS now,
    press Y. To exit Setup without installing MS-DOS,
    press F3. To review your configuration selections,
    press any other key.
    ```

14. Press Y to continue or press F3 to cancel the installation proce-
    dure. Press any other key to return to the preceding on-screen
    box.

    After you confirm that you want Setup to continue with the
    installation procedure, Setup displays a message instructing you to
    label a disk `UNINSTALL #1` and to insert the disk into the floppy
    disk drive.

15. Place the disk UNINSTALL #1 in the indicated floppy drive and press Enter. Any data on the disk is erased.

    Setup copies files from the hard disk to the UNINSTALL disk and copies other files to a new directory on the hard disk named \OLD_DOS.1.

16. If instructed to do so, label a disk UNINSTALL #2, place this disk in the floppy disk drive and press Enter.

    The files on the UNINSTALL disk(s), and in the \OLD_DOS.1 directory are used later only if you decide to remove DOS Version 5.0 from the system and return to the preceding version of the operating system.

    After Setup finishes creating the UNINSTALL disk(s), Setup instructs you to insert the DOS Version 5.0 disk labeled Disk 1 into the floppy disk drive.

17. Insert Disk 1 into the specified drive and press Enter.

    Setup begins copying files to the hard disk.

18. Remove and insert disks only when prompted to do so.

    During the installation procedure, Setup indicates progress by displaying a number that denotes the percentage completed. Setup also shows a vertical bar graph that expands according to the number of files copied to the hard disk.

19. When Setup is finished, remove the last disk from the floppy drive and press Enter.

    Setup reboots the computer. If you indicated that you want the Shell to run at startup, the DOS Shell screen appears. Otherwise, you see the following prompt:

    ```
    C:\>
    ```

The installation process is complete.

Caution: When you use Setup to install DOS Version 5.0 on the hard disk, Setup modifies any existing CONFIG.SYS and AUTOEXEC.BAT files (configuration files are discussed in Chapter 15). If Setup cannot correctly update the existing CONFIG.SYS and AUTOEXEC.BAT files, Setup renames these files with a numeric extension (CONFIG.0, for example).

Upgrading Version 5.0 to Floppy Disks

Use the following instructions to upgrade DOS Version 5.0 to floppy disks or to create a set of bootable DOS Version 5.0 disks:

1. At the initial screen, press Enter to continue with installation or press F3 to Exit. (If you have a black-and-white display or a mono-chrome LCD display—such as on a portable computer—press F5 to make the screens more readable.)

   After you press Enter at the initial screen, Setup displays an on-screen box that lists the following settings:

   - `Install to Drive`: Indicates the drive to which Setup installs DOS files, unless you specify otherwise. The default drive is A.

   - `Display Type`: Denotes the display type Setup expects the system to have, based on Setup's initial analysis of the system.

2. To change the drive to which Setup installs DOS, press the up-arrow key to highlight the `Install to Drive` line and press Enter. Setup displays an on-screen box that lists the disk drives available on the system. Use the up- or down-arrow keys to select the drive you want to use and press Enter.

3. To change the display type, use the up-arrow key to highlight the `Display Type` line and press Enter. Setup displays the following choices:

   ```
   Monochrome
   CGA
   EGA
   EGA Monochrome
   VGA
   VGA Monochrome
   Hercules
   MCGA
   ```

4. Use the up- and down-arrow keys to highlight the video display type that matches the video adapter used in the computer and press Enter.

5. After you have selected or confirmed disk drive and display type, highlight the `Continue Setup` line and press Enter.

   Setup begins reading files into memory.

6. Remove and insert disks only when prompted to do so. Be particularly careful to note which disk and drive Setup specifies when you remove and insert disks.

During the installation procedure, Setup indicates progress by displaying a number that denotes the percentage completed. Setup also shows a vertical bar graph that expands according to the number of files copied to the disks.

Note: If you already have installed DOS to a hard disk and want merely to create a bootable floppy disk, you can press F3 to quit from the installation procedure after Setup creates the disk labeled Startup. The Startup disk is the only bootable disk in the set of installed DOS disks.

You also can create a bootable disk by using the SYS command, discussed in Chapter 5 and in the command reference. Bootable disks do not, however, contain all the DOS files contained on the Startup disk.

7. When Setup is finished reading and copying files, remove the last disk from the floppy drive, replace it with the disk labeled Startup, and press Enter.

   Setup reboots the computer. You see the following prompt:

   ```
   A:\>
   ```

The installation process is complete. Use the Startup disk each time you need to start the computer.

Using UNINSTALL

When you use the upgrade version of DOS Version 5.0 to install the operating system to a hard disk, Setup creates one or two disks labeled UNINSTALL #1 and UNINSTALL #2 (if the second disk is needed). These two disks contain files that enable you to remove DOS Version 5.0 from the system and to return to the preceding version of DOS. Returning to the old version of DOS is possible only if you have not repartitioned the hard disk.

To UNINSTALL DOS Version 5.0, perform the following steps:

1. Place the disk labeled UNINSTALL #1 in drive A and reboot the computer (press and hold down the Ctrl and Alt keys while pressing the Del key).

   After the computer finishes self-test procedures, DOS begins the UNINSTALL procedure and displays the following message:

```
YOUR HARD DISK INSTALLATION WAS SUCCESSFULLY COMPLETED.
Continuing with the UNINSTALL program removes MS-DOS
Version 5.0 system files from the hard disk and
replaces them with the original DOS. To restore
the original DOS, press R. To exit, remove the
UNINSTALL disk from drive A and press E.
```

2. To continue with UNINSTALL, press **R**.

Note: To exit and return to DOS, remove the UNINSTALL disk from the floppy disk drive and press E. The UNINSTALL program reboots the computer.

---

3. Replace the disk labeled UNINSTALL #1 with UNINSTALL #2 only when prompted to do so. (Skip this step if Setup created only one UNINSTALL disk.)

   The UNINSTALL program deletes the DOS Version 5.0 files, copies necessary files from the UNINSTALL disk(s) to the hard disk, and copies the old DOS files from the \OLD_DOS.1 directory to the original DOS directory on the hard disk.

   When the UNINSTALL procedure is complete, the following message appears on-screen:

   ```
   UNINSTALL is now complete
   Please remove any disks from the floppy disk
   drives and press any key to restart the original
   DOS.
   ```

4. Remove the UNINSTALL disk from the floppy drive and press any key.

   The UNINSTALL program reboots the computer. DOS Version 5.0 is gone, and the original version of DOS is installed in its place.

Deleting Old DOS Files

After you determine that DOS Version 5.0 meets your needs and you don't want to return to the preceding version of DOS, you may want to delete the old version of DOS from the hard disk. Taking this action recovers disk space. After you perform this cleanup, however, you no longer may run the UNINSTALL procedure, described earlier in this appendix. Files needed by the UNINSTALL program are erased.

1. To delete the old DOS files from the hard disk, access the DOS prompt, type the following command, and then press Enter:

   DELOLDOS

   The program displays the following warning message:

   ```
   Running DELOLDOS removes all old DOS files from
   the system, making it impossible to recover the
   previous DOS. To continue with DELOLDOS, press Y.
   To exit, press any other key.
   ```

2. To continue with DELOLDOS, press Y. Press any other key to return to the DOS prompt without deleting the old DOS files.

   After you confirm that you want to delete all old DOS files, DELOLDOS displays a message that it is DELETING OLD_DOS.1 as it deletes the files from the hard disk. When all files have been erased, the program displays a message indicating that the program has finished removing the old DOS files.

3. Press Enter to return to the DOS prompt.

Repartitioning the Hard Disk

If your hard drive is larger than 32M, and you have been using a version of DOS earlier than Version 4.0, you may want to use Version 5.0 to repartition the hard disk before installing the Version 5.0 files to the disk. Versions of DOS before Version 4.0 do not recognize a hard disk drive larger than 32M. To use larger hard disks with pre-Version 4.0 DOS, you have to use FDISK to create several *logical* partitions (DOS Version 3.3 enabled users to divide a hard disk into multiple partitions, each of which was 32M or fewer; DOS then treated each partition as if it were a separate physical disk drive—referred to as a *logical* drive) or use a special partitioning program supplied by the manufacturer of the hard disk. DOS Versions 4.0 and later enables you to create a primary DOS partition up to 2 gigabytes (2,000 megabytes).

Note: With DOS Version 4.0, you have to run the program SHARE.EXE to use a partition larger than 32M. DOS Version 5.0 does not use the program SHARE.EXE in this manner and does not require you to load any other special utility to take advantage of large hard disks.

To repartition the hard disk before installing DOS Version 5.0, perform the following steps:

1. Back up all the programs and data on the hard disk.

   Repartitioning the hard disk deletes all data. You need this backup copy to restore all files to the hard disk after repartitioning and reformatting the disk.

   After you repartition the hard disk, you cannot boot the computer from the hard disk. The DOS Version 5.0 upgrade distribution disks are not bootable; the programs contained on the distribution disks are in a compressed and nonexecutable format. You need the DOS Version 5.0 floppy disk set to reboot the computer and to repartition the hard disk.

2. Follow the instructions in the "Upgrading DOS to Floppy Disks" section of this appendix to create a set of DOS Version 5.0 floppy disks.

   After you have a complete backup of all files on the hard disk and after you have a bootable set of DOS Version 5.0 disks, you are almost ready to repartition the hard disk. First, you have to remove the existing partition information by using the program that installed the current partitions.

3. Use the partitioning program that created the present hard disk partitions to remove all DOS partitions.

   Before you can use the DOS Version 5.0 partitioning program, you need to boot the computer by using DOS Version 5.0.

4. Place the disk labeled Startup into drive A and reboot the computer.

   DOS Version 5.0 starts and displays the following prompt:

   ```
   A:\>
   ```

   You finally are ready to repartition the disk.

5. Place the disk labeled Support into drive A. Type the following command and press Enter:

   ```
   FDISK
   ```

   FDISK starts and displays a menu of the following options:

   ```
   1. Create DOS partition or Logical DOS Drive
   2. Set active partition
   3. Delete partition of Logical DOS Drive
   4. Display partition information
   ```

FDISK prompts you to enter a choice and suggests option 1.

6. Press Enter to select option 1—Create DOS partition or Logical DOS Drive.

   FDISK displays a second menu with the following options:

   1. Create Primary DOS Partition
   2. Create Extended DOS Partition
   3. Create Logical DOS Drive(s) in the Extended DOS Partition

   FDISK, again, suggests option 1 as your choice.

7. Press Enter to select option 1—Create Primary DOS Partition.

   FDISK asks whether you want to use the maximum available size for the primary DOS partition. The default answer is yes, which creates a partition equal in size to the entire hard disk.

8. To create a partition that includes the entire hard disk, press Enter at the suggested response—Y.

   FDISK indicates that the system will now restart. The program further instructs you to place a system disk into drive A and press any key.

9. Place the Startup disk in drive A and press a key on the keyboard.

   The computer restarts and displays the A:\> prompt. The next step is to format the primary hard disk partition.

10. With the startup disk inserted in drive A, type the following command and press Enter:

    FORMAT C: /S

    FORMAT warns you that all data on drive C will be lost and asks whether you want to proceed with formatting.

11. Press Y and Enter to proceed.

    FORMAT displays a message indicating the size of the disk that begins the formatting process. Finally, FORMAT indicates that the process is complete and prompts you to enter a volume label.

12. Type up to 11 characters (including spaces), as a volume label, and press Enter.

    FORMAT informs you of the total number of bytes on the disk, the space used by the operating system, and the number of bytes free for storage of programs and data. You now are ready to restore to the hard disk the backup copy of the data that originally was on the disk.

13. Restore the backup copy to the hard disk. If you used the DOS command BACKUP to create the copy, use RESTORE from the same version of DOS to copy the files back to the hard disk.

    After you have restored the programs and data files, you are ready to install DOS Version 5.0 to the hard disk.

14. Place the DOS Version 5.0 distribution disk labeled Disk 1 into drive A. Follow the instructions for upgrading to a hard disk described earlier in this appendix to complete the installation procedure.

E

ANSI Terminal Codes

All ANSI terminal codes are preceded by an Escape (ESC) character and a left bracket ([). The Escape character is 27 decimal or 1B hexadecimal. ANSI codes often are referred to as *ANSI escape sequences* or just *ANSI sequences*.

Using Cursor-Control Sequences

ANSI sequences are used to control the cursor on-screen. For the cursor-control sequences, if a value is omitted, use the default value of 1. The following ANSI codes are used to position the cursor on-screen:

Horizontal and Vertical Position

ESC[#;#H   The first # is the row (vertical coordinate).

ESC[#;#f   The second # is the column (horizontal coordinate). The starting value for either coordinate is 1 (also the default value).

Cursor Up

ESC[#A   # is the number of rows to move up.

Cursor Down

ESC[#B   # is the number of rows to move down.

Cursor Forward

ESC[#C   # is the number of columns to move forward (right).

Cursor Backward

ESC[#D   # is the number of columns to move backward (left).

Device Status Report

ESC[6n   Causes the ANSI console driver to output a Cursor
            Position Report escape code sequence indicating the
            position saved by the Save Cursor Position sequence

Cursor Position Report

ESC[#;#R   Reports the cursor position. The string is returned by
            the ANSI console to the device and is eight characters
            long. The first # is the two-digit row number; the
            second # is the two-digit column number. For
            example, the Device Status sequence causes the
            console to generate a Cursor Position Report
            sequence.

Save Cursor Position

ESC[s   Saves the current cursor position in memory. The
            position is restored by using the Restore Cursor
            Position sequence.

Restore Cursor Position

ESC[u   Sets the cursor to the horizontal and vertical position
            saved when the Save Cursor Position sequence was
            issued

Erasing

The following ANSI sequences are used to erase portions of the display:

Erase Display

ESC[2J   Erases the display and moves the cursor to the Home
            position (the upper left corner of the screen)

Erase to End of Line

ESC[K   Erases from the current cursor position to the end of
            the current line

Controlling Modes of Operation

The following ANSI sequences control screen color and video mode. For these codes, if a parameter is omitted, use the default value of 0.

Set Graphics Mode

ESC[#;...;#m   Sets the character attributes by the following parameters. The attributes remain in effect until the next graphics mode command.

Parameter	Meaning
0	All attributes off (normally white on black)
1	Bold on (high intensity)
4	Underscore on (monochrome display adapter only)
5	Blink on
7	Reverse (inverse) video on
8	Cancel on (invisible characters black on black)
30	Black foreground
31	Red foreground
32	Green foreground
33	Yellow foreground
34	Blue foreground
35	Magenta foreground
36	Cyan foreground
37	White foreground
40	Black background
41	Red background
42	Green background
43	Yellow background

44	Blue background
45	Magenta background
46	Cyan background
47	White background

Set Screen Mode

Esc[=#h   Sets the screen width or type based on #

Reset Screen Mode

Esc[=#1   Resets the screen width or type based on # (in the following list). Available with DOS Version 4.0 or later.

Parameter	*Meaning*
0	40 × 25 monochrome
1	40 × 25 color
2	80 × 25 monochrome
3	80 × 25 color
4	320 × 200 color
5	320 × 200 monochrome
6	640 × 200 monochrome
7	Wrap at end-of-line (set mode); or do not wrap and discard characters past end of line (reset mode)
14	640 × 200 color
15	640 × 350 monochrome
16	640 × 350 color
17	640 × 480 monochrome
18	640 × 480 color
19	320 × 200 color

Reassigning Keyboard Keys

The following sequences are used to reassign keys on the keyboard:

Esc[*sequence*p   Sets the sequence typed by the named key

The parameter *sequence* can be in the form of #;#;⌐# (where # represents the one-, two-, or three-digit code for an ASCII character), or "string" (a string of characters within double quotation marks), or any combination of the two provided that # and "string" are separated by a semicolon.

Esc[#;#;⌐;p

or

Esc["string"p

or

Esc[#;"string";#;#;"string";#p

The first ASCII code (the first #) defines which key or keystrokes (such as a Ctrl-character combination) are being reassigned. However, if the first code in the sequence is 0 (ASCII Nul), the first and second codes designate an Extended ASCII key sequence.

The remaining numbers (#) or characters within the "string" are the replacement characters typed when that key or keystroke combination is pressed. Any nonnumeric characters used in the replacement must be placed within double quotation marks.

Enabling/Disabling Extended Keys on Enhanced Keyboards

To enable or disable extended keys on enhanced keyboards, use the following commands:

Esc[1q   Enables assignment of the extended keys on the
           Enhanced Keyboard. The sequence is the same as using
           the /X switch for the ANSI.SYS configuration command.

Esc[0q   Disables assignment of the extended keys on the
           Enhanced Keyboard

Using EDLIN

EDLIN is a mini text editor provided with every copy of DOS. It is a line-oriented editor, enabling you to work on only one line at a time. EDLIN is quite useful, however, when you need to create a short note or write a simple batch file.

You can use EDLIN to make changes in special configuration files used by DOS and many applications programs. The DOS CONFIG.SYS and AUTOEXEC.BAT files, the Microsoft Windows WIN.INI file, and similar files for other programs are simple ASCII files you can edit with EDLIN. In Chapter 12, you learn that EDLIN can be useful for typing or editing a series of commands in special batch files.

Starting EDLIN

To run EDLIN, you type **EDLIN**, followed by the name of the file you want to create or edit. EDLIN.EXE must be located in the current directory or in one of the directories listed in your DOS path.

Creating a Memo with EDLIN

In this section, you learn to use EDLIN to create a simple memo. Type the following command at the DOS prompt to start EDLIN with the file MEMO.TXT:

EDLIN MEMO.TXT

This command loads EDLIN (no matter which directory is the current one) and begins work with a batch file called MEMO.TXT.

After EDLIN is started, you see the EDLIN prompt. Although the default DOS prompt is the drive name and greater-than symbol (such as A>, C>, and so on), EDLIN's prompt is a simple asterisk:

```
New file
*
```

When you see this prompt, EDLIN is waiting for your instructions. Each EDLIN command consists of a letter (upper- or lowercase) which can be preceded or followed by numbers that tell EDLIN the number of lines you want to work with or the line numbers you are referring to. Some commands also enable you to specify strings of characters to search for or replace.

Inserting Text

Because the MEMO.TXT document you created in the preceding section is empty, you first need to enter some text. The I (Insert Lines) command is used for inserting text (even when the file is empty, text is inserted). To tell EDLIN that you want to insert text into the current file, type the following at EDLIN's prompt:

*I

EDLIN responds with the following:

1:*

Notice that the colon is preceded by a line number, which tells you that EDLIN is currently in Insert Lines mode. If a line number, a colon, and an asterisk are the only things shown on a line, EDLIN is waiting for you to enter text. Now type the first line of the memo:

1:*MEMO TO: Scott N. Hollerith, President

Press Enter at the end of the line. EDLIN responds with the following:

2:*

Don't confuse the asterisk shown after the line number with EDLIN's prompt. When shown with a line number, the asterisk marks the current line. The current line is the line currently being entered or, when you are editing lines, the line most recently edited.

EDLIN is now ready for you to enter a second line. Type the rest of the following memo, pressing Enter at the end of each line:

```
 2:*From: Otto Wirk, Research Chief
 3:*Subject: New Dual Processor Micro
 4:*Date: Sunday
 5:*
 6:*Our testing confirms that we should indeed
 7:*include two microprocessors in the next model
 8:*TLS-8E. This increases the odds that one will
 9:*work. If both happen to function, they can
10:*take turns
```

To leave line 5 blank, press Enter without typing anything. When you are finished with the memo, stop inserting text at line 10 by pressing Enter to finish the line. (Don't add a period to the end of the sentence on line 10; you fix that later.) Then press Ctrl-C or Ctrl-Break. The EDLIN asterisk prompt returns. You also can press a list of items, the F6 key, and then Enter to exit the Insert mode. (EDLIN types ^C on line 11 when you press Ctrl-C or types ^Z on line 11 when you press F6; these characters, however, do not become a part of the file.)

Even though you haven't saved the memo to disk yet, suppose that you forgot to include several other staffers on the distribution item. The I command enables you to fix this error quickly.

Type the following and press Enter:

5I

EDLIN responds with the following:

```
 5:*
```

If you type a number in front of the I command, EDLIN enables you to enter text beginning with a new line preceding the line you specify. In this example, EDLIN inserts a new line 5 in front of the old line 5. EDLIN renumbers the lines as necessary to accommodate the new line or lines. The line numbers aren't part of the memo you are creating; EDLIN uses line numbers only to help you keep track of the various lines currently in memory. The line numbers are not included in the file you store to disk.

At the I (Insert Lines) prompt, type the following line:

```
 5:* CC: Bill Kem, Marketing; Betty Site, Testing
```

Press Enter at the end of the line. A new blank line 6 appears. Because you don't want to add another line to the file, press Ctrl-C, Ctrl-Break, or F6 and Enter to stop inserting lines.

Listing Text

To see what the memo looks like with the addition, you can use EDLIN's L (List Lines) command to display the lines currently in memory. You can use the L command to look at a line or a range of lines. Up to 23 lines can be shown on-screen at one time. Because the sample memo is shorter than 23 lines, you don't have to type in a range of line numbers to be displayed. Instead, specify only the first line you want displayed. Type the following:

s*1L

EDLIN responds by showing you the entire file so far:

```
 1 : MEMO TO: Scott N. Hollerith, President
 2 : From: Otto Wirk, Research Chief
 3 : Subject: New Dual Processor Micro
 4 : Date: Sunday
 5 : CC: Bill Kem, Marketing; Betty Site, Testing
 6 :*
 7 : Our testing confirms that we should indeed
 8 : include two microprocessors in the next model
 9 : TLS-8E. This increases the odds that one will
10: work. If both happen to function, they can
11: take turns
```

Notice that the original blank line 5 has become line 6. In addition, the asterisks that followed each line number when the text was entered are gone. They, like the line numbers, appear on-screen only to guide you. The asterisk on line 6 shows that line 6 is the current line.

For practice, list only a few lines at a time using the L command. Type the following:

*1,5L

EDLIN displays the first five lines of the memo—lines 1 to 5. Notice that when you type a line range, you separate the numbers with a comma instead of a hyphen, space, or other character.

You can list one line by typing that line as the range. For example, you can type the following to list only line 1:

*1,1L

Editing a Line

If you listed the entire memo, you may have noticed that no period was typed at the end of the last sentence (line 11). This error easily can be fixed.

At EDLIN's * prompt, type the following:

> *11

Notice that you do not type a specific command in this instance; you type just a line number at the EDLIN prompt to indicate that you want to edit line 11 of the current file. EDLIN responds by displaying the text of the specified line with the line number, colon, and asterisk prompt on the following line:

```
11:* take turns
11:*
```

No text is displayed on the second line. You can type a new line to replace the old one. Because you want to make only a small change at the end of the line, however, press F3. EDLIN displays the entire line:

```
11:* take turns
11:* take turns
```

Press the period key (.); then press Enter. EDLIN displays line 12 just as it did line 11. Press Ctrl-C or Ctrl-Break to stop editing.

The same function keys used as DOS editing keys are used with EDLIN. Recall that F3 is used to redisplay an entire command line. In the example you just worked through, F3 enables you to begin editing at the end of the specified line. To replace the final word in the line, press Backspace four times and then type a new word. Later in this section, you see how the other DOS editing keys are used with EDLIN.

For now, type **1L** at the EDLIN * prompt to list the memo. It looks much like it did before, with two changes:

```
 1 : MEMO TO: Scott N. Hollerith, President
 2 : From: Otto Wirk, Research Chief
 3 : Subject: New Dual Processor Micro
 4 : Date: Sunday
 5 : CC: Bill Kem, Marketing; Betty Site, Testing
 6 :
 7 : Our testing confirms that we should indeed
 8 : include two microprocessors in the next model
 9 : TLS-8E. This increases the odds that one will
10: work. If both happen to function, they can
11:*take turns.
```

The period you typed at the end of line 11 is added, and line 11 now has an asterisk following the colon. The asterisk indicates that line 11 has been marked by EDLIN as the current line. Several EDLIN functions use the current line as a default if you don't enter a new value when you type the command. Use the L (List Lines) command and look for the asterisk after the line number to discover which line is the current line.

Saving Text

Before you modify the memo further, save it to disk so that you can retrieve it in this finished form later. To save the current file, end the EDLIN session with EDLIN's E (End Edit) command. The DOS prompt then returns. EDLIN writes the file to the disk with the changes you made in the current session.

Try this technique now for practice. At the EDLIN prompt, type the following:

*E

Remember to press Enter to activate the EDLIN command, and the DOS prompt reappears. Notice that you don't get any feedback, such as a message like Saving file to disk. No such message is needed: when you exit EDLIN with the E command, the text always is stored. To exit EDLIN without saving the changes to your file, use EDLIN's Q (Quit) command to end the EDLIN session. The Q (Quit) command is discussed in a later section in this Appendix.

Printing the Memo

While you are at the DOS prompt, you can practice printing the memo. EDLIN does not have a specific print command, but to print a text file, you can use one of several DOS commands: PRINT, COPY, and TYPE.

You can use the PRINT command to print the file. You also can use the COPY command to copy the file to the printer. The TYPE command also can be used to redirect the file to the printer.

To print your memo, type one of the following commands at the DOS prompt:

PRINT MEMO.TXT

TYPE MEMO.TXT > PRN

COPY MEMO.TXT PRN

If you use the TYPE or COPY command, only the text is sent to the printer. A form-feed character is not sent with these two commands. Use the form feed button on your printer to eject the printed page. If you use PRINT, a form-feed command is sent to the printer.

Because you still have some work to do with MEMO.TXT, reload the file into EDLIN. To start EDLIN with an existing file, type the following:

EDLIN MEMO.TXT

The message End of input file and the asterisk prompt appear. Typing **L** after you load a file is good practice so that you can list the file and confirm that EDLIN has indeed loaded the text you intend to edit.

Deleting Lines

The last of EDLIN's basic commands is D (Delete Lines). As with the L (List Lines) command, you can work with one line or a range of lines. The syntax is the same. Delete lines 5 and 6 of the memo by typing the following line at the EDLIN prompt:

*5,6D

List the lines of the memo (type **1,11L**) to see what has happened. The memo now looks like the following:

```
1 : MEMO TO: Scott N. Hollerith, President
2 : From: Otto Wirk, Research Chief
3 : Subject: New Dual Processor Micro
4 : Date: Sunday
5 :*Our testing confirms that we should indeed
6 : include two microprocessors in the next model
7 : TLS-8E. This increases the odds that one will
8 : work. If both happen to function, they can
9 : take turns.
```

EDLIN renumbers the lines to accommodate the changes. Line 5, the line marked by the asterisk, is the current line because it is the first line that follows the lines you removed.

You can end this practice EDLIN session by typing **Q**. EDLIN asks whether you want to abort the session. Respond by pressing Y. Because you used the Q command, the changes you made (deleting two lines) are not saved. The original version of MEMO.TXT remains on disk. You can verify this by using the command **TYPE MEMO.TXT** at the DOS prompt.

Learning More about EDLIN's Features

In the process of creating a memo with EDLIN, you learned some of the program's basic features. EDLIN also includes some additional editing features and commands, which are discussed in the remaining sections of this appendix.

Using EDLIN's /B Switch

EDLIN has an additional parameter, the /B switch, that can be used when you start the program. You add the /B switch to the initial EDLIN command at the DOS prompt, as in the following example:

EDLIN MEMO.TXT /B

The /B switch tells EDLIN to read the entire file, based on its size as listed in the disk directory.

In its normal mode, EDLIN loads the file up to the first Ctrl-Z character found in the file (within limitations of available memory). By using the /B switch, you tell EDLIN to load the entire file, ignoring any Ctrl-Z characters it encounters in the file. You also can load program files (files that have the extension COM or EXE). Because program files also are called binary files, the switch is called /B. You have little reason to load such binary files; other tools like DEBUG are better suited for editing true binary files.

Using the Editing Keys

You can use the function keys F1 through F6 with EDLIN to reenter and correct text lines. The function keys available for editing in EDLIN are explained in table F.1.

Table F.1
EDLIN Key Combinations

Key	Function
F1 or →	Copies one character from the edited line to the current line
F2 *char*	Copies all the characters from the edited line to the first occurrence of the character *char*
F3	Copies all the remaining characters from the edited line to the current line. By pressing F3 without first typing anything on the current line, all characters from the edited line are copied to the current line. If you already have started to edit the current line, pressing F3 copies the remaining characters.
F4 *char*	Copies all the characters from the edited line found after the value of the character char
F5	Copies all the characters typed on the current line into the keyboard buffer. When you press F3, the copied characters transfer to the edited line.
F6	Creates a Ctrl-Z, (^Z) end-of-file, character
F7	Creates a null character, Ctrl-@
Ins	Acts as a toggle switch between insert and overtype modes. After you press Ins, you can insert characters at the current cursor position. Press Ins again to turn off insert capabilities.
Del	Erases one character to the right of the current cursor position
Esc	Causes the current line to be ignored

Using the EDLIN Commands

Table F.2 is a complete list of the commands available with EDLIN. Each command is listed with its function and any available parameters.

Table F.2
EDLIN Commands

Command	Syntax	Function
Append Lines	*n*A	Loads the next *n* lines of a file into memory if the file is too large to fit into memory
Copy Lines	*sline,eline,* **dline**,*count*/**C**	Copies lines from line *sline* to line *eline*, inserting them before **dline**, and repeats the copy *count* times
Delete Lines	*sline,eline,***D**	Deletes the lines from line *sline* to line *eline* from the file
End edit	**E**	Ends EDLIN and saves the edited file
Insert Lines	*n***I**	Inserts new lines of text into the file starting at the line *n*
List Lines	*sline,eline***L**	Lists the file's contents from line *sline* to line *eline*
Move Lines	*sline,eline,* **dlineM**	Moves a block of text from line *sline* to line *eline* and inserts them before line **dline**
Page	*sline,eline***P**	Lists the file's contents one page (screen full) at a time, from line *sline* to line *eline*
Quit Edit	**Q**	Quits the EDLIN session without saving any changes you made to the file
Replace Text	*sline,eline?* **Rstext<F6>rtext**	Replaces text, *stext*, with text, *rtext*, from line *sline* to line *eline*
Search Text	*sline,eline?***Sstext**	Searches the text file for the character string **stext** from line *sline* to line *eline*
Transfer Lines	*n***T***d:***path** **filename.ext**	Transfers the entire contents of the file **filename.ext** into the current file
Write Lines	*n***W**	Writes *n* lines to the file

Index

E

J

K

NO POSTAGE
NECESSARY
IF MAILED
IN THE
UNITED STATES

BUSINESS REPLY MAIL
First Class Permit No. 9918   Indianapolis, IN

Postage will be paid by addressee

11711 N. College
Carmel, IN 46032

NO POSTAGE
NECESSARY
IF MAILED
IN THE
UNITED STATES

BUSINESS REPLY MAIL
First Class Permit No. 9918   Indianapolis, IN

Postage will be paid by addressee

11711 N. College
Carmel, IN 46032